D0145866

Apparel Merchandising

The Line Starts Here

Apparel Merchandising

The Line Starts Here
Second Edition

Jeremy A. Rosenau/David L. Wilson

Fairchild Publications, Inc.
New York

Executive Editor: Olga Kontzias
Senior Development Editor: Jennifer Crane
Production Editor: Elizabeth Marotta
Art Director: Adam B. Bohannon
Production Manager: Ginger Hillman
Copy Editor: Chernow Editorial Services, Inc.
Cover Design: Adam B. Bohannon

Second Edition, Copyright © 2006
Fairchild Publications, Inc.

First Edition, Copyright © 2001

Library of Congress Catalog Card Number: 2006921454

ISBN-13: 978-1-56367-448-8

ISBN-10: 1-56367-448-3

GST R 133004424

Printed in the United States of America

CH01, TP13

Contents

Extended Contents

Chapter 2   Modern Merchandising   51

PART 2 MERCHANDISING: THE PLANNING

Chapter 3   Market Knowledge   81

Chapter 4   Planning and Control   **117**

PART 3 MERCHANDISING: THE EXECUTION

Preface

Apparel Merchandising: The Line Starts Here analyzes the evolution and development of the merchandising function in branded apparel companies and retail private label apparel. The text presents an academic discussion as well as practical applications of the management philosophies and technologies used by apparel merchandisers and their retail counterparts who provide private label or private brand merchandise in today's fast-paced global fashion industry. Throughout this textbook, the title "merchandiser" will be used to refer to both merchandisers in apparel companies and their retail private label or private brand counterparts whom our survey has shown to be referred to as product managers, merchandisers, or buyers. Executive perspectives from a broad spectrum of industry leaders are used to bring into focus the implementation of merchandising principles in different sectors of the apparel supply chain. These perspectives present the points of view of the individuals based upon their industry credentials.

This text is targeted for junior or senior year college students majoring in fashion design, fashion merchandising, apparel management, or any fashion-related curriculum. This text could also be used for graduate courses in fashion and apparel as well as in continuing education programs and seminars for industry personnel.

Interviews with executives from each segment of the industry are included to provide their real-world views to the concepts discussed in the text. Photographs of merchandising activities and examples of company forms and tools used by merchandisers are provided to aid students in understanding the complexities of this important function. At the end of each chapter, discussion questions and suggested learning activities allow students to analyze the principles presented in the chapter and stimulate critical thinking.

To determine the specific needs of the industry, an extensive survey of 675 companies in the men's, women's, and children's markets covering all price points from budget through designer was conducted. A second survey of a similar population was conducted in 2002 to identify what, if any, changes had taken place since 1996. The results of these surveys determined the focal points for each chapter and provided valuable insight into the differences of merchandising responsibilities in each market segment. The survey also emphasized how the industry is actually utilizing the apparel merchandiser in all areas of the business, from defining the target market through line development and manufacturing. In many companies, critical marketing and sourcing decisions fall to the merchandiser. The interface of merchandising with the marketing and manufacturing departments and how these functions integrate in an effective team concept is evaluated. A profile of the "ideal" merchandiser is presented to allow students to take personal inventory of their strengths and weaknesses when considering apparel merchandising as a career.

The role of merchandising is analyzed relative to market research, planning and control, line development, costing and pricing strategies, quality assurance, supply chain management, and sourcing. Special attention is paid to modern computing and advancements in communications. Industry consultants were used as resources for evaluating the future direction of the industry and the role of merchandising.

A companion survey of 526 retail companies was conducted at the same time by Professor Doreen Burdalski, Coordinator of the Fashion Merchandising program at Philadelphia University. This survey found that the responsibilities of retail product managers or merchandisers overlapped those of apparel merchandisers. The results from all of these surveys have been incorporated into this edition of the textbook.

Acknowledgments

The second edition of *Apparel Merchandising: The Line Starts Here* is the result of continuous research and writing since the first edition was published in 2000. Once again we have received the support and assistance of many people and organizations who we acknowledge at this time. As before, we first want to thank the staff and administration at Philadelphia University. In particular, we want to thank David Brookstein, Dean of the School of Engineering and Textiles, and Professors Herb Barndt, Janet Brady, Doreen Burdalski, Jack Carnell, Celia Frank, Steven Frumkin, Muthu Govindaraj, Peggy Goutmann, Anne Hand, Clara Henry, Jane Likens, Matthew London, and Melvin Wiener. In addition, we thank Stan Gorski from the Gutman Library and Margaret Cuches, our Research Assistant. We are also appreciative of the advice, information, and materials that we received from Steve Lamar and Nate Herman of the American Apparel and Footwear Association, Kathy DesMarteau of *Apparel Magazine*, Aroq Ltd, Freeborders, Bud Staples of Gerber Technology, JustWin Technology, The Thread, and the Textile Clothing Technology Corporation.

Our book would not be a success without the interviews that were granted by the many leading executives in the apparel and retail industries. Each "Executive Perspective" is a unique opportunity for our readers to explore, experience, and understand the philosophies and dynamics and response to global events that continue to guide the planning and operations of the apparel and retail industries. We are most grateful to (in alphabetical order) David Baron, Norton Binder, Jay Bornstein, William Calvert, Lynn Duckworth, M. Lederle Eberhardt, Andrea Engel, Bryan Eshelman, Joe Feczko, Brian Ford, Mike Fralix, Jay Gardner, Lori Greenawalt, E. Lee Griffith III, Andrew Kahn, Bud Konheim, Mario Lerias, Jack Listanowsky, Walter Loeb, Jim Lovejoy, Peter McGrath, Cheryl Nash, Colombe Nicholas, Laura O'Connor, Gary Simmons, Lorraine Trocino, Gus Whalen, Bob Zane, and Howard Ziplow.

Once again our final acknowledgement is to our wives and families. Without their complete understanding, enduring patience, advice, guidance, and unwavering support, the second edition of *Apparel Merchandising: The Line Starts Here* would not have been written.

As style became more important to the purchasing decisions of apparel customers and the frequency of style
changes increased, the apparel industry needed a new
level of management to plan and control product development and global manufacturing. Merchandising has
evolved to fill that need and plays a very important role in
the success of today's apparel companies. When retailers
added a style component to their private label merchandise, the same need emerged which was met by the creation of a staff of product managers.

Part 1 focuses on the evolution and multifaceted responsibilities of merchandising in the apparel industry and product managing of private label in the retail industry. An understanding of the historical developments that increased
the complexity of the apparel and retail industries provides
a perspective for the structural changes that occurred in apparel and retail organizations. These changes resulted in
the growing importance of both the merchandising and
product managing functions.

MERCHANDISING: THE CONCEPT

Evolution of Merchandising in the Apparel Industry and Managing Private Label Apparel in the Retail Industry

OBJECTIVES

- Discuss the historical changes in the apparel industry and the effect on the merchandising function.

- Identify the stages of change in management structure in the apparel industry.

- Identify the various models in developing and producing private label apparel.

- Trace the rise in importance of private label apparel in the retail sector from the mid-20th Century until the early 21st Century.

- Understand the possible roles of the participants in developing, executing, and delivering private label apparel.

- Recognize the retailer's advantages and disadvantages with private label merchandise.

Fashion is excitement. Fashion is glamour. Fashion is change. Fashion is art. Fashion is also a high-stakes business. It requires talented executives with a keen sense of the marketplace and finely honed management skills that enable them to make the critical decisions needed to keep a company profitable. The driving and central force in today's apparel business is merchandising.

The term **merchandising** means simply to buy and sell commodities for a profit. In the fashion business, the role of merchandising may vary depending on whether it is performed in a retail or manufacturing context. In the retail environment, **retail fashion merchandising** is the buying of apparel products and selling them to the ultimate consumer for a profit. In the manufacturing environment, **apparel merchandising** involves the conceptualization, development, procurement of raw materials, **sourcing** (the process of deciding where and how to manufacture a product) of production, and delivery of apparel products to retailers. Major retailers develop and have produced their own **private label** apparel (products that are developed and produced exclusively for their store) and some manufacturers have opened their own retail stores. While this textbook focuses primarily on the process of apparel merchandising as it relates to the apparel sector, it also applies to the process of product managing in the retail sector.

We follow the evolution of the merchandising function from its historic roots of two **seasons,** or product offerings, per year with minimal style changes and emphasis on production efficiency, to today's season-less, consumer-driven, fashion oriented, computerized, global environment. Also included is the evolution of retail private label from inexpensive basics to styles with fashion flair. The focus is to provide the management philosophies, business strategies, technical tools and problem solving skills needed by apparel merchandisers and private label product managers in today's demanding and quickly changing global business climate.

■ Historical Perspective

During the first half of the twentieth century, the U.S. apparel industry had very little foreign competition. Domestically produced apparel products dominated the market. After World War II the United States transferred many of the manufacturing technologies developed to support the war effort to the private sector. The apparel industry focused on industrial engineering principles in order to improve production efficiency. Some of the larger apparel businesses hired industrial engineers in the hope of increasing productivity and reducing costs.

■ A Changing Apparel Industry

During the period immediately following World War II, the apparel industry had two seasons per year: spring/summer and fall/winter. There were minimal changes in style. Raw materials consisted primarily of natural fiber fabrics such as cotton, wool, linen, and silk. Product development evolved over a number of seasons, thereby allowing stock to be carried over from year to year without risk of obsolescence. Most companies maintained large warehouse inventories. They produced to stock and sold from stock. Companies struggled internally as the manufacturing divisions tried to keep the warehouses full, and the sales forces tried to empty them. The period between 1960 and the early 2000s saw dramatic changes in the structure, focus, and content of U.S. apparel companies.

Dramatic Growth

Many of the emerging apparel companies of the 1950s started fighting for market share in the 1960s, the decade of change. In 1962 the largest publicly owned apparel firms still produced mostly basic apparel products. The top five apparel companies in 1962 represented net sales of only $635,700,000. The U.S. apparel industry was still a large fraternity of small and medium-size companies.

The 1970s brought a dramatic growth spurt to the apparel industry, which continued through the 1980s and 1990s and established large, billion dollar corporations as the industry leaders. (See Table 1.1 and Figure 1.1.) Growth of apparel sales by public companies in the 1970s was 1,310 percent. In the 1980s, growth was 24 percent, and the 1990s experienced 38 percent growth. It is important to note that Figure 1.1 includes only public companies and that privately held companies like Levi Strauss with sales of over $7 billion are not included. By 1999 the net sales of the top five publicly owned apparel companies reached a staggering $24,127,000,000 and rose to $25,089,400,000 in 2004. This increase was generated in large part by consolidation and mergers as well as by the emergence of American megadesigners such as Liz Claiborne. The merger mania continued through the early 2000s with smaller to medium-sized apparel companies tempted to merge so as to become more competitive with larger companies. On the other hand, the large, publicly held firms were forced to keep growing in order to justify asking investors for higher stock prices (Ryan, 1998).

During this period of rapid growth in the United States, apparel sales kept pace with personal consumption of all **nondurable goods**, those products that have a short utility and must be replaced periodically. Retail apparel sales increased by 74 percent in the 1970s, by 153 percent in the 1980s, and by 39.6 percent in the 1990s. In the first three years of the 21st Century, the increase has slowed dramatically. Sales only grew from 240,928,000 to 256,544,000 or 6.48 percent. According to the U.S. Bureau of Labor Statistics, "The 6.2 percent decrease in spending on apparel and services in 2003 was similar to the 6.1 percent decrease in 2001. Spending on that component in 2002 was essentially unchanged, rising just 0.3 percent. The trend

TABLE 1.1

Leading Apparel Manufacturers (public corporations)
Net Sales (rounded to nearest thousand dollars)

1962

1.	Cluett, Peabody & Co., Inc.	$169,300,000
2.	Kayser-Roth Corporation	154,300,000
3.	Spartans Industries, Inc.	116,500,000
4.	Kellwood Company	97,800,000
5.	Hart Schaffner & Marx	97,800,000
	TOTAL	$635,700,000

1977

1.	Burlington	$2,388,200,000
2.	Northwest Industries	1,876,500,000
3.	Interco Incorporated	1,666,700,000
4.	Levi Strauss	1,559,300,000
5.	Melville Corporation	1,473,600,000
	TOTAL	$8,964,300,000

1987

1.	Wickes	$3,776,500,000
2.	VF Corporation	2,573,800,000
3.	Interco Incorporated	1,996,000,000
4.	West Point-Pepperell	1,703,500,000
5.	Hartmarx	1,080,400,000
	TOTAL	$11,130,200,000

1995

1.	VF Corporation	$5,062,300,000
2.	Fruit of the Loom	2,403,100,000
3.	Liz Claiborne Inc.	2,081,600,000
4.	West Point Stevens	1,649,900,000
5.	Kellwood Company	1,466,000,000
	TOTAL	$12,662,900,000

1999

1.	Sara Lee Corporation	$7,440,000,000
2.	VF Corporation	5,552,000,000
3.	Calvin Klein Inc.	5,200,000,000
4.	Jones Apparel Group	3,129,000,000
5.	Liz Claiborne Inc.	2,806,000,000
	TOTAL	$24,127,000,000

2004

1.	Sara Lee Branded Apparel	$6,449,000,000
2.	VF Corporation	6,054,500,000
3.	Jones Apparel Group	4,649,700,000
4.	Liz Claiborne Inc.	4,632,800,000
5.	Polo Ralph Lauren	3,303,400,000
	TOTAL	$25,089,400,000

The net sales of the top five public apparel companies in 1962, 1977, 1987, 1995, 1999, and 2004.

Sources: Fairchild's 1963 Textile & Apparel Financial Fact Book & Directory; Fairchild's 1978, 1980, & 1997 Textile & Apparel Financial Directory; *Apparel Industry Magazine,* August 2000; Hoover's Online, July 3, 2005.

| FIGURE 1.1 | NET ANNUAL SALES OF TOP FIVE PUBLICLY OWNED APPAREL COMPANIES |

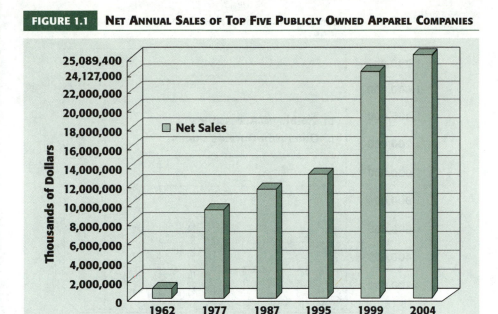

Growth in the apparel industry parallels the growth of the top five public apparel companies in the representative years 1962, 1977, 1987, 1995, 1999, and 2004.

in the share of total expenditures spent on apparel and services has been downward over the past several years possibly due to the competition of cheaper imported clothing, as well as a shift to more casual, less expensive styles." In addition, consumers are buying less of their apparel at the more expensive department store channel and more of their apparel at mass merchants and discounters. Furthermore, as reported on February 5, 2005, in the *Wall Street Journal* article "As Consumers Find Other Ways to Splurge, Apparel Hits a Snag," spending for electronics, home furnishings, home improvements, education, and healthcare has taken dollars away from spending for apparel. (See Figure 1.2.)

The extraordinary growth of the apparel industry during the last half of the twentieth century brought with it a heightened level of professional management. The industry shifted from an entrepreneurial generalist structure in which company owners made the critical marketing, product development, and manufacturing decisions to a professional specialist structure with marketing specialists, product development specialists, and manufacturing specialists. The larger, more complex businesses require highly trained executive specialists to manage the intricacies of the sophisticated apparel supply chain.

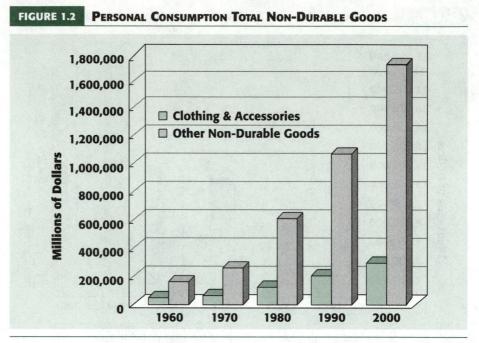

FIGURE 1.2 **PERSONAL CONSUMPTION TOTAL NON-DURABLE GOODS**

Personal consumption expenditures for clothing and accessories excluding luggage and shoes has increased dramatically during the past four decades rising from 21.4 billion dollars in 1961 to 250.7 billion dollars in 2000.

Supply Chain

To appreciate the complexities of the apparel industry, it is important to have a basic understanding of the industry **supply chain**, the system that provides the raw materials and processes necessary to get apparel products from concept to consumers. (See Figure 1.3.) There are five distinct sectors in the apparel supply chain.

1. The **fiber sector** includes the agro-industry for natural fiber production and petrochemicals for manufactured fibers also known as manmade fibers or synthetic fibers.
2. The **textile sector** includes yarn preparation, weaving or knitting, and fabric dyeing and finishing.
3. The **findings sector** covers a broad range of products that are integral to apparel production, such as buttons, zippers, labels, interfacings, pads, hook and loop fasteners, and thread.
4. The **apparel sector** is made up of companies that develop, manufacture, and distribute garments to the retail sector.

FIGURE 1.3 **APPAREL SUPPLY CHAIN**

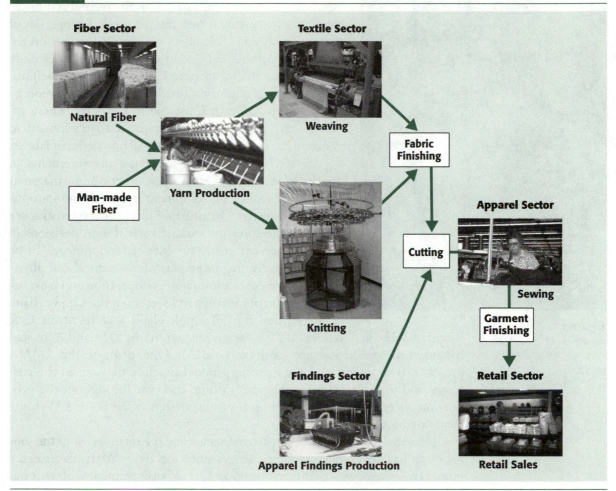

Apparel supply chain sectors from production of natural or man-made fibers through to the purchase of apparel by the consumer at retail.

5. It is the **retail sector** that must merchandise, promote, display, and sell products to the consumer.

The raw materials used in apparel products can create a technical nightmare for all sectors of the apparel supply chain. Fabrics have an unstable nature and complex **mechanical properties** (the properties of fabric created by the forces generated by the interaction of the fibers, yarns, and the fabric structure) such as stretch, slipperiness, stiffness, compressibility, abrasion resistance, shear, bending, and tensile strength. In addition, the physical properties of fab-

Figure 1.4 The expansion of the private label has led to the popularity of retailers such as Banana Republic.

rics (weight and thickness) combined with factors such as heat and moisture shrinkage add to the technical difficulties. Intensive research into the mechanical properties of raw materials and their effect on garments is performed by highly specialized facilities such as the Grundy Laboratories at Philadelphia University in Philadelphia, Pennsylvania, and the Textile Clothing Technology Corporation (TC)[2] in Cary, North Carolina. These research labs use specialized, sophisticated equipment to measure the mechanical and physical properties of fabrics.

Apparel manufacturers use these measurements to specify fabric requirements when ordering raw materials and to adjust stitching equipment in production for optimal performance. Quantifiable fabric characteristics are also valuable tools for making early design decisions in order to prevent costly product redevelopment. To be used effectively, measurements of mechanical and physical properties of fabrics require cooperation and trust between the textile and apparel sectors of the supply chain.

A detailed apparel supply chain analysis of the U.S. Integrated Textile Complex (ITC) was performed by the Demand Activated Manufacturing Architecture project (DAMA). One goal of the DAMA project was to understand the existing product pipeline that serves the customer and to look for potential gains in time and cost throughout the production system. Results of this project can be viewed at the DAMA Web site (**www.dama.tc2.com**).

The relationship between the apparel sector and the retail sector of the supply chain has undergone dramatic changes since the 1960s. Mergers created a more aggressive buyer-seller relationship and led to boring sameness of what was being produced. Leading industry executives share their views on the changes that the supply chain has undergone in "Quotes From The Pros" (see Page 11).

Advent of Style

The customers of the 1950s bought what the manufacturers produced. Style changes were subtle and slow to evolve until the baby boomers became the flower children in the early 1960s. What the apparel industry didn't provide, the younger generation filled in with feathers, beads, and tie-dyed clothing.

Teenage fashion became a new, rapidly growing category in the 1960s as Americans focused on doing their own thing. The 1960s had a dramatic effect on the apparel industry by transforming it into a consumer-driven market. Bertrand Frank of Bertrand Frank Associates, Inc., a management consultant, stressed the role of styled wear in focusing apparel companies on shortening product development cycles in an April 1969 article for *Bobbin* magazine.

Quotes From The Pros

"The relationships we developed over the years with the accounts no longer exist. Business is conducted in an entirely different way. Computers have more impact, and maybe rightly so, than a relationship that has been built between supplier and retailer. It's a numbers game. You have to play the game in order to exist. Before they even look at the line, the buyers want to know what kind of a markdown allowance they are getting. Adding to the difficulty is the fact that there are only about a dozen important suppliers. Today you have to be large, and you have to want to deal badly. You have to give your soul away in order to sell your merchandise. One must be able to provide good salable merchandise and then be prepared to sell it at very low margins.

"I think there is a new era coming where the little guy will have a chance again because the major suppliers are all producing very similar merchandise. If somebody can come up with something original and can catch the consumer's eye, he or she has a chance."

Max Raab—President, Villager and J. G. Hook

"In the past, merchandising was very removed from dealing with buyers and merchandise managers in stores. Today, sales and merchandising review with store executives merchandise opportunities that can be added to store assortments. For example, Dillards would like to have a colored cotton shirt program; Neiman Marcus would like to have a cashmere twin set sweater program. This item business is planned outside the regular line plan. For the most part, merchandising would source and plan the unit for a program requested by the store."

Colombe Nicholas—President, Anne Klein

"Large retailers got really comfortable with getting rebates from the manufacturers. The stores understood that everything was negotiable so they started asking for advertising; they started asking for sales help; they started asking for rebates. So a sale was actually never completed because it was negotiated after the product was sold. You kept negotiating.

"The buyers moved from the back of the sales floors. They moved to an ivory tower someplace where there is a computer that monitors point-of-purchase sales. Now they're not interested if the merchandise fits or doesn't fit. They're not interested if the colors don't match. All they're interested in is **sell-through** [the percentage of items purchased from a specific manufacturer that are sold to consumers during a specific period of time]. They call up the manufacturer and say, 'Your sell-through is no good. You want to do business with us, you have to give us a rebate.' That's kind of the rule right now, and retail stores have reengineered themselves to work this way. This is how they work now. This is how they think. They always have a fallback position to get something from their suppliers. They think they can negotiate themselves into profit no matter what happens. Everything is based on willingness to negotiate. The buyers keep negotiating their profits on your back. The result at the end of the century is that apparel at retail has become boring."

Bud Konheim—CEO, Nicole Miller

Case in Point 1.1

"Profits in Apparel, a New View"

The key to profits today is market acceptance. You have to produce what people will buy now, today, and do so in a way that at least brings you your proper profit margin, regularly.

Profit, sustained sound profit, is the goal of every apparel company, indeed every business. Profitability in the apparel industry long has been equated with efficiency and to some degree this still is true. But today, efficiency does not necessarily yield profits. It can, and sometimes does, bring huge losses, particularly when the efficiently produced garment cannot be marketed at the right price.

What do people buy today? They buy fewer staple or unchanging garments and more and more styled wear.

Staples are under attack from abroad. If you produce basic, staple apparel with exceptional efficiency, you may survive as domestic production shrinks. But Taiwan, Hong Kong, Portugal and some of the emerging nations even now land staple apparel here much cheaper than U.S. producers. They use the best equipment, pay pitiful wages and ship inexpensively.

How can you compete? Simple. The manufacturing cycle of 4, 8 or 10 months of foreign firms works against them. That long cycle can work for you if you let it. But you must make styled wear. Styled wear invites the relative uniqueness of product that minimizes competition and outflanks foreign production. The apparel industry trades, with fashion-oriented seasons—and certainly item business—turn those long cycles against imports and smother them. Foreign competition simply has too long a manufac-turing cycle to compete with fast-moving, style changes.

However, some better, styled garments now are flown over from Hong Kong and Milan yet undercut competition. So, either you move into low to medium priced styled wear (possibly into better goods) with its admitted risks but proven profits, or you battle for pennies on basics.

It works almost everywhere in apparel, The men's and boys' shirt industry is rapidly moving to fancies, knits, almost a costume look—all timed to stimulate consumer desires. This merchandise sells at abnormal prices that profitably cover the risk of close-outs. Others, such as lingerie, house dresses, and even staid men's clothing have begun to parallel this move.

Style then, is the focal point and a marketing orientation to rapid change throughout the Company, is the answer.

Speed Is Essential

New styles however, must move quickly from acceptance of the season's line through production to shipping. The cycle time, the time for the entire procedure, must be short, or the risk of style failure skyrockets.

Short cycles hedge risk; long ones lengthen the pipeline risk, geometrically.

Cycle time falls into two categories: Pre-production and Production.

(continued)

Preproduction cycle is normally defined as either that time taken from starting to design a style or a line, or from style acceptance by merchandising, to the time that it is in a position to be manufactured. **Production cycle** is defined as the time from availability for marking in of garment patterns and fabric cutting through finishing and delivery to the stock room for shipping.

Preproduction cycles of six or even ten months are not unusual and, indeed, may in the past have not been too important. Today though, the advent of ever more style and the necessity to be as close to the needs of the market as possible (three or four weeks) have shown that the preproduction cycle is now perhaps one of the most important and vital areas of potential improvement in the apparel company.

The shorter the cycle time, the more likely it is that the merchandising function will be effective. This is simply because the needs of the market are better known two or three months from a delivery date then they are ten or twelve months before. A long cycle time often results in heavier than desirable close-outs of garments and excessive piece goods holdings, because of the need to order and commit fabrics early.

To complicate matters, all too many companies not only have a long preproduction cycle, but often incorrectly perform some of the major elements in it. A fairly representative example of this would be the often halfhearted attempt at pre-costing the line prior to selection. Another would be the relative absence of value engineering prior to and immediately after merchandise acceptance. It is important that if a company's profits are to be optimized, every effort be made to build as much profit into an individual style as is possible. This is a far more complex technique than simply relying on a merchandiser's or president's intuition.

It is by no means uncommon to find companies with long pre-production cycles also having a long production cycle. This, of course simply compounds the risks and problems inherent in playing, the "style and fashion game." (Production cycles repeatedly have been discussed by us. We have engineered several styled wear shops for a normal, three-week delivery from fabric release onward, with five to seven day normal stitch time.)

It is, of course, difficult to quantify in terms of dollars the exact benefits which result from shortening the pre-production and production cycle times. Yet, few companies would doubt that it is perhaps one of the most important profit-making endeavors available to them.

Bertrand Frank Associates, Inc., have, over the past several years, developed investigative analyses to apply a systems approach to the shortening of the pre-production and production cycles. The results have in many companies, been spectacular. To reduce the time by one-third or even one-half is by no means unique. However, it is a complex proposition, for it calls not alone for the application of cold engineering or operations research techniques. It also calls for intimate understanding of the garment business. Many of the problems are at least as much emotional as they are technical, for those functions which are a part of the pre-production cycle are prone to the development of individual empires supported by rationalizations by the people involved.

One example of this tendency to take excess time—perhaps as added insurance against

(continued)

errors—can be found in the designing function itself. Often, designers claim the sacrosanct right of creativity. Meanwhile, for all practical purposes, the company needs deadline styling. Ways have to be found in which both of these needs can be satisfied within the profit structure of the individual company.

We have found that many companies with the best of intentions, develop time targets showing the dates by which the various parts of the preproduction cycle should be completed. On close analysis, these times are more often based on when the style is needed to be finished rather than reflecting the time that each function actually should take. This produces a position where the maximum permissible times are almost always taken. People proceed not to try to reduce the amount of time involved in each of their jobs, but are simply satisfied to achieve the company's schedule. Therefore, the beginning of the production cycle is evermore distant from the end of it.

We use as a part of this analysis technique, PERT (Critical Path) and comparable procedures, tied to operations research techniques, such as queuing, etc. The first step is to define, using these techniques, precisely the time now being used for each function. Next, we analyze the validity and the quality of the information produced.

Then, charting study and experience produce new or changed sequences among and within jobs. Finally, parallel activities, work elimination, combination or simplification yield sharply shorter and far less costly pre-production and production cycles.

Short cycles clearly save money in capital costs, pre-production executive and clerical labor, and in smooth handling of production in swiftly flowing, well established plants. However, the major result of short cycles is in more assured profits. Merchandising risks are truly narrowed by taking decisions on styling and cuttings only a few weeks, rather than several months, prior to actual completion of the pre-production and production phases. Anyone can put the wrong merchandise into work. But lengthy cycles amplify the commitment and risk to resounding proportions with potentially huge closeouts that can end profits and mount losses.

So, fast cycles of preproduction sharply cut merchandising risks. They also limit foreign competition and truly save money. Repeatedly, their introduction has substantially enhanced profits. ∎

From Bertrand Frank, Bertrand Frank Associates, Inc., Management Consultants, New York. April 1969. *Bobbin*, pp. 101–103.

Case in Point 1.1   Summary

This case in point identifies the importance of controlling the pre-production and production cycles to enhance profitability. "Deadline styling" requires skillful, disciplined management control. In many companies it is the responsibility of the merchandiser to control the elements of the product development process as well

as sourcing the production. The constant change and subtle shifts in consumer fashion tastes require merchandisers to be constantly tuned in to their target market. With change comes *risk*. The rapidly evolving function of apparel merchandising could be compared to risk management with the added requirement of extreme creativity. A successful merchandiser must possess keen business skills as well as a creative eye for design. The varied functions and attributes of an apparel merchandiser are analyzed in detail in subsequent chapters. ■

"The key to profits today is market acceptance. You have to produce what people will buy now, today, and do so in a way that at least brings you your proper profit margin, regularly . . . What do people buy today? They buy fewer staple or unchanging garments and more and more styled wear. . . . Styled wear invites the relative uniqueness of product that minimizes competition and outflanks foreign production" (Frank, 1969).

As the 1960s progressed, the country's growing fascination with style generated a new crop of designers—Oleg Cassini, Anne Klein, Halston, and Bill Blass. By the late 1960s Calvin Klein, Ralph Lauren, and a retail casual wear chain that developed big name recognition, Gap, entered the fashion scene.

The 1960s and 1970s saw an explosion of U.S. apparel company mergers and the rapid growth of the new "designer" labels. The apparel industry experienced the emergence of giant publicly owned corporations. In 1971 a 28-year-old designer, Diane Von Furstenberg, made a big splash on the fashion scene with her jersey wrap dress. In 1975 Geoffrey Beene made his indelible mark on the fashion world as one of the first American designers to be featured in European runway shows. Liz Claiborne entered the fashion wars in 1976 with the concept of clothing America's working women in style and color. Her company shot to the top of the fashion marketplace where it remained among the top five apparel corporations throughout the last decade of the twentieth century.

To help serve the growing need for lower-priced apparel for the baby boomers, a new category of discount department stores, Kmart, Woolco, Target, and Wal-Mart, became major retail players. These retail giants created a new demand for more and more apparel product lines providing fresh new silhouettes, fabrics, prints, and colors.

The 1980s and 1990s added Donna Karan, Nicole Miller, Betsey Johnson, Perry Ellis, Tommy Hilfiger, Ann Taylor, Albert Nipon, Rena Rowan, Marc Jacobs, and a host of other new designers to the growing cadre of U.S. fashion names. In the 1980s the maturing tastes of some of the baby boomers, who metamorphosed into yuppies, ushered in a new style category, contemporary fashions.

The growth of shopping centers and suburban malls as well as the revitalization of urban shopping districts that started in the 1970s was an enor-

Figure 1.5
Abercrombie and Fitch is an example of successful retailers that are represented in many of the suburban malls.

mous boon to retail fashion outlets. This in turn increased the demand for more fashion products.

Brands and the concept of the private label proliferated during this period. Retailers such as the Gap, Banana Republic, the Limited, Express, and Old Navy developed, produced, and sold their own product lines. JCPenney created Arizona Jeans, Worthington, and Hunt Club. Federated Department Stores developed its I.N.C. and Alfani lines, while Sears came out with Canyon River Blues. Kmart called on actress Jaclyn Smith to represent its own line of clothes, and Wal-Mart introduced its highly successful Kathie Lee Gifford, Mary Kate and Ashley, and George lines.

Jeans are a perfect example of the dramatic growth of styles, brands, and companies that entered this popular market. In the 1960s there were few brands and styles to choose from. Levi's®, Wranglers®, and Lee® were the major purveyors of blue jeans. Today the list has grown dramatically and includes: Levi, Wrangler, Lee, Calvin Klein, Polo Jeans Co., Gloria Vanderbilt, Liz Sport, Claiborne, DKNY, Guess, JNCO, Fubu, Mudd, Bugle Boy, Eddie Bauer, Paris Blues, LEI, Tommy Hilfiger, Express, Abercrombie and Fitch, American Outfitter, Union Bay, Canyon River Blues, Faded Glory, Arizona, the Gap, Blue Cult, Paige Denim, and Frankie B.

The tail end of the millenium redefined the product category **active sportswear** or **activewear**, which is functional as well as stylish clothing designed to improve the performance or comfort of the wearer while participating in a particular sport or activity. This category grew to support the running, biking, tennis, in-line skating, and fitness crazes. Brand names like Adidas, Nike, Nautica, Fila, Champion, Russell, Columbia, Prince, Converse, Reebok, Moving Comfort, Everlast, and hundreds of innovative new companies were added to the exploding apparel industry.

In the late 1990s this new market raised the bar another notch with a fashion category for "extreme sports." Specialized gear for rock climbing, mountain biking, snowboarding, triathlons, extreme skiing, sea kayaking, and roller hockey added a new dimension to design criteria: protection from extreme conditions of climate and terrain. Waterproof, breathable fabrics; shock resistant, neoprene, body clinging, spandex and microfiber blends; performance fleeces; and other exotic high-tech fabrics and constructions became new requirements in the ever-expanding technology base for active sportswear.

Gerard P. Mandry, vice president of marketing planning for the Arrow Company summed it up nicely in an *Apparel Industry Magazine* article. "There was a time when an Arrow shirt salesman could walk into an account with advance proofs for Arrow ads in *The Saturday Evening Post* and walk out with the next season's orders. In those days, the art of marketing men's shirts was at a stage where a quality product at the right price, advertising dominance in a leading national medium, plus a little advance planning could keep a major brand like Arrow on top of the heap.

"Today it's a different market," Mandry stressed. "Shirts are offered in countless fabrics—knit, woven, 100 percent Qiana, dozens of different fiber blends, plus the strong entry of a new 100 percent cotton called Sanfor-set™. Collars that stayed the same for years are suddenly exploding in dimension and shape on a monthly basis. Then there is the question of exact sleeve lengths vs. average sleeve lengths. And finally, today's customer demands an incredible variety of color, texture, and pattern from which to choose." Mr. Mandry's comments weren't made to usher in space-age fabrics of the twenty-first century or the 1990s style explosion; his article appeared in 1978 (Mandry, 1978).

In the beginning of the 21st Century, mega apparel companies increased their presence in the retailing sector of the apparel supply chain. Polo Ralph Lauren and Nike opened additional stores. Gloria Vanderbilt has plans for boutiques in Los Angeles, Hong Kong, and Paris to join those in New York, Miami, and London. VF Corporation has opened stores in China. Guess expanded in Europe and is now looking to Asia. American Apparel will have 50 stores by 2007. Jones Apparel group bought Nine West and Barneys New York. Liz Claiborne purchased Mexx, an international retailer with 600 stores, and also added to their locations of Lucky Brand, Sigrid Olsen, Ellen Tracy, and Juicy Couture. Retailers also diversified as exemplified by Sears buying Lands' End and May Company purchasing David's Bridal.

Figure 1.6 An example of store brands is Sears' Canyon River Blues.

The beginnings of the 21st Century also brought consumer dissatisfaction with the sameness of the merchandise from one store to another. When consumers can find value priced apparel in stores such as Wal-Mart and Target, they need added incentive to buy apparel in department and specialty stores. These incentives are fashion and assortment. Both national branded merchandisers and private branded product developers must meet the twin challenges of providing a broad assortment of fashionable garments to their targeted market.

Textile Innovation

The textile industry added a new dimension to the complex decisions facing product developers in the apparel industry. Up until the 1950s most garments were made of natural fibers such as cotton, wool, linen, and silk. This all

Figure 1.7 Extreme sportswear includes apparel for aggressive outdoor activities such as mountain biking.

changed when nylon, aramid, and acrylic fibers were produced commercially after World War II. Brand-name synthetic fibers began flooding the market starting in the 1950s. Acrilan™, Creslan™, Dynel™, Lycra™, Dacron™, Kodel™, Trevira™, and Fortrel™ are just a few of the commercially successful brand-name fibers that revolutionized the apparel industry. In the 1970s and 1980s texturizing and special finishes created hundreds of new fabric options. In 1991 DuPont introduced the first microdenier fiber with the trade name Micromattique (Hudson, Clapp, and Kness, 1993).

Malden Mills hit a grand slam with its Polartec™ brand of polyester fleece, which took the 1990s' activewear and casual sportswear markets by storm, then expanded into all categories of rtw (ready-to-wear), even lightweight fleece for summer garments. Tactel™ nylon by DuPont and Ultra Touch™ by BASF entered the U.S. intimate apparel market in 1997. Increasing demand for comfortable foundation garments has targeted microfibers as a boom category for the new century (Monget, 1998).

The last 2 years of the twentieth century introduced branded DyerTech fabric from Dyersburg. It was designed for moisture control, thermal retention, and windproofing. DuPont's marketing focused on its high-performance MicroSupplex. Tactel™ SuperMatte provided a supersoft microfiber, and Tactel Diablo brought a silk-type luster and ease of care to intimate apparel and rtw programs. BASF kept pace with its soft Ultra Touch high-filament product (Chirls, 1998).

Kinder, gentler synthetics with the look and feel of natural fibers further expanded the rapidly growing fabric market. Westridge Naturals, a 500-denier Cordura nylon, was introduced by Brookwood to emulate cotton canvas.

Finishes have also complicated the fabric decisions of apparel companies. The branded chemical finish Intera adds moisture-management properties to fabric, allowing perspiration to pass through the fabric and evaporate while claiming to add mildew resistance and odor resistance. New finishes also focus on natural fiber fabrics like cotton, providing wrinkle and soil resistance, color retention, shrinkage control, and ultraviolet protection (Holch, 1998).

These innovative technologies opened up exciting options for apparel designers: fabrics with the drape and feel of silk; fabrics with incredible thermal qualities; and new options for water-resistant, wind-proof, breathable fabrics.

The application of nanotechnology to the manufacture of fabrics used in apparel allows for greatly improved performance. In the April 2005 issue of *Worth Magazine*, Steven Frumpkin, a professor at Philadelphia University, wrote an article called "Smartly Dressed." In it he mentions that nanotechnology applications created fabrics that resist spills, wrinkles, odor and bacteria, and the formation of static electricity. Also, the fabrics repel and release stains, and increase moisture wicking, which keeps your body dry and cool. To date, Levi Strauss, Haggar, Eddie Bauer, and Gap have offered apparel that promote these attributes. He refers to Nano-Tex (**www.nano-tex.com**) and Crypton Fabrics, which are behind the use of nanotechnology.

At the same time, the technologies dramatically increased the number of options for creating exciting new fashion styles. The task of sorting through the myriad of options fell to the ever-expanding responsibilities of the apparel merchandiser.

Computer Applications

The microprocessor revolution has permanently altered the apparel industry landscape. Macs, PCs, and proprietary computer hardware and software have changed the way fashion styles are created, garment patterns are designed, markers are made, fabric is cut, work-in-process is transported and monitored, sewing machines are controlled, finished garments are selected and packed, invoices are created, and retail sales are monitored.

Today, in every phase of supply chain management, the computer plays a very important role. **Electronic data interchange** (**EDI**), the transfer of information between computers, eliminates the need for paper purchase orders, manual data input for ordering and receiving raw materials, manual logging of manufacturing production orders, manual processing of worker piece-rate earnings, manual recording and monitoring of production bundles, and preparation of shipping documents. Even when garments are sold at retail, EDI plays an important function for many companies. **Point-of-sale** (at the cash register in a retail store) capture of critical style, size, and color information on bar-coded hangtags is transmitted in **real time** (the actual point in time that the event takes place) to the apparel manufacturer. Retailers' computer databases maintain complete supplier histories containing quality performance, delivery records, product sell-through analyses, average maintained markups—in short, a complete report card of an apparel company's performance.

Liz Claiborne began using point-of-sale information as its own best market analysis (Owens, 1998). Levi Strauss uses the computer to reach consumers through its **levi.com** Web site where a visitor can browse through Levi products or determine his or her style preferences. The jeans giant also created the Levi's Original Spin™ program, which allowed consumers to design their own jeans using computer kiosks in select stores. Lands' End added My Virtual Model™ to their Web site, which allows consumers to see how various styles would look based upon their individual measurements.

"The major change that I saw in the apparel industry in the past half century was the advent of the computer . . . The important decisions from 1980 to the present have been based upon the computer printout of your perfor-

Figure 1.8 The home page of the levi.com Web site where a visitor can browse through Levi's® products online.

mance report card. Do you deliver on time? Does your product sell-through at retail?" This is how Andrew Kahn, chief executive officer of Kahn Lucas Lancaster, Inc., rates the importance of the computer.

Global Transition

Since the apparel industry is **labor-intensive** (requiring a large expenditure of labor in comparison to capital) and start-up costs for manufacturing apparel products are relatively inexpensive, this industry is very attractive to emerging third world countries. Most apparel products require a lot of skilled hand labor to manufacture. Due to the complex variable mechanical properties of fabric (also referred to as soft goods), the apparel industry has had only marginal success in automating sewing operations. The handling of limp, flexible, slippery, stretchy fabric has made picking up and positioning a single ply and controlling it under the needle and feed dog of a sewing machine a task that has stymied even the expertise of the scientists who put a man on the moon. Technology has not been able to duplicate the sensitivity of human fingers. Therefore, the workers in most emerging countries who possess high levels of manual dexterity have proven to be ideal candidates for apparel manufacturing employment.

Starting in the early 1960s, apparel companies began moving production to the Far East. Apparel employment in the United States fell by one-quarter from 1967 to 1987 (Taplin, 1997). Domestic employment continued to drop as apparel companies chased low-cost labor in every corner of the world. (See Table 1.2.) By the 1990s apparel imports caught up to and surpassed domestic production.

Not only are apparel companies manufacturing their products in the far reaches of the globe, but they are also finding new markets in which to sell those products. Andrea Engel, vice president of production and merchandising at Eagle's Eye, is amazed by the changes. "The U.S. is a declining market with the baby boomers fading. China and India and South America are becoming the great new middle-class markets. It blows you away. It is unbelievable. As an American, you could be working for a company like Nike, sourcing product in Mexico that's shipped to and sold in Costa Rica."

Apparel has become a global industry requiring executives who understand the international business environment as well as the technical complexities of garment manufacturing.

■ Structural Changes in the Apparel Industry

Societal changes, such as more women in the workplace and an expanding middle class, brought about an increased demand in people's clothing needs, which in turn created a consumer-driven marketplace. The apparel industry experienced dramatic growth, and new technologies provided manufacturers with the ability to respond quickly to change. The textile industry created new generations of fabrics from **microfibers** (modified, extremely fine denier, synthetic yarns that often have the feel and functionality of natural fibers), weeds,

TABLE 1.2

Apparel Employment

1990	929,100	1998	639,000
1991	902,600	1999	555,600
1992	905,200	2000	496,800
1993	882,500	2001	426,500
1994	856,300	2002	359,700
1995	814,100	2003	312,300
1996	743,100	2004	284,800
1997	703,200		

Employment statistics in the apparel manufacturing industry continued their steady decline in the 1990s and the early 2000s.

Source: Bureau of Labor Statistics, **http://data.bls.gov/cgi-bin/srgate**

and even recycled soft drink bottles. Apparel manufacturing went global as it searched for cheaper labor. The two seasons per year of the early 1960s became seasonless years with new styles being presented to retailers almost monthly. All these factors created turmoil in the fashion business. Fashion trends changed faster than the speed of hype. Gone were the days of manufacturing departments tweaking every penny to achieve company profits. Today's successful apparel company must determine what the consumers want and see to it that they get it when they want it and at a competitive price that still allows for profit. Overproduction of a particular style can result in **markdowns** (a reduction of the original wholesale or retail price), which cut into company profits. On the other hand, if too little of a particular style is produced, the result is lost sales, which also reduces company profits.

James Oesterreicher, chairman and CEO of JCPenney Co., told AAMA (American Apparel Manufacturers Association) members that consumers' demands seem impossible to fulfill, noting that they want products that are constantly innovative, immediately available, in styles and colors that fit their whims, and only if they "can get it for as close to zero as possible" (Ostroff, 1998).

The complex job of developing, executing, and delivering a product line based upon the needs of a target market is the responsibility of the apparel merchandiser. The task must be performed with a focus on meeting the overall objectives of the merchandiser's firm. The individual with the responsibility for this function may be given many different titles: merchandiser, product development manager, design manager, merchandising director, design director, creative director, product manager. In many of today's larger companies this function may be broken down into more specialized areas of responsibility such as general merchandising, creative design, technical design, sourcing, and quality management. However, there is one common denominator. In every company someone must make the decisions concerning design direction and which garment styles get adopted into the product line. This same someone must see to it that the garments get made in time to meet customer demand. Thus, the process of **apparel merchandising** may be defined as the development, execution, and delivery of a product line based upon the needs of a target market.

The position, responsibilities, and authority of the apparel merchandiser evolved as apparel companies made the transition from the traditional focus on production efficiency to the more recent focus on changing consumer needs. This evolution took place over 50 years and involved five distinct structural changes in the typical apparel organization.

Stage 1

The structure in Stage 1 represents the immediate post-World War II era where sales representatives took orders and the manufacturing division of a company maintained stock positions. The profitability of the company was dependent primarily on efficient manufacturing. Under this structure manufacturing executives wielded tremendous power within the organization and within the industry. (See Figure 1.9a)

Stage 2

In the early 1960s, brand recognition became very important. The concept of marketing was embraced by the apparel industry to evaluate consumer needs and strengthen the image of growing apparel companies through advertising and promotion. The marketing function was added to company structures. The rapid growth of many apparel companies also created a new focus on finance and cost containment, introducing the function of finance and administration. (See Figure 1.9b)

Stage 3

In the late 1960s the companies that embraced modern marketing concepts prospered, and the marketing executives took on increased responsibilities and authority within the organization. Understanding the need to fulfill consumer demands, product development departments were established with creative design capabilities. In many companies the marketing executive absorbed the responsibility for product development along with sales. Since marketing was primarily a business function, the responsibility for the creative aspect of design brought with it a new management challenge. To bridge the gap between rigid business structure and creativity, a new function emerged: merchandising. Early merchandisers focused on overseeing the design function to ensure that market data were interpreted into desirable product lines in a timely manner. (See Figure 1.9c)

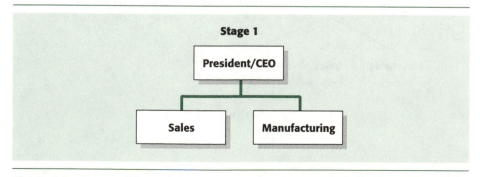

Figure 1.9a Stage 1 of the evolution of the merchandising function during which sales took the customers' orders and manufacturing provided the finished garments to fill the orders.

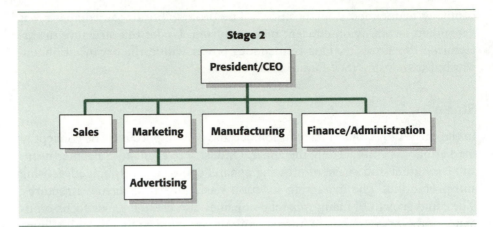

Figure 1.9b Stage 2 of the evolution of the merchandising function adds marketing to evaluate consumer needs and to strengthen a company's image. Finance and administration was established as a separate management function to focus on financing and cost containment.

Stage 4

In the 1970s and 1980s those companies that were able to successfully interpret the rapidly changing whims of the fashion-buying public into fresh new styles prospered. This prosperity depended on the talents of the new breed of professional apparel merchandisers. In some companies or in the product di-

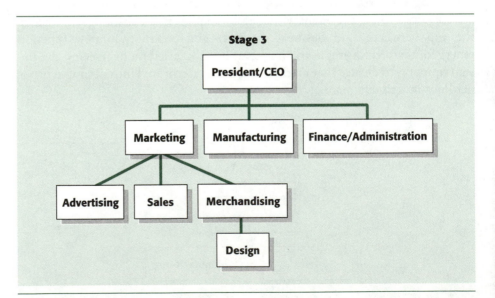

Figure 1.9c Stage 3 of the evolution of the merchandising function shows the emergence of product development with creative design capabilities to meet the needs of the consumer. Merchandising was established to oversee and control the design function.

visions of larger companies, the management skills and creative abilities of merchandisers enabled them to become presidents. At this point, most established manufacturing companies were looking to **global sourcing** (contracting production in factories worldwide) in order to lower prices. In fact, many new designer labels did not have their own manufacturing facilities. In many companies sourcing fell under the purview of the merchandiser. During this period the merchandiser rose to a level equal to marketing in the management hierarchy. Product development became vital to the success of apparel companies, and the merchandiser was the key to that success. (See Figure 1.9d)

Norton Binder, former executive vice president at Joan Vass, USA, sums up the transition of merchandising well. "The role of the merchandiser has always been important, but I think now they are finally getting recognition. In the early years the sales manager used to be the god. If he brought in the business, that's all you needed. But as competition increased and stores combined into larger conglomerates with fewer buyers, the merchandiser became more important. What to make became more important than how much of it to make."

Stage 5

Due to the increasing complexities of product development and global sourcing as well as the extraordinary amount of time required to set up and monitor the sourcing process, some companies have established sourcing as a separate function. This allows merchandisers to focus all their efforts on the creative process and on product development. In some companies, this also in-

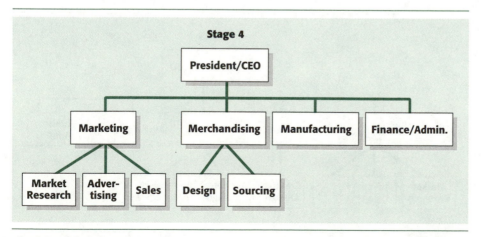

Figure 1.9d Stage 4 of the evolution of the merchandising function witnessed product development and global sourcing becoming vital to the success of apparel companies. As the key to this success, the merchandising function rose to equal the importance of the marketing function.

cluded the functions of technical design. In recent years, with the increase in **full-package sourcing** (contracting to purchase a style where the contractor provides fabrics, trims, supplies, and labor), the contractor may also do the technical design. Under these circumstances, the apparel company has still retained the role of approving the prototype before the beginning of production.

The current initiative of companies within the apparel supply chain is to strive to reduce the cycle time to develop and bring products to the selling floor from an average of 12 months to an average of 6 months. In his presentation to the Enterprise Competitive Council of the American Apparel and Footwear Association in January 2005, David Bassuk, Principal at Kurt Salmon Associates, spoke of "The 7 Habits of Highly Effective Product Development." In his approach to reducing cycle time, he mentioned the application of the newest technologies, such as Product Life Cycle Management. He also mentioned the collaboration of spec development and the ultimate transfer of these activities to Asia, including the approval of the prototype, complete transparency and visibility of the product development and production to all partners in the supply chain, and the elimination of separate product development and sourcing groups. The future evolution of the role of the merchandiser might once again include sourcing, as was the case in Stage 4.

The direction in larger companies is frequently toward higher levels of management specialization, utilizing a team approach for critical decision making. Even under this more specialized structure, the functions of development, execution, and delivery of the product line based upon the needs of the target market remain central to the success of an apparel company. (See Figure 1.9e)

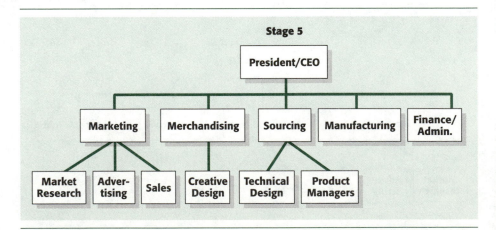

Figure 1.9e Stage 5 of the evolution of the merchandising function responds to the increasing complexities of global sourcing by establishing this function as a separate management responsibility. This allows merchandising to dedicate all of its attention to the creative process and product development.

■ Private Label and Private Brand Apparel

Retailers have moved rapidly into developing their own apparel products. These apparel lines are referred to as **private labels** or **private brands,** which are exclusive to a specific retailer.

The concept of private label was first introduced by retailers in basic or generic products that could be offered at lower prices than the brands. These products were used by retailers as pricing incentives during promotional periods and provided higher margins than branded merchandise. Private label products were often inexpensive knockoffs of designer fashions, often a year behind the runway styles. As the use of private label products expanded in importance to the retailer, many of them invested in merchandising teams to add more style content to their offerings.

The success of private label apparel spawned the emergence of an important new concept for retailers. Today we are seeing more and more emphasis on private brands. The primary difference between private labels and private brands is that private brands are categories of apparel that completely commit to a certain lifestyle and a specific customer demographic. They are given the star treatment as if they were designer labels, advertised in newspapers like national brands, and heavily promoted in the stores. This allows consumers to develop a commitment to a private brand that has its own design integrity and identity. Private brands are designed to compete head-to-head with national brands.

Examples of apparel merchandise concepts exclusive to a specific retailer:

- All merchandise in the store carries the name of the retailer such as GAP, Brooks Brothers, Banana Republic, and Eddie Bauer.
- A retailer develops their own private brand. Federated Department Stores has INC and Charter Club. JCPenney has Arizona and Stafford. Kohl's has Sonoma.
- Branded apparel companies develop special brands for specific retailers. Liz Claiborne sells Axcess, Russ, and Villager brands. Levi sells Signature brand.
- A retailer may license a name and then develop the brand on its own with assistance from a third party or an apparel company. Target uses this process with their Todd Oldham and Mossimo brands. Kmart has Joe Boxer and Martha Stewart.
- A buying office can develop a private brand and sell it to its clients. At one time the Doneger Group offered Spectacle Repertoire and Greg Adams to their members.

Examples of private label and private brands:

- Wal-Mart   Faded Glory, Mary-Kate and Ashley, Kathie Lee Gifford
- Target   Cherokee, Isaac Mizrahi, Mossimo

- Sears*   Canyon River Blues, Lands' End, Covington
- Kmart*   Joe Boxer, Jaclyn Smith, Martha Stewart
- JCPenney   Arizona, Stafford, St. John's Bay
- Federated   Alfani, Jennifer Moore, INC, Charter Club
- Kohl's   Sonoma, Croft and Borrow, Daisy Fuentes
- Gap   All of their merchandise
- Nordstrom   Halogen, Classics Entier, Pure Stuff, Nordstrom

*Before merger into Sears Holdings

History of Private Label and Private Brand Apparel

Until the final decades of the 20th Century, apparel companies refused to sell their national brands to national chains such as JCPenney and Sears. Establishing private labels was the solution for both mass merchants and manufacturers. National chains could stock their shelves with private label garments from branded manufacturers and the branded manufacturers could supply these stores without endangering loss of their branded sales to their department store and specialty store accounts.

Private label was also a strategy that allowed department stores to offer better value to their consumers without cannibalizing their national branded business. Branded manufacturers could offer private label products at lower prices because there were no marketing and advertising costs.

When large retailing organizations began to develop their own private label products, they focused on basic apparel with little or no fashion content. As private label developed and became an important part of retail apparel sales, retailers began adding fashion content by developing their own merchandising and design capabilities. As retailers initiated their own sourcing either directly with a manufacturing contractor or by using a third party, they also had to assume all of the risks associated with producing fashion merchandise. To reduce these risks, their early private label lines became repeats of previous seasons' successes. National brands were adding to the sameness by flooding the marketplace with similar styles. The result was that each retailing organization had the same looks on their selling floors at the same time.

At the beginning of the 21st Century, the largest retailing organizations were looking for product differentiation as well as value to attract consumers. Federated, JCPenney, and, to some degree, Target committed their resources (fixtures, floor space, advertising) to market and position their private label products to compete side-by-side with the national brands. Their consumer research determined that having a product at a good price was not enough. The consumer either demands the lowest price and is willing to wait for the lowest price for national brands at store, discounter, or manufacturers' outlets, or wants a product that expresses "fashion freshness."

Since research showed that shoppers do not care who owns the brand, as long as the label gives them what they want, retailers realized they had an opportunity to develop and promote their own private brand merchandise to compete with branded labels. A July 21, 2003 press release by NPD Fashionworld indicated that private brand merchandise represented 36 percent of the apparel market. In the January 20, 2005 edition of *WWD*, Terry Lundgren, the chairman, CEO, and president of Federated Department Stores, states, "Private brands have been the most successful business in our stores"—including INC, Alfani, and Charter Club which does more volume than any other brand sold at Macy's.

The evolution of the proprietary labels developed by retailers allows them to differentiate themselves from their competitors and achieve above-average margins, usually around 10 percent higher than well-known national brands. Private brands allow retailers to stand out with a freshness and distinctiveness that creates the same consumer loyalty to a retailer as to the exclusive brands that they carry.

Today there is a need for retailers to have a constant flow of private label, private brand, and national branded apparel, which demands renewed efforts to reduce the time of bringing fresh products to market. As the proprietary programs grow, retailers are redefining their roles in market research, design, product development, sourcing and logistics. This requires a staff that is qualified to perform the functions this text ascribes to *Apparel Merchandising*: the development, execution, and delivery of a product line.

Role of Traditional Manufacturers

The traditional manufacturer is responsible for developing an exclusive line to meet the seasonal needs of a retailer according to predetermined prices and specifications. An exclusive label can be owned by a manufacturer such as Villager by Liz Claiborne, nicole by Nicole Miller, Riders by VF Corporation, and A Line by Jones. Isaac Mizrahi, Mossimo, and Cherokee are examples of labels provided to retailers through a licensing arrangement.

The manufacturers meet in advance with their retailer partners to plan the line. They then design their lines and present them to the retailers for their selection. Once confirmed orders are received, production takes place either in company owned or contractor facilities. The manufacturers hold the inventory until agreed upon shipping dates. Excess inventory is held until the retailer gives instructions for its disposition.

Frank Bracken, president and chief operating officer of Haggar, says, "Success in the private label business depends on three issues: global sourcing capabilities, product leadership, and the ability to keep customers in-stock."

The success of private labels and private brands puts pressure on branded apparel producers to show consumers effective product differentiation. Branded manufacturers must understand that private label, private brand, and branded products can co-exist, but there must be reasons for both. Consumers will have the final word when they choose the products that meet their styling and pricing needs.

Role of Retailers

Retailers must determine strategies for private labels and private brands as compared to national brands. Today's shoppers are not concerned about who owns the brand, whether it's a manufacturer or a retailer. Their focus is on whether a garment style meets their fashion needs at a price that they are willing to pay. A style must resonate with the consumer. This requires a thorough understanding of a retailer's target customer: age group, fit requirements, lifestyle, geographic considerations, and all demographic factors. It's not enough for a retailer to have the same products as their competitors. They must present products that stand out as unique and attractive in the eyes of their customers.

A department store may have multiple private brands that relate to different segments of their customer base. Joe Feczko, executive vice president and chief creative officer of Macy's Corporate Marketing, identifies four lifestyle buckets for his company's private brands. They cover traditional, neo-traditional, contemporary, and fashion customers. Charter Club is geared toward the classic, traditional market. The Style & Company private brand is a centered, neo-traditional brand, which caters to more moderate price points, while the INC line targets a neo-traditional to contemporary class of customer.

The retailer must determine a strategy for their private label and private brand products relative to the national brands. This strategy must include the volume private label and private brand merchandise represents as a percentage of sales. A 2005 Just-style.com report shows the importance private labels and private brands represent to a sampling of major retailers:

TABLE 1.3

Company	Private/Exclusive Brand as % of Sales	Policy
Wal-Mart	70-80%	Private label: Bobbie Brooks, George Licensed brands: Faded Glory, Mary-Kate and Ashley, No Boundaries, White Stag
Gap	100%	All Gap products are sold under the brand of the fascia concerned. Virtually 100% internally designed

TABLE 1.3 (*continued*)

Company	Private/exclusive brand as % of sales	Policy
Target	60-70%	Cherokee, Isaac Mizrahi, Liz Lange, Merona, Mossimo, Todd Oldham
May Department Stores	25%	Identity, i.e., Ideology, Valerie Stevens, Exceed, Kate Hill, Metropolitan by Lord & Taylor
JCPenney	40%	Penney-branded clothing. Exclusive: Arizona Jeans, Delicates, St. John's Bay, Stafford, Worthington
Sears	40-50%	Exclusive brands: Lands' End, Covington, Canyon River Basics, Apostrophe, and Lucy Pereda
Federated Department Stores	30%	Private label, plus exclusive brands: Greendog, Alfani, American Rags, First Impressions, Style & Co.

To achieve successful private label and private brand programs, retailers must carefully research their target markets and utilize their point-of-sale data to develop apparel lines that meet the needs of their customers. They must develop accurate line plans for their exclusive product lines either in-house, with apparel company providers such as Kellwood, Haggar, and Carol Hochman Designs, or with third-party providers such as Li and Fung and Luen Thai. They must then contract production through their retail buying offices, with apparel companies providing them exclusive labels, directly with outside contractors, or through third-party providers. Throughout the entire process, they must monitor point-of-sale data to make adjustments to pricing and deliveries.

In the arena of private label and private brands, retailers take responsibility for the hidden costs related to developing, sourcing, executing, delivering, and promoting their exclusive apparel lines. When retailers enter this arena, they are playing the role of manufacturer and retailer and must shoulder the responsibilities associated with this dual role. They no longer have a national brand manufacturer to share some of the burden of overruns, markdowns, and excess costs.

Role of Sourcing Organizations

To be successful in providing retailers with private label and private brand products, sourcing organizations must expand their services beyond simply acting as a middle man between the retailer and contract factories. Third-party providers such as Li and Fung or Luen Thai can provide everything from concept to delivery, or produce and deliver styles at contracted prices.

TAL, an apparel supplier that produces one in every eight men's dress shirts sold in the United States, also assumes the role of replenishment for JCPenney's Stafford shirt collection. Their Hong Kong office receives point-of-sale information from Penney stores and through a custom-designed computer model issues automated production and shipping orders to their factories. This streamlined supply chain system allows TAL to respond quickly to consumer needs and provides Penney's with a valuable service. Penney's is able to maintain a lean dress shirt inventory. Prior to this replenishment system, Penney's had to maintain inventories of thousands of dress shirts in warehouses across the United States, tying up valuable capital resources and creating the risk of markdowns.

Tarrant Apparel Group is a leading provider of men's, women's and children's casual, private label apparel. They are a value-added supplier that maintains an in-depth understanding of the fashion and pricing strategies of their customers that include specialty retail, mass merchants, and national department stores, such as Abercrombie and Fitch, Chico's, Federated, Kohl's, The Limited, JCPenney, Kmart, Sears, Target, Mervyn's, and Wal-Mart. Their own teams of expert designers, sample-making capability, and the ability to assist customers in market-testing designs with quick-turnaround production of "test-order" products make them an important asset in providing private label and private brand products to retailers. As the demands of the market changed, Tarrant leased most of their manufacturing facilities in Mexico to a third party and returned to their previous strategy of being solely a trading company with strong product development and sourcing capabilities.

To be successful in today's changing market, sourcing companies must become value-added suppliers, developing strong design, merchandising, and sourcing capabilities so they can match trends and grow with their customers.

Advantages

Developing private label and private brand merchandise provides special advantages for fashion retailers.

- Lines can be developed specifically for the retailer's targeted consumer. This provides a much more highly defined product that meets the specific needs of that retailer's customers. This also includes producing size scales that relate directly to the retailer's sales history. National brand manufacturers must focus on a larger population of consumers.

- Retailers can develop consumer loyalty through their private label and private brand programs. The exclusivity of their products brings consumers into their stores for repeat business.
- Price independence is an important aspect of these programs. The retailer is not forced to reduce prices to meet competitors' prices for national brands or meet restrictive policies established by branded suppliers.
- Initial mark-ups are higher because the retailer eliminates the profits and higher marketing and promotional costs of the branded supplier.
- Absence of requirements from branded suppliers for maintained retail selling prices, advertising and promotional activities, and required order quantities.
- Retailers can provide new fashions at affordable prices.
- Licensing arrangements for exclusive use of popular brands or designer names give the retailer added prestige in the marketplace.

Disadvantages

There are also certain risks and disadvantages associated with retailers developing their own private labels or private brands.

- Any problems with merchandise are the full responsibility of the retailer and cannot be shared with a branded supplier including late deliveries and markdowns.
- Cost of investment in inventory might offset initial higher margins.
- Hidden costs of generating a store brand. A substantial investment in technology and staffing is required to establish an effective capability to do market research, develop, execute, and deliver apparel lines to compete with national brands.
- The added costs of marketing and promoting exclusive brands.
- The risk of markdowns or having to dispose of excess inventories for styles that do not meet the expectations of consumers.

"National Brands Battle Private Label"

NEW YORK – Marc Gobé, chairman and chief executive officer of brand-image consultant desgrippes gobé, said national brands will face mounting competition in the next several years from a growing number of store-created brands.

"Private label brands are clearly competing with national brands and retailers have the advantage of a better understanding of their customers, and how to brand their own products," Gobé said. "Retailers have learned that the private label route, if well executed, will increase traffic and loyalty.

"Consumers are seeing the same national brands everywhere and private labels have the advantage to be a unique signature you can find only at stores that make them, like Alfani, Mossimo and Arizona, and retailers are increasingly going directly to designers for partnerships, as Target has done with Mossimo and Isaac Mizrahi," he said.

Allan Ellinger, senior managing director at MMG, an investment banking and apparel consulting firm, disagreed about the status of national brands.

"I think national brands who have carved a niche for themselves have given the consumer a point of view," Ellinger said. "A brand of that size has a loyal following because multiple retail stores gives them credibility. But I do think some smaller guys need to be concerned as stores get bigger and apply more pressure on brands to support the stores' needs."

Arnold Aronson, managing director of retail strategies at Kurt Salmon Associates, said, "It's really about private label versus national brands and designer brands. There has to be a proper assortment and mix. Whether good, better, or designer; a Warner's, Maidenform, Natori, or Lejaby label, those companies are betting 24/7 on creating fashion and value for the department stores to sell."

Aronson said positioning a national name as a store brand may be tricky, depending on the brand's image, integrity and how it's been marketed. He cited Sara Lee Corp.'s Hanes, Hanes Her Way, Playtex and Champion brands as prime candidates for a licensing partnership with a major retailer.

"There's nothing to keep Sara Lee from licensing its brands," he said. "It's an option they have. But it would have to be in big quantities and there are only a few retailers around who could offer the quantities that would justify such a move. But if a brand still has a lot of juice in it, it would be a question of would a brand want to limit opportunities to one store. There's also an afterglow period when some brands are not doing as well right now, but still have enough energy left for the mass market. Mossimo had trouble succeeding in the better bridge area, but it's been a success at Target."

Paul Cohen, an industry consultant and former president of the licensed Ralph

(continued)

Lauren Intimates at Sara Lee, said, "I could see department stores becoming much more aggressive in acquiring and developing established innerwear brands, either by licensing or simply buying a brand, particularly if the brand is established and [is] a relatively strong brand that consumers know and understand, like Gilligan & O'Malley at Target or Joe Boxer at Kmart."

Anne DiGiovanna, vice president of marketing at the Warnaco Group, said, "Private label brands bring clear identity to the retailers and help to draw in more consumers, which is good for all brands in the department. The consumer doesn't know that the private label brands are developed by the retailer. She only knows what she likes and where to find it. When the brand story is right, it can only help the retailer grow its share."

DiGiovanna added that for a brand to be popular with consumers, it doesn't have to be a long established name.

"There's a certain cachet to little-known brands with great style," she said. "If the product is great, consumers will buy it."

Despite the hunger for fashion and interesting new names, Gobé said retail consolidation will affect the flow of new ideas and product.

"[Commodification] based on performance is hurting most brands today," he said. "National brands can be the best ambassadors of change and they have to rise up to the challenge. I believe national brands have a great future, but not necessarily the brands we know today."

John Schulman, senior vice president and general merchandise manager at Frederick's of Hollywood, said established brands can compete effectively with store-created fashion brands and commodity labels if the marketing is effective.

"It depends on the [established] brand and the marketplace," Schulman said. "A fashion brand in a high-end environment needs to be known among the fashion crowd that it is appealing through the right marketing and [public relations], and the product has to show up in the right magazines and at the right places. A brand that is defining its niche based on price and selling in a mass market environment is less constricted in those same areas and price becomes the driver of the brand."

Regarding the production of branded goods and private label on the part of the manufacturer, Howard Radziminsky, senior vice president of sales and merchandising at Movie Star Inc., said, "There has always been a market for [U.S.] manufacturers to design or manufacture private label goods. Many of us have pursued private label, as well as [maintained] a branded presence. The national brands in some cases resisted private label and concentrated on their brands."

No matter what consumers want —national brands or private brands—Stan Herman, designer of robes bearing his name at the Carole Hochman Group and president of the Council of Fashion Designers of America, summed it up this way: "I still strongly believe the designers are the messenger. Bury their taste and vitality and we are all in trouble. The branding iron has been too hard at work outside the corral. To make this work, the stores need to come back and focus on relevant product that continues to stimulate the consumer." ■

Excerpt from Karyn Monget. April 25, 2005. *Women's Wear Daily.*

Case in Point 1.2 | Summary

National brands are facing mounting competition from store-created brands. Private label brands are competing with national brands and retailers have the advantage of a better understanding of their customers. Private labels have the advantage to be a unique signature you can find only at stores that make them, like Alfani, Mossimo and Arizona.

Retailers need to provide a proper assortment and mix of private label versus national brands and designer brands. Department stores are becoming much more aggressive in acquiring and developing established brands, either by licensing or simply buying a brand, particularly if the brand is established like Gilligan & O'Malley at Target or Joe Boxer at Kmart. Private label brands bring clear identity to the retailer and help to draw in more consumers, which is good for all brands in the department. Established brands can compete effectively with store-created fashion brands and commodity labels if the marketing is effective.

No matter what consumers want—national brands or private brands—designers are the messenger. Their taste and vitality in producing relevant products are what continue to stimulate the consumer. ∎

Andrew Kahn Experience—Chairman, Kahn Lucas Lancaster, Inc.

Advent of the Computer

"The major change that I saw in the apparel industry in the past half century was the advent of the computer. Up until the 1980s the important decision making between the manufacturer and retailer was made either over a drink or at a golf club. The important decisions from 1980 to the present have been based upon the computer printout of your performance report card. Do you deliver on time? Does your product sell-through at retail? Retail buyers have less input as to what is bought and whom they buy from. Everyone in the retail management chain sees all the factors. That's the way it is at Penney's. It's that way certainly at Sears and certainly at Wal-Mart. And where we've had some problems with some retailers, if our report card shows that our goods sell-through, they have to come back to us. And, conversely, if our goods have terrible performance, the buyers will respond appropriately."

Direct Imports

"The buyers are also torn between our products and their own products. Since the retailer must always have an eye on margin, one of the primary goals of a buyer is to determine [if the] products they are buying can be bought directly and eliminate the importer. This move to go straight to the source has accelerated with the continuous retail merger activity. They are getting bigger, generating more buying power and taking more of a vertical approach to their business. Retailers are acquiring certain business processes that traditionally had been in the hands of the importers. By going upstream and expanding their design and merchandising staffs, they are able to develop their own private brands. This is completely different from the way it was in the 1950s, 1960s, 1970s, 1980s, and even the 1990s."

Quality Control

"In the period of the 1950s through the 1970s you didn't need to have tight quality control. From the 1980s to today you need to have very sophisticated quality control systems. It's getting more difficult every year and more complicated with imports coming from the far reaches of the globe. Merchandisers must build tight quality specifications into every garment. Everyone inspects what they get, and they evaluate and return it if it doesn't meet their rigid specifications, whereas in the earlier period that was not really an issue.

"The famous story that I have is of a buyer who was very friendly

(continued)

with my father. This was a buyer who had in today's terms a $500,000,000 open-to-buy, you know, a big, big, big buyer. This guy was called in by his senior management and told he was giving too much business to Kahn and that he had to review the factory. He and my father went to Lancaster, Pa, to see the factory and their schedule was they'd play golf in the morning and then review the quality of the Kahn production in the afternoon. So they played golf in the morning, had lunch, a few drinks, and went over to the factory at around three. As it was told to me, as they were walking up the steps to the factory, the buyer turned to my father and said, 'Can't you send samples to me in New York?' My father said, 'Yeah, of course.' The buyer turned around and said, 'Let's get out of here and go home.' They never got into the factory.

"That was a very different era. Today they look at your performance with a microscope. Look at your AQL [acceptable quality level]. Look at your quality performance record. Look at your on-time delivery history. Look at your human rights issues and your labor compliance. They've got a computer database with every detail. If the buyer doesn't handle it correctly, his boss will have him on the line. Why are you doing business with these people? You're not doing your job . . . and you're out."

Merchandisers Are Becoming Technicians Rather than Mere Creators

"Our company structure has changed more in function rather than form. We had merchandisers then. We have merchandisers now. What they do has changed dramatically. Apparel is a much more sophisticated business today and therefore so are the people. It's much more staff-driven. Merchandisers are looking at many more computer printouts on last year's performance by style, size, color, and customer base. The tools that are used today are from a different world than what they were in the 1950s and 1960s. Decisions are based more on fact than on gut. Merchandisers are becoming technicians rather than mere creators. The job functions have changed dramatically, while the structure is similar."

Development of the Merchandising Function

"Going back to the 1950s, we had sales and manufacturing. During the 1960s the market created a greater demand for product development. Merchandising developed as sort of a bridge between design and sales. Merchandising worked for sales and was part of the sales organization. The merchandising function didn't have the significance that it has today. The merchandiser is

(continued)

now a top-level executive, and back then it was a staff support function."

The Merchandiser Needs to Be a World Player

"The most significant change in this decade is that we source globally. In 1988 we owned and operated nine facilities. Today we own and operate two in the United States. In 1985 we did no production in Central America. Today we have our core production in Guatemala. And we are going to do 40 percent of our business in the Orient, and that's too small a number. There have been significant changes in the way we source, and our customer base is now spreading out as well. We are not as aggressive as we should be in international sales, but certainly we now have customers all over the world where in the past we did not. I think we are lagging the market, and we could do a much better job in international selling. The stronger our Orient manufacturing becomes, the better our ability to have strategic alliances all over the world.

"The merchandiser needs to be a world player. He or she needs to think globally and translate into local needs, rather than thinking locally and trying to translate that into worldwide needs. That's a major difference. Seasonal changes are a factor in every country and that becomes a tricky issue on a world scale of supplying product.

"Merchandisers also need to be aware of social and ethical issues. With most retailers placing more emphasis on corporate social responsibility, merchandisers must factor human rights into the selection of their sources of supply. One of the best examples is Wal-Mart. They are under a microscope and they are taking an aggressive stance concerning social and ethical issues that ripples through the entire buying process."

The Right Style at the Right Time

"I think execution will always be a key factor in sales. Being able to get better information on a timely basis and turn it around into product for our customers is how we stay ahead of our competition. And we must deliver these products to the consumer before our competitors do. We need to continue shortening time frames for product development and getting the product to market.

"Up until 1980 there were three or four lines a year, period. Now we basically come out with a new line every month. The 1970s through the early 1990s was a period of evolution where we moved away from four seasons to regular monthly shipments. Merchandising is closer to the actual point of sale than it used to be. The retailer gives you a selling performance on every style and you need to understand what it is by week and where it's going. *Getting the right style at the right time, that's the measure of a good merchandiser.*"

Andrea Engel Experience—vice president, production and merchandising, Eagle's Eye

Set the Line Plan

"The function of merchandiser in our company is to set the line plan. I want 86 styles for the spring line, this many knits, this many wovens. This is the price range. These are the target wholesale prices. This is what we're trying to appeal to. This is our target customer. The design and sourcing functions are separate responsibilities. I suppose you could say our company has a specialist structure. We're more departmentalized. Merchandising focuses on analyzing the market and sales results to set the line plan, design understands color and silhouette and creates the new styles, and production interfaces with design from a technical viewpoint and then sources the product. The design department works with merchandising on concepts, themes. Production is heavily involved at this point. I need to know if the fabrics will price out and if the construction can technically be executed. Our production department is heavily involved in product development and also deciding where to make it."

Merchandising Should Be Responsible for Design

"I think merchandisers should be more focused on the actual product development. They should be the ones who know where the fabric can be bought, know what kind of yarn to use. Merchandisers should not just be doing the line plan; they should be guiding the design department on fabric constructions and what they should be creating. Designers will always want to design a Mercedes and then the sales people want to sell a Volkswagen and the production people want to make surfboards. Merchandising should be responsible for design and put the whole package together. This would allow designing into a plan. You can't have a design that you find out six months later isn't manufacturable."

Understand What the Buyers Want

"A merchandiser's got to understand what the buyers want, not the customers, but the buyers. Regardless of what we think, our customer is the buyer. But buyers are trained to look at last year's performance. So buyers are your least forward thinking people of the entire matrix in the apparel industry. Designers are very forward thinking and buyers can be backward thinking. So the merchandiser must be the arbiter of good taste and fashion and keep the process moving in a positive direction."

(continued)

Production Sourcing

"In this company production sourcing is a lot more creative. In a lot of companies it's just taking an order. They get the order and they follow up on it. Here we source materials and manufacturing capabilities, as well as pricing, as well as monitoring manufacturing, and importing it back into the country. We're responsible really from design concepts through finished production into the warehouse on time to ship to our customers."

Good Organization and Excellent Communication Are Musts

"A merchandiser, product development manager, director of production, and a sourcing director in an apparel company should all be excellent communicators. That's number one. They should have the ability to manage a thousand things at once. They must be able to react quickly to changing conditions. Sometimes a not so good decision today is better than a perfect decision tomorrow. In this business you must be able to make a decision and move on it. Fashion is very fast paced. An understanding of the global marketplace and an appreciation of cultural differences are critical today. To succeed in this competitive business you must be administratively strong and a very good delegator. Good organization and excellent communication are musts."

Executive Perspective 1.3

Bryan Eshelman
Experience—partner,
Kurt Salmon
Associates

Focus on Product Development

"I'm seeing a definite focus in the product development areas by our wholesale apparel and retail specialty clients in order to improve their product lines. Many of these companies are improving their speed to market. They want to be closer to the market instead of having nine to 12-month cycle times from concept to shelf. One of the tactics that a lot of these companies are taking is moving some of the activities that traditionally occurred on-shore in the U.S., in the product development cycle, offshore to their sourcing partners.

"One of the reasons for moving the product development process offshore has been the removal of quota, which has allowed companies to start to concentrate their manufacturing with fewer, more capable players. These sourcing partners are providing more value added services around the product development process. Initially we saw, years ago, marker making go offshore to the manufacturer. Now we're seeing some tasks that are a little bit more design-oriented move offshore, such as technical spec writing, pattern-making, even the initial prototyping for design and fit purposes, and possibly the ultimate production prototyping and production sampling.

"I don't think we'll see the designer moving offshore to the sourcing partner. The designer needs to be someone who has intimate knowledge of the brand and the culture of the market they are designing into. The designers haven't given up the approval authority to their sourcing base, but rather are spending more and more time taking trips overseas and working on prototype approval in the factories. However, as more trust develops between these players, a lot more authority will be given to the sourcing base on making approval decisions, even fit approval around the standard fit blocks or measurements that the manufacturer or the branded player has. I see the next stage of merchandising development to be where the product development function really ends up more in the sourcing realm. In this scenario the sourcing realm will be broadly defined as both the internal employees of the brand or the retailer and the third party employees of the factory base.

"I think the high fashion, low volume companies that are very design-driven are going to be less likely to let go of that approval process. But I think that the larger branded players that still have a pretty high fashion content, like Liz Claiborne,

(continued)

Jones Apparel Group, Ann Taylor, and Talbots, are more likely to give up some of that approval process to their sourcing partners."

Speed to Market

"In order to support this shift in product development activities going off-shore, we have seen Product Lifecycle Management (PLM) players from other industries enter the apparel market. They have experience solving some of these same problems relating to extended multiple country, multiple party, complex product development processes. Their technologies and strategies allow the apparel private brands or national brands to be closer to the market to reduce cycle times and collaborate with their sourcing base.

"Some of the big brands and some big retailers are beginning some very large initiatives aimed at improving their speed to market, their productivity, their staff capabilities, and product development. The macroeconomic shifts in the market, consumers wanting brand and fashion content at every price point, and the changes in technology that are occurring are really altering how apparel companies and retailers are getting their products to the market."

Replenishing versus Constant Change

"I think a company that has its own brand—and wants that brand to be something the consumer knows is going to have freshness and newness—will not be focused on replenishment, but rather will bring in fresh new styles. They will take a stand on what the product design should look like and not continually look in the rearview mirror and chase the best sellers. Instead, they will try to focus more forward and have a new line for the consumer.

"The consumers have been trained to wait for discounts and know that they don't have to buy something when it first appears on the rack because either the garment or something like it will be on the rack two or three months from now and likely be marked down. Companies are trying to change that dynamic and get away from the training that we've gone through for the past five years and really train the consumers that if they want a garment, they better buy it now, because something else will be in its place and not months from now, but weeks from now.

"Markdown money is still a negotiation. The importance of the brand, how effective the brand is, not only at delivering or developing good merchandise, but servicing good merchandise and keeping the floor section packed is critical. Running a tight ship with replenishment or providing fresh new merchandise on a timely basis enters into the equation. A company that executes well has more leverage in the markdown conversation

(*continued*)

than a company that doesn't execute well."

Product Development in Apparel Companies versus Retailers

"I think the product development function in retail companies is generally the same as in apparel companies. Retailers that sell their own products and other brands, such as department stores or specialty retailers in certain markets, such as "outdoor," treat their own product development organizations almost as if they're another brand.

"The reason that these companies are doing their own product lines is that the margin on their own products is usually five to ten points greater than buying someone's outside brand. Being a part of the retail mother ship gives them insight into what the buyers are going to want for the next season and it also gives them insight into what's selling well in the other brands that they are essentially competing with on the retail floor.

"Retailers in some ways have a little bit more of a leg up on the tra-

ditional wholesale manufacturers in that they have always operated more in a buying mode than in a manufacturing mode and therefore have less of a legacy organization, systems, and processes."

Brand Name Licensors

"There are brand name licensors who do a lot of the product development process, but they get blessings from the retail design organizations along the way at key milestones. Their design staff does a concept or theme meeting with the retailer and then the retailer's staff fleshes that out and converts it into potential garment designs. The brand name licensor's staff then works with the retailer's team to finalize the line. This type of model works well for many retail brand name licensors.

"There are brand name licensors who create a label and make it exclusive for a specific retail operation. In this case, the product development process is the same as for the rest of the brand name licensor's products."

Walter Loeb
Experience—president, Loeb Associates

Private Label

 "In today's market, private label apparel is very important. For many retailers, the only way they can distinguish themselves from their competition is by having exclusive, well-designed brands. Federated Department Stores has developed a number of private labels including INC, Charter Club, and Tools of the Trade. Private label merchandise is designed for specific target groups. The Bloomingdale's buyer may be buying separate INC merchandise than the Macy's buyer.

"It is important to have fresh new merchandise in the stores. Every month the styles are replaced with new designs. For private label, you have to have the right designer, the right backup by senior management, and you need to provide the right fashion at the right time at the right price.

"Private label started with more basic styles. The buying offices represented the stores and bought a label from the manufacturer. It was initially more of a label than a brand. There was no advertising and most stores used private label as a basic product and as a promotional item during sale periods.

"The fashion part of private label is something new. Today, the private label programs may represent as much as 40 percent of the total fashion business. That doesn't mean that Ralph Lauren and Liz Claiborne don't have their place in department stores. They are an important segment of the overall business, but private label fills a need for having a well-designed brand that gives better margins, exclusivity, and opportunity for growth.

"One company that really stands out is Target with an almost exclusive private label program, be it Exhilaration, Mossimo, or any of their other private labels. The use of the famous designer names in Target, such as Michael Graves, Todd Oldham, and Mossimo, is really a terrific support of design ingenuity and innovativeness that Target has used for its customers. JCPenney has also done a great job in developing its own private label fashion programs to maintain its own identity that is exclusive and a look that is its own. Sears has acquired Lands' End to be its exclusive brand."

Merchandising

"Merchandising is very important in making the consumer aware of apparel quality, look, timeliness, and value. Today, private label programs are merchandised intelligently in an effort to have the styles delivered at the same time so they can be fashion coordinated and delivered to the stores in an effective way.

(*continued*)

"I've seen how designs are created on computers in the United States, sent electronically to manufacturers in a given country, and garments are back in the United States in a few days. Communications have become faster, and through collaborative efforts with sourcing partners there is more confidence that a garment will be properly manufactured.

"Private label programs for some retailers are being developed exactly as if they were a national brand. Some of these programs have the strength, the design capabilities, and the characteristics of a national brand. Many private label designs are developed by design teams with a long range view of the merchandising requirements. They provide their sourcing partners with a full specification package. Victoria's Secret is a private label that has grown by leaps and bounds and has done that excellently through its marketing and merchandising expertise. To be successful in today's market you have to be in synch with the fashion, not ahead or behind the fashion trends."

Private Label versus National Brands

"In today's market you have to have the same knowledge base whether you are going to produce a private label or a national brand. Students preparing for an apparel merchandising career need the same knowledge whether they go to work for a private label or a national brand. The only differential is that for a private label program there is a much more focused customer.

"I think that students who go into today's private label field may have good opportunities for growth. A well-developed private label program has opportunity to explode and many of the brands are at a saturation point.

"With the many mergers and acquisitions, today's industry is shrinking in number of companies. I see fewer companies running bigger organizations. Right now Federated and May Company combined are at $30 billion. I think the future will be in the hands of the large complex companies and as a result there will be very interesting developments in the future. I think the private label programs will be more sophisticated, will be done with more emphasis, and will account for 40-plus-percent in most stores for total sales in apparel."

Summary

During the second half of the twentieth century, the U.S. apparel industry evolved from creating two product offerings per year with minimum style changes to providing almost continuous new product offerings with dramatic style changes. During the 1970s through the 1990s a number of multi-billion-dollar apparel companies emerged as apparel sales increased significantly each decade. This same period saw a dramatic growth in the entire apparel industry supply chain including the fiber sector, textile sector, findings sector, apparel sector, and retail sector.

New fashion categories and a growing emphasis on the importance of styling brought a new dynamic to the apparel industry. The emergence of a growing number of U.S. designers, fashion brands, and retailers developing their own brands through private label placed an increased emphasis on product development. A staggering number of new synthetic fibers, finishes, and fabrics further complicated the process of making styling decisions that met the needs of a company's target market.

Advancements in computer technology affected every segment of the apparel industry supply chain. Market data can be evaluated, styles can be created, fabric can be ordered and cut, garments produced and shipped to retailers, and retail sales can be monitored all by computer hardware and software systems. Computer databases allow retailers to evaluate the performance of individual garment styles as well as entire apparel companies. The advent of the computer revolution required a new set of skills for apparel executives.

The apparel industry underwent a globalization during the last 40 years of the twentieth century. Production was moved throughout the world to countries with low-cost labor. By the 1990s apparel imports surpassed domestic production. This global expansion created a need within apparel companies for executives knowledgeable in international business as well as in garment manufacturing technology.

Apparel companies experienced five stages of structural change from after World War II through to the end of the twentieth century. Societal and economic changes created a consumer-driven fashion marketplace requiring changes in the management structure of the apparel industry. The industry moved from a manufacturing focus on production efficiency to a focus on product development and effective sourcing to meet rapidly changing consumer needs. Out of these structural changes emerged the function of apparel merchandising, which is responsible for the development, execution, and delivery of a product line based upon the needs of a target market.

Key Terms

active sportswear
activewear
apparel merchandising
apparel sector
electronic data interchange (EDI)
fiber sector
findings sector
full-package sourcing
global sourcing
labor-intensive
markdowns
mechanical properties
merchandising
microfibers

nondurable goods
point-of-sale
preproduction cycle
private brand
private labels
production cycle
real time
retail fashion merchandising
retail sector
seasons
sell-through
sourcing
supply chain
textile sector

Discussion Questions and Learning Activities

1. What do you believe is the most important change in the apparel industry in the past 25 years that has had the greatest impact on the role of merchandising? Has this change also affected private label development? Explain your answer.

2. Explain today's relationships among the participants in the apparel supply chain and explain how their interaction influences the function of apparel merchandising.

3. How has the computer increased the effectiveness and efficiency of the apparel merchandiser? How has it affected the role of product manager of private label apparel?

4. Research three or more articles in trade publications such as *WWD*, *DNR*, or *Apparel Magazine* relating to a function of merchandising. In each case, identify how the merchandising decisions affect the entire company.

5. Visit your local JCPenney store and compare Arizona with a comparable branded product. Which would you buy and why?

6. What do you feel are the most important reasons for retailers to develop private label apparel?

7. What can a national brand apparel company do to compete with a retailer's private label apparel products?

8. What percentage of a retailer's apparel inventory should be devoted to private label merchandise? Explain your answer.

References and Resources

Chirls, Stuart. January 27, 1998. New Plans for Fibers, Fabrics. *Women's Wear Daily*, p. 12.

Frank, Bertrand. April 1969. Profits in Apparel, A New View. *Bobbin*, pp. 101–103.

Holch, Allegra. February 3, 1998. High Tech Goes Natural. *Women's Wear Daily*, p. 12.

Hudson, Peyton B.; Clapp, Anne C.; Kness, Darlene. 1993. *Joseph's Introductory Textile Science*. New York: Holt, Rinehart and Winston.

Mandry, Gerard P. October 1978. Giving Retailers What the Customer Wants. *Apparel Industry Magazine*, pp. 40–41.

Monget, Karyn. June 22, 1998. Microfiber for the Millennium. *Women's Wear Daily*, p. 8.

Ostroff, Jim. May 12, 1998. AAMA Paley Told: Satisfy Customers. *Women's Wear Daily*, p. 2.

Owens, Jennifer. January 22, 1998. Claiborne's Thompson Tells NRF of Revamping. *Women's Wear Daily*, p. 14.

Ryan, Thomas. December 7, 1998. Merger Fever Raging. *Women's Wear Daily*. pp. 22–23.

Taplin, Ian M. Spring 1997. Struggling to Compete: Post-War Changes in the U.S. Clothing Industry. *Textile History*, pp. 94–95.

Modern Merchandising

OBJECTIVES

- Examine the profile of a successful merchandiser (product manager).

- Identify the responsibilities of a merchandiser (product manager).

- Discuss the personal traits required of a merchandiser (product manager) in the high-tech, competitive, global apparel industry.

Marketing focuses on broadly defining a company's target market and the characteristics of that market. Merchandisers must understand the nuances of the target market so that they can develop specific products for it. In order to be successful in today's complex and rapidly changing fashion marketplace, merchandisers must be immersed in their target markets. Because of intense product and brand competition, merchandising and product management have evolved into more than nine-to-five jobs—they have become lifestyles in which these executives must constantly be aware of the fashion environment in which they live.

■ Profile of Today's Merchandiser

Today's apparel merchandisers must be constantly aware of subtle changes occurring in their target market and be acutely sensitive to the market environment. Societal changes, work ethics, leisure-time activities, music, movies, the arts, physical fitness, vacation choices, eating trends, attitudes, philosophies of life, geopolitics, reading habits, language, the global economy, and even climatic changes all have an effect on fashion preferences. The merchandiser must be able to tune in to all these factors and project how they will affect next year's fashion choices.

The role of merchandising was redefined in the late 1970s. Apparel companies could no longer focus solely on efficient manufacturing to be successful. Target market analysis, product development, sourcing manufacturing throughout the world, and inventory management had to be under effective and positive control.

To achieve this level of control while developing, executing, and delivering a product line that meets the rapidly changing needs of a target market requires a very special management professional. Today's apparel merchandiser must be a blend of a logical, analytical thinker and an intuitive, expressive, creative individual. He or she must have the capability of utilizing the integrated activity of right-brain and left-brain functions to attain both analytical and creative thought processes (see Figure 2.1) (Myers, 1998). The merchandiser must be able to rigorously plan and control the functions involved in developing product, sourcing it, and getting it to the customer on time, as well as have a keen understanding and appreciation for creative design. It is this balance of solid analytical thinking and abstract creative expression that makes the ideal merchandiser such a unique individual.

"In fashion we preach one gospel today and another tomorrow, with no apologies for our inconsistency. The consumer expects change and demands it. Today's successful man or woman in the fashion industry must be social scientist, a computer and a magician with the understanding of his customer's lifestyle—because fashion apparel is based on a woman's desire and need for change" (Miller, 1972).

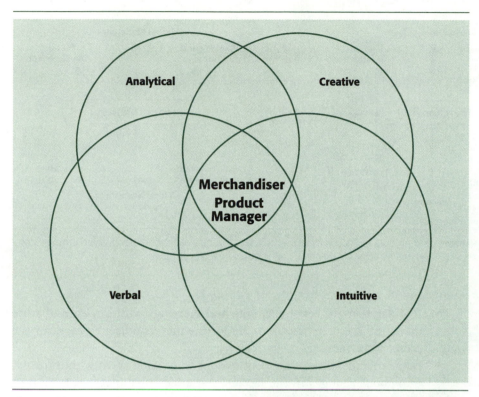

Figure 2.1 The merchandising executive must combine logical and analytical thinking with intuitive and expressive creativity.

■ Responsibilities of the Merchandiser

In order to fully appreciate the blend of characteristics and traits that are needed for an effective merchandiser, it is important to understand the responsibilities the job entails. Depending upon the size and structure of a company, the merchandiser may be responsible for some or all of the functions shown in Figure 2.2. The following functions are discussed in detail in subsequent chapters.

Market Knowledge

A merchandiser must have an intimate and comprehensive knowledge of his or her company's target market. In 100 percent of the companies surveyed (see 2002 Merchandising Survey, Appendix), the merchandisers in apparel companies and product managers in retail have responsibilities for knowledge of consumer preferences for silhouettes, colors, fabrics, and trims.

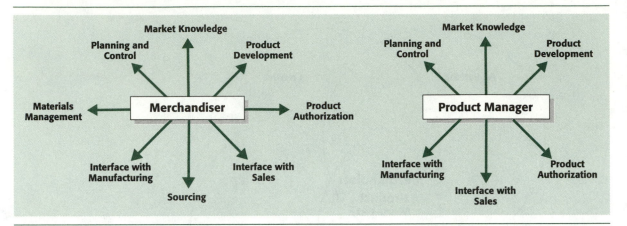

Figure 2.2 Modern merchandisers and product managers must be multi-faceted individuals who are involved in many company functions that result in the creation, development, execution, and delivery of a product line.

- Regular visits to retail accounts and meetings with buyers and store managers are necessary in order for the merchandiser to monitor the pulse of the market.
- Some merchandisers use focus groups to provide them with information about changes in the factors that affect customer satisfaction or to test new styling concepts. **Focus groups** are a cross section of consumers from a specific target market who meet with market research professionals to discuss their preferences.
- Shopping the competition is also an effective means of evaluating styling strengths and weaknesses. This involves the merchandiser visiting retail stores that carry competitors' products to analyze their design trends and pricing.
- **Styling services** and **styling consultants** can dramatically reduce the amount of time required of a merchandiser in researching a target market. These services may utilize large staffs located in key geographical areas to perform market research and summarize the results in customized reports for a merchandiser. They may also provide styling suggestions concerning silhouette, fabric, and color direction. Of course, paying for these research services usually can be quite costly—a price tag of $10,000 to $30,000 per year per product category is not unusual.
- Researching past sales records is also an effective means of detecting styling trends. Analyzing the past sales history of style categories, silhouettes, fabrics, and colors may provide insight into shifts in consumer preferences.
- Progressive companies create Web sites targeted at their consumers as a way of monitoring trend shifts. Consumers can log on to the company's Web site to see new styles and provide instantaneous feedback.

Figure 2.3 A focus group convenes at the Bala Cynwyd, PA offices of Group Dynamics in Focus, Inc., a qualitative market research company. Under the direction of a trained facilitator, members of the focus group who are representative of the target market, will evaluate several apparel products.

Merchandisers must also stay current with the textile markets. They must keep up with the newest fiber developments, fabric constructions, fabric finishes, color trends, and print direction in order to guide the product development process. *Apparel Magazine* along with a myriad of other textile and fashion magazines and journals provide updates on new fabrics designed for specific apparel applications.

Changes in the retailing environment can have a profound effect on merchandising decisions. Retail strategies and retail opportunities for growth must be under the constant scrutiny of merchandisers. "Apparel makers are revving up the retail scene with their own stand-alone collection areas and more in-store shop concepts. Their efforts have doubled volume per square foot for many sellers, and the race is on to pump the space for all its worth" (Abend, 1998). Major men's wear brands such as Tommy Hilfiger, Nautica, and Ralph Lauren each have over 1,200 high-focus, **in-store shops**, where these brands control and provide fixtures for the retail spaces within a department store in which their products are displayed and sold. Women's wear leaders Liz Claiborne, Jones New York, and Donna Karan have also embraced the in-store shop concept and have established their own retail stores as well.

The merchandiser must always be aware of special conditions that affect the marketplace. Good examples are Olympiads or the end of the millennium. Olympic games produce increased sales of active sportswear. In addition, as the end of the millennium approached, there were dramatic changes in fashion buying patterns that market savvy merchandisers capitalized on. There was a great surge in sales of formal fashions for men and women in preparation for the global New Year's Eve spectacular. (See Case in Point 2.1.)

Planning and Control

Another important function of merchandising and product managing is planning effectively and maintaining control. These actions encompass all departments of an apparel company. In nearly all the companies surveyed (Appendix), merchandising is responsible for critical planning and control functions, such as the following:

- The merchandiser plays a vital role in **strategic planning** (identifying where and how a company's resources should be allocated) along with marketing, sales, production, finance, and administration.
- The merchandiser must ensure timely line development in accordance with market needs and the company's capacities and capabilities.
- The merchandiser must integrate company functions within the total supply chain, which is very complex in connection with global sourcing of both raw materials and finished products.
- In larger companies, the merchandiser coordinates intracompany activities with other departments.

The tools used to accomplish planning and control are:

- The **marketing calendar** is the basis for all other apparel company planning. It establishes the **line preview date**, which is the date when management will review proposed styles with sales; the **line release date**, which is when the line will be available for sale to retailers; the sales plan; and the shipping plan. The line release date is the pivotal point for each season's activities. It is the one date that is etched in stone and cannot be delayed or postponed since it usually coincides with major market weeks, industry shows, and sales presentations to key accounts.
- The **merchandising calendar** or **line calendar** is the primary control tool in an apparel company and retail company that develops private label merchandise. It establishes responsibilities for, and sets forth, starting dates and deadlines for completion of all key events for a season.

"Formalwear Fever Jump-Starts Tailored Clothing at MAGIC"

Dressing for millennium spurs tuxedo buying and even more black suit business.

Las Vegas—The millennium is giving the tailored clothing market a shot in the arm for the second half of '99. There has been a tremendous surge in tuxedo bookings along with dressy three- and four-button black suits for the party circuit.

And retailers and manufacturers are talking big numbers at MAGIC (Men's Apparel Guild in California annual menswear trade show). Typical is Jim Zimmer, executive vice-president, Men's Wearhouse, who said the huge chain predicted the tux boom last year and posted a 20 percent increase in this category. He said, "We expect another 30 percent hike in tux sales for fall and holiday."

Steve Sockolov, president, Rochester Big & Tall, reported the specialist has always counted tuxedos as part of its basics assortment and said, "We're going to use more for this fall and winter. We're adding more fancies and I estimate this business will be about 25 percent ahead of a year ago."

According to Brian Lefko, owner of the store of the same name in Baltimore, Md., the spurt in tuxes also gave his black suit business a boost. "We're buying more black and not just any black suits, but more fashion models, like four- and five-button single-breasteds and fly-fronts."

Most retailers, meanwhile, aren't buying formalwear as a sometimes thing but as an integrated part of their stock with EDI backup. On the other hand, Men's Wearhouse carries two-button, notched-collar tuxes as regular stock and Zimmer expected to add more fancies for millennium selling.

Black suits, meanwhile, he added, have been selling briskly for the last year and a half. "This year black will be even bigger than it was. It's now 10 percent of our business," he pointed out.

Commenting on the formalwear business at the show, Ronnie Wurtzburger, president, Peerless International, said, "If formalwear was ever going to happen, this is the year. Stores are planning for a black-tie New Year's Eve along with a super-dressy fall. And remember, all this will be followed by 2000, which will be an election year and more dressing up." The company is showing tuxedos for all of its major labels at the show.

This time around, retailers are building their standing stock of tuxedos and not confining their buys to basic, he noted. "They want super 100s and all the fashion models. Stores are committing to formalwear and not just tuxes for weddings. It's a joy trip."

Other exhibitors also gave thumbs-up for formalwear at MAGIC and among them was Pincus Bros.-Maxwell, which has a thriving tuxedo business, stated Joel Cohen, vice-president of the division. "This season there's a lot of conversation about tuxedos and, from all the phone calls we're getting, it looks like many department and specialty stores, also off-pricers, which never thought about formalwear, are jumping into the business for fall. Or they're increasing their buys." ■

From Stan Gellers, March 3, 1999; *Daily New Record*, p. 2.

- The **line plan** focuses the efforts of the design team in one cohesive direction. It establishes the number of fabrics, styles, constructions, and stock keeping units (SKUs) in a line by product group.
- The **shelf stock plan** is made up of the styles and quantities by color and size that should be in stock on a weekly basis. The six-month merchandise plan is the retailer's counterpart to the shelf stock plan. A refinement is the model stock plan.

Merchandisers use computers for developing their plans and for tracking progress in various departments. Spreadsheet, relational database, project management, and task scheduling software have greatly aided the merchandiser in accomplishing the complex responsibilities of planning and control.

Product Development

Many apparel and retail companies offer new styles nearly every month. The number of increased offerings creates an almost continuous styling mode in most design departments. In 98 percent of the companies surveyed (in Appendix), the merchandiser is responsible for coordinating design activities. Merchandising must provide rigorous controls of the product development process to ensure that balanced groupings of styles are ready for each offering. Interviews with retailing executives indicated that product managers coordinated the designing activities for private label apparel.

At the same time, companies are also trying to compress the product development time-line to allow fabric and styling decisions to be made as close to product releases as possible. This allows the product line to be totally responsive to the needs and wants of the target consumer, thereby improving retail sell-through and reducing the risk of markdowns. Careful control of the product development process is vital to the success of an apparel company and retail private label. (See Figure 2.4.)

M. Lederle Eberhardt, vice president design and merchandising Woolrich, Inc., sees the merchandiser as a technically skilled visionary. "As far as merchandising, you have to be somewhat of a visionary. You should also take courses in pattern making. You do have to understand how the product goes together. You have to understand where you can cut cost out of a garment. A merchandiser must keep the designers on track and on time. They have to be sure that each style the company creates is salable."

The product development process includes many interrelated functions that affect one another. A poor decision or a delay in fabric selection, creating a prototype, developing patterns, or preliminary costing could eventually require redefining the line plan or development of new style concepts. The merchandiser must keep a tight rein on the entire process if a company is to have the most effective styles ready for line release. The merchandising cal-

FIGURE 2.4   **PRODUCT DEVELOPMENT PROCESS**

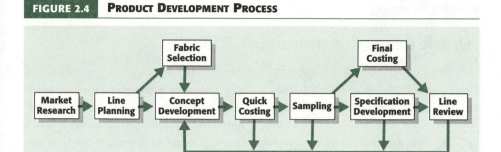

The product development process begins with market and fashion research and ends with the final adoption session of line review.

endar is used to establish time schedules and accountability for each function of product development. The merchandiser must monitor the calendar to see that each function is completed on time or must make adjustments for any missed deadlines.

Andrea Engel, former vice president of production and merchandising for Eagle's Eye, believed it was important for merchandisers to be responsible for product development. "I think merchandisers should be more focused on the actual product development. They should be the ones who know where the fabric can be bought, know what kind of yarn to use. Merchandisers should not just be doing the line plan; they should be guiding the design department on fabric constructions and what they should be creating. Designers will always want to design a Mercedes and then the sales people want to sell a Volkswagen and the production people want to make surfboards. Merchandising should be responsible for design and put the whole package together. This would allow designing into a plan. You can't have a design that you find out six months later isn't manufacturable."

In order to unleash the full creativity of a designer or stylist, it is important to have a "business mind" organizing and controlling the product development process. The merchandiser performs this function by providing a creative environment and positive direction for the design team without losing sight of the marketability of the line. After all, merchandising is responsible for the end product being salable and profitable. The entire process must be accomplished while the critical timetables necessary to get the line completed by the line release date are maintained.

Costing

Developing accurate cost estimates for new products is a critical merchandising function. This cannot be done without a thorough understanding of the

"Quick Response Mandates Today"

The Impact of Quick Response on Product Development Efforts

Quick Response initiatives provide benefits throughout an organization—from product development through distribution. Apparel firms focus a great deal of effort on back-end functions such as inventory management and shipping. But much less attention has been paid to the front end, and, to attain QR [quick response] goals and remain competitive, companies are discovering through QR that they must place an equal emphasis on product development.

Benefits that can be realized by applying QR strategies to the product development process include:

- **Shorter Development Cycle Time:** QR strategies allow an apparel manufacturer to design key fashion items closer to market.
- **Maximized Sales Volume and Margin:** Quick development of market-right products helps maximize retail sell-through and reduce markdowns.
- **Reduced Product Development Expense:** Creating on-target styles the first time minimizes last minute changes, thus decreasing the overall cost of developing a product.
- **Improved Customer Service:** An efficient, on-time development process builds a foundation for QR production and distribution—improving the apparel manufacturer's ability to deliver product in a timely manner.

The product development process consists of six key steps: Line Planning & Consumer Research, Concept Development, Quick Costing, Sampling, Specifications Development, and Line Reviews. Following is a discussion of each step and the QR innovations utilized by today's leading organizations.

1. **Line Planning & Consumer Research**—Effective line planning is grounded in fundamental knowledge of an apparel firm's target market. QR companies analyze retail point-of-sale (POS) data to gain an understanding of their consumer base, to determine key sales trends and quickly develop market-right products.
   - **QR Technologies**
     - **Data Warehouse** of POS and consumer profile data
     - **Data Mining** tools to extract sales trend and consumer information
2. **Concept Development**—The stage of line planning and consumer research consists of shopping the marketplace, creating concept boards, and translating a merchandising-driven line plan into a well-targeted product assortment. QR initiatives are supported through the use of computer-aided design [CAD] technology for developing fabrics and silhouettes.

   Using CAD technology is faster and more efficient than the creation of physical samples: physical samples are sewn only after a CAD concept is approved. CAD technology also enables an apparel

(continued)

firm to develop and maintain fabric and silhouette libraries from which new seasonal concepts are developed.

During this stage, initial fabric and production sources are chosen. Leading organizations avoid the mistake of sourcing sample fabrics with a mill that cannot produce the quantities necessary for line production in the required timeframe. Today's most responsive manufacturers are electronically linked to their fabric mills and other suppliers for fast, flexible delivery of raw materials.

- **QR Technologies**
  - CAD technology to support the creation of fabrics and silhouettes
  - Historical database of company designs
  - EDI links with mills and suppliers

3. **Quick Costing**—Quick Costing is a tool that enables designers to calculate a rough cost estimate for the materials and labor required to produce a concept, avoiding development of concepts—whether fabrics, trims, or body styles—that will not fit retail price point targets.
   - **QR Technologies**
     - Preliminary costing software

4. **Sampling**—Sampling is a critical part of production approval. Production sources prove they understand the product concept by effectively creating a first sample. Leading apparel firms use input from this process as a key variable to measure the competitiveness of a resource.
   - **QR Technologies**
     - A database of contractor performance statistics

5. **Specification Development**—Once a first sample is approved, all production-related tools are created—including a specifications sheet, pattern and marker.

A computer-aided system for pattern making, grading and marker-making increases both the speed of developing and the efficiency of these tools. In addition, QR firms keep libraries of garment specifications, patterns and markers to provide a starting point for new product development.

- **QR Technologies**
  - CAD software to speed the development of patterns and markers, and to aid in efficient fabric utilization in the cutting process
  - A relational database to hold garment specifications, patterns and markers in a well-organized, easy-to-copy format

6. **Line Reviews**—To minimize costly late changes in the development process, QR firms make sure they conduct line reviews with the manufacturing and merchandising departments throughout the five earlier steps. The next step is a critical review of the line with the sales department. Leading companies use applications software that supports the presentation of the final line to the sales team, as well as to retail customers. This tool presents a clear picture of the line visually and financially. Styles are pulled together in coordinated groups; target margins and retail price points are outlined.
   - **QR Technologies**
     - Software to support line review at style and coordinated level

It is clear that Quick Response goals cannot be achieved without a focus on improving the product development process. The front end is fundamental to QR efforts—for example, if the development

(continued)

team does not provide product specifications to the manufacturer or contractor on time, production will be late.

Leading organizations use a computer-automated, enterprise-wide merchandising calendar where deadlines and current status of each step in the process are organized in one chart that is accessible to everyone in the organization. The calendar automatically generates daily "to do" lists for each

development team member, enabling them to manage their work and meet key deadlines. This system increases the efficiency of product development by making it easier for the organization's members to work together as a team. ■

From Kurt Salmon Associates. (March 1997). *Apparel Industry Magazine*, pp. 45,54.

Case in Point 2.2 **Summary**

Case in Point 2.2 emphasizes the importance of shortening response time in the product development process. To achieve quick response within all phases of the supply chain requires an effective merchandiser. Maintaining up-to-date market knowledge; careful planning and control of the entire apparel process; dynamic product development; quality communications with sales, marketing, and manufacturing; efficient authorization of production; cost-effective materials management; and profitable sourcing of product are the measurement of a successful apparel merchandiser. ■

manufacturing process and a command of math. M. Lederle Eberhardt, of Woolrich, stresses the importance of understanding math. "If you want to be a merchandiser, you had better be good with numbers and math. Designers are usually not focused on price and statistics. Merchandisers have to apply the business sense to the line. This is a numbers game. This really is a numbers game coming down to pricing and to volume."

Merchandisers must be capable of calculating the cost of producing each garment, determining selling prices, preparing statistical forecasts based upon incoming sales data, analyzing spreadsheets that are used to follow the status of fabric and production orders, and evaluating financial statements. These processes require a merchandiser to be comfortable working with math and statistics.

Interfacing with Sales and Marketing

Line planning, style selection, and line presentation require a close working relationship among merchandising, sales, and marketing. Throughout the entire product development process, merchandising should be obtaining valuable input from sales and marketing as to how current styles are selling at retail and trend projections from retail buyers. Periodic style preview meetings to discuss line direction and line adoption meetings allow sales and marketing to "buy" into the final line. A good sales staff maintains constant communication with key accounts and can therefore provide valuable current information on changing market trends in retail sales.

In 87 percent of the apparel companies surveyed in 2002, the merchandiser participates in line presentations to the sales force during seasonal sales meetings. Merchandising has molded the line plan and developed the concepts that hold the product themes and groupings together.

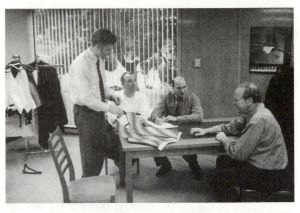

Figure 2.5 Design and Marketing executives of Lord West meet to evaluate the salability of new styles.

It is important for the merchandiser to be able to guide the sales force in how best to clearly present these concepts to the buyers. According to the 2002 survey, in 100 percent of retailers, the product manager participates in the presentation of the private label seasonal line to their buyers and their sales associates. (See Appendix)

Merchandisers may attend a few sales presentations during a season to get a firsthand understanding of how the buyers respond to the line. Attending sales presentations may be difficult for merchandisers because of their hectic schedules, but this opportunity to see buyers' reaction to the line can be quite valuable in helping to maintain a clear understanding of the target market. It is frequently heard that many designers and merchandisers spend too much time in their "ivory towers" and lose touch with their retail buyers and the ultimate consumers.

It is also critical for the merchandiser to maintain close communications with sales throughout the season in order to receive advance sales advice. This information may be in the form of:

- Early sales estimates—estimates of sales potentials for each style gleaned by sales reps from reliable retail customers.
- Early sales promises—commitments from key accounts that are not yet confirmed orders.
- Early sales orders—confirmed orders that may not yet be entered into the order processing system. Many companies are focusing on capturing these orders at point-of-sale by equipping their sales forces with notebook computers and modems.

In 100 percent of the retailers surveyed, the product manager monitors the POS of private label styles. In 94 percent of the companies surveyed (see Appendix), the merchandiser is responsible for fashion forecasts. The merchandiser often uses these forecasts to commit early production authorizations. This is especially critical for off-shore production, which requires a longer lead time than domestic production. Many times these commitments must be made well in advance of the line release date.

Production Authorization

Since many apparel companies must commit to production before meaningful sales have been generated, someone must decide what and how much to manufacture. In 41 percent of the companies surveyed (see Appendix), the merchandiser is directly responsible for production authorization. Merchandisers use past sales histories, current market research, advance sales advice, and sales forecasting models to make production authorization commitments. Unfortunately, there are no magic crystal ball forecasting models that can zero in on the exact styles by sizes and colors that will be sold in any given season.

An increasing focus is being placed on forecasting systems. Apparel firms and retailers are striving to build effective decision support systems (DSS), fueled by **data warehouses** (databases containing massive amounts of digital data on a company's products and sales), to capture and analyze their data, and provide them with completely new ways to look at their vast amounts of data on sales, customers, and operations (Bloom, Bunasky, and Kurtz, 1998). The high cost of data warehouse technology has caused most apparel companies to shy away from this high-tech approach to forecasting. Companies like Exact Software, Computer Generated Solutions, GEAC, i2 Technologies, Intentia Americas Inc., Logility, New Generation Computing, Porini U.S.A., and SAP have developed cost effective and user friendly interface tools to meet the broader needs of the apparel industry.

Interfacing with Manufacturing

The number of U.S. apparel companies that maintain their own manufacturing facilities decreased dramatically during the 1990s and early 2000s. Most firms have opted to source their production with domestic or off-shore contract manufacturers. For those companies that do have their own facilities, maintaining low levels of **work-in-process** (WIP, the number of garments that have been cut but are not finished and available for shipping) and still providing a **shippable-mix** (the necessary assortment of styles including all sizes and colors for each style required to make a shipment) is critical to risk reduction and optimal customer service.

Since in many companies the merchandiser authorizes production, it is important for the merchandiser to maintain close communications with manufacturing. A mix of styles must be issued that can optimize manufacturing capabilities as well as satisfy customer requirements. The goal of the merchandiser must be to maintain a mix of styles in the factories that will achieve low production costs and still meet shippability criteria. This requires the merchandiser to have a solid understanding of manufacturing processes and a keen sense of marketing and sales requirements.

Whether a company manufactures its own products or sources its production domestically or globally, it is very important for the styles developed by merchandising to have carefully defined garment specifications with measurable quality standards. **Garment specifications** are lists of raw materials, patterns, cutting instructions, construction guidelines, finished garment measurements, and quality expectations. The garment specification package should also include a detailed sketch of the garment showing seam and stitching requirements as well as exploded views of special details such as patch and flap constructions. Quality considerations such as finished garment measurements, positioning of parts, and fabric pattern matching should be detailed with acceptable measurable tolerances.

Some of the more sophisticated product development software systems provide applications that can create product drawings and capture detailed manufacturing and quality specifications during the design process. Gerber's PDM and WebPDM 5.0 systems (**www.gerbertechnology.com**), Freeborders' FB Product Manager (**www.freeborders.com**), and Lectra's Mikalis VIR 1 (**www.lectra.com**) provide comprehensive features to assist in these functions.

Materials Management

Raw materials, including fabric, findings, and trim, can represent from one-third to one-half the total cost of a garment. The purchasing and scheduling of these raw materials must be programmed for delivery as close to their required usage as possible. This is the business philosophy of **just-in-time (JIT)** manufacturing, which greatly reduces inventory carrying costs and warehousing requirements by scheduling the delivery of raw materials precisely at the time they are to be used in the production process. One major branded jeans manufacturer schedules trailer loads of denim fabric to be delivered daily to its cutting facility with the rolls loaded in the order in which it is planned that they will be spread for cutting. This allowed the manufacturer to eliminate a half million square foot fabric warehouse and reduce handling costs by 50 percent. In 81 percent of the apparel companies surveyed (see Appendix), merchandisers select all raw materials; in 40 percent, merchandising is responsible for purchasing raw materials for the design function; and in 25 percent, the merchandiser actually purchases raw materials for stock. The responses from retailers were different. In 69 percent of the companies, product managers select the raw materials, and when it comes to purchasing the materials for the design or production stages, the product manager has no responsibility whatsoever.

The rapid growth of new developments in fibers, yarns, and fabrics has further complicated the materials management function, which is a critical concern for many merchandisers. The use of effective computer database management systems is crucial to the success of this area of merchandising responsibility. Accurate **bills of materials**, which provide detailed listings of material requirements for each style; effective **style status reports** showing sales versus forecasts, authorized fabric purchases and receipts, and authorized production for each style; **master production plans** showing, by style, the fabric needs by time period per available factory production capacity; and accurate raw materials and finished goods inventory reports are vital merchandising tools.

In many companies, **materials management**, the planning, ordering, and follow-up of delivery and utilization of materials, is an entry-level job that enables future merchandisers to gain valuable knowledge of the operations of the merchandising department.

Sourcing

With more than 50 percent of U.S. apparel products being imported from around the globe and fewer and fewer companies manufacturing in their own factories, sourcing is a growing responsibility. Depending upon the size and departmentalized structure of an apparel company, sourcing may be the sole responsibility of merchandising; it may be an independent, senior-level management function; or it may be a shared responsibility. Whichever the case, the merchandiser must understand the complexities of domestic and international sourcing.

Determining how and where to manufacture apparel products has become a major concern for most companies. A good sourcing executive must have a working knowledge of manufacturing processes, quality assurance procedures, garment costing, product development, government quota and import legislation, international cultural and business practices, and international banking and legal procedures. In addition, the sourcing executive must be an excellent negotiator.

When the responsibility for sourcing falls upon the shoulders of merchandisers, it becomes extremely difficult for them to fulfill this responsibility while dealing with the demanding task of product development and meeting production deadlines. In many companies some of the product development responsibilities such as **prototyping** (the creation of the initial garment sample of a style in either the actual fabric or in a muslin for evaluation purposes) and fabric procurement are transferred to the sourcing contractor as a **value-added** (any activity, over and above the direct cost of producing a garment, that adds to the value of the garment) function. This occurs in the more highly developed sourcing countries such as Hong Kong, Taiwan, and Korea. The merchandiser and a member of the design team may visit the sourcing contractor to review the progress of the current production orders and also to work on developing the new product line.

In most retailing organizations, the product manager will not be directly responsible for sourcing. There may be some involvement when the private label merchandise is produced by an apparel company. However, in those cases where retailers have their own offices that deal directly with the producer or go through a third party, their involvement might be limited to developing the prototype. (Refer to Jay Gardner's Executive Perspective 6.4)

■ Traits of a Merchandiser

In today's high-tech, competitive, global apparel industry, a merchandiser must possess a rare blend of traits, skills, and experience. He or she must be part designer, part engineer, part computer expert, part marketer, part business management guru, and part entrepreneur.

In addition to experience, a successful merchandising candidate should be:

- An independent thinker with the ability to maintain a steady course toward the long-term company objectives while under pressure from sales, marketing, and manufacturing requirements.
- An entrepreneur by being assertive in leading the company in new directions while taking risks based upon an innate feel for the market.
- Flexible with the ability to adjust to the changing demands and timetables of the marketplace.
- A leader demonstrating the ability to gain the respect and cooperation of other members of the management team while making the critical decisions needed to keep the company ahead of the competition.
- A communicator with the ability to express new ideas and concepts clearly and persuasively and also being capable of convincing the design staff to translate subtle styling indicators into firm style trends.
- Dedicated with a focused commitment on maintaining a clear vision of the company's target market and styling direction.
- Organized, exhibiting the ability to maintain a disciplined business atmosphere while managing many functions simultaneously and meeting critical deadlines.

Market knowledge and solid apparel experience are essential for merchandisers. These credentials can be gained from manufacturing experience combined with extensive customer contact and intimate styling and design involvement or from a retail buying or selling background within the target market. Learning the market is an ongoing experience that requires dedication and constant research and involvement with the target market.

Andrea Engel, defined her ideal merchandiser, "A merchandiser in an apparel company should be an excellent communicator. That's number one. He or she should have the ability to manage a thousand things at once. He or she must be able to react quickly to changing conditions. Sometimes a not so good decision today is better than a perfect decision tomorrow. In this business you must be able to make a decision and move on it. Fashion is very fast paced. An understanding of the global marketplace and an appreciation of cultural differences are critical today. To succeed in this competitive business, you must be administratively strong and a very good delegator. Good organization and excellent communication are musts."

Lynn Duckworth, former vice president of merchandising at Little Me, stressed that a good merchandiser should possess "thoroughness, retail experience, and selling and design experience." In addition, Ms. Duckworth stated that a good merchandiser should "be well organized, have the ability to keep everyone on track, be a visionary, have the ability to sell ideas to the sales force, have experience in sourcing, know how to travel overseas, understand manufacturing processes, be knowledgeable in patternmaking, and have a working knowledge of costing."

Norton Binder Experience—executive vice president and director of operations, Joan Vass, USA; president, HOM Sportswear

Merchandising, the Key to Success

"My first job was as assistant to the president of Robert Bruce. It was really an elevated title for, 'go get him lunch.' The first thing they assigned me to do was to prepare the product description sheets for manufacturing. I created the detail on how to make the product from fiber, machinery, finishing, trimming, color range, and size range. I was in charge of seeing that the spec sheet was correct and delivered to the manufacturing division in time to make the production. That brought me into the mill where I learned what the machines could do and what kind of work was involved in preparing a line.

"I did that for a year or two and then went to my boss and said, 'it's very nice to know process and procedure. I want to get involved in determining what you're making.' To me that was the key to success, the merchandising department. I recognized that very early on. Unfortunately I couldn't get into merchan-

dising for another ten years, because I needed background and manufacturing experience first.

"In the interim I was in the glamour area of marketing and sales promotion, but I still always recognized that *what* to make was more important. During the early days it was the owners of the company who determined the product line. But as the companies grew, they needed professional assistance, and the merchandiser became the key to their success. This was true in almost every company I was with."

Team Effort for Product Development

"My background was more of a generalist. In the beginning of my career at Robert Bruce I was in charge of the description sheets and sample manufacturing. I then worked my way into the marketing department. This gave me a taste of merchandising. There was a team effort for product development. No one person had the total responsibility. There was a merchandise manager. We worked with him, and he would assign us various parts of the line to feed him information. I was in charge of the active sportswear line working with Arnold Palmer in golf and the tennis line working with Jimmy Connors. I provided information, market research if you will. I analyzed our competition, sales, and product history. I visited the stores to find out what was happening on the selling floor. I researched

(continued)

why some products sold well, while others sold poorly so I could get a better idea of what the market was looking for.

"My knowledge of the factory operations and machinery capabilities allowed me to join the market research and factory capabilities together to suggest new products that met both criteria. I also researched the fiber producers to develop new products. For instance, DuPont was promoting texturized Dacron™ polyester. Another company, Puritan, had developed a sweater shirt using this fabric, and I brought it in for our golf line. The production department created the actual product that was approved by the merchandiser. The product took off like crazy. This merchandising team approach to product development was very effective."

Produce a Product that Meets the Needs of Your Target Market

"When I joined Joan Vass, the company was just starting. After the first year the company was doing about $750,000. After 10 years the bookings were close to $30 million. The smaller the company, the less departmentalized it gets, but the principles are the same. You have to do the same amount of research no matter the size of the company because the decisions are the same. You must develop a product that meets the needs of your target market.

"We were looking for upscale consumers. So we went into the mar-

ket and interviewed better sportswear buyers at about 25 key stores throughout the country in major market areas. We also had a list of better smaller retailers and interviewed many of them. We did focus groups in better malls to find shoppers' impressions of what we were showing from our product sampling. That's how we continued development of our line plan."

Continuing Market Research

"In all the various firms I was with, the process was the same. Once the line was developed, we had our salespeople in the field fill out questionnaires. They would go out on the floor at maybe 30 or 40 of their stores and analyze what was selling, what colors were hot, what fibers were doing well, what prices customers were looking for, what was our competition doing. Continuous market research is critical to successful merchandising.

"We would go to the trade shows to see what was being shown. We would search for new ideas from overseas in the import lines. We'd buy samples from stores of the best selling items so we could either adapt them or innovate on our own. We used color services and fiber company ideas. The Wool Bureau and the Cotton Council were very helpful. Then our designers would come up with original ideas and we'd evaluate them to see where they would dovetail based upon our ability to manufacture and our pricing structure."

(*continued*)

Computer Skills Are Vital

"Today with point-of-sale capture of data and computer linkages, you get information a lot faster. A lot of companies use quick response systems to analyze current trends and speed production through their factories.

"The key to knowing what should go into a line is recognizing what kind of market positioning you are capable of attaining.

"Today I would use a lot more computer information to give me a better picture of changes in the marketplace more quickly. And CAD systems have reduced the design cycle from days to hours for developing a new idea. The computer is a major factor in our industry since it saves a lot of time and gives merchandisers more tools. Today's students must realize that computer skills are vital to becoming a successful merchandiser."

World Markets Have Expanded

"Today, world markets have expanded so that they no longer are just contract sources for production. They're idea spinners themselves, and you go into those overseas markets and see things that are being developed from a fresh point of view, especially in China and Southeast Asia.

"I would suggest that students learn geopolitical information because worldwide sourcing is going to be a much bigger factor than it

ever was. You have to know what is going on and what countries to look at. Sourcing is a vital part of merchandising and you have to understand the global political situations, whether it's long term or short term. You have to know that you are going to a country that's stable if you are going to invest money and time and effort."

Interface with Sales

"The merchandiser also plays a major role in determining how the products should be presented. The flow of presentation is no longer the sole purview of sales. Merchandising develops the concept and direction for the line and therefore is in the best position to determine the most effective format for presentation and advertising. Today, merchandising must interface with sales in preparation for sales meetings and shows. Many buyers attend national and regional shows where they can make their purchases at one time and see all the styles from many manufacturers in one venue. The ability to mount a show becomes critical for the manufacturer."

Blend of Many Skills

"Merchandising is a unique function in that it requires a blend of many skills. *A good merchandiser should have an understanding of production methods, marketing techniques, styling and design functions, costing criteria, and also be a meticulous planner.*"

Colombe Nicholas Experience—president, CEO, Anne Klein Company; president, CEO, Healthtex; president, Christian Dior USA

Merchandising at Anne Klein Is the Bridge between Sales and Design

"In the designer world we have three seasons: fall, resort and spring. The season is broken down into individual monthly deliveries, and then into number of styles/units, i.e., short jacket, long skirt, pleated pants, etc. Sales determines a line plan for a season. This sales/unit plan is passed to merchandising who then starts to work by setting up a merchandising calendar in order to have the line ready for sale during the appropriate market.

"Design following the outlined merchandising calendar draws the sketches, selects the fabric, puts together the groups, and starts designing what will be the season's look and theme.

"How many groups need to be executed in the season? How do the groups relate to each other? How do the deliveries flow? For example, does the gray fabric, which is going to be on the floor first delivery, look okay with the tan group that's coming in the next delivery? Merchandising is the orchestra leader. It is acting as the coordinator between design's concepts and ideas and sales' requirements."

Merchandising Balances the Styles in the Line

"Once the sales/unit plan has been completed and design has designed product according to the plan, merchandising then reviews the line. As a merchandiser, you have to be organized and analytical. For example, if there are too many long jackets—no slim pants—only double-breasted jackets, merchandising will go back to design and request short jackets, etc. This same analytical skill applies to fabrics and colors that are used in the line."

Merchandising Is Responsible for Getting Quick Costs

"You have to have some knowledge of manufacturing. Merchandising has to look at the garment—and review cost of fabrics, details added to the garment such as pockets, zippers, pleats, etc., all of which create the manufacturing cost. Merchandising is responsible therefore for getting quick costs because as beautiful as a garment might be, if it's too expensive to manufacture, it might have to be dropped."

Peter McGrath Experience—executive vice president, director of product development, trend quality and sourcing, JCPenney

Changing Model for Private Label Product Development

"The profiles of the brands and private labels are much more specific, much more targeted than they were years ago. The model of building a line and the buyer comes in and picks and chooses is gone. We work with the merchants to develop a particular theme. We provide a look book, which is a theme for a season, and in some cases outsource through an importer. Their designers work with the look book to develop particular styles. There is a variation on this model, overseas sample rooms, which began about four years ago and is a version of outsourcing of design out of the United States to foreign countries. The designers are schooled in design and have access to computer research as well as shopping the European stores. The difference is, instead of being from New Jersey, the designer may be from Bangladesh.

"Years ago the private label brands were cheaper and inferior to the national brands. Private label has evolved to where we're attempting to build in better product features and benefits greater than the national brands. Pricing our private label brands comparable to national brands but with more intrinsic value is a formula that has worked very well. Consumers recognize value and understand the association of value and price. That has been the fundamental change in the history of product development and brand management over the past 20 years.

"Another factor is that the upper-end, branded manufacturers provided a cache of fashion that was the most relevant to the time. The consumer had to by their products because they were the fashion leaders. Liz Claiborne is a good example. The Claiborne line was dominant. Today, we are able to fully interpret, analyze, and execute runway fashion into our private label products so that they can compete with the national brands.

"Cycle time reduction is key to keeping up with fashion trends. We have a company-wide initiative on cycle time reduction and expect to be in the first quartile performance on concept to selling floor. We are working on the systems to regularly produce large volumes of product in a 60-day period from concept to in our stores."

(*continued*)

Product Development and Sourcing

"Our designers create the styles and turn them over to our merchants. For us, a merchant and a buyer are the same thing. The merchant determines if each style is right for the customer on the selling floor. They are the sole authority as to what goes on the floor in the store. How it's designed resides with the designer. The merchants understand what the key items are going to be, what the table items are going to be, what the wall items are going to be. Then planning and allocation executes the plan to a rack level. There are planning and allocation departments in all of the major retailers in the U.S. They do more of the number crunching than the merchants do."

"We have a central sourcing department staffed by professionals who source by category. It is their job to get the products to our stores at the best price and on time. We are developing more efficient systems to control the sourcing process. The nature of retailing in the United States is forcing greater and greater efficiency in cycle times. Anyone who has a win in our industry has that win alone for only a short period of time, because if it works well, it's going to be quickly emulated by others and that just sets the bar higher and higher.

"Our goal is to react closer to customer demand. Becoming a demand chain is one of the profound changes that will occur in our industry over the next decade. The whole industry will migrate away from a demand push system to a pull system based upon what the consumer wants. You have to satisfy customers more effectively today than ever before. They are very demanding."

Post Quota Environment

"In the post quota environment, when Vietnam gets into the WTO, together with China, they will be very strong competitors in exporting apparel. Because nobody wants to put all their business in one country, India, Pakistan, Bangladesh, Indonesia, and a few other countries will remain strong in the sewing trade.

"As you evolve into a relationship with a business partner or manufacturer in the post quota environment, you create basically a verticalization of the two companies. Whether it's fabric or garment design, or technical design, you integrate the process to support the cycle time reduction. The factory receives a basic sloper and tries to achieve a consistent record of hitting your fit model standards. You're responsible for final fit approval. As you fully verticalize, you build what is called a mega-relationship with suppliers who totally understand your fit requirements. This can also extend to color approval and other design aspects."

(continued)

Educational Needs

"To meet the changing needs of the industry, universities should visit and dialogue on an ongoing basis with the apparel manufacturers and retailers as to what they view as their particular needs. It is a challenge for all apparel related higher education providers to understand the dynamics of the industry. Whether it's design or technical design or merchandising, there are specific skill sets required to operate effectively. For graduates to meet the requirements of entry-level jobs, they need to have mastered those skill sets."

Summary

E. Lee Griffith III of the Context Group sees the background for merchandisers changing. "I think the days of the merchandiser/designer who dictates trends, and who has a sort of black magic idea of what the public wants is no longer there. The apparel industry is very much a business that is relying more and more on technology; using information, analyzing information, working with available data to decide what the next styling direction is going to be based on consumer buying patterns. Merchandisers need technological backgrounds, highly quantitative problem solving backgrounds, basic business skills, international business sense, and at the same time they need the design and creative aspect combined with all that. The successful merchandiser needs a little bit of everything, they have to be a fashion superhero."

Key Terms

bills of materials

data warehouses

focus groups

garment specifications

in-store shops

just-in-time (JIT)

line plan

line preview date

line release date

marketing calendar

master production plans

materials management

merchandising calendar

prototyping

shelf stock plan

shippable-mix

strategic planning

style status report

styling consultants

styling services

value-added

work-in-process (WIP)

Discussion Questions and Learning Activities

1. Describe the principal differences between the approach to product development at Anne Klein and Joan Vass.
2. In Case in Point 2.2, which merchandising function is most critical to achieving the shortened development cycle time? What actions should the merchandiser take to ensure that all deadlines are met? Is the same true for the retail product manager of a private label?
3. Use the Internet to research the latest software systems that are available to aid the apparel merchandiser's and product manager's functions. Select one system for each and discuss which area of responsibility it affects and what advantages it offers.
4. Create a want ad for either an apparel merchandiser or product manager.

5. Discuss the possible differences in a merchandiser's responsibilities in a small active sportswear company versus a very large, active sportswear company like Nike.
6. What changes can you envision for the merchandising function in the next 10 years. Will these same changes occur in the retail product manager's function? How will these changes affect the requirements for these positions?

References and Resources

Abend, Jules. September 1998. In-Store Shops Up the Ante for Apparel Brands. *Bobbin*, pp. 32–40.

Bloom, David; Bunasky, Don; Kurtz, Matt; CFT Consulting. September 1998. Getting a Grip on the Evolving IT Environment. *Bobbin*, pp. 98–99.

Flake, Bill; Frank, Bertrand. March 1978. Consumer Buying Patterns Force Market Change. *Apparel Industry Magazine*, p. 68.

Kurt Salmon Associates. March 1997. Quick Response Mandates Today. *Apparel Industry Magazine*, pp. 45–54.

Miller, Lynn Scott. February 1972. *Mademoiselle Magazine*.

Myers, David G. 1998. *Psychology*. New York: Worth.

Being properly prepared to make the multitude of decisions that are needed to develop, execute, and deliver profitable apparel lines requires effective planning. Merchandisers and product managers must obtain an intimate knowledge of their company's target market in order to prepare effective company plans and timetables.

Part 2 analyzes the market factors that must be understood by merchandisers and product managers and the methods of obtaining and evaluating that information. Part 2 also examines the planning and control tools that can be used by merchandisers and product managers to develop company strategic plans, achieve company objectives and establish control over the functions involved in the timely development and execution needed to provide a constant flow of new apparel products to the selling floor. It is important to keep in mind that in this textbook, the title "merchandiser" will be used to refer to both merchandisers in apparel companies and product managers of private label apparel in retail companies.

PART **2**

MERCHANDISING: THE PLANNING

Market Knowledge

- Examine the factors involved in developing a detailed understanding of target markets.

- Evaluate the importance of market segmentation and alternate marketing.

- Explore methods of data collection and industry information sources.

Market knowledge is the comprehensive understanding of a company's market and products. This knowledge is the foundation upon which a successful merchandising effort is built. In order to obtain market knowledge, a merchandiser and product manager must master the available technologies, research techniques, and management principles that can monitor changes in that market. This requires a combination of technical knowledge and practical experience. Technical knowledge can be obtained through academic courses or industry seminars and workshops. Practical experience may be acquired through retail or manufacturing training in a wide variety of jobs. Some companies view retail buyers as potential apparel merchandisers. Others prefer candidates with job experience in design, apparel merchandising, marketing, or manufacturing. No matter how a company selects its merchandisers, the critical element for a successful merchandiser is a thorough knowledge of that company's apparel market and products.

To obtain and update their market knowledge, merchandisers and product managers utilize the following resources:

- Shopping the market—visiting retail stores.
- Meeting with retail buyers and store managers.
- Researching the consumer market by utilizing focus groups, consumer panels, mall intercepts, surveys, and point-of-sale data capture.
- Shopping fabric and trim markets.
- Reading trade and business journals and periodicals.
- Observing lifestyles and tastes within the market community.
- Utilizing the services of styling consultants and forecasting services.
- Using the Internet for research.
- Industry associations.
- Attend national and international trade shows.

■ Target Markets

Apparel merchandisers make key decisions that create next year's fashion trends. These decisions must be based upon an in-depth understanding of their companies' **target markets** (the ultimate consumers who will purchase their products, usually a homogeneous group of customers to whom a company wishes to appeal). Successful merchandisers constantly monitor the pulse of their markets, sensing any subtle changes in consumer preferences. They must be in tune with market shifts at all times. This requires current, accurate, and reliable information.

It is easy for an apparel company with a solid market image to become complacent and lose sight of its target market customers. This was the case with jeans giant Levi Strauss in 1998 when it continued to lose important

market share (the percent of the total sales in a product category that a company generates) in its primary jeans division. Levi's sales had declined by 4 percent to $6.9 billion in 1997.

The young shoppers Levi's once had in its back pocket had moved on to fresher, more exciting brands. The company had been notoriously insular and inert as the competitive environment around it intensified. However, when confronted with lost sales and revenues, the company mapped out important strategic changes including:

1. Paying closer attention to the consumer.
2. Organizing the company around consumer segments instead of brands, while focusing initially on teenagers and young adults.
3. Conducting forward-looking research instead of the "rear-view mirror" approach.
4. Enlarging its portfolio of brands through acquisitions, brand extensions, and brand creation.

> Levi's was so busy maintaining the status quo that it took the consumer for granted. It was so blinded by its success it could not see the tarnish accruing to its image. Meanwhile, a host of powerful and jazzy new competitors arrived, including designer brands like Tommy Jeans and DKNY Jeans, private brands like JCPenney's Arizona and Sears' Canyon River Blues, powerful specialty retailers like Gap Inc. and a host of hot junior names like Mudd, Paris Blues, LEI, JNCO and Fubu. Levi's was being squeezed on all sides [Socha, 1998].

This wake-up call required Levi's to take a closer look at its target market and listen to its ultimate consumers who were no longer satisfied with classic five-pocket jeans.

The Gap went through a similar experience. After many years of successfully meeting the needs of their consumers, comparable store sales began a steady decline. In order to revive their lagging sales, GAP dramatically changed their merchandising assortment. When they introduced trendier styles to attract new customers, their historic shopper could no longer find what they were looking for. As sales continued to drop, GAP once again returned to the style mix that originally brought them success. They also brought in Paul Pressler in 2002 as part of a new management team to restore their tarnished position in the retail world. While their comparative store sales increased consistently for the next two years, it has only happened three times between March 2004 and June 2005. According to some analysts, Gap has still not put forth a comprehensive presentation that is in touch with their customers. In August 2005 the company opened the first of many Forth and Towne stores that caters to the over-35 crowd who were the original GAP consumers. In a unique approach, the store is divided into four segments, each aimed at a different clientele. In his August 23, 2005 *WWD* article, David Moen describes these segments, "Allegory is for classic, conservative, tailored men's wear. Vocabulary is for an individual with her own sense of style. Prize is for the most feminine and flirtatious. Gap Edition is for the most casual and bright."

The Four Ps

Apparel merchandisers must participate in developing the proper marketing mix for their target markets. This mix includes the controllable variables needed to satisfy the target market and develop a line of clothing that will have a high percentage sell-through (the number of units sold at initial selling price divided by the number of units a retailer purchased). The primary variables involved in the marketing mix can be expressed by the four "Ps" of marketing, which are:

Product: creating the "right" garments in terms of silhouette, fabric, color, and fit for the current needs of the target market. "Product" also includes the proper product mix within a line of clothing. In 1998 Levi Strauss realized that part of the reason for its loss of jeans market share was due to the fact that bottoms represented more than 75 percent of Levi's business. According to department stores, denim bottoms represent only about 20 percent of the business in the status jeanswear category. Knits, sweaters, outerwear, and bottoms in nondenim fabrics make up most of the volume in what is increasingly a lifestyle business (Socha, 1998). Levi's restructured its merchandising and marketing efforts to get back on track in producing the "right" garments for its target market.

Place: getting the "right" garment to the target market's "place," which is the retail outlet used by the target market consumers. This may be a retail store or a direct purchase through catalog or Internet sales. The garment reaches the customers through the **channel of distribution**, the process that moves it from the producer to the ultimate consumer. In today's fast-paced society, timing is critical. Therefore quick response methods of sourcing are gaining importance for merchandisers. **Quick response** (**QR**) in the apparel industry is a business strategy that is designed to promote responsiveness to rapidly changing consumer demand. QR utilizes collaborative business partnerships, electronic data interchange, and other computer technologies to link the members of the apparel supply chain in order to reduce inventories and speed the process of supplying products to consumers.

Promotion: informing the target market about the product. The promotional function usually falls under the purview of the marketing department. However, the merchandiser in an apparel company is frequently responsible for the theme and direction for presenting the "right" product to retailers and consumers. Most retail product managers will collaborate with their advertising and visual merchandising departments.

As part of its turnaround strategy, troubled Levi Strauss & Co. vowed that it would focus single-mindedly on young consumers, tuning in to their interests and talking their language. So it wasn't a huge leap to actually let young people create and star in the jeanswear giant's marketing effort to regain market share (Socha, 1998). Merchandisers worked with the teens to assemble their own outfits for the ad campaign.

In many apparel companies, the merchandiser also presents new apparel lines to the marketing department at seasonal meetings, emphasizing how to best sell the salient features of the line. The role of private label managers is to present the new styles to their retail buyers.

Price: establishing the right price for the right product. The merchandiser must consider the competition in the target market and the cost of producing each garment as well as manufacturing overhead and general and administrative costs. The complexities of establishing the price of apparel products are addressed in detail in Chapter 7, Costing and Pricing Strategies.

The consumer is the key to the target market equation but is not an actual part of the marketing mix. The consumer is the target for all marketing and merchandising efforts and is therefore the central focus of the four Ps as shown in Figure 3.1. The needs of the target market establish the marketing mix; therefore, it is critical for merchandisers and product managers to perform their target market research with great care.

FIGURE 3.1 **FOUR Ps**

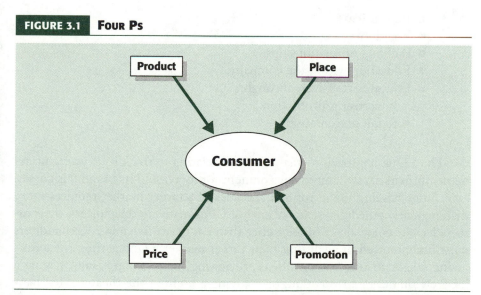

The marketing mix consists of four controllable variables, which are blended to meet the needs of the target market.

Understanding Target Markets

In order to better understand its target market and develop growth opportunities, VF Playwear created the following strategic analysis process: focus, discover, innovate, and communicate (FDIC):

- **Focus**
  - Market size/growth pattern.
  - Volume trend.
  - Consumer opportunity.
  - Target consumer.

- **Discover**
  - Consumer needs.
  - Brand attributes.
  - Product attributes.
  - Customer opportunity/alignment.
  - Consumer profile.
  - Primary/secondary research.
  - Competition.
  - Pricing.

- **Innovate**
  - Product attributes.
  - Styling.
  - Added value.

- **Communicate**
  - Brand imagery.
  - Building of relationships.
  - Education within the company.
  - Educate extensively through:
    - Advertising/promotion.
    - Retail presentation.

The FDIC approach to analyzing and relating to the VF Playwear target market provides a structured environment for increasing its brand businesses.

Understanding the needs and attitudes of a target market requires more than regularly scheduled seasonal analyses. For many merchandisers, their careers have become a way of life rather than a nine-to-five job. Merchandisers must be immersed in analyzing their target market whether they are scrutinizing sales statistics in their offices, reviewing focus group results, having a leisurely dinner at a restaurant, or enjoying a night at the theater. Merchandisers must be constantly aware of what is happening around them and how it may affect their target market.

Merchandisers must understand their consumers in order to develop products that meet the consumers' needs. The most successful merchandisers and designers have one thing in common—they design for their target market customer, not for themselves. Few merchandisers are fortunate enough to work for a company whose target market customer matches their own profile. Therefore, most merchandisers must be able to tune in to their target consumers and project what styling features will attract them as far as a year in the future.

Changing Target Markets

Target markets are shrinking in scope as they become more specialized. In the 1970s U.S. Olympic successes in long-distance running firmly established an active sportswear market for jogging clothes. Olympic champion Frank Shorter and Boston and New York City marathon champion Bill Rogers established their own lines of running gear. This was followed by biking, surfing, basketball (led by the Michael Jordan phenomenon), bodybuilding, aerobics, volleyball, triathlon training, and in-line skating trends complete with their associated highly specialized target markets.

Figure 3.2 Senior citizens have become a target market for active wear. At the Weston Health Club in suburban Philadelphia, a senior citizen wears stretch leotards and cross trainers when using an elliptical exerciser.

In the late 1990s activewear added the adjective "extreme" to its target market definitions. Specialized clothing for skateboarding, mountain biking, roller hockey, snowboarding, and rock climbing incorporated protective padding, reflective materials, and waterproof, windproof, and abrasion resistant fabrications.

As the competition has sharpened for the consumer's apparel expenditures, both retailers and apparel companies alike have identified and pursued smaller and smaller segments of the consuming public. First, there was interest in the baby boomers; next, Generation X, then Generation Y, followed by the Millenniums, and most recently back to the baby boomers—each one having their own needs which are met by successful apparel and retail companies. The plus-size woman has been receiving increased attention. Sears, Wal-Mart, and Kmart have developed merchandise specifically for their Hispanic customers.

The teen market has exploded. Retailers such as Abercrombie/Hollister, American Eagle Outfitters, Forever 21, H and M, and Urban Outfitters, and apparel lines such as Billabong, Juicy Couture, Lucky Brand, Quicksilver, and XOXO offer the trendiest styles demanded by this ever-changing market. The national obsession with physical fitness affects all age groups. Children, ages 6–17, have become increasingly active in both team and individual sports. They are most active in basketball, in-line skating, softball, volleyball, touch football, and roller hockey. Seniors, age 55+, have been blazing fitness trails with over 6.5 million seniors indulging in fitness walking 100 or more days per year. Golf, recreational vehicle camping, weight training, stationary biking, tennis, and bowling are other popular pastimes for this growing demographic group (Sports Apparel Products Council). These research data are critical for the merchandisers who make the decisions aimed at hitting the moving targets of style, color, mix, price, and timing for these specialized target markets.

The increasing number of target markets requires merchandisers to have a more detailed and refined knowledge of market segments and specialized products.

■ Market Segmentation

As markets change, companies must adjust their product lines to accommodate the new needs and desires of their ultimate consumers.

Redefining Markets

In 1996 Donna Karan realized it was time to refine her Collection to meet the changing requirements of her target market. A September 11, 1996, *Women's Wear Daily* article by Janet Ozzard titled, "The Great Divide," summed up her strategy. (See Quotes From The Pros, page 66.)

A similar strategy was embraced by Tommy Hilfiger in 1997 when he unveiled "operation clean-up," a wide-ranging marketing and design strategy that called for cleaner logos and definitive segmenting of his core men's sportswear business into two distinct fashion categories: flag and crest. (See Quotes From The Pros, page 66.)

The process of redefining a target market into smaller more specialized segments is called **market segmentation**. For many companies this process isn't well defined or completely understood. Consumer behavior is extremely complex and is affected by many **demographic** (related to human populations) characteristics. The task of breaking a total market down into homogeneous segments that have a meaningful relationship to a company's product mix is a formidable one. Some factors that are analyzed when a market is segmented are:

- *Demographic trends*: changing age distributions, gender, ethnicity, salaries, social class, geographic populations, family size, education, occupation, spending patterns.

The designer is refining her Collection, renaming her Essentials line to Signature and splitting up her DKNY bridge and casual line into five new labels: D by DKNY, DKNY, Classics, Jeanswear, and Active.

The moves are designed to target the Karan consumer more efficiently and ultimately increase the company's sell-throughs at all price points.

"It's about the potentiality of segmentation," Karan told WWD. "For example, right now DKNY is very diffused; we have everything from high-tech nylon to embroidered dresses to sweatshirts under the same name."

Karan has even worked out a chart showing the demarcations between the various labels, and demonstrating that the company now covers the entire women's market.

"If you're talking about a jacket, the designer line goes from $1,200 to $1,500, Signature is $750 to $850, D is $450 to $650, and DKNY is $295 to $350. Classics is $220 to $365, and jeanswear and activewear will be priced competitively."

The moves were inspired by the education Karan said she is getting from her own stores.

"I'm designing as a retailer now," she said. "I tell my staff, this is no longer about designing as a designer. We're all designing as retailers. I'm learning so much with my retail stores.

"A key part of the whole corporate strategy right now is segmentation," she added. "In this way, we're thinking like retailers, to clarify each brand for the consumer. Isn't that the next stage? It's just cleaner, simpler, nonconfusing" [Ozzard, 1996].

Donna Karan is dividing to conquer.

Hilfiger said his flag sportswear will be modern, fresh, crisp, clean, young in spirit, and full of color. Flag will be marked by the familiar and distinctive red, white, and blue semaphore based on Hilfiger's initials.

Crest would be traditional, subdued, less blatantly logoed, and slightly older. The crest is movable and more subtle and may appear on the chest, or the shirt tail, or may be barely visible in a color on color presentation.

"Our true sportswear is undergoing an evolutionary change," Hilfiger said. "Our customer is growing up. We want to grow up with him."

After building an apparel and accessories empire around a foundation of heavily logoed red-white-and-blue sportswear, Hilfiger said the segmentation was part of an overall strategy of developing new tiers within existing businesses, "filling in all the slots, all the way up to collection," he said [Curan and Lohrer, 1997].

In 2004 Hilfiger unveiled his "H Hilfiger" collection. "This is the first time we've done dressy in a more sophisticated and more grown up way—with no visible logos," Hilfiger explains. H, Mr. Hilfiger adds, layers a new identity onto the Tommy Hilfiger name, providing "a new halo for the brand." [Agins, 2004]

After launching H Hilfiger with much fanfare, including fashion shows and ads featuring David Bowie and Iman, H Hilfiger is retreating from department stores. Tommy Hilfiger Corp. decided to stop delivering the better line to department stores and moved the collection into a new specialty store concept the firm developed. "This will allow us to have greater control over product and presentation," said David Dyer, president and chief executive officer. [Clark, 2005]

Tommy Hilfiger creates three distinct fashion categories: flag, crest, and H Hilfiger.

- *Psychographics*: attitudes of a population, patterns of living, interests, opinions.
- *Social force trends*: religion, family standards.
- *Government influences*: legislation, international agreements, quotas.
- *Economic trends*: stock market fluctuations, inflation, balance of trade, unemployment, consumer spending.

Segmentation Strategies

A major difficulty with market segmentation is that not every potential customer fits neatly into a particular market segment. This poses the problem of adding additional segments or combining segments. The number of segments that a company should develop is a qualitative decision rather than one governed by a scientific rule.

For example, two possible apparel market segments could be:

- 20–50-year-old males, blue-collar workers, live in the Midwest, conservative, sports-oriented, avid TV viewers, drive pickup trucks, interested in durable garments at budget prices, comfort is important, shop discount department stores.
- 25–45-year-old males, white-collar workers, live in the Northeast, liberal, fashion-oriented, drive status autos, interested in quality fabrics and construction details, fit is very important, active sportswear orientation, price is not important, shop specialty stores.

These segments obviously require very different merchandising efforts relative to the 4Ps. The importance of market segmentation is to increase the probable success of matching your product to the needs of the customer. In these two examples, by carefully defining the target market customers, the merchandisers can perform the appropriate market research to determine the "right" product for each market segment. Another example is the difference between the private brands INC and Charter Club as discussed in Executive Perspective 3.2, Joe Feczko.

Figure 3.3 shows the brand action plan formula used by VF Corporation to develop its brand strategies. This 10P approach (people, product, positioning, placement, pricing, packaging, presentation, processing, pull-thru, and push-thru) is the basis of its market segmentation strategy. By providing a market segmentation focus for its marketing and merchandising teams, VF Corporation increases the probable success of matching its products to its customer requirements. Its 10P approach concentrates the efforts of its merchandising teams on common objectives throughout the entire process of development, execution, and delivery of its product lines.

FIGURE 3.3	BRAND ACTION PLAN 10 Ps

1. People	**2. Product**	**3. Positioning**	**4. Placement**	**5. Pricing**
Age	Product categories	Positioning statement	Distribution channels	Pricing strategy
Income	Competitive advantages	Promise	Key stores/ accounts	Price range
Family status	Unique features & benefits	Critical attributes	Geographic penetration	Promotional plan
Geography	Important fabrics & finishes	Rank Vanity Fair Mills' versus competitors' attributes	Penetration focus, target doors to open	Special terms
Attitude/lifestyle				
Fashion style/ motivation	Important silhouettes			
Activities				
Size/shape				
Purchase occasion				
Product Requirements				

6. Packaging	**7. Presentation**	**8. Processing**	**9. Pull-thru**	**10. Push-thru**
Special requirements	Floor positioning strategy	Essential services	Brand awareness goal	Sales material needs
Label strategy	Preferred location on floor	Increase retailer turn	Advertising budget	Sampling strategy
Hang tag strategy	Preferred fixturing	Floor ready requirements	Media plan	Show ads for regional shows
Packaging requirements	POS signage and poster strategy	Planned percentage of business	The message to the consumer is...	Key market dates/ major account meetings
Hanger Requirements	Sales floor education and communication strategy	Basic reorder business as percent of total business	Promotional tie-in	
Poly bag requirements	Store display strategy	Planned floor replenishment as percentage of total business	Sponsorships/ endorsees	
	Technology related presentation ideas		Pedestal product	

The Brand Action Plan of VF Corporation is the basis for the development of their brand strategies. The 10P approach allows its merchandising teams to focus on common objectives throughout the development, execution, and delivery of its product lines.

Segmentation Approach

There are many approaches to market segmentation depending on a company's target market, product category, and competition. The following steps suggest a general approach to market segmentation that can be revised and fine-tuned depending on a company's needs.

1. *Define the broad product market.* This is usually stated in the company's strategic plan; for example, denim jeans.

2. *List potential consumer needs.* In this step it is critical to consider all potential consumers of the broad product market. Review the factors that are analyzed when segmenting a market as a guide; for example, utility and wearability for workers and children, style features for the fashion conscious, fit for the body conscious, uniqueness for teens who want to be different, price for the budget conscious, availability at various retail outlets, comfort for the older jeans customers, brand recognition for the status conscious, and so on.

3. *Create submarkets.* Group potential consumers from step two into submarkets by similar needs and characteristics. It is important to create homogeneous groups that can be satisfied by the same marketing mix and that have common segmentation criteria; for example, lower- to middle-income family teens looking to differentiate themselves from their peers; higher-income family teens who want to make a status statement; construction workers who are looking for reasonable price, comfort, durability, and special features such as utility pockets; horsewomen looking for special features that will provide comfort for riding while not sacrificing style and fit; retirees who want a durable loose-fitting jean that will not bind them while gardening and doing household chores; and so on.

4. *Research the attitudes and behavior of each market segment.* Why do these market segments behave the way the do? What criteria does each segment use to differentiate itself from other segments? What motivates the segments? What exactly drives their purchasing decisions? Getting the answers to these questions will require using market research tools such as focus groups, consumer panels, mall intercepts, and mail and telephone surveys. As more information is gathered on each market segment, new segments may be revealed which may require splitting and identifying additional segments; for example, 18–30-year-old utilitarians may also be concerned about fit and style, thereby creating another submarket—utilitarian-hip. This new market segment may be willing to pay a bit more for the appropriate style and fit.

5. *Identify the consumer needs that drive the purchasing decision.* Review the list of potential consumer needs and highlight those needs that will drive the purchasing decision of the target market consumer for each submarket. Try to rank these needs in order of impact on the final purchasing decision; for example, price, fit, unique styling features, availability at customary retail outlets, status brand recognition, and the like.

6. *Create unique consumer segment identifiers.* Review the list of needs that drive the purchasing decision and determine a unique identifier for each submarket; for example, status teens, utilitarians, generation Xers, fashionphiles, weekend warriors, gray foxes, and so on.

7. *Determine the approximate size of each market segment.* Demographic data from market research such as U.S. census statistics can be utilized to estimate the size of market segments. These data can be helpful in determining which segments offer sufficient potential for a company's sales and distribution capabilities to make them viable targets for new product or brand development; for example, if the "gray fox" segment targets millions of potential customers in the Florida retirement communities for which a jeans company has distribution outlets through large department store chains, that may warrant developing a new brand identification for this market segment.

Market segmentation directs a merchandiser to decide which product market criteria are most important for planning marketing mixes and garment design features. Creating a consistent formula for determining the economic feasibility of developing product lines for specific market segments provides solid justification for complex merchandising decisions. Used effectively, market segmentation can be the driving force behind an apparel line that increases market share for a progressive company.

■ Alternate Marketing

A well-executed market segmentation analysis may provide opportunities for **alternate marketing**, which is increasing market share or developing new products or new markets for an apparel company. Alternate marketing provides opportunities for companies to grow by:

- *Market penetration*: increasing the company's share of market for current products in current markets.
- *Market development*: finding new markets for current products.
- *Product development*: creating new products for current markets.
- *Diversification*: developing new products for new markets.

This concept of alternate marketing is vital in the ever-changing apparel marketplace. In today's marketing-driven business environment, some companies have even found a fifth alternative—the "name game"—in which they increase market penetration by providing the same products under new, catchy, designer-sounding names.

The classic example of alternate marketing occurred in 1850 when Levi Strauss, then 20 years old, left New York on a selling trip to the West. When he reached San Francisco with rolls of canvas intended for gold miners' tents, he found there was no great demand for new tents. What the miners really needed were pants that wouldn't wear out. Levi's alternate marketing decision to make pants out of the tent canvas was the start of one of the most successful apparel ventures in the world. Demand for his pants soared. In order to keep pace with his target market needs, he added rivets at stress points and changed from canvas to a durable fabric from Nimes, France, known as denim. The rest is history.

Recent examples of Alternate Marketing:

- *Market Development:* In 2003 Levi Strauss launched Signature in Wal-Mart and later at Target in an effort to move down-market. Nicole Miller created a line, "nicole by Nicole Miller," for the mid-tier retailer JCPenney.
- *Product Development:* In 2003 Juicy Couture introduced a line of 70 styles of shoes. In 2005 Hugo Boss announced plans to develop Boss Orange for Women to compliment Boss Orange for Men that was first introduced in 1999. The Carole Hochman Design Group, primarily an innerwear company, has plans to enter the foundations business. Donna Karan added accessories in 2004. In 2005 Levi Strauss introduced a line of underwear, loungewear, sleepwear, and daywear.
- *Diversification:* Woolrich began selling bottled water in 2005 to Mid-Atlantic grocery stores and is investigating the potential of selling luggage and backpacks.

Listening to Consumers

In order to effectively use alternate marketing, merchandisers must listen carefully to the changing needs of their customers. This is well illustrated by examples of alternate marketing from Liz Claiborne, Levi Strauss, and Tommy Hilfiger.

Liz Claiborne

In 1996 Paul R. Charron, chairman and CEO of Liz Claiborne Inc., reported to the American Apparel Manufacturers Association's Outlook seminar that, "We have spoken to 6,000 customers since 1995, in what we believe to be the most ambitious research program ever undertaken within the women's fashion apparel industry."

The study, which according to Charron comprised Claiborne's "core sportswear audience, which represents 50 percent of sales and 60 percent of profits," showed that women think there are too many choices, too little time, and too many roles that they must play in the course of a hectic and demanding day.

"We also learned," Charron continued, "that in order to simplify life, women are dressing more casually than ever. But that doesn't mean . . . sloppy or nonwork attire. Rather, 'casualization' is best described as versatility—

clothing that serves multiple uses. Versatility is the new added value woman's apparel."

Citing data that indicate that 25 percent of the consumer population shops in stores like Wal-Mart at least once a week and that in the communities in which the store is located, fully 90 percent shop there with some frequency, Charron said, "Loyalty is disappearing as increased dissatisfaction with the department store shopping experience, and renewed interest in value moves the consumer to consider alternate venues."

Laying the groundwork for that reality, Claiborne stated that its "special markets" activity would reach $200 million within 2 years. It had just moved its Russ division products from department stores initially to Wal-Mart, because, "We think it's the right brand to lead our mass merchant initiative. And we've already had a dialogue with Kmart," Charron said. Another line, the company's First Issue division, would be an exclusive in Sears Roebuck for the first year.

Charron emphasized, "When I'm asked, 'Why in the world would you want to sell Wal-Mart? They're so demanding,' that's exactly why. If we can meet their value equation, if we can be sufficiently sophisticated to address their needs, think of what we can be as a company" (Abend, 1997).

Levi Strauss

In 1998 Levi Strauss & Co. said it was no longer targeting "everyman." Instead, the $6.9 billion jeans giant was intent on building a portfolio of youth-oriented brands and aggressively micromarketing to a younger consumer. Levi's is apparently developing a subbrand of retroinspired jeans under the name Red Line (Knight, 1998).

In 1999 acknowledging that it needed more brands to reach more consumer segments, Levi Strauss had said it planned to build a portfolio of names by launching new brands and more subbrands like Red Line, or through acquisitions.

In 2000, Robert D. Haas, chairman and CEO, said Levi's short-term priority was "extension of our strong megabrands in order to target specific product categories, channels of distribution, or consumer preferences" (Socha, 1999).

Tommy Hilfiger

Tommy Hilfiger announced plans to launch Tommy by Tommy Hilfiger, a more dressy and less logo-driven junior sportswear line, for spring 2000 retailing.

"This will be sexier and more feminine," Hilfiger said of his latest venture. "It will include more dresses, more outfits, more skirts. It'll be more female-driven items and coordinates."

Hilfiger said he planned to bring quality to a category that is not known for it, as well as more modern styling. "Perhaps some designers stay away from the junior business because it is too young," he said, "but we feel strongly that we are a young brand, and we attract a young audience" (Socha, 1999).

These efforts by industry giants Claiborne, Levi's, and Hilfiger show how effective use of alternate marketing can provide continued growth for companies that have matured in their primary target market categories. Without these new opportunities for growth, these companies would experience declining sales.

■ Market Research

Gathering, validating, interpreting, and evaluating information can represent 30 percent to 40 percent of a merchandiser's time. Many apparel merchandisers have administrative assistants whose full-time job is maintaining merchandising information systems.

M. Lederle Eberhardt, vice president design and merchandising at Woolrich, Inc., is no exception. "I have to track what's going on in the market as far as trends are concerned. I have an assistant who does a lot of that for me. The women's business tends to be a little more trendy than the men's business anywhere from fit to styling. My assistant will track what is selling and get information from the stores as to what is being purchased at full price because those are the items that are pulled out first from the stores. We also subscribe to *Women's Wear Daily* and some of the other publications out there, like *Sports Style*, things that are relevant to our industry so we know what's going on. Our positioning in the market is rugged outdoors. We don't produce the high-performance, extreme activewear garments that are worn to go up Mount Everest. We want to be for the people who like the outdoors and if they did climb Mount Everest, they'd come home and put on Woolrich."

The market knowledge necessary for the merchandising function comes from two main sources—primary data collection and general market information.

Data Collection

An ongoing process for merchandisers is the interpretation of data collected to gather statistics about a market, learn what customers think about a company and its products, and learn how customers behave under various conditions. There are a number of methods for gathering data. They fall into two basic categories—quantitative and qualitative research.

Quantitative research focuses on responses to questions that can be summarized by objective, statistical results such as percentages, averages, or

"In Search of Jeans that Fit!"

So you've finally resigned yourself to the fact that your most beloved pair of jeans—those that have memorized exactly where your hips are and how you like to sit when you watch TV—are on their last leg, so to speak. Unfortunately, you now face the daunting task of actually replacing them, or finding another pair in the universe of styles, cuts, colors and brands, that will have star potential. And you're not terribly optimistic.

You're not alone. The Cotton Incorporated *Lifestyle Monitor*™ shows that women are indeed having a tough time when it comes to finding clothes that fit. In fact, 45 percent of women surveyed said that, in general, they could not find clothes that they liked in the correct size. *Monitor* data also shows that, within the last calendar year, the number of women who cited appearance versus practicality as the major concern when buying denim increased by 4 percent to total 50 percent of all responses. And, when it comes to price, 55 percent of women said that they would pay between $21–$40 for a pair of jeans that fit, a figure higher than the $20 average price paid for a pair of women's jeans (according to NPD data as of June 1998).

Back in 1994, Levi Strauss & Co. launched a program called Levi's "Personal Pair" Jeans for Women, which helped customers find the right pair of Levi's jeans to suit their particular body type. The program, which was well received, is currently being re-launched for both men and women under the name Levi's Original Spin™ which, while still giving attention to fit, focuses more on style issues by allowing customers to create their own unique pair of jeans. The customer does this by modifying a basic, five-pocket jean based on a multitude of available options.

From Cotton Incorporated. October 29, 1998. *Women's Wear Daily*, Lifestyle Monitor™.

degrees of agreement or disagreement. Ranking of styles in a line from most salable to least salable is an example of quantitative data gathering. Another form of quantitative analysis is asking respondents how much they agree or disagree with a questionnaire statement.

Qualitative research seeks open-ended responses to questions such as, "What do you think about when making your garment purchasing decisions?" Another example is, "What would be your reaction to a friend's well-tailored suit when she shows you the label, and it is a Fruit of the Loom suit?" Qualitative questions often require follow-up questions so that the researcher can fully understand the motivations behind the interviewee's responses.

Case in Point 3.2

"Levi Strauss Puts a New Spin on Brand Management"

Levi hopes to scramble back up the slippery slope of declining market share and keep its number-one slot by reorganizing the company around the consumer segments that wear its products rather than around the brands themselves.

Levi Strauss's closure of more than 50 percent of its U.S. sewing plants in January 1998 solved the company's long-time problems with excess manufacturing capacity with a $200 million severance package for 6,400 employees. But while the company enthusiastically detailed its generous severance packages and transition programs for its former employees, it was much more sketchy about its plans for its own future.

While its market share had been shrinking for years—down from approximately 48 percent in 1990 to 15.4 percent in spring 1998—in November 1997 Clarence Grebey, director of corporate communications for the San Francisco based company asserted, "We are still the leading brand—we have the lion's share." At the same time, however, Gordon Shank, then-president of Levi Strauss, the Americas, alluded to "a shift in the company's brand management strategy." The company declined to discuss it further then, but on August 20, 1997, John Ermatinger, who replaced Shank as president in April 1998, announced internally a corporate reorganization based on a "consumer-focused brand management business model."

Long criticized for clinging to its heritage five-pocket jean and a philosophy best described in its corporate brochure as a "long-term focus on what it made famous in the first place," Levi Strauss appears to be singing a new song with its revamped corporate structure, which organized the company around two consumer segments—Youth (ages 13–25) and Young Adults (25–35). The Youth segment currently encompasses the Levi brand, while Dockers and Slates fall under Young Adults.

"What a consumer-focused structure does is keep all the work areas in the company focused on what the consumer needs. The result is going to be more trend-right and market-right products in a more timely fashion," says Jeff Beckman, manager of communications.

As an example, Beckman cites Levi's identification of a trend toward dark, hard denim in certain markets, and he says the company has responded with new silhouettes that reinterpret the hard, dark look in two finishes, including one with a soft finish. "We believe there's a huge opportunity in hard jeans, as kids are looking for new ways to wear denim," he notes. "Levi wants to take ownership of this trend."

"Before, we were organized around functions like merchandising and sales and operations under the brands," Beckman says of the company's previous structure. "For example, we had a merchandising department for Dockers. Now, [those] people will think about merchandising for their category of consumers rather than about mer-

(continued)

chandising for Dockers. This has everybody singularly focused on what we're doing for [Young Adults] and how we're meeting their needs and expectations and delivering products that are relevant to [them]."

"This is a business model used by premier marketing companies, but we're making it unique for us by taking the best practices from packaged goods companies and then looking at what other apparel companies are doing and combining the best practices with what we're already doing here that works," Beckman continues.

"In packaged goods, we see a real discipline around business analysis and managing resources and product development. It's a real analytical, business based approach to developing and marketing product. But in apparel there's a creative and intuitive element that's trend-sensitive to meet the changing needs of consumers. Procter & Gamble may test 50 kinds of laundry detergent to deliver two, but we aren't going to do that because our timeline is so much faster in terms of delivering trend-right products to market."

While Beckman claims that the structure is still unfolding and its impact on product development is still unknown, he emphasizes the industry will see "more fashion-forward product, more trend-right product, and faster product development that delivers these products [to retail] much more quickly."

Two areas Levi might use to anticipate new trends and consumer wants and needs are its Web sites and its new Levi's Original Spin program, which replaces the Personal Pairs program. Several industry experts have noted that Levi has invested heavily in new data warehouses and decision-support technology, for which it may leverage both of these programs to enhance point-of-sale (POS) data and other information it collects.

"Our digital marketing has already begun to play a significant role in this new relationship [with the consumer]," Beckman notes. "For example, on levis.com, there is an area where consumers can register with the brand. The Be In Club opens a dialogue with consumers and lets us provide them with information about activities in their area that are relevant to their lifestyle. It also lets us understand what they want from the Levi brand."

Levi's Original Spin program, which launched in select markets last summer, reaches consumers with computerized kiosks where consumers can work their way through a touch-screen menu that explains the program and their options, and walks them through the process of designing their own jeans.

"Personal Pairs was about being a fit solution for women," Beckman explains. "Original Spin is all about providing choices to men and women that allow them to express their personal style. This [Young] consumer group has told us individualized fashion is very important to them because it tells people who they are. For example, if I express myself though loose-fit dark jeans, then I can do that in a way that's special to me with Levi's Original Spin."

"Although initially it's a small program, it's the best one we have right now to develop intimate relationships with consumers," he observes. "Working with consumers to design a product gives us a great place to get direct feedback. We can monitor the requests they're making, and not only can we consider adding the elements they request, but it gives us information useful to all the Levi's brands." ■

From Suzette Hill. December 22, 1998. *Apparel Industry Magazine*, pp. 1–3.

| Cases in Point 3.1 and 3.2 | **Summary** |

Cases in Point 3.1 and 3.2 focus on the importance Levi Strauss has placed on targeting specific market segments. The giant jeans company has integrated market segmentation, alternate marketing, and many multiple research techniques into its strategic plan to restructure the company around two consumer segments. Developing and maintaining a comprehensive understanding of its critical target market is the basis of its new strategy. Market knowledge and research are the pivotal functions that will form the foundation of Levi's new "consumer-focused brand management business model." ∎

Focus Groups

A popular form of qualitative analysis is the focus group. A focus group involves 6 to 12 consumers chosen from a target market segment who are interviewed as a group in an informal setting by a skilled group leader. Questions are open-ended with the leader trying to stimulate group interaction. The sessions are frequently videotaped so they can be carefully analyzed by the merchandising team. Visual reactions to questions by the group members are observed as well as the members' verbal responses.

Gary Simmons, former president of VF Playwear, used focus groups as a meaningful element of his market research. "While we're building a line, we talk to the consumers. We do 50 focus groups a year. We also do about 16 to 20 mall intercepts a year. So we try to constantly get information from the consumer who we listen to in concert with the retailer."

Luxury brands also use this method for consumer research. For example, in 2005 Robert Polet requested that his designers at Gucci keep in touch with consumers by conducting focus groups.

Mall Intercepts

An increasingly popular form of data collection is done at shopping malls. Interviewers stop shoppers who fit a market segment profile and ask them to participate in a short survey. This form of market research is called **mall intercepts** (see Figure 3.4). An advantage of this type of research is that the interviewers can approach consumers coming out of a particular store that carries the interviewer's company's products. A disadvantage is that during a personal interview the interviewer may influence the response or the interviewee may not give a candid response if the true answer is negative.

Consumer Panels

Some companies use **consumer panels**—a select group of consumers who provides information on a continuing basis. A popular form of consumer panel is a teen fashion council made up of local teens from selected schools.

Figure 3.4 A professional surveyor interviews a shopper in a regional mall to gather consumer preference information about an apparel product.

They meet periodically and review styles being considered for next year's line. VF Corporation sponsors a Lee's Trend Leaders panel, which is composed of 35 young men and women who are peer-group fashion leaders. They share their views with the product development staff.

Mail Surveys

Mail questionnaires are used for extensive surveys. The response rate is usually low, 20 percent or lower, and the results may be skewed because respondents tend to be those people most interested in the topic, thereby minimizing negative responses. Multiple-choice and fill-in-the-blank questions are the most effective since they are easiest for the respondents to answer. A key factor in the success of mail surveys is the quality of the mailing list. The survey recipients must meet the target market criteria of the company. This method of market research is usually the most economical.

Telephone Surveys

Telephone surveys provide quick results and allow interviewers to probe the respondents to determine the scope of their feelings and attitudes. National surveys of over 1,000 interviews can be performed and logged into computer databases in one evening by reliable research firms.

Point-of-Sale Data

Today's bar-coded garment labels and scanners at retail checkout stations allow for point-of-sale (POS) data capture of garments by style, color, and size. With computer interfaces, this information can be transmitted in real time to apparel manufacturers from retail partners throughout the United States. These data can provide valuable sell-through information for apparel manufacturers and retail product managers.

Corporate Sales Records

Charting past sales records by style classification provides trend analyses that can guide merchandisers in the product development process. Many companies have applied data mining to their management information systems (MIS). **Data mining** is a process of using a variety of data analysis tools to discover patterns and relationships in customer and product data that may be used to make valid predictions. Computers and database applications have made it relatively easy to search out, interpret, and evaluate important data imbedded in company records.

Web Sites

The Internet has become a powerful business tool that can provide instant access to important government statistics and useful industry data.

Gary Simmons, former president of VF Playwear, finds the Internet a valuable resource, "We get our fashion direction from traditional sources: fashion forecasting services, fashion trade publications, but we've also added a new resource. We subscribe to Global Style Network from WORTH. It's an Internet service that keeps us up to date on everything that's happening in fashion anywhere in the world. If there was a fashion show yesterday in Milan, we go on the Internet and we can see what was in the fashion show. If I want to see what happened at retail in San Francisco, I can click on the Internet, go to San Francisco through the Global Style Network, and see what was shopped there this week. It's fabulous."

Industry Information Sources

In addition to target market data, merchandisers need to stay up to date on industry and fashion direction. With fashion constantly changing, keeping up with the industry is a challenging task.

Trade Shows

The textile and apparel industries sponsor national and international trade shows, fairs, and seminars. Merchandisers can shop their competition almost any week of the year somewhere around the globe.

In addition to international shows, there are regularly scheduled market weeks at the regional apparel marts. The shows and market weeks are highlighted by extravagant fashion shows, parties, and events designed to capture the allure and imagination of the latest collections for the retail buyers eager to place their initial orders for a new season.

Figure 3.5 The Worth Global Style Network provides current intelligence about the global apparel supply chain.

Vanna Longwell, former vice president of merchandising for Motherswork, utilizes the major shows as a primary industry information source, "We do our market research at major shows such as the Missy and Junior shows at the LA Mart, the New York shows, which are one week earlier, London, Paris, and sometimes Italy. We try to go to Premiere Vision, Prado export, and the Pitti Filatti for high-end knits and yarns. Traveling to the major fashion cities and asking a lot of questions is a good way to keep up with the market direction. We shop the stores and have a California buying office that provides us with West Coast trends. We also get good input from the predictive services: Cottonworks, Wool Bureau, Promostyl, Tobe [retail], and Colour Authority."

Trade Publications

Another valuable resource for merchandisers is trade publications. (See Figure 3.7.) These periodicals provide in-depth reporting on the latest events in each segment of the apparel industry. General industry magazines include *Bobbin*, and *Lectra*. Publications related to women's wear include *Women's Wear Daily, California Apparel News, Mode, Contours, Sportswear and Knitting Times, Beachwear and Skinwear, Hong Kong Apparel News, Forecast International Fashion, Clothing World, Trends, Collezioni*, and *Sportswear International. Earnshaws, Children's Business, Kids Creations*, and *Bambini Collezioni* are some periodicals that focus on children's wear. The men's wear sector is serviced by *Menswear* and *Daily News Record*. Magazines focusing on fabrics include *Printwear, DuPont*, and *Textile World*.

Subscriptive Services

There are a number of specialty forecasting services available to merchandisers on a subscription basis. Such services may cost as much as $20,000 or more per year. These subscriptive services provide periodic reporting on yarn, fabric, color, silhouette, and retail sales trends. The high cost of these services can often be justified because acquiring the information the services provide would require a full-time staff of market researchers and stylists. A sampling of these services follows:

TRADE SHOWS

Hong Kong Fashion Week, Hong Kong Convention & Exhibition Center, Wanchai, Hong Kong. Organizer: Hong Kong Trade Development Council, 38th Floor, Office Tower, Convention Plaza, 1 Harbour Road, Wanchai, Hong Kong.

Bangkok International Fashion Fair, Bangkok International Trade & Exhibition Center, Bangkok, Thailand. Organizer: Department of Export Promotion, Ministry of Commerce, Royal Thai Government, 22/77 Rachadapisek Road, Chatuchak, Bangkok 10900, Thailand.

International Kids Fashion Show, Jacob K. Javits Convention Center, New York City. Organizer: The Larkin Group, 485 Seventh Avenue, Suite 1400, New York, NY 10018.

Pret a Porter, Paris, Porte de Versailles, Hall 7. Organizer: SODES, 5 rue de Caumartin, 75009 Paris.

Herren Mode/Inter-Jeans, Koln Messe, Messeplatz 1, 50679 Cologne, Germany. Organizer: Koln Messe, Messe und Austellungs Ges.mb.h., Koln, Messerplatz 1, D-50679 Koln, Postfach 210760 D-50523 Koln, Germany.

CPD Dusseldorf, Dusseldorf, Germany. Organizer: Igedo Company, Stockumer Kirchstrasse 61, D-40474 Dusseldorf, Germany.

ISPO, New Munich Trade Fair Center, Germany. Organizer: Messe Munchen GmbH, Messeqelande, D-81823, Munchen, Germany.

Pitti Filatti (fabrics), Fierra Milano, Italy. Organizer: Pitti Immagine, Via Faenza, 109, 50123 Florence, Italy.

MAGIC West, Las Vegas Convention Center, Las Vegas, NV; **WWDMagic**, Sands Expo Center, Las Vegas, NV. Organizer: MAGIC International, 6200 Canoga Avenue, Suite 303, Woodland Hills, CA 91367.

UK Fashion Fair, London, England. Organizer: Igedo Company, Stockumer Kirchstrasse 61, D-40474 Dusseldorf, Germany.

Intermezzo Collections, Piers 90 and 92 at the Show Piers on Hudson, 12th Avenue and 55th Street, New York City. Organizer: ENK International, 3 East 54th Street, New York, NY 10022.

Figure 3.6 The WWD Magic Show is held twice a year in Las Vegas attracting large numbers of apparel manufacturers and retailers.

Figure 3.7 Trade publications communicate vital information to all members of the textile and apparel supply chain and provide a valuable resource for merchandisers to maintain their knowledge of the market.

REGIONAL APPAREL MARTS

AmericasMart Apparel, Atlanta, GA. (800) ATL-MART.

California Mart, Los Angeles, CA. (213) 630-3600.

Chicago Apparel Center, Chicago, IL. (312) 527-7610.

Concourse Exhibition Center, San Franciso, CA. (925) 328-1122.

Denver Merchandise Mart, Denver, CO. (303) 292-6278.

Hyatt Merchandise Mart, Minneapolis, MN. (800) 272-6972.

Miami International Merchandise Mart, Miami, FL. (561) 753-6490.

- Color Association of the United States, (212) 947-7774.
- The Color Council, (212) 473-0692.
- Concepts in Colour, (212) 967-5688.
- Sharon Gray, (212) 944-9079.
- Promostyl, (212) 921-7930.
- The Doneger Group, Inc., (212) 564-1266.
- Cottonworks, Cotton Incorporated, (919) 678-2220.
- Margit Publications, (212) 302-5137.
- Worth Global Style Network, (212) 946-2738.

Web Sites

It seems that every day more Web sites are established that focus on the apparel industry. These Web sites are a rich source of free information. There are sites that cover every area of fashion and apparel.

- **General apparel sources**: American Apparel Producers' Network, Apparel Design, Apparel News, Apparel Online, Apparel Net, Apparel Strategist, Canada Apparel Network, National Textile Center.
- **Apparel associations**: American Apparel and Footwear Association, American Textile Manufacturers Institute, Atlantic Apparel Contractor's Association, International Apparel Federation, International Swimwear and Activewear Market, International Textile and Apparel Association.
- **Apparel industry**: Apparel & Textile Network, Apparel Exchange, Apparel Industry International, Apparel Information Management System, Apparel Manufacturing Software.
- **Fashion sources**: Angel of Fashion, CJLutz Fashion, Clothing & Textiles Home Page Brigham Young University, Denim Survival Guide, Fashion Canada, Fashion Central, Fashion China, Fashion Di-

rectory, Fashion Internet, Fashion Line, Fashion Live, Fashion Navigator, Fashion Net, Fashion Trends Forecast, Firstview, Inside Fashion, 7th on Sixth.

- **Fashion designers**: Etienne Aigner, Giorgio Armani, Jhane Barnes, Hugo Boss, Thomas Brent, Kenneth Cole, Dolce & Gabbana, Raoul Duty, Fendi, Gianfranco Ferre, Egon von Furstenberg, Jean Paul Gautier, Gucci, Donna Karan, Krizia, Mary McFadden, Nicole Miller, Missoni, Moshino, Todd Oldham, Emilio Pucci, Sonia Rykiel, Valentino.
- **Fashion history**: Boys' Historical Clothing, Costume Gallery, Costume Imagebase, Costume Site, La Couturiere Parisienne, Past Patterns, Regency Fashion, Victorian Fashion.
- **Fashion magazines**: *Accent, Allure, Catwalk, Cosmopolitan Fashion— UK, Cosmopolitan Italia, Cosmopolitan Magazine, Elle, Elle* (France), *Fashion Icon, Fashion Planet, Fashion UK, Flare Online, Glamour Magazine, Hint Fashion Magazine, The Look, Lucire, Lumiere, Mademoiselle, NY Style, NYW, Passion, Sportswear International, Viabazaar* (Harpers), *Vogue, Women's Wear Daily, World of Style*.

Bud Konheim Experience—CEO, Nicole Miller

Niche Business

"In 1982 when I started Nicole Miller, I was focused on developing a very credible one-price, one-level, brand-name business. I wanted a niche business, and it was not going to be the biggest because the biggest is actually the most vulnerable. There are very few people who get away with that. And you can name them. It's Ralph Lauren and Calvin Klein who today are really licensing businesses. Liz Claiborne is a combination of really well structured businesses that are also successful commercial brands. They have Dana Buchman; they have Liz, Liz Sport; they have Claiborne; they have Russ Togs. And they are all well run businesses making commercial stuff. They don't pretend to be designers. They're really merchandisers and mainstream suppliers.

"What we've done at Nicole Miller is taken niches that we really understand. One of the niches is of course Nicole herself. Her niche is that she doesn't do market research. She designs for her lifestyle. And the customers buy into that. And her lifestyle has stayed about twenty-two years old. She's always mentally twenty-two. If you do one thing and do it well, you can have a very healthy business without selling everybody. The key word is loyalty. If you can develop loyalty in your niche, you have a very successful business that doesn't have to do sales in the billions."

That's Merchandising

"The structure of our company has stayed the same from its inception to today. Nicole is the designer, and she's responsible for that part of the business, and I'm responsible basically for all the rest. I'm kind of 'Mister Outside' because I understand our retailers. I'm very sales oriented. In a specialty niche company like ours we must work together as a team to do the merchandising. When Nicole shows me the latest thing she wants to do, I have to put on my merchandising hat. I might say I get the idea but it's overdesigned for our marketplace. My suggestion may be to simplify it. Or she shows me something and I'll say, you know, it's out there already. Then she tweaks it and comes up with a fresh approach. That's merchandising.

"Merchandising is what big businesses are all about in the United States today. It's not about designing. Jones is merchandising. Liz Claiborne is merchandising. Ralph Lauren is not about designing. Ralph himself is not a designer.

(continued)

Tommy Hilfiger is not a designer. Liz Claiborne was a designer, but she's not there anymore. So what they do is merchandise those businesses to have so many suits and so many of this and so many of that. They merchandise a certain look. It requires a very focused analysis of their markets. The country is not really fashion-oriented."

Today, the Customer Is King

"We do our merchandising with everybody in the loop all the time—Nicole, myself, our sales force, our retail stores. We have our own 30 stores. The stores act as a promotional tool, making the brand credible. We have a store on Madison Avenue and a store in SoHo.

"Today, the customer is king. Customers can buy on the Internet or buy on QVC or run around to a discount store or go to a regular store or go anyplace they want to. Today you have to start with what appeals to the customer. You work backwards to what you are going to supply, and you'll figure it out pretty fast. It's important to listen to your customers. We just came up with an interesting result. We're constantly looking for feedback from our customers through our 30 stores. What came up was that customers today really prefer comfort over anything. Comfort over fashion. We're still making fashion, but it's gotta be comfortable fashion."

Joe Feczko Experience—executive vice president, chief creative officer, Macy's Corporate Marketing

Two-Part Marketing Strategy

"We have a two-part marketing strategy. We have both private label and private brand product lines. Our private brands are categorized into four lifestyle buckets. The first is traditional, which speaks for itself. The second is neo-traditional, which is a traditional brand that has a nod towards a little more fashion direction or a bit more of a contemporary lifestyle. The third is the contemporary lifestyle, which clearly is for the fashion-forward customer. The fourth is the fashion customer who is only interested in the hottest new fashion trends. Most of our business falls into either the neo-traditional or the traditional lifestyle buckets.

"Private brands are defined as categories of goods that completely commit to a certain lifestyle and a certain customer demographic. Our INC line is a neo-traditional to a contemporary class of customer at a specific price point. Our Style & Company private brand is basically a centered neo-traditional brand, which caters to more moderate price points, but a customer who still wants neo-traditional fashion styling.

"Private label is used for opportunities that come about when a new fashion trend or possibly a special price point doesn't fit into one of our private brand strategies. We create the item because we don't want to miss the sales revenue and the opportunity, but we create it under a private label that does not tarnish the image of one of our private brands.

"We want our private brands to have the same design sensibilities as competitive national brands with the same quality at a relative or better value for our customers. We want them to stand on their own in terms of design.

"A typical model for many retailers in the private label business is to take last season's styles and manufacture them at a lower price for the next season. To be in the private brand business, you need design teams, and you need to take some risks betting on upcoming trends. We have become very successful at being fashion risk takers, which is important for you to be successful in the fashion business.

"Our private brand business has created true differentiation between ourselves and our competition. We offer products that are exclusive and not available at our competitors."

(*continued*)

Executive Perspective 3.2 (*continued*)

Marketing and Advertising

"It was a lot easier when you could use a one-size-fits-all strategy for your advertising. There was a time when you could run a 30-second spot on the Ed Sullivan Show and target nearly 100 percent of your audiences. Today the business of advertising has gotten very fragmented. You need different messages for different age groups and ethnically diverse customers. You must be aware of your media outlets. Broadcast is now fragmented between network and cable channels as well as the new complexities of Internet advertising, outbound e-mail and text messaging. Getting your message to the right consumers is much more complicated than ever before.

"Through our private brand marketing efforts, we are gaining confidence on how to sell better goods with little or no resistance to price points. Our merchants are becoming much more confident and more competent in terms of how to work with better fabrics, more sophisticated designs and updated styles. We are truly private brand designers in a broad array of categories from basic promotional price points to better, and we touch on the fringe of luxury price points."

Preparing Students

"To prepare students for careers in retail private label and private brands, they have to be taught to be critical thinkers. They have to gain experience in all aspects of the apparel business. Today's market requires a global perspective and a holistic approach to the business. Students must learn the different aspects of design, sourcing, manufacturing and marketing, and understand how the different parts of the process work and how they rely on each other.

"Students who want to be successful in today's market must not get caught up in a solo mentality where they are just concerned about the design process or the manufacturing process. They must keep their eye on the total business picture, because those who do are the ones who are the most successful. These future leaders are sensitive to their partners in the team process and understand the big picture."

Summary

Successful merchandisers and product managers must have a comprehensive understanding of their companies' market and products. This knowledge requires in-depth research and analysis of a company's target market. The merchandiser's ultimate objective is to provide the "right" product at the "right" price in the "right" place using effective promotion to obtain a high percentage sell-through at retail. To achieve these four "Ps" of marketing, a merchandiser must focus the efforts of the design department on developing products that meet the needs of the target market.

Target markets are getting smaller in size and are increasing in number, thereby making the job of merchandising more difficult. Market segmentation is an effective strategy for analyzing the effects of demographic, psychographic, social, government, and economic factors on a target market. Market segmentation allows a merchandiser to focus product development efforts on the specific design factors that will meet the needs of their target market and thereby increase market share.

Merchandisers can develop new opportunities for growth by carefully analyzing the market segments within a target market. Alternate marketing focuses on developing new markets, new products, or increasing market share for current products in current markets. It requires constant communication with consumers and careful analysis of their changing needs. Alternate marketing is a vital tool to prevent declining sales for companies with product categories that have reached a mature stage of development.

To obtain a high level of market knowledge requires comprehensive and sophisticated market research. Merchandisers must gather, validate, interpret, and evaluate large amounts of data. Data is collected through quantitative and qualitative research and is analyzed using data mining techniques and other market research tools. Merchandisers complement market research with a growing number of industry information sources that allow them to spot raw material, styling, and consumer trends. Successful apparel merchandisers in today's global marketplace must stay tuned in to their target market. This requires developing a constantly evolving knowledge base and using the latest computer technologies to tap into that information to make timely, critical, merchandising decisions.

Key Terms

alternate marketing

channel of distribution

consumer panels

data mining

demographic

mall intercepts

market knowledge

market segmentation

market share

qualitative research

quantitative research

quick response (QR)

target market

Discussion Questions and Learning Activities

1. Discuss the importance of market knowledge to today's apparel merchandisers and retail private label product managers.
2. What method of data collection provides the quickest results for either apparel merchandisers or private label product managers?

3. What do you think Levi Strauss could have done to prevent the erosion of its primary jeans market? Could the GAP have used the same approach to keep its customer base intact?

4. Discuss what factors in the current apparel market may affect the ability to acquire market knowledge.

5. Investigate U.S. government Web sites or publications and locate data that would provide merchandisers and product managers with target market information. Discuss how this data could be used in making product development discussions.

6. Research fashion Web sites to discover a change in styling direction for a specific target market. (Hint: Use a Web search engine to locate sites on fashion or fashion design.) Be sure to find at least three resources that support the change.

7. What type of market knowledge was enhanced by Donna Karan's retail experiences? Explain how other apparel designer's retail stores can change their merchandising focus today.

8. Visit an apparel store at which you normally do not shop. Analyze a product category within the store and develop a segmentation profile of the consumers (target market) who shop there.

9. Discuss the common technique of Donna Karan, Tommy Hilfiger, Liz Claiborne, and Levi Strauss to increase their volume. Can this same strategy be used by JCPenney or Federated Department Stores to increase the sales of their private brands?

10. Explain which data collection method would be the most effective for a children's wear company that wants to develop a line of clothing in a children's wear category that it currently does not service. Which data collection method would be the most effective for a retailer who wants to develop a new category of private brand apparel?

11. From the Bud Konheim Executive Perspective 3.1, explain how the company maintains a thorough knowledge of its target market.

12. Give examples of apparel companies using three different forms of alternate marketing.

References and Resources

Abend, Jules. February 1997. Levi's, Claiborne, Kmart Getting Refocused. *Bobbin*, p. 22.

Agins, Teri. March 19, 2004. Tommy Hilfiger Brings the Runway to Retailers for 'H'. *Wall Street Journal*, pp. B1–B2.

Clark, Evan. February 3, 2005. H Hilfiger to Leave Department Stores. *www.wwd.com*.

Cotton Incorporated. October 29, 1998. In Search of Jeans That Fit! *Women's Wear Daily*, Lifestyle Monitor™.

Curan, Catherine; Lohrer, Robert. August 4, 1997. Hilfiger Maps Segmentation of Men's Sportwear Business. *Women's Wear Daily*, p. 27.

Galloni, Alessandra. August 9, 2005. At Gucci, Mr. Polet's New Design Upends Rules for High Fashion. *Wall Street Journal*, p. 1.

Hill, Suzette. December 22, 1998. Levi Strauss Puts a New Spin on Brand Management. *Apparel Industry Magazine*, pp. 1–3.

Knight, Molly. November 23, 1998. Levi's to Acquire, Develop Youth Brand in Effort to Win Over Kids, Teens. *Daily News Record*, pp. 1–4.

Ozzard, Janet. September 11, 1996. Donna Karan The Great Divide. *Women's Wear Daily*, p. 1.

Socha, Miles. January 22, 1998. Levi's Shifts into Fashion Cycle. *Women's Wear Daily*, p. 1.

Socha, Miles. September 17, 1998. Shank's Aim: Reclaim Levi's Luster. *Women's Wear Daily*, p. 1.

Socha, Miles. November 17, 1998. Levi's New Campaign Is Youth Driven. *Women's Wear Daily*, p. 17.

Socha, Miles. January 5, 1999. Hilfiger Plans to Launch Junior Division in 2000. *Women's Wear Daily*, p. 1.

Socha, Miles. January 12, 1999. Jacobi Will Retire as Levi's President, Operating Chief. *Women's Wear Daily*, p. 9.

Sports Apparel Products Council. 1996. Activewear Trends Report. *Sporting Goods Manufacturers Association*.

CHAPTER 4

Planning and Control

OBJECTIVES

■ Examine the importance of planning and control to effective merchandising.

■ Identify the planning and control tools used by merchandisers.

■ Understand the merchandiser's responsibility in managing the interaction of planning and control tools and interfacing with other departments.

Effective planning and control are vital to the success of today's apparel companies. The function of development, execution, and delivery of apparel product lines is becoming increasingly complex and time-critical. To be consistently successful season after season, apparel merchandisers must utilize powerful planning and control tools.

■ The Importance of Planning and Control in Today's Global Environment

The apparel industry is totally global. Many U.S. companies have established alliances in almost every developing country with locally owned factories that serve as subcontractors to produce an entire range of apparel products. These production relationships can be, and are, moved from country to country, producer to producer, with increasing speed as apparel companies search for the best tax deals and the most efficient and lowest-cost labor forces. Nike first established its Asian production facilities in Japan, but when costs became too high, it hopped over to Korea and then went to Thailand, China, the Philippines, Indonesia, and Vietnam (Friedman, 1998). This scenario is frequently replayed by many apparel manufacturers and private label retailers.

In order to be effective in this global marketplace, there are many factors that must be overcome:

- Communication is difficult because of language differences.
- Complex product specifications and quality requirements create difficulties because of differences in cultural and business paradigms.
- Travel to the far reaches of the globe to visit factories and negotiate prices is arduous and time-consuming.
- Varying production lead times, logistic capacities, and shipping schedules create scheduling problems.
- Stability of foreign governments, international economic conditions, and human rights must be constantly monitored.
- U.S. government regulations and terrorism concerns complicate the import process.

Detailed planning and fail-safe control systems are vital for successful apparel merchandising in this complex global environment.

■ Changing Consumer Demands

To further complicate the task of planning and controlling the apparel product development and production processes, merchandisers and product managers are faced with retailers and consumers demanding more frequent offerings of more and more styles. Merchandisers are confronted with "seasonless" seasons. The spring, summer, fall, and winter (holiday) offerings have evolved into product lines that for many companies change on a monthly basis. Retailers want a constant flow of fresh new products to draw customers into their stores, and consumers eagerly anticipate the next fashion change. The result is a planning nightmare.

With two seasons per year (spring/summer and fall/winter), merchandisers of the past could lay out a standard six-month product development plan for each season. This allowed the design team to complete the line development process for one season before starting the process for the next season. Table 4.1 shows the orderly planning that existed for two seasons per year.

When the number of seasons per year increased to four seasons (spring, summer, fall, and winter/holiday), design teams had to work on two seasons simultaneously. Figure 4.1 shows the increasing complexity of planning for four seasons per year. The design teams developed prototypes for one season while beginning color, fabric, and silhouette research on the next season.

With 12 offerings per year and a six month development cycle, the line development functions would overlap so that the design team would be simultaneously working on six lines. Through the use of computer-aided design (CAD) equipment (see Figure 4.3) and by streamlining the design function, many companies have compressed the product development cycle to one to two months. Under this scenario the design team must juggle three different lines at the same time.

With today's rigorous consumer demands, merchandisers must establish clearly defined operating plans and utilize precise methods of control or they will be courting disaster. Without careful planning, merchandisers will fulfill the old adage, "by failing to plan, you are planning to fail."

■ Planning and Control Tools

Apparel merchandisers must utilize effective tools to perform the complex planning and control functions necessary to deliver apparel product lines under today's compressed time constraints. With greater competition and less time to develop products that meet rapidly changing consumer demands, merchandisers must perform their responsibilities with greater precision. This requires well-defined planning and disciplined execution of all merchandising functions.

The need for new systems of planning and control was evident as long ago as 1973 when the main theme of the Bobbin Show/AAMA (American Apparel Manufacturers Association) Convention opening seminar was the means of achieving closer coordination and control with regard to merchandising and manufacturing activities. A *Bobbin* magazine article reviewing that seminar stressed the importance of planning and control systems. "Only the swiftest

---

TABLE 4.1

Men's Clothing Manufacturer's Merchandising Calendar
Two Seasons per Year

Spring 2005

Start		Finish		Activity	Responsibility
Mon.	1/12/04	Mon.	1/12/04	Preliminary Meeting Spring 2005	JL
Tues.	1/13	Wed.	3/3	Design and cut prototypes	RT
Tues.	2/10	Tues.	2/10	Piece Goods and line meeting	JL
Thurs.	3/4	Thurs.	3/4	Review meeting of design and cut prototypes	RT
Mon.	3/8	Fri.	3/26	Select models for photo shoots	GK
Mon.	3/15	Fri.	4/9	Order piece goods for sales rep samples	CW
Tues.	4/6	Wed.	4/7	Finalize line	JL
Wed.	4/7	Wed.	4/7	Decide on advertising samples	TW
Thurs.	4/8	Fri.	4/16	Prepare all manufacturing and spec sheets	RT
Thurs.	4/8	Tues.	4/13	Fabric and trim tests	RT
Mon.	4/12	Mon.	4/12	Authorize sales rep samples	TW
Wed.	4/14	Wed.	4/14	Cut advertising samples	SC/RT
Wed.	4/21	Fri.	5/7	Receive sales rep sample goods	CW
Wed.	4/21	Wed.	4/21	Finalize all manufacturing and spec sheets	RT
Mon.	4/26	Fri.	5/7	Initial sales forecast	TW
Mon.	5/3	Fri.	5/7	Order production piece goods and trim	CW
Mon.	5/3	Fri.	5/21	Cut sales rep samples	SC/RT
Mon.	5/10	Fri.	5/21	Complete advertising samples	SC/RT
Thurs.	5/20	Wed.	5/26	Photograph advertising samples	GK
Mon.	5/24	Fri.	5/28	Product costing of old styles	SC
Mon.	5/31	Fri.	6/4	Develop new yields	SC
Mon.	6/7	Fri.	6/11	Product costing of new styles	SC
Mon.	6/14	Fri.	6/18	Price line	KM
Thurs.	7/1	Fri.	7/9	Complete sales rep samples	SC/RT
Thurs.	7/1	Fri.	7/9	Complete advertising materials	GK
Mon.	7/12	Wed.	7/21	Key customers view line and place advance orders	TW
Thurs.	7/22	Fri.	7/23	Sales meeting (Line Preview)	TW
Mon.	8/2	Mon.	8/2	Second sales forecast	TW
Mon.	8/9	Fri.	8/13	Supply projected mix to manufacturing	CW
Mon.	8/16	Fri.	11/19	Receive first production piece goods	CW
Mon.	8/23	Fri.	12/17	Advance sales orders	TW
Mon.	8/30	Mon.	8/30	Project first cuttings	CW
Mon.	9/13	Fri.	3/4/05	Cutting	SC
Mon.	9/27	Fri.	3/18/05	Manufacturing	SC
Fri.	11/5	Fri.	4/22/05	Finished goods to inventory	SC

Merchandising calendars from an apparel company that produces tailored clothing for spring and fall seasons.

(continued)

TABLE 4.1	*Continued*

**Men's Clothing Manufacturer's Merchandising Calendar
Two Seasons per Year**

Fall 2005

	Start		Finish	Activity	Responsibility
Mon.	8/6/04	Mon.	8/6/04	Preliminary Meeting Fall 2005	JL
Tues.	8/17	Fri.	10/1	Design and cut prototypes	RT
Tues.	8/31	Tues.	8/31	Piece Goods and line meeting	JL
Thurs.	9/30	Thurs.	9/30	Review meeting of design and cut prototypes	RT
Fri.	10/1	Fri.	10/15	Select models for photo shoots	GK
Mon.	10/4	Fri.	10/29	Order piece goods for sales rep samples	CW
Tues.	10/26	Wed.	10/27	Finalize line	JL
Wed.	10/27	Wed.	10/27	Decide on advertising samples	TW
Mon.	10/25	Fri.	10/29	Prepare all manufacturing and spec sheets	RT
Mon.	10/25	Thurs.	10/28	Fabric and trim tests	RT
Wed.	11/3	Wed.	11/3	Authorize sales rep samples	TW
Mon.	11/8	Mon.	11/8	Cut advertising samples	SC/RT
Wed.	11/10	Mon .	11/22	Receive sales rep sample goods	CW
Wed.	12/1	Wed.	12/1	Finalize all manufacturing and spec sheets	RT
Fri.	12/3	Fri.	12/10	Initial sales forecast	TW
Mon.	12/6	Fri.	12/10	Order production piece goods and trim	CW
Mon.	11/15	Mon.	11/22	Cut sales rep samples	SC/RT
Wed.	11/17	Wed.	11/17	Complete advertising samples	SC/RT
Fri.	11/19	Fri.	11/19	Photograph advertising samples	GK
Fri.	12/3	Fri.	12/10	Initial sales forecast	TW
Mon.	12/6	Fri.	12/10	Order production piece goods and trim	CW
Fri.	12/17	Tues.	12/21	Product costing of old styles	SC
Wed.	12/22	Fri.	12/31	Develop new yields	SC
Tues.	1/4/05	Thurs.	1/6/05	Product costing of new styles	SC
Fri.	1/7	Fri.	1/7	Price line	KM
Mon.	1/10	Thurs.	1/13	Complete sales rep samples	SC/RT
Mon.	1/10	Thurs.	1/13	Complete advertising materials	GK
Wed.	1/12	Wed.	1/13	Key customers view line and place advance orders	TW
Fri.	1/14	Fri.	1/14	Sales meeting (Line Preview)	TW
Mon.	1/31	Mon	5/2	Advance sales orders	TW
Thurs.	2/10	Thurs.	2/10	Second sales forecast	TW
Mon.	2/14	Wed.	2/16	Supply projected mix to manufacturing	CW
Mon.	2/21	Fri.	4/25	Receive first production piece goods	CW
Mon.	2/28	Mon.	2/28	Project first cuttings	CW
Mon.	3/7	Fri.	4/29	Cutting	SC
Mon.	3/21	Fri.	5/13	Manufacturing	SC
Mon	5/16	Fri.	6/24	Finished goods to inventory	SC

Merchandising calendars from an apparel company that produces tailored clothing for spring and fall seasons.

FIGURE 4.1 MERCHANDISING CALENDAR FOR A CHILDREN'S SPORTSWEAR COMPANY THAT HAS FOUR COLLECTIONS A YEAR

2005	JANUARY 7 14 21 28	FEBRUARY 4 11 18 25	MARCH 3 10 17 24 31	APRIL 7 14 21 28	MAY 5 12 19 26	JUNE 2 9 16 23 30	JULY 7 14 21 28	AUGUST 4 11 18 25	SEPTEMBER 1 8 15 22 29	OCTOBER 6 13 20 27	NOVEMBER 3 10 17 24	DECEMBER 1 8 15 22
2004	8 15 22 29	5 12 19 26	5 12 19 26	2 9 17 23 30	7 14 21 28	4 11 18 25	2 9 16 23 30	6 13 20 27	3 10 17 25	1 8 15 22 29	1 8 15 22	3 10 17 24

ACTIVITY

- Market Research
- Fashion Research
- Fabric Research
- Color Research
- Collection Research
- Initial Fabric Selection
- Review Previous Sales
- Line Plan Meeting
- Line Plan Approval
- Order fabric sample cuts
- Concept boards
- Style development
- Spec sheet/tech drawings
- Pre-cost
- First pattern/prototype
- Fit model session
- Pattern revisions
- Final cost
- First adoption
- Order fabrics for samples
- Revisions
- Final adoption
- Review with top accounts
- Initial sales forecast
- Order production fabric
- Receive fabric for samples
- Cut and sew samples
- Line preview (sales mtg)
- Grade/production marker
- Line release (start selling)
- Receive production fabric
- Cut, sew production
- Sales forecast adjustment
- Order additional fabric
- Receive additional fabric
- Cut/sew additional quantity
- Begin shipping
- Complete shipping
- Season critique

"SP" represents the Spring Line, "SU" represents the Summer Line, "F" represents the Fall Line, and "H" represents the Holiday Line.

The merchandising calendar from the Kid's Creations Ltd. Company that produces four collections each year: Spring, Summer, Fall, and Holiday.

FIGURE 4.2   PRIVATE BRAND DEVELOPMENT CALENDAR FOR MODERATE TIME ACTION

	JAN	FEB	MAR	MAR	APRIL	MAY	MAY	JUNE
DESIGN DEVELOPMENT	SPRING 06				SUMMER 06			
Research and Development/Concept	2/7–2/21							
Color Overseas	3/2							
Start Development Packages/Build Blocks & Styles								
Development Packages ex NY to PO								
Samples due to NY	5/25				7/22			
MERCHANDISING								
Product Team Travel	4/13							
Style Count *Plans*								
Buy Meeting/International Meeting (3 wks)	6/13–6/17				8/1–8/5			
International Buy Meeting	6/20–6/24				8/18–8/12			
Finalize Orders/Total Style Count Confirmed (1 wk)	6/17							
Team meetings	6/6–6/10							
FIT APPROVAL								
Early turn over on repeat known styles			8/1–8/5		8/5–8/15			
Style Adopt/Turnover/PE review (1 wk)	6/27	7/19	8/15		8/29			10/10
First Fitting (Style/initial Fits) (1 wk)	7/5–7/8	7/20–7/29	8/16–8/23	8/16–8/30	8/30–9/9			10/17–10/28
First PDM Due Date/Factory Allocation (2 wks)	7/25	8/12	9/9	9/9	9/23			11/11
Approval Deadline (8 wks)	8/25	9/30	10/14	10/31	11/9			1/6
PRODUCTION WINDOW								
Production Start (1 wk)	9/1	10/7	10/21	11/7	11/16			1/13
Production Complete Transit to Consolidate (8 wks)	10/6	11/7	12/5	12/19	1/16			3/3
Ship Window (1 wk)	10/13–10/19	11/14–11/18	12/12–12/16	12/26–12/30	1/23–1/27	2/13–2/17	2/27–3/3	3/13–3/17
In DC (8 wks)	12/5	1/2	1/30	2/13	3/13	4/3	4/17	5/1
On Floor (3 wks)	Jan	Feb	Mar	Mar	April	May	May	June

The private brand development calendar for a retailer's spring and summer collections.

Figure 4.3 The introduction of twelve collections per year requires a much shorter development cycle. The application of computer-aided design (CAD) software reduces the time needed to bring new styles to the marketplace.

apparel companies will be able to survive the changing conditions of our industry. Companies that are able to introduce new systems of planning and controlling their operations, that are able to develop the management skills such systems will require will be able to respond with greater speed and accuracy to the demands of changing markets" (Kurt Salmon Associates, Inc., 1973).

Strategic Planning

The broadest type of planning done by any company is strategic planning, which identifies where and how a company's resources should be allocated. A strategic plan sets forth the overall company vision. Each department should develop its own action plan to support the company's strategic plan and coordinate with other department plans. Strategic planning is a total company commitment to achieve a coordinated vision.

Strategic planning should raise the following questions:

- Where are we now?
- Where do we want to go?
- How do we get there?

Answering these broad-based questions allows a company to develop realistic objectives and goals. It requires projecting economic, social, and political conditions that will affect a company's future. An effective strategic plan involves formulating alternative courses of action to reach a company's goals. The hardest question is "Where are we now?" because the answer requires an unbiased evaluation of one's own company. Many firms utilize consultants to evaluate the current position of their company.

The executive planning team must choose the most feasible alternatives to where they want to go and how they will get there. They must address these questions in light of the company's resources (strengths and weaknesses). The key to the effectiveness of a plan is devising methods for measuring progress toward the overall goals and periodically evaluating outcomes.

For apparel companies the plan should specify:

- Target markets through market segmentation.
- Marketing mix by product categories.
- Company resource allocations by time periods.
- Expected results relative to sales and profits by time periods.

The standard time frame for a strategic plan in many industries is three to five years. This is beyond the horizon for many apparel and retail companies, which find it difficult to look further than next season's product line offerings. In order to be successful in the highly competitive fashion business, companies must take the time and make the effort to create effective strategic plans. The need for establishing and reviewing strategic plans has increased dramatically as companies respond to the swift structural changes in the global apparel and retail sectors.

Industry Examples

Levi Strauss   In 1992 Levi Strauss evaluated where it was and where it wanted to go based upon surveys of its 21 largest customers and on-site interviews with medium and small retailers. How Levi's would get there resulted in a corporate reengineering program designed to move decision making closer to the customer, which by 1997 had grown into an $850 million project called the Customer Service Supply Chain (Abend, 1997).

Liz Claiborne   Liz Claiborne started a new initiative in 1995 to evaluate the needs of its changing consumer. After interviewing 6,000 customers, it found that women were dressing more casually, with 25 percent of them shopping at least once a week at discounters. Claiborne developed a strategic plan to focus on developing this new market (alternate marketing). It repositioned its Russ brand from department stores to Wal-Mart, began a 3- to 5-year plan that included developing programs for Kmart and Sears, and also put into action plans to reduce general and administrative expenses by $100 million. To prepare for this progressive strategic plan, top management had to evaluate the company's resources and allocate the appropriate personnel and budgets to achieve the desired results. By December 1998 Claiborne reached its cost reduction and mass merchant initiative strategic marketing goals.

In 2005 Liz Claiborne announced the company was set to launch exclusive moderate lines at key national chains and create international "power brands" from its existing portfolio. The company is planning to roll out six "mid-tier" brands in 2005 at stores such as Sears, JCPenney, and Kohl's. These would be similar to the way Claiborne sells its Axcess brand at Kohl's. The firm is embarking on a program of creating "power brands," citing Juicy Couture, Mexx, Lucky Brand, and Sigrid Olsen as among its cadre of 38 labels that have the potential to become "global, multi-channel, multi-category brands that reach consumers when, where, and how they shop" (Greenberg, 2005).

VF Corporation   In 1998 apparel giant VF Corporation undertook an aggressive plan to micromerchandise its jeanswear assortments to accommodate regional differences and individual store needs. The company made targeted consumer research and cutting-edge market-response systems its strategic focus. Its strategic plan was to build its $5.2 billion business to $7 billion by

Figure 4.4 The Evan Picone Line is prominently displayed at Strawbridges, a May Company store in the Philadelphia area.

2000. "The most important thing we are doing is 'consumerization,' to be the best in the business in delivering products customized for what the consumer wants," said Mackey J. McDonald, president and chief executive officer of VF Corporation (Lewis, 1998).

Jones Apparel Group   In 1999 Jones Apparel Group announced a plan to move its Evan-Picone label from the better-price distribution channel into the moderate arena and begin distributing the brand in JCPenney and May department stores. The Jones Apparel Group strategic plan of targeting a different customer involved slashing prices about 50 percent, but it allowed Picone to move out of the very competitive better women's department store floor. By repositioning the label, the company aimed to develop it into a megabrand. This alternate marketing approach enabled Jones Apparel Group to pursue much larger revenues in the mass market channel and at the same time create additional **open-to-buy** (the dollar amount a buyer can spend on purchases for a specific delivery period minus the dollar amount allocated to orders not yet delivered) money in the better channel for its existing brands (Kletter, 1999). In 1999 Jones Apparel Group purchased Nine West, a highly successful shoe retailer, as part of its strategic plan to introduce clothing products into the Nine West retail outlets.

Reebok   Reebok made a bold move to offer a consolidated global apparel collection for spring 2000. The active sportswear company's strategic plan involved creating a global apparel business unit to eliminate its separate designs for the United States, Europe, and the Far East. The goal was to eliminate 65 percent of its **stock keeping units** (**SKUs**) (a garment inventory unit identified by style, color, and size) in an effort to clean up the line (McKinney, 1999).

Hartmarx Corp.   In 1992 clothing maker Hartmarx Corp. manufactured only men's tailored suits. It undertook a strategic plan to change with the times and expand into new products including sportswear and slacks. By 1997 the company had eight divisions that produced a product mix ranging from $65 knit shirts to $1,000 formal suits (Gellers, 1997). By 1999 Hartmarx expanded its markets by adding brands such as Burberry, Tommy Hilfiger casual slacks, and Kenneth Cole. Its golfwear business was led by Bobby Jones and Jack Nicklaus brands. The company positioned itself to grow the under $350 retail suit business with Claiborne and Perry Ellis and the "upper moderate" category, between $350 and $450 with Kenneth Cole and Krizia (Brumback, 1999).

Gap   Paul Pressler, president and chief executive officer of Gap, outlined a five-step approach to beef up the company's financial performance, including:

- Providing trend-right and appropriate products in easy-to-shop environments.

- Improving the supply chain to increase cost savings and operating efficiencies via consolidating vendors and "aggregating category buys."
- Expanding its efforts to get the right sizes in the right stores in Gap and Old Navy to improve margins.
- Growing existing brands through two initiatives: the opening of 175 stores, and the expansion of product initiatives. Most of the square-footage growth will be at Old Navy, with 75 new stores and more product extensions, such as maternity and plus sizes. In addition, maternity offerings will be increased to 70 Gap stores and petites will be offered at Banana Republic in 26 locations.
- Returning excess cash to shareholders via dividends and share repurchases. For example, the company has doubled its first-quarter dividend to 18 cents and it announced Thursday a new $1.5 billion share-repurchase program (Derby, 2005).

Penney's "JCPenney Co. wants to be the preferred shopping choice for middle America," said Chairman and Chief Executive Myron E. Ullman, III. "Our long-range plan is focused on serving our customers and growing our business. Working together, we will take our performance to an industry leadership level. All the mergers taking place in retailing now are creating turmoil for the consumer, and we see this as being an even more important time to focus on and make an emotional connection with middle-income customers, which are the sweet spot of our business. At least half of Penney's volume is generated by shoppers who are 35 to 54 years old, with annual incomes of $35,000 to $85,000," Ullman said. Penney's is committed to new-store growth and plans to build 12 to 20 off-the-mall stores each year over the next five years, with $2.4 billion earmarked to remodel units and $270 million a year to build stores (Williamson, 2005).

Each of these industry examples required major planning and control efforts by the merchandisers. Some companies had to establish new merchandising product development teams to address new markets or new product lines. Others had to create more effective decision-making structures and streamline the merchandising process to reduce costs and respond more quickly to consumer needs. The key factors in achieving these strategic plans were careful allocation of company resources, the development of detailed planning strategies, and the establishment of clearly defined goals and periodic evaluations of outcomes.

Cost Elements

The most important element in evaluating business decisions is the effect of those decisions on the short- and long-term profitability of a company. The

"Consumer Buying Patterns Force Marketing Change"

A redefinition of the role of merchandiser has been forced onto the apparel industry by the buying public. For many years, the customer bought what the manufacturer produced. Now, we, the producers, must manufacture what the customer will buy. Superimposed on this dramatic shift is the forceful entry of foreign goods, manufactured with good quality and cheap labor, into the United States market.

In short, we can no longer turn on the switch to manufacture and, in effect, walk away. Product development, cost inventory, delivery, manufacture and timeliness must be under firm, effective and positive control.

This change in roles and responsibility has not reduced in any manner the stature of sales and manufacturing. It has merely provided in a single staff agency the responsibilities and tools necessary to provide the right apparel product, at the suitable price and quality, to the customer in proper shipping sequence and without degradation of planned markup due to markup erosion or markdown of finished goods or material.

Marketing Calendar

In conjunction with Sales, the marketing calendar is developed. This calendar shows the number of seasons (or group offerings) in which a product line will be presented. The calendar, among other things, shows the date on which a line will be released to the salesmen and the start and completion dates of shipment of the goods to the customers.

Key Event Calendar

In conjunction with manufacturing, the merchandiser develops a merchandising key event calendar. This calendar, among other things, determines the optimum scheduling of manufacturing to provide the necessary shelf stock position to support shipping in full, on time to the customer. By proper scheduling of manufacturing, the maximum percentage of the season will be produced "under paper," to solid sales information such as orders with a minimum fluctuation of the plant loading.

Merchandising Calendar

Derived from the marketing and key event calendar, the merchandiser, in conjunction with sales, manufacturing and customer service develops and monitors the merchandising calendar.

Line Plan Development

At the appropriate time for each season, the merchandiser develops the line plan for that season. Normally, we would expect the season objectives in dollars and dozens or units to have been provided as a part of the annual financial plan. If this is not the case, he develops a proposed season's objective. In addition, he must make a determination of where and if new seasons should be added to the marketing year.

The plan includes, but is not limited to, the number of styles which will constitute the line, the number of fabrics for knitting, yarns, the number of colors per style, any

(continued)

coordination of garments, and the anticipated number of stock keeping units which will be in the line. In addition, the yarn/fabric necessary to support the category is computed, and the cash flow for the season's purchases is calculated.

Product Development

In conjunction with sales (for market acceptability), manufacturing (for costing, garment engineering and manufacturability), and design (if separate design function exits), the merchandiser develops the product line for the season.

Product development is not only a function of putting together the line for a season, but the necessary market research and garment construction research and development necessary to ensure fresh products being offered at the proper time. This is a continuous function and only indirectly tied to seasonal product development.

Style Adoption

The merchandiser is responsible for the overall style adoption procedure. This includes, but is not limited to, designer sample preparation, precosting, garment specifications, quality specifications and designer pattern preparation. He ensures the timely scheduling of product engineering and the provision of appropriate advance information to manufacturing.

Forecasting

As soon as styles are adopted, the merchandiser will, in conjunction with Sales, estimate the sales for each style to align the merchandising planning. After final adoption and line review, in conjunction with Sales, he makes a more sure-footed season forecast by style. The forecasts are not at all

authorizations to produce. They are only plans; they are not commitments.

Shelf Stock Planning

With the season forecast completed, the merchandiser puts together the season shelf stock plan.

Manufacturing Plan

As soon as the line of garments for the season is completed, the forecast by style is made and the shelf stock plan developed. The merchandiser participates with manufacturing in the development of the season manufacturing plan.

Salesmen's Duplicates

When styles are adopted, the merchandiser initiates the necessary action to ensure that the salesmen's duplicates (sales samples) are completed in time for the line release.

Fabric and Yarn Requirements

The merchandiser is responsible for the timely procurement and delivery of yarn and fabric. In this regard, he ensures that yarn and fabric is available for maintaining the proper level of manufacturing and a shippable mix of finished goods is going on the shelf. While it is necessary to ensure that material is available, he must strive for optimum use of capital invested in material by control of the material turns and minimization of loss due to markdown of obsolete yarns and fabrics.

Production Authorization

In accordance with the initial shelf stock plan and advance information from sales, the merchandiser authorizes the "mix modules" of finished garments that he wants on

(continued)

the shelf by time frame. He should authorize only garments for which yarn or fabric and trim is on hand. This is the "cuttable cut."

Inventory Management

The merchandiser continuously monitors the inventory levels for both style and in-stock garments to maintain the predetermined level of customer support while achieving an acceptable level of finished goods turns.

Control of Loss Due to Markdowns or Carryover of Excess Inventory

The merchandiser is the businessman in that he assures the profitability of the division or company and brings about the most effective utilization of capital.

Work-in-Process Inventory

While the control of work-in-process is a direct manufacturing function, it is pivotal to proper delivery. So the merchandiser remains aware of these levels and will consult, as appropriate, with Manufacturing about them.

Manufacturing Throughput

As with work-in-process, manufacturing throughput is a manufacturing function. However, throughput in style mix rather than as single lots of garments not only directly affects the level of finished goods inventory of stock items, but is pivotal to proper customer service in the case of seasonal styles. Because of this, the merchandiser must be aware of throughput time and be prepared to consult here as well with Manufacturing when necessary.

Customer Service

The merchandiser keeps in contact with customer service personnel to assure the desired level of customer service.

Season Critique

The merchandiser prepares an informal critique of each season to assist in future season planning and execution. ■

From Bill Flake and Bertrand Frank. March 1978. *Apparel Industry Magazine*, pp. 68, 70.

Case in Point 4.1   ## Summary

Case in Point 4.1 outlines the complexity of merchandising, which includes many planning and control functions that were required of a merchandiser even as far back as 1978. Since that time, the number of seasonal offerings per year has increased, product development cycle times have been reduced, and the volume of global sourcing has dramatically increased, which contrib-ute to complicating the production process. The need for precise planning and accurate controls in every phase of the merchandising process is much greater in today's fast-paced global marketplace. Merchandisers must use powerful computer applications and communications tools to keep pace with the rapid changes in the fashion industry. ■

expanding global nature and fashion volatility of the apparel industry make it difficult to evaluate the net effect of many strategic plans on a company's bottom line. This is especially critical for the merchandising function where product development costs and global sourcing create complex cost issues.

A good strategic plan must include a careful analysis of all affected costs. It is difficult to allocate design and general and administrative costs to strategic plans that involve creating new product development teams or developing global sourcing partnerships for new products. No matter how difficult the task, a good strategic plan must reexamine all elements of the business, getting an accurate compilation of current costs and obtaining accurate costs for implementing the strategic plan. "Good strategic planning requires good cost information so that sound and prudent decisions can be based on some quantifiable basis" (Weintraub, 1986).

Marketing Calendar

The basis for all merchandising planning in apparel companies is the marketing calendar. This calendar is the central mechanism from which all other marketing schedules and all merchandising and manufacturing plans evolve (Bertrand Frank Associates, 1985).

This planning tool is the clock that drives merchandising product development schedules, sales appointments with important customers, manufacturing planning, and shipping schedules. Not every company has an official document called a marketing calendar, but every company deals with the components of this important planning instrument. The key elements of the marketing calendar are:

- Line preview dates by season.
- Line release dates by season.
- **Start ship date** (the first date when a season's orders can begin to be shipped to retailers).
- **End ship date** (the last date that a season's orders can be shipped without incurring discounts or penalties from retailers).
- Weekly sales plans in dollar amounts of goods to be sold and units to be sold (actual vs. planned). Some companies plan on a monthly basis.
- Weekly shipping plans in dollar amounts of goods to be shipped and units to be shipped (actual vs. planned). Some companies plan on a monthly basis.

The **line preview date** is the merchandisers' deadline for having all prototypes and pricing for a new product line completed. Merchandisers work backwards from this date to create their product development plans. The line preview date is often the date of the seasonal sales meeting where the merchandising team presents the line to the sales force. The final line adoption committee meets prior to the line preview date to select those styles that will make up the final seasonal line.

The line release date is the merchandisers' deadline for having all sales samples ready for the sales team to begin presenting the new line to customers. Since most sales representatives schedule their earliest appointments with their most important customers, this deadline is crucial to the success of the sales effort. If a sales appointment with a retailer is cancelled due to late delivery of samples, the retailer will most likely reschedule the sales appointment at the end of the buying season when there will be minimal if any open-to-buy available.

The **weekly sales plan** is a barometer for the sales department, financial planning, and manufacturing schedules. (Some companies may plan on a monthly rather than a weekly basis.) This plan shows season-to-date as well as sales statistics for a specific weekly or monthly time period. It also measures the effectiveness of a product line for the merchandising department. A graphic analysis of this plan can project increases or decreases in overall sales for a season, thereby allowing manufacturing, product sourcing, and finance to make appropriate adjustments in production and **cash flow** (a statement of changes in a company's cash position) analyses. The sales plan is usually based upon past sales trends that incorporate seasonal adjustments for holidays and special events.

The **weekly shipping plan** is another barometer for manufacturing, product sourcing, and finance. (Some companies may plan on a monthly rather than a weekly basis.) This plan also shows season-to-date as well as shipping statistics for a specific weekly or monthly time period. It allows manufacturing and sourcing to determine whether or not the product mixes being delivered to distribution meet the **shippability** (whether or not a sufficient mix of SKUs are available to meet customer order minimum shipping requirements) criteria. The plan also alerts finance of any changes in cash flow.

Figure 4.5 shows a sample marketing calendar for a four-season women's sportswear company. If a company offers product lines for catalog, chain, and specialty retail customers or produces lines for different markets (men's, women's, children's), it may have multiple marketing calendars for the differing buying and delivery cycles of these customers or markets. This further complicates the planning process and requires effective controls to meet the myriad of deadlines.

The marketing calendar is the responsibility of the marketing department but requires careful collaboration with sales, merchandising, finance, and manufacturing in order to meet the overall objectives of the company. It is important that all departments be committed to meeting the deadlines and achieving the goals of the marketing calendar.

FIGURE 4.5	LADY RAMS MARKETING CALENDAR 2006

	Spring	Summer	Fall	Holiday
Line Preview	Oct 3	Jan 4	Feb 17	June 19
Line Release	Oct 17	Jan 17	Mar 3	July 3
Start Shipping	Jan 17	April 17	June 19	Sept 18
End Shipping	Mar 17	May 19	Aug 17	Nov 17

	JAN	FEB	MAR	APR	MAY	JUN	JUL	AUG	SEP	OCT	NOV	DEC
Sales (000 units)	15	10	20	15	10	5	5	10	10	10	25	5
Shipments (000 units)	20	20	10	10	10	10	30	10	8	15	7	0

The marketing calendar for The Lady Rams Sportswear Company shows the critical deadlines and anticipated sales and shipment quantities by month.

Merchandising Calendar

The primary control tool when developing a seasonal line in an apparel company is the merchandising calendar or line plan calendar. This very critical instrument is designed to control the key events needed to get the right apparel products, in the right mix, at the right price, to the customer at the right time. Some companies may call the merchandising calendar a key events calendar, line development calendar, critical path calendar, critical task calendar, or line calendar. No matter what the title, the important factor is that this control tool sets forth the starting and completion dates for all critical events necessary to achieve a successful season. The basic ingredients of a successful apparel season are:

- Manufacture what the consumer wants relating to style, quality, and cost.
- Deliver the proper product mix on a timely basis.
- Maintain low raw material, work-in-process, and finished goods inventories. This increases inventory turns, which reduces the amount of operating capital needed to run the company. **Inventory turns** equal the annual value of total inventory created divided by the average value of inventory throughout the year. For example, if a company generates $5 million in total inventory during a year and the average value of finished goods inventory is $1.5 million, then the number of finished goods inventory turns would be 5 divided by 1.5 or 3.3. This means that the company had an investment in each piece of inventory for 15.8 weeks throughout the year (52 divided by 3.3).
- Accommodate changes with split-second timing.

These elements may seem basic, but under the compressed time frame and rapidly changing trends of the fashion industry, what was once a rather straightforward, step-by-step activity has become a complex function requiring intricate planning of many simultaneous steps. If used effectively, a good merchandising calendar can help a company to meet product development deadlines, increase inventory turns, improve customer service, and enhance profits.

Critical Path Method (CPM)

The critical path method (CPM) of planning is the key to a successful merchandising calendar. **Critical path method** (CPM) planning involves determining the critical functions necessary to perform an activity or series of activities required to achieve an overall objective. The activities involved in the development, execution, and delivery of an apparel product line must be analyzed to determine the critical functions necessary to achieve a successful season. What determines a critical function is whether an activity that follows a particular function can successfully take place without the critical function being accomplished. For example, a prototype cannot be made without a pattern being created or fabric being ordered. Fabric cannot be ordered without researching fabric suppliers. A pattern cannot be created without a silhouette. Each of these functions is critical to the succeeding activity and to the final objective of development of a product line.

After the critical functions are selected, each one must be analyzed to determine the time required to accomplish it. The critical functions are then interfaced into a master calendar in the form of a **Gantt chart** (a series of parallel horizontal graphs which show schedules for functions plotted against time). The relationships between critical functions determine the positioning on the chart and the overall time for completion.

Some companies use a chart that lists start and stop dates for each function or an actual large-size monthly calendar with function start and function stop notations written in the date squares of the calendar. An interactive computer database can handle this calendaring more effectively since it can highlight functions that are running behind schedule and print out exception reports to allow management to take corrective action.

A typical merchandising calendar may have 35 to 60 functions for a product line. At four seasons per year, this represents 140 to 240 tasks that must be performed within a year. If a company has four product lines and ten offerings per year, the number of tasks jumps to 1,400 to 2,400 tasks per year (4 lines × 10 offerings × 35 functions). Consider the shorter time spans, the number of personnel involved in product development and sourcing, seasonal overlaps, interdepartmental responsibilities, employee holidays and vacations, and the occasional missed deadline, and you begin to appreciate the complexities involved in achieving a successful season.

Figure 4.6 shows the enormous task involved in controlling the line development functions for a children's wear company with three delivery pe-

FIGURE 4.6 — HEALTHTEX AND LEE 2005 LINE DEVELOPMENT CALENDAR

#	DEVELOPMENT TASK	JAN 3	JAN 10	JAN 17	JAN 24	FEB 7	FEB 14	FEB 21	FEB 28	MAR 7	MAR 14	MAR 21	MAR 28	APR 4	APR 11	APR 18	APR 25	MAY 2	MAY 9	MAY 16	MAY 23	JUN 6	JUN 13	JUN 20	JUN 27
	2005	3	10	17	24	7	14	21	28	7	14	21	28	4	11	18	25	2	9	16	23	6	13	20	27
	2004	5	12	19	26	2	9	16	23	1	8	15	22	5	12	19	26	3	10	17	24	7	14	21	28
1	MARKET RESEARCH	SPRING	2005											SUMMER	2005							FALL	2005		
	BUSINESS ANALYSIS												F										H		
	BUSINESS ACTION PLAN MEETING	SP																							
	FOCUS GROUP									SP										SU					
	COLOR/PRINT/FASHION SERVICES						SP							SU							F				
2	VENDOR WEEK		SP												SU									F	
3	CONCEPT ACTION PLAN																								
	COLOR/THEMES/FABRICS/PRINTS					SP	SP	SP	SP	SP					SU	SU	SU					F	F	F	F
	TRIMS/REOS/CONCEPT BOARDS					SP	SP	SP	SP	SP					SU	SU	SU					F	F	F	F
4	SUBMIT COLORS, SEW & EMBR. THREADS						SP	SP	SP	SP					SU	X	SU	SU					F	F	
5	PRELINE WITH TARGET ACCT.									SP															
6	YARN DYE DEVELOPMENT						1/2			3					1/2			3							
7	FILL BODIES/MDSE BY DEL.									1	1	1	2	2	2	3	3	1	2	2	3	3	3		
8	MENDING FABRIC TO MEADOWVIEW										1		2	2	3			1	2		3				
9	SUBMIT PRINTS IN REPEAT & I.D.									1	1	1	2	2	2	3	3	1	1	1	2	2	3	3	3
10	ID YARN DYE WOVENS									1/2	1/2		3	3			1/2	1/2			3				
11	ID PC DYE WOVENS/YD STRP./SP. PFP									1	1		2	2	3	3		1	1	2	2	3	3		
12	ID PC DYE KNITS									1	1		2	2		3	3	1	1	2	2	3	3		
13	ID TRIMS (SPECIAL)									(1)	1		(2)	2		(3)	3	(1)	1	(2)	2	(3)	3		
14	ORDER PIECE GOODS/TRIM (PFP)	3							(1)	1	1/(2)	1/2	2	2/(3)	2/3	3	3	3	(1)	1/2	1/2	2	2	(3)	3
15	ENTER S.C.s IN KARAT (DAILY GOAL)									1	1	1	2	2	2	3	3	1	1	1	2	2	3	3	3
16	APP. PROTO./1ST COST MARKERS									1	1	1	1	2	2	3	3	1	1	1	2	2	3		
17	SUBMIT EMR./(HEAT SEAL I.D.)								(1)	(1)	1	1	(2)	(2)	2	2	(3)	3		(1)	1	(2)	2	(3)	3
18	APPROVE MEDINGS									1	1	1	2	2	2	2	3	3		1	2	2	3		
19	1ST COSTS									1	1	1	2	2	2	2	3	3		1	2	2	3		
20	STYLE SET UPS									1	1	1	2	3	3			1		2	2				
21	LINE SHEETS IN DDS/KARAT									1	1	1	1	2	2	2	3	3		1	2	2	3		
22	SUBMIT SCREEN PRINTS (PATCHES)	3	3							(1)	1	1	1	(2)	2	2	(3)	3	3		(1)	1	(2)	2	
23	SPEC. DEV. BY ENG. IN KARAT	3	3	3							1	1	1	2	2	2	3	3	3	3			1	1	1/2
24	SAMPLE PLANT ASSIGNMENT										1			2			3			1		2			
25	PRINT STRIKEOFFS		2	3	3	3								1	1	1	2	2	3	3	3		1	1	2
26	SAMPLE PC. GOODS READY AT MILL		2	2	3	3	3							1	X	1	2	2	2	3	3	3		1	1
27	SAMPLE PIECE GOODS IN HOUSE	X	2	2	2	3	3								X	1	1	2	2	2	3	3	3		1
28	ISSUE/CUT SAMPLES	X	2	2		3	3	3	3						X	1	1	2	2	2	3	3	3		1
29	SUBMIT QUALITY GUARANTEE					3									X	1		2			3				1
30	RELEASE PRICE LIST FOR TICKETS					3									X	1		2			3				1
31	APPROVE SCREEN PRINTS	X	2	2	2	2	3	3	3	3					1	1	1	1	2	2	2	3	3	3	3
32	SEW SAMPLES	X	2	2	2	2	3	3	3	3	3				X	1	1	2	2	2	2	3	3	3	3
33	6 SETS OF PRE. BOARDS FOR SP. 3 REL.																					3	3	3	
34	REVIEW KARAT PRICES		H															3							
35	PREPARE RANKING DISKS/VERIFY PMS #								H '04						1/2										
36	RANKING TRIP TOP 6 RETAILERS						H		H '04	'04						1/2									
37	RANKING REVIEW MEETING									H '04							1/2								
38	MARGIN REVIEW							H		H '04								1/2							3
39	DISTRIBUTE PLA						H												1/2						
40	DEVELOP ORDER PADS						H	H										1/2	1/2						
41	DEVELOP CAD SALES CATALOGS					H	H	H										SP	SP	SP					
42	CADS TO DUPLICATING (BOX MAIL)								H	(H)											SP	(SP)			
43	DISTRO SALES SAMPLES						H	H	H	H									1/2	1/2	1/2	3	3		
44	SALES MEETINGS								H					H '04											
45	ON SALE									H					H '04	'04								1/2	
46	SELL IN REVIEW/OVERAGES						F							H				H '04							
47	OFF SALE								F									H				H '04			
48	CUT-UPS									F								H					H '04		
	2004	5	12	19	26	2	9	14	23	1	8	15	22	29	5	12	19	26	3	10	17	24	7	14	21	28
	2005	3	10	17	24	7	14	21	28	7	14	21	28	4	11	18	25	2	9	16	23	6	13	20	27

S:\PUBLIC\CAL_2000\LDCAL_OO.WK4

DEVELOPMENT TASK CALENDAR

#	DEVELOPMENT TASK	Jul 4	11	18	25	Aug 1	8	15	22	Sep 5	12	19	26	Oct 3	10	17	24	Nov 7	14	21	28	Dec 5	12	19	26
	2005 →	4	11	18	25	1	8	15	22	5	12	19	26	3	10	17	24	7	14	21	28	5	12	19	26
	2004 →	5	12	19	26	2	9	16	23	6	13	20	27	4	11	18	25	1	8	15	22	6	13	20	27
1	MARKET RESEARCH								HOL. 2005																
	BUSINESS ANALYSIS																			SP					
	BUSINESS ACTION PLAN MEETING	F																							
	FOCUS GROUP				F														H						
	COLOR/PRINT/FASHION SERVICES										H														
2	VENDOR WEEK											H													
3	CONCEPT ACTION PLAN																								
	COLOR/THEMES/FABRICS/PRINTS	F									H	H	H	H											
	TRIMS/REOS/CONCEPT BOARDS	F									H	H	H	H											
4	SUBMIT COLORS, SEW & EMBR. THREADS	F	F									H	H	H											
5	PRELINE WITH TARGET ACCT.				F										H										
6	YARN DYE DEVELOPMENT	1/2		3										1/2		3									
7	FILL BODIES/MDSE BY DEL.		1	1	1	2	2	3	3	3								1	1	1	2	2	3	3	3
8	MENDING FABRIC TO MEADOWVIEW		1				2		3									1			2			3	
9	SUBMIT PRINTS IN REPEAT & I.D.			1	1	2	2	2	2	3	3	3						1	1	1	2	2	3	3	3
10	ID YARN DYE WOVENS			1/2	1/2		3	3								1/2	1/2		3	3					
11	ID PC DYE WOVENS/YD STRP./SP. PFP		1	1		2	2		3	3					1	1		2	2		3	3			
12	ID PC DYE KNITS		1	1		2	2			3	3				1	1		2	2			3	3		
13	ID TRIMS (SPECIAL)			(1)	1	(2)				3	3					(1)	1	(2)	2		(3)	3			
14	ORDER PIECE GOODS/TRIM (PFP)	3		(1)	1/2	1/2	(2)	2/3	2/3	2/(3)	3	3	3		(1)	1/2	1/2	1/(2)	2/3	2/3	2/(3)	3	3	3	
15	ENTER S.C.s IN KARAT (DAILY GOAL)		1	1	1	1	2	2	2	3	3	3			1	1	1	1	2	2	3	3	3		
16	APP. PROTO./1ST COST MARKERS	3			1	1	1	2	2	2	3	3		3			1	1	1	2	2	3	3		
17	SUBMIT EMR./(HEAT SEAL I.D.)	3		(1)	(1)	1	(2)	(2)	2	2	(3)	3	3	3			(1)	1	1	(2)	2	2	(3)	3	3
18	APPROVE MEDINGS	3	3			1	1	2	2	2	2	3	3	3				1	1	1	2	2	2	3	3	3
19	1ST COSTS	3	3			1	1	1	2	2	2	3	3	3				1	1	1	2	2	2	3	3
20	STYLE SET UPS				1	1		2	2	3	3							1	1		2	2		3	
21	LINE SHEETS IN DDS/KARAT	3			1	1	2	2	3	3	3	3						1	1	2	2	3	3	3	
22	SUBMIT SCREEN PRINTS (PATCHES)	(3)	3		(1)	1	(2)	2	2	(3)	3	3	3	3		(1)	1	1	(2)	2	2	2	(3)	3	
23	SPEC. DEV. BY ENG. IN KARAT	2	2/3	3	3	1	1	1	1	2	2	2	3	3	3	3		1	1	2	2	2	2	3	
24	SAMPLE PLANT ASSIGNMENT	3				1			2		3						1		2			3			
25	PRINT STRIKEOFFS	2	X	2	3	3	3		1	1	1	2	2	2	3	3	3		1	1	1	2	2	2	
26	SAMPLE PC. GOODS READY AT MILL	2	X	2	2	3	3	3		1	1	1	2	2	2	3	3	3		1	1	1	2	2	
27	SAMPLE PIECE GOODS IN HOUSE	1	X	2	2	2	3	3		1	1	1	2	2	2	2	3	3	3		1	1	1	2	
28	ISSUE/CUT SAMPLES	1	X	2	2	2	3	3	3	1	1	1	2	2	2	2	3	3	3		1	1	1	2	
29	SUBMIT QUALITY GUARANTEE		X	2			3			1			2		3					1				2	
30	RELEASE PRICE LIST FOR TICKETS		X	2			3			1			2		3					1				2	
31	APPROVE SCREEN PRINTS	1	X	1	2	2	3	3	3	1	1	1	2	2	3	3	3	3			1	1	1		
32	SEW SAMPLES	3	X	1	1	2	2	3	3	3	1	1	1	2	2	2	2	3	3	3		1	1	1	X
33	6 SETS OF PRE. BOARDS FOR SP. 3 REL.																								
34	REVIEW KARAT PRICES		SU										F												
35	PREPARE RANKING DISKS/VERIFY PMS #			SU											F										
36	RANKING TRIP TOP 6 RETAILERS				SU											F									
37	RANKING REVIEW MEETING					SU											F								
38	MARGIN REVIEW					SU											F								
39	DISTRIBUTE PLA		3					SU											F						
40	DEVELOP ORDER PADS	3	3				SU	SU										F	F						
41	DEVELOP CAD SALES CATALOGS						SU	SU	SU										F	F	F				
42	CADS TO DUPLICATING (BOX MAIL)									SU	(SU)									F	(F)				
43	DISTRO SALES SAMPLES	3	3							SU	SU	SU							F	F	F	F			
44	SALES MEETINGS		SP								SU											F			
45	ON SALE			SP								SU												F	
46	SELL IN REVIEW/OVERAGES	1/2				SP									SU										
47	OFF SALE						SP											SU							
48	CUT-UPS							SP										SU							
	2004 →	5	12	19	26	2	9	16	23	6	13	20	27	4	11	18	25	1	8	15	22	6	13	20	27
	2005 →	4	11	18	25	1	8	15	22	5	12	19	26	3	10	17	24	7	14	21	28	5	12	19	26

JULY | AUGUST | SEPTEMBER | OCTOBER | NOVEMBER | DECEMBER

riods for each of four seasons per year. During any one week the merchandiser may have to monitor 20 to 25 separate functions being performed by the line development team.

Figure 4.7 shows a merchandising calendar for a popular women's sportswear company with five seasonal offerings. This calendar is developed in two parts, a Line Development Calendar and a Production Calendar.

Computer Applications

Database and spreadsheet computer programs are a necessity that enable merchandisers to keep up with the complex task of controlling merchandising functions. There are also many project scheduling programs on the market that can be easily customized to display merchandising calendar tasks in colorful timelines. The presentation-quality schedules clearly illustrate merchandising objectives and deadlines, keeping team members informed and up to date. This software allows for the creation of weekly or daily task lists which allocate tasks for departments or personnel responsible for their on-time completion. Automated computer systems allow merchandisers much greater flexibility in scheduling and controlling the complex tasks that must be completed to achieve a successful season.

Gary Simmons, former president of VF Playwear, understands the importance of the computer in developing and tracking the tasks on a merchandising calendar. "We include a marketing calendar within our line development calendar. There are 40 steps within our line development calendar. The line development calendar is developed by the merchandisers and signed off by the senior team. It also blends into the marketing department and operational calendars. We have different calendars for each brand. Healthtex and Lee is on one calendar and Nike has a different one, because they do a little more importing. We use computers to develop and keep track of our information. The computer allows us to be more flexible and maintain tighter controls over our business tasks."

Development, Execution, and Maintenance

Developing, executing, and maintaining an effective merchandising calendar is a merchandising responsibility. It is an important element of **pre-season planning**, which is the activity that coordinates product development and sales expectations with material purchases and production capacities. Pre-season planning of an apparel line has always been one of the most critical activities in the entire manufacturing process. This is where decisions are made that have the greatest impact upon the ultimate success or failure of the company's efforts (Cole, 1970).

During a season the merchandiser should track the progress of each task against the appropriate timeline in the merchandising calendar. It is very important to make every effort to achieve each deadline. A proper plan of ac-

LINE DEVELOPMENT CALENDAR

	Spring	Summer	Fall 1	Fall 2	Holiday/Cruise
RESEARCH-FAB/YARN/COLORS	2/15-3/31	4/1-5/15	6/10-7/25	7/25-9/10	11/1-12/15
ORDER SAMPLE FAB/YARN/SWEATERS	4/1	5/15	7/25	9/10	12/15
RECEIVE SAMPLE FAB/YARN	6/15-7/15	8/1-9/5	10/10-11/10	11/25-1/5	3/1-4/15
COMMIT STOCK FAB/YARN	4/20-7/20	7/20-9/5	9/15-11/20	11/5-1/20	1/25-4/5
ASSORT STOCK FAB/YARN	6/20-9/20	9/20-11/5	11/15-1/20	1/5-3/20	3/25-6/5
RECEIVE STOCK FAB/YARN	8/5-11/25	11/25-1/10	1/20-3/25	3/10-5/25	6/1-8/10
DESIGN LINE	5/25-7/20	8/10-9/10	9/15-10/31	11/15-1/15	2/5-4/5
LOCK-IN MEETINGS	6/10-7/25	8/15-9/15	10/1-11/15	11/30-1/20	3/15-4/15
POST LOCK-IN MEETINGS	6/10-7/25	8/15-9/15	10/1-11/15	11/30-1/20	3/15-4/15
FINAL COSTING	8/10	10/1	12/5	2/1	5/1
PRICE LINE	8/20	10/10	12/15	2/10	5/10
DUPLICATES OUT	7/5-8/5	8/25-9/25	11/1-11/30	12/15-1/25	3/5-4/25
DUPLICATES BACK	8/5-9/5	9/25-10/25	12/1-12/31	1/25-2/25	4/25-5/25
LINE OPENS	9/10	11/1	1/5	3/1	6/1

PRODUCTION CALENDAR

	Spring	Summer	Fall 1	Fall 2	Holiday/Cruise
POST LOCK-IN MEETINGS	6/10-7/25	8/15-9/15	10/1-11/15	11/30-1/20	3/15-4/15
DUPLICATES OUT	7/5-8/5	8/25-9/25	11/1-11/30	12/15-1/25	3/5-4/25
DUPLICATES BACK	8/5-9/5	9/25-10/25	12/1-12/31	1/25-2/25	4/25-5/25
LINE OPENS	9/10	11/1	1/5	3/1	6/1
PATTERNS/SPECS/SAMPLES COMPLETE	8/20-11/20	11/20-1/5	1/15-3/20	3/5-5/20	5/25-8/5
MARKERS SENT	8/25-11/25	11/25-1/10	1/20-3/25	3/10-5/25	6/10-8/10
FABRIC DELIVERY	8/25-11/25	11/25-1/10	1/20-3/25	3/10-5/25	6/10-8/10
CUTTING ORDER SENT	9/1-11/30	12/1-1/15	2/1-4/1	3/15-5/30	6/5-8/15
PRE-PRODUCTION SAMPLES RECEIVED	9/8-12/8	12/8-1/23	2/8-4/8	3/23-6/8	6/13-8/23
CUT	9/10-12/10	12/10-1/25	2/10-4/10	3/25-6/10	6/15-8/25
CUTTING TICKET RECEIVED	9/25-12/25	12/25-2/10	2/25-4/25	4/10-6/25	7/1-9/10
STOCK SHIPPED-BOAT	9/20-11/20	12/10-2/5	2/20-4/20	4/5-6/20	6/25-9/5
STOCK SHIPPED-AIR	11/10-2/10	2/10-3/25	4/10-6/10	5/25-8/10	8/15-10/25
STOCK RECEIVED	11/20-2/20	2/10-4/5	4/20-6/20	6/5-8/20	8/25-11/5
SHIP TO STORES	12/1-2/28	3/1-4/15	5/1-6/30	6/15-8/30	9/5-11/15

Figure 4.7 The line development and line production calendars for a women's sportswear company that has five collections per year. The last six events of the line development calendar are also the first six events of the production calendar. This emphasizes the continuity, collaboration, and cooperation required among departments in the development, execution, and delivery of a product line.

tion is only as good as its execution. When a critical task is delayed, it forces all subsequent tasks to be delayed, which results in the critical season objectives not being met. For this reason the merchandiser must monitor each task to determine its progress and to identify delays as soon as possible so corrective action can be taken. Weekly progress meetings are a good means of identifying potential problems early enough to allow for corrective action. If a company has an intranet, the merchandising calendar can be updated in real time through the network. This allows the merchandiser to maintain a constant vigil on the progress of each critical task.

A merchandising calendar should be reevaluated after each season and adjusted when necessary. This critical control tool should become more accurate each year with the input from previous seasons.

Line Plan Summary

The merchandising planning and control tool that provides guidelines for the line development team is the line plan summary. The line plan summary focuses the efforts of the design team in one cohesive direction by providing the number of styles, fabrics, colors, and sizes that should be developed for each product group. Instead of designers creating new styles in a vacuum, the line plan summary provides guidelines that point designers in the right direction based upon the company's marketing and merchandising objectives. Evolving out of each seasonal line plan meeting, which includes input from marketing, sales, manufacturing, and finance, the line plan summary is critical to achieving optimal results from the product development effort. The elements of the line plan summary include:

- The number of fabrics in the line by product group, i.e,. knit sportswear blouses, woven sportswear blouses, and woven dressy blouses. This statistic takes into account minimum order quantities for fabrics and allows merchandisers to force fabrics into other styles if needed to meet these minimum quantities.
- The number of styles in the line by product group (fabric + silhouette). Merchandisers base the number of styles upon estimated minimum sales, i.e., $100,000 per style. This affects product development time, sampling and design costs, and sales presentations.
- The number of constructions in the line by product group (fabric + silhouette + color). Merchandisers establish guidelines for the maximum number of colors, i.e., four to five per style. This affects the number of manufacturing bundles, thread changes during production, and overall product cost.
- The number of stock keeping units (SKUs) per product group (fabric + silhouette + color + size). Merchandisers base SKUs on ex-

pected sales, i.e., 160 SKUs per $1 million in sales. The more SKUs, the higher the costs involved in manufacturing, warehousing, and distribution.

Retailers might use an **assortment plan,** which first determines the dollar amount and quantities that should be invested in each classification, and then refines these figures into specific styles and indicates when they should be in stock on a monthly basis.

The ultimate goal of a line plan summary is to maximize sales and profits per square foot of space or per SKU. If a company has too few SKUs, it may not meet the needs of its consumers; if it has too many SKUs, it generates excessive costs. Other factors that affect the decisions in creating the line plan summary are competition, economic conditions, the raw materials markets, and fashion trends.

Sales Forecasts

Since most apparel companies must place production orders before initial sales orders have been received, sales forecasts must be developed. A **sales forecast** is a projection of sales by category, style, color, and size based upon historical data and statistical analysis. It is one of the most difficult planning and control tools for an apparel merchandiser to successfully implement. Due to the complex nature and rapid changes of style trends, forecasting sales of apparel product lines is less than accurate. A retailer would develop a **merchandising plan,** which forecasts sales by category within a specific time period.

Many methods of forecasting have been tested in the apparel industry but none has proven to be highly effective. The most widely used process is a **style ranking** system that uses key company personnel to rank styles from the top seller to the styles projected to generate the least sales. The personnel who participate in the ranking sessions have their past results charted, and their ranking statistics are weighted based upon their success rate and consistency. Sales curves are developed for styles based upon historical sales patterns and style ranking. This tells the merchandiser what sales should be accumulated by style along a timeline for the selling season.

There are also complex statistical sampling systems that use input from key accounts who preview the new lines. Some companies use sophisticated mathematical models that simulate risk factors associated with various style categories. Many companies begin with minimal forecasts to start a season and focus on tracking orders against expected sales curves. This conservative approach can highlight potential exceptions to the standard sales curves, but this usually occurs too late to achieve required production levels, especially for styles sourced offshore.

No matter what system of sales forecasting is used, the merchandiser is often responsible for making the ultimate decision about what styles in what quantities will be produced. In the final analysis, merchandisers usually rely upon **pragmatic forecasting**, which applies their experience to computer forecasting and style ranking to create adjusted projections. Experienced merchandisers must trust their knowledge of the market and their sense of market direction to make the ultimate decisions for fabric purchases and production authorizations.

Shelf Stock Plan

Once a realistic sales forecast is developed, the merchandiser must apply the forecast to providing customers with an appropriate mix of products on a timely basis. This requires integration with the marketing plan, which establishes the desired weekly shipments. The resulting shelf stock plan establishes a schedule of product by style and quantity that must be available for shipping on a monthly and weekly basis. A proper style mix by SKU to provide shippability is critical to an effective shelf stock plan. The goal of a well-executed shelf stock plan is to provide maximum shipment of customer orders with minimum inventory. Ideally, every garment that is received in shipping should be immediately applied to an outstanding order and shipped to a customer.

The accuracy of a shelf stock plan directly effects:

- Production scheduling.
- Shipping.
- Fabric purchasing.
- Raw materials and finished goods inventories.

The shelf stock plan is critical to good customer service and maintaining low inventory, which results in high inventory turns and low inventory carrying costs. The retailer would develop this information as part of their Assortment Plan.

Style Status Report

Once the pre-production process is complete, it is time to schedule and monitor the production process. Whether or not merchandising is responsible for sourcing production, it has a vested interest in the results of the processes that take place after the line has been developed and put on sale. The report that monitors the progress of sales and manufacturing is the style status report. This report takes many different forms in different companies. In some companies it is a series of reports, while in others it is a comprehensive database.

No matter how the report is developed, the functions that it covers must be carefully planned and monitored. The functions that must be covered are:

- Actual sales against forecast by style and time period.
- Piece goods, findings, and trim purchases, delivery status, and inventory positions against forecast by time period.
- Production authorizations, garments in process, and finished goods inventories by style and time period.
- Shipments against orders by style and time period.

The style status report acts as the central data bank for all production information and scheduling relative to each style in the line. The purpose of this report is to monitor and evaluate actual versus projected activities and to indicate when corrective action should be taken. Fabric orders and production authorizations may often be adjusted up or down to minimize excess inventories or missed sales opportunities. An interactive database is a necessity for accurate and timely development and maintenance of this report. It can be handled by merchandising, manufacturing, or a liaison department such as production control. This report is the master planning and control tool for the production phase. It should be updated daily or in real time to reflect the most current status of each style.

A retailer's **style sales report** indicates inventory on hand, inventory on order, sales for the past one, two, or three weeks, and sales-to-date. It alerts the buyer when action should be taken just as the Style Status Report indicates corrective action needed by the apparel merchandiser.

Order Tracking

With the continued globalization of the sourcing of apparel products, tracking the progress of orders has become more complex than it used to be. When production is scattered around the globe, it is often too costly and time-consuming to send personnel to each factory to monitor production on a daily or even a weekly basis. However, with decreasing windows of opportunity for sell-through at retail, timely deliveries are critical.

Some merchandisers responsible for global sourcing have turned to computer technology and the Internet to track orders that are being processed thousands of miles away. Through electronic data interchange (EDI) technology, daily updates of production progress can be transmitted to merchandisers in the United States from anywhere via the Internet. Even more progressive companies are using real-time data capture through computer controlled unit production systems or bar-code readers at operator workstations to track orders through factories. As an operator swipes a bundle ticket

"1999 TAC Report—Case Study #1, Tanner Companies"

This case study relates to Tanner Companies' use of databases, data mining techniques, and scanners to develop line plans and merchandising planning documents. These plans are electronically communicated to all other functional areas to speed the process.

The need for effective merchandising can be no more critical than in the ever-changing world of women's fashions. Tanner Companies, a North Carolina-based firm that designs, manufactures, and retails its own product, places a strategic importance on the merchandising process. With two major seasons' and two minor seasons' lines introduced each year, this ongoing process is fraught with tight deadlines.

Tanner's design decisions begin 12 months prior to a line's introduction to the retail market. At this time, the color and general silhouette direction are set. The design team reaches its decisions after careful study of information including that provided by fashion services and fabric shows.

Then, merchandising conducts an in-depth analysis of sales history. This analysis takes the general direction from the design team to a much more specific level of fabric, styling/silhouette, price targets, and line size. This step takes place 10 months prior to line introduction. It requires an accurate database of the sales for the prior year/same season. It is important that this database is capable of being viewed in many different ways such as: a) fabric construction type (knit, woven, etc.), b) fiber content, c) silhouette type, d) color, e) price points, etc.

In addition to analyzing prior year/same season, merchandising will also review the databases containing the sales histories leading up to the current season. The ability to manipulate this data in many ways can help to detect trends that are seasonal as well as seasonless in nature.

The result of this key process is the merchandising line plan. The line plan is the company's "bible," indicating each item to be included in that season's product offering.

Silhouette sketches are an important visual tool within the line plan. After the sketches are complete, they are scanned into a computer. Once scanned, the sketches can be reduced, enlarged, and moved as needed to create the document itself. The document includes a sketch of each silhouette, fabric description, color, and assigned style number. This line plan is electronically communicated to various areas of the company. For example, the Product Development area uses the line plan as the tracking tool for styles that need to be developed into patterns and resulting specifications. The Sourcing area uses the plan to finalize the process of placing work into different factories around the world. The Planning area uses the plan for specific direction in the initial forecast of volumes for the season.

The merchandising line plan is *the* plan that communicates to the entire company

(continued)

what the product line will consist of in specific detail. It is pertinent to have good data that can be manipulated for many different looks to understand the consumers' buying patterns, and therefore their desires, as accurately as possible. When developing the plan, it is also important to be able to communicate the resulting plan easily and quickly, through electronic capability, so the subsequent processes throughout the company can begin their critical tasks to meet the deadlines of the upcoming season. ■

From American Apparel Manufacturers Association, 1999.

Case in Point 4.2   ## Summary

Case in Point 4.2 highlights the importance of using detailed analyses of sales histories and careful planning to create a comprehensive merchandising line plan. The line plan becomes a company's "bible," which communicates each season's product line in specific detail. The plan focuses the efforts of the design team in a coherent direction, is used as an important tracking tool for product development, guides the planning department in preparing initial forecasts, and directs the sourcing function in placing production orders. ■

through a bar-code reader or a bar-coded unit production hanger drops into place at a workstation, the factory computer system identifies that bundle or garment at that workstation. With these state-of-the-art systems a merchandiser can access the status screen for a factory in Thailand or Korea and monitor production orders over the Internet.

■ Interfacing with Other Departments

The process of planning and control cannot be performed by a merchandiser in a vacuum. For the process to be effective, it must involve the cooperation of all departments in an apparel or retail company. Proper communications and coordination among marketing, merchandising, manufacturing, sourcing, finance, and administration are necessary to develop effective, realistic systems to plan and control the complex functions required to achieve a successful season.

Gary Simmons
Experience—president, VF Playwear; president, Gerber Childrenswear

Line Development Structure

"At VF Playwear we had general managers (GMs) of merchandising. In Lee we had a brand manager responsible for merchandising and sales because of the size of the business. In the case of Nike there was a VP of merchandising responsible for infants, toddlers, boys, and girls. These individual managers are the drivers of the product. A designer works with an assistant designer and works in concert with a merchandising associate (MA) and the merchandising specialist (MS). You can liken it to two pillars. The designer and assistant designer and the MA and MS report to the GM of merchandising. You have the design pillar and you have the analyst and paperwork pillar. One pillar analyzes the business opportunities and the other pillar designs to those business opportunities and the general manager coordinates both.

"At Gerber Childrenswear, a division of Kellwood, Gerber only focuses on the Newborn to Toddler sizes. We have a merchandising area that has a VP of Merchandising, four designers, four assistant designers, one graphic artist, one packaging expert, and two product engineers. This team develops unique prints and art for our top three clients (Wal-Mart, Target, and BRU) working closely with sales and sourcing to get the best value with the best margins. Unlike VF Playwear where we did multiple size ranges splitting our merchandising group into Newborn/Infants, Boys 2-8, and Girls 2-14, this is not required at Gerber due to our more narrow focus."

Product Marketing Strategy

"At VF Playwear we did a three-year strategic plan, and what we called a one-year concentration. We looked out three years, but we focused on one year. VF has a very focused process with second, third, and fourth quarter reviews. At our first review we'd go through the initial plan for the current year, which was presented the first week of August and the detail plan was presented the first week of November, and the final plan was signed off on in January.

"The company is very planning oriented. We developed a product marketing strategy or PMS. It set the initial sales goals tying back to the line plan. The business opportunities were set by client or product categories at strategy meetings. Sales, in concert with merchandising, said we can sell this much. From that initial plan, a formalized

(continued)

product marketing strategy sheet came out which said that not only could we sell $10 million, but we'll sell $2.5 million in this product category and $1.5 million in rompers. The PMS is developed down to the product category level so we can drive those categories by season. We did our line plan and from that we projected our gross margins and our production planning forecasts for our plants.

"At Gerber Childrenswear we just completed a three-year plan which outlines the following key strategies:

1. Brand Focus – What do we need to do to protect our core business and what categories should be added over the next three years? Tied into this focus we review the current brand positioning versus our competitors and the overall market.

2. Sales, Margin, and SG&A Targets—Developing an initial three-year P&L.

3. A.S.W.O.T. (Assumptions, Strengths, Weaknesses, Opportunities, & Threats) for internal and external review.

4. Developed a strategy for licensing and potential acquisitions to be used as the basis for all future opportunities."

Line Plan

"As part of the initial strategy at VF Playwear, the line plan told the company how much volume we were going to do, here's how many

styles we needed and we looked very closely at the productivity per style. We hardly ever let the productivity per style decrease. If our business was going to go up 10 percent, we didn't add 10 percent more styles. We may have added two percent or three percent more styles. Our goal was to increase the dozens per style. After the initial plan at the first forecast (30 days before on-sale) we dropped some styles. At the sales meeting we dropped more styles. After four weeks of sales when we had 50 percent to 55 percent of total sales, we dropped more styles. Throughout the entire process we cut styles, so from the initial line plan onward we always increased our productivity per style. This allowed us to include a fashion injection of a new style anywhere in the process without greatly diluting our per style volume.

"At VF Playwear, because of our focus on six major clients driving a substantial portion of our business, instead of developing a line plan, we analyze extensively our floor set planograms for areas of opportunity for next year. We also set targets for areas of growth outside of the planogram.

"In 2005 we established strict criteria for accepting new initiatives that tie back to sourcing requirements and profit goals."

Sales Forecasts

"At VF Playwear, as we develop our product line, our PMS sheets came

(*continued*)

in concert. Then about 30 days before on-sale, we forecasted the line with the merchants and with key sales people. At the sales meeting we re-ranked the line with actual sales samples. The initial ranking was done with the manager of the business unit, the merchandising associate, the designer, the head of sales, one or two key sales people, a financial person, and the head of production planning and our forecasting person. We worked together to plan our market strategy. With this information we did our initial up-front order buy (issue purchase orders for product before any sales have been generated), which was a substantial portion of our total business. Within three to five weeks of going on sale, we had 50 percent to 60 percent of our business in. We then moved away from the initial forecasts and went to orders. Our sales force was good at estimating our business volume. I also reviewed our position with them every week. Our goal was to get the right initial mix so we could move the forecast to actual sales. That's how we did our initial product planning and forecasting.

"We did a separate plan for our reorderables. It was developed all at the same time, but we did a lot of analysis on how much shelf stock we should carry. That was based on rate of sale. We were totally computerized. We captured sales at retail by style and colors from our top 18 clients. Our merchandisers actually saw what was really selling at retail.

We had a triangle approach. We'd take sell-throughs by the customer, we had line reviews during our line development process, and then we'd also get our sales department input. That's the triangle that drove our forecasting. We were very involved in forecasting along the entire process.

"Because the majority of Gerber Childrenswear business is done on six-month or 12-month planogram sets, the planning department reports to the Senior VP of Manufacturing and Operations. He and his team have established four planning areas:

1. Wal-Mart
2. Target, Dollar General, Sears-Kmart
3. TRU/BRU
4. Open Line

"These planning teams review weekly POS data adjusting current and future forecasts on a continuous basis in order to balance inventory for Gerber and to deliver the client on time and complete. The result of this work is impressive in that we are carrying an average of 75 days of inventory and have delivered an average of 99.5 percent on time."

Merchandising Calendar

"The VF Playwear merchandising or line development calendar had 40 steps. We included a marketing calendar within our line development calendar—line plan, start ship, end ship. The line development calendar

(*continued*)

was developed by the merchandisers and signed off on by our senior team. It also blended into the marketing department and operational calendars. We took a lot of time developing our calendars. We used this system to develop and track our information and progress.

"The biggest challenge we had in product development was staying on our calendar. We were constantly challenged to stay on the calendar schedule. The big reason why we got off a calendar, quite frankly, was changes. We started in this direction, and then we had to go back and start in another direction.

"If we could have gotten better and earlier information for our line development, then we would have had a better chance of staying on calendar. We worked on that with our Web site. We had a business-to-business site and a business-to-consumer site. One of the goals of our business-to-consumer site was to develop a range of folks on the Internet who would be our consumer panel. These people would be targeted demographically, psychographically, and geographically. If we used them right and received good consumer feedback, we'd get some valuable input for line development. We used The NPD Group for panel research and we used focus groups. All that was great but what you sometimes needed was immediate input to determine what consumers would think about a new product offering. In 24 hours, you could have enough responses to get quantifiable answers. We had gotten kudos on our site, **www.health tex.com**, because it was a clean, clear site. We had done our digital photography different from anyone else. You could go to our site and see this outfit, and you could click on it and see a close-up of the fabric, the pattern, and any detailing such as buttons, appliques or embroidery treatments.

"Gerber merchandising in concert with all appropriate departments follows a strict merchandising calendar. This calendar is reviewed weekly, every Friday from 8:45–10:30. Included in this meeting are all responsible VPs and me. Everyone is aware it is crucial they stay on time and we, in fact, review line by line by key client and open line anywhere from 40-50 active projects. The benefit of this intense review is a more collegic work place. Since this calendar was implemented, "redos and errors" have fallen substantially, and it also allows for improved communication throughout the company."

Lorraine Trocino Experience—merchandiser, Jones Apparel Group

Classic Merchandising Functions

"As Jones Apparel Group grew, the classic merchandising functions became divided into specialized positions among various departments. The division presidents are responsible for the bottom line, the profitability of their division. Each division design department handles product development, and the design director, along with the division president, develops the line plan. The textile purchasing department negotiates prices with the fabric suppliers for blanket greige goods based upon the line plan. Then the design coordinators place the actual detailed fabric purchase orders. We also have a trim purchasing department that handles all trim purchases.

"My merchandising department is the liaison between design, sales, and production. We develop the schedule that is followed to assure that knits are purchased with enough lead time to meet planned deliveries. We schedule weekly cut meetings with the division presidents to review which woven and knit orders have to be placed. We also issue all cutting tickets. The import production department then takes over and follows up to make sure that the factories have everything they need to begin production."

Line Plan

"It all starts with a vision. The design director will say, 'We're going to have tweed, we're going to have argyles.' The director hands the concept plan to the division president who allocates projected sales dollars to each group. The design director develops individual styles and works together with the president to balance the line and make sure that it is marketable. The result is the initial line plan. A design coordinator then communicates the line plan via computer to the rest of the company.

"Merchandising works with design throughout the entire product development process to assure that the design objectives are met without jeopardizing delivery or profit margins. Is design planning any mercerized cotton sweaters? Are they developing crocheted sweaters? Are they using any fancy yarn? Design shows us the protos that they send out and we get feedback from the factories to determine when we have to give them specific orders. We feed information back and forth

(continued)

on those styles that are time sensitive due to longer lead times or the nature of the yarn. It's our job to see that the line plan can be produced on time with minimum problems."

Production Planning and Control

"We must make sure that all the information is in place before we issue the cutting tickets. My merchandisers communicate with our agents in Hong Kong, Taiwan, and Korea. The agents then go to the factories to determine lead times and deliveries. When we have all our schedules for knit and woven production, we give the division presidents a cutting plan for their product lines. It tells them what orders have to be placed each week to meet deliveries.

"We use a style color worksheet to plan our cutting tickets. It's a fabric worksheet that lists all the styles that are being offered in a fabric range, along with the yardage yields and sales projections for each style and the total yards that are required at that moment. For example, we may have a utilization requirement of 10,000 yards of a particular fabric, but we only own 8,000 yards. We then have to present a proposal to the division head, this is how we think you should cut back your projections. When the division heads sign off on the plan, we prepare cutting tickets by size.

"After we issue the cutting tickets, the production department fol-

lows up to assure deliveries are on time. We only get involved again if there is a problem that would cause us to miss our shipping window."

Merchandising Calendar

"We have a very extensive report that lists all of the events that must take place in order to develop the line and meet deliveries. It includes the target dates for each event such as pre-production garment approval, lab dip approval, pattern approvals, and when graded sets of patterns must be sent out. The person who is responsible for an event must sign it off in the system when the event has been completed so that everyone can monitor the status of the line development. It's a very fine-tuned merchandising calendar.

"The schedule is handled on our mainframe computer by a software system that was developed by a systems consultant. Everyone is able to print out reports to see where we stand on a particular season or style. Our company is too big and our functions are too complex to handle scheduling any other way."

Educational Background

"In order to work in our merchandising department, someone needs the right educational background. They need strong math skills. No calculus or anything sophisticated, just algebra. You have to be able to solve word problems. For example, if the sales projections show that we

(*continued*)

need 10,000 yards but we only have 8,000 yards, and we are running three styles, each with a different yield, how do you manipulate that?

"They also have to be able to look at a number generated by the computer and say, 'No, that's not right.' It's hard to teach someone to double check what the computer is telling them. It requires basic logic and an understanding of fundamental apparel and textile functions. A merchandising candidate should also know basic garment construction. They should know how many yards it takes to make a garment.

The basics, for example, a long plaid skirt utilizes more fabric than a solid color blouse does. That knowledge is important as well as an understanding of textiles. Courses like Textile Technology, Fabric Structures, and Fabrics and Their Uses will provide valuable insight into the raw materials that we use in developing a line.

"Work-study is also very important for students. Most of the college interns who work here are very surprised to see what goes on in the real business world. It's an eye opener and a great experience for them."

Summary

The global nature of the apparel industry and the increased frequency of seasonal product offerings require complex planning and control procedures. Merchandisers must develop carefully structured planning strategies and effective controls to meet the rigid time constraints for development, execution, and delivery of the many seasonal product lines that are required for apparel companies to be competitive in today's market.

The planning and control process is driven by the objectives established by a company's strategic plan, which identifies where and how the company's resources should be allocated. Answering the questions, where a company is now, where the company wants to go, and how the company will get there, establishes many goals and objectives that require specific time frames for completion and effective allocation of the company's resources.

The marketing calendar establishes timetables for the completion of each season's line, sales objectives for the products in the line, and start and stop dates for shipping customer orders. The merchandising calendar creates detailed time frames and assigns responsibility for each key event required to achieve the objectives of the marketing calendar. Project scheduling software is a necessity for creating task lists and keeping track of the status of the many functions that are required to deliver the right product to the right customers at the right time.

Another important aspect of a merchandiser's role in effective planning and control involves interfacing with other departments. Information must be shared and communicated quickly and accurately through all departments to successfully achieve the goals of the company's strategic plan.

Key Terms

assortment plan

cash flow

critical path method (CPM)

end ship date

Gantt chart

inventory turns

line preview date

merchandising plan

open-to-buy

pragmatic forecasting

pre-season planning

sales forecast

shippability

start ship date

stock keeping unit (SKU)

style ranking

style sales report

weekly sales plan

weekly shipping plan

Discussion Questions and Learning Activities

1. Discuss the effect that changing consumer demands has had on the planning function performed by merchandisers.
2. Discuss the role of the merchandiser in developing a company's strategic plan.
3. What effect did Liz Claiborne's decision to develop a mass merchant initiative have on the merchandising function of its Russ brand division?
4. Have the strategic initiatives of Macy's, JCPenney, and Sears to fully develop their private brands successfully improved their sales performance?
5. Analyze the Web sites of three different apparel companies that produce the same category of products. Discuss any perceived differences in strategic plans based upon the structure and content of the Web sites.
6. How might changes in apparel distribution channels affect the marketing calendar?
7. How might the current direction of the apparel industry affect merchandising calendars? Do you believe that merchandising calendars of the future will be more complex or more simplified? Explain your answer.
8. Create a computer database sample merchandising calendar for one season of a children's wear company that outsources its production.
9. Discuss how a line plan summary for a couture women's wear company might differ from that of a popular priced women's sportswear company.
10. Explain how the personnel structure of the planning and control functions of a large apparel company like Donna Karan might differ from that of a smaller specialty company like Nicole Miller.
11. Which planning and control tool discussed in this chapter would relate to the sales/unit plan mentioned in the Colombe Nicholas executive perspective? Explain your answer.

References and Resources

Abend, Jules. February 1997. Levi's, Claiborne, Kmart Getting Refocuses. *Bobbin*, pp. 21–22.

Bertrand Frank Associates. 1985. *Profitable Merchandising of Apparel*, 2nd ed., p. 31. New York: National Knitwear & Sportswear Association.

Brumback, Nancy. April 16, 1999. Hartmarx Deemphasizing $200 to $300 Suits, Revving Up Sportswear. *Daily News Record*, p. 6.

Cole, David. December 1970. Pre-Season Planning. *Bobbin*, p. 79.

Derby, Meredith. February 25, 2005. Gap's Five-Step Growth Plan. *www.wwd.com*.

Flake, Bill, and Frank, Bertrand. March 1978. Consumer Buying Patterns Force Marketing Change. *Apparel Industry Magazine*, pps. 68, 70.

Friedman, Thomas L. 1998. *The Lexus and the Olive Tree*, p. 112. New York: Ferrar Straus Giroux.

Gellers, Stan. September 12, 1997. A Tailored Clothing Giant Changes with the Times. *Daily News Record*, p. 5.

Greenberg, Julee. May 20, 2005. Claiborne Sets Brand Plan. *www.wwd.com*.

Kletter, Melanie. February 11, 1999. Jones Scores 34% Net Hike, Plans Picone Move to Moderate. *Women's Wear Daily*, p. 18.

Kurt Salmon Associates, Inc. November 1973. Survival of the Swiftest. *Bobbin*, pp. 128–129.

Lewis, Robin. February 12, 1998. Consumers at Apex of VF Vision. *Women's Wear Daily*, p. 8.

McKinney, Melonee. June 28, 1999. Reebok to Consolidate Global Apparel. *Daily News Record*, p. 24.

Weintraub, Emanuel. December 1986. Strategic Planning Needs Better Cost Information. *Bobbin*, p. 20, 22.

Williamson, Rusty. May 23, 2005. Ullman Lays Out Penney's Plan. *www.wwd.com*.

Part 3 explores the functions involved in the execution of apparel product lines. Consumers want garment styles that meet their design expectations at acceptable quality levels and reasonable prices.

Merchandisers and product managers must understand the design process in order to manage line development. The elements and principles of design and the processes used to integrate those factors into garment styles that meet the needs of a company's target consumer are carefully evaluated.

Increased competition in the fashion industry has forced apparel and retail companies to make dramatic changes in product development and manufacturing processes. These changes have affected the strategies required to maintain effective cost controls and competitive pricing. Part 3 evaluates pricing strategies based upon sound costing principles used in the apparel industry to adapt to changing conditions.

Quality continues to play an important role in consumer purchasing decisions. Part 3 analyzes consumers' perception of quality, how acceptable quality is designed into each style, and the inspection and sampling procedures used to assure the end product meets consumer expectations.

The development, production, and retail sales of apparel products involves a complex supply chain including fiber, fabric, findings, supplies, apparel, and retail. Part 3 analyzes the factors that affect the supply chain and discusses various strategies to achieve quick response in developing and supplying apparel products to the consumers.

Apparel manufacturing is a labor-intensive industry. Price competition has sent many apparel manufacturers to all parts of the globe in the quest for low cost labor while others have focused on the advantages of quick response technologies for producing their products in or near the United States. Part 3 discusses and evaluates the strategies and processes for sourcing production domestically or offshore.

MERCHANDISING: THE EXECUTION

CHAPTER 5

Line Development: Principles and Technologies

OBJECTIVES

- Understand the concept of line development.

- Examine the creative process and the role of the merchandiser and product manager as facilitators.

- Identify design elements and design principles and their role in line development.

- Discuss the role of computer technology in the line development process.

The U.S. marketplace has changed from being centered around production to being centered around the customer. Ken Sharma, senior partner of i2 Technologies, focused on the change at his company's 1998 Greensboro, NC, conference on Excellence in Supply Chain Management for Textiles and Apparel. "Today, the entire life span of a product is four months," he explained. "It's estimated that this will drop to three months. And the customers' insatiable greed for new products will drive the supply chain." (Rabon, 1998.)

Today's rapidly changing fashion marketplace is driven by fresh new styles. A **style** is an identifiable garment produced in a specific **silhouette** or body (the three-dimensional outline or shape) from a specific fabric and trims. Apparel companies usually identify styles by a unique **style number** or alphanumeric code. To be successful, apparel and retail companies must introduce many more new products, or styles, than its competitors. This was underscored by a 1998 study of public apparel companies by A. T. Kearney's consumer products and retail office, which targeted companies that:

- Manufactured apparel exclusively.
- Were publicly traded for at least 5 years.
- Earned more than $300 million in sales.
- Showed consistent performance in sales and profitability over the past 10 years.

The top-performing companies studied—Tommy Hilfiger, Nine West, Nautica, Jones Apparel Group, and Nike—introduced more than ten times as many new designs annually than underperformers. In addition, their design efforts are heavily supported by market research and frequent design reviews, a highly market-oriented research and development (R&D) approach, and a tendency to use **licensing** (an agreement for a **licensee** to use intellectual property such as a designer name, brand name, or design owned by the **licensor** in return for payment of royalties to the licensor) to introduce new products with a minimum of risk.

■ The Concept of Line Development

"The success of retailers is location, location, location. For today's apparel companies success is product, product, product." Hal Upbin, CEO of Kellwood Company, made this observation at the October 1999 University of Missouri joint session of the Professional Leadership Council of the American Apparel Manufacturers Association and the Missouri Textile Apparel Council. The focus on product styling becomes more important each year. Developing new and exciting styles is the responsibility of merchandising through the line development process.

Line development is the creation of a line, also referred to as a **collection** (a group of garment styles that is presented to consumers for sale and delivery during a specific time period). The term collection is frequently used in Europe and by higher-priced designer and couture businesses such as Yves St. Laurent, Versace, Christian Dior, Chloe, and Armani. Large companies may have a number of different lines, each targeted to specific customer categories such as evening wear, sportswear, outerwear, active sportswear, or even petite or women's large size lines. Some of these companies have men's, women's, and children's divisions, each offering a number of different lines.

The number of times per year that companies offer their lines for sale varies greatly. The number of offerings or releases have increased throughout the last half of the twentieth century. In the 1950s and 1960s most apparel companies had two releases per year—warm, long-sleeved garments for winter and lightweight, short-sleeved garments for summer. In the 1970s the offerings increased to four, following the seasons: fall, winter, spring, and summer. Then some apparel companies added back-to-school, holiday, and cruise or resort lines. Beginning in the 1990s with pressure from consumers for more frequent releases, many companies started presenting additional offerings, some reaching 10 or 12 per year. This was often accomplished by dividing a season such as spring or fall into two or three delivery periods with unique styling groups offered for each release.

The expanding number of line releases has increased the importance of effective line development. Decreased cycle times and increased fashion competition have put tremendous pressure on the line development process, which has become a focal point for merchandisers. The process must be carefully controlled to focus the design direction so that a line will be created that will capture the wants and needs of a target market in a reduced time frame. Apparel merchandisers play the pivotal role of planning and controlling the line development process. They must provide competent, creative direction, and they must manage the timely completion of each function required to prepare a salable line for presentation to customers and for preparation for manufacturing.

To consistently create new designs that meet the expectations of consumers and sell-through at retail, the line development team must achieve the following:

- **Understanding**: acquire and maintain a thorough sense of the market and target consumer by the line development team.
- **Conceptualization**: be able to quickly and effectively visualize new styling ideas and communicate the concepts.
- **Creation**: the ability to develop finished garment styles that meet the expectations set forth in the conceptualization stage through an efficient design process.

■ The Creative Process

The driving force behind effective line development is **creativity**. This ability to visualize a concept that will capture the essence of a consumer's buying urge almost a year in advance is not easily quantifiable. Creativity is also not easily understood. Many academicians believe that creativity cannot be taught, that all we can do is provide a supportive environment for people to tap into their creativity. In this respect creativity is affected by the design environment and corporate product development philosophy, which is often established, interpreted, and controlled by the merchandiser.

Merchandiser as Facilitator

In many ways creativity is in the eye of the beholder. For apparel companies it is vital for merchandisers to share the critical eye of their target market customers. Good merchandisers must also be able to understand the creative abilities of their designers and provide a healthy environment that enables the designers to achieve the most effective styling results. From this perspective the merchandiser is a facilitator of the design process. The merchandiser provides the environment and control for effective line development, thereby allowing the designers to focus their energies on creativity. In 1999 Liz Claiborne consolidated its line development efforts for all divisions in a renovated facility at its New York offices at 1441 Broadway. "It will be specially constructed to encourage independent thinking and cross-pollination of design content," said Denise Seegal, Claiborne's president, adding that the three-level area will feature a resource center, as well (D'Innocenzio 1999).

Controlling line development is difficult because of the creative element. Award winning designer Gordon Henderson told *The Wall Street Journal* concerning his financial backers, "They always want to set a formula. . . . They want things to work on a timetable, for me to pick the colors first or the fabric before I know what I'm going to design. It's hard for a creative person to work that way."

Some executives believe that management discipline cannot be applied to the design process because it inhibits creativity. This is a dangerous philosophy that can lead to incongruous styling, large expensive lines, and late samples. The line development process should not operate without defined criteria (the line plan), measurable performance standards, and critical timetables (merchandising calendar). It is the task of an effective merchandiser to see that these important management controls operate yet without stifling creativity.

In order to function as a facilitator, a merchandiser must possess a thorough understanding of the creative elements of design and also have a good foundation in business principles. It is this unique blend of right-brain and left-brain abilities that allows merchandisers to maintain the necessary balance between business management controls and creativity. This makes apparel merchandising a difficult position to fill. Successful merchandisers come from a broad range of backgrounds. Some have undergraduate degrees in fashion design, apparel management, retail fashion merchandising, and retail buying. Others have majors in textile design or textile technology. These educational backgrounds are often combined with industry experience in retail buying, fashion design, apparel manufacturing, or entry-level positions within an apparel merchandising department. Those who exhibit a combination of excellent management skills and creativity eventually rise through the ranks to become successful apparel merchandisers.

Styling versus Design

In fashion as in most creative endeavors, there are two elements that affect creativity—craft and art. In order to release the art, or that which affects the sense of beauty, it is critical to have mastered the craft, the skill in using the tools that create the art. In fashion, this involves drawing, pattern making, and garment construction techniques. Depending on the size of a company, the art and craft may be expressed through the positions of stylist and designer.

The functions of stylist and designer are often confused. "Garrick Anderson is best thought of as a stylist. Why everyone who has something to do with the way clothes look (rather than how they are made) should be called a designer is something we might ask" (Boyer, 1990). In simplest terms the stylist's talents may be weighted more toward art, while the designer's skills may be weighted more toward craft.

Styling

Styling involves creating concepts and theme direction for each line. Some large corporations may have the luxury of having **stylists** on staff who create the styling concepts and theme directions for each line. This usually takes the form of **storyboards**, which are also referred to as **trend boards**, **inspiration boards**, or **concept boards**. These are large presentation boards that are created for themes. They contain photos, magazine clippings, 3-D elements, or sketches depicting the theme concept along with color palettes, fabric swatches, and stylized silhouette sketches. The storyboards establish the mood and styling direction from the standpoint of the artistic elements that will drive the line (see Figure 5.1). Music, art, cinema, television, sports, and world events may inspire trend direction.

"Trend boards make everything click. For its licensed Kenneth Cole Reaction line, DML Marketing spelled out its younger customers' interests—home, news, music, rituals, jobs, entertainment, food, spiritualism and adventure—and used photos to illustrate them. Images of sushi, surfers, beer bottles, 'South Park' characters, and rainbow-color condoms were used to illustrate their varied interests" (Feitelberg, 1998). The storyboards have become powerful sales tools during line presentations to important retail buyers. "It makes buying the line easier. It helps them understand how their category relates to the realm of fashion," said Deborah Boria, executive director of design and merchandising for Hanes Hosiery. "It gives them more confidence about why they bought what they did."

An effective stylist must be highly skilled in fashion illustration techniques, thus providing clear conceptual presentations of a company's styling direction. The critical areas that affect styling direction are color, fabric, and silhouette. The stylist must also be tuned in to the company's target customer and have an acute sense of market direction and changes. In a sense, stylists are the fashion antennae for an apparel company. They must focus all their attention on the company's particular fashion niche to detect the subtle elements that promote style change.

Designer William Calvert sees this creative process as the key to a successful line. "Communicating styling ideas quickly and accurately is the key to developing exciting lines. One idea becomes the germ for another. Creativity is often a synergy generated by our design team. I provide the styling direction and my assistant, Lina, provides the technical expertise. She creates the first pattern, and we work very closely every step of the way."

Design

Once the styling direction is established, **designers** interpret the concepts communicated by the stylists into actual garments. This involves many of the craft aspects that affect product development, such as pattern design and grading, garment construction techniques, and the interplay of fabric, **findings** (functional, nonfabric items such as zippers, buttons, and elastic), and trims. A skilled designer creates prototypes for the silhouettes presented on the story boards for a specific line. The interpretation of the stylist's illustrations by the designer must meet the practical expectations of the target market consumer without minimizing the stylized concepts that drive the company image.

Most medium-sized and small apparel companies do not have the luxury of having both a stylist and designer on staff. For these companies the designer usually performs the function of stylist by establishing the creative concepts and trends as well as being the technical designer and developing the patterns and prototypes for all new styles. This often results in a tradeoff between creative talent and technical skill. When the two are in conflict, it is usually creativity that is jeopardized.

Hinda Miller, who cocreated the first sports bra in 1977 by sewing together two athletic supporters, expressed concern about the danger of designers stifling creativity. "Sometimes we get such tunnel vision when we're designing. We need to stop and step out to see how these products fit into the big picture" (Feitelberg, 1998). Some companies use styling services or styling consultants to provide the initial styling direction, which allows the designer to focus on the technical creation of the line.

Design Elements

To oversee the creative process and develop successful lines, an apparel merchandiser should have a thorough understanding of the elements of design. A merchandiser can learn the elements of design by taking academic courses. However, mastering these elements requires years of industry experience evaluating what works and what doesn't. The elements of design, specifically those that affect the visual and tactile senses, must be properly integrated to create garments that are aesthetically pleasing to the consumer.

Color

Color has an immediate and powerful impact on our perception. It plays a key role in the aesthetic appeal of apparel. Selecting the proper color palette or color story when creating a trend board can be a key element in establishing an effective direction for the line development process.

Color plays a vital and complicated role in the development of apparel products. Color measurement and color appearance are not the same. Differing materials will create different color appearances even when dyed using the same color measurement criteria. This is a critical issue for trim and findings like buttons, lace, piping, and thread. Different weaves can create different shades even when the weaving is done with the same lot of dyed yarn.

There is powerful computer hardware and software available today that measure color characteristics, but even if they are calibrated between apparel manufacturer and suppliers, management design decisions must be made. The equipment can then provide consistent, accurate results after color standards are agreed upon. Companies specializing in color measurement equipment are Datacolor International, Hunterlab, and Minolta Corporation. A quality line development team must have a quality color management system that provides the process and controls necessary to maintain color consistency throughout a product line.

Understanding color theory is a complex science involving many factors. It is highly recommended that anyone seriously considering a career in merchandising or design take at least one course in color science.

Analysis of a company's sales histories can identify the effect of color on product success. Certain colors consistently sell better than others in different target markets. Most companies create sales profiles that capture the relationship of sales to color. This does not mean that low sales histories should automatically eliminate certain colors from a new **color story** or **colorway** (the array of color choices available for each style). Some colors may be needed to complete a balanced line presentation even though records show that they do not generate substantial sales.

The color that is chosen for a sales sample can have a dramatic effect on the sale of a particular style. The sample color is usually selected by buyers when they make a purchase, and a poor sample color could eliminate a style from a buyer's selection. It is therefore important to choose colors that have excellent past sales histories for sales samples.

The three dimensions that determine color are hue, value, and intensity.

Hue Hue is the dimension of color that refers to a scale of perceptions that range from red through yellow, green, and blue and circularly back to red. Hue is based upon pure pigment colors and equal mixes of pure pigment colors. Hues are created by single wavelengths or small bands of wavelengths of light.

Examples of hues that affect our perception of fabrics, which absorb light, are the **subtractive** (or pigment) **primary colors** yellow, blue, and red. When equal quantities of the subtractive primary colors are combined, the result is black. For the purpose of discussing apparel, the term "primary colors" refers to the subtractive or pigment primary colors.

The colors produced by a computer monitor are from emitted light and therefore are the **additive primary colors** red, green, and blue. When equal quantities of additive primary colors are combined, the result is white. When using a CAD system to emulate a garment color, the term "primary colors" refers to the additive primary colors.

Secondary colors are a combination of two primary colors, and tertiary colors are combinations of a primary and secondary color. The basic subtractive hues for subtractive primary colors are presented in Figure 5.2.

Colors (hues) can be classified as warm such as reds, yellows, and oranges. These colors can be stimulating, exciting, aggressive, cheerful, or lively. Cool colors such as blues, greens, and purples are quiet, peaceful, refreshing, or reserved. Neutral colors such as tans, browns, grays, black, or white express sophistication and do not detract from other colors. A color story may focus on one classification or provide a blend of key colors from different classifications, but there must be a meaningful relationship among the colors for the story to be effective. A nautical theme can be created with only a few colors—royal blue, red, gold, and white—while a garden theme would invoke a much broader spectrum.

Value Value is the variation of the strength of light in a color. White is the total presence of light, and black is the total absence of light. The lightest values are **tints**—colors mixed with white. Darker values are **tones**—colors mixed with gray. The darkest values are **shades**—colors mixed with black. Value contrasts can create subtle nuances in garments, such as the use of a light purple tint with a darker purple tone, or dramatic effects with the use of black and white.

The contrast of low- and high-value colors when applied to garments can create illusions that can emphasize or downplay parts of the body. Low value or light colors draw attention and can make areas on the body seem larger than they are, while higher value or darker colors create the illusion of something being smaller. When light is contrasted with dark, the eye is drawn away from the dark areas to the light areas, which visually seem to be larger. Combining a dark-colored bodice with light-colored pants can minimize a large bust or broad shoulders. A light-colored sweater or blouse combined with dark slacks can minimize broad hips and make the wearer seem taller.

Intensity   **Intensity** is the strength or weakness of a color determined by its saturation or vividness of hue. Pure primary colors are the most intense. Intensity can be lowered by mixing the primary color with another hue or by mixing it with gray, which will not change its value. Intensity can also be lowered by mixing a color with white, which will increase its value. Mixing a color with black will lower its intensity and will also lower its value. Lowering the intensity of a color can be compared to adding water to paint. Royal blue is a high-intensity color, while sky blue is a lower-intensity color.

Color Names   The Inter-Society Color Council of the National Bureau of Standards (ISCC-NBS) has developed a standardized method for designating color. It has standardized the terms *light*, *medium*, and *dark* (which can be extended by adding the adverb *very*), which are used to designate varying degrees of value. *Grayish*, *moderate*, *strong*, and *vivid* identify varying degrees of intensity. *Brilliant* relates to light and strong; *pale* relates to light and grayish; *deep* refers to dark and strong. These terms, when combined with white, gray, or black, can be applied to color names to create descriptive color identifiers relative to the three attributes of hue, value, and intensity. An example of the application of this system to the color pink is shown in Figure 5.3. The National Bureau of Standards Special Publication 440, *Color: Universal Language and Dictionary of Names* is an excellent reference for researching the color name system.

Color Notation   Standard systems for referencing colors have been developed to allow designers to effectively communicate color requirements. The Munsell and Pantone color notation systems are widely used to communicate color preferences. Each system uses a specialized series of color chips or swatches of various materials. The color chips are identified by unique notations, some of which relate to hue, value, and intensity, for identifying each color relative to the material medium it is presented on. Some systems specify the formulas for mixing pigments or formulating dyes to achieve colors on dyed or printed fabrics that match those displayed on the color chips or swatches. Merchandisers must establish consistent standards for communicating color requirements with their vendors. The major advances in digital color management software have given merchandisers the necessary tools to source apparel globally and still meet their specific requirements in a timely manner.

Consider what would happen if a merchandiser told three vendors to produce a garment in the color teal. The results could very well be three different colored garments. However, if the merchandiser specifies Pantone No. 327 to the three vendors, the result will be three garments of the same color.

There are many computer software applications available that are linked to the Pantone and Munsell color systems. These computer applications allow accurate simulation of colors on computer monitors and various output devices by accounting for the differences between additive and subtractive color systems. The use of this software allows a designer to create accurate color sketches or even accurately drape computer-generated fabrics over three-dimensional CAD silhouettes.

Light Light conditions greatly affect the way we perceive color. In bright light, garment colors may appear different from the way they do in dim light. A similar phenomenon relates to how colors appear when they are next to other colors. Many colors appear to change in value or intensity when placed next to other colors. In fashion design, color combinations are frequently used in a single style, and therefore the effect of light changes and surrounding colors must be carefully evaluated.

Different lighting such as fluorescent, incandescent, or natural sunlight can cause fabric colors to take on different hues, which is a **metameric** effect. This can be caused by the use of different dyeing and printing processes and formulas. During the line development process as fabrics are selected, they should be compared using a controlled viewing light that can duplicate fluorescent or halogen store lighting conditions as well as daylight and incandescent home light. This is especially critical with coordinated sportswear and matching separates sportswear groups.

Range A line is created in a range of colors to satisfy the needs of the target market without generating excessive development and inventory carrying costs. The merchandising process targets the appropriate colors for a color story. The selection should accommodate the current fashion color trend projections and also be the most flattering to the target consumer. A range of colors for a style is commonly called a colorway. The merchandiser must achieve a delicate balance by carefully controlling the number of colors in each colorway. Too few colors may jeopardize sales potential, and too many colors will drive up costs.

Stock keeping units (SKUs) equal the number of styles in a line times the number of sizes times the number of colors. A line with 40 styles, 6 sizes, and

6 colors creates 1,440 SKUs ($40 \times 6 \times 6 = 1,440$). Each color represents 240 individual SKUs that must be produced and inventoried at considerable cost and risk. The merchandiser has to analyze a number of factors when making critical color range decisions:

- Sales histories.
- Fashion trends.
- Color forecasts.
- Requirements for coordinates and matching separates.
- Needs for basic or classic styles.
- Effect on total SKUs.
- Line presentation considerations.

The final decision usually involves a conflict between styling, design, sales (wanting more color options), and finance and manufacturing (wanting fewer colors in the line). The merchandiser must weigh all the factors and make the decision based upon what is best for the overall profitability of the company.

Line

As a design element in product development, line determines the direction of visual interest in a garment. **Line** is the visual path the eye follows when viewing a garment. Line can be created by the placement and shape of garment parts, fabric prints or patterns, use of color, seam positioning, pleats, darts, tucks, folds, gathers, trims, or even topstitching.

A long skirt, shirtdress, shirt placket, princess seams, and bold double-stitched lap seam on a pair of jeans are examples of actual lines created on garments that move the eye along a vertical path. These techniques use vertical lines to create a long, lean appearance for the wearer. A vertical line can be implied by a long row of small buttons; a horizontal line may be created by two wide breast pockets.

It is important to remember that thin vertical lines or long diagonal lines add height and slenderize while broad horizontal lines widen the figure or cut it into shorter segments. Lines have length, width, weight, and direction, which work together to determine the ultimate direction of visual interest in a garment.

Shape

While line is a direction viewed on a two-dimensional plane, **shape** is an enclosed space or boundary produced in two or three dimensions. A garment silhouette or a body style in three dimensions is a typical example of shape. Silhouettes may be fitted to follow the natural curves of the body, be oversized or tubular to hide the body, or be triangular with padded, exaggerated shoulders to create the illusion of strength and power. A soft look can be achieved by the use of relaxed shapes with curves and layers. Angular lines created by structured tailoring and stiff interfacings can create a more rigid, formal look.

Various parts of a garment may utilize shape to make a design statement. For example, wide raglan sleeves, broad peaked lapels, a cowl neck, pleated bellows pockets, or bold oversized French cuffs create detailed shapes that can make dramatic fashion statements. Shapes can focus attention or distract the eye. Repeating a shape can carry a fashion statement throughout an apparel line.

Texture

Texture is surface variations in fabric that can be used as an effective element of design. Fiber type, yarn structure, fabric construction, and fabric finishes can create infinite varieties of texture. From the luxurious smooth surface of crepe de Chine to the rough texture of linen and ramie, the options are limitless.

Similar textures can be combined to form fluid graceful styles, while contrasting textures can create an interesting dissonance. Designer William Calvert uses textures to create excitement in his eveningwear line. "Fall was about mixture of perfection and imperfection. The highest sheen and technically precise silks mixed with the crudest, most imperfect hand-woven cashmere and angora fabrics. Some of them almost looked like rugs. They were tweedy, complicated."

A skilled creative stylist and designer can use texture to create dramatic contrasts or fluid continuity in garment styling.

Design Principles

Gestalt psychology deals mainly with the concept of perception, with the eye and brain defining visual images as a pattern or a whole rather than the sum of finite component parts. For example, a city skyline is perceived as a pattern rather than merely a sum of distinct building silhouettes. This perceptual philosophy has a profound effect on fashion design. The elements of design provide the building blocks of the apparel product development process. The proper integration of these elements creates the visual perception that is the essence of an aesthetically pleasing garment style. The integration of the elements of design involves the principles of:

- Proportion
- Balance
- Rhythm
- Emphasis
- Harmony

Proportion

Proportion is the relationship between the garment as a whole and the size and placement of parts and shapes. This principle is also referred to as **scale**. Proportion can be equal and balanced or unequal and contrasting. The principle of proportion is affected by the design elements of line and shape. Construction seams and trim items can divide a garment silhouette into component shapes. During the creation of a new style, the relationship of these evolving shapes must be carefully evaluated. The relative size of pockets, sleeves, cuffs, yokes, pant legs, waistbands, and collars have a dramatic impact on garment proportions. Proportion must also be carefully considered when creating coordinates or matching separates so that the ensemble meets the aesthetic objectives of this design principle.

The perceived relative mass as well as the height and width of a garment part can affect proportion. This is especially critical when different fabrics and trims are combined. Fabrics such as silk voile give a perception of airiness, while fabrics such as denim and corduroy evoke a feeling of bulk. Fabric print dimensions also play a very important role in proportion. The subtle difference between a 3/8-inch and a 5/16-inch fabric stripe can be the difference between a style that works and a style that doesn't. When asked what contributed to his ability to succeed in the highly competitive women's wear market, a successful designer responded, "The fact that I'm detail-oriented to a level of nitpicking insanity. Either it's right or it's wrong. End of discussion."

A centuries old Greek mathematical formula has determined that the ratios of 3:5:8 and 5:8:13 can be translated into what is most visually pleasing to Western civilization. Even though these ratios create classic, aesthetically appealing relationships between the length of a bodice and a skirt or between the length of a jacket and pants, there are no hard and fast rules for determining the best proportional fashion relationships. The many variables of fabric, trims, seams, colors, and shapes all affect proportion. Fashion trends often deviate greatly from the classic ratios to create extremes such as the miniskirt of the 1960s or the drooping jeans of the hip hop craze in the late 1990s. Apparel merchandisers and designers must develop a sensitivity to and awareness of the most effective interrelationships of parts to the whole. This requires years of experience and constant experimentation with different variations of the elements that affect proportion until a desired aesthetic effect is achieved (see Figure 5.4).

Balance

The equal distribution of visual weight on a garment is **balance**. The visual weight of the different elements of a garment are evaluated relative to the vertical and horizontal axes of the garment.

Horizontal balance refers to the relationship between the top and the bottom of a garment. A shirt or blouse with wide shoulders and a narrow waist may give the impression of being top-heavy. Baggy pants and a body hugging T-shirt would result in a bottom-heavy look. Body types that are not balanced horizontally can be compensated for in garments that visually enlarge the smaller area and visually deemphasize the larger area thus creating the illusion of a balanced figure. For example, a person with a narrow chest and shoulders and wide hips could wear an oversized top with large breast pockets to visually enlarge the upper body and deemphasize the hips.

Vertical balance relates one side of a garment to another. The human body is symmetrical along a vertical axis. Garments are usually vertically symmetrical, which presents a stable, balanced, visual expression. Each side is a mirror image of the other, providing perfect symmetry. Balance can also be achieved when one side of a garment is different from the other. This asymmetrical balance is created by a small focal concentration on one side balanced by a larger less striking area on the other side. The contrast to create the visual illusion of asymmetrical balance is usually achieved through the use of color or shape. To create successful asymmetrical balance requires much thought and experimentation by a highly skilled designer (see Figure 5.5).

Rhythm

Rhythm is the sense of movement and continuity created by repetition. **Repetition** is the repeated use of a design element to create a unified look in a garment. The repeated element is the design thread that binds the entire composition into a coherent whole. Repetition of print, color, line, shape, or texture can be used to create interesting styling effects. Rhythm creates a visually smooth transition through the repeated design elements. A print motif repeated in different scales on a sweater and skirt; the use of binding or trim on collars, cuffs, and pockets; a sequence of buttons; interesting color blocking; contrasting topstitching on various garment parts; or the repeated use of pleats or tucks are examples of rhythm.

The rhythm of a design must be meticulously planned to create a harmonious result. A haphazard or disconnected use of repetition can create discord. The relative size or proportion of the repeated design elements and the distance separating them contribute to the resulting sense of rhythm. The rhythm can be alternating, using a regular occurrence of a design element, or progressive using a gradual change in the size or placement of a design element (see Figure 5.6).

Emphasis

The design principle that directs the viewer's attention to a specific area of a garment is **emphasis**. A splash of color, converging lines, dramatic shapes, or sharp contrast can be used to create emphasis. This focal point on a garment creates visual interest and design excitement.

Emphasis can direct the eye to a positive part of the body or lead the eye away from a problem area. A garment may be designed to draw attention to the face by using a contrasting collar or a vee neck. Light colors around the face are used to create a pleasing effect. Bold belts on slacks or skirts bring attention to the waist, while large contrasting jacket pockets at hip level or bust line draw the eye to those areas. Emphasis in garment styles should be designed to flatter the figure.

There can be multiple points of emphasis on a garment but, too many points of emphasis can create confusion and may detract from the overall aesthetic of a style. Emphasis can be created through the use of contrast, placement, or isolation.

Contrast   **Contrast** is utilizing dramatically different design elements to develop emphasis and attract the attention of the observer. Contrasting colors, values, sizes, or shapes of an element of the style can create a point of emphasis.

Placement   The prominent **placement** of a styling element or garment part can create emphasis in a design. Other elements may be used to direct or lead the eye toward the point of emphasis. Two converging style lines, a row of buttons, pockets, piping, or print placement can draw the eye to a point of emphasis.

Isolation   A styling element placed apart from other elements can be a point of emphasis because of its **isolation**. The element of emphasis takes on a special visual importance when it is separated from other elements.

For emphasis to be effective, it must be an integral part of the overall design. Emphasis should be intentionally incorporated into a design with subtlety and not merely be added for effect. A sophisticated embroidered pocket patch on a navy blazer or a bow at the neck of a women's dress are examples of creating emphasis using contrast and placement (see Figure 5.7).

Harmony

A garment style is created to produce a positive effect for the wearer. When customers view a garment on a rack in a store, they may touch the fabric, look at its styling features, and even analyze its construction. The decision to buy the garment is often made when customers try it on and look in a mirror to see the overall effect it has when it is on their body. This overall effect is the combined result of the individual elements of design and their integration through the effective use of design principles. This final **harmony**, or unity of design, determines the ultimate visual aesthetic.

It is the merchandiser's responsibility to focus the efforts of the design team to create a line that meets the requirements of the line plan and sells-through at retail. At every step of the line development process, each style must be evaluated against the fashion trends evolving for the target market as well as how effectively they utilize design principles. Harmony is achieved when all the elements of design and the design principles work together to create an aesthetically pleasing garment style (see Figure 5.8).

Since design principles are not hard and fast scientific rules, they can be modified or breached to achieve specific creative objectives. But harmony can be achieved only when the line development team makes design decisions intentionally, not in error. The merchandisers and designers can achieve a harmonious effect only if they have mastered the design elements and principles.

A case in point occurred in the early 1980s when Liz Claiborne, during a European trip, was inspired to create a group of women's coordinated separates using a unique combination of fabric designs. She developed a group of skirts in a large, bold, buffalo plaid and coordinated blouses in a small paisley print. When Claiborne merchandisers and sales executives first previewed the styles, they were not enthusiastic about the combination. The design principles of proportion and harmony did not seem to have been taken into account in these styles. The combination also broke with the accepted paradigm that fashion designs should not mix radically different prints.

Liz Claiborne stuck by her styling decision. After a few weeks, the merchandisers and sales executives began commenting that the styles were growing on them. The styles did very well at retail and were expanded into other styles that combined different print designs. A careful evaluation of the plaid and paisley combinations revealed that the delicate paisley blouses were in pleasing aesthetic proportion to the bold plaid skirts. The sophisticated colorways for these fabrics and the smooth transition from the different scales of the print motifs also provided a sense of continuity and rhythm for the styles. Liz Claiborne had intentionally taken two discordant print patterns and, through the skillful use of color, proportion, balance, and rhythm, created harmony in the resulting garment styles.

Merchandisers should continually hone their creative skills and their mastery of the elements and principles of design. This can be done by analyzing competitors' and their own styles relative to the design principles. Maintaining an awareness of the impact of the principles of design on the aesthetic properties of successful garment styles will heighten sensitivity to this important concept. Effective merchandisers must be inquisitive, highly perceptive, and motivated to reach for a higher standard of design excellence.

■ Line Development and Computer Technology

Decreasing line development cycle times and increasing consumer demands result in the need for quick response from the design team. Such a response can be achieved only through the use of sophisticated computer technology.

Computers are becoming the critical nucleus of tomorrow's line development process.

The computer revolution was slow to catch hold in the apparel industry, but it picked up momentum by the end of the twentieth century. Computer applications for apparel manufacturing first gained acceptance with computer-aided design (CAD) systems for pattern grading and marker making in the early 1980s. The real impact on line and product development came during the 1990s with the evolution of:

- Sophisticated color illustration systems.
- CAD systems that realistically drape computer generated fabrics on three-dimensional garment bodies.
- Advanced pattern design systems (PDS).
- Product information management systems (PIMs) using relational databases.
- Videoconferencing.
- Interactive, on-line fashion information services.
- Web-based data management systems.

Advanced computer systems have changed the design paradigm for many forward-thinking manufacturers. Stylists and designers have found a powerful tool in computer technology that allows them to create, organize, and communicate design ideas more quickly and accurately than was previously possible. Researching styling trends on-line, creating accurate color illustrations, developing garment and textile designs, draping computer-generated fabrics onto CAD sketches and photographs, designing and grading precise patterns, developing detailed garment specifications, and instantly communicating on an international basis have dramatically increased designer productivity.

These computer applications have allowed companies to:

- Shrink the line development cycle time.
- Expand designer creativity.
- Improve effective design communications.
- Enhance process controls.
- Smooth integration of product development and manufacturing and sourcing.
- Reduce line development costs.
- Increase responsiveness in a global environment.

The increased demand for computer-aided design solutions for the textile and apparel industries has even created specialized CAD service consultants such as FabriCAD at **www.fabricad.com**. These consultants provide customized system design, CAD newsletters for the fashion industry, specialized conferences, and Web sites featuring the latest CAD innovations and news briefs.

Interactive Online Fashion Information Services

The Internet and the World Wide Web have created a perfect vehicle for bringing the latest global fashion news and styling advice directly into the design studio. By using specialized software, merchandisers, stylists, and designers can create personalized Internet search capabilities that provide up-to-the-minute news updates from their favorite World Wide Web fashion news resources. Subscriber services such as Worth Global Style Network at **www.worthstyle.com** have emerged, offering a growing index of research tools.

Men's, Women's, Youth, and Children's Trend Reports

Professional colorists, stylists, and designers track the trends emerging from developments at leading fiber and textile producers, analyze designer collections, and interpret changing retail buying habits and consumer attitudes. These design professionals provide color trends for each product category, new fabric developments, graphics and print directions, and silhouette predictions.

Daily Fashion News Updates

Daily highlights of industry news from the fashion capitals of the world are created by staffs of leading trade journalists. Interviews with key fashion executives are featured. Many sources provide calendars of international fashion shows and trade events complete with contact information. Archives of featured articles referenced by subject and date are available for easy access to important research data.

Many of the top fashion trade publications such as *Women's Wear Daily* at **www.wwd.com** offer direct access to their extensive archives through subscription services.

Store Reports

Monthly and seasonal reports of what is selling at retail are summarized for international fashion capitals and key U.S. cities. Photo reporting and brand focus by category and market level are featured. This information is ideal for enabling users to spot changing consumer preferences and forecast the effect of such changes on future lines.

Fashion and Trade Events

Up-to-the-minute calendars and reports on international fashion shows and trade events save valuable time in planning and scheduling. These services frequently provide in-depth reports with photographs and videos of the shows. Staff journalists attend many of the events and interview trend-setting designers or prepare comprehensive analyses of seasonal color, fabric, and silhouette directions.

Organizations that specialize in coordinating international fashion events like the Igedo Company at **www.igedo.com** maintain Web sites that provide updates on exhibitions and markets, shows, important dates, projects, news, and the people to contact.

Resource Libraries

Resource library services providing color, silhouette, and print libraries are maintained by stylists, textile designers, and graphic designers. These resources can be accessed through sophisticated database searches by market category or season or by a descriptive phrase.

More and more museums, educational institutions, and service bureaus are digitizing works of art and graphics, thus making them available through their Web sites. The amount of inspirational material available on the Web for styling and design is growing exponentially.

Resource Listings

Comprehensive listings of fashion resources, Web sites, manufacturers, suppliers, service providers, and technical specialists are available from a growing number of on-line fashion information services such as Worth Global Style Network.

Integrated Graphics Systems

Computer technology plays a large role in the creative aspect of line development. Powerful PC graphics tools allow designers to develop more styles in less time. These integrated systems enable designers to:

- Create rough styling sketches or finished color-correct fashion illustrations using electronic tools that simulate pencil, chalk, charcoal, pen, felt-tip pen, crayon, airbrush, oils, or water colors.
- Create technical or mechanical garment drawings.
- Develop accurate color storyboards using sophisticated spectrophotometry and industry standard color matching systems.
- Use powerful graphic design tools to create logos, labels, embroidery, appliqués, and detailed product specification drawings.
- Create woven, knit, and print textile designs.
- Drape the textile designs or scanned fabrics onto illustrations or photographs for realistic line reviews. Some more sophisticated systems can map fabric patterns and textures onto a digital body that can be viewed in three dimensions.
- Print textile designs onto fabric using specialized ink-jet printing systems for instant prototyping.
- Create digital 24-bit true color separations.

Examples of these popular graphic design systems are Vision Fashion Studio by Gerber Technology at **www.gerbertechnology.com**, Vision Studio by

Nedgraphics at **www.nedgraphics.com**, and Computer Design Inc. U4ia and PrimaVision TCX by Lectra at **www.lectra.com**. Sample fabrics can be printed in the design studio using specially treated fabrics from DigiFab at **www.digifab.net** and 12-color DisplayMaker digital ink-jet printers from Mimaki at **www.mimakiusa.com** and ColorSpan at **www.colorspan.com**. These graphic tools and print capabilities allow designers and merchandisers to experiment with new styling concepts by creating prototypes in hours rather than days (see Figure 5.9). The result is:

- Enhanced creativity.
- Quick response.
- Increased productivity.
- Improved design communications.

Pattern Design Systems

Pattern design systems (PDS) have evolved since the mid-1980s into sophisticated expert systems that automate many complex pattern-making functions. There are systems that allow designers to work on full-scale patterns on computer drafting tables or in miniature by creating patterns on a computer monitor using a mouse, stylus, or trackball. The advantages of computer-aided pattern design systems are:

- Accuracy.
- Speed.
- Flexibility.
- Ability to optimize the use of fabric.

Patterns can be created within one tenth of a millimeter of accuracy. Once **grade rules** (the formula for creating patterns of every size from the initial sample size patterns) have been established, patterns can be graded in all sizes in seconds with the same accuracy. Repetitive tasks such as deriving facings and linings for existing fronts, armholes, or neck openings can be automated and performed quickly, easily, and accurately. Notches, pins, darts, folds, and pleats can also be added to patterns with a simple click on system icons. Seam lines can be added to patterns or adjustments dictated by fit sessions can be made with only a few mouse clicks or keystrokes.

Technology has been developed that generates 2-D patterns from 3-D images and 3-D images from 2-D patterns. There is ongoing research to develop technology that will allow a designer to create a three-dimensional garment image on a sample size body form that can be rotated and viewed from all perspectives. This garment image would then be translated into two-dimensional patterns through the use of expert computer system technology. A sample cutter can cut out the garment parts from fabric printed on a digital ink-jet printer for construction of a prototype. This process will allow designers to create a prototype of a garment in less than 1 hour.

Examples of pattern design systems for apparel are Accumark by Gerber Technology at **www.gerbertechnology.com**, Modaris by Lectra at **www.lectra.com**, Investronica at **www.investronica-sis.es**, Scanvec Garment Systems at **www.optitex.com**, and TUKATECH at **www.tukatech.com** (see Figure 5.10).

Product Information Management Systems

Critical functions for merchandisers are the control of the line development process and the communication of accurate product data to their manufacturing or sourcing partners. These functions are time-consuming and generate an enormous amount of paperwork. Product information management (PIM) systems utilize relational databases, technical drawing software, and Internet interfaces to allow merchandisers to perform these functions electronically. Style information must be accurate, up to date, and instantly available in order to streamline the product development process.

The sophisticated software packages available to apparel companies are comprehensive and flexible systems that can customize forms to the individual user's needs. Product information management systems provide:

- Product development calendars, which detail workflow functions and personnel responsibilities as well as provide E-mail notification of function progress.
- Creation of **technical drawings**, which are flat line drawings of a garment showing design details such as stitch locations and critical measurements, as well as special manufacturing instructions.
- Colorways.
- Style or model description sheets.
- Bills of materials.
- Packaging details.
- Costing data.
- Detailed garment specification sheets.
- Tables of measurements.
- Quality control information.
- Vendor quote sheets.
- Centralized file management to provide authorized users with all the data related to a style updated in real time.
- Internet integration to transmit forms and data worldwide.

Examples of available systems are Freeborders PLM Suite by Freeborders at **www.freeborders.com**, Product Data Management (PDM) and WebPDM

5.0 by Gerber Technology at **www.gerbertechnology.com**, Justwin WebConnect at **www.justwin.com**, and GalleryWeb by Lectra at **www.lectra.com** (see Figure 5.11).

A by-product of automating the line development process is a reduction in the number of errors. Sears was one of the early adopters of PIM applications. It reduced errors by as much as 30 percent and increased productivity by as much as 50 percent (Hill, 1999).

With the proliferation of global sourcing, accuracy of information and speedy communications are paramount. The newest generation of product information management systems supports Web-based communications. The systems provide information access from virtually anywhere in the world over the Internet. Encryption technology and partner licenses ensure secure Internet or direct-dial communications of confidential styling and costing information. These systems provide total integrated control over the line development process from image management and cataloging through control of the specification processes and maintenance of a complete revision history for each style.

When selecting a product information management system, it is important to evaluate how well the system can incorporate the many manual and computer processes that the company is currently using. Unless all elements of the line development function are integrated into the system, the cycle time cannot be optimized.

VF Playwear understood the importance of total integration when it developed its product information management system. Merchandisers should carefully coordinate any effort to automate the product information process to ensure smooth system integration with every element of line development from concept through communications with manufacturing or sourcing.

Videoconferencing

Many medium- and larger-sized companies have multiple locations. Marketing and sales, merchandising and design, and manufacturing may each be in different cities or even different countries. Merchandising is often required to communicate visual information to marketing and sales for product and line reviews and to manufacturing for construction or specification changes and quality analyses. In order to discuss visual-based problems, many merchandisers get on a plane with sample garments and travel to remote locations. Another option is to ship samples between locations, transmit drawings by fax, and then discuss the details on the telephone. These solutions often result in delays, confusion, or critical manufacturing errors.

Videoconferencing provides a fast, efficient solution to audiovisual communications. Whether it is over the Internet or through direct communications over high-speed digital phone lines, new videoconferencing systems can provide high-quality video. Companies such as Levi Strauss, the GAP, JCPenney, Wal-Mart, and VF Corporation have been using videoconferencing effectively since the mid-1990s to communicate with their global satellite offices and trading partners.

In conjunction with product information management systems, videoconferencing allows apparel companies to review new styles and discuss worldwide manufacturing problems face to face. Some of the more sophisticated systems have cameras that automatically track the speaker's voice, as well as pan, zoom, tilt, and autofocus. Many companies have videoconferencing setups in their conference rooms, which are equipped with large screen monitors and second close-up cameras mounted above the center of the conference table to capture garment and fabric sample details.

"1999 TAC REPORT—Case Study #6, Oshkosh B'Gosh"

This case study demonstrates how children's apparel manufacturer Oshkosh B'Gosh has used computer-aided design (CAD), computer-aided engineering (CAE), and manufacturing resource planning (MRP) to communicate its product specifications to suppliers and factories all over the world.

It is increasingly common, yet no less challenging, for an apparel manufacturer to design a product in the United States, develop and purchase the fabric in the Far East, assemble the garment in Central America, finish the garment back in the United States, and finally ship the product to a customer in Europe. Indeed, synchronizing the activities in a company's supply chain to accomplish the above scenario requires considerable cooperation, coordination, and the right set of tools.

Those are exactly the pieces of the puzzle that have been put in place by Oshkosh B'Gosh. Founded in 1895, the company has its own manufacturing sites in the United States and Honduras. It also uses contractors in the United States and Honduras, as well as in Mexico, Guatemala, El Salvador, and several Far East countries. The company operates more than 100 retail stores in the Unites States and Europe, and has many key wholesale customers including JCPenney, Sears, and Kids 'R' Us. All critical processes such as product development, purchasing, planning, and contractor management are centralized in the Oshkosh, WI, offices.

Like other apparel manufacturers in today's era of intensified global competition, Oshkosh B'Gosh has encountered the constant pressure of declining margins and higher customer expectations. The need to supply new, fresh, and affordable products multiple times throughout the year puts extreme pressure on a company's product development processes. In addition, competition comes not only from imported goods that are produced under dramatically different labor and capital structures, it can even come from a company's own customers, with their private label goods.

During the past decade, Oshkosh B'Gosh has used technology and teamwork to compete in today's changed business environment. As competitive pressures increase and as worldwide suppliers offer higher-quality and lower-cost products, the imperative to source internationally is greatly heightened. The company recognized that in order to compete successfully in such a global environment, an apparel manufacturer must have some of the following practices in place:

- Managerial support, especially from senior managers.
- Good communication skills.
- Cross-cultural awareness.
- Long-term relationships with important suppliers.
- Global sourcing skills.
- Knowledge of foreign business practices.
- Supplier certification/qualification programs.

(continued)

- Use of third-party logistics services.
- Adequate information technology and business systems.
- E-mail and Internet.

For Oshkosh B'Gosh, it starts in the product development area. The company does its line planning using information from marketing, sales, customers, and other resources. It has developed a PC-based, time-phased, line planning calendar to coordinate and guide all of the functional areas from color, fabric, and style development to sample production and final delivery of product to its customers. In the past, each functional area kept its own calendar, and many times core events were not completed on time, which led to poor downstream execution and, ultimately, poor on-time delivery.

In addition to the coordinated planning calendar, Oshkosh B'Gosh has implemented a number of other technologies for line planning and product development in recent years, all of which have greatly facilitated the development of color, fabrics, and garments. Among them are color control technology, computer aided design (CAD), computer aided engineering (CAE), and manufacturing resource planning (MRP).

Establishing a seasonal color story is one of the starting points for product development. Making sure the red top from Kentucky, the red jeans from Honduras, and the red sweater from Hong Kong match is very important to customers. In the past, because OBG used domestic fabric suppliers exclusively, getting consistent color across multiple fabrics from multiple suppliers was challenging but not impossible. With the addition of global fabric sourcing, however, color consistency was becoming impossible to manage. As a result, the company established a color matching process using color control software. This color control tech-

nology coordinates the process worldwide, solving color problems, and measuring the timeliness and effectiveness of suppliers.

CAD systems have also played a very important role in product development. With these graphic arts tools, Oshkosh B'Gosh has the ability to central design its fabrics, trims, screen prints, embroideries, and garments, which has made the product development process extremely efficient. Being able to electronically communicate this information among suppliers, factories, and contractors has had significant impact on avoiding problems, reducing product development lead times, and reducing costs.

CAE tools have also been instrumental, from product development to producing samples through bulk production. Product data management, pattern design, and marking software provide for engineered specifications, product/pattern measurements, drawings, assembly specifications, parts lists/bills of material, and cutting information. All of these tools can be shared with suppliers, contractors, and Oshkosh B'Gosh's own factories through internal systems, e-mail, and the Internet. CAE also allows corporate engineering, plant engineering, remote processing sites, shop floor supervisors, and suppliers to act as engineering partners. Plus, it enables the product development process to move away from sequential department input, which consumes much time and creates numerous changes.

Ideally, all of this preparation leads to the successful manufacturing of the finished product. To manage production, Oshkosh B'Gosh uses an MRP system. Based on a master production schedule, raw materials are purchased and scheduled for delivery; work orders or purchase orders are released to factories and contractors; and garments are pro-

(continued)

duced and delivered to a distribution center on time for delivery to their customers.

As a result of all these new technologies, Oshkosh B'Gosh has realized many benefits, including:

- Reduced product development cycle time.
- Improved quality of samples to show customers.
- Reduced costs in sample production due to rework.
- Reduction in errors on screen print and embroidery development.
- Improved color matching.
- Improved communication between functional areas, suppliers, contractors, and factories.

- Improved inventory turns (and less obsolete inventory).
- Improved fabric utilization.
- Improved on-time delivery.
- Improved quality.

Developing new products and producing them any place in the world requires the right tools, the right skill sets in people, establishing partnerships with your suppliers, as well as sound and flexible processes. For Oshkosh B'Gosh, technology has played a major role in meeting those requirements. ■

From American Apparel Manufacturers Association, 1999.

Case in Point 5.1   ## Summary

Formulating a successful line development process requires progressive management strategies based upon sound design and business principles. Oshkosh B'Gosh was faced with the classic apparel merchandising dilemma of supplying frequent offerings of fresh, new, cost-effective products while coordinating manufacturing in the United States, Mexico, Central America, and the Far East. Its management strategy involved utilizing new technologies and teamwork to synchronize the company's product development process. It incorporated:

- Computer integration of data from marketing, sales, research, and its customer base.
- A PC-based, time-phased, fully integrated line planning calendar to coordinate the merchandising process of development, execution, and delivery of its product line.
- Sophisticated color control technology to ensure consistent, color-matched fabrics from multiple suppliers on a timely basis.

- CAD systems with graphic arts tools to centralize the design of fabrics, trims, screen prints, embroideries, and garments.
- Computer-aided engineering (CAE) tools to provide MIS controls over the total line development process.
- PC communications with suppliers, contractors, and its own factories through internal systems, E-mail, and the Internet.
- A PC-based manufacturing resource planning (MRP) system to control production planning, raw materials purchasing, and production control through to timely product delivery to its customers.

Oshkosh B'Gosh has embraced new technologies to reduce its product development cycle time and improve the quality of its products while reducing costs. It is this integration of people and technology into the critical marketing, merchandising, and manufacturing decision-making processes that provides companies with a competitive edge in the changing apparel marketplace. ■

Mario Lerias Experience—vice president of design and quality, Lord West

Team Approach

"At Lord West we have a little different method of design development than at other companies I have worked at. Here at Lord West we do it as a team. We get the merchandising team and representatives from our sales office and we thrash ideas around as to what we feel the market needs. That's our concept meeting. I take notes from that meeting and blend in some of my own ideas. I try to add new fashion direction or a twist into some of the ideas from the concept meeting. The next step is to produce prototypes for our team to review in the first phase of the adoption process.

"My work in creating our product line is based upon a line plan of the number of silhouettes and fabrics established by our development team. In my position I have to be very close to the sales arm of the business and merchandising because they know the customers better than I do and no matter what I think is right, the customer is always right.

"Our timetable is also put together by a team of the senior executives of the company. Our president establishes an itinerary that he thinks we should hit. Then we adjust our dates if there is any conflict so that everybody is on the same page. Timing is very critical in men's wear. I put together our fall line from June to late August. This line starts selling in January of the following year, so everything must be ready.

"The final line adoption is also handled by our team. The group will discuss each style. We each present our case and like with anything else, there's a referee. Our CEO makes the final decision."

CAD

"When they give me an idea of what styling they are looking for, I get to my table and start creating. I add my own flare to it, and when we have the prototype finished, they'll either think it's too far to the right or too far to the left and I'll manipulate it a bit. CAD has really made that process a lot easier. We use Gerber's Accumark pattern design system. I can work from a regular picture, a sketch, or take an existing model from our warehouse, look at it, and create the patterns in a fraction of the time it used to take doing it manually. If it's a change to an existing model, I bring the original up on CAD, manipulate the patterns, and in minutes I have the new style.

"Today designers would be lost without computers. Patterns are more accurate. Grading is done automatically. A designer can even

(continued)

map a computer image of a new fabric onto an image of a suit silhouette and see what the finished product will look like. Computers are a real time saver and help stretch the creativity of a designer."

Design and Merchandising Skills

"In today's market the most important skill for a designer and merchandiser is being able to deal with people. If you can deal with people on a professional level, you can get twice as much accomplished.

"In line development it's important to be able to envision what you want your product to look like. Whether it's a concept in a sketch or a drawing, or a picture, or only an image in your mind, a good designer must be able to envision what the final garment will look like.

"An understanding of cost is also very important. While the line is being put together, it is my job to be cognizant of what the cost is going to be to achieve this new model. Every company has price constraints. I can't afford to spend a lot of time developing a new product and have it pulled out of the line because it's too expensive.

"A knowledge of textiles is another important area for designers and merchandisers. Today there are so many new fabrics and fibers. Thankfully there are not that many fabrics for tuxedos. But our fabrics have to withstand at least 50 dry cleanings because of our rental business. We send our fabrics out to a lab to verify that the tests performed by our suppliers meet our high standards."

Interface with Sales and Manufacturing

"There are certain things that we can do and certain things that we can't do feasibly in manufacturing. It's my job to tell the product development team, 'You guys have great ideas, but we're never going to be able to achieve this in manufacturing.' I've got to be the one to draw the line. If you're making one single tuxedo for one single customer—you can do anything you want. But when you have to be able to set it up for mass production at ten or fifteen thousand units, you're limited by the capabilities of the factories.

"The most challenging part of my job is trying to walk the fine line between sales and manufacturing. I'm really in the middle because I understand both sides of the business a little better than most people. Those in the manufacturing end of the business are focused on how many units they can produce in a given period of time. I must also understand the sales side of it when they walk into a store and they're bombarded about what the store's needs are and we are not delivering. The most challenging part of my job is to be between sales and manufacturing and say, 'Yes, we can ship them this, but we can't do that,' and try to work out a compromise that works for the overall good of our company."

William Calvert Experience—CEO/ designer, William Calvert

Fashion Niche

"I started designing into a fashion niche the Americans call 'couture price-points,' which is slightly more expensive than designer. You can always work down, but you can't always work back up the market. If I'm going to strut my fashion design talent, the easiest way to do that is in evening wear; it's the best place to show off ability. I had haute couture training in Paris. I worked there for three years, and I wanted to bring some of that training back with me in a slightly easier to market product.

"We retail between one and five thousand dollars. We also do a lot of custom work where really the sky's the limit. I have one customer who's always pushing me. 'Go for it. Be wacky. I want people to remember this.' This type of customer gives me the incentive to push the envelope. After all, it's the product that makes us successful. You can spend big money on a fashion show, but if there're no outstanding pieces there, forget it."

Team Effort

"I have an incredible circle of people around me who are experts in their fields. Lina, my assistant, does all of what in America we call the first patterns. She's my hands. I'm the eyeballs and the mouth, maybe. Lina worked for Halston, for Pauline Trigere, for Oscar, for John Anthony. She knows her stuff. She has a sense of line that's often younger than mine. It's not just, 'Oh, it curves from center front to center back and dips over the hip.' There's a grace to that line when she does it. When someone else does it you say, 'Yeah, that's the line I drew.' With her you look and go, 'That's the line I meant. That's the line I felt.' That's the difference that allows us to compete in the 'couture price points.'

"We're two halves of the whole. I trust her implicitly. I give her some ideas and some inspiration. I have to give her a lot of credit. I couldn't do it without her and she couldn't do it without me. It's a team effort. But the final decision has to be mine."

Inspiration Is a Real Challenge

"Inspiration is a real challenge for me because I am really adamant about doing nonderivative clothes. Do you look at all the magazines so you really know what's going on? Do you go to all the stores to really know what's going on? That's a real dilemma because if you do, you're influenced by all those other designers. The other option is to not open a fashion magazine and just wander around the world and try and put your finger on the pulse of fashion

(*continued*)

direction so to speak. I really try for that. I am aware of trends, but I use them just to double-check myself.

"I listen to and look at the environment around me, but in the end I do my own thing. This is what I'm about. It's much more about ergonomic lines and origami and hard with soft or that dichotomy of male to female.

"My first season it was shiny with matte. Then we evolved into hard with soft. And then it became sleek with fuzzy. Not every garment has two textures in it but maybe the cut is very hard and the fabric is very drippy. This approach can lead to real construction problems. To get those sharp clean lines in silk jersey or matte jersey, good luck.

"For me, finding inspiration is easy. I don't wait for it to find me. I just have to keep my eyes and my mind open. Inspiration is all around me, whether I'm in Manhattan or in the country."

Planning and Control

"Because we're small, we work a season at a time. In the beginning it was easy. I designed, then I produced, then I designed, and then I produced. But now as the lines have grown and become more sophisticated, I'm not able to do that. There's overlap. I've got to start the next season before the last one is complete. I'm checking on the sample sewers, checking on fabrics, running down to the factory. It's a little nutty. We're experiencing those growing pains where it's just about the time to have people take care of the planning and control. I guess I may need a merchandising type to keep track of everything.

"As far as starting a line, I'm slowly getting into the groove. This is the first or second time that I've put ideas on a styling board to keep track of myself. I usually did sketches and handed them to Lina. Now I'm starting to organize them because I don't have time otherwise.

"Initially I had written a business plan and a friend lent me her sample room for six weeks to put a line together. We put together six dresses, not a huge collection, four gray, two black. We called Bergdorf's and Barney's. They showed up, they both ordered, and I was in business. The next season it was 12 dresses and the next season it was 20, and I started to mix in sportswear. I don't mean less expensive separates, I mean separate pieces. Now we shoot for 25 outfits. I have to pay much more attention to planning, because of our private client work, especially wedding dresses.

"I even have to develop a line plan for each collection. Right now we do two collections per year, fall/winter and spring/summer. Before I start designing, I work out what I need. I need a short skirt, I need a wide skirt, I need a long skirt, I need a wide pant, I need a skinny pant, I need a rock 'n' roll pant, I need a

(continued)

Figure 5.1 A concept board is created to establish the theme or styling direction for a new collection. This women's product category is lingerie and the luxurious palette has been communicated by the lace, pearls, and pictures of ornate furnishings.

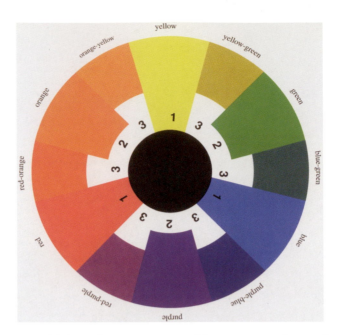

Figure 5.2 A color wheel for subtractive (or pigment) hues presents primary colors indicated by the numeral 1; secondary colors, which are combinations of equal parts of primary colors, are indicated by the numeral 2; and tertiary colors, which are combinations of a primary and a secondary color, are indicated by the numeral 3.

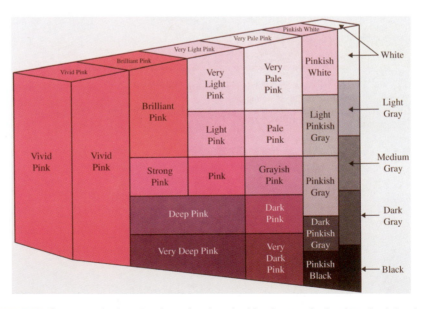

Figure 5.3 The many shades of pink can be described by the standardized method developed by the Inter-Society Color Council of the National Bureau of Standards.

Figure 5.4 Gianfranco Ferre's design illustrates proportion by combinig a wide flowing coat with much narrower pants.

Figure 5.5 Two examples of balance are represented by (a) Yves Saint Laurent's symmetrical balance in his jacket design and the asymmetrical balance of (b) Giorgio Armani's jacket..

Figure 5.6 Repetitive rows of feathers on this Christian Dior jacket is an excellent example of the principle of rhythm.

Figure 5.7 The accentuated shoulders and the bow at the neck in Karl Lagerfeld's design is a perfect example of the principle of emphasis.

Figure 5.8 Emanuel Ungaro brings together in harmony the asymmetrical hemline of the top, emphasis created by the military influence of epaulets, the proportion of the long coat with the shawl collar, and contrasting bound seams that match the color of the blouse.

Figure 5.9 A designer uses Artworks, Gerber Technology's comuter-aided design (CAD) program. This software enables designers to create and edit sketches, design fabrics, and drape fabrics onto sketches or photographs.

Figure 5.10 Pattern design software supports the function of the pattern maker. Shown is the computer screen of Gerber Technology's Pattern Design 2000, which allows for the design and edit of the pattern for multiple styles simultaneously in separate work areas.

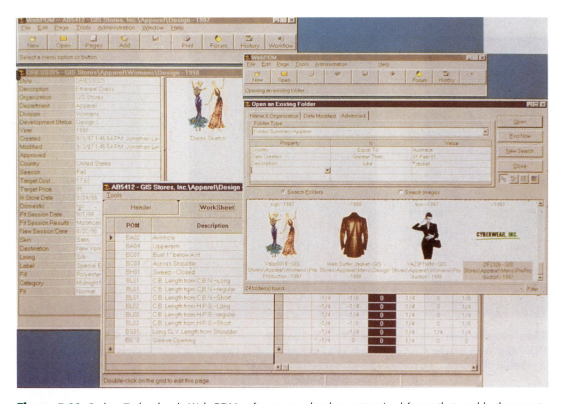

Figure 5.11 Gerber Technology's Web PDM software can develop customized forms that enable the user to organize construction, cost, and measurement information in a central database. This software streamlines the entire product development process.

pant that can go to the office. It's not a sophisticated line plan, but it steers me in the right direction."

Fabric and Color

"I initially picked one to four fabrics, and did the whole collection based upon them. I design into fabrics. Once I choose my fabrics, I group my concepts around colors. The first collection was black and gray. The second collection was black, gray, navy, and stone.

"One day I came into the studio and said, 'This place looks so drab. Enough!' I went out and bought all these wacky colored fabrics, and my interns were like, 'Okay, sure, how are you going to make that look cool. It's turquoise and it looks like some scary prom dress with bows all over it.' We really worked on that by combining the turquoise with a shape that was really hard and had an edging of navy. So for the last couple of seasons I've been really fascinated by color. We are now into turquoise, orange, red, coral, and electric blue. For spring it's almost going to be monochromatic. There will be pink, orange, and red and levels of that. When I say levels I mean you have heavily saturated silk that looks like the skin of an orange or you have fabrics that have yarns of that color in them but they're also mixed back with a white, so that mutes them.

"So that's where we were in the planning process. I sort of laid out all the colors. Each sheet had a different color, black, tan, gray, white, cream, orange, reds, blue, pink. Black looks old. Gray looks old. And then it came down to just the white and the creams and the pink, orange, and reds. We lumped them all together and said, 'Okay, this is your hard, this is your soft, this is your liquid, this is your shiny, this is your dull.' Then I started ordering fabrics and crossed my fingers. I do that a lot. I order based upon instinct. I guess that's what makes couture special.

"I go to the fabric shows in Paris twice a year. I start gathering up swatches, and we cut the swatches and stick them on card stock with Velcro dots, and they get organized by what category they're going to be in. Sometimes we do it by gown, dress, coat, top, bottom, or sometimes we do it strictly by color."

Everything Gets Draped

"Then everything gets draped in real fabric. You can't use muslin for a jersey or a charmeuse because they're too liquid. And you can't use muslin for double-faced satin because it acts like leather, and you're yanking on it and it doesn't respond. We don't use seam allowance. Usually there's two inches around every seam. All sew lines get transferred onto the backside of the fabric using tailor's chalk in white and all that tailor's chalk gets thread traced in white thread. All the notches, every line. Then it gets put together by

(*continued*)

hand with white cotton thread because it breaks easily. The garment gets fitted, and all the corrections get pinned on one side. They get retraced in another color. The whole fit garment gets opened up. Those corrections go onto the pattern. The garment gets put back together by hand, and you do another fitting. That may happen once. It may happen seven times.

"Some people say that's a waste of time and expense. I say, 'See how graceful that dress is. That's why it looks like that.' If that dress was stitched up from the first patterns it would never look like that. That's why I appreciate this way of working. There's the short long way or the long short way and anyone who will tell you otherwise doesn't know what they're talking about."

Cost

"I try and shoot for a range of price points. I set limits for fabric unless it's something I can pitch as very special. I try not to go above $80 per yard. Cost is always in the back of my mind. I can't make a ball gown out of $250 per yard fabric, but I could make a little tiny dress out of that fabric and stay within my price range. I have to balance the fabric usage and the labor.

Visual Elements of Design

"To create aesthetically pleasing garments, it's so important to understand the basic visual elements of design; color and light, line and shape. They must become second nature to you as you work. If you're creating a gown in silk chiffon, you want it to flow effortlessly, sensuously around the body. No tension, no pull lines, no drag lines, just grace. You can't be in this business without a great sense of line and shape."

Design Advice

"I learned in Italy draw, draw, draw, draw. After thousands of sketches, eventually your pen becomes an extension of your vision. Then you can focus on creating the ideal form in your mind's eye, and it will flow onto the paper. If you can't draw then drape, drape, drape. I don't care what you have to do, but you must practice interpreting your ideas and visions into wearable garments. Make mistakes, fumble. One mistake leads to seven masterpieces. You must learn to communicate your ideas into reality because that's what it's all about. It's all about presenting your thoughts in a way that can simultaneously shock and inspire people.

"I would recommend that fashion design students should go after jobs that are related to the market niche that they ultimately want to specialize in. If they want to work for Donna Karan but can't get a job there, they should work for a company that has a similar ideology to hers. The aesthetic doesn't necessar-

(continued)

ily have to be the same, but where they produce, how they produce, what fabrics they use, what price points they're in, you want to be as close to that as possible.

"I try and keep the design process as artistic as possible. Yes the garment has to fit, and yes it has to be graceful and flattering and wear-able. But the bottom line is the feeling someone has when they try on your garment. That comes from what's in your gut. *My job as a designer is to walk around like a big sponge absorbing those feelings and find some graceful way to exhale all of that. That's what design is all about.*"

Summary

The change from a production-centric society to a consumer-centric society has had a profound effect on the U.S. apparel industry. Consumers want more styles more frequently. This has forced apparel companies to focus on reducing the line development cycle time and improving the effectiveness of the line development process. Apparel merchandisers play the pivotal role in planning and controlling line development activities and making critical styling decisions. They must have an intimate knowledge of their target market, a thorough understanding of the elements and principles of design, and a solid foundation in business management strategies.

Styling creates the concepts, themes, and fashion direction for an apparel line or collection under the direction of the apparel merchandiser. Design then interprets the concepts into actual garment styles. Stylists may be more focused on creativity, while designers require technical expertise in pattern design and garment construction. In many companies the designer is responsible for both the styling and design of the line. The merchandiser is faced with maintaining control of the line development process to meet company line plan objectives and timetables while still providing an environment conducive to maximizing creativity.

Successful apparel companies develop and implement strategies that utilize new technologies and teamwork to synchronize their product development processes. These strategies focus on advanced communications and computer integration of data and process controls with their suppliers, contractors, and their own factories. Many companies utilize interactive on-line fashion information services, integrated graphics systems for development of fabric and garment styles, pattern design systems, product information management systems, and videoconferencing to improve their line development functions.

Key Terms

additive primary colors	line development
balance	metameric
collection	placement
color story	proportion
colorway	repetition
concept boards	rhythm
conceptualization	scale
contrast	shades
creation	shape
creativity	silhouette
designers	storyboards
emphasis	style
findings	style number
Gestalt psychology	stylists
grade rules	subtractive primary colors
harmony	technical drawings
hue	texture
inspiration boards	tints
intensity	tones
isolation	trend boards
licensee	understanding
licensing	value
licensor	videoconferencing
line	

Discussion Questions and Learning Activities

1. Discuss which societal changes and industry practices have resulted in consumer demand for more frequent offerings of fresh new styles.
2. What factors should merchandisers consider when developing planning and control strategies for the line development process?
3. Discuss the management practices and philosophies that would create the proper environment for a successful line development team.
4. Considering the current direction of the apparel industry, what educational background and work experience would best prepare someone for a successful career as an apparel merchandiser?
5. Discuss the differences in skills and education required for a stylist and a designer. What similar skills and education should they both share?
6. Visit a department store or apparel retailer and select a garment in a unique color. Describe the color using subtractive primary colors and the Inter-Society Color Council of the National Bureau of Standards' descriptive color identifiers.

7. Discuss the factors that would support an argument to minimize the number of colors in a colorway. What effect does the number of colors in a colorway have on SKUs?
8. Select three garments within the same product category from an apparel specialty store. Analyze each garment and discuss how design elements were used to make a design statement.
9. Using fashion magazines as your resource, select photographs of garments that exemplify the effective use of each of the design principles.
10. Research fashion trends on the World Wide Web and locate two different Web sites that highlight the same trend direction for either color, fabric, or silhouette.
11. Discuss the role videoconferencing can play in improving the line development process.
12. Discuss how children's wear manufacturer Oshkosh B'Gosh in Case in Point 5.1 resolved the difficult task of matching colors from its global fabric suppliers. How can the technology it adopted to resolve this problem be used to speed up other functions within the line development process?
13. Discuss the primary differences in the approaches to product development used by Lord West and William Calvert Designs.

References and Resources

Agins, Teri. September 18, 1990. In Fashion, the Talent and His Money Man Make Promising Team. *The Wall Street Journal*, p. A1.

Boyer, Bruce G. 1990. *Eminently Suitable*. New York: W.W. Norton & Company, Inc., p. 134.

Burns, Leslie Davis; Bryant, Nancy O. 1997. *The Business of Fashion*. New York: Fairchild Publications.

D'Innocenzio, Anne. May 21, 1999. Liz Claiborne Shifting Merchandising Focus. *Women's Wear Daily*, p. 2,14.

Feitelberg, Rosemary. June 1998. Designers Told: Vary The Vision. *Women's Wear Daily*, p. 10.

Feitelberg, Rosemary. August 17, 1998. Trends Boards Make Everything Click. *Women's Wear Daily*, p. 16.

Hill, Suzette. February 1999. Product Development: The Next QR Initiative? *Apparel Industry Magazine*, p. 71.

Rabon, Lisa C. September 1998. Industry Looking to Squeeze Fat from the Supply Chain, *Bobbin*, p. 10.

Tate, Sharon Lee. 1999. *Inside Fashion Design*. New York: Addison Wesley Longman, Inc.

Welling, Holly. September 1999. Color Blind? Rethink Your Color Processes!, *Apparel Industry Magazine*, pp. 136–140.

Line Development: The Process

- Analyze the line development process and the role of the merchandiser in that process.

- Examine the importance of establishing a creative environment for design while maintaining efficient controls over the process.

- Understand the value of market and fashion research.

- Examine the importance of a line plan in an effective line development process.

- Identify the steps involved in line development.

- Discuss the adoption process as it relates to finalizing a product line.

The process of line development consists of many complex interrelated functions that build on one another and that must be carefully monitored and controlled. In medium- to large-size companies, the merchandiser is often responsible for the planning, monitoring, and control of line development. In many smaller companies, the designer or even the chief executive may shoulder the responsibility for this function as well as provide the styling and technical design expertise.

Gary Simmons, president of Gerber Childrenswear emphasizes the importance of line development. "Nothing happens without line development. It is essential to everything we do. Because if the line's not on target, you won't meet your sales objectives."

■ Response Time

Response time is the time it takes from beginning the line development process through to shipment of the styles in that line to retailers. Continued pressure by retailers to increase the number of product offerings and reduce response time has shifted corporate attention to line development. Leading apparel companies and many **vertical retailers** (retailers that develop and manufacture their own private label product lines) have focused on the line development process in their quest to shorten response times. To maintain a competitive edge, merchandisers continually analyze and reevaluate each element of line development in search of ways to streamline the process.

This initiative, which brings the quick response (QR) philosophy to line development, has been effective because of advances in computer-aided design and graphic systems, Internet Web-based research capabilities, PIM systems based on relational databases, and improved communications through E-mail and videoconferencing. Web-based product information systems even allow merchandisers, designers, and manufacturing sourcing facilities to have access to important product information 24-hours every day anywhere around the globe. Applying QR strategies to the line development process has allowed companies to cut 26- to 40-week cycles to as few as 2 weeks.

■ Design Environment

A critical role of merchandising in the line development process is to establish an effective, creative environment. This involves developing design spaces where all creative personnel can interact and share inspirations and ideas outside the bounds of corporate structures, confining offices, and rigid controls. Merchandisers must establish this environment of free expression but still maintain control of the line development process in order to meet

"1999 TAC Report—Case Study #4, VF Corporation"

This study details VF's reengineering of the product development process and how CAD, product data management, and business process software are used to support the new processes. This reengineering has enabled VF to develop a process that can be used across all brands and divisions, worldwide, to deliver the products that the market wants, when they are required.

As recently as 1995, apparel giant VF Corp. was using a business strategy that allowed its 17 divisions to operate as independent business units. This independence allowed each division to grow by developing its own way of doing business; but it precluded the sharing of best practices among the divisions—and it also made it very difficult to leverage VF's capabilities and size to gain competitive advantages.

At the same time, the company's markets were becoming more unpredictable, product life cycles were getting shorter, and the supply chain was becoming more complex. So it became imperative for VF to completely rethink its business processes and supporting technology in order to maintain and strengthen its position as a global apparel leader.

The reengineering effort that would change its modus operandi began in 1995, when a team of VF employees was formed to analyze both the company's internal operations as well as the operations of companies outside the apparel business. Over 700 U.S. and European employees were interviewed to document "the good, the bad, and the ugly" they faced in their everyday working environment. Also, more than 30 innovative "best practice" companies were visited to help inspire "out-of-the-box" thinking. For example, VF went to Caterpillar Corp. to determine if any best practices used in the development of new bulldozers and tractors could be used in the development of new apparel products.

Knowing that much can be learned from a past relationship, VF also interviewed 80 of its top suppliers and over 200 senior-level executives at top retailers in the U.S. and abroad.

One of the results of the research and subsequent reengineering was a set of best practices to be embedded in a common product development process that would be deployed across the corporation. This new product and service development process is a simplistic approach founded on the principles of marketing intelligence, clearly defined and detailed plans, process-focused teams, and discipline. The process begins with the building of a well-defined brand business plan, developed from a comprehensive analysis of consumers' needs and identified attributes, and identifying the necessary actions, expected results, and rationale for the plan itself. The foundation for the plan is a brand positioning strategy, one for each in VF's portfolio of brands. Ultimately, each brand's positioning strategy, as well as the action plans, are formally communicated to the entire VF organization.

Product and service concepts are not planned in a detailed manner until the positioning strategy and action plan are developed and communicated to all involved. Then each concept is detailed regarding the goals and targets it should achieve, as well as the why, the how, and the when that will support the brand's positioning and action

(continued)

plans. After the building of the three types of plans, the execution of products and/or services can begin.

A new organizational structure was also necessary to implement and achieve VF's corporate goals. High-performance, process-focused teams were organized to significantly reduce both product and service development cycle times and cost. Two types of teams, one strategic and one product-focused, were formed to enable the process to work both efficiently and effectively. The strategic teams focus on consumer segments, brands, and distribution channels, and "own" the positioning strategy of the brand, the action plan, as well as the strategic elements of building both products and services. The product-focused teams are responsible for building the products and services as defined by the strategic teams. These teams, made up of individuals with all the necessary skills needed to bring the corporate vision to fruition, are empowered by established decision points, or "Stage Gates." For example, product costing cannot begin until the strategic team has provided the target financials for that product.

Both teams are driven by predefined line development calendar dates. However, the new process is more flexible because of its more disciplined approach. In other words, clearly defined plans, along with the established decision points in the process (Stage Gates) and on-time, actionable market intelligence, allow the teams to react to changes with both an understanding of the consequences and an ability to make informed decisions.

After a common process and organizational structure were determined, technology was the third and critical link in the product development reengineering effort. VF's goal was to develop a PDM (product data management) solution that would:

- Permit the integration of all the previously deployed CAD/CAM tools into the new business system to be implemented across the entire VF enterprise.
- Store, control, and manage information about its products.
- Enforce and manage the process of creating these documents.
- Enable VF's product development teams to quickly process and share product information with consistent accuracy.

Today, the new PDM solution is being implemented at VF to enable its new product and service development process. Its anticipated benefits include: reduced engineering costs; shorter product and service development cycles; reduction in time required to process product and service changes; fewer product and service changes; and reduction in the overall time to market.

In the end, many lessons have been learned and many factors are considered by VF to have been critical to the success of the project.

Those key points are:

- The process should be defined first, organization and technology second.
- The majority of the benefits will be driven by process improvement.
- Organization and technology changes may be required to enable the process and leverage the benefits.
- People, not technology, will prove to be the biggest obstacle.
- Top management support is a requirement.
- A project team composed of business and technical associates is vital. ■

From American Apparel Manufacturers Association, 1999.

Case in Point 6.1   ## Summary

Market fluctuations, shorter product life cycles, and the increasing complexity of the supply chain have caused apparel companies to reevaluate their line development processes. VF Corp. analyzed company environments to determine the "best practices" to be used in reengineering its product development process. These best practices were founded on the principles of:

- Market intelligence.
- Clearly defined and detailed plans.
- Process-focused teams.
- Discipline.

The foundation of its plan was an aggressive brand positioning strategy with the goal of reducing product development cycle times.

VF Corp. created strategic and product-focused teams driven by predefined line development calendar dates. The strategic team focus is on consumer segments, brands, and distribution channels, while the product-focused team is responsible for building the products and services as defined by the strategic team.

VF Corp. developed a computer-based product data management (PDM) solution to achieve effective results for its reengineering effort. The company combined the benefits of clearly defined process, organization, and technology to improve its line development process. The results were:

- Reduced engineering cost.
- Shorter product and service development cycles.
- Reduction in time required to process product and service changes.
- Fewer product and service changes.
- Reduction in the overall time to market. ■

deadlines and line plan objectives. In performing this function, the merchandiser must establish a very delicate balance between relieving the creative personnel of the pressures of deadlines and design restrictions and still meeting the needs of the market, the line plan, and the company's strategic plan.

Establishing a creative environment may be especially difficult when it involves integrating the efforts of a design or product development team whose members are in various locations across the country. Some companies have gone to great expense to achieve the synergy that results from the interaction of members of the line development process. Liz Claiborne's consolidation of line development for all divisions at 1441 Broadway in New York in 1999 is a prime example of that commitment to quality merchandising.

To achieve this cross-pollination of ideas and creative thought, smaller companies have a distinct advantage. Designer William Calvert runs his couture price-point women's wear business from his Manhattan offices. He stresses that "Creativity is often a synergy generated by our design team." His showroom, design studio, and sample department are all on the same floor. He can receive input on design ideas from buyers, showroom staff, his assistant, or sample hands without having to leave his suite of offices. This opportunity to receive immediate feedback from all functions of his company and his customers provides an ideal environment for creative stimulation.

■ Elements of Line Development

The size of a company does not affect the basic elements of line development. Every critical function within the process must be accomplished on time in order for a line to be presented to retail buyers and be ready for production. Figure 6.1 shows a flow chart of the critical functions typically involved in line development.

In companies with frequent product offerings, the line development team works simultaneously on two or more lines. One line may be in the styling concept stage, while another may be in the prototyping stage and still another is being considered for final adoption. This requires that the stylists and designers be able to make constant transitions between different themes and concepts. The merchandiser must be able to keep all these developmental functions moving forward and under control. Line development is a complex juggling act that requires very careful planning and constant monitoring and control. If the merchandiser drops one ball (misses one deadline), the whole line development process can collapse, sending shock waves through sales and manufacturing or sourcing. For these reasons, effective apparel merchandisers must incorporate the latest and most efficient planning and control tools in order to meet the changing needs of the industry.

■ Planning and Control

As discussed in Chapter 4, the proper planning and intricate timing of each critical line development function often means the difference between a successful season and a disaster. The merchandising calendar is the vehicle used by merchandisers to maintain control of the complex line development process. Gary Simmons of Gerber Childrenswear stresses the role played by this important planning and control tool. "If your merchandising calendar is not cross-coordinated with all other departments and the timetables are not met, you have serious problems. We focus a lot of effort on line development because if that process is under control, everything else flows on schedule."

Sophisticated computer scheduling applications can monitor functional progress and notify the responsible management personnel of off-schedule activities and the resulting effects on sample completion and line opening dates. The merchandiser must follow up on all off-schedule activities and take whatever action is appropriate to bring the total merchandising calendar back on target.

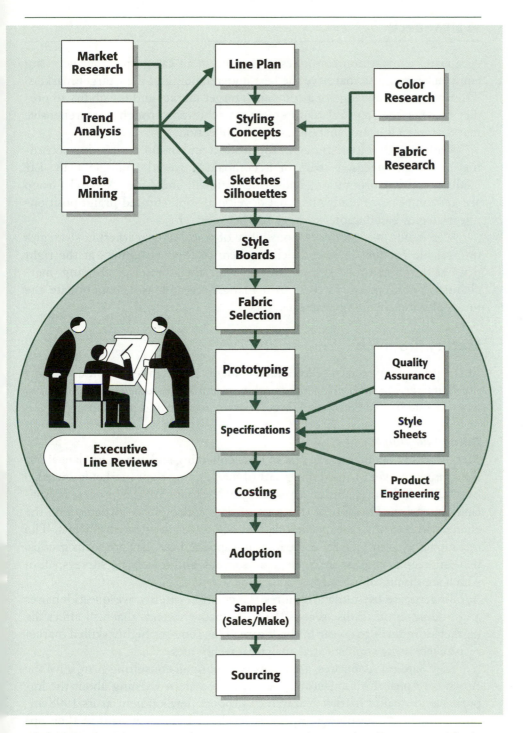

Figure 6.1 This flow chart shows the many critical steps that must be taken to successfully develop an apparel product line.

■ Research

As apparel competition continues to heat up in all categories, the successful companies are those that have the best understanding of their target markets. This intimate knowledge of a company's target market and the ability to predict that market's apparel requirements is achieved through comprehensive market research, trend analysis, and data collection.

Marketing develops strategies for product and brand positioning according to market needs as part of a company's overall strategic plan. Liz Claiborne, VF Corporation, Bally International, and Jones Apparel Group are key examples of companies that developed sophisticated brand positioning strategies based upon extensive market research.

Merchandising has the responsibility of translating marketing strategies into salable product lines and deliver them to their customers at the right price at the right time. As companies change their brand positioning, merchandisers must perform their own market research to accommodate the needs of these changing target markets.

Market Research

In the preliminary stages of line development, merchandisers can determine the characteristics of a market through segmentation studies or by collecting data directly from a company's target market as discussed in Chapter 3.

Data Collection

Merchandisers spend a great deal of time collecting and analyzing data about their target market as an ongoing part of maintaining their market knowledge base. During the preparation phase of line development, this process is especially intensive. The aim of this type of data collection is to determine the changes in consumers' expectations that will affect their buying habits. The techniques used by apparel companies to capture these data are focus groups, mall intercepts, consumer panels, mail surveys, and telephone surveys, all of which are discussed in Chapter 3.

To generate useful data requires the creation of effective questionnaires and leading intuitive discussions that can uncover trends that will affect the market six months to a year in the future. This requires highly skilled market researchers using sophisticated analytical techniques.

Kurt Salmon Associates, a top apparel and retail consulting firm, gave the American Apparel Manufacturers Association a stern warning about the importance of quality market research to product development at its 1998 annual conclave. "Consumers' expectations about what they want in their apparel and their shopping experiences are rising," said David Cole, chairman and chief executive officer of KSA.

"Only a small number of makers and retailers do regular research to ascertain consumer preferences, track consumer purchases, or test potential new products," said Adele Kirk, KSA's consumer marketing manager. "Over the last decade, consumers have become more savvy and changed their requirements of what they want in apparel and shopping. Yet the industry has focused on cost reductions instead of finding ways to create value in their products," Kirk said. "Some may say they can't afford this research . . . which costs maybe 1 percent of sales, but the response is that they can't afford not to. It's that important," Kirk said (Ostroff, 1998). In the past eight years, this requirement for success has become more important than ever before. Designers and merchandisers must know the consumers and offer unique products to meet their fashion needs.

Fashion Research

Once a market has been clearly defined through market segmentation, merchandisers then perform in-depth research to determine the styling that will affect line development. Fashion research analyzes the future direction for colors, fabrics, trims, and silhouettes. This research becomes the foundation for effective line development.

Fashion Trend Research

Merchandisers must keep a constant eye on the fashion marketplace. Keeping abreast of developing trends can be achieved through:

- Reading trade publications.
- Reading international fashion magazines.
- Using predictive services.
- Using consumer software such as Consumer Outlook!
- Shopping the competition.
- Interviewing retailers and buyers.
- Attending European and American designer fashion shows.
- Researching fashion Web sites.

European couture collections often provide the fashion spark that begins a trend in U.S. ready-to-wear. Therefore it is important for merchandisers to carefully monitor the European high-fashion designers. Videotapes and digital video clips of top European shows are available from subscription fashion services. Examples of these resources are discussed in Chapter 3.

Above all, merchandisers must have a keen understanding of what their target market consumers are wearing and be sensitive to their changing attitudes. Periodic focus groups and scheduled meetings with consumer panels are good methods for detecting the subtle changes that may affect buying trends.

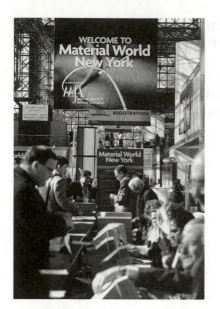

Figure 6.2 The Material World Show is held once a year in Miami and once a year at the Jacob Javits Center in New York City. It is an opportunity for apparel companies to see the new collections of both domestic and foreign fabric producers.

To keep the designers and line development team on track with fashion trend research, merchandisers should schedule periodic trend meetings and require designers to prepare trend reports. These functions should be integrated into the merchandising calendar since this research is a critical element of the line development process.

Color Research

Color trends play a key role in the line development process. The color palettes that evolve for a specific season can have a direct influence on fabric choices and silhouette development. Most apparel lines contain both basic, or staple, colors and fashion colors. The earlier that the line development team can establish a color story, the easier it will be to select fabrics and create styles that rely upon color integration for their fashion focus.

Color forecasts are provided by fiber and textile companies as well as forecasting services such as the Color Association of the United States (CAUS), the Color Council, International Colour Authority, Color Marketing Group, Concepts in Colour, and Promostyl. These services provide forecasts for various categories of men's, women's, and children's apparel. Many apparel companies subscribe to multiple services as a means of refining their forecasts to minimize missing out on important color trends.

Some fashion-forward companies rely on their own sense of fashion direction in developing color stories. The merchandiser and line development team may embrace a theme that dictates the color direction for a particular line. For example, a Southwestern theme could inspire a color palette of turquoise, sand, copper, rose, and azure.

Fabric and Trim Research

Fiber companies like DuPont, fiber organizations such as the Woolmark and Cotton Incorporated, and fabric producers like Milliken and Burlington Mills provide valuable forecasting information. A fabric company's sales presentations at its showroom or at an apparel company's design studio provide fabric swatches and sample cuts (3- to 5-yard fabric samples) to stimulate the line development process.

International fabric shows such as International Fashion Fabric Exhibition, Pitti Filatti, Yarn Expo, Premier Vision, Ideacomo, and Interstoff are excellent venues for evaluating trends in fabric and trim. Trade publications often have special issues that focus on fabric and trim direction.

For some apparel companies the line development process evolves from fabric development. These companies work directly with fabric manufacturers to develop exclusive fabrics, especially prints and knits. For companies like Missoni or Nicole Miller, fabrics or print designs make their fashion statement. For them fabric and print research and development is the focus of their creative efforts and therefore critical to the success of their apparel lines.

Just as in the case of color, a theme could inspire fabric and trim choices. Rugged denims, cool pastel cotton shirtings in Southwestern print motifs, beads, faux metallic buttons, and silver buckles could be a natural extension of the Southwestern theme.

Since fabric and trim are half of the style equation (silhouette + fabric = style), merchandisers must impress upon the line development team the importance of gathering the best possible research about these critical components. When crucial deadlines for ordering fabrics, finishing prototypes, or completing specification sheets are looming, it is frequently the more esoteric elements of the line development process, such as research, that are sacrificed. As consumer fashion demands become more specific, carefully executed research is the only way to capture the styling trends that will meet a company's target market's expectations.

■ Line Plan

The line plan or assortment plan sets the parameters for a company's product line. The format for a line plan is a detailed chart organized by product category that shows the number of styles, fabrics, colors, and sizes that are expected to be included in a line. The line plan is based upon a company's market strategies for product and brand positioning. It sets forth the company's annual and seasonal sales goals and distribution of sales by product category. The line plan provides the foundation and directional guidelines for the line development process. It is an integral part of a company's strategic plan and reflects any changes in direction relative to target market or product lines.

The line plan evolves from a dollar sales volume goal, which is established by top management and marketing based upon prior years' actual sales and market forecast analyses. Merchandisers establish style groups and the number of styles within each group that are needed to meet the objectives of the company sales plan and the requirements of the consumer. Line plans often further establish parameters for the optimal number of colors, fabrics, silhouettes, and sizes that will be incorporated into the line. Merchandising develops these criteria from a cost/value analysis that evaluates the cost of adding SKUs to the line versus the expected additional sales. This analysis is complex because there are many variables that affect ultimate sales. In the June 20, 2005 issue of *Women's Wear Daily*, Sharon Edelson reported, "After price, consumers' next priority was that stores offer a wide assortment of styles." She also referred to Zara and H&M who quickly introduce new styles every few days as a way to bring consumers into their stores. The evaluation of many seasons' sales statistics and line content is necessary to establish reliable data. Figure 6.3 shows the typical data included in a line plan for a children's wear manufacturer.

The line plan should take into account the following:

- Brand or product positioning.
- Projected sales for the season including sufficient styles to generate anticipated sales volume (historic ratios).
- Economic conditions.
- Balance by price ranges.

FIGURE 6.3 **FUN KIDS' LINE PLAN—FALL 2005**

Fall '05 SKU Plan		#Sizes	# Styles	#Colors	#SKUs
Transition:	Infant Prams	3	4	1	12
	Infant Jackets	3	5 (2G + 3B)	1	15
	2/4T Boy	3	4	2	24
	4/7 Boy	4	4	2	32
	8/20 Boy	7	3	2	42
	2/4T Girl	3	4	3	36
	4/6X Girl	4	4	3	48
	7/16 Girl	6	3	3	54
Coats:	Infant	3	1	1	3
	2/4T	3	4	2	24
	4/6X	4	4	2	32
	7/12	4	3	2	24
Heavyweights:	Infant Prams	3	8 (4G + 4B)	1	24
	Infant Jackets	3	6 (3G + 3B)	1	18
	2/4T Boy Jacket	3	6	2	36
	Snowsuits 2/4 B	3	3	1	9
	4/7 Boy Jacket	4	6	2	48
	8/20 Boy Jacket	7	6	2	84
	2/4T Girl Jacket	3	6	2	36
	Snowsuits 2/4T G	3	3	1	9
	4/6X Girl Jacket	4	8	2	64
	Snowsuits 4/6X G	4	2	1	8
	7/16 Girl Jacket	6	8	2	96
	Total		105 Styles		778 SKU's

The Fun Kids' line plan for Fall 2005 indicates the number of product groups, styles, and SKUs in each group, and the colors and sizes in each style.

- Balance to accommodate geographic climate differences (for example, fabric weights and sleeve lengths).
- Balance for fashion content based upon position of the target market.

The merchandiser then fits interim product development goals within the merchandising or line development calendar. If a line is planned for 80 total styles within four style groups, there may be eight deadlines of 10 styles due for prototype completion. These interim goals allow merchandising to make adjustments early in the line development process rather than waiting until the line is scheduled for final adoption only to realize that 18 styles have not yet been completed.

The line plan establishes the benchmarks for the line development team, which must be adhered to in order for the company to achieve its sales objectives without generating excessive product development costs. The merchandiser must closely monitor the progress of line development to prevent the line from deviating from the established benchmarks. Designers frequently tend to expand the number of styles, fabrics, or colors for some groupings without compensating with equivalent reductions in other style groups. Through regularly scheduled progress meetings, merchandising can redirect the efforts of the line development team to those styling areas that are still open within the line plan.

The structure of many line plans has changed with the increased number of offerings. Jay Margolis, a veteran top apparel executive from Liz Claiborne and Tommy Hilfiger USA, took on the challenge of rebuilding Esprit de Corp sportswear in the late 1990s. He restructured its line plans by offering smaller, but more frequent, groups. "When lines get bigger and bigger and get overassorted, and there is too much stuff out there and too much to choose from, I find that you are not getting a design vision across to the consumer," said Margolis. He noted that the company used to sell a group a month in sportswear, but now sells two groups a month. "It's the same number of SKUs, but they are tighter offerings that make a more focused statement to the consumer" (Ellis 1999).

■ Styling Direction

The first critical step in developing new styles is the establishment of a styling direction. This involves creating styling concepts that meet the needs of the target market and that will stimulate the creative efforts of the design team. The primary factors to consider in establishing styling direction are color, fabric, and silhouette. Styling direction should also focus on group concepts, that is, themes for styling groups that should be included in the line. These groups can be coordinated through theme, color, fabric, or silhouette. For example, a nature concept could include groups that represent wildflowers, woods, and mountain stream themes. Input from market research and fashion research provides the foundation for this important step in the line development process.

Inspiration is the catalyst that drives the creative process. It can be derived from the arts, European fashions, music, sports, history, ethnic trends, or even from zeitgeist, the spirit of the times.

The vehicles for communicating styling concepts or themes for a product line are storyboards (trend boards, concept boards). These graphic examples of colors, stylized sketches or paintings, and inspirational collages mounted on foam core boards set the tone for the creative direction of a product line. Each stylist or designer has his or her own technique for presenting styling concepts. An example of a typical concept board is shown in Figure 6.4.

The merchandiser reviews the line concepts to be sure that they meet the needs of the target market and can fit within the guidelines set forth in the line plan. If the line development team goes off course, critical time can be lost, which could jeopardize the success of a line. The merchandising function provides a valuable check and balance for the creative process.

Figure 6.4 A concept board is created to establish the theme or styling direction for a new collection. This board targets young boys' shirt, tie, and vest ensembles.

■ Product Development

Product development is the process of creating each individual style within the line. After the research phase of line development is completed, silhouettes are developed, fabrics and trim selected, prototypes made, and specifications created. The resulting styles are analyzed to determine manufacturing costs. These steps are all part of the product development phase of the line development process.

The first steps of silhouette development and fabric selection are approached in different ways by different designers and companies. Many companies base their lines around fabric and print designs. Their designers start by selecting fabrics and then create silhouettes for those fabrics. These designers are **fabric-driven**. Other designers are **silhouette-driven**. They design silhouettes and then select fabrics that are compatible with the silhouettes. Both processes achieve the same end result—unique garment styles. The sequence used is a factor of company philosophy and designer preference.

Figure 6.5 The choice of fabrics to be used in a new collection can take place in the textile suppliers' showrooms, at the apparel company's design studio, or at a trade show.

Fabric Selection

Fabric selection involves the designer either visiting textile supplier showrooms, attending fabric shows, or having textile sales representatives present their lines at the apparel company. The designer must not only evaluate the aesthetic characteristics of the fabrics but must also take into consideration the following factors:

- Fiber content.
- Fabric construction—basic structure.
- Texture and engineered effects created by weave configurations and yarn selections.
- Prints.
- Color range.
- Performance characteristics—wear factors, care requirements, sewing compatibility, and drape.
- Versatility for use in multiple styles.
- Price and terms.
- Availability.
- Minimum order quantities.

When selecting fabrics, designers must always be aware of the intended end use. This is especially critical for garments that will be subjected to extreme conditions such as swimwear, which requires that it be colorfast in chlorine and extreme sunlight, and active sportswear, which may require special thermal properties, abrasion resistance, or the ability to wick moisture away from the body.

There are many guide books and reference services available for merchandisers and designers that can assist them in finding special fabrics and trims. One example is the Apparel and Textile Information Services division of JanMar Enterprises, Inc., of New Providence, New Jersey. Another good source of information is the World Wide Web under the listing *textiles*.

Silhouettes

Silhouette development involves transforming garment ideas into final garment sketches or technical drawings, which are hand or CAD renderings of the front and back of a garment, including stitching details. Technical drawings usually do not include body silhouettes and are used where construction and styling details are critical to the design. CAD drawings are being used more frequently nowadays because they provide a consistent basis for communicating design ideas throughout the entire line development process. Sportswear companies find it convenient to duplicate previous CAD silhouettes and make changes to the drawings to quickly create new silhouettes. Some companies have CAD specialists on their product development staff to take designer sketches and transform them into a technical drawing format (see Figure 6.6).

Many designers use computer graphics software to create their garment sketches. These programs allow the designer to prepare and store a database of body silhouettes, sometimes called **croquis**, in many different poses, duplicate a pose, and draw a garment sketch onto the croquis. Once a silhouette has been created, it can be transformed into different garment styles by applying computer-generated, or scanned, scaled fabric images. This use of computer technology is streamlining the product development process. It allows designers greater latitude in stretching their creative boundaries. Instead of spending hours creating color illustrations of style concepts, a designer can test ideas using computer graphics in a matter of minutes. These graphic images can be electronically transmitted to a merchandiser or other members of the product development team for review and comments.

Line Sheets

As designers select fabrics and develop silhouettes, they are focusing on filling the requirements of the line plan. **Line sheets** are created for each style

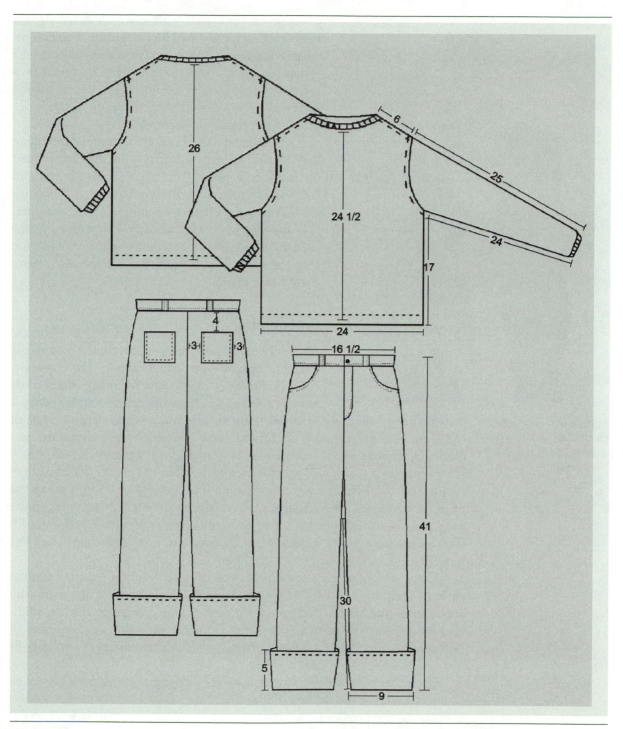

Figure 6.6 A technical drawing of a top and pants that has been developed by free-lance designer Katie McKensie using Primavision software by Lectra.

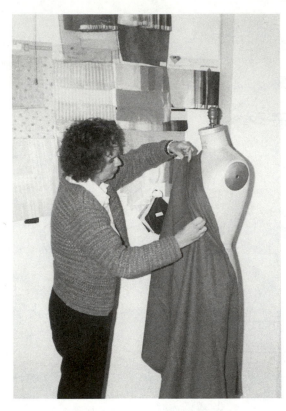

Figure 6.7 A designer creates her prototype by draping fabric on a mannequin.

group in the line plan with space allocated for the number of styles planned for the group. The designers provide sketches of each style that is added to the group along with fabric swatches and pertinent prototype information. These line sheets are constantly reviewed by merchandising to keep the product development process on schedule.

Designers also use style boards for reviewing line development groups. **Style boards** are created on foam core boards and show color sketches or color CAD printouts of styles within a group including fabric and color swatches. These presentation boards along with the trend boards are often used in merchandising reviews and line adoption sessions since they capture the creative essence of each theme group.

Prototyping

After silhouettes have been approved, the next step is to create a **prototype** or first sample. The prototype is the first critical opportunity for the product development team to see an actual garment style and try it on a **fit model** (a model who has body measurements equivalent to those of the company's target market consumer). This opportunity to evaluate the aesthetics of the style on the human body is an important step, especially for fashion garments. It is also an opportunity to see if the style meets the company's standards for quality. For basic sportswear, it is also important in refining the fit of the garments. Merchandisers must strive to maintain consistency in the fit of their company's products. Apparel brand loyalty is often based upon fit. This is especially critical in underwear, foundations, jeans, dress shirts, and tailored clothing.

There are two primary methods for creating prototypes—draping and flat pattern. **Draping** is usually used by couture and ready-to-wear designers who create garments for the designer price range. This process of cutting, shaping, and draping fabric on a dress form or mannequin allows the designer to evaluate the way a fabric performs when it is shaped to conform to a three-dimensional shape (see Figure 6.7).

Flat pattern is a process that involves altering basic pattern blocks or slopers to achieve the desired silhouette. It is more frequently used in ready-to-wear apparel companies to create prototypes. **Slopers** or **blocks** are sets of patterns for each basic garment type produced by the company. They have been refined over a period of many seasons to provide the exact fit desired by the target market consumer. Today's CAD pattern design systems (PDS) are the most efficient method of flat pattern design. They achieve a high degree of accuracy and speed when creating new patterns for a prototype. They also easily interface with single-ply, automated sample cutters to allow the designer to quickly construct a prototype to check proper fit. After the fit sample is tested, pattern adjustments can be made quickly and easily.

With the proliferation of global sourcing, the sample-making process is often transferred to a manufacturer who may be located halfway around the world. The cost and time required to make and deliver prototypes from global sourcing partners make controlling the product development process a challenge. It requires that merchandisers monitor the initial phases of product development carefully in order to weed out any potential styles that may not fulfill the needs of the line plan. Accurate communications of prototype requirements is another critical issue for merchandisers. Computer-based PIM systems provide a consistent, accurate method of creating and communicating prototype requests, whether they are transmitted to a factory in the United States or to a sourcing contractor in South America or Southeast Asia. The following data are critical for a prototype request:

- Company name.
- Season and date.
- Style code.
- Product identification.
- Prototype identification code.
- Detailed description of garment.
- Technical drawing of garment.
- Sample pattern identification codes.
- Sample size measurements with tolerances.
- Fabric description.
- Bill of materials.
- Cutting instructions.
- Sewing construction details.
- Labeling instructions.
- Finishing instructions.
- Packaging instructions.
- Target price.

Figure 6.8 shows a sample prototype request.

A prototype also can be made using a form that is an exact replica of the company's fit model. Shapely Shadow is a company that utilizes 3-D scanning in their five-step process called "Customization" that creates a clone of the fit model's body. When a contractor makes the prototypes the contractor will be supplied with a copy of the form. After the prototype has been sewn, it is placed on the contractor's form and a digital video is made. Using software that converts the 2-D video to 3-D, one can rotate the prototype 360 degrees,

Style Definition/ Prototype request:

Identifiers::

Style/Var. Code: SH714004 / 00011   **Company:** Karat BZa Products   **Division:** Mens Shirts
Descriptions : Classic long sleeve, button down collar, false placket, straight bottom mens shirt   **Variation:** Neutral linen
Prototype No. : PR22342   **Pattern Number:** SP93134LG   **Construction Number:** 0444

General Conditions:

Product : Classic mens shirt   **Season:** Spring06   **Status:** Final   **Approved By:** G. Williams

User Identification:

Merchandiser: S. Sklar	**Account** : JCPenney	**Sales Rep.** : G. Roll	**Est.Cost Com:** yes **Det.Cost Com:** No
Outside ID : Performance +	**Fit Approved:** yes	**Target Price:** $24.95	**Finish Instr.** : Hanging **Coord. Group:** Chaps
Cutting Inst. : Block fronts/slvs- FF/NOW		**Fabric Type**	: Basket weave 8 oz linen check **Packing Instr.** : Butterfly collar / pin slvs

Size Ratio:

Size Range: Mens Classic

	14	14 1/2	15	15 1/2	16	16 1/2	17	17 1/2	18	18 1/2	19
	1	2	4	4	3	2	1	1			

Sample Size Measurements:

Sample Size	Neck opening	Chest 1" fr arm	Waist 8" fr arm	Bottom sweep	Shoulder	Ctr back length	Ctr front length	Bk yk fr ctr back	Fr yk fr should
15	15 "	43 1/2 "	42 1/2 "	42 "	20 "	32 "	27 "	4 1/2 "	2 1/4 "

Notes:
3.5 % shrinkage - length
2.7 % shrinkage - width

Materials:

Class/Type	Wh Used	Code	Description	Vendor	Size/wdt	Usage	Black	Red	Navy	Green
Fabric/Shell	Body	SHL00345	100% Linen	Harrison Mills	58 "	1.25 yd	Black	Red	Navy	Green
Fabric/Lining	Body	LIN6873	Satin Taffeta	Consolidated	45 "	0.5 yd	Grey	Rose	Sky Blue	Mint Green
Trim/Buttons	Cuffs	BUT001	4 hole flat	ABC Buttons	18 line	4 ea	Black	Red	Navy	Green
Trim/Buttons	Placket	BUT002	4 hole flat	ABC Buttons	24 line	6 ea	Black	Red	Navy	Green
Label/Care	Neckline	LBCR223	Care Label - cotton	Lucky Labels		1 ea	No Color	No Color	No Color	No Color
Label/Logo	Neckline	LBLG011	Woven Chaps	Universal		1 ea	No Color	No Color	No Color	No Color
Package/Polybag		PKBG12	Polybag	Delta	12" x 16 "	1 ea	No Color	No Color	No Color	No Color

Detail Garment Description:

Topstitching	Pockets	Pleats	Collar
☐ 1 Needle	☐ 1 Sq Ptch 5"x6"	☐ 1 Ctr Back	☐ 2pc Lined
☐ 2 Needle	☐ 2 Sq Ptch 5"x6"	☐ 2 Ctr Back	☐ 2pc Unlined
☐ 1/4 "	☐ 1 Rd Ptch 6"x8"	☐ 2 Cuffs	☐ 1pc Lined
☐ 1/16 "	☐ 1 Rd Ptch 6"x8"	☐ 4 Cuffs	☐ 1pc Unlined

Sideseam	Sleeveset	Shoulderseam
☐ 2Needle Felled	☐ 2Needle Felled	☐ 2Needle Felled
☐ 1Needle Busted	☐ 1Needle Felled	☐ 1Needle Busted
☐ 3/8" Safety stitch	☐ 1Needle Busted	☐ 3/8" Safety stitch
☐ Topstitch	☐ 3/8" Safety stitch	☐ Topstitch
	☐ Topstitch	

Product/Development Specifications:

Inside lining- sewn in, set at neck, sleeve finish, center front
Onseam sleeve placket- 3 1/4" length, horizontal tack at end
Backtab- 1 pce folded, 1/16" edge stitched with horizontal buttonhole + 2buttons sewn
     into back yoke seam

Figure 6.8 Computer PIM systems can accurately and consistently communicate prototype requirements.

as well as zoom in and out to inspect quality. When these images are transmitted electronically from the producer of the prototype to the product development staff, adjustments can be made immediately. This increases efficiency and saves both time and money. According to a Shapely Shadow spokesperson, American Eagle Outfitters, GAP, and Donna Karan have adopted this approach.

Precosting

The prototype process provides an opportunity for the development of data that will determine the estimated manufacturing cost for each new style. In today's highly competitive apparel marketplace, selling price plays an important role in the sales potential for garment styles. Merchandisers should have comprehensive databases of product costs and effective cost accounting or cost engineering support. These data along with feedback from prototype production can provide valuable information for estimating the manufacturing cost of a new style. This process of preparing a cost estimate is called **precosting** or **quick costing** by some companies.

The precost formula must cover all costs of manufacturing a garment, including materials, labor, overhead, design and distribution, general and administrative costs, and markup. Materials and labor are the cost areas that must be estimated during the precosting process since the other cost categories are usually allocated based upon a standard cost formula. (See Chapter 7 for a detailed discussion of precosting.) CAD pattern design systems allow for quick pattern grading, preparation of sample markers, and calculation of fabric utilization in determining the material costs. Labor costs are estimated by factory engineers, cost engineers, quality personnel, or quoted by sourcing contractors. With these data, reasonable manufacturing cost estimates can be developed.

If it turns out that the estimated cost of a style is going to be too high to meet the price point required for it to be marketable, it is important to stop wasting valuable product development time. The recommendation to delete a style in process is usually presented by the line review committee, and the final decision is made by the merchandiser in concert with the designer. At this stage, product engineering may be brought in to determine if any changes can be made to the style to reduce manufacturing costs and still achieve the desired aesthetic results envisioned by the designer. This may involve slight pattern changes to improve fabric utilization or construction changes to reduce labor costs.

Specifications

For the styles that are estimated to meet acceptable price points and are approved by the review committee, preliminary manufacturing specifications are prepared. Final production patterns are created that accommodate all fit adjustments and production construction requirements. The patterns are then graded and prepared to be sent to the source of production. Today, many companies have transferred this responsibility to their "full package" suppliers.

Detailed production specification sheets are prepared. These may differ according to the factory that will be making the style. Sequence of operations and detailed manufacturing procedures are determined so that final costs can be calculated. It is during this process that final product engineering is performed. **Product engineering** is the analysis of a style to determine whether any pattern adjustments or construction changes can reduce the cost of producing the style while still achieving the desired design results. Companies that source their production with contract manufacturers negotiate final pricing at this stage of the product development process. (See Chapters 10 and 11 for detailed discussions of the sourcing process.)

Another important element of the specification process is providing the proper **care label** instructions for each garment style based upon apparel testing (see Figure 6.9). The Federal Trade Commission established the Care Labeling Rule, which requires manufacturers and importers of textile wearing apparel to provide regular care label instructions when these products are sold. These instructions must provide warnings if a garment cannot be cleaned without harm to the product. The companies must also ensure that the care labeling instructions, if followed, will cause no substantial harm to the product. This label must remain legible throughout the useful life of the product. Merchandising must not overlook this important function in product development.

Computer-based product information managers (PIMs) provide a consistent platform for creating specification sheets and transmitting the information to manufacturing or sourcing contractors. The process often starts with a design work sheet, then progresses to a prototype request, and finally the garment specifications which have been updated and expanded to include all changes derived from prototype production and fit sessions. This integration of data from a central database eliminates duplication of effort and paperwork.

Calvin Klein is testing a new version of a product data management system that provides factory personnel on-line around the world with access to product specifications via the Internet (Zimmermann 1998). The use of integrated PIM systems takes the bits and pieces of data that were created by word processing, spreadsheet, and database programs and places all the data about a product in one easy to manage location. From the designer worksheet to the final specification sheet, all the data are generated through the PIM system. When any one piece of information is updated, all files utilizing that bit of information are automatically updated. This type of integration minimizes the chances of errors in manufacturing and ensures consistent quality.

Figure 6.9 The federal government requires that care instructions be permanently attached to a garment. The care labels shown here use symbols to indicate the individual care that is required for each garment.

Final Costing

Another critical step of the product development phase is **final costing** or **costing for sale**. This process is a detailed calculation of the costs required to manufacture a style based upon available data. The cost accounting or cost engineering department makes a detailed analysis of the material requirements based upon sample markers and prototype reports. The garment is broken down into each production operation, and manufacturing costs are synthesized using elemental work measurement standards or are based upon time studies performed during prototype construction. It is important that costing at this level be as accurate as possible because style adoption and selling prices will be based upon the results. (See Chapter 7 for a detailed discussion of costing strategies.)

■ Adoption

The culmination of the complex line development process is final line adoption. Throughout the process there are frequent **executive line reviews**. These are performed by the merchandiser and members of the design team and sometimes include input from sales, marketing, and key retail buyers. Merchandising uses these reviews to focus the direction of the design team on products that have the greatest chance of being adopted in the line. Executive

"1999 TAC Report—Case Study #5, Kellwood"

This study, supplemented with sample forms, shows how Kellwood has accomplished the task of communicating its product development process output to manufacturing facilities all over the world, both owned and contracted.

One of Kellwood's larger divisions is its Sportwear Division. And it is there that one can see the Product Development department at the center of activities—from the creation of a product to the release of production information to the factory or contractor that will manufacture it.

The Product Development department is involved with design and merchandising from sketch, to prototype specifications and prototype garment, to pricing, evaluation for inclusion in the line, and final acceptance in the line. Because production information is a by-product of a comprehensive development process, data is constantly generated and accumulated; and once a style is adopted, data is updated and refined to create the information package for production of that product.

Kellwood's Sportswear Division has years of experience in contracting domestically and internationally, both value added and full package. In addition, it operates its own factories both domestically and internationally. From this experience, the Product Development team knows that comprehensive information must be provided if an acceptable product is to be produced. Over the years, the division has created an information format it calls a "Style Package," which it provides to the producer. This package has evolved from a manual compilation to today's computer-generated reports.

The primary purpose of the Style Package is to provide a clear, graphic description of a product. Its components are:

- Style Adoption Sheet—Identifies the style and the date the package is created.
- Revision History Log—Identifies changes chronologically and indicates updates to other package components.
- Pattern Sketch—A front and back pictorial representation of the product.
- Label Placement—Pictorial of all positions in the garment.
- Folding/Hanging Instructions—Depiction of product as it is packaged.
- All Views—Appearance of product, all sizes, with prominent features shown.
- Style Color List—Listing of all styles and colors or other appearance characteristics.
- General Specifications—Written instructions for critical garment features, components, or construction details.
- Style Color Specifications—Written information for color coordination of fabric, thread, or other color-dependent items on the garment.
- Pattern/Piece Goods Cross-Reference—Information to correlate pattern numbers, style/color, and piece goods numbers.
- Graded Measurements—Matrix of sizes, measurements at all points of measurement, and tolerances of measurement vs. specification.

(continued)

- How to Measure—Depiction of points of critical measurement, with indications of how to measure correctly to correspond to the Graded Measurement specifications.
- Construction Specifications—Chart of all major operations by part required to construct the garment. Also included are stitches per inch, seam margins, seam allowances, stitch type, and number of needles.
- Mini-Marker—Plot of one size marker. Sample size is used.
- Graded Pattern Approval—Description of markers needed, spreading method, and any fabric characteristics requiring special spreading techniques.
- Pattern Parts List—Listing of parts and the number of each part required to make garment, with indication of orientation of part in marker to achieve desired result.
- Trim Card—Pictorial representation of all trim items.
- Process Flow Analysis—Illustration of operations by part and assembly operations once parts are completed.

- Detailed Construction Diagram—Diagram by part and operation, presenting visually all operations by part and assembly, with critical aspects of the operation highlighted.

If necessary, based on the contractor's ability, the Style Package can also include a garment made to specification and a plot of the full set of patterns. What's more, Kellwood is working on enhancements that would allow Style Packages to be transmitted over the Internet; challenges that must be overcome are the incompatibility of computer systems and their ability to translate pattern information. Translation of data into several key languages is advancing, as well.

As global contracting becomes even more a way of life for today's apparel manufacturer, Kellwood is demonstrating how the refinement and ease of transmitting the Style Package is critical to accurate, concise, and timely information of product components for production. ■

From Apparel Manufacturers Association, 1999.

Case in Point 6.2   ## Summary

Kellwood's Sportswear Division created a computer generated "Style Package" for its apparel producers. This Style Package contains all the detailed specifications and instructions needed to produce a garment that meets all Kellwood's merchandising and quality requirements.

To accommodate its diverse sourcing contractors, Kellwood is designing this information package to be translated into several languages and to be capable of being transmitted over the Internet. This application of technology to its product development process has improved Kellwood's ability to communicate with its global manufacturing resources. ■

line reviews are designed to keep the line development process on track and determine as soon as possible if the design team is deviating from the merchandiser's intended styling direction. These reviews provide the opportunity for the top company executives to buy in to each style as it is developed. This prevents any surprises when it is time for final line adoption.

Final line adoption is the last critical event on the line development time line. It is usually performed by a team of top company executives and is coordinated by the merchandiser. This is the point at which the company decides which styles will become part of the line and which styles will be dropped. The guidelines for the final selection process are derived from the same line plan that controlled the product development process. During the final line adoption, each style is evaluated on its merits within the context of the overall line plan requirements. Has each style group been fully developed to make a good sales presentation? Has each group stayed within the maximum number of styles, fabrics, and colors? Does the line stay within the guidelines of the maximum number of SKUs?

Final line adoption is the first opportunity for the line to be viewed in its entirety and be evaluated in terms of the line plan. In most companies the merchandiser allows the line development team to create approximately 10 percent more styles than are called for in the line plan. This allows the line adoption committee to select the styles that will meet the criteria of the line plan and that they feel will generate the greatest volume of sales. Sometimes, during final line adoption, last minute adjustments are made to the line that deviate from the original line plan. This may be due to some style groups not meeting the overall expectations of the final adoption committee and others surpassing their expectations. The merchandiser must maintain control over this process to keep the line within the acceptable limits of the overall line plan. If styles are added, other styles must be dropped. Without this control, the size of the line would grow and costs would escalate.

The line adoption committee often ranks the line according to its evaluation of the relative salability of each style. These data can be weighted by the historical accuracy of each committee member to provide the initial sales forecasts by style.

M. Lederle Eberhardt Experience—vice president design and merchandising, Woolrich, Inc.

Controlling Line Development

"At Woolrich we have a fall release, a small holiday season, and a spring season. Within each of the fall and spring seasons there are four smaller groups, which gives us nine groups to develop. The retailers today want to flow merchandise. There has to be a reason for the consumers to buy, so every month the retailers want freshness on the floor. For nine months they receive our nine groups, and for the other three months of the year they like to buy off-price products so they can help boost their margins.

"There are 30 to 35 styles within each of the major seasons. That gives us 125 total styles for each of the major spring and fall releases. Sixty percent of our business is what we call fashion. It's in the line for a year and then out. Forty percent of our styles are repeats. I have to keep a close eye on the total SKUs in the line. It's quite a balancing act keeping line development under control.

"I set the direction for our New York design staff. I get my input from buyers, from consumers, from trends in the market, from where Woolrich wants to be, and what sold last year."

Color, Print, and Fabrication Drive Design Process

"The designers start sketching ideas for prototypes. We start setting color direction, and then we set print direction.

"We have just installed a CAD system in New York so the designers can do their sketches in CAD or scan them into our computer system. I try to keep abreast of their progress to keep them on track with my line plan.

"Color, print, and fabrication drive our design process. Within our current spring line there are four color stories. The first color story has a lot of leaf prints and is focused around linen fabrics. The next group is built around twill fabric and florals. We have other groups based on gardening and camping/hiking themes."

Market Dictates

"I came from a manufacturing-driven company, Sara Lee—Hanes Her Way. There we developed the product line into the capabilities of their manufacturing. Here we're focusing on market-right products. Let the market dictate what the product is going to be and then figure out where you're going to source it and make it. There's two

(*continued*)

different approaches to product development, whether the market dictates what the product is going to be or whether manufacturing dictates what the product needs to be."

Specifications

"After the designers sketch the silhouettes, their prototype requests are sent here to Woolrich headquarters to a centralized spec department. They have a coordinator who's dedicated to women's sportswear. She will take the sketches and fill out a whole prototype specification package. That department reports to the VP of manufacturing. There are people over there looking at how the garment should best be constructed. They put down as much detail as they can on that garment, and then it is sent out to sourcing."

Prototypes

"The prototypes will either get made here at Woolrich or in Hong Kong or Taiwan. The prototype spec package is sent out to where I want it sourced. The manufacturer makes patterns, sews up prototypes, and we do fit sessions here to make final adjustments. When the prototypes get signed off on in our product development group, they're ready for the adoption meetings."

Price Points

"I'm responsible for hitting price points. The designers and merchandisers in New York report to me.

I review everything and decide whether a garment will fall within the right price point or whether I have to tweak it. My designer in sportswear likes everything super long and I always have to knock two inches off her skirts and jumpers. That's where you can eat up fabric and increase prices. Designers often loose sight of price, and it's my job to rein them in.

"You have to understand where you can cut cost out of a product without degrading the product. I have to be sure that each style we create is salable. I am responsible for controlling SKUs and for the bottom line."

Paper Trail

"We have an extensive paper trail. We have a document called the craft section, which is generated out of the spec department, which is our central communication point. It is a working document that is continually updated as the line is being developed. When a prototype is submitted, it gets put into this document, which is our bible.

"The craft section document lists the fabrics by picks and warps, yarn counts, the garment process (Is it garment-washed? Is it enzyme-washed? Is it not washed?), who's manufacturing it. All colors that are lab dipped are in the document and as we weed them out they are removed.

"We use Freeborders software to compare specs and communicate these specs to the factories. This is a

(continued)

Web-based system that is very flexible and allows me and anyone else involved in the process to make changes and then instantly communicate these changes to everyone else. I did a search for styles that were using a particular River Shell button. I got three pages of styles, and didn't realize the designer was using that button that much. It is a button that really communicates femininity and that was her group focus.

"The craft document is continually updated, and I can receive the documents while I am in the Orient via E-mail. New York design is networked to Freeborders so they can submit prototypes directly into the system."

Line Reviews

"Throughout the entire process there are meetings with management for reviews, which analyze what men's is doing versus what we're doing in women's. We want to have one message. We are Woolrich. The vice president of merchandising, the VP of marketing and sales, the VP of manufacturing, two or three key sales reps, and the inventory control manager participate in the meetings.

"When we go into a line select meeting, we probably have one and one-half times the number of items that will eventually become the final line. The items begin as prototype numbers, and, then when they are adopted, they are given style numbers."

Qualifications

"A merchandiser needs to be somewhat creative, and you do need to take classes in design and patternmaking and understand the design process. You should also take some textile courses to understand fabrics. If a designer wants to use a particular fabric, it has to be tested, and I need to make sure that it lives up to Woolrich standards.

"Merchandisers have to be somewhat visionary. Today they come from such different backgrounds. Some come from retail, some from design. I came from manufacturing. One thing for sure is that you have to be very team-oriented. In today's business environment, team orientation is a must. It's not about me, me, me. It's about we, we, we. And I have a great team."

Lynn Duckworth Experience—vice president, merchandising, Little Me

Substitutions

"Sometimes we've asked for a certain texture to be used and the factory just can not supply it, but they've got a great substitute. We may accept the substitution and change the entire design package during the negotiating meetings to accommodate the new fabric. All information on changes that occur during the price negotiation process are relayed back to the product managers in Cumberland, Md. where they correct the master design packages to reflect the new information."

Approvals

"One of the most time-consuming and critical parts of the design cycle is the approval process. Every lab dip, embroidery thread color, screen print, decorative label, fabric swatch, print strike-off, embroidery mending, button, and bow per style is sent to the New York design department for approval. Each style in the line has a folder with its own information. Every approval sent from the factory is matched up to its file and checked for accuracy against what it is supposed to look like. Many times items are rejected three or four times until a maker gets it right. This process is highly critical in determining how good the sales samples will look and ultimately how good your stock will look. Every style has a fit sample made by the maker, which is also sent to the New York design department and pattern-making to be fit and adjusted. Every time an approval on a style or component part of a style is rejected, it further delays the making of the sales sample. At some point you have to know when to accept and when to continue to reject approvals. It's a very fine line."

Sales Samples

"Orders for sales samples are placed during the overseas sourcing trips. We need 36 pieces of each style for the sales force, showrooms, advertising, and quality control department. Sometimes while in Asia, we can select substitute fabrics that are very similar to expedite the sample process. If we need a yarn dye mini-check for instance, and the factory has one the right color but a slightly different size, we will approve it just for sales samples. It is critical to have sales samples on time for market week, so every effort is made to expedite the process."

Review Process

"Once the design director and I have approved a category of designs or fashion grouping of designs, they

(continued)

go through a sales editing review process. The sales department and president of the division review each style and fashion group. The approved styles go into finalized presentation boards and they, along with the original concept boards, are then used for key customer line reviews prior to line opening."

Specifications and Data Packages are Thorough

"Our garment specification packages that are sent to each overseas maker are very thorough and detailed. We try to include every bit of information that they will need to make our garments accurately and on time. It is the primary function of the product managers to prepare these packages for every style in the line. We include a color drawing of the design, a technical black and white sketch, which indicates the pattern departments' measuring points for fit specs, black and white line drawings for all artwork, colored artwork drawings, embroidery information, screen print information, embroidery thread colors, trim information, label information, fabric specs, color information, print layout, and color pegs. The fabric spec pages include every single fabric used for each garment part, including weight or construction to color combinations. Trim pages identify all trim components including sewing thread colors, button sizes, type and color, bows, snaps

size and color, elastic, logo labels, etc., every last detail. We indicate for the maker which label, hangtag, hanger, and plastic bag to use on each garment. We include all required completion dates for prototype samples, revised samples, and sales samples.

"Each embroidery gets a colored artwork page that shows the design plus the information on thread color and number of stitches to be used. If we know a specific style will be in Hong Kong or Thailand, we even indicate the maker of the thread as it differs from country to country. Each print used will have a page showing the 'repeat' and color pegs. We develop all our own prints rather than using 'market' prints. Each print design is copyrighted to The Schwab Company.

"Some companies are using computer interactive databases to transmit their specifications to their overseas makers. Unfortunately you cannot electronically transmit a swatch of color or a swatch of fabric for texture, and you cannot electronically transmit a sample garment. When the overseas maker receives a design package from Little Me, it is 100 percent complete. He has everything to begin garment production without having to go back and forth and wait for additional information that could not come via computer. Computerized transmission of initial design packages are faster, and I am sure we will all be using them very soon."

(*continued*)

Make versus Buy Meetings

"We have 'make versus buy meetings,' which are really production sourcing meetings, since the company has fundamentally moved away from United States based manufacturing. In these meetings the product managers and I meet with the sourcing departments via videoconference between New York and Cumberland, Md. We collectively decide which factory is the best suited for each group, individual style, or category of product. Decisions are based on type of product, difficulty, and fabrication, i.e., knit versus woven. Some factories are better suited for knit/woven combinations, some are strictly knits, and others are strictly wovens. We try to keep individual fashion groups in the same factory, sometimes in two factories within the same country. It is rare when we have to split a fashion-coordinated group between two countries. It is a logistical nightmare. When we do split groups between makers, it is our agents' or our buying office's responsibility to coordinate the efforts of the two makers."

We Design to Price Points

"I know what our price point parameters are for the company by product category. I can pretty well determine what a vendor is going to charge before a product goes overseas. We design to price points that are predetermined. We try to get as many design packages as possible sent overseas before the trip so each maker has time to get back to us with preliminary costs. We review these costs before the trip and alert the maker of potential costing problems or changes that can be made to facilitate costs before we arrive.

"During the trip, when we are actually negotiating the prices, I can make changes to price points or garments can be adjusted to ease the cost. It is critical for a merchandiser to go on these trips to make critical and necessary garment changes or corrections. For instance, approving the use of embroidery instead of screen printing if the printing is going to cause a problem for the maker and drive the price up. All negotiating of prices is done on the sourcing trip. When we return to the office, cost and wholesale prices are reviewed again, and margins are checked and finalized."

Concept Boards

"Every season we develop concept boards based on prints we like, specific color stories, stripes, and themes that we have identified as being important for that season. A concept board will have color swatches, three or four related (companion) prints, and pictures from magazines to illustrate the theme. It creates the feeling and mood for the group that we want the designer to stay within.

(*continued*)

"Once a theme is identified, we allow it to drive the fabric decisions. Some themes drive themselves toward fabrics very easily like 'polar bears and polar fleece.' Others take time to develop. Once we determine the fabrications, the information is plugged into the line plan. Lightweight fabrics generally deliver first, corduroy in the middle, and heavyweights toward the end of a typical fall season. We design the groups in their order of delivery."

Color CAD

"In the New York office, our designers prepare black and white rough sketches, which are refined by computer and transformed into color technical drawings. Some designers prefer to work directly on the computer and start with color sketches. We are constantly reviewing and editing at every phase of the process. We must cull everything down to approximately 10 or 12 designs per group. At this point, everything is still on paper and we do not make design samples.

"We use the computer to generate our black and white technical sketches from the designers' pencil sketches, which are standardized for the company to use over and over again. (This is all changing rapidly as more and more of our designers are working directly on the computer-aided design system or CAD). I'm from the old school though. I still prefer black and white pencil sketches; they're more fluid and less stiff. All sketches are transmitted to Cumberland, Md., where we have one person whose sole job it is to turn designers' sketches into color, technical drawings. We use U4ia software to do our CAD work. New York and Cumberland are networked, so the designers can send designs back and forth via the system. It works great!"

Six Months for Line Development

"In the design cycle, we allow ourselves 6 months for line development per season, 1 month for research, 4 months for design, and 1 month for sourcing. The company has two major seasons per year. A typical season begins with 1 month for shopping the stores, previewing and developing color stories, buying original artwork for prints, and developing theme concept boards. The actual design process takes about 4 months to complete. This would include working with designers, merchandising and editing the designs to fit our plan, and reviewing with sales.

"As designs are finished, and sales and merchandising have signed off on them, they go immediately to our product mangers in Cumberland, Md., where the design packages are completed, including technical specifications, patterns, fabric and trim specs, color tabs, and final artwork."

(continued)

Importance of Proper Planning and Control

"I use a Gantt chart as my primary tool. Every critical event that we need to complete on time to stay on track for the season is indicated. I have beginning dates and 'drop-dead' ending dates. We follow it to the letter. We use a spreadsheet for tracking and highlight in red when a date goes off track. Years and years of working with KSA (Kurt Salmon Associates) have taught me the value of such a tool. They indoctrinated me in the importance of proper planning, control, and tracking. We adjust the plan dates seasonally to the calendar, but it stays pretty consistent.

"Once a season starts, the line development calendar is locked in stone. The real drop-dead date is when we have to leave for the Orient. We know that by that date every step in developing the line must be done. Period!"

Line Plan

"My line plan lays out by month the planned deliveries by dollars and SKUs. We know how many styles are girl, boy, or neutral in certain categories, and we know how many styles are fashion versus basic per shipping month. This is critical information to dovetail with the receipts plans for the major stores. It does no good to plan to ship more than your major stores are planning for their receipts. A typical line size is 535 styles. This requires a tremendous amount of prep and coordination."

We've Got the Process Working Really Well

"Right now I wouldn't change much of anything. We've got the process really fine-tuned and working well. I have a great group of people who work for me, and that makes all the difference."

Laura O'Connor Experience—general merchandise manager, Urban Outfitters

Private Label Product Development

"For our private label products, the buyers and the designers work together on developing concepts for the total season, but we deliver products on a constant basis. They meet every week to review the progress of what's being developed. The weekly progress meetings continue through to the finalization meeting. At this meeting we look at samples and decide what we are going to buy, what needs to be edited, and write purchase orders for those products that will be put into production. From that meeting, it is usually six to nine months until the merchandise hits the selling floor.

"In the meantime there is an ongoing process we call 'chase,' which involves quick response to current consumer demand. Designers update best selling items and the buyers place orders that get these items on the floor within 60-90 days. All these efforts focus on getting the right products in front of our customers as quickly as possible. "The divisional merchandise man-ager manages both the buyers and the designers and is responsible for the business of a division. The buyers and designers are equal partners in the process."

Design Calendar

"We maintain constant delivery flow to our stores involving both our own private label merchandise and branded products. There are different products flowing from different sources into our business at all times. The scheduling is quite complex and for that we use a design calendar.

"For each delivery date we set up a series of trigger dates. Trigger dates are defined as the last possible date to make a decision before on-time delivery is jeopardized. There is a date to purchase the raw materials, a date to dye the fabric, and finally a date to cut and sew the garment. The final option to reduce lead time is to ship the order via boat or via airfreight. Shipping via air can be very costly, but air can save up to 14 days of transit time. By managing our calendar around these critical dates we are able to give the designers and buyers more time to react to the immediate need/want of our customer."

Line Plan

"We have standards by classification that govern how many styles we should have on the sales floor at any given time to be profitable. The line

(*continued*)

plan is a chart that details the number of styles and color choice that are required to meet the business objectives for each classification. The divisional merchandise managers work with each of the buyers to develop a line plan for each season. The designers use this line plan as their checklist as they're developing products to make sure they are putting enough time into the categories targeted for growth."

Market Research

"Our market research process is non-traditional. We do very little work with professional consultants although we do employ the creative services of freelance artists and fledgling fashion designers to enrich our collections. Our primary source of research material is our own core customer. The buyers and designers closely follow the lifestyle of our target customers and develop the ability to anticipate their needs and desires. The trick is to maintain the balance between our youngest target customer who is 18 and the nearly 25-30-year olds who are still shopping with us."

Qualifications for Buyer and Designer

"The most important qualification for those who want to be either a buyer or designer is to be very enthusiastic about the customer they will be servicing. You have to understand the customer and be passionate about their interests. You have to know the customer well enough to know what they want before they do. Success in this business requires the ability to make the distinction between an idea that is merely 'trendy' and a trend that is truly relevant to your customer.

"A buyer needs to be left and right brain-oriented. They must be able to manage a business that has competing priorities while simultaneously exerting a good deal of creative energy. It requires an unusual skill balance to be a person who can really do both, but that's the person who will be the most successful. A successful designer needs to be focused and reasonably well organized, but a high level of creativity is the most required skill. The ability to manage creative flow into the constraints of the design calendar is the most linear aspect of our design work. We also expect our designers to excel at teamwork. They need to be able to work successfully in tandem with the buyer to meet the needs of the business."

Technology

"In today's market you need the systems support to be able to quickly and continuously service your customers. For a business that operates in multiple and diverse markets it is imperative to use allocation and planning tools that can provide exception reporting. Isolating the hits and the misses on a weekly basis allows a buyer to capitalize on suc-

(continued)

cesses and correct weaknesses to maximize profitability.

"Technology also plays an important role in design and production work. Tools such as Web-based PDM and CAD help to significantly streamline the more technical aspects of the design and manufacturing process. Web-based PDM functions as an on-line database. The design and production teams as well as agents and manufacturers are all able to view the most up-to-date status of a product simultaneously. This significantly reduces the amount of mistakes, streamlines the communication flow, and ultimately increases the speed of product to market."

Executive Perspective 6.4

Jay Gardner Experience—senior vice president of production, QA and NBD, Macy's Merchandising Group

Process of Private Label Product Development

"Our product development process is basically the same as an apparel manufacturer. The only difference is that we have a lot more input from retail because we're a retailer. We have more studies and more information available to us than an apparel manufacturer does.

"Each of our business areas has a vice president who has a full design staff, full merchandising staff, full product development staff, and its own technical design staff for support in areas like spec-ing and grading. We have design teams for every family of business. We have a fashion office that's like a major retailing or designing consultant that a manufacturer would have. This is where we get our fashion direction along with the design services and color services."

Product Managers

"Our product managers perform the same basic functions as the merchandisers in an apparel company. They must keep a pulse on what's selling in the marketplace from competitors as well as knowing the fashion direction for each of our five divisions. They must understand regional demands and needs because we have stores in Florida and Seattle and there's a different mindset and different product requirements for those areas of the country.

"The product managers are responsible for determining what the line should be as far as categories of product and the number of styles in the line. We have deliveries twice a month and create five seasons a year: spring, summer, holiday, fall I, and fall II.

"Product managers give the designers direction based upon what's selling in the marketplace and feedback on color, fabrication, and price points. Once the lines are developed, the product managers work collectively with our seven major overseas offices in sourcing the products to determine who can best produce each style at the optimum price points."

Costing

"The product managers are involved in the costing of each style. We don't have a cost sheet that's as intense as those used by merchandisers at apparel manufacturers. We don't go down to yardage yields and specific trim and findings costs. We compare FOB prices to previous similar styles, but we're working on

(continued)

making ourselves more of a manufacturer when it comes to costing."

Control Tools

"We utilize a merchandising or development calendar to keep our product development and sourcing activities on schedule. We also provide a line plan summary to our design staff so they don't over assort.

"We very carefully determine the correct balance of goods for our store assortments. The buyers place their orders a week after each buy meeting at which they are presented the lines. Then there is a collaborative effort to assure the orders meet the needs of each division. Once we accumulate the orders, we look at the assortments to decide whether each division has the right product mixes, right quantity mix, right color mix. This is usually a three-week process. After the orders are entered, we analyze them for a week; then, during the second week, we discuss them with each division; and during the third week, the orders are finalized and placed with the factories overseas."

Sourcing

"Ninety-eight percent of our products are sourced full-package. We are currently working on buying fabric and developing some new products from the ground up. We supply our sourcing partners with pattern blocks by category or family of business. We have five different ladies' fits for our brands. These fit standards relate to each brand because the brands deal with different lifestyles.

"We have our own quality control people. They inspect the goods at the factory sites, getting our merchandise over here—and if it doesn't meet our quality standards, it is of no value to us or our sourcing partners.

"Sourcing is a collaboration with our vendors. For our everyday value program there are replenishment items. These products can be replenished from within our own warehouse or through quick response with the factory producing them. Then there are hot items, which sell very quickly. If we decide to replenish these, due to time constraints we may go to a special importer or make the products here domestically so we can get them back into our stores quickly. Three-quarters of the line we get in and get out of. There's only 25 percent that we try to replenish or what we call back tracking.

"Sourcing in today's market is truly a collaboration. Twice a year we develop a schematic called a supplier categorization where we prepare analysis reports on each factory for the entire year. We use that to control our vendor base so that we don't have an excessive number of vendors. We want to be important to a small, but high quality vendor group."

Skills Needed

"We bring in recent college graduates as product assistants. In this

(continued)

entry-level position, it is very important for them to understand how to operate using an event calendar and scheduling techniques. The ability to partner and work in a team environment is critical. They also need to have a basic knowledge of the manufacturing process. Factory visits would be an important part of that education.

"Our staff should have mastered the skills needed for computerized pattern making. We don't do any manual pattern making today. Everything's done by computer. Our pattern makers know both manual and computerized pattern making, but they prepare all of our patterns via computer so we can e-mail the patterns to the factories the next day.

"New technologies are important to be successful in today's market. To us, speed to market is key. We are working with computer systems specialists to develop 2-D and 3-D software to eventually allow us to do fittings online. We are also working with computerized measuring tapes. We're heavily into color management where all of our color matching is done digitally. If we can turn products faster and get things moving quicker, we're going to take every new avenue we can."

Logistics

"We're very sophisticated in logistics. We have to deliver products to five different areas of the country. We have a tight shipping schedule that's very complex. We have deadlines at each area of the country that we must meet every Friday.

"All of the factories we work with are already up to speed or ahead of Homeland Security guidelines. Our requirements for compliance cover all government regulations. Whatever requirements customs has in place from port of exit, our containers have it. From the time they leave a facility, they're locked with a seal, with a code, and they're not opened until they get here. They're in full compliance."

Summary

Efforts to shorten cycle times and the complex nature of the process have made planning and controlling line development more difficult. Computer-based merchandising calendars utilizing CPM planning methods are necessary tools for the effective merchandiser. Relational database PIMs are another sophisticated tool used by merchandisers to control the development and flow of data throughout the line development process. It has become apparent that today's apparel merchandisers must be adept at using computer applications to keep up with the rapid pace of product changes and increasing consumer demands.

The line development process begins with comprehensive market research, trend analysis, and data collection. Merchandisers must spend a part of every workday gathering and analyzing data about their target market. They must determine consumer preferences, track consumer purchases, and test new products concepts.

Merchandisers must also perform in-depth research to determine styling direction for colors, fabrics, trims, and silhouettes. This fashion trend research is the foundation for effective line development.

Merchandising oversees and directs the line development process. To keep the line development design team focused on the company's market strategies for product and brand positioning, the merchandiser creates a line plan. This detailed formula sets forth the parameters for the product line. The plan is based upon the ideal number of SKUs that should be in the line to achieve the company's projected dollar sales volume. It is further broken down by product group into the number of styles, fabrics, colors, and sizes per group. The plan must be balanced by price ranges, geographic sales areas, and fashion content. The line plan becomes the road map for the product development team to create new styles for the line.

The creative process involved in line development is influenced by the work environment, which is established by the merchandiser. Providing ease of interaction between line development team members and proper studio space can result in synergy and more enhanced product styling. Through periodic executive line reviews and constant monitoring of the progress of the design team, the merchandiser can allow the designers to focus on the creative aspects of product development. This role of applying business sense and control to the creative process without stifling creativity is an important merchandising responsibility.

Throughout the product development phase of line development, accurate and speedy information flow is critical. This information begins with designer style sheets, which are created when silhouettes and fabrics are combined, and continues through prototyping, pre-costing, product engineering, specification development, final costing, and final adoption. In today's fast-paced computer-driven marketplace, apparel merchandising must embrace the latest technologies in order to maintain a competitive edge in line development.

Key Terms

blocks	fabric-driven
care label	final costing
costing for sale	final line adoption
croquis	fit model
draping	flat pattern
executive line reviews	line sheet
precosting	silhouette-driven
product development	slopers
product engineering	style boards
prototype	vertical retailers
quick costing	

Discussion Questions and Learning Activities

1. What factors make controlling the line development process so difficult? Explain why this is the case.
2. Discuss the differences in the line development process for a small, designer price-range fashion company such as William Calvert (Chapter 5) and a large megacompany such as Liz Claiborne or Macy's.
3. As the merchandiser for a small to midsized, rapidly growing apparel company with one designer, two sample hands, and a shared secretary, what staffing changes might you consider to cope with your company's growth?
4. What could be sources of inspiration for a design team for an active sportswear company focusing on soccer clothing? Explain your reasoning.
5. Based upon the direction of today's apparel industry, what areas of expertise do you think will gain in importance for apparel merchandisers or product managers?
6. Visit a department store and locate a group of products from a single apparel company or private label that represents a specific theme. Identify the theme and the design elements that carry that theme throughout the group.
7. Discuss the importance of staying within the line plan when creating an apparel line.

8. Discuss the different problems associated with prototyping for a company that manufactures in its own domestic factories versus a company that sources all its production to global contractors. What steps can be taken by a global sourcing company to make its prototyping process easier and faster?

9. Discuss the effect on the line development process if the prototyping function has fallen behind schedule by two weeks. What steps can be taken by the merchandiser to keep the process on schedule for final adoption?

10. Discuss the differences in merchandising philosophy and practice between the merchandisers in Executive Perspectives 6.1 and 6.2.

11. Research the World Wide Web for technologies that could improve the cycle time or control of the line development process.

References and Resources

Burns, Leslie Davis; Bryant, Nancy O. 1997. *The Business of Fashion*. New York: Fairchild Publications.

D'Innocenzio, Anne. May 21, 1999. Liz Claiborne Shifting Merchandising Focus. *Women's Wear Daily*, p. 2, 14.

Edelson, Sharon. June 20, 2005. What Drives Consumers In? *www.wwd.com*.

Ellis, Kristi. January 21, 1999. Esprit Turns It Around, Outlines Aggressive Program for Growth. *Women's Wear Daily*, p. 18.

Frings, Gini Stephens. 1996. *Fashion from Concept to Consumer*. New Jersey: Prentice-Hall, Inc.

Kletter, Melanie. February 11, 1999. Jones Scores 34% Net Hike, Plans Picone Move to Moderate. *Women's Wear Daily*, p. 18.

Lewis, Robin. February 12, 1998. Consumers at Apex of VF Vision. *Women's Wear Daily*, p. 8–9.

Ostroff, Jim. May 12, 1998. AAMA Paley Told: Satisfy Consumers. *Women's Wear Daily*, p. 2, 4.

Tate, Sharon Lee. 1999. *Inside Fashion Design*. New York: Addison Wesley Longman, Inc.

Zimmerman, Kim Ann. November 4, 1998. Calvin: Specs Go On Line. *Women's Wear Daily*, p. 16.

CHAPTER 7

Costing and Pricing Strategies

OBJECTIVES

- Examine the pricing formula.

- Discuss the strategies used to determine wholesale and retail selling prices of garment styles.

- Analyze the costing principles and the elements that make up cost of goods and general operating expenses.

- Explore costing strategies and their effects on product mixes.

The pace of the fashion business continues to quicken as styles change rapidly and competition heats up in all product categories. The pressure on merchandisers to create successful lines increases with each new season. There is a wide variety of measurements used to determine the success of apparel lines. For example some companies focus on:

- **Gross margin (GM)**, also referred to as **markup**, is net sales minus the total cost of goods sold.
- **Gross margin return on inventory (GMROI)** is gross margin divided by average inventory investment.
- **Adjusted gross margin (AGM)** is gross margin minus inventory carrying costs plus distribution costs.
- **Maintained (margin) markup** is the final markup that is based upon all of the merchandise that has been sold at all prices compared to the cost of the merchandise.
- **Required departmental markup** is the required markup for the department that establishes the profit that must be generated after deducting the costs of the merchandise and the cost of all other expenses.
- Sell-through is the percentage of the units in a line that sold through the normal distribution channel to the ultimate consumers at the suggested retail selling price before being marked down. This measure of success captures the desirability of an apparel line to the retail merchants and the ultimate consumers, but does not directly address profitability.

Unfortunately, gross margins and sell-through are only individual elements in determining the ultimate success of an apparel company. As with most business enterprises, **net income**, or the amount of revenue earned beyond the related costs incurred for an accounting period, is the prime determinant of success.

Total sales for a period determine revenues, but it is often the related costs that determine the profit or loss generated by an apparel line. The apparel merchandiser usually has the responsibility for **pricing**, establishing the wholesale selling price for each garment style in the line. In order to effectively determine price, the merchandiser must accurately perform **costing**, calculating how much each style costs to produce. The product manager of private brands is also involved in determining price. According to the Research Study of 2002 (Appendix 3), the product manager had a higher degree of responsibility for maintaining profit margins than the apparel merchandiser.

"The costing of a product for apparel manufacturing is one of the most important planning functions performed within a company. Direct and indirect costs have a definite influence on the quantity of products sold, and in turn, profits and losses are directly proportional to the quantities produced and the accuracy of the product costing" (Faber, 1991).

Mastery of pricing and costing is critical to success for an apparel merchandiser in today's fast-paced, global marketplace. E. Lee Griffith III, formerly a principal at Kurt Salmon Associates, identifies bottom line financial responsibility as a key component of the merchandiser's job. "A merchandiser should be responsible for a few key elements of a company's success. Gross margin and profit are important. I like to see merchandisers responsible for inventory and essentially be an SBU [strategic business unit] manager of a part of the business. They're responsible for putting together a line, adopting it, making it coherent to have a statement to the market place, forecasting it, procuring it, inventorying it, marking it down, disposing of the inventory at the end of the season, and achieving the company target gross margin on the line as well. I think it's very important for the merchant to have gross profit or financial responsibility. Danger signs are when you've got merchants that don't have to answer to a bottom line, don't have to answer to a profit or gross margin goal."

■ The Pricing Formula

The formula for success in the apparel industry is governed by the pricing formula: *cost of goods + markup = wholesale selling price*.

1. **Cost of goods** includes materials plus direct labor plus factory overhead. Cost of goods includes all costs required to produce a garment. For companies that use domestic contractors to manufacture their garments, the cost of goods is the full package price charged by the contractor or the **cut, make, and trim** (**CMT**) price plus the cost of materials. Companies that manufacture their garments offshore must use the **landed duty paid** (**LDP**) cost of each style. This cost includes the price paid to the contract manufacturer for CMT plus materials or the full package of labor and materials, plus the freight cost to get the product from the foreign factory to the U.S. distribution center, plus import duties and any associated brokerage expenses. Most private brand merchandise today is sourced as full-package and the retailer's sourcing department will negotiate the cost of goods. Some companies use **807**, the original title of the U.S. Customs category that allows garments to be cut in the United States from U.S. textiles and assembled in a foreign country with duty charged only on the value added in the foreign country. This 807-type assembly requires a combination of domestic cutting and offshore contract manufacturing cost calculations.

2. **Markup** (**gross margin**) includes marketing and selling costs plus product development costs plus distribution costs plus general and

administrative costs plus profit. The costs involved in markup can be represented as a percentage of the wholesale selling price. The sales commission is based upon a percentage (2 percent to 10 percent) of the selling price. Profit is planned as a percentage of gross sales, which is the sum of the wholesale selling prices of all garments sold. Marketing, product development, distribution, and general and administrative costs are budgeted expenses that can also be represented as a percentage of gross sales, which again can be related to the wholesale selling price.

3. **Wholesale selling price** is the price the manufacturer or contractor charges the retailer or wholesaler for each garment. To complicate the pricing process, some garment categories, especially women's wear, include a discount in the wholesale selling price, which results in a **wholesale net selling price**. These discounts are included in the **payment terms** such as "8/10 net 30" offered by traditional women's wear companies. This means that an 8 percent discount is given if the total invoice amount is paid within 10 days; the total invoice net amount is due within 30 days. There is also a policy of dating used by some companies. **Dating** delays payment for 60 or even 90 days. Companies must be extremely careful when determining the effect of discounts or dating on their pricing formula. Discounts could reduce total revenues, and dating could increase administrative costs that are needed for paying interest on operating capital.

Figure 7.1 shows an example of wholesale selling price calculations for a product without a sales discount. Figure 7.2 shows the calculations for the same product with a sales discount. A shortcut to calculating the wholesale selling price using the pricing formula is: cost of goods ÷ reciprocal of markup = wholesale selling price. The reciprocal of markup is 100 percent minus the markup percentage, that is, the reciprocal of a 33 percent markup is 100 percent minus 33 percent = 67 percent. Therefore, the wholesale selling price of a garment with a cost of goods equal to $18 and a markup of 33 percent is $18 ÷ 67 percent = $27.

No matter how the pricing formula is adjusted to accommodate different manufacturing methods, sales discounts, and company structures, it must always cover all the costs that are generated within the company. If all associated costs are not covered in the pricing formula, the result is reduced profit or possibly a financial loss. The merchandiser must work closely with the financial department and manufacturing in structuring the formula to address the needs of marketing, product development, and manufacturing as well as the overall financial accounting requirements of the company. The end result of this effort can be analyzed in the profit or loss generated by the company.

FIGURE 7.1   **PRICING FORMULA—NO SALES DISCOUNT**

A women's dress has the following cost of goods:

1. Fabric	$ 6.27
2. Trimming	1.33
3. Labor and overhead	6.85
Cost of goods	$14.45

The company markup, or gross profit margin, is 34%.

The merchandiser uses the pricing formula: **cost of goods + markup = wholesale selling price (WSP).** Since the markup is a percent of the wholesale selling price (34% markup = 34% wholesale selling price), the formula becomes:

Cost of goods + 34% WSP = WSP

$$\underline{\qquad\qquad -34\% \text{ WSP} = -34\% \text{ WSP}}$$

Cost of goods   = 66% WSP

$14.45   = 66% WSP

$$\underline{\div 66\% \qquad = \div 66\%}$$

$14.45 ÷ .66 = WSP

Wholesale selling price = $21.90

Calculation of the wholesale selling price with no sales discount using the formula: Cost of Goods + Markup = Wholesale Selling Price.

The company **income statement** or **profit and loss statement** is the financial statement that relates the company's sales revenues (the sum of the wholesale selling prices multiplied by the number of units sold) to expenses (the sum of the cost of goods and markup less profit) resulting in a profit or loss for a specific period. The simplified income statement in Figure 7.3 illustrates the effect of the elements covered in our sample pricing formula on the profitability of the company.

The actual gross profit margin (markup) of 38 percent achieved by the company during the period of the profit and loss statement is greater than the 34 percent markup used in the pricing formula. This indicates that either the cost of goods or the general operating expenses could be lower than were estimated when the pricing formula was established, or that sales were greater than anticipated for that period. Increased sales volume creates additional revenue that may not be needed to absorb certain fixed costs and therefore results in increased profit. The effect of sales volume on the pricing formula used by a company is an important factor in pricing strategies.

FIGURE 7.2	**PRICING FORMULA—SALES DISCOUNT**

A women's dress has the following cost of goods:

1. Fabric $ 6.27
2. Trimming   1.33
3. Labor and overhead   6.85
   Cost of goods $14.45

The company markup, or gross profit margin, is 34%.

The retail buyers expect an 8% discount on all orders.

The company's 8% discount must be included in the wholesale selling price (WSP) calculation. The company will actually be paid a **wholesale net selling price,** which is the WSP − 8% WSP. Because the 8% discount must be included in the wholesale selling price calculation, the formula becomes:

Cost of goods + 34% (WSP − 8% WSP) = WSP − 8%WSP

Cost of goods + 34% (.92WSP) = .92WSP

Cost of goods + .3128WSP = .92WSP
                   −.3128WSP = −.3128WSP
Cost of goods   = .6072WSP

$14.45   = .6072WSP
÷.6072   = ÷.6072
$14.45 ÷ .6072 = WSP

$23.80 = WSP

The wholesale net selling price = $23.80 − 8% = $21.90
[The actual revenue from the sale of the garment in Figures 7.1 and 7.2 is the same amount, $21.90, yielding the same gross profit ($21.90 − $14.45) of $7.45 and gross profit margin ($7.45 ÷ $21.90) of 34%.]

Calculation of the wholesale selling price with an 8 percent discount using the formula: Cost of Goods + Markup = Wholesale Selling Price.

■ Pricing Strategies

Garment pricing in apparel companies is the calculation and determination of a wholesale selling price for a garment style that will meet the needs and expectations of customers and generate the intended profit for the company. This process involves both calculation, which is objective, and determination, which contains a subjective element.

FIGURE 7.3	SIMPLIFIED PROFIT AND LOSS STATEMENT

Category		Period Amount	% of Net Sales
Net sales		$25,800,000	100%
Cost of goods			
Materials	$8,320,000		
Direct labor	4,160,000		
Indirect labor	420,000		
Factory overhead	3,210,000		
Total		$16,110,000	62%
Gross profit margin (markup)		$ 9,690,000	38%
General operating expenses			
Selling costs	$2,064,000		
Design costs	2,322,000		
Distribution costs	1,032,000		
General and admin.	2,064,000		
Total		$ 7,482,000	29%
Net operating profit or (loss) for period		$ 2,208,000	9%

A simplified profit and loss statement showing net sales, cost of goods, gross profit margin, general operating expenses, and net profit or loss. The figures are shown in both dollars and percentages of net sales.

Garment pricing of private brands is somewhat different. Product managers will establish their retailing selling price based upon the needs of their consumers; and from there they determine what they can pay suppliers based upon their required margin.

Rigid Calculation

Some apparel companies abide by a calculation process that incorporates a rigid pricing formula to determine prices similar to those in the examples in Figures 7.1 and 7.2. This method assumes all cost data and sales expectations will be consistent with the estimates used to develop:

- Variable direct labor and material costs.
- Variable and fixed factory overhead.
- Variable and fixed costs included in markup or gross margin.

This process is often adequate for basic styles. However, as companies move toward alternate marketing, looking to expand their current market or add new markets and products, this formulaic approach may not be the most effective means of pricing new products.

Later in this chapter we discuss a process involving a more detailed analysis of all activities related to a specific style or group of styles that is used to allocate the cost of these activities in determining product pricing.

Subjective Pricing

When evaluating new products or developing strategies for increasing and protecting market share, merchandisers could consider **subjective pricing**, or pricing according to what the market will bear. This process allows the merchandiser to evaluate the following market factors when setting the price of a new garment style:

- The current selling prices of similar competitive styles.
- The uniqueness of the style compared to competitors' products.
- The current value of the product brand as it influences consumer willingness to pay a premium for brand status.
- Current consumer advertising or packaging plans for the style that could result in powerful **pull-through marketing** (promotion designed to get customers to search out and request specific products).
- The relative effect of price on potential sales volume.
- Current market trends.

Product managers must also consider these factors when establishing their retail selling prices.

When using subjective pricing, the merchandiser calculates the price of a product using the company's pricing formula and then adjusts the price up or down depending on market conditions. Adjusting a price upward can increase the earned markup and potential profits. Adjusting a price downward can increase the sales volume of marginal products and therefore increase revenues, which enables the company to absorb more fixed costs and thus increase potential profits. If, however, the merchandiser does not have an intimate knowledge of a particular market, errors in subjective pricing can lead to either reduced sales (if the price is higher than what the market can bear) or decreased markup (if a lowered price does not result in the expected increase in sales).

Merchandisers must be extremely careful to evaluate the effect of subjective pricing on both the product being priced and overhead and fixed gross margin costs. Because subjective pricing deviates from the rigid calculation process that takes into consideration all costs and expected profits based upon specific sales expectations, careful evaluation of the overall effect of this process on covering all fixed costs must be made. The merchandiser must calculate the effect of each subjective pricing decision on the projected gross margin contribution made by the adjusted expected sales. Figure 7.4

FIGURE 7.4	SUBJECTIVE PRICING EXAMPLE

Shirt style 1001:

Wholesale selling price	$20
Gross margin contribution of $6.80	34%
Expected sales volume	10,000 units
Total projected gross margin contribution	$68,000

Using subjective pricing, the merchandiser decides the wholesale selling price of style 1001 should be $18 to be competitive in the current market.

At a wholesale selling price of $18, the gross margin contribution would be reduced to $4.80 per unit or $48,000 for 10,000 units resulting in a $20,000 shortfall to cover budgeted fixed costs.

To price style 1001 at $18 and still meet earnings objectives requires one of the following:

1. Style 1001 must sell at least 14,167 units at the reduced price to make up for the lost gross margin contribution of $20,000 (14,167 x $4.80 = $68,000).

or

2. Other styles in the line must be priced higher than the standard pricing calculation to generate an additional gross margin contribution of $20,000.

If the pricing of an apparel product is reduced below the calculated wholesale selling price based on the competition, a merchandiser must consider effects on the gross margin contribution of that style and the entire line. In order to maintain planned seasonal earnings, either an increased quantity must be sold or the balance of the line must be priced higher to generate additional gross margins.

shows an example of the decisions that must be made to effectively use subjective pricing.

Subjective pricing can be a dangerous practice when it is applied by someone without an intimate knowledge of a company's market and should be used only by highly skilled merchandisers as part of a comprehensive company strategic plan.

Pricing Variables

The variables that have the greatest effect on pricing are *volume* and *costing*. If actual sales volume is less than the volume estimated to calculate selling prices, the result is lower revenues. Lower revenues in turn do not generate expected gross margin contributions or absorb all fixed factory overhead. Similarly, if costs are not accurately calculated or estimated, the result will be inappropriate prices. Prices that are higher than what the market can bear can result in reduced sales. Prices that are too low may not generate expected gross margin contributions. All these conditions can result in less than expected profits or even losses.

Merchandisers must be able to accurately project sales volumes by style and precisely estimate company costs in order to competitively price their product lines. This requires an effective system for sales forecasting and comprehensive accounting procedures for capturing and allocating costs.

■ Costing Principles

Pricing strategies can be effective only if the underlying cost bases are accurate. This requires precise accumulation and allocation of all costs that are reported in a company's financial statements. These costs are summarized in *cost of goods* and *general operating expenses*.

Cost of Goods

Cost of goods is all expenses involved in the manufacture of an apparel product. Under generally accepted accounting principles, the manufacturing costs are regarded as measures of assets and therefore can be viewed as inventory. If a company is sourcing its products through domestic or international contract manufacturers, as is the case with most private brands, the cost of goods is based upon the contract agreement. If a company is buying a finished package including labor and materials, the landed duty paid (LDP) price becomes the cost of goods. If a company is contracting for cut, make, and trim (CMT) only, the cost of goods would be the CMT price plus the cost of materials. If a company is using its own factories for manufacturing, it must determine the cost of goods based upon the company cost basis as defined by its accounting system. The cost of goods is summarized under the categories of *direct materials*, *direct labor*, and *manufacturing overhead*.

Direct Materials
Direct materials include fabric, thread, trim, and findings. The quantity of each material required for a garment style must be accurately measured. The prototyping process provides an opportunity for determining the quantities for each direct material. The results are recorded in the bill of materials as part of developing a style sheet or specification sheet for new garment styles.

Fabric is the most costly material in most garment styles. Accurately determining the amount of fabric required for a new style is essential. The most accurate method is to create a cutting marker using the appropriate size scale. The **size scale** is the ratio of sales per size for a style. A size scale of $2 \cdot 3 \cdot 2 \cdot 1$ indicates that for every 2 smalls that are sold, 3 mediums, 2 larges, and 1 extra large are sold. The size scale usually determines how many sets of each size pattern are included in a typical marker. To accurately determine the average amount of fabric needed for a garment style requires creating a marker for the style using the size scale and the fabric width. With today's computer-aided pattern design software (PDS) and marker making systems, this process has become relatively easy. With appropriate grade rules for creating all pattern sizes based upon the sample size, when the sample pattern set has been created, the PDS system can quickly create sets of all patterns for each size and a marker maker can create a sample marker from which the average fabric requirements can be determined. The software also calculates the **material utilization**, the percentage of fabric utilized in cutting the garment parts. By analyzing the material utilization against the company standards for similar styles, a merchandiser can decide whether a new style should be reviewed for possible pattern engineering to reduce the fabric requirements.

There are many garment pattern design systems and product development software packages available for calculating materials requirements and creating garment specification databases. Gerber Garment Technology and Lectra Systèmes provide suites of programs to create and grade patterns, develop markers to determine material utilization for shell and lining fabrics, and create data management databases of material requirements for each style in a line. Freeborders, Justwin Apparel, New Generation Computing, Byte Software, Porini, and Exact Software also market data management systems for developing garment specification databases.

Another factor that must be considered by merchandisers when determining fabric costs is **minimum order quantities**. Most textile companies require minimum order quantities for each style and color. If a specific fabric requires 1.5 yards per garment and the minimum order quantity is 1,000 yards, then the merchandiser must be confident that each color ordered in that style will sell at least 667 units ($1,000 \div 1.5$). For this reason, many merchandisers use a specific fabric style and the same range of colors for multiple garment styles.

For all other direct materials such as trim, thread, buttons, zippers, labels, shoulder pads, and poly bags, quantities per garment are measured in units, sets, or yards. For these materials, minimum order quantities must also be considered. Waste factors are calculated to accommodate buttons that are dropped or broken and materials that get soiled or damaged during the manufacturing process. Most companies establish a waste percentage that gets applied to the total cost of these direct materials.

Season: SPRING 2005

Control	Date	Initial	Garment:		Sample	Style
Submitted			1 Piece Dress		No. 1007	No. 4260
Received			Description:			
Estimated			Zipper back princess line shift w/tie			
Adopted						

Piece Goods: / **MATERIAL COST**

Description	Mill Number	Width	Unit Cost	Yardage Est.	Std.	Actual	Cost Est.	Std.	Actual
Sunflower Print									
100% Rayon	10097	54"	$2.85	2.2			$6.27		
				Total Piece Goods Cost			$6.27		

Trim and Findings:

Item	Source	Style No.	Unit	Unit Cost	Quantity Est.	Std.	Actual	Cost Est.	Std.	Actual
Zipper	ABC	22"	100	$48.00	1			0.48		
Ribbon Tie	XYZ	3244	Yd.	$0.45	1.3			0.59		
Label	Trimco	8650	1	$0.15	1			0.15		
Care Label	Trimco	2285	1	$0.02	1			0.02		
Thread	Threadco	2685	6000yd	$5.25	22			0.02		

Garment Sketch

	Total	$1.26	
	Add: Waste Factor	5%	
	Total Trim and Findings	$1.33	

MANUFACTURING COST

Dept.	O.H. Factor	Direct Labor Est.	Std.	Actual	Direct Labor + Overhead Est.	Std.	Actual
Cut	160%						
Sew	205%						
Finish	170%						
Total Manufacturing Cost							

TOTAL COST OF GOODS

GROSS MARGIN CALCULATION

	Est.	Std.	Actual
Wholesale Selling Price			
Less 8% Discount			
Wholesale Net Selling Price			
Gross Margin $			
Gross Margin %			

Comments

Figure 7.5 A cost calculation sheet showing the cost of all material and trim for style 4260.

The cost calculation sheet in Figure 7.5 shows the direct materials calculations for a sleeveless shift dress.

Direct Labor

Direct labor includes those costs that change the condition or physical appearance of raw materials. Examples of direct labor functions are cutting, bundling, folding, sewing, and finishing. Under this definition, bundle handling or moving a bundle of garment parts from one workstation to another would not be considered direct labor because the raw materials are in the same condition when they arrive at the second workstation as they were when they left the first workstation.

Labor standards should be determined for each style. These standards are calculated in time units as **standard allowed minutes (SAMs)** for each operation required to produce a specific style. The standard time for a given operation in SAMs is the time required for an average operator, fully qualified, trained, and working at a normal pace, to perform the operation (Niebel, 1960).

SAMs include allowances for personal time, reduction in production performance due to fatigue, and normally expected work delays, which are classified as **personal, fatigue, and delay (PF&D)** time. The SAMs required to perform an operation should not change unless methods or equipment change. SAMs can easily be converted to costs by applying earnings objectives. For example, if an operation is calculated to take .86 SAMs per unit to complete and the earnings objective is $9.00 per hour, the direct labor cost for that operation is $9.00 per hour ÷ 60 minutes × .86 SAM = $0.129 per unit. For operations that are on **piece rate**, the operators are paid a fixed price for each piece they produce. Using the example above, the operators would be paid a piece rate of $0.129 per unit for that operation. For costing purposes, the advantage of a piece-rate payment system is that the direct labor cost per unit is fixed as opposed to an hourly wage system where the labor cost per unit varies depending on worker productivity.

When measuring direct labor costs using standard labor hours and piece rates, it is important to make adjustments to account for off-standard manufacturing time and ancillary costs. Operator training, machine downtime, waiting for work, and overtime premiums are examples of these cost adjustments. Many companies use historical company accounting data to determine the amount of off-standard direct labor costs as a percentage of earned direct labor. This percentage is then included in the overall factory overhead percentage.

Software packages have been developed to assist in the labor estimate for new garments. Methods Workshop (**www.methodsworkshop.com**) offers Quick TruCost©, which provides labor costs within 10 percent accuracy based upon answers to 8-16 questions about the construction of the individual style.

Season: SPRING 2005		**COST CALCULATION SHEET**

Control	Date	Initial	Garment:		Sample		Style	
Submitted			1 Piece Dress		No.	1007	No.	4260
Received			Description:					
Estimated			Zipper back princess line shift w/tie					
Adopted								

MATERIAL COST

Piece Goods:									
Description	Mill Number	Width	Unit Cost	Yardage Est.	Std.	Actual	Cost Est.	Std.	Actual
Sunflower Print									
100% Rayon	10097	54"	$2.85	2.2			$6.27		
				Total Piece Goods Cost			$6.27		

Trim and Findings:									
Item	Source	Style No.	Unit	Unit Cost	Quantity Est.	Std.	Actual	Cost Est.	Std.	Actual
Zipper	ABC	22"	100	$48.00	1			0.48		
Ribbon Tie	XYZ	3244	Yd.	$0.45	1.3			0.59		
Label	Trimco	8650	1	$0.15	1			0.15		
Care Label	Trimco	2285	1	$0.02	1			0.02		
Thread	Threadco	2685	6000yd	$5.25	22			0.02		
Garment Sketch			Total					$1.26		
			Add: Waste Factor					5%		
			Total Trim and Findings					$1.33		

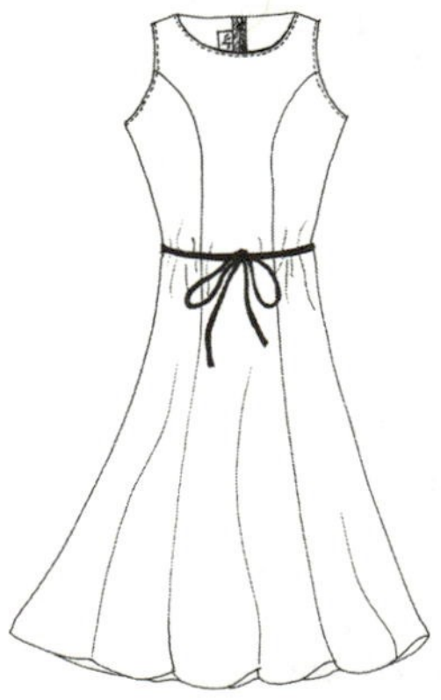

MANUFACTURING COST

Dept.	O.H. Factor	Direct Labor Est.	Std.	Actual	Direct Labor + Overhead Est.	Std.	Actual
Cut	160%	0.62			0.99		
Sew	205%	2.40			4.92		
Finish	170%	0.55			0.94		
Total Manufacturing Cost					$6.85		

TOTAL COST OF GOODS	$14.45		

GROSS MARGIN CALCULATION

	Est.	Std.	Actual
Wholesale Selling Price			
Less 8% Discount			
Wholesale Net Selling Price			
Gross Margin $			
Gross Margin %			

Comments

Figure 7.6 A cost calculation sheet showing the total cost of material, trim, and labor (including factory overhead) for style 4260.

Manufacturing Overhead

Manufacturing overhead includes all the costs of manufacturing except direct materials and direct labor. Some of these costs are variable in that they increase or decrease in direct proportion to production volume, and some are fixed in that they remain unchanged relative to production volume. The fixed portion of manufacturing overhead is more closely related to the capacity to produce than to the production of specific garments. Examples of variable manufacturing overhead are machine oil, sewing needles, a portion of power, and machine parts. Fixed overhead costs are property taxes, depreciation of factory facilities, light, heat, indirect labor such as supervision and bundle handlers, building maintenance, and other costs of operating the factory. In reality, some of these costs are part fixed and part variable. At some point during increased production volume, additional bundle handlers or supervisors may be necessary. Management must ultimately decide how to categorize and allocate these types of costs.

There is a variety of methods available for allocating manufacturing overhead. It is difficult in apparel manufacturing to accurately allocate variable overhead to specific products. Many companies combine variable and fixed manufacturing overhead in one overhead pool, which is allocated to products either on a per unit basis or as a percentage of direct labor.

Figure 7.6 shows the manufacturing cost of the sleeveless shift dress (from Figure 7.5) by calculating direct labor and overhead percentages by department and allocating overhead as a percentage of direct labor. The sum of total piece goods costs, total trim and findings, and total manufacturing costs equals the total cost of goods for the sleeveless shift dress.

General Operating Expenses

All costs over and above those included in the total cost of goods of a product are **general operating expenses**, which are referred to by some companies as **general and administrative expenses** (**G&A**). These costs can be broken down into *marketing and selling expenses*; *merchandising, design*, or *product development expenses*; *distribution expenses*; and *administrative expenses*.

Marketing and Selling Expenses

Marketing and selling expenses include all costs required to secure garment orders and deliver the garments to the customer. Some examples are advertising, sales salaries and commissions, sales travel and entertainment, showroom expenses, finished goods warehousing, and shipping. For many apparel companies that do business with large retail chains, this category of costs has grown to include compensation for certain markdowns taken by their customers, special in-store department expenses, advertising rebates, and a growing list of guarantees requested by the retailers to protect them from eroding gross retail margins.

Merchandising, Design, or Product Development Expenses

Merchandising includes a wide variety of costs associated with the development, execution, and delivery of the product line. Product development costs for design and sampling, product engineering, quality assurance, specification writing, sourcing, and costing may all fall under this category. This category is one of the most difficult to budget since constantly changing market demands can dramatically alter product development costs and global sourcing requirements.

Distribution Expenses

Warehousing the finished goods inventory, picking and packing customer orders, and shipping are included in distribution expenses. Quick response and just-in-time manufacturing systems are dramatically reducing distribution costs for many companies by shrinking warehouse space and allowing some manufacturers to pack and hold garments directly from the production floor.

Administrative Expenses

Administrative expenses include executive, organizational, and clerical costs that do not logically fit under cost of goods, marketing, merchandising, or distribution. These costs include executive compensation and accounting, secretarial, legal, public relations, and human resources expenses.

Figure 7.7 shows a completed cost calculation sheet for the sleeveless shift dress, which includes the general operating expenses accounted for under the gross margin calculation. In this case the company determined that it needed a gross margin of 34 percent to cover general operating expenses plus its profit objective. Periodic financial statements such as the simplified income statement in Figure 7.3 are generated to compare the actual periodic costs to the estimates used in the pricing formula. Merchandisers must constantly analyze, compare, and adjust the cost estimates to meet the changing needs of their company and the marketplace.

■ Costing Strategies

As discussed, the cost of a new style must be calculated as accurately as possible so that a marketable price can be established for the product. The merchandiser and the accountant must work together to develop a system that will allow for making effective costing and pricing decisions. **Cost accounting** bridges the gap between financial accounting and managerial accounting.

Season: SPRING 2005

COST CALCULATION SHEET

Control	Date	Initial	Garment:		Sample		Style	
Submitted				1 Piece Dress	No.	1007	No.	4260
Received			Description:					
Estimated				Zipper back princess line shift w/tie				
Adopted								

MATERIAL COST

Piece Goods:									
Description	Mill Number	Width	Unit Cost	Yardage			Cost		
				Est.	Std.	Actual	Est.	Std.	Actual
Sunflower Print									
100% Rayon	10097	54"	$2.85	2.2			$6.27		
				Total Piece Goods Cost			$6.27		

Trim and Findings:										
Item	Source	Style No.	Unit	Unit Cost	Quantity			Cost		
					Est.	Std.	Actual	Est.	Std.	Actual
Zipper	ABC	22"	100	$48.00	1			0.48		
Ribbon Tie	XYZ	3244	Yd.	$0.45	1.3			0.59		
Label	Trimco	8650	1	$0.15	1			0.15		
Care Label	Trimco	2285	1	$0.02	1			0.02		
Thread	Threadco	2685	6000yd	$5.25	22			0.02		
				Total				$1.26		
				Add: Waste Factor				5%		
				Total Trim and Findings				$1.33		

MANUFACTURING COST

Dept.	O.H. Factor	Direct Labor			Direct Labor + Overhead		
		Est.	Std.	Actual	Est.	Std.	Actual
Cut	160%	0.62			0.99		
Sew	205%	2.40			4.92		
Finish	170%	0.55			0.94		
Total Manufacturing Cost					$6.85		

TOTAL COST OF GOODS $14.45

GROSS MARGIN CALCULATION

	Est.	Std.	Actual
Wholesale Selling Price	$23.80		
Less 8% Discount	$1.90		
Wholesale Net Selling Price	$21.90	$21.90	
Gross Margin $		$7.45	
Gross Margin %		34%	

Garment Sketch

Comments

Figure 7.7 A cost calculation sheet showing the net wholesale selling price of style 4260 based upon an 8 percent discount.

Managerial accounting is concerned with providing information to *managers*—that is, to those who are *inside* an organization and who are charged with directing and controlling its operations. Contrast managerial accounting with **financial accounting**, which is concerned with providing information to stockholders, creditors, and others who are *outside* an organization (Garrison, 1994).

Cost accounting satisfies the requirements of generally accepted accounting principles required by financial accounting as well as provides important cost information used to identify, measure, and allocate costs in the costing process. In order for merchandisers to establish effective prices for new garment styles, they must have appropriate cost accounting information to establish accurate cost bases upon which to make their pricing decisions. The following are three cost accounting strategies for identification, measurement, and allocation of costs.

Direct Costing

One of the first costing strategies to be used by apparel companies was **direct costing**, sometimes referred to as **variable costing**. This method of costing applies only the variable costs directly related to labor and materials as product costs or cost of goods. All other costs such as nonvariable factory expenses, marketing, product development, and general and administrative costs are allocated through gross margins as either a fixed cost per garment or as a target gross margin percentage. This form of costing is effective for companies that manufacture staple product lines with little variation in labor, product development, and marketing costs. Basic T-shirts, dress shirts, jeans, khakis, or classic suits are candidates for this costing strategy.

Figure 7.8 shows the effect of using direct costing to price a new product being added to a basic T-shirt line. Direct costing is easy to use because it requires measuring only the variable expenses directly related to materials and labor and accumulates the rest of the costs in one large cost pool where those costs are often applied to a product on a per unit basis.

Absorption Costing

Another costing strategy is **absorption costing**, which allocates fixed manufacturing overhead to each unit of production along with variable manufacturing costs. Absorption costing treats all costs of production as product costs and therefore is also referred to as the **whole cost method**. This method of costing absorbs all fixed and variable manufacturing costs into the cost of goods, which is used to establish inventory values.

Absorption costing focuses on differentiating between manufacturing and nonmanufacturing functions. It takes into account the relative effect of vari-

| FIGURE 7.8 | **DIRECT OR VARIABLE COSTING** |

The Avant Garde T-shirt company has been using direct costing. It applies its factory overhead, general and administrative costs, and profit, which totals $472,000 for its projected 400,000 unit sales at $1.18 per unit. The cost of goods contains only direct variable costs for materials and labor.

A T-shirt has the following cost of goods:

Fabric	$ 1.10
Trimming	.50
Labor	.47
Cost of goods	$ 2.07

Markup or gross margin contribution for factory overhead, general and administrative costs, and profit	$ 1.18
Wholesale selling price	$ 3.25
Retail selling price	**$ 6.50**

The company decides to add a 3-button placket polo shirt to its product line. This transition requires new capital investment for equipment and additional marketing and product development costs of $268,000, which increases its gross margin contribution to $740,000 or $1.48 per unit at projected sales of 400,000 T-shirts and 100,000 polo shirts. Under its current direct costing system the two products would price out at:

T-shirt		Polo shirt	
Fabric	$ 1.10	Fabric	$ 1.90
Trimming	.50	Trimming	.70
Labor	.47	Labor	1.38
Cost of Goods	$ 2.07	Cost of goods	$ 3.98
Gross margin contribution	$ 1.48	Gross margin contribution	$ 1.48
Wholesale selling price	$ 3.55	Wholesale selling price	$ 5.46
Retail selling price	**$ 7.10**	Retail selling price	**$10.92**

Using direct costing to price these products would result in a 10 percent increase in the retail price of the T-shirts and therefore could price them out of the market.

This common adaptation of the method of costing known as variable or direct costing calculates the variable costs of materials and labor for each style and applies the rest of the costs including variable and fixed factory overhead on a per unit basis.

able and fixed manufacturing overhead to each style produced. Allocating these costs to the products that generate the costs gives a more equitable distribution of manufacturing overhead and doesn't burden low direct labor products with overhead generated by high direct labor products.

Figure 7.9 shows the effect of absorption costing on the new product being added to the basic T-shirt line. In this example, the variable manufacturing overhead is applied to each product as a percentage of the direct labor

---

FIGURE 7.9 **ABSORPTION COSTING**

The Avant Garde T-shirt company decides to evaluate absorption costing in introducing its 3-button placket polo shirt into its product line. This transition requires new capital investment for equipment and additional factory overhead, marketing, and product development costs.

The company calculates its variable factory overhead to be $341,000, which can be absorbed by the total direct labor cost of $326,000 for projected sales of 400,000 T-shirts and 100,000 polo shirts at the rate of 105 percent of direct labor. The cost of goods contains direct variable costs for materials and labor plus variable factory overhead.

The gross margin contribution of $400,000 for 500,000 unit sales will require increasing the markup to $ .80 per unit.

Under the absorption costing system the two products would price out at:

T-shirt		Polo shirt	
Fabric	$ 1.10	Fabric	$ 1.90
Trimming	.50	Trimming	.70
Labor	.47	Labor	1.38
Factory O.H.	.49	Factory O.H.	1.45
Cost of Goods	$ 2.56	Cost of goods	$ 5.43
Gross margin contribution	$ .80	Gross margin contribution	$ .80
Wholesale selling price	$ 3.36	Wholesale selling price	$ 6.23
Retail selling price	$ 6.72	Retail selling price	$12.46

Using absorption costing to price these products would result in a 3 percent increase in the retail price of the T-shirts, which could reduce total sales of the product depending on market conditions.

Another method of costing is absorption costing. In this strategy the cost of goods for each style includes variable materials, labor, and fixed and variable factory overhead that is allocated as a percentage of direct labor. The gross margin contribution including general and administrative costs is applied on a per unit basis. Absorption costing provides a more equitable distribution of manufacturing overhead.

generated by the product. Under absorption costing, the basic T-shirt is not carrying the overhead burden created by adding the polo shirt to the line but is still equally sharing the fixed manufacturing overhead and general and administrative costs generated by the polo shirt.

Activity-Based Costing

Activity-based costing is a multistage process. First the manufacturing overhead and the general operating expenses are assigned to multiple cost pools rather than simply being assigned to departments. These pools represent activities such as supervision, machine maintenance, pattern design, fabric selection, materials management, engineering, operator training, production planning, quality assurance, advertising, and market research. A cost pool is created for each activity that generates cost and then is assigned to garments styles based upon their use of the cost pool.

This costing strategy requires very expensive processes to capture and allocate costs to specific products. The apparel industry has complex indirect manufacturing costs and product development processes that make it difficult to allocate costs effectively to each product style or category. Defining the correlation between a cost pool and the actual utilization of that pool by a particular garment style or category is critical to achieving accurate costing results.

Activity-based costing focuses on these key activities or cost pools as the bases for allocating cost. Department managers must carefully evaluate the use of the cost pools within their departments and justify their expenditures directly to the benefit of product styles or categories. This direct relationship between cost and product forces managers to evaluate the cause (activities) and effects (costs) of their decisions on the short-term and long-term economic well-being of the company. The decision to purchase a computer-aided pattern design system will be based upon the direct effect it will have on the cost of each product and will not place an additional burden on basic carryover styles that do not require new pattern design work.

Figure 7.10 shows the effect of activity-based costing on the new product being added to the T-shirt line. In this example, the basic T-shirt is not carrying the overhead burden or the additional general and administrative costs generated by the polo shirt. The T-shirt is also benefiting from the fact that some of the fixed costs that it was totally absorbing are now being partially absorbed by the new polo shirt.

Blended Costing

Gary Simmons, as president of VF Playwear, had a unique approach to costing.

We do something unique in the industry called **blended costing**. Assume we have plants that are very efficient and cost-effective in El Salvador, the Do-

FIGURE 7.10 ACTIVITY BASED COSTING

The Avant Garde T-shirt company decides to evaluate activity based costing by introducing its 3-button placket polo shirt into its product line. The new capital investment for equipment and additional factory overhead, marketing, and product development costs are carefully analyzed and assessed to the styles that create the demand for those resources.

T-Shirt (400,000 units)

O.H.	$190,000	absorption rate at $188,000 D.L. = 101%
G.M. Contribution	$216,000	allocated to 400,000 units = $0.54 per unit

Polo Shirt (100,000 units)

O.H.	$151,000	absorption rate at $138,000 D.L. = 109%
G.M. Contribution	$184,000	allocated to 100,000 units = $1.84 per unit

Under the activity-based costing system, the two products would price out at:

T-shirt		Polo shirt	
Fabric	$ 1.10	Fabric	$ 1.90
Trimming	.50	Trimming	.70
Labor	.47	Labor	1.38
Factory O.H.	.48	Factory O.H.	1.50
Cost of Goods	$ 2.55	Cost of goods	$ 5.48
Gross margin contribution	$ .54	Gross margin contribution	$ 1.84
Wholesale selling price	$ 3.09	Wholesale selling price	$ 7.32
Retail selling price	$ 6.18	Retail selling price	$14.64

Using activity based costing to price these products would result in a 04.9 percent decrease in the retail price of T-shirts due to the overall increase in projected sales volume, which increases absorption of nonvariable costs. This costing method results in a more realistic allocation of costs based upon actual use of each resource and could result in increased sales of T-shirts or increased T-shirt profits, depending on market conditions.

Activity based costing assigns manufacturing overhead and general operating expenses to pools that represent activities and are assigned to styles based upon the activities required by each style. In this example, the basic T-shirt is not burdened by the additional fixed overhead, general, and administrative costs created by the polo shirt.

minican Republic, Mexico, and Asia, and we have one major facility in the United States for quick response. We happen to believe, even though it's debated constantly, that if we put a garment in the least costly plant, here's where my margin is, that's really not true. In reality, we might or might not put the garment there for any number of reasons. It is our position that no matter where the garment is being made, we blend all the costs together into one cost formula.

We use a standard from a budget that ties into a sewing cost, an embroidery cost, an overhead absorption cost, reserve costs (reserves for markdowns), and it all comes down to one cost. We set the standard once a year, but we tweak it whenever necessary. That cost is then blended into the best cost. Even if you're making all your garments in the lowest-cost factory, you don't get the benefit because the costs are all blended together. That way it doesn't matter where it's made, and that gives us much more flexibility. We can then focus on what the competition is doing to determine if our prices will work. We're able to do subjective pricing to match our competition.

As can be seen from this industry example, there can be many different strategies for product costing. Apparel merchandisers must review their strategic plan, evaluate their resources, and analyze the characteristics of their product lines to determine which costing strategy is best for their company.

Costing Levels

The increased number of seasons or offerings per year has put tremendous pressure on product development and the costing process. Constant style changes require constant feedback and adjustments for whichever costing strategy a company chooses to adopt. This has resulted in a multilevel costing process, which includes:

- Quickie costing (cost estimating).
- Costing for sale (cost calculating).
- Production costing (cost monitoring).
- Accounting costing (cost reporting).

Quickie costing, also referred to as quick costing, involves preliminary cost estimates used by merchandising to evaluate different style alternatives during the early stages of product development. Cost engineers use summarized standard cost data, previous garment cost sheets, and fabric requirement approximations to prepare cost estimates for a proposed new style. These estimates allow merchandisers to cull the styles that will have little chance for adoption and focus the attention of the design team on styles with a greater likelihood of adoption.

Costing for sale involves accurate cost calculations used by merchandising in consideration for adoption and the ultimate pricing of a style. This level of costing is based upon an actual garment sample. Fabric requirements are

"Product Costing to Win Profit Margin"

Increases in flexible production, global sourcing and full package importing reveal a need for more advanced costing systems. Those companies unwilling to revamp their methods risk dramatic inaccuracies that could send profit margins crashing.

As the sewn products industry is faced with an ever-increasing maze of production variables and retail pressures, manufacturers no longer can view product costing as a simple, cut-and-dried formula with enough padding to cushion overhead wherever it may fall. On the contrary, today it's imperative to understand and move beyond the limitations of traditional costing systems or risk dramatic inaccuracies that could shrink profit margins.

For U.S. sewn products firms, the need for more advanced costing systems follows on the heels of several trends, including an increase in flexible domestic production and growth in global sourcing and full package importing. If this is not enough to consider, add to the mix U.S.-based cutting followed by 807-type assembly. This complexity has given rise to many costing dilemmas: Should a company blend the costs for offshore and U.S. manufacturing, use an average or separate offshore costs, hoping to make the most of lower-cost production? It doesn't end here. Quick response initiatives, floor ready merchandise requirements and vendor managed inventory programs also put stress on traditional costing systems. And from the retail side, manufacturers are faced with "cherry picking," a practice whereby retailers select the most favorably priced goods and skip over higher-priced items, particularly in commodity categories.

Faced with these pressures, sewn products companies using inaccurate costing systems are hard-pressed to garner acceptable gross margins. In this case, the old adage "the more we sell, the broker we get" is becoming a reality for many in the industry. However, there are solutions.

As a starting point, and to provide a comparative perspective, it is helpful to take a brief look at traditional sewn products costing. This method calculates manufacturing overhead as a percentage of direct labor. Fabric and trim costs and administrative overhead are added to determine total manufacturing cost. Gross margin is the percent difference between the designated selling price and the total manufacturing cost.

The following example approximates traditional costing figures:

Cut and sew labor $3.54 × 1.13 (excesses)	$4.00
Overhead at 64% of labor cost	$2.56
Material and trim	$7.88
Total manufacturing cost	$14.44
Selling price	$21.20
Gross margin	**32%**

Gross margin = selling price (21.20) − manufacturing cost (14.44) divided by selling price (21.20) = 32%

(continued)

Today, the biggest pitfall of this method is a relatively low labor cost in comparison with total manufacturing cost. In the past, when labor typically was a steady 40 percent of total cost, this straightforward system had a fairly high level of accuracy—or at least sufficient accuracy. However, many companies now are achieving direct labor ratios from 12 percent to 15 percent, and thus there is a significant potential for error when overhead recovery is based on such a small number. Moreover, this percentage continually is reduced with the adoption of more advanced technology and increased production in low-wage countries. Keep this in mind as you evaluate the following scenarios.

QUESTION: We are a small outerwear manufacturing company. At the end of the year—when all the costs are totaled—we are satisfied with the bottom line and our overall gross margin. However, we find it difficult to maintain a steady gross margin because we work with some customers on a cut, make and trim (CMT) basis, whereby they supply the fabric. The balance of our production is done on a private label basis, whereby we purchase the fabric. How should we cost our products using varying overhead recovery formulas?

SOLUTION: As with most costing problems, there are no simple solutions. One possible approach is to concentrate first on establishing the gross margin for CMT sales. It may be beneficial to use a traditional method of costing here, whereby 2.5 times labor is used to establish total cost, including overhead. This will serve as a check to determine if your overhead is in line.

For the private label business, start with the CMT gross margin. Add in the cost of the fabric and a small percentage, say 10 percent, to cover the carrying charges.

Recalculate the cost using this formula and evaluate if the gross margin seems appropriate based on your experience.

QUESTION: My business has gradually changed over time to include smaller lot sizes and many additional SKUs. I have been using the same costing approach for 40 years, and I know the system is now generating individual product costs that are incorrect. What should I change?

SOLUTION: Your cost system probably has a large number of averages built into it that were perfectly valid when your production runs were long and styling was fairly simple. You should take a close look at each process and identify the cost drivers. Also evaluate construction, materials, labor content and services offered (i.e., quick response replenishment, floor ready programs). These factors must be identified for each SKU and calculated when developing standard costs.

QUESTION: Several years ago I purchased a very expensive piece of automated equipment to produce a fairly unique product. Unfortunately, market conditions have changed and this unit remains idle 50 percent of the time. When our cost accountants rebuilt the company's budget, the fixed overhead cost for this piece of equipment went sky-high, making it impossible to produce the product even close to market price. Is there any way around this problem?

SOLUTION: With the fixed expenses of owning (depreciation, insurance, taxes, etc.) and operating highly automated equipment spread among a smaller number of units, the cost per unit has nowhere to go but up. In this situation, every penny counts. Hence, it is important to review all overhead allocations and determine if they are

(continued)

distributed properly. For example, make sure that management time earmarked to the equipment has been adjusted to reflect less production.

Second, examine the actual out-of-pocket expenses associated with the equipment and determine if the market price per unit can cover these costs. Typically, a large portion of the fixed cost associated with the equipment is in noncash expenditures, such as depreciation. Hence, if the market price for the product allows for full recovery of out-of-pocket expenses, you should be able to continue to produce the product.

QUESTION: I've heard that activity-based costing (ABC) is more accurate than traditional costing systems. I'd like to adopt the approach, but I'm concerned my company may not be able to handle the transition. What is the best way to implement ABC?

SOLUTION: As a first step, I suggest keeping the existing system intact and using ABC as an analytical tool to determine if current overhead costs are accurately allocated for activities including order entry, design, sample making, maintenance and supervision. (You'll probably be surprised to find that the company has not been covering expenses for these activities.) This approach will establish a comfort level with ABC. Once employees are accustomed to ABC, the next step is to operate it in conjunction with your existing system, Once ABC is running smoothly, drop the older system. Looking down the road to future projects, you may want to consider activity-based management in conjunction with ABC. Combined they are a powerful tool in today's manufacturing environment. ∎

From Gene Barbee. July 1998. *Bobbin*, pp. 26, 28.

Case in Point 7.1 | Summary

A rapidly changing sewn products industry requires a move beyond traditional costing systems to more sophisticated systems that accurately account for production variables, global sourcing, quick response initiatives, and retail pressures. Today's relatively low labor costs in comparison with total manufacturing costs create a significant potential for error in capturing overhead as a percent of labor cost.

There are no simple solutions to the myriad of cost-related problems. Some companies have customer bases that provide fabric and others that don't; some have increasing SKUs and smaller lot sizes; others have requirements for expensive specialized equipment; still others are concerned with their ability to handle advanced activity-based costing systems. Each company must evaluate its particular costing requirements and custom design a costing and pricing system that meets its individual needs relative to the rapid changes taking place in the industry. ∎

calculated from a test marker using the appropriate size scale, actual fabric widths, and actual completed pattern sets. Labor costs are calculated from detailed predetermined time standards or proven piece rates. During this level of costing, the garment is engineered to take into consideration any alternative construction possibilities that might lower costs. Appropriate costing strategies are used when all fixed and variable costs are calculated. This level of costing is incorporated into the pricing formula for determining the eventual wholesale selling price.

Production costing is the measure of actual variable manufacturing expenses for labor and materials. At this costing level, adjusted piece rates are substituted for any calculated standards and actual material utilization is calculated from the cutting process. An evaluation of off-standard manufacturing costs may be made at this level to adjust overhead rates. Production costing depicts the actual cost of production but does not take into consideration all the aspects of sales volume relating to absorption of overhead and gross margin. This level of costing is a monitoring function for the manufacturing process and provides valuable feedback for quickie costing and costing for sale.

Accounting costing is a measure of the actual costs derived from the cost control process of accounting used to create a company's financial statements. This level of costing measures cost of goods, both variable and fixed portions of manufacturing overhead, as well as variable and fixed general operating expenses and is the basis for evaluating the profit or loss for the company for a specific accounting period. Accounting costing is used to make final adjustments to all elements of the costing and pricing processes.

■ Computer Applications

There are numerous computer software applications available to automate the maintenance of data and the calculations required to determine costs and selling prices. Some companies create their own software applications using interactive databases or standard spreadsheet programs. Others use proprietary programs designed for apparel applications. A typical software application allows a company to create a number of cost-related reports that are linked together to generate valuable cost analysis sheets as well as cost evaluation summaries.

A bill of materials for a specific style showing all materials required by quantity and cost with allowances for wastage and handling is created by product development. (See Figure 7.11.) The bill of materials is generated as prototypes are developed, and it becomes an integral part of the style specification package.

Fabrics
Header | Trims | Labels | Packaging | Finishing | Assembly | Total Cost | Details | Attachments

New Fabric

			Fabric ID	Description	Fabric Type	Placement	Quantity	Quantity UOM	Price	
☐			*Peach Taslan	S-Series 5000 ...	Woven	Garment	2.90	Meter	12.70	3
☐			Printed Taffeta...	Confettis Print	Woven	Body & Hood L...	2.50	Meter	0.75	1
☐			Solid Taffeta N...	Taffeta lining	Woven	Sleeves lining	0.75	Meter	0.75	0
☐			N210 Cire	Cire fabric	Woven	Gaiter	0.17	Meter	2.90	0
☐			Brushes Tricot	Plain brushed ...	Knit	Pockets Lining	0.25	Meter	2.00	0

Trims
Header | Fabrics | Labels | Packaging | Finishing | Assembly | Total Cost | Details | Attachments

New Trim

		Trim ID	Description	Type	Placement	Quantity	Quantity UOM	Price	Total
☐		4TAW024	Swingtag Rosy...	Hangtag	Attached on si...	1.00	Each	0.0500	0.0500
☐		4TAW026	Swingtag S-Se...	Hangtag	Inside back on...	1.00	Each	0.0300	0.0300
☐		4PCA016	Rosy Transpar...	Snap	Gaiter	4.00	Each	0.0800	0.3200
☐		4PUW005	Rosy WSD Gu...	Zipper Pull	1 Collar+ 2 fr P...	3.00	Each	0.0900	0.2700
☐		4PUW008	Rosy WSD Gu...	Zipper Pull	Hood	1.00	Each	0.0600	0.0600

Labels
Header | Fabrics | Trims | Packaging | Finishing | Assembly | Total Cost | Details | Attachments

New Label

		Label ID	Description	Label Name	Placement	Quantity	Quantity UOM	Price	Total
☐		4LAW063	ROSY WSD S-...	ROSY S-series	Inside back-on...	1.00	Each	0.2500	0.2500
☐		4LAW062	ROSY WSD S-...	ROSY WSD S-...	Left of main in...	1.00	Each	0.0500	0.0500
☐		4LAW060	ROSY WSD S-...	ROSY WSD S-...	Left fr pocket fl...	3.00	Each	0.0500	0.1500
☐		4LAX079	ROSY WSD S-...	ROSY WSD S-...	Cuffs	2.00	Each	0.1300	0.2600
☐		Black woven c...	Black Woven	Black woven c...	Left Side seam	1.00	Each	0.0400	0.0400

Figure 7.11 A bill of materials that has been developed using Freeborders Product Manager.

A bill of labor is created by engineering, showing each manufacturing operation required to produce the style with standard allowed minutes and cost per unit. (See Figure 7.12.)

A cost sheet is then generated that uses data from the style database, which is established by the bills of materials and labor with factors added for seconds, handling, freight, excess costs, fringe benefits, indirect labor, factory overhead, selling, and operating costs. The cost sheet provides a calculation of a total cost of goods that is compared to various selling prices to determine potential gross margins. Retail selling prices and retail markup potential can also be analyzed. In Figure 7.13 the company includes variable operating costs and a selling commission of 3 percent in determining its total cost of goods.

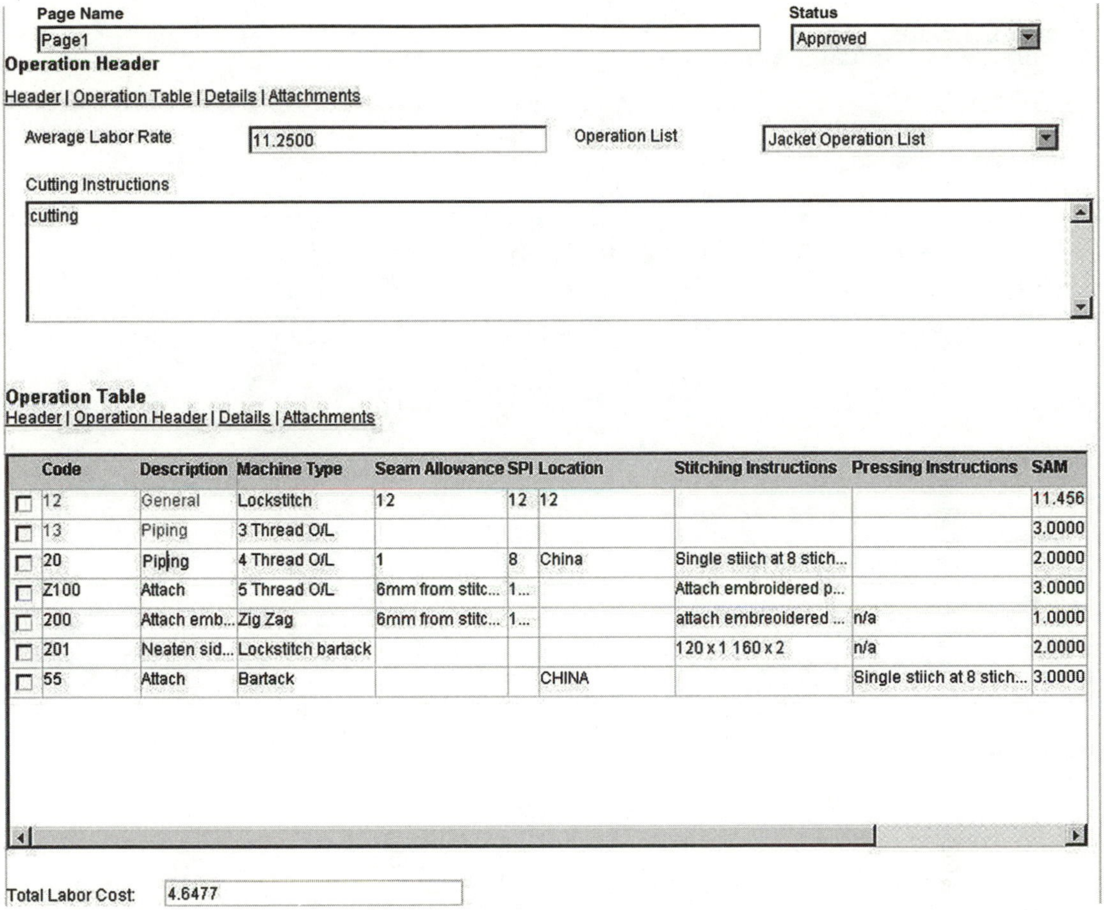

Page Name

Page1

Status

Approved ▼

Operation Header

Header | Operation Table | Details | Attachments

Average Labor Rate   11.2500

Operation List   Jacket Operation List ▼

Cutting Instructions

cutting

Operation Table

Header | Operation Header | Details | Attachments

	Code	Description	Machine Type	Seam Allowance	SPI	Location	Stitching Instructions	Pressing Instructions	SAM
☐	12	General	Lockstitch	12	12	12			11.456
☐	13	Piping	3 Thread O/L						3.0000
☐	20	Piping	4 Thread O/L	1	8	China	Single stiich at 8 stich...		2.0000
☐	Z100	Attach	5 Thread O/L	6mm from stitc...	1...		Attach embroidered p...		3.0000
☐	200	Attach emb...	Zig Zag	6mm from stitc...	1...		attach embreoidered ...	n/a	1.0000
☐	201	Neaten sid...	Lockstitch bartack				120 x 1 160 x 2	n/a	2.0000
☐	55	Attach	Bartack			CHINA		Single stiich at 8 stich...	3.0000

Total Labor Cost: 4.6477

Figure 7.12 A bill of labor that has been developed using Freeborders Product Manager.

These same cost sheet data can be used in cost summaries to evaluate various manufacturing options. The company can evaluate making the style in either an 807 offshore facility or in a domestic factory. Since all data are captured in a master database, comparisons and "what if" scenarios can be evaluated quickly and accurately. This allows merchandisers to make informed sourcing and pricing decisions.

Examples of software applications for apparel costing are: Product Data Management in GERBERsuite from Gerber Technology, Gallery from Lectra Systems, Justwin Apparel from Justwin Technologies, and Freeborders of Canada.

Color/Size Matrix

Cost Request Details | Quote Details | Attachments

⦿ Color Size Matrix
◯ Color Size Prepacks Matrix

Size Category Combination Women's XS-XXL

Colorway ID	Colorway Name	XS	S	M	L	Color Total
14W01	Graphite/Redstone	200	200	500	450	1550
14W02	Dark rust/Sharkskin	200	200	500	450	1550
14W03	Alpine green/Shamrock	100	100	225	175	705
						0
	Size Total	500	500	1225	1075	3805

Sizes   Next >

Request Total 3805

Quote Details

Cost Request Details | Color/Size Martrix | Attachments

Quote Number	**Date Submitted**
72	03/20/2006
Submitter	**Number of Units ***
Chantal Agent	3,805
Factory *	**First Ship Date ***
China	09/27/2006
Shipping Method *	**In House Date ***
Sea	10/18/2006
Assumptions	
All fabrics and trims are available no later than June 25	
Origin	**FOB**
China	FOB
Fabric Cost	**Fabric Cost Calculated**
42.3400	35.9750
Trim Cost	**Trim Cost Calculated**
7.7500	9.0900
Label Cost	**Label Cost Calculated**
2.5500	2.1300
Packaging Cost	**Packaging Cost Calculated**
1.0000	0.7000
Labor Cost	**Finishing Cost**
4.0859	0
First Cost *	**First Cost Calculated ***
73.0559	67.3109
Duty Category	**Duty %**
Outerwear	8.340
HTS Code	**Quote Currency**
	USD
Freight	**Misc Cost**
12.4300	4.3300
Estimated Landed Cost	
95.9088	

Figure 7.13 A cost sheet that has been developed using Freeborders Product Manager. This software program calculates the landed cost for a style, and the anticipated retail price.

Lori Greenawalt
Experience—partner,
KPMG LLP

Apparel Cost Accounting

"For apparel companies, measurement of labor content and understanding performance standards and production measures are very significant. Due to fashion changing styles and fabrics on a seasonal basis, most of the specific products manufactured in the apparel industry are manufactured only once. An apparel manufacturer often does not have the benefit of [adjusting], and ability to, adjust standards and the resulting sales price of their garments. They must be able to accurately establish standards in order to run a profitable business.

"In the apparel industry there is quite a diversity among what costs are actually capitalized in the cost accounting model. Many of the domestic apparel manufacturers are old-line companies who set up their policies, procedures, and systems ages ago. When they were set up, I think they were very good at capturing raw data but not good at utilizing this information for enhancing or measuring performance.

"From an accounting perspective, the older or more established manufacturers tend to capitalize only specific direct costs of production into inventory. The newer, and often more aggressive, companies will bring in ancillary costs that they identify as direct costs of manufacturing. This often results in very different overhead pools and therefore different margins between companies. For instance, is there any portion of the design function that truly is a cost required to get an item to manufacture, or is it always R&D? The newer companies may consider the designers and the product sourcers, and other functions that are important to procurement and production as a part of the overhead pool. The accounting rules provide a set of general principles that clearly state that all direct costs of manufacture are to be capitalized into inventory. Interpretation of these principles is where the diversity comes into play. Accounting is full of judgment calls that management has to apply. The capitalization process can become highly judgmental as it relates to the overhead pool and unfortunately diversity in practice has developed."

Costing Responsibility

"Most companies have a cost accounting department to track actual against standards. Someone out of the production or sourcing area will do the bottoms-up costing on a per unit basis. There is a formalized costing sheet that starts with how much material, with what type of waste, with how many minutes of labor, at what level of proficiency, at

(*continued*)

what payroll cost, with what associated benefits and overhead go into a garment.

"Most manufacturers have mastered the art of capturing all costs of production associated with a unit and tying these costs back to actual invoices and labor costs incurred. However, the problem often occurs in the follow-up after production. This is where the system often breaks down. There is a disconnect in getting the actual cost of production into the system and back to the merchandisers at an item level so they can use that information in their future line development. This is where the problem perpetuates itself. If responsibility for variances is not tracked and clearly communicated, the manufacturer may continue to price its products at a price where it will not be able to maintain profitability."

Classifying Costs

"I encourage apparel companies to have a very pure cost accounting system and to periodically analyze how they classify the costs in each of the overhead pools. Design is a good example. Design could be pure R&D or it might be the cost of tweaking an old stable style into a new style that's more salable. Taking the same pair of jeans that a company has made for years and widening the leg or changing the flare could transform it into a fresh new style that could generate substantial sales. That minor tweak in design is often not considered R&D; it is preparing a design for manufacturing by adjusting some of the patterns and therefore can reasonably be classified as part of manufacturing overhead.

"The problems we see in accounting is that once an overhead category is established, over the years all sorts of costs get thrown into it that weren't intended in its original purity. The things that end up being classified in each of those categories get blurred over the years. All of a sudden the buying trip to Paris ends up being absorbed in that functional design overhead category. Expenses that start out as minor can end up growing into accounting monsters because of improper allocations within account categories. I believe that apparel manufacturers need to review their categories more often than they do to ensure purity. The objective is to allocate costs to the categories that directly affect each style that is produced. If a cost is not directly related to a style, then it should be classified in a category that it directly effects. The buying trip to Paris could be classified as a product development function that may be absorbed in a general and administrative [G&A] category that is not part of the cost of goods sold [COGS].

"All companies should reevaluate the components of their costing pools every season. What new items

(continued)

have developed and what new functions have been added that are classified into an account that is included in the accounting pool? Is the manufacturer reevaluating those components, even down to the basics of what percent of the building is allocated to manufacturing, in light of an expanded product development department? These are important questions that must be addressed. I'd prefer to see this with every season of production. More realistically, it needs to happen on an annual basis.

"We're in a different economy and a different mindset today than we were 20 years ago. If you started a company 20 years ago, your policies and procedures are probably far more conservative than those of a new entrepreneur starting out today. You will have many more different cost classifications today than you had 20 years ago."

Costing Formula

"The components and methodology of costing formulas will vary by apparel manufacturer depending on what they are manufacturing, how stable their product mix is, and the size of their production runs. These factors will change the matrix a company uses. The basic elements of direct labor, materials, and overhead are all there. It's how they are calculated and applied that varies. Some companies are very system-savvy, have sophisticated cost accounting systems, and are thor-

oughly integrated. They capture actual production costs per style, detailed payroll costs, and overhead costs that directly relate to each style. These companies vary greatly from the ones that do their costing from a best-guess approach. 'The extras on this garment probably cost 5 cents. The overhead is about 80 cents. We've always used 80 cents.' There are even companies that base their overhead rates on the wholesale cost of the garment or the cost of the fabric. I can't find the correlation between the wholesale cost of a garment or the fabric cost and overhead. I prefer to see overhead based on production time or labor content.

"I am often questioned about whether an apparel company should use direct costing or absorption costing. If a company is a true manufacturer with overhead, then it should use absorption costing. As a rule of thumb, as soon as there is an overhead, by default you have absorption costing. That's the only way to know the true effect of overhead on each style."

Variances

"Standard costing systems generate variances, and the accounting department books them. Most companies do that right. Where they fail is when they don't have proper integration or accurate allocation of variances. A manufacturer must know at the end of the day after all markdowns, after all advertising

(*continued*)

credits, after all money gets exchanged, how profitable each style was. A monthly variance may not be very large, but it may consist of large variances up and down on different styles. In reality, the manufacturer may be selling certain products at a loss and others at a profit and not really know it. Access to accurate and timely information may dramatically change the products designed for future selling seasons.

"Over and under capacity are another variance problem for most manufacturers. Costing based on the accounting principle guidelines assumes full capacity. Allocations typically aren't adjusted for minor over/underutilization. Those are period costs that get expensed. The profitability of a company can change dramatically based on utilization, but the costing methodology should be relatively stable if you use standard costing because it assumes no unusual utilization problems. It is management's responsibility to see that a company is running at full capacity. Management establishes sales targets to keep manufacturing at full production and should adjust capacity levels to meet company expectations. Practically speaking, labor is immediately adjusted, but overall capacity is rarely adjusted due to facility obligations and the hope of increased capacity."

"Variance information at the style level is critical to the decisions made by merchandisers as they are developing the next product line.

They must be able to update standards and reflect them in the costing system so that they really know what a style costs and actually sells for at the end of the day."

Selling Price

"Cost accounting methodology builds up what it will cost to make the product, but setting the selling price is a separate decision. Some companies may take their standard cost and double it. That is not the way to establish selling prices. You must always ask yourself, what will the market bear?

"There are excellent sophisticated computer modeling tools available to perform what-if analyses. If I believe the capacity is X and if I price a style at $10, I can sell this many. But if I price it at $8, I can sell three times as many. Using these modeling programs, I can build into the matrices what I can produce, in what time frame, at what overhead absorption rate, the effect on the total style mix, markdown exposure, and the effect on my gross margin. I can analyze all the variables and determine how these decisions will affect my bottom line.

"You must ultimately look at the retail consumer. You have to start at the beginning of the manufacturing cycle and say, 'What will the ultimate consumer buy this for?' Merchandisers must take everything into account when developing, costing, and pricing apparel lines. This

(*continued*)

includes accepting returns, giving markdown money, and other promotions regularly given to retailers after the retail selling season. Merchandisers will do what they are motivated to do based upon compensation. Companies need to keep this in mind when designing their compensation systems. Initial margin realized is not an appropriate measurement in the current apparel environment; maintained customer margin is a far better measurement as it includes all promotional moneys given after the initial sale. Selling prices established must take into account all of the costs related to each style as well as the effect of the selling price on ultimate sales."

Quick Response

"Increasingly important to apparel manufacturers are quick response and just-in-time manufacturing. There are some vertical retailers in the United States that are manufacturing domestically using quick response. They do a production run that will put five garments in every store that will be carefully monitored to determine how quickly they sell during the first weekend of sales. If they don't sell, they [the manufacturers] don't produce another run. If they do sell well, they resupply their chain in X number of days using quick response technology. This involves a sophisticated EDI environment from point-of-sale through to the manufacturing plants and fabric suppliers. I've only seen this work successfully for domestically manufactured goods.

"This test market approach is designed to reduce markdowns and inventory carrying costs. Unfortunately if you get into products that are highly stylized or the social movements are changing too quickly, you can still miss the moving target."

Art and Intuition

"At the end of the day, the CEO must make the final decision. A part of the costing and pricing philosophy will always be art and intuition. Always."

Howard Ziplow Experience—chief financial officer, Westmill Clothes

Garment Costing for Sale

"We typically don't do a formal precosting. We do the final costing or costing for sale of our products after they have been adopted into our line. Our labor for a coat or a pair of trousers does not change dramatically. The merchandisers in our company who perform the selection know what piece goods the garment is being processed in and are able to reasonably judge what the approximate cost will be. If they're considering very high-priced piece goods, they are able to reasonably judge the garment cost and may look for lower-priced piece goods to stay within our price points. From this perspective we do precosting as our new styles are being developed."

Standard Cost Analysis (Production Costing)

"Our costing for sale becomes our standard cost. The garment has been processed through engineering. We have identified what the yield of the cloth is and the yields of the different trim components. Engineering has provided us with the direct labor cost. We know our approximate indirect labor cost, percentages for excesses, and overhead. We then derive our standard cost for each garment. On a quarterly basis, we look at our variances versus our standard and make adjustments.

"We determine our variances from reports based on the actual costs of manufacturing. Our labor is based on piece work so that should be accurate except for overtime and off-standard manufacturing conditions, which we try to keep to a minimum. We analyze the actual yield of piece goods and trim and determine any variances. It is important for us to capture variances and determine why they occurred. I suppose you would call this production costing. This allows us to revise our standards going forward."

Overhead

"A certain portion of our cost we figure as a percentage of our direct labor. For example, this percentage covers factory overhead, supervisors, and factory managers. There is another component that is fixed, which covers such items as depreciation of the building and electricity. We treat these costs as hard, fixed costs applied to each garment."

Pricing

"In costing you want to get as close as you can, knowing full well that

(continued)

you're not going to be 100 percent accurate. From the standpoint of pricing, you attempt to maximize the price you can get within the market place without going over what the market will accept. You try to maximize your price without losing market share. It's easy to price a garment very high, but if your competition is significantly lower than your price, you're not going to sell the garment. You can have the greatest costing system, but in the end you must be able to price your products at what the market will bear.

"You have to be very conscious from a pricing standpoint where your competition is. Once you go through a costing, there may be ways to reduce those costs that should be implemented prior to the manufacturing process so that you can perhaps get a better margin or lower your price and increase market share."

Improving the Costing System

"We currently use a basic spreadsheet software package to do our costing. We could improve our costing system by better monitoring the piece goods, trim, and labor variances and modify our standards more quickly. We need to better control the tracking, particularly of our labor within the factory. When it comes to labor, we don't look at it on a per style basis. We really only look at it in the overall shop, and that's one area that we really could improve upon."

Merchandiser Costing Knowledge

"I'd expect a merchandiser with responsibility for product development to know how to develop a cost sheet on a particular product with all the different components that go into a cost sheet. They'd have to know the theory behind what goes into a product cost because as you go from company to company, things may change slightly. They should have a very strong understanding of the costing process, what costs are variable costs, what costs are fixed costs, and how to develop their own costing standard.

"Because this is a very labor intensive business, there are many variables that affect product cost, and those variables must be carefully monitored, analyzed, and adjusted to maintain the profitability of a company."

Jay Bornstein
Experience—tax partner, Ernst & Young

Brian Ford
Experience—audit partner, retail distribution and manufacturing, Ernst & Young

Today, Consumers Are in Control

"At one time the manufacturer was in control. At one time the distributor was in control. In another phase of American retailing, the retailer was in control. Today, the consumers are in control. There is about 8,000 square feet of retail space today for each consumer compared to about 1,000 square feet of retail space 15 years ago. In any pricing model, you can't lose sight of what the customer is willing to pay for your products."

Liquidation of Overhead

"Costing and pricing models should be sensitive to the complete liquidation of overhead. Typically in any of the garment manufacturing situations, whether production is in-house or done by a third party, at the end of the day, the factor that seems to facilitate increased profit is liquidating overhead over a larger volume base. The standard cost model is based upon a projected number of labor hours and adjusted periodically to true it up based upon actual usage.

"It is important to design your pricing model to accommodate what the customer is willing to pay, and then hope that sales volumes will be greater than the forecasted base used in the model. If you are at 100 percent production capacity with your pricing model where your factory is working 24 hours a day, then you can't take advantage of increased volume. Most factories are not modeled on 100 percent production capacity, so increased sales and reorders requiring a few hours of overtime liquidates a lot of overhead costs over the larger production. It is important for factories to have capacity elasticity so they can have the ability to increase production when needed. These companies make their real hits in a higher level of liquidation of fixed costs or the costs of operating their factories after the variable expenses of labor and power consumption."

Charge Backs and Markdowns

"The wholesale selling price has to be set to include charge backs and

(continued)

markdowns. Whether they come somewhere below the gross margin line or are incorporated as a reduction of gross revenues, they must be accounted for. Any negotiated adjustments such as cash discounts, advertising, and markdown money must be accounted for in your pricing formula. From an operational cost accounting function, these adjustments might go into the difference between gross margin and net income, but from a financial accounting perspective, some of these items may end up as reported reductions of sales revenue.

"Today, markdowns may be tied right into the retailers' point of sale (POS) system. The manufacturer and the retailer can be looking at the same data on a real-time basis so they can see the movement of goods through the store and the sales prices of all the merchandise showing what's been marked up and what's been marked down. It sounds kind of cliché when you say it, but you can do all the costing you want. If the retailer isn't going to make a margin when he sells the product to the customer for what the customer is willing to pay, then you aren't going to get many orders."

Retailers and Private Label

"The number one barometer for retailers today is sales. They use a business model that takes them through what they call responsible usage of their stores to achieve a margin. Today more and more retailers are taking control over the

manufacturing process through private label. Even if a retailer doesn't invest in physical production facilities and outsources production, they still have the infused investment in design and sourcing infrastructure, which is also a fairly expensive undertaking.

"This brings up the concept of transfer pricing, which is the mechanism of dividing the profit so you can evaluate the product development and sourcing operation or internal manufacturing, and the retail operation. If it costs a retailer six dollars to make a garment and they can sell it for 15 dollars, there's a nine dollar profit. It is important to determine a fair transfer price between the manufacturing operation and the retail operation to cover both the selling effort and the production effort. The development of equitable costing and pricing models are critical to the success of private label operations.

"The private label winners of the future are going to be the companies that can create vertical information flows so that they not only know what the sales are, but which styles, which sizes, and which colors are selling. They must be able to react very quickly to sales trends and keep fresh, saleable merchandise in the stores for their customers.

"Retailers today know that the price elasticity is better in their private label product lines than in their national brands. A customer can look at a Dockers pant in different stores and see who has the best price.

(*continued*)

Executive Perspective 7.3 (*continued*)

This cannot be done with a private label pant. A retailer can have it priced two or three dollars lower, even though the cost of it may have been five or six dollars lower. This allows for price elasticity."

Gross Margin

"In the 70s, retailers used the concept of keystoning, which was designed to achieve an average gross margin of 50 percent. Today, due to consumer pricing pressure, retailers are achieving gross margins in the 35 percent range, even with the advent of private label products.

"The most difficult cost factor to control for both apparel manufacturers and retailers in achieving desired gross margin is the liquidation of overhead. Forecasting is really the bottom line in accurate liquidation of overhead. An accurate system of forecasting sales volumes over a period of time and average margins is the key to being successful in establishing a pricing structure."

Summary

The success of today's apparel companies is dependent upon their developing salable product lines that meet the rapidly changing needs of the global marketplace. During each phase of the product development process, merchandisers must be aware of the impact that costing and pricing will have on the successful marketing of their product lines. A keen understanding of costs and their impact on the ultimate selling price guide successful merchandisers in making important styling decisions.

The basic pricing formula, cost of goods + markup = wholesale selling price, is the foundation for determining the price of each style in a product line. The accumulation of cost data and the allocation of the cost elements that go into the pricing formula are the critical functions that control the accuracy of garment pricing. Costing strategies include direct costing, absorption costing, activity-based costing, and blended costing. Merchandisers must carefully select the strategy that meets the needs of their particular company, products, and market. Each of these strategies requires careful planning and control through timely feedback, modification, and decisive management action.

Key Terms

absorption costing

accounting costing

activity-based costing

adjusted gross margin (AGM)

blended costing

cost accounting

cost of goods

costing

cut, make, & trim (CMT)

dating

direct costing

direct labor

direct materials

807

financial accounting

garment pricing

general and administrative
   expenses (G&A)

general operating expenses

gross margin (GM)

gross margin return on inventory
   (GMROI)

income statement

landed duty paid (LDP)

maintained (margin) markup

managerial accounting

manufacturing overhead

markup (gross margin)

material utilization

minimum order quantities

net income

payment terms

personal, fatigue, and delay (PF&D)

piece rate

pricing

production costing

profit and loss statement

pull-through marketing

quickie costing

required departmental markup

size scale

standard allowed minutes

subjective pricing

variable costing

whole cost method

wholesale net selling price

wholesale selling price

Discussion Questions and Learning Activities

1. Discuss why net income is often the prime determinant of success in the apparel industry.
2. What is the prime determinant of the success of private brands?
3. Compare the value and the retail selling price of a retailer's private brand garment with a similar national brand garment. Which do you feel is superior?
4. In the pricing formula, what element of markup is not a true cost?
5. Give an example of a product line that could effectively use the rigid calculation method of garment pricing. Explain why.
6. Using the pricing formula, calculate the markup (gross margin) percentage of a garment with a cost of goods equal to $6.00 and a wholesale selling price of $10.00.
7. For the same product in question 4, apply the following: If the com-

pany needed to achieve a markup of 45 percent, what would the wholesale selling price be?

8. If the customers of the above company require an 8 percent sales discount, what would be the wholesale selling price of this same product in order to maintain the 45 percent markup on the wholesale net selling price?

9. What additional information would you need to determine whether the company that created the cost calculation sheet in Figure 7.7 was using direct costing or absorption costing?

10. Discuss two dangers in using subjective pricing.

11. Which of the three costing methods—direct costing, absorption costing, or activity-based costing—would be the most costly to maintain? Explain why.

12. One of the companies discussed in Case in Point 7.1 was concerned about the effect of smaller lot sizes and many additional SKUs on its individual product costs. Under these conditions, which costing strategy would be the most effective? Why?

13. Present an example of how certain design costs could be classified as part of manufacturing overhead and therefore capitalized into inventory.

References and Resources

Bertrand Frank Associates. 1985. *Profitable Merchandising of Apparel.* National Knitwear & Sportswear Association.

Faber, Ed Jr. June 1991. Finding the Right Price, *Bobbin*, pp. 82–83.

Garrison, Ray H.; Noreen, Eric W. 1994. *Managerial Accounting.* Richard D. Irwin, Inc., p. 4.

Horngren, Charles T.; Foster, George. 1991. *Cost Accounting—A Managerial Emphasis.* New Jersey: Prentice-Hall, Inc.

Horngren, Charles T.; Sundem, Gary L. 1987. *Introduction to Management Accounting.* New Jersey: Prentice-Hall, Inc.

Niebel, Benjamin W. 1960. *Motion and Time Study.* Richard D. Irwin, Inc. p. 312.

Quality

- Understand the role of quality in apparel products.

- Identify consumers' quality expectations.

- Identify the apparel and retail company's role in meeting the needs of its targeted consumer.

- Explore the responsibilities of the merchandiser in establishing and implementing quality standards during the development and execution of product lines.

- Analyze the importance of specifications in communicating quality standards.

- Examine inspection and sampling procedures used to ensure consistent quality throughout the manufacturing process.

Quality can be defined in many different ways and seen from various perspectives. It is a difficult concept to quantify for apparel because it may mean one thing to one consumer and something else to another. For example, a fashion forward blouse that is expected to be passé within several months does not have to be serviceable beyond its limited life span. On the other hand, a basic blouse must last much longer, therefore serviceability is a critical quality consideration. For apparel products, quality can be the determining factor that makes a sale at retail or brings consumers back to purchase additional garments from the same brand.

Even within an apparel company, views may differ with respect to quality. A designer may have one view, a pattern maker or sewing supervisor another, while sales and marketing may have yet another. The merchandiser must fill the role of interpreter, translating the quality needs of a company's target consumer into concepts that can be easily understood by all members of the management team. The proper interpretation of quality can have a profound effect on the success of an apparel company. After a company's quality objectives are established, the responsibility for creating and maintaining a consistent level of quality must be shared by all employees.

Up until the past few years, the making of a high-quality product was considered a strategic, competitive advantage. However, in today's global marketplace, quality is a requirement for staying in business. In a recent study it was shown that "international competition, mandatory and voluntary product standards, and consumer knowledge have considerably reduced the amount of poor-quality merchandise . . . Thus the risks in consumer choice owing to poor substantive quality have been reduced" (Carsky, Dickinson, and Camedy, 1998).

■ Consumers' Perception of Quality

Consumers measure quality in many different ways. "Customer perceptions of quality consider the materials and production techniques used in the product, the uniformity or consistency across similar products, the fashion statement inherent in the design of the product, and the cost or price of the product" (Kadolph, 1998). The first assessment takes place when the consumer is in the process of deciding whether to buy the apparel product. At this time the focus is on aesthetics, which include style, color, fabric, trim items, fit, and construction details such as seams, stitches, and the matching of geometric patterns including stripes and plaids. The second assessment takes place after the garment has been worn and is based upon the following performance criteria:

- **Durability** is determined by how long the garment will be used for its intended purpose and how well it will retain its original look and shape. Fabric durability refers to the strength and structural integrity such as resistance to abrasion, pilling, snagging, and color permanence. The importance of durability also applies to findings and supplies.

- **Comfort** relates to how the body feels in response to the garment. This property includes whether or not body heat is retained as in ski-wear; whether moisture is absorbed or repelled, especially in warm climates; fabric hand (softness, harshness, smooth, silky, etc.) and the use of either bulky, covered, or flat seams. The design of the garment can either restrict or allow for ease of movement thus affecting comfort.

- **Care** refers to a garment's response to the recommended procedures for cleaning. How did cleaning (either machine washing, hand washing, or professional dry cleaning) affect its dimensions, its color, and its surface characteristics. Does the garment resist staining, soiling, or wrinkles?

- **Appearance retention** is the quality that describes how the garment keeps its original appearance and shape during use, storage, and care. For example, did knit sweaters stretch out of shape? Did **fusibles** (fabrics or interlinings with resin dots that are applied with heat and pressed to the outer fabric) **delaminate** (separate from the fabric shell)?

Aesthetic criteria will attract a customer and performance criteria will retain a customer. The merchandiser must determine the specific criteria that are important to the target consumer. Quality and its effect on the consumer is important in all sectors of the apparel industry. According to Jack Ward, chairman, president, and CEO of Russell Corporation, an established and highly respected manufacturer of active wear, "We have to insure that we are providing the highest quality product at the lowest possible price" (Fairchild Publications, 1998).

■ Company Responsibility

In order for an apparel company to survive in today's global environment, it must be responsive to its target market. Defining product quality criteria and establishing effective controls are among a company's most important policy decisions. When an apparel company focuses all its activities to deliver a quality product that satisfies the needs of its target market by creating a culture or philosophy of management in which all personnel are involved in identifying and resolving quality problems, it is practicing **total quality management (TQM).** Each department within the company must focus on meeting the perceived needs of its targeted consumer. The responsibility of the merchandising department in TQM is to understand the dimensions of quality that are important to its target market and build these attributes into its products.

"Simplicity Is the Key"

As Calvin Klein, the pre-eminent American among the world's fashion modernists, has built one of the largest apparel and accessories brands in the world today, a key part of his strategy has been picking the right partners. . . . Recognizing that his strength lies in the design and marketing areas, Klein carefully enters business partnerships cultivated and managed by a top-rate executive team led by Gabriella Forte, president and COO, and backed up by a global business infrastructure.

While bold changes and aggressive expansion have made Calvin Klein into the powerhouse it is today, the creative inspiration has stayed the same through its 29 years of existence, resting in the signature Calvin Klein Collection with its simple, elegant point of view. The Collection is the purest reflection of Calvin Klein and the extraordinary designers who collaborate with him. . . .

The key to Calvin Klein's success is its core product and the care the company takes with its design and execution. Quality is not given lip service here. With freestanding stores in New York, Seoul, Paris, London, Hong Kong . . . quality is everything. An obsessive attention to quality is integral to the company's identity and image, and because of this, the Collection line has become ambassador, epitome, . . . that represents company philosophy. "We would be disloyal to our customers if we allowed less than the highest quality in the line," says Susan Longo, the firm's director of production CAD systems. A sweater in the line sells for approximately $600 and evening gowns run as high as $4000. But Collection customers do not expect to return merchandise because of product defects of any kind, Quality assurance teams are "everywhere, at every stage of production," says Longo, whose unique position in the company allows her to see both up and downstream from the company's midpoint.

The quality process begins with fabric inspection and continues through all phases of construction. Microscopically uneven buttonholes, snags, runs, ungenerous hems and seams, and bad top-stitching are not allowed. "When you are selling garments at this price range, the customer expects stringent attention to every detail," Longo says. "Quality is part of our process at every stage. We guarantee it to win and keep our customers' loyalty."

Quality in terms of exactness and ability to produce perfectly constructed garments has been much enhanced by Lectra's Modaris pattern-making and Diamino marker-making software. . . . "Every facet of production from pattern-making to manufacturing, is stored on the Lectra CAD and database management systems," says Longo. This includes both runway and production patterns. Sample and production cutting is done both in house and by subcontractors in the United States and Italy.

Many of the company's subcontractors are equipped with CAD and CAM tools, and are sent patterns by modem, floppy disc, or via the Internet. The firm provides its own markers for domestic cuts or for styles with strict quality standards. The Lec-

(continued)

tra software allows for improvement in both productivity and quality. The system enables the pattern maker to make alterations for fit or design such as narrowing lapels on suits or adding fullness to the chest.

Every alteration to a pattern piece is automatically carried over to its associated marker. The altered pattern can then be sent to a contractor in Italy, for immediate use in production.

Certain garments might require sacrificing fabric efficiency for quality. "While mass manufacturers are looking for a high percentage of fabric usage and efficiency, we are looking for a perfect garment, which may not always be your most efficient yield," says Longo. "If we were putting price before quality, we wouldn't be making a high-end garment anymore. We often do things that won't give us the best fabric usage but are critical for quality, and yet we definitely wouldn't be as efficient with fabric consumption if we didn't have the CAD system.

But quality not quantity is still the main concern—the technology ensures a high degree of accuracy in pattern-making, allowing users to make precise changes on form fitting styles. "If the fabric reacts differently than we expected, we can alter our patterns to match," says Longo. "Some manufacturers are only focused on the money they'll save by using a CAD system, but for us, the point isn't just savings, its quality."

The Calvin Klein brand name manages to transcend wildly diverse customer bases. . . . Still, Klein's cornerstone Collection is designed with a specific customer in mind—an affluent woman who appreciates quality.

These are important lessons no apparel manufacturer should dare disregard. Today's consumer demands value, but is no less exacting about quality. ■

From *Apparel Industry Magazine*, December 1997.

Case in Point 8.1 ## Summary

Calvin Klein's Collection epitomizes a product that meets the quality expectations of its targeted consumer. Its product development and pre-production processes reflect the attention to detail that is required to deliver quality apparel to the consumer. The degree of care that Calvin Klein Collection takes to maintain the highest level of quality at the expense of the lowest cost of production should serve as a role model for the apparel industry. It reinforces the concept that quality is not an activity that takes place at the end, but is a constant pursuit throughout the entire process. ■

W. Edwards Deming was a pioneer in recognizing the need to focus on quality in the development and manufacturing of a product. Deming stressed the importance of management initiative and responsibility in achieving TQM. His beliefs are synthesized in a 14 point plan.

Another original proponent of quality improvement was Joseph M. Juran who initiated a 10-step philosophy that focused on understanding and maintaining a dialogue between the company and the target market, communicat-

DEMING'S 14 POINTS

1. Create constancy of purpose for improvement of product and service.
2. Adopt the new philosophy.
3. Cease dependence on mass inspection.
4. End the practice of awarding business on the basis of the price tag alone.
5. Improve constantly and forever the system of production and service.
6. Institute training.
7. Adopt and institute leadership.
8. Drive out fear.
9. Break down barriers between staff areas.
10. Eliminate slogans, exhortations, and targets for the work force.
11. Eliminate numerical quotas for the work force.
12. Remove barriers that rob people of the pride of workmanship.
13. Encourage education and self-improvement for everyone.
14. Take action to accomplish the transformation.

Reprinted from *Out of the Crisis* by W. Edwards Deming by permission of MIT and The W. Edwards Deming Institute. Published by MIT, Center for Advanced Educational Services, Cambridge MA. Copyright © 1986 by The W. Edwards Deming Institute.

Deming's 14 Points laid the foundation for Total Quality Management.

JURAN'S 10 STEPS TO QUALITY IMPROVEMENT

1. Build awareness of both the need for improvement and opportunities for improvement.
2. Set goals for improvement.
3. Organize to meet the goals that have been set.
4. Provide training.
5. Implement projects aimed at solving problems.
6. Report progress.
7. Give recognition.
8. Communicate results.
9. Keep score.
10. Maintain by building improvement into the company's regular systems.

Published by permission of Stephen Uzelac and Mohican Publishing Company.

Dr. Jospeh Juran's philosophies can be expressed in 10 Steps as stated by Stephen Uzelac.

ing the target market needs within the company, and then continuously improving the company's response to meet these needs.

In the 1990s Mikel Harry, Ph.D., established the Six Sigma Breakthrough Strategy as a quality improvement project based upon customer feedback and potential cost savings. The Breakthrough Strategy reaches across the entire corporation in a unified and focused manner to give highest priority to improvements that have the largest impacts on customer needs and revenues. The Breakthrough Strategy affects six areas fundamental to improving a company's value. (Harry, 2000.)

In order to reach the Six Sigma goal of 3.4 defects per million points of

---

SIGMA SIX BREAKTHROUGH STRATEGY: SIX AREAS FUNDAMENTAL TO IMPROVING A COMPANY'S VALUE.

1. Process improvements.
2. Product and services improvement.
3. Investor relations.
4. Design methodology.
5. Supplier improvement.
6. Training and recruitment.

Reprinted from *SIX SIGMA: The Breakthrough Management Strategy Revolutionizing the World's Top Corporations* by Mikel Harry, Ph.D., and Richard Schroeder with permission from Currency Books published by Doubleday. Copyright © 2000 by Mikel Harry, Ph.D., and Richard Schroeder.

---

inspection, one must define, measure, analyze, improve, and control (DMAIC). The purpose is to solve problems at the beginning or root of the process (the inputs), which will reduce the need to repair and inspect (the outputs). Richard Atwell of [TC]² feels that while most apparel companies have not achieved a six sigma level in their operating procedures, any company can profit from focusing on quality using available statistical tools and established standards. Management and employees must be involved, accountable, and committed to continuous improvement.

The following principles in Deming's, Juran's, and Harry's concepts concerning the role of quality should be embraced by apparel merchandisers:

- Involve top management.
- Encourage training and education of all employees.
- Continuously improve processes.
- Understand that the dedication to quality is a positive contributor to the growth and prosperity of the company.

- Measure quality attributes.
- Analyze the variables that cause quality defects.
- Improve processes to create and produce quality products.
- Control processes so that the same problems do not reoccur.

The responsibility of an apparel company relative to quality is to gain and keep the trust of the consumers who purchase its products. This involves building quality into each garment style; developing and using effective quality systems, controls, and procedures; selecting and training inspectors; and the proper installation and maintenance of inspection equipment. Effective specifications must be created for each style and accurate measures of quality must be made at the critical stages in the production process.

■ Standards

Apparel companies that have recognized the need to instill quality throughout their business operations have established expectations for the garments they produce and sell. **Standards** are descriptions of acceptable measures of comparison for quantitative or qualitative value that are communicated to all involved in the development and execution of a product. These descriptions are expectations for a variety of apparel factors such as dimensions, materials, style components, appearance, and performance. These factors apply to raw materials, design, production, and packaging. It is critical that standards be expressed in language that is clearly understood by all personnel that could affect the quality of a garment style. At times this requires the use of illustrations, photographs, diagrams, definitions, and samples.

Quality expectations should be communicated in written form such as a quality assurance manual that is distributed to company personnel and outside suppliers and contractors. Quality assurance manuals should state the precise and exact characteristics of a product including minimum levels of performance and expectations.

Standardization is the process of establishing rules for compliance with the standards a company has developed for its products. Standardization requires cooperation among all company personnel as well as suppliers, contractors, and consumers. When an entire industry adopts a standard, it is referred to as an **industry standard**. An example of an apparel industry standard is the use of a one-quarter-inch seem allowance when sewing a collar to a shirt. When the need for a standard exists but not all companies choose to develop or follow that standard, it is known as a **voluntary standard**. An example of a voluntary standard is when many shirt manufacturers establish a standard of using fusible linings in cuffs rather than sewn-in linings and some manufacturers continue to use sewn-in linings. When the issue of public

"An International Boss"

*A*im's first-ever International All-Star, Hugo Boss USA is uniquely international: Italian-owned, the company operates with German management and technology, and has chosen to manufacture *for* the United States, its second largest market.

"As its base of manufacturing, Hugo Boss has bought the largest and oldest apparel factory in the United States, the Joseph and Feiss Co. in Cleveland. It seemed a brilliant solution at the time, and it certainly put people on notice that Hugo Boss was manufacturing in the United States. But as senior vice president of manufacturing Wolf Schneider says, "We could have built a fabulous new factory from the ground up for the amount we have spent on this place."

The decision to manufacture in the Joseph and Feiss Co. plant was anything but an immediate, unqualified success. In fact, things went so poorly at first that Neiman Marcus dropped Hugo Boss on the excuse that it did not sell suits under $1000. It was a crushing blow and humiliating embarrassment for a line that proclaimed itself the *crème de la crème* of men's tailored clothing.

Hugo Boss regrouped, under the strategically important tutelage of corporate technical director Leo Oppe, who was made president of The Joseph and Feiss Co. for his pains, and the company's quality improved dramatically over the next five years. But, after seeing most U.S. manufacturing moving offshore, the company's six directors met last year to decide whether to continue its production here and deadlocked in a three-to-three tie. Andreas Kurz, the president of Hugo Boss USA, and Oppe, as Hugo Boss's worldwide production manager and technical director and president of the Cleveland facility, eventually persuaded the opposition not to abandon manufacturing in the United States. The solution would be to give up the Joseph and Feiss plant and invest between $10 and $12 million remodeling a slightly smaller warehouse in nearby Brooklyn into a high-tech manufacturing facility and distribution center.

An obsession with quality is just plain common sense. Hugo Boss lost its Neiman Marcus account because of quality complaints. "No manufacturer can make $200 suits one week and $800 suits the next," says Oppe of the original Joseph and Feiss system, which made mass market suits and top quality suits on the same production line. "The operator's natural inclination is to make a $200 suit all the time, because it's easier."

"The Cleveland facility today is staffed by very experienced workers, 500 of them, whose entire approach to manufacturing is filled with enthusiasm associated with making a respected world product to standards that are also world class. They have what Oppe and Schneider call the "Hugo Boss mentality."

"At all of our facilities," says Oppe, "we start by training the management, the production manager, the supervisors, the quality control people. We provide three weeks to three months training on what is behind

(continued)

the name of Hugo Boss, our philosophy and vision. We go in with a special training team for cutting, sewing, pressing, organizing the floor. We train everybody onsite in our production equipment and methods, which are exactly the same worldwide."

Operators can at any time refer to two-inch-thick handbooks (written in German and the local language) placed next to each piece of equipment or function. The manuals detail the cutting, sewing, and pressing process for each garment, listing the minimum and optimum equipment required for each task's completion, and actual movements the operator should use. As an example, arrows indicate the direction in which a presser must push his or her hands to smooth a jacket before pressing

"Yet the purpose of the manuals and intensive training is not to achieve ISO status. It's to achieve perfect quality and also trouble-free communication, which saves millions of dollars. Hugo Boss has to implement style changes in 20 different plants almost overnight.

"While training takes place in each manufacturing facility, an international team of production managers and technicians converge on Cologne's Herren Mode Woche, MAGIC's much larger European counterpart, to see Hugo Boss's new collections inside and out. Production managers are asked questions such as, "What investments would you like your facility to make in new equipment? Do you need more training?" Then the team goes on retreat to places like the Swiss Alps to discuss common problems and solutions. "We build a family, a team that will stay together over long distances," says Oppe.

"Whatever the Hugo Boss style, its quality must be impeccable." Oppe's chief goal for the U.S. operation is to have a line efficient enough to offset the high cost of a UNITE labor force, while maintaining top quality production.

Oppe emphasizes, "The perfection of a Hugo Boss suit is in the sewing;—you cannot improve bad sewing with good pressing. Just as you must produce quality, you cannot check it. All of the quality we have today is due to our superb operators, who are experts at each step of production."

Having virtually eliminated every quality problem Cleveland ever had, Oppe is well aware that, in a world hungry for fashion, no production solution can be permanent. "The most important thing for the future is to be flexible, to be fast, good and flexible," says Oppe.

Two weeks before *AIM* toured the brand-new facility nearing completion in Brooklyn with Kurz and Oppe, Daryl Osborne, director of men's furnishings at Neiman Marcus, told Andreas Kurz he thought the new Hugo Boss collection was quite wonderful, and invited Hugo Boss to rejoin the Neiman Marcus fold. The six-year struggle back into the luxe retailer's good graces ended happily. ■

From *Apparel Industry Magazine*, December 1997.

Case in Point 8.2   ## Summary

Hugo Boss encountered quality problems when it began to manufacture its men's tailored clothing line in the United States. In order to overcome their quality hurdle, the international company applied their proven methods of emphasizing training, investing in new machinery, building quality into every product, giving pride of workmanship to its employees, and involving management in all phases of the quality process.

The "Hugo Boss mentality" focused on making a respected world product to world-class standards. Production managers, supervisors, and quality control personnel attended extensive three weeks to three months training in the Hugo Boss philosophy and vision. Handbooks were prepared for each piece of equipment and function detailing the process and the quality concerns. By embracing the same tenets of quality that were identified by W. Edwards Deming, Hugo Boss transformed their U.S. manufacturing operations into a quality success story. ■

safety is raised, as for example, in the case of the flammability of infant's sleepwear, the use of drawstrings, or the use of small parts, the federal government becomes the primary partner in the process. If the standard is one that is required by statute, it is known as a **mandatory standard**.

Before any standards are acceptable to all the affected participants, they will be examined, evaluated, and probably revised several times. Since standards provide a means for the entire supply chain to evaluate and compare similar products, standards encourage competition. For example, in sewing the center placket of an expensive shirt 22 stitches per inch is used as compared to using 10 or 12 stitches per inch for sewing a less expensive shirt. The merchandiser must pay careful attention to the role of standards and standardization in the development and manufacture of their product lines.

There are several national and international organizations that develop and promote standards used within the textile and apparel industries. The following four organizations are key contributors to establishing quality standards and testing procedures that affect the apparel industry:

1. The American Association of Textile Chemists and Colorists (AATCC) is recognized around the world for its standard methods of testing dyed and chemically treated fibers and fabrics, which measure such performance characteristics as colorfastness to light and laundering, durable press, dimensional stability, and water repellency. Today, practically all the dyes and finishes and many chemicals produced in the United States are evaluated by AATCC methods (AATCC.org).

2. The American Society for Testing and Materials (ASTM) is the largest nongovernmental organization in the world that writes stan-

dards for materials used in many industries. ASTM Committee D-13 is responsible for establishing and maintaining textile and apparel standards and specifications. ASTM is the foremost developer of voluntary consensus standards, related technical information, and services having internationally recognized quality and applicability that:

- Promote public health and safety.
- Contribute to the reliability of materials, products, systems, and services.
- Facilitate national, regional, and international commerce (ASTM, 1999).

3. The American National Standards Institute (ANSI) maintains as its primary goal the enhancement of global competitiveness of U.S. business and the American quality of life by promoting and facilitating voluntary consensus standards and conformity assessment systems and promoting their integrity. Many ASTM procedures have been accredited through the ANSI certification program.

4. The International Organization for Standardization (ISO) is composed of national standards institutes from large and small countries, industrialized and developing countries, in all regions of the world. ISO develops voluntary standards that represent an international consensus in state-of-the-art technology.

In recent years many companies throughout the world have sought and obtained ISO 9000 certification, which affirms their implementation of the proper strategies, systems, and programs to measure, manage, audit, and continuously improve quality. As many countries around the world as well as neighboring Mexico continue to solicit apparel business from companies in the United States, "to demonstrate their diversification beyond simply 'commodity' apparel production to high-quality fashion merchandise, more firms are adopting quality systems such as ISO 9000" (Kalman, 1999). ISO 14000, as an extension of ISO 9000, certifies that the certified organization has established quality management systems that recognize the need to protect the environment.

■ Specifications

Specifications are exact criteria that must be met by a product or service. Apparel specifications define raw material requirements and how a garment is to be made to achieve the company's established quality standards. In order for specifications to be meaningful, they are expressed in terms of numeric values. There can be a minimum or maximum acceptable value or a range of ac-

ceptable values called **tolerances**, which are allowable deviations from specified values. For example, in the case of fabric performance, the expectations
for properties must meet a measurable maximum such as 2 percent shrinkage.
With respect to dimensions, a tolerance is commonly used. For example, the
length of the sleeve seam on a man's shirt could be 32 inches with an acceptable tolerance of ½ inch (it can be as long as 32½ inches or as short as 31½
inches).

An apparel manufacturer must exercise care when using tolerances. For
instance, if all of the dimensions of a garment are just within the upper tolerance limits, the entire garment may be too large. In order to prevent this
problem, a manufacturer can warn its suppliers that although the individual
dimensions for a garment fall within allowable tolerances, the garment might
be rejected if the overall measurements are not within tolerances. This warning must be stated in terms of a specific measurable quantity or percentage.

As in the case of standards, the writing of specifications must be exact,
consistent, and absolutely clear to both supplier and purchaser. In order to
achieve such precision, individuals known as **specification** or **spec writers**
who are specially trained to perform this task may be hired. Spec writers must
have superior knowledge of all dimensions of their product, be detail-oriented, exacting, and have the ability to write clearly and concisely. Spec writers who are involved with fabrics require a mastery of fibers, spinning, knitting, weaving, color science, chemicals, and finishes. Those who oversee fit
and patterns must have a full understanding of the geometric relationships of
the human body and how to translate two dimensional drawings into three dimensional garments. Spec writers who deal with the manufacturing process
are required to know seams, stitches, and the sequence of operations.

A **specification sheet** is the document that communicates a garment's
specifications both within and outside the company. The format for the specification sheet can come from a variety of sources. For example, an apparel
company might choose one of the many standard forms that are commercially
available, a proprietary form developed by its own personnel, or a form that
is electronically generated as part of a PIM package (see Figure 8.1).

A specification sheet is first used in the product development process
when the prototype is created. At this time the designer needs to communicate to the pattern maker and sample maker exactly how the prototype should
look. When a contractor or third party provider is responsible for making the
prototype, it is even more critical that the spec sheet be accurate, clear, and
complete. Otherwise, there will be unnecessary delays and expenditures, both
of which are unacceptable in the time now allocated for product development.
This specification sheet should include the following information:

- Style and/or design number.
- Sketch.
- Swatches of fabrics.

Exact Knitting Mills
Frogfish Apparel
Measurement Specifications

| Created By | : | Mike Piombino | 2/27/06 12:59 PM |
| Last Modified By | : | Mike Piombino | 2/28/06 9:49 AM |

Style	T992	Cap Sleeve 9-Button Tee		Description	Sample BP111		
Sample Dimensions	XS			Color	ASSORTED	Version	1
Season	All Year			Class	Junior Tops	Approved By	Bob Smith
Customer	Clair Casuals			Status	Development	Style Copied	new

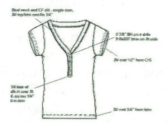

POM Item	Description	Low TOL	High TOL	Measure Base	XS	S	M	L	XL
T100	Front Body Length Fr HPS	0.00	1.00	Inches	23.50	24.00	24.50	25.25	26.00
T200	Chest Width 1" Below Armhole	-0.50	0.50	Inches	10.00	11.00	12.00	13.25	14.50
T212	Sweep	-0.75	0.75	Inches	11.75	12.75	13.75	14.75	15.75
T231	Waist	-0.50	0.50	Inches	8.50	9.50	10.50	11.75	13.00
T185	SHLDR Width	-0.25	0.25	Inches	3.125	3.25	3.50	3.625	3.75
T187	SHLDR Width Pt. to Pt. - Straight	-0.375	0.375	Inches	12.50	13.00	13.50	14.00	14.50
T704	Neck Width Edge To Edge	-0.125	0.125	Inches	7.50	7.75	8.00	8.125	8.25
T230	Waist Position Fr HPS	-0.001	0.001	Inches	13.75	14.125	14.50	15.00	15.50
T222	Across Frt. 6" Fr HPS (Raglan)	-0.50	0.50	Inches	10.75	11.25	11.75	12.375	13.00
T223	Across Bk 6" Fr HPS (Raglan)	-0.50	0.50	Inches	11.50	12.00	12.50	13.125	13.75
T301	Sleeve Length fr CB - Short	-0.25	0.25	Inches	9.75	10.00	10.25	10.625	11.00
T311	AH Depth - Raglan	-0.25	0.25	Inches	7.875	8.125	8.375	8.75	9.25
T335	Sleeve Opening - Short Sleeve	-0.25	0.25	Inches	4.125	4.375	4.75	5.25	5.75
T713	Front Neck Drop From HPS to Edge- AA	-0.125	0.125	Inches	7.75	7.875	8.00	8.125	8.25
T714	Back Neck Drop From HPS To Edge	-0.125	0.125	Inches	0.25	0.375	0.50	0.625	0.75
T180	Underarm Sleeve Length	-0.25	0.25	Inches	0.625	0.625	0.625	0.625	0.625

Figure 8.1 An example of a specification sheet that defines the graded measurements for a women's tee shirt. This form has been created using the ApparelIT Software from Exact Software Company.

- Usage and cost of fabric, trim, and findings.
- Identification of pattern pieces.
- Special sewing instructions.
- Notations regarding placement of parts.

A specification sheet would be used again to convey important information to the manufacturing facility. Normally this specification sheet is part of a package that would also include a production sample, a set of patterns, and possibly a production marker. Regardless of whether the actual production takes place at the apparel company's production facilities or at a contractor's facilities, the need for correct and accurate information is a prerequisite for the manufacturing of a product that meets the company's quality standards. This specification sheet should include the following information:

- Style identification.
- Sketch or photograph.
- Sizes, the measurements for each size, and tolerances.
- Colorways.
- Usage of fabric, trim, and findings.
- Swatch of fabric, samples of trims and findings.
- Construction details including seams and seam allowances, stitches, stitches per inch (spi), placement of parts such as labels, pockets, etc.
- A suggested sequence of manufacturing operations.
- Information that is to be included on the care label (if the care label has not already been produced).

It must be emphasized that in today's global environment, the spec sheet is even more critical in meeting a company's standard of quality when using a contractor or third-party provider.

■ Merchandisers' Responsibilities for Quality Assurance

Merchandisers must research and analyze the quality demands of their target market as the first stage of product development. Based upon the end use of the garment, the merchandiser needs to understand the various quality attributes that determine consumer satisfaction. This may be difficult to determine because the consumer may not always be able to name or to describe these product attributes. There are times when a consumer's perception of quality is different from the inherent quality (actual quality of materials, components, and construction). The merchandiser must be aware that in these situations the perceived quality becomes the real quality.

Quality Determinants During Product Development

Merchandisers must consider quality from the very beginning of the product development cycle. Quality must be built into each style. Quality is not a determinant that can be added during or after the production cycle. Merchandisers must be consistent with regard to quality in their selection of the raw materials, designs, fit, construction details, and finishing that are to be included in a product line. (See Figure 8.2.) When tests on raw materials or prototypes indicate that the company's quality standards will be breached, the

FIGURE 8.2 QUALITY CONCERNS OF MERCHANDISER

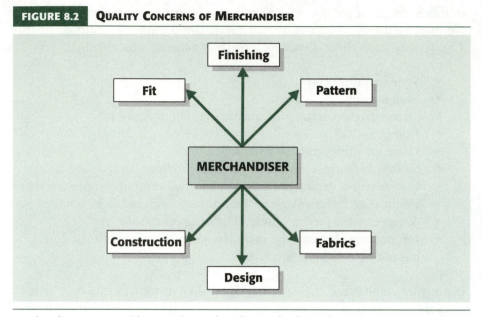

Merchandisers must consider many factors that affect quality during the product development cycle.

merchandiser must either reject that component or style or reevaluate the validity of that specific standard for the target market.

Raw Materials

Merchandisers must meet consumers' expectations of quality as well as ASTM standards, which must be met and guaranteed by the textile mills and converters. When merchandisers investigate and select fabrics, they should receive samples from the supplier accompanied by a data sheet which describes:

- Fiber.
- Size of yarn for both warp and fill.
- Number of turns per inch for yarns.
- Fabric **count**, or number of yarns in the lengthwise and crosswise direction of the fabric (for woven materials, the warp is listed first).
- Fabric **gauge** or **cut** in knit fabrics (needles per inch in the knitting machine used to knit the fabric).
- Weight per square yard and/or linear yard.
- Finished width.
- End use of fabric.
- Finishes that are used and their effectiveness.
- Average and minimum performance levels and the test method used for determining tensile, tear, and bursting strengths.
- Average and minimum performance levels and the test method used for determining stretch.

- Average and minimum performance levels and the test method used for determining abrasion.
- Average and minimum performance levels and the test methods used for determining shrinkage and colorfastness with respect to laundering, dry cleaning, gases, and light sources. (See Figure 8.3.)

At the time the materials are selected, merchandisers may test them to make sure that they meet the company's standards. They may also compare the materials to those of the competition. The tests evaluate the quality, the characteristics, the performance demands, and the reliability of the textile materials. When more than one fabric is used in a garment, all components must be tested for compatibility. For example, do the properties of color react when a 100 percent cotton fabric is attached to a fabric, finding, or trim that is a blend of cotton and synthetic fibers? When two fabrics of different fibers are combined, do both fabrics have the same degree of shrinkage? Can both fabrics be laundered using the same setting on the washing machine? Can both fabrics be dried using the same settings on the drier?

It is always preferable to test materials *before* they are selected and used. This will protect the apparel company in those situations when materials arrive late and do not allow the time required for proper testing. Testing can be performed by the apparel company, by the vendor, or by an independent laboratory. Some of the best independent laboratories are found at schools that specialize in textiles. One of the world's foremost laboratories is the Grundy Center For Textile Product Evaluation at Philadelphia University, formerly Philadelphia College of Textiles and Science. (See Figure 8.4.)

Only **standard test methods**, those approved by organizations such as the ASTM and the AATCC, should be used. Standard test methods are established only after much time and effort have been devoted to their development, evaluation, and refinement. They have to be precise, accurate, reliable, and reproducible.

When applying various materials to different silhouettes, the merchandiser must make sure that these two elements of design are compatible. For example, it is hard to put knife pleats in a heavy fabric such as 12-ounce denim or 5-wale corduroy, and it is equally difficult to hem a circular skirt made of nylon organza. In both cases it would be a challenge to maintain a high level of quality without paying a price in either excessive direct labor or rejected garments. The merchandiser must also take into account how different fibers interact with each other. When various materials are combined for their aesthetic appeal, the consumer will be satisfied only if all the garment's components perform according to their expectations.

Pattern and Fit

Each company has developed its sloper, which is the basis for the pattern for each part of the garment. As each style is created, the patterns for that indi-

---

FIGURE 8.3	**FABRIC SPECIFICATION SHEET**

To be prepared by the fabric supplier at the time of submission.

Manufacturer:_____   Date:_____
Brand Name:_____   Construction Name:_____
Fiber Content:_____   Finish:_____

Yarn Construction/Ply:_____   Warp:_____ Fill:_____
Twist/Inch: Warp:_____   Fill:_____

Fabric Construction: Ends/Inch:_____ Picks/Inch:_____
Width +–:_____inches   Weight: oz/sq yd:_____ oz/linear yd:_____

PROPERTY	PERFORMANCE	METHOD
Tensile Strength:		
Warp_____	Lbs:_____	ASTM-D5034
Fill_____	Lbs:_____	
Tear Strength:		
Warp_____	Ozs:_____	ASTM-D1424
Fill_____	Ozs:_____	
STRETCH:		
Warp:	%_____	ASTM-D 2594
Fill:	%_____	
RECOVERY (for elastomeric construction):		
Warp:	%_____	As agreed to between buyer & seller
Fill:	%_____	
Fabric Care Instructions:		
Wash Temperature,oF:	_____	AATCC-124
Iron: Temperature,oF:	_____	
Bleach:	Y_____ N_____	
Dry Method:		

An example of a data sheet that should be submitted by suppliers when sending samples of fabric.

Figure 8.4 The Grundy Center For Textile Product Evaluation at Philadelphia University is a world famous textile testing facility.

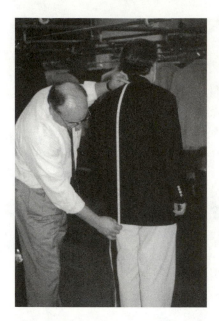

Figure 8.5 A prototype is measured on a fit model to check for the proper measurements.

vidual style are made taking into account the fashion element, the fabric, and the end use of the garment. A prototype is then made and checked on a fit model by the merchandiser, the designer, and the pattern maker. (See Figure 8.5.) All the necessary adjustments must be made to each pattern so that the final production patterns and their size gradations result in the proper garment dimensions and fit.

Construction

The selection of seams and stitches must be consistent with the company's standards. The use of chain, lock, overlock, mock safety, or safety stitches should be decided as well as the application of fully bound, partially bound, or raw seams. The need to include linings and interlinings, hand-stitched or machine-stitched buttonholes, or fused or sewn appliqués must also be determined. The design that is created in a sample room environment must be capable of being reproduced in a production facility. This is one of the reasons why it is always preferable to make samples in the same factory where the production will take place. The merchandiser will be able to analyze any production difficulties with each sample style including the attendant quality assurance issues if the manufacturing facilities do not have the equipment, the trained personnel, or the production expertise needed to meet the product specifications.

Quality Procedures after Line Development

If as a result of Deming's, Juran's, and Harry's philosophies, all the quality assurance processes and procedures are in place during product development and production, only minimal final inspection will be necessary. Nevertheless, many apparel companies perform some type of in-process inspection on their garments.

Inspection of Fabrics, Trims, and Findings

If an apparel company has a long-standing positive relationship with a vendor, the need for quality inspections by the company is greatly reduced. In the partnership approach of quick response (a business strategy that considerably reduces the length of time it takes to replenish retail inventories) raw materials must be shipped free of imperfections. This business practice transfers to the supplier the responsibility for quality assurance and eliminates the need for the apparel company to inspect the raw materials when they are received, thus saving valuable time. However, for purchases from vendors other than strategic partners, inspection should take place immediately upon receipt. When the inspection is delayed, the time to receive a replacement or substitute material is reduced, and the vendor might challenge the validity of the claim. (See Figure 8.6.)

There are two types of raw material defects. The first is known as a **patent defect** because it can be detected by examination, inspection, or testing; the second is known as a **latent defect** because it cannot be seen through normal testing and inspection and will become apparent only over the course of

Figure 8.6 Fabric should be inspected by apparel manufacturers upon receipt. Machines such as the one shown here are used to perform the inspection.

time. Finding patent defects is aided by the use of a machine that moves the fabric across the viewing area lengthwise, from the beginning to the end of the roll. This inspection focuses on:

- Misweaves.
- Distortions of the yarn from the perpendicular such as **bow** when the crosswise yarns arc as they go across the fabric, or **skew** when the filling yarn forms some angle other than 90 degrees with the warp.
- Holes and cuts.
- Color deviations known as **shading**.

Once defects are discovered, the apparel manufacturer must determine whether or not the degree of the imperfection will have a negative impact on the acceptability of the finished product. For this purpose a numeric value or grade is assigned to the fabric. The grade is based upon size, severity, and number of defects on either a 4-point or a 10-point system. Two ASTM standards, ASTM D 3990-93 for Standard Terminology Relating to Fabric Defects and ASTM 5430-93 for Standard Test Methods for Visually Inspecting and Grading Fabrics, are used to make this evaluation.

Some apparel manufacturers also perform source inspections, which are inspections at the vendor's location. The purpose of such inspections is to assess the testing procedures and documentation used by the vendor or to evaluate product quality and take corrective action before shipping to the apparel production facility, thereby minimizing delays caused by defects. To provide high quality raw materials, textile mills must perform effective finished goods inspections. Textile mills must identify and map fabric defects so apparel manufacturers can achieve optimal material utilization and minimum garment fallout due to fabric defects during manufacturing.

Proper Marking, Spreading, and Cutting Operations

A second opportunity for visual inspection is during the spreading of the material in advance of the cutting operation. Once again the spreader looks for holes, cuts, misweaves, distortions, misprints, and shading. If defects are found, they are cut out. There are some inspecting machines that will indicate the exact location of holes, cuts, misprints, shade variances, and minimum widths. The information gathered in this process, known as **mapping**, can be fed into a computerized spreading machine that will stop at the defect location. The spreader can then determine whether to remove the defect, to mark the location, or to include the defect in the layer of the fabric if it will fall in the waste area.

The spreader must be careful to properly align the marker within the cuttable width of the fabric, to spread the materials smoothly, and to keep the material free from tension. All manual cuts should be inspected to make sure that they are within prescribed tolerances of the outlines on the marker. If the parts are not cut accurately, they cannot be assembled without distortion or within the tolerances of the size specifications. This problem is eliminated with computerized cutting because of its accuracy.

During each of these operations, inspections must be performed to ensure that the quality standards are being met. If an unacceptable number of defects are found, the cause must be determined and remedial action must be taken immediately.

Sewing and Assembly of Cut Parts

It is imperative that once the sequence of operations has been established, it be followed and that the proper seams and stitches be used in each operation. However, even when the instructions are meticulously followed, it is still possible for the sewing operator to make mistakes. In order to control these situations, either roving or stationary inspections can be performed.

In a **roving inspection**, the inspector randomly goes from one sewing operator to another inspecting seam allowances, the number of stitches per inch, the alignment of parts, and critical specifications. For example, since the proper measurement of the armhole of a blouse is a prerequisite for the proper sleeve cap attachment, the inspector will focus on this element. In a **stationary inspection**, garment parts are brought to the inspector who visually assesses the critical points at a well-lit and properly equipped inspection station. Under both types of inspection, when the supervisor is immediately informed of any deficiency, she or he immediately takes remedial action. The remedial action would include meeting with the individual sewing operator to solve the problem and repairing or discarding the defective parts before any additional sewing operations are performed.

FOUR POINT SYSTEM

The Four Point System is used to determine if a piece of knitted fabric is to be classified as first quality or as a second. It was established, subject to annual review, by the Knitted Textile Association and the Textile Distributors Association Inc., on June 24, 1971.

The knitted fabric should be inspected on the face side for defects with penalty points being assessed according to the length of the defect. A maximum of four points can be charged against any one linear yard of knitted fabric which is 64-66 inches in width. The quality shall be expressed in the number of points that such quality would have in a 100 yard length (e.g. 5 penalty points in 20 yards would be rated as 25 points for 100 yards). For knitted fabrics that are wider than 64-66 inches, the maximum is increased proportionately with 64 inches as the basis for the calculation.

The penalty points are as follows:

Size of Defect (length in inches)	Number of Penalty Points
3 inches or less	1
over 3 but not over 6 inches	2
over 6 but not over 9 inches	3
over 9 inches	4

The identification and rating of the defects shall be subject to the following:

1. Defects within one inch of either edge shall not be considered.
2. Irregularities normal to the existing state of the art or beyond the reasonable control of the manufacturer or inherent in any specified type of construction, shall not be considered for penalty.
3. Any hole other than a pin hole shall be considered a major defect and assigned the maximum number of points.
4. Unless otherwise specified and agreed to by buyer and seller, the knitted fabric is to be examined for defects only on its face.
5. Conditions such as barre, bowing and pin holes cannot be assigned penalty points and must be judged based upon the degree and extent to which they occur and their probable effect upon the type of garment being cut.

Knitted fabrics having a width up to 64–66 inches shall be classified as first quality if the number of penalty points does not exceed 50 points on the assumed basis of 100 yards. When the width of the knitted fabric is greater than 64–66 inches, the number of allowable penalty points shall be increased proportionately with the number of 64 being the basis for the calculation.

Source: Textiles Distributors Association, Inc.

The Four Point System is used to determine if a piece of knitted fabric is to be classified as first or second quality.

TEN POINT SYSTEM

The ten point system, a standard for the examination of finished goods, was established by the Textile Directors Institute, Inc. and The National Federation of Textiles Inc. They cover all marketwide fabrics of manmade and/or natural fibers alone or in combination and apply to all fabrics regardless of width or construction. While primarily intended for finished materials, they can also be used for grey or unfinished goods. These standards explain the penalties to be assigned to both warp and filling defects and conditions, what constitutes defects, and the penalties in points to be applied against each defect.

The grading shall apply to every imperfection according to size, but in the case of fabrics that are over 50 inches in finished width, an increase of not more than 10 percent in penalty points will be allowed in "first" quality. If the total number of penalty points is less than the number of yards in the piece, the piece is graded a first; if the total points exceed the yardage, the piece is graded as second. With print cloth, any piece of grey goods which contains less than 50 percent more penalty points than the yardage may be passed for printing purposes. No single yard should be penalized more than 10 points. Any warp or filling defect occurring repeatedly throughout the entire piece makes it a second.

The face side of finished goods should be examined in one complete piece and in full width either by a machine or over a perch. Inspection shall be made using north daylight free from reflections or shadows or an approved type of lighting system. The machine or perch shall be placed perpendicular to rays of light, and the material shall be run at an angle of 45 percent to the vertical.

Imperfections are defects which can be prevented under normal conditions and with normal care. Normal irregularities, which are defects beyond the reasonable control of the manufacturer or natural to any particular quality or construction, should not be considered as a defect. Imperfections appearing within one half inch from either edge should be disregarded. Imperfections are classified as follows:

- Vertical imperfections or those running parallel to the warp.
- Horizontal imperfections or those running parallel to the filling thread.

Warp Defects		Filling Defects	
0 to 36 inches	10 points	Full width	10 points
5 to 10 inches	5 points	5 inches to half width	5 points
1 to 5 inches	3 points	1 to 5 inches	3 points
Up to one inch	1 point	Up to one inch	1 point

Source: Textile Distributors Association, Inc.

The Ten Point System is used to determine primarily whether finished woven fabrics are to be graded as a first or second quality. Under this system, standards for defects are explained and then penalty points are applied against defects.

Finishing

Finishing inspections focus on the following:

- Correct hangtags and labels.
- Absence of loose threads.
- Acceptable pressing and pinning and packaging.
- Inclusion of all required components such as both the skirt and jacket or both the gloves and scarf that are part of an ensemble.

■ Inspection Procedures

The actual process of inspection can be performed in several places and at different times during the manufacturing process. The purpose of the inspection is to compare the raw materials, components, and manufacturing work-in-process to the established standards, specifications, and requirements of the company. In order to initiate and maintain a successful inspection system, the following elements must be in place:

- Standards and specifications with tolerances must be created for each style.
- The inspection must be conducted in a well-lit, unobstructed area.
- The inspection must be performed by properly trained, properly equipped, and properly compensated personnel.
- All findings must be properly documented and communicated to all the interested parties.

The precepts of both Deming and Juran have influenced apparel companies to conduct their examinations as early in the process as possible. According to *Apparel Industry Magazine* "the difference between a plant with consistent quality and one with questionable quality often depends upon who assumes responsibility for quality and when it is assumed. Today's more successful plants rely more on building quality into their product from the beginning of the production process. They also rely on and reward the efforts of their associates in assuring quality, rather than relying on and paying inspectors to look for defects. By keeping responsibility for quality products within the plant itself, the company makes the need for quality first priority, rather than the desire to produce a higher volume of products at a lower quality" (AAMA, 1995).

The American Apparel and Footwear Association has developed a chart that illustrates the differences in quality control between the old inspection-based method and the new production-based method. The new approach demonstrates the influence of W. Edwards Deming. (See Figure 8.7.)

Old Way 100 Inspection	New Way Quality Assurance/Empowerment
Acceptable Quality Level (AQL)	Zero defects
Inspector dominant	Associate responsibility
Attempt to inspect quality into the product	Build quality into the product
Justification for equipment investment based solely on reduction in labor content	Justification for equipment investment based on quality improvement
Need to produce volume first priority	Need to make a quality product first priority
Quality inspector given responsibility for product quality	Associate accepts ownership of quality process
Operator punishment for creating defects	Associate rewarded for recognizing and correcting the cause of defects
No incentive for quality production, inspector paid based on pieces processed	Incentive for quality production, associates paid based on number of first quality products produced
Inspectors paid for finding defects (non-value-added activity)	No need for inspectors, as associates paid for producing quality the first time (value-added activity)
Limited after-the-fact reporting	Casual analysis by statistical process control and other measurement tools (reporting of defects by type, quantity, area, associate)
Repair an integral part of the process	Low or no need for repair and cost of repair not justifiable
Standards are what the supervisor says they are	Standards are based on specifications developed with consideration for process capability

Figure 8.7 The American Apparel and Footwear Association clearly identifies the differences between the older inspection based method and the newer production based method. It is easy to recognize the application of the teachings of W. Edwards Deming.

Raw Materials

The first place to conduct an inspection is at the source of the raw materials before they are shipped. This allows fabric to be moved directly to the cutting table when it is received by the cutting facility, thereby reducing the total time it takes to replenish inventory. This inspection at the source also serves to eliminate the time and effort needed to negotiate and complete the return of the defective material to the vendor. With the development of buyer/seller partnerships and the substitution of a mutually beneficial alliance for an adversarial relationship, both parties work together to develop and deliver an acceptable product. A vendor partnership might lead to the formal certification known as a **vendor** or **supplier certification**, which reduces the need for material inspections. If an inspection at the vendor's location is not possible, the next best alternative is to examine the goods as soon as they are received.

Components

Parts of garments, such as cuffs, embroidered collars, and pockets, and individual components, such as hats, gloves, and socks, can be manufactured by the apparel producer, a vendor, or by a contractor. After the components are completed, they are shipped to the apparel producer to be combined with other parts in the assembly of the garment. The same inspection opportunities exist for components as they do for materials.

Work-in-Process (Assembly)

Operators can perform inspections in a progressive system (bundle or unit production system) when they inspect the work of the operator who just completed the previous step in the process. (See Figure 8.8.) In addition roving or stationary inspectors may also be involved in the process.

Figure 8.8 Inspectors check sewing quality to identify any imperfections. This should be done before garments move to the next phase of the manufacturing process.

The number of garments inspected can vary: in some cases, every garment is inspected (100 percent inspection); in others, a predetermined number (sampling inspection) are inspected. Some apparel companies might inspect or examine the first group of samples. This allows them to make minor adjustments in order to solve potential production problems before they occur.

When garments are manufactured by outside contractors, apparel companies should make every effort to monitor the production process. They can assign their own employees to conduct the inspections, or they can engage an independent agent. Independent agents are normally used when production takes place in another country or when the contractor's facility is a great distance from the apparel company. There also are situations where the foreign contractor performs an audit inspection before the merchandise is shipped to the domestic distribution center. Liz Claiborne has established "Quality Assurance Centers located in the regional headquarters of its world-wide sourcing network, with the objective of identifying and correcting quality problems closer to the manufacturing source" (DesMarteau, 1999).

Finished Goods

The final inspection of merchandise is to ensure that the completed garment meets the company's required specifications and standards. While this procedure normally is performed in the production facility, it can also take place at the distribution or shipping point. Finished goods can also be inspected after they have arrived at their destination. Several apparel companies have adopted the practice of shipping merchandise to fictitious customers and then performing their own inspection when the garments are returned. This gives the apparel company the opportunity to see exactly what the customer would see when receiving its products. It is a way to evaluate all components of the garment, beginning with the selection of the materials and ending with the packaging and shipping operations.

■ Sampling Procedures

Regardless of where and when an inspection takes place, an effective sampling process must be used to assure the apparel order or lot being inspected meets the company's quality standards. While the safest method would be to examine each garment at each stage of production, this approach would be very expensive and time consuming. Most companies, therefore, employ a sampling method, in which a predetermined number of garments, or a specified portion of a production lot, are selected for inspection. In the apparel industry Federal Military Standard 105 E (MIL-STD-105E) and commercial standard

ANSI/ASQ Z1.4-1993 are typically used to establish sampling procedures and acceptable quality levels (AQL). This standard sets out the required number of samples to be examined based on lot size and the number of non-conforming samples that determine whether to accept or reject the lot. The lower the AQL number, the fewer the non-conforming samples needed to reject the lot. In other words, the lower the AQL, the greater the effort to insure delivery of a quality product.

For example, in a lot of 501 to 1,200 pieces, 80 garments must be inspected. If the company uses an AQL of 2.5, only 6 non-conforming samples will cause the lot to be rejected. If the company uses an AQL of 4.0, the number of non-conforming samples increases to 8.

When inspection reveals that the quality of production is questionable, a greater number of garments may then be inspected. When inspection reveals few if any quality defects, fewer garments may be inspected. When inspection results in a number of defects that the sampling plan determines is critical, each garment in a production lot may be inspected.

Types of Samples

There are various methods for selecting the number of garments to inspect. A **random sample** is when each garment in a production lot has an equal chance of being examined regardless of style, size, or color. Most apparel companies prefer to inspect a **representative sample**, which is a specific number of garments and includes samplings of each style, size, and color. Sometimes a constant percentage of each production lot is inspected, no matter how many garments are in the lot. This type of sample, known as a **constant percentage sample**, causes two sets of problems. With small production lots, this inspection method does not provide for the examination of a sufficient number of garments, which challenges the validity of the inspection; with large production lots, it can result in the examination of too many garments thereby increasing the cost and time of the inspection.

Another approach is to select samples from each production lot, which is referred to as **lot-by-lot sampling**. This method is used when the production facility is new to the sourcer or when a style is new and the sourcer has no previous experience with the style to gauge the potential for quality problems caused by specific construction or fabric attributes. The company may also choose to examine only some of the production lots once a consistent level of quality has been proven over a period of time, when a high level of production has been reached, or when there has been a constant use of the same materials, construction, or design features. This is known as **skip-lot sampling**. When there is continuous production of a style over a long period of time, a **continuous production sample** will be inspected to ensure that the quality has been maintained.

Determination of Acceptance or Rejection

When any part of an apparel product does not meet the standards and specifications of the company, the garment is considered defective. Since each company sets its own standards and specifications, what might be considered a defect at one company might not be considered a defect at another. There are various degrees of defects. A **critical defect** is one that would cause harm to the consumer when either worn or maintained. This might include material finishes that could cause skin irritation. A **major defect** is one that detracts from the attractiveness or the performance of a garment as with the misalignment or the malfunction of parts such as buttons and buttonholes. A **minor defect** is one that will not greatly affect the intended use or the performance of the garment. A minor defect may be a pocket that is slightly larger or smaller than the specified tolerance allows.

The location of the defect can also determine whether it is major or minor. For example, the bowing in a plaid part that is in the front of the garment where it is highly visible would be graded differently from a situation in which the bowing was in the back or in the hem of the garment. Each company has to determine its **acceptable quality level (AQL)**, which is the maximum number of each type of defect that would not bring about the rejection of a garment. Each company also must determine how many defects would cause the rejection of a total production lot of a particular style.

Merchandisers can make a major contribution in establishing acceptance levels. They know what qualifies as a critical, major, and minor defect and how each would affect the consumer's purchasing decision.

■ Statistical Process Control

Statistical process control (**SPC**) is the use of statistics and control charts in monitoring variations in the manufacturing process. While it is relatively new in the apparel industry, SPC has been used previously in other manufacturing and service industries as an analytical tool for continuous quality improvement. SPC employs the use of control charts to determine whether the variations in a company's products or processes fall within the acceptable upper and lower limits. Most variations are a natural occurrence because no two products or processes are exactly the same. This type of variation, referred to as **normal variation**, can be measured, and these measurements normally follow a definite pattern called a **frequency distribution**. When the measurements are plotted, they form a **normal distribution curve**, which shows that most of the measurements fall close to the middle of the range of variations. It is when variations fall outside this curve or pattern that they are called **abnormal variations**. Abnormal variations are unacceptable and require investigation to determine the probable cause and formulate the possible solution.

For example, the normal distribution curve for the setting of a shirt's collar shows that a range between 3 percent and 4.5 percent of the collars will be set improperly. If the percentage of imperfect settings jumps to 5 percent, this is an abnormal variation. The cause of the abnormal variation must be found and a solution applied.

When an apparel company adopts SPC, it determines the critical features of its garment that meet the specific needs of the consumer. After this selection process, the company must next identify the production factors that affect these characteristics. They then can determine the upper and lower control limits or normal variations in measurement. As a result of monitoring the critical processes, the company can detect when the limits have been breached. It knows to look for the following special causes of the abnormal variations:

- Training of machine operators.
- Machine failure or malfunction.
- Improper procedures.
- Use of improper materials.
- Poor working environment.

Having previously devised possible solutions, the company can remedy the situation before it becomes a major problem.

David Baron Experience—vice president, Quality Assurance, Liz Claiborne, Inc.

Definition of Quality

"Quality can be defined in many different ways. The current popular definition is centered on customer expectation. Certainly this is valid, but in terms of our work environment, we have to define and communicate our expectations to our suppliers in more definitive terms. We use our written specification sheet and an approved garment to achieve a mutual understanding of our expectations. The approved garment or sealed sample, with any written comments attached, is the tool we use to define specifications in terms of the garment aesthetics, fit, construction and measurements."

Defining Standards of Quality

"Each business unit at Liz Claiborne determines product design and aesthetic, as well as the quality standard. From a corporate perspective, we have to provide fabric performance guidelines that conform to industry standards and protect the reputation of Liz Claiborne. These guidelines address issues of fabric safety, durability, and performance.

"A balance has to be achieved between the creative elements of our business, which is often searching for uniqueness, and the concerns regarding consumer performance expectations. Some fabrics have inherent limitations due to the physical properties of the yarns, dye stuffs, and finishes. We have to determine where creativity and newness cross the boundaries of reasonable performance. Subjectivity occasionally becomes part of the decision-making process, as all products have limitations. For example, an iridescent fabric in certain colors has light color-fastness limitations. If the hot trend is this product, do we forsake it because of these limitations, or inform the consumer via educational information attached to the product? This is a business decision."

Quality Assurance as a Corporate Responsibility

"The quality function at Liz Claiborne is the responsibility of everyone who touches and supervises the development and manufacturing of any product. From a corporate perspective, the quality assurance organization deploys assets in the field to monitor the systems and processes of our suppliers. In addition, we support the efforts of agents to ensure that their approach to quality

(continued)

assurance mirrors the principles that we embrace as an organization."

Input of Designers and Merchandisers

"We have to understand the point of view of the designer and merchandiser and reach a compromise between their vision, cost constraints, margin goals, and other criteria we deem important in the eyes of our retail customers and the ultimate consumer. Once we've merged this information together, guidelines for standards and performance are developed. It's the responsibility of the business unit to communicate performance and construction standards in the specifications package that is forwarded to the supplier.

"We can also view quality on many different levels within the organization. Quality of work and communications is an important consideration within the company. There are many internal customers that expect correct information communicated on a timely basis. In this regard, we are looking at quality of execution and a clean hand off to the next internal customer."

Relationship Between Quality and Price

"If the goal is to achieve a specific price point and you're also attempting to achieve a certain margin, then you have to work within parameters. Raw material costs and sewing construction issues are important con-

siderations. Often, a trade-off is necessary when attempting to achieve a certain price point for a specific consumer.

"Suppose we are having difficulty in achieving our margin goals. We may have to compromise our desire to have full plaid matching on a garment. We may be confined to matching only the fronts and pockets. We might decide to balance the sleeves and collars, but give up our desire to match the side seams. Constraints will result in compromise. A business unit that is seeking to achieve a target price point is best served by establishing standard methods of construction that are compatible with its objectives."

Information Provided to Suppliers

"The package that goes to the manufacturing facility is generally a pattern, a sample, spec sheets, and trims, which are used to produce the first counter sample. As we look toward the future, we are expecting our suppliers to develop product on our behalf, from a sketch. The vision is to supply slopers as building blocks that reflect the appropriate fit for our customer. The fabric development and selection will remain a part of our internal core competency. Verification of fabric quality is the responsibility of the garment supplier. We expect our garment suppliers to use the four point fabric evaluation system, which is identical to the inspection systems used by

(*continued*)

our textile mills. Each shipment is expected to average 13 points per 100 linear yards, with none to exceed 26 points. Fabric specifications to the textile mills and converters are clearly defined by our terms of engagement and the specifications on any purchase orders. Textile suppliers are required to include fabric inspection and testing reports in all shipments. The garment supplier validates the authenticity of these reports. If there is a quality issue, the textile mill and garment supplier are expected to negotiate a settlement. As a last resort, we will intercede to mediate a situation.

"As product development responsibility is shifted to our suppliers, we have to gauge the capability of their staffs to perform this role. Our goal is to buy the finished product, instead of elements of the process. This approach is both time- and cost-efficient for both Liz and our suppliers, assuming our suppliers own the necessary skill sets. This intimate understanding of the product from the inception reduces the length of the product development process, provided that design clearly defines its goal."

The Importance of ISO 9000

"ISO 9000 accreditation is a reasonable objective. It reshapes an organization through the requirements of procedural documentation and formalized training. If properly developed and applied in a disciplined manner, it will strengthen an orga-

nization. Too often, what you see is companies going for the accreditation and then failing to abide by the principles and disciplines embraced in their documented systems and procedures. ISO certification is not a panacea or a guarantee that a supplier can consistently achieve your standards. It's a good start."

The Importance of Statistical Process Control (SPC) at Liz Claiborne

"We believe that SPC is the most effective tool available to ensure our quality standards. SPC is a method of measuring process variance and predictability. Observing and recording data on a control chart at regular intervals brings a process to life. Process deficiencies can have multiple causes. It's a combination of management responsiveness and operator awareness that results in corrective action to improve a process. The goal is to establish processes in manufacturing that are predictable, stable, and exceed a customer's specification, consistently. If the process doesn't meet your customers' specification, then you're obliged to change the process until it meets or exceeds the specification. The goal is continuous process improvement.

"At Liz Claiborne we have begun to apply statistical process control to our internal processes. We are concerned about the accuracy, completeness, and timeliness of information throughout the orga-

(continued)

nization. There is significant money to be saved if we do things right the first time. We're actually using SPC to evaluate the performance of pattern makers, counter sample technicians, and technical designers. We can improve performance by identifying areas to target for further education and training. We hope to expand the use of this tool to evaluate calendar disciplines, logistics, transportation, and performance in our finance department. Beyond this, the potential is unlimited for other applications.

"SPC is also a requirement to be classified as a Certified Supplier of Liz Claiborne. Suppliers that don't embrace SPC are likely to jeopardize their future business with our company. However, the vision we have shared is that the use of the tool benefits the supplier, in terms of increasing its productivity and profitability. Hearing this from a competitor, who has benefited from SPC, and a visit to their facility to share a best practice, has resulted in the effective leveraging of our early success stories. This has aided our organization to expand the use of this tool into supplier facilities that produce the majority of our apparel products."

Summary

Merchandisers must look to the company's target market to see what factors consumers apply when they assess the quality of their apparel purchases. Most consumers are concerned with aesthetics (design, fit, and construction) and performance (durability, care, comfort, and appearance retention). The company needs to set standards that meet or surpass the expectations of its target market. When an apparel company directs all the activities in all of its departments to delivering a quality product that will satisfy its target market and at the same time reach its own business objectives, it is practicing total quality management (TQM).

Merchandisers must know the expectations of their target market and then incorporate these real or perceived needs into each garment. They need to develop consistent criteria, standards and specifications when deciding which materials, designs, and construction details to include in their line. Specification sheets communicate critical quality information, which can include minimum acceptable quality levels or a range of acceptable quality values known as tolerances.

Raw materials should be tested by the methods approved by the ASTM and AATCC and then evaluated for their quality, characteristics, performance demands, and reliability. Patterns must provide for the proper fit for all sizes of the style. The selection of fabrics must be compatible with the design of the garment, the seams and stitches must be consistent with company standards, and the sample must be reproducible in mass production.

Apparel companies continuously conduct inspections during the manufacturing processes. The examination begins with the receipt of raw materials and then continues through the marking, spreading, cutting, sewing, and finishing operations. Decisions must be made on the number of garments to inspect at each phase of production. Since 100 percent inspection is too expensive and time consuming, a sampling of the production is normally examined. Sampling can be random or a constant percentage of each production lot, of only some of the production lots, or on a continuous basis.

A defect is determined when any part of the apparel product does not meet the established standards and specifications. Critical, major, and minor defects are the various levels of defects. The merchandiser participates in a company's determination of its acceptance level, which is the number of each type of defect that would cause a garment to be rejected by the consumer.

Statistical process control (SPC) is used by some companies to meet the specific quality needs of their consumers. The system monitors production to determine when quality limits have been exceeded and appropriate action must be taken to assure consistent product quality.

Key Terms

abnormal variations

acceptable quality level (AQL)

appearance retention

bow

care

comfort

constant percentage sample

continuous production sample

count

critical defect

cut

delaminate

durability

frequency distribution

fusibles

gauge

industry standard

latent defect

lot-by-lot sampling

major defect

mandatory standard

mapping

minor defect

normal distribution curve

normal variation

patent defect

random sample

representative sample

roving inspection

shading

skew

skip-lot sampling

spec writer

specification sheet

specification writer

specifications

standard test methods

standardization

standards

stationary inspection

statistical process control (SPC)

supplier certification

tolerances

total quality management (TQM)

vendor certification

voluntary standard

Discussion Questions and Learning Activities

1. What are the two measures that consumers use when they assess the quality of apparel products? How do the measures differ from each other?

2. Why do apparel companies establish standards for their products? Why do apparel companies issue specifications? What is the relationship between a company's set of standards and its specifications?

3. What actions can the merchandiser take to maintain the company's level of quality in a global environment?

4. What is the purpose of inspection? When should inspections be performed? Where should inspections be performed? Who should perform the inspections?

5. Enumerate the various alternatives to inspecting every garment.

6. What is statistical process control? Do you believe that this practice will grow in importance in the apparel industry? Explain your answer.

7. What could be the impact upon an apparel company's quality assurance program when it becomes certified for ISO 9000?

8. Select one of your favorite garments and then ask several of your friends to judge its quality. How do their assessments compare to each other? Do you agree with their opinions? Why or why not?

9. Imagine that you have been assigned the responsibility for establishing a set of quality standards for your apparel company. What steps would you take when developing these standards?

10. List all the components that would be found on a specification sheet that an apparel company would give to its contractor. Create a form that would include all this information.

11. Visit a clothing store and compare the quality of two identical garments from the same national brand manufacturer. What are the differences between the two? Now select two of the same type of garment from the store's private brand and compare one to the other. Evaluate the quality of each garment and determine if the difference in quality would influence your purchase decision.

12. Talk to a student in a fashion design class and find out what quality factors are considered when creating a style. Do you feel that enough attention is given to prevent potential quality problems?

References and Resources

AAMA, Continuing Education Subcommittee. December 1995. Education Update. *Apparel Industry Magazine*, p. 54.

Bonner, Staci. December 1997. Simplicity Is the Key. *Apparel Industry Magazine*, pp. AS 20–26.

Carsky, Mary L.; Dickinson, Roger A.; and Canedy III, Charles R. 1998. The Evolution of Quality in Consumer Goods. *Journal of Macromarketing*, pp. 132–144.

Conrad, Andree. December 1997. An International Boss. *Apparel Industry Magazine*, pp. AS 12–18.

DesMarteau, Kathleen. May 1999. Liz Launches Global Quality Coup. *Bobbin*, pp. 34–38.

Fairchild Publications Staff Report. July 23, 1998. Russell to Take Charge on Quarter. *Womens Wear Daily*, p. 9.

Hamel, Gary, and Prahalad, C. K. 1994. Competing for the Future. *Harvard Business Review* 72 (4), pp. 122–28.

Harry, Mikel, Ph.D., and Schroeder, Richard. (2000). *Sigma Six*. New York. Currency, p. 21.

Kadolph, Sara J. 1998. *Quality Assurance for Textiles and Apparel*. New York. Fairchild Publications, p. 32.

Kalman, Jordan. May 1999. Partnering Made Easy: Inaugural Bobbin Expo Mexico and Central America. *Bobbin*, pp. 22–25.

Levine, Gene. August 1997. Implementing Cost Effective Quality Assurance Programs. *Bobbin*, pp. 116–118.

Williamson, Rusty. July 9, 1998. Breaking Through. *Womens Wear Daily*, pp. 4, 48.

Web sites

http://www.aatcc.org/membership/corp%20memb.htm
http://web.ansi/public/about.htm
http://www.astm.org SRAQ/texweb.htm
http://www.iso.ch/htm

CHAPTER 9

Supply Chain Management

OBJECTIVES

- Explore the evolution of supply chain management.

- Discuss the effect of demand-activated manufacturing architecture on the apparel industry.

- Explore the concept of quick response relative to the full scope of the apparel merchandising process.

- Examine the role of control, communication, and collaboration in supply chain management.

Short interval scheduling (SIS), quick response (QR), just-in-time (JIT), theory of constraints (TOC), electronic data interchange (EDI), vendor-managed inventory (VMI), collaborative planning, forecasting and replenishment (CPFR), enterprise resource planning (ERP), supply chain management (SCM), Radio Frequency Identification (RFID), Product Lifecycle Management (PLM). The buzz words and acronyms keep changing, but the underlying principle remains basically the same: apparel merchandisers must get the desired product to the customer as quickly as possible, at the best quality, and at the lowest possible price. What has changed, however, is the focus of the management systems and philosophies used to achieve those results.

■ Evolution of Supply Chain Management

In the 1970s and 1980s apparel managers focused on reducing manufacturing costs. They reduced the manufacturing cycle through **short interval scheduling (SIS)**, which establishes tight production control systems to decrease work-in-process inventories, thereby creating a leaner manufacturing process. SIS decreased **inventory carrying costs** (the costs to maintain inventories, such as interest charges on capital needed to purchase the materials and labor expended on inventory and the overhead expenses created by the space required to store inventory) and enabled companies to respond more quickly to customer demands. During this same period, many apparel companies started importing garments. This led to intense sourcing efforts to find the lowest possible manufacturing costs by scouring the globe for developing countries with low labor rates and sufficient infrastructure to support apparel manufacturing.

In 1984, in response to increasing imports, the fiber, textile, apparel, and home furnishings industries formed the Crafted With Pride in U.S.A. Council, Inc., to strengthen the competitive position of U.S.-made products. As part of its program, the council promoted quick response (QR) manufacturing practices, which encouraged apparel companies to develop working relationships with their retail customers and their raw material suppliers in order to reduce product development and manufacturing cycle times and to respond more quickly to consumer demands. When the quick response initiative was launched in 1985, it was projected that $25 billion was being lost annually within the **soft goods supply chain** (the system that provides the raw materials and processes for getting textiles and apparel products from concept to consumer). This lost revenue was caused by decreasing margin dollars through markdowns on garments that did not meet the needs of the market; through lost sales due to stock outs, where consumers couldn't find the style they wanted in their size and desired color; and high inventory carrying costs. (See Figure 9.1.)

In order to support the QR initiative, different sectors of the textile and apparel supply chains established voluntary interindustry organizations. The **Voluntary Interindustry Commerce Standards (VICS)** council was estab-

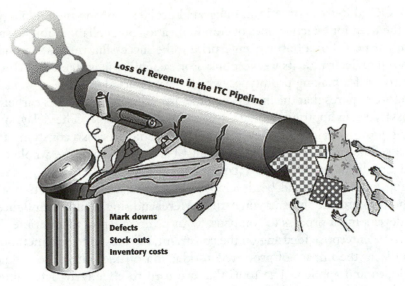

Mark downs
Defects
Stock outs
Inventory costs

Figure 9.1 The dramatic loss of revenue in the U.S. Integrated Textile Complex supply chain can be traced to mark downs at both the wholesale and retail sectors, defects, lost sales due to stock outs or not having exactly what the consumer wanted, and the high costs of carrying inventory.

lished by retail, apparel, and textile firms to institute standards for product marking, computer-to-computer communications, and shipping container marking. The **Textile Apparel Linkage Council (TALC)** was established to develop voluntary standards that would support QR and just-in-time delivery between textile and apparel companies. The **Fabric and Suppliers Linkage Council (FASLINC)** was created to improve communications and cooperation between textile companies and their fiber suppliers. The **Sundries and Apparel Findings Linkage Council (SAFLINC)** was formed by apparel companies and their trim and findings suppliers to establish EDI standards to improve communications and product identification between their industry sectors. These voluntary councils were successful in supporting and fostering the growth of the QR movement.

At the same time that the Crafted With Pride in U.S.A. Council began stressing quick response and collaboration to reduce apparel product throughput time, Dr. Eliyahu M. Goldratt developed the **theory of constraints (TOC)**, a portfolio of management philosophies, management disciplines, and industry-specific "best practices." In his theory, Dr. Goldratt notes that management traditionally emphasized reduction of operating expenses first, followed by improving throughput and, finally, inventory reduction. His theory stresses that the greatest gains will be realized by first increasing throughput, then by reducing inventory, and the last priority—not the first—should be reducing operating expenses. In order to achieve increased throughput, total enterprisewide solutions should focus on the business functions of marketing, supplier relations, production, and distribution.

TOC addresses not only an integrated problem-solving methodology but also the need for effective lines of communication and collaboration by supply chain partners. For a business enterprise to be successful, the system must be analyzed to determine its weakest link. For example, the weakest link could be the process for making prototypes, which delays line adoption by 2 weeks and therefore requires that the line development process begin 2 weeks earlier than necessary when appropriate market data are not available. The delay in producing prototypes impacts the entire system and therefore is a constraint to the process. The cause of the constraint must be identified and the whole enterprise must be managed with that constraint in mind. An alternative process for making prototypes could be developed. Marketing could adjust its research methods to provide information earlier. Merchandising could reconfigure the line development process to compensate for prototype production time. With the whole enterprise focusing on the constraint, the most effective methods for minimizing the impact of prototype production on the enterprise should be developed and applied. The tools that are used to effectively determine the best alternatives and implement enterprisewide solutions are:

- Win-win conflict resolution.
- Idea evaluation and feedback.
- Team building.
- Empowerment and delegation.

Many apparel companies adopted the TOC philosophy as part of their efforts to achieve quick response manufacturing. In recent years, software systems have been developed to implement TOC. In 2005, Intentia (**www.intentia.com**), a Swedish global enterprise solutions provider, introduced its TOC Production Planning Solution which permits apparel manufacturers to reach optimum production levels by overcoming their critical bottlenecks.

By 1997 consumers were saving $35 billion annually from improvements in the efficiency of the soft goods supply chain, of which $13 billion was attributed to quick response (KSA 1997). In order to achieve these dramatic results, the apparel industry has broadened its focus to encompass the total soft goods supply chain, which requires companies to embrace new digital technologies. As a partner of Kurt Salmon Associates E. Lee Griffith III stressed the importance of technology, "Technology's the name of the game in today's apparel industry. . . . The whole chain needs to be run by automatic systems rather than a whole lot of manual intervention."

■ Demand-Activated Manufacturing Architecture

In 1993 the **demand-activated manufacturing architecture (DAMA)** project was initiated by a collaborative research consortium of soft goods industry members, the Department of Energy national laboratories, other federal agencies, textile universities, and industry associations to work on shrinking the supply chain, which links the U.S. fiber, textile, sewn products, and retail industries. This dynamic project is part of the American Textile (AMTEX™) Partnership (**www.amtex.sandia.gov**) to improve the effectiveness of the U.S. **integrated textile complex (ITC)**, which is the soft goods supply chain including fiber, yarn, textile, and apparel producers. The DAMA project laid the groundwork for many of the developments that led to growing improvements in the soft goods supply chain. A history and detailed analysis of the DAMA project can be found at the Textile Clothing Technology Corporation's Web site: **www.dama.tc2.com**.

One of the first challenges for the DAMA project was to prepare an in-depth analysis of the soft goods supply chain. Participants chose to analyze the process steps for men's cotton slacks. They documented these steps through the business network that prepares the product for retail sale. The resulting process flow chart is represented in Figure 9.2. The total production pipeline for men's cotton slacks was estimated to be 58 weeks, consisting of 11 weeks of actual process time, 45 weeks of wait time during which no processing occurred, and 2 weeks of transportation time. These results clearly identified the potential for dramatically reducing the cycle time and costs inherent in the pipeline, thereby increasing the effectiveness of the fiber, textile, apparel, and retail industries.

The DAMA project consisted of two phases. The initial phase included:

- *Enterprise modeling and simulation (EM&S)* of existing processes. Strategic changes and business tools were then recommended for the U.S. Integrated Textile Complex (ITC).
- *Connectivity and infrastructure (C&I)* to electronically connect the industry partners and educate them on Internet and intranet capabilities.
- *Cooperative business management (CBM)* to develop and demonstrate the required software business tools such as DAME (data modeling), TEXNET (textile network of secure and selective information sharing over the Web), SCIP (supply chain integration program), PA (pipeline analysis), SS (sourcing simulator), and NSDB (a national sourcing database).
- *Education, outreach, and commercialization (EO&C)* to educate and engage the industry and to commercialize innovative products to improve the ITC supply chain.

The second phase of the DAMA project focused on:

- Developing a *Supply Chain Architecture* standard for collaborative business across the interenterprise supply chain including standardized document formats and electronic data interchange standards.
- Developing the methodology for performing *supply chain analysis* leading to cost, time, and quality improvements in the ITC.
- *Commercialization* of DAMA tools and methodologies.

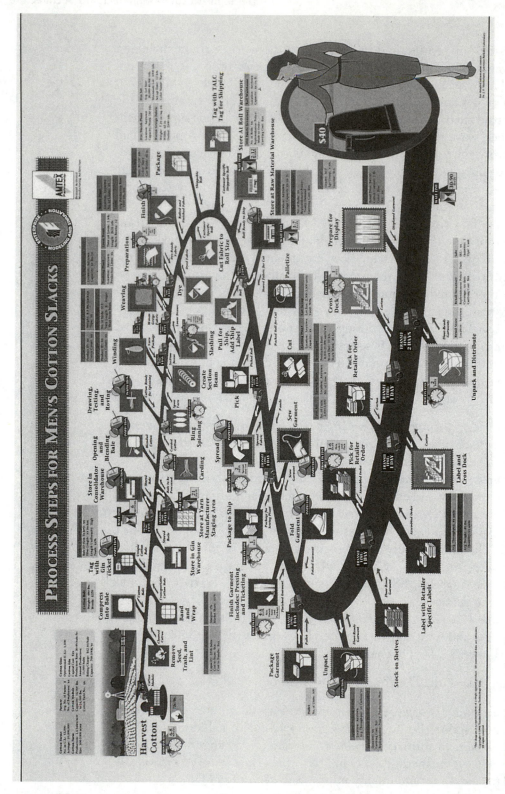

Figure 9.2 This DAMA flowchart created by the AMTEX Partnership illustrates the process of manufacturing a pair of men's cotton slacks. It estimates the amount of time required for each process step.

FIGURE 9.3 **MAGNITUDE OF ITC SUPPLY CHAIN COMPLEXITY**

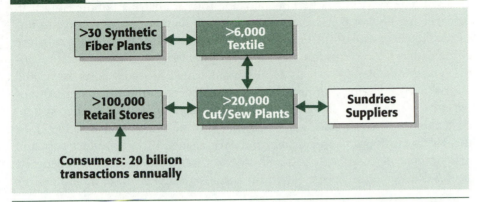

The complexity of the Integrated Textile Complex supply chain can be shown by the number of participating companies and consumers.

The complexity and magnitude of the ITC supply chain provided a fertile opportunity for dramatic improvements in efficiency and costs. (See Figure 9.3.) With over 125,000 different business enterprises and over 20 billion transactions per year, the U.S. ITC supply chain provided an ideal laboratory for DAMA. The project was completed in early 2001. It determined that collaborative business practices can reduce both the amount of time and the amount of inventory in the soft goods pipeline by almost 50 percent. The results are slightly lower when offshore sourcing is factored into the equation. The results of the project have been published in a paper entitled "Supply Chain Simulation: An Analysis of Traditional versus Collaborative Supply Chains in the Softgoods Industry," by Tim Curran and Jim Lovejoy of Textile Clothing Technology Corporation [TC]². Studies continue today under the auspices of the **Voluntary Inter-Industry Commerce Standards (VICS) Council**. The dynamic outcomes of data, tools, and methodologies from DAMA coupled with the rapid development and growth of information technology laid the foundation for the U.S. apparel industry to take full advantage of quick response strategies.

■ Quick Response

One of the most important elements in establishing and maintaining a successful apparel company is time. In the product development process, merchandisers are constantly faced with determining what consumers will want to purchase at some time in the future. The longer the time frame between developing a styling concept and delivering the completed style to retail stores, the greater the risk of error and associated markdowns.

In the apparel industry, time often directly affects costs. Gus Whalen, the CEO of The Warren Featherbone Co. and former chairman of the American Apparel and Footwear Association, finds this is quite apparent relative to imports. "I believe one of the reasons many companies are sending jobs offshore is the result of a very narrow view of 'costs.' *Component* cost has become confused with *total system* cost. By total system cost, I mean all costs associated with the manufacture and distribution of products to the consumer. An apparent lower offshore labor cost may in fact contribute to a higher system cost, due to expenses associated with time and distance" (Whalen 1997). In the 1990s the focus of the apparel industry changed from product cost and production time to process cost and process time. In the twenty-first century, time has become the new standard for success: design it, make it, and deliver it faster than the competition.

Quick response addresses this time element relative to the full scope of the apparel merchandising process: the development, execution, and delivery of a product line based upon the needs of a target market. One of the first QR pilot programs, organized by the Crafted With Pride in U.S.A. Council, Inc.; Wal-Mart Stores; Seminole Manufacturing; and Milliken & Company experienced substantial success (Frazier 1985). Basic improvements after only 3 months included:

- Increasing the frequency of replenishment orders from monthly to bi-weekly, thus enabling stock outs to be avoided or detected earlier and reducing the size of reorder shipments.
- Cutting reorder cycle time, from counting inventory on the selling floor to receipt of the replenishment order, by 33 percent.
- Shortening the cut–authorization-to-finished–goods availability by 30 percent through changing from monthly to weekly planning.
- Reducing the time from color assortment to shipment by 50 percent.

The concept of QR was developed as a business strategy for the domestic textile, apparel, and retail sectors to reduce inventories, shorten cycle times, and respond rapidly to changing consumer demands. In essence, one of the primary objectives of QR is risk reduction. Purchasing the wrong styles and quantities of raw materials and producing SKUs that do not sell and generate large markdown losses create the greatest opportunity for cost reduction and profit improvement for apparel companies. The QR strategy involves using developing technologies in data processing and communications, evolving software applications, and effective collaboration among business partners in the integrated textile complex supply chain. QR is in a constant state of evolution and development, and, therefore, companies must be committed to the process and be ready to make the changes necessary to reap the benefits of increased sales and greater profits.

The elements required for effective QR can be summarized by the three Cs:

- Control
- Communication
- Collaboration

Control

In order to respond quickly to the rapidly changing complex fashion marketplace, well-defined, effective control systems must be in place throughout all areas of an apparel company, especially in merchandising. Merchandising calendars; product data management; merchandise planning, forecasting and adoption; line management analysis; materials management; product sourcing; manufacturing systems; inventory management; and point-of-sale product performance must all be carefully controlled with accurate and responsive systems. Management must be able to monitor each function within the company in order to make effective decisions and take necessary corrective action.

In a QR environment, the product development process must be capable of reacting to subtle and rapid changes in the marketplace so that styles that are in the pipeline can be adjusted and new concepts can be injected into the process in time to meet production deadlines. Manufacturing and sourcing must likewise be able to perform with low work-in-process inventories to respond quickly to change and provide a consistent flow of merchandise for distribution to retail customers. Precise timetables must be established, integrated, and rigidly maintained for a company to be successful using QR strategies. For all these processes, costs must be captured, allocated, and analyzed. This can be accomplished only if efficient control systems are in place to monitor processes, capture data, and communicate critical information to the decision makers on the management team.

For any control system to be effective, management, starting at the top, must work together in a well-structured, team environment. Since QR relies on intra- and intercompany coordination, effective, reliable control systems are paramount for successful implementation of QR strategies. When a number of company departments and supply chain participants are working together to achieve a common goal of increasing inventory turns, reducing costs, reducing lead times, and improving new product success ratios, control systems play a very important role. Each participant in the process must rely on other team members to complete their responsibilities accurately and on time. This makes it possible to compensate for any corrections or delays, which is essential for the entire process to be successful. Efficient, responsive control systems are necessary to ensure QR success.

Figure 9.4 The 12-digit Universal Product Code (UPC) is used to identify apparel products.

Computer technologies enable apparel companies to coordinate the efforts of product development, product manufacturing, and product distribution with real-time data capture and information sharing to make control a proactive process. The days of speculative forecasts are nearly gone, replaced by well-tuned control and communication systems that can move critical product decisions closer to actual retail sales. QR can be effective only if apparel companies have the controls in place for merchandisers and top management to maintain rigorous timetables and make quick and accurate decisions.

Communication

Effective communication within an apparel company and with that company's supply chain partners is critical to attaining QR benefits. Much of the wait time documented by the DAMA project's supply chain analyses was caused by raw material or finished product inventory remaining idle until decisions were made concerning styles to produce or which SKUs to ship to retailers. Fast digital communications through the use of bar codes for product and shipping container identification, and electronic data interchange for fast, accurate transfer of data and exchange of business documents are necessary elements for QR communications. The **Universal Product Code (UPC)** is used for product identification. It is a 12-digit number that identifies the product category, manufacturer, and merchandise item. (See Figure 9.4.)

- One digit identifies the general category of merchandise.
- A five-digit manufacturer identification number is issued by the **Uniform Code Council (UCC)**, which is the administrative council that oversees issuance of manufacturer identification numbers and assists in implementing bar code systems.
- A five-digit item code is for use of the manufacturers to identify their products.
- A check digit is provided at the far right of the bar code for error detection. The check digit is created by performing a series of arithmetic operations on the first eleven digits that creates a single digit result.

Bar codes provide rapid, accurate identification of products, and EDI allows the simultaneous electronic transmission of the bar-code data to any global location. These technologies eliminate the need for paper transactions that require manual logging of data that contains the inherent risk of human error. QR partners routinely utilize EDI to communicate purchase orders, order entries, purchase order confirmations, order status, advance shipping notices (ASN) that alert customers that a shipment will be made shortly, invoices, transfers of funds, and many other types of transactions. EDI allows this information to be translated into a standard format that can be exchanged electronically with other companies in the chain easily and economically over the Internet.

The UPC on a dress sold in a New York City department store can be transmitted via EDI to the apparel manufacturer who produced the garment and the textile mill that created the fabric. The 12-digit UPC contains the manufacturer code and the product code that can identify the garment along with a check digit to verify that the code transmitted by the retailer's computer and the code that was received by the QR partners' computers is identical. EDI requires that the parties involved in the transmission and reception of electronic data use the same digital format. The Voluntary Inter-Industry Commerce Standards Council established barcoding and EDI standards for retailers and apparel manufacturers.

Transmitting point-of-sale data accurately and rapidly from retail stores to apparel manufacturers and communicating raw materials requirements throughout the textile supply chain is essential for successful implementation of QR strategies. This data transfer also allows manufacturers or private label retail merchants like The Limited to perfect style testing at key stores and fine-tune styles before making their final sourcing decisions.

The nature of the U.S. ITC supply chain creates a serial information flow environment in which data in each segment of the chain rely upon data from previous segments. Due to the time involved in the serial transmission of data, changes in the retail or apparel manufacturing channel could change dramatically by the time the information reaches the apparel merchandiser, textile mills, or fiber producers. For this reason, the communication channels in the ITC supply chain should be parallel, whereby data flow to all segments of the chain simultaneously instead of being transferred through the system serially, one link at a time. (See Figure 9.6.) Software systems from companies such as The Thread and Justwin make parallel information flow possible.

Effective communications must provide meaningful, accurate data and transfer the data as quickly as possible. Real-time data capture and transmission are the ultimate goals of QR communications. When a garment is sold at retail, the SKU should be transmitted to each partner in the supply chain. When a garment is cut and then progresses through each step in the manufacturing cycle, it is desirable for information about that garment to be made available to all departments within the apparel company as well as to the retailer, who awaits the ultimate delivery of the garment. If all members of the supply chain who have a vested interest in a particular SKU know the status of that SKU, they can make important decisions that affect their ultimate profits.

Figure 9.5 The UPC on the pair of pants and sweater is read or scanned by the sales clerk at the point of sale. Information about the transaction that has been captured by the retailer can be transmitted via electronic data interchange to the pants and sweater manufacturers.

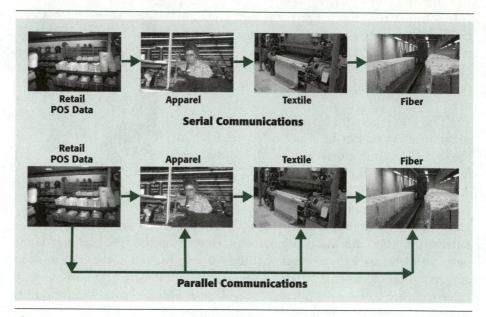

Figure 9.6 The compression of time in the apparel supply chain necessitates immediate sharing of information. This is accomplished through parallel channels of communication where each member of the supply chain receives information simultaneously. When using serial channels of communication each member must wait for the previous member to pass on the information.

Collaboration

From the initial pilot QR programs in 1985 to the current QR initiatives, a vital factor has been collaboration. The foundation of QR is built on partnerships among the links in the integrated textile supply chain. This partnership approach is stressed by some of the key executives who participated in the development of QR (see Page 292).

Each participant in a QR partnership must be dedicated to sharing information and establishing decision-making models that function within the supply chain management system. With this collaboration comes the need for trust and confidence that your supply chain partners will live up to each of their commitments. Since any chain is only as strong as its weakest link, if one partner in the collaborative effort does not fulfill its obligations, the entire QR partnership fails. Establishing reliable, effective, responsive partnerships throughout the entire supply chain is the cornerstone of successful QR initiatives.

Expanding Scope

Early QR efforts focused on reducing production cycle times and establishing vendor and user partnerships that guaranteed weekly production volumes while delaying detailed orders until the retail selling season was nearer. Dur-

Quotes From The Pros

"We can optimize our processes internally, but to maximize returns and responsiveness, we must collaborate in truly meaningful ways with our trading partners."

Paul Charron, chairman and CEO, Liz Claiborne, Inc.

"The most important ingredient in our flow replenishment system is the new form of alliance we must establish with our retail partners . . . without this alliance, all the technology in the world won't accomplish Quick Response."

Larry Pugh, chairman, VF Corporation

"Streamlining distribution between retailer and vendor creates financial gains for both partners."

Tom Sample, vice president, information systems, Haggar Apparel

"Adding Quick Response partnerships changes your investments in VICS technologies from good to great."

William Dillard II, president, Dillard's

"We have achieved excellent results, and are accelerating implementation of VICS technologies and Quick Response with our retail partners."

Bob Haas, CEO, Levi Strauss

"Warren Featherbone has proven that small and large companies succeed when working as QR partners to truly serve the consumer."

Gus Whalen, CEO, The Warren Featherbone Co.

ing the late 1990s and the early 2000s, QR has expanded to play a major role in all phases of supply chain management. Today's successful apparel companies are focusing on three major areas of QR:

- Line development.
- Product sourcing.
- Logistics.

Line Development

The process of line development, one of the major responsibilities of a merchandiser, involves many complex functions that fall into the basic categories of research, line planning, product development, costing, specifications development, review and adoption, and sample making. To develop effective QR for line development requires addressing each function relative to new

"TSI Built to Win"

Tropical Sportswear Int'l. Corp.'s sales have grown from $25 million to $400 million in just nine years, and as it skillfully maneuvers its private label and branded businesses, the firm continues to raise the bar for best practices in customer service.

A bank that sells bananas: Tropical Sportswear Int'l. Corp. (TSI) often views it's business with this concept in mind—a bank because it carries its customers' inventories, and bananas because they are something that must be turned every week, lest they go bad.

This type of unusual "out of the box" thinking has been critical as the Tampa, FL-based casual pants firm has driven its sales from $25 million to more than $400 million in just nine years . . . and brought its turn times down to an average of 36 days, from piece goods to finished product . . . and the list goes on.

TSI now has set its sights on achieving much higher sales and expanding its brands to include everything from shirts to cologne—all while improving customer service with an eight-hour turn, from the time it receives a customer's order until the goods are shipped out, labeled to specifications and ready for the retail floor.

How have they done it, and how are they approaching the road ahead? It's all about having a can-do attitude, its top executives emphasize, and following a solid blueprint for success. . . .

Inventory Orchestration

At the heart of TSI's success is inventory management, and the ability to quickly and accurately "fill in"—in other words, to adjust production and shipping mid-stream according to demand at retail.

As (Michael) Kagan, who serves as the firm's executive vice president and CFO, says: "Inventories have been the cause of more failures in the apparel industry than anything else. . . . We use our systems, our reporting capabilities and our procedures to keep inventories in line. We do things with inventory that no other company in the industry does."

As an example, the company keeps no more and no less than five days of piece goods inventory in its cutting facility in Tampa.

"We operate by the minute," says Kagan. "We know you can no longer do something in two weeks. We know that when a truck pulls in with a shipment of goods from the Dominican Republic, it takes one hour and 42 minutes to unload that truck. Every process is measured."

TSI's leanness also is closely tied to its "chassis" manufacturing strategy, whereby most styles the company produces are based on six basic pant styles. These models are built to strict specifications—most specification packages run 20 pages to 40 pages in length, including instructions in both English and Spanish—that adhere to TSI's "good-better-best" product philosophy. The good, better, and best categories are distinguished from each other by the quality of fabric and level of workmanship and de-

(continued)

tail used in the different styles, which are geared to different retail channels and price-point ranges.

The basic chassis may be altered with a different cuff here or an extra pocket there, but in general, the six chassis fit the bill for more than 90 percent of TSI's slacks demand from retailers. And once a TSI sewing contractor masters one or two of the chassis, efficiencies increase and turn times quicken, creating higher profits all around.

"Some of our competitors come in and change styles on the contractors fairly often, and the learning curve can be very tough," observes executive vice president of finance and operations Larry McPherson. "We promise a steady flow of work in a particular style so that they can get very good at it, and that's what sets us apart."

Moreover, 90 percent of the goods flowing into TSI's 190,000-square-foot Tampa warehousing and distribution center are unlabeled, which provides the company great flexibility in terms of selling slacks from a common inventory to a vast array of different customers and across multiple distribution channels. Extensive employee training and quality control procedures, combined with the latest in Paxar Corp. and Avery Dennison label printing equipment and software, are instrumental in assuring products are labeled properly with customer-specific care labels, hangtags, pocket flashers, UPC-coded price tags, etc.

Staying on Top of Systems

Information systems, of course, also play a vital role in TSI's masterful orchestration of its inventory. . . .

Elaborating on TSI's information technology approach, executive vice president and chief information officer Brent Pulsipher explains: "You have to build a solid technology infrastructure, and that means you have an architecture for hardware, software, telecommunications, desktop computing and business functionality. . . . Our objective is to get a common infrastructure that is reasonably uniform, which gives us better leverage to do two things: 1. Get the cost of ownership down because we don't have to maintain a lot of different systems; and 2. Put us in a better position to do acquisitions and integrate them more quickly."

. . . TSI's emphasis on using its data to its fullest potential is what enables the company to achieve "as close to just-in-time manufacturing as you can get in the apparel industry," Pulsipher continues. For example, the firm is in the process of rolling out an inventory management program, developed collaboratively by Savane in conjunction with a retailer, whereby, he explains: "The customer tells us the beginning inventory, we keep track of the movement of our products through the retailer's point-of-sale system, and we keep track of what we're shipping so that at any given time we should know the assortment of our products on the retailer's floor."

TSI's systems have been known to identify inventory inaccuracies in retailers' data, triggering corrective action on the retailer's part. "Our approach helps the retailers use their own information," Pulsipher says. "We summarize the data at the retailer's regional, district, and store levels. When inventory looks out of balance, the system suggests, by a comment at the end of a summary report, what ought to be done. . . . We can then ship product in the right sizes and quantities to meet demand, and they sell more product."

(continued)

The ultimate driver behind TSI's Herculean systems endeavor is its goal of offering the best value in a full package program that a retailer can find. And the company is finding that the service side of a program is just as important, if not more so, than the product, especially as retailers develop their own in-house sourcing capabilities.

As president Richard Domino asserts: "When I have an opportunity to sit down, one on one, with any retailer, I can show that retailer why it is more profitable for him to do business with me than it is for him to do a program himself."

The Western Hemisphere Sourcing Strategy

Another essential element in TSI's ability to maintain a steady stream of on-time shipments to its retail customers is its focus on the Western Hemisphere in its sourcing. Ninety percent of its products are produced by contractors in the Dominican Republic and Mexico. TSI currently uses between 11 and 15 contractors in the Dominican Republic and approximately six in Mexico.

"As far as we're concerned, they're U.S.-based," Domino states, pointing to TSI's 36-days-and-falling average turn time. "That is about as quick as anybody is doing [work] here in the United States."

The remaining 10 percent of the firm's goods, usually products that call for a higher level of needlework, are imported from the Far East or other regions. Yet even for this one-tenth of production that is sourced from afar, TSI always has contingency plans in place to supply to goods closer to home. "Whatever we do in the Orient, we also do [through an 807 program] as a safety mechanism so as not to hurt our customers. We're the only company I know of that aggressively goes after that approach," says Elliott Lightman, executive vice president of sales, marketing and merchandising, who oversees TSI's non-Western Hemisphere import programs.

The firm's sourcing strategy is paying off nicely. Case in point: JCPenney recently had a need for 100,000 pair of Arizona flat-front twills. The retailer was not able to acquire these units from its supplier on time. TSI stepped to the plate, and provided the goods (from piece goods to finished product) within 28 days. "If we weren't around to service that program for them, things are too competitive to just lose sales because your supplier can't deliver on time," Lightman emphasizes.

. . . The firm currently is working with its contractors to ensure they have the right technology in place. . . .

"Basically it's a joint venture," Pulsipher says of the IT investment required at the contractor level. "We will often make the investment [in their systems] and amortize it over some period of time against the work that they do for us. So it's very much a partnership. . . ."

By 2001 TSI reduced their turn times to 30 days. Their objectives and philosophies for continued improvement in the management of their supply chain include:

- Reducing production cycle time.
- Reducing distribution cycle time.
- Increasing order fulfillment rates.
- Meticulous management of forecast/ production schedules.
- Form long-term partnerships with key suppliers.
- Share business plans and promote trust and fairness with suppliers and customers.

(continued)

- Ensure partner profitability while obtaining the best value for TSI.
- Treat inventory as a liability rather than an asset.
- Identify ideal inventory levels at each stage in the production cycle.
- Electronic processing of receipt of fabric.
- Electronic transfer of width information to marking.
- Computerized real time in-process control.

- Forecast and production teams meet weekly to review demand changes.
- Communication and synchronization of efforts allows for quick response.
- High-level decisions are made as a team. ■

From Kathleen DesMarteau. January 1999. *Bobbin.*

Case in Point 9.1   **Summary**

Tropical Sportswear Int. Corp. (TSI) turned to quick response to carve out a successful niche in the casual pants market. By achieving turn times from piece goods to finished product of 36 days in 1999 and 30 days in 2001, TSI provided a valuable service to their customers.

The key to TSI's success in reducing its turn time is successful management of its supply chain through control over inventories and quick response strategies for processing customer orders. By labeling 90 percent of its products at its distribution center using in-house printing systems, TSI can provide customer-specific labeling with an eight-hour turn from receipt of customer orders until the goods are shipped to specific retail stores.

TSI's sophisticated information technology systems using a common infrastructure, allows them to achieve close to just-in-time manufacturing capabilities. A collaborative inventory management program with retailers allows TSI to track its products through retailers' point-of-sale systems, make adjustments to their production and inventories, and even suggest corrective action when retail inventories look out of balance.

TSI's focus on Western Hemisphere sourcing and its use of information technology to communicate with its sourcing partners allow the company to respond quickly to special customer needs. Reducing production and distribution cycle times, electronic processing of raw materials, and computerized real time in-process controls are examples of philosophies and systems that allow TSI to effectively manage their total supply chain. ■

Case in Point 9.2

"Zara's Secret for Fast Fashion"

Spanish retailer Zara has hit on a formula for supply chain success that works. By defying conventional wisdom, Zara can design and distribute a garment to market in just fifteen days. From Harvard Business Review.

In Zara stores, customers can always find new products—but they're in limited supply. There is a sense of tantalizing exclusivity, since only a few items are on display even though stores are spacious (the average size is around 1,000 square meters). A customer thinks, "This green shirt fits me, and there is one on the rack. If I don't buy it now, I'll lose my chance."

Such a retail concept depends on the regular creation and rapid replenishment of small batches of new goods. Zara's designers create approximately 40,000 new designs annually, from which 10,000 are selected for production. Some of them resemble the latest couture creations. But Zara often beats the high-fashion houses to the market and offers almost the same products, made with less expensive fabric, at much lower prices. Since most garments come in five to six colors and five to seven sizes, Zara's system has to deal with something in the realm of 300,000 new stock-keeping units (SKUs), on average, every year.

This "fast fashion" system depends on a constant exchange of information throughout every part of Zara's supply chain—from customers to store managers, from store managers to market specialists and designers, from designers to production staff, from buyers to subcontractors, from warehouse managers to distributors, and so on. Most companies insert layers of bureaucracy that can bog down communication between departments. But Zara's organization, operational procedures, performance measures, and even its office layouts are all designed to make information transfer easy.

Zara's single, centralized design and production center is attached to Inditex (Zara's parent company) headquarters in La Coruña. It consists of three spacious halls—one for women's clothing lines, one for men's, and one for children's. Unlike most companies, which try to excise redundant labor to cut costs, Zara makes a point of running three parallel, but operationally distinct, product families. Accordingly, separate design, sales, and procurement and production-planning staffs are dedicated to each clothing line. A store may receive three different calls from La Coruña in one week from a market specialist in each channel; a factory making shirts may deal simultaneously with two Zara managers, one for men's shirts and another for children's shirts. Though it's more expensive to operate three channels, the information flow for each channel is fast, direct, and unencumbered by problems in other channels—making the overall supply chain more responsive.

In each hall, floor to ceiling windows overlooking the Spanish countryside reinforce a sense of cheery informality and openness. Unlike companies that sequester their design staffs, Zara's cadre of 200 de-

(continued)

signers sits right in the midst of the production process. Split among the three lines, these mostly twentysomething designers—hired because of their enthusiasm and talent, no prima donnas allowed—work next to the market specialists and procurement and production planners. Large circular tables play host to impromptu meetings. Racks of the latest fashion magazines and catalogs fill the walls. A small prototype shop has been set up in the corner of each hall, which encourages everyone to comment on new garments as they evolve.

The physical and organizational proximity of the three groups increases both the speed and the quality of the design process. Designers can quickly and informally check initial sketches with colleagues. Market specialists, who are in constant touch with store managers (and many of whom have been store managers themselves), provide quick feedback about the look of the new designs (style, color, fabric, and so on) and suggest possible market price points. Procurement and production planners make preliminary, but crucial, estimates of manufacturing costs and available capacity. The cross-functional teams can examine prototypes in the hall, choose a design, and commit resources for its production and introduction in a few hours, if necessary.

Zara is careful about the way it deploys the latest information technology tools to facilitate these informal exchanges. Customized handheld computers support the connection between the retail stores and La Coruña. These PDAs augment regular (often weekly) phone conversations between the store managers and the market specialists assigned to them. Through the PDAs and telephone conver-

sations, stores transmit all kinds of information to La Coruña—such hard data as orders and sales trends and such soft data as customer reactions and the "buzz" around a new style. While any company can use PDAs to communicate, Zara's flat organization ensures that important conversations don't fall through the bureaucratic cracks.

Once the team selects a prototype for production, the designers refine colors and textures on a computer-aided design system. If the item is to be made in one of Zara's factories, they transmit the specs directly to the relevant cutting machines and other systems in that factory. Bar codes track the cut pieces as they are converted into garments through the various steps involved in production (including sewing operations usually done by subcontractors), distribution, and delivery to the stores, where the communication cycle began.

The constant flow of updated data mitigates the so-called bullwhip effect—the tendency of supply chains (and all open-loop information systems) to amplify small disturbances. A small change in retail orders, for example, can result in wide fluctuations in factory orders after it's transmitted through wholesalers and distributors. In an industry that traditionally allows retailers to change a maximum of 20 percent of their orders once the season has started, Zara lets them adjust 40 percent to 50 percent. In this way, Zara avoids costly overproduction and the subsequent sales and discounting prevalent in the industry.

The relentless introduction of new products in small quantities, ironically, reduces the usual costs associated with run-

(continued)

ning out of any particular item. Indeed, Zara makes a virtue of stock-outs. Empty racks don't drive customers to other stores because shoppers always have new things to choose from. Being out of stock in one item helps sell another, since people are often happy to snatch what they can. In fact, Zara has an informal policy of moving unsold items after two or three weeks. This can be an expensive practice for a typical store, but since Zara stores receive small shipments and carry little inventory, the risks are small; unsold items account for less than 10 percent of stock, compared with the industry average of 17 percent to 20 percent. Furthermore, new merchandise displayed in limited quan-

tities and the short window of opportunity for purchasing items motivate people to visit Zara's shops more frequently than they might other stores. Consumers in central London, for example, visit the average store four times annually, but Zara's customers visit its shops an average of 17 times a year. The high traffic in the stores circumvents the need for advertising: Zara devotes just 0.3 percent of its sales on ads, far less than the 3 percent to 4 percent its rivals spend. ■

Excerpt from Kasra Ferdows, Michael A. Lewis, and Jose A.D. Machuca. November 2004. *Harvard Business Review*, Vol. 82, No. 11.

Case in Point 9.2 ## Summary

Zara is the premier example of fast fashion supply chain management. They have developed a unique method to constantly replenish their stock with new and fashionable merchandise. The foundation of their success is the continuous exchange of information among all of the members of the supply chain. It begins with the consumer and easily flows upstream through store managers and merchandise specialists to the design staff, and then back downstream through buyers, production personnel, manufacturers, and distributors. Throughout its organization, Zara has embraced technology that facilitates the flow of information, creates new styles, and monitors the progress. By establishing cross-functioning product development staff and flattening the organizational structure, the company provides their consumer with the right product, at the right place, at the right time . . . the true role of apparel merchandising. While every apparel and retail organization cannot duplicate the "fast fashion" model of Zara, many companies in the apparel supply chain can adopt those policies and procedures that reduce the time from concept to consumer. ■

technologies in order to shorten the process cycle and improve communications with QR partners. Examples of QR line development technologies are:

- *Internet*: New and innovative Internet fashion research sites can shorten market and fashion research time by transferring data and product information among product development teams and sampling locations.
- *POS*: Point-of-sale data capture provides up-to-the-minute consumer information from retail QR partners.
- *Data mining*: Data mining is a process that allows computers to search for patterns in consumer or product information. It is a valuable tool that can aid merchandisers in spotting sales or styling trends. Sophisticated algorithms and data extraction software can locate subtle trends hidden in company records. The automated data mining process collects, explores, and selects critical decision-making data.
- *CAD*: CAD systems are used to create computer-generated fabrics and silhouettes. This technology allows line development teams to establish and maintain extensive computer fabric and silhouette libraries. CAD is also used for rapid pattern and marker creation, thus minimizing product development errors.
- *EDI*: Electronic data interchange links with textile mills and sundries and findings suppliers allow designers to review vendor inventories and place sample orders on-line.
- *Costing*: Software that utilizes predetermined time standards and material utilization data is being used to provide cost estimates that guide merchandising product decisions.
- *PIM*: Product information management software allows the rapid and accurate creation of electronic specification packages that can be immediately shared among the members of the line development team and sampling and production facilities.
- *Line review*: Presentation software systems can speed up the line review process by enabling managers to sort the line by coordinated groups, margins, and retail price points. This same software can be used for sales presentations.
- *Sampling*: Computer-aided pattern design and marker making systems linked to automated sample cutters can speed up the prototyping process. These same computer-aided systems combined with product development software and linked via the Internet to manufacturing facilities can cut many days off the process of making sales samples.
- *Merchandising calendars*: Computer integrated, companywide merchandising calendars provide timetables for each line development function, identifying responsibilities and showing current status and the effect of delays on other departments and functions. These real-

time planning and control tools improve total company efficiency and establish the foundation for effective team building.

Many companies have been able to reduce product development cycles of 3–6 months down to 3–6 weeks, and in some companies to as little as 1-2 weeks. Zara has been the leader in **fast fashion,** which collapses the time required to create a style and then deliver it to their selling floor to less than three weeks. Fast fashion is responding to consumer demand and replaces the typical two-season approach to weekly or monthly delivery of new merchandise. This can be achieved only by integrating all the line development functions through a comprehensive, interactive database and linking each function with fast, accurate electronic communications.

Sourcing

To allow time for production of reorders without excessively inflating prices, many U.S. companies are turning to **blended sourcing**. This process involves placing initial orders with Southeast Asian manufacturers to obtain low initial costs. Then, if sales are greater than expected, follow-up orders are placed with domestic manufacturers or with Mexican or Caribbean suppliers with shorter lead times and higher prices. Typical process times are 60–90 days for Southeast Asia, 14–21 days for Latin America, and 3–5 days for short-cycle domestic producers. (See Figure 9.7.) This allows a company that utilizes blended sourcing to achieve price point objectives and establish appropriate response times for replenishment programs. These changes have put great pressure on developing QR initiatives that address the multifaceted demands of global sourcing.

- *Automation*: Preproduction processes have been automated to eliminate redundancies and reduce cycle times. Computer applications for product data management help to coordinate the efforts of the entire product development team and provide accurate, up-to-date information for sourcing partners.
- *EDI*: Electronic data interchange allows companies to transmit specifications to their domestic factories and global sourcing partners and monitor the progress of orders through real-time data capture.
- *Short-cycle manufacturing*: Many apparel companies have adopted flexible, short-cycle unit production or modular manufacturing systems to reduce the production cycle time from weeks to days or even hours. This improved response time allows for rapid replenishment and minimizes forecasting errors by moving order commitments closer to retail selling time.
- *Consolidation*: Some apparel companies have consolidated their sourcing efforts by making major commitments to fewer factories. These

FIGURE 9.7	**APPAREL PROCESS TIMES**

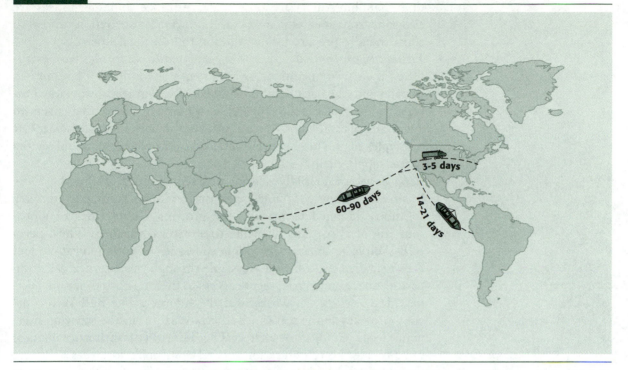

The time required to process an order from the date the order is placed until the time the merchandise is received varies from one global location to another. In order to allow time for the production of reorders while taking advantage of lower costs of off shore manufacturers, U.S. apparel companies are using blended sourcing.

strategic alliances reduce the number of transactions, record keeping requirements, and plant visits, and allow for the development of consistent, effective quality standards.

• *Customizing orders*: More and more companies are collaborating with their sundries and findings suppliers to produce labels, tags, and packaging materials for each individual production order and drop shipping them to the appropriate assembly factory. This cuts valuable days from the supply chain process compared to purchasing bulk materials, having them shipped to a company warehouse, compiling the materials for each production order, and shipping them to the appropriate assembly factory.

• *Advance shipping notices*: Some companies are arranging for fabric mills to send advance shipping notices of fabric shipments, including individual roll information such as shade and yardage, by EDI so they can direct the sequence of loading rolls onto trucks for direct shipment to cutting facilities. The rolls can then be assigned in sequence directly to cutting tables for just-in-time manufacturing, thus saving valuable time, handling, and warehouse space. Advance shipping notices are also sent from apparel manufacturers to retail distribution centers to allow them to prepare for distribution to individual stores.

- *Vertical integration*: Some U.S. fiber and textile companies have established their own operations or joint ventures for apparel assembly in Mexico and the Caribbean. This **vertical integration** provides complete product packages to apparel customers for a price that covers all raw materials and labor. Vertical integration uses state-of-the-art QR principles to provide enhanced service to the apparel and retail sectors of the supply chain.

- *B2B Commerce*: A rapidly growing new segment of **B2B (business-to-business)** commerce is aimed at apparel sourcing. Automated turnkey solutions designed to manage the growing complexities of global sourcing are becoming available to apparel companies. Third party B2B Web companies are providing sophisticated communications and data management software accessible through the Internet. Sourcing partners have immediate, secure access to their up-to-the-minute business data anytime, anywhere over the Internet. The B2B Web company provides all the software and customizes it to the sourcing partners' needs. Companies such as The Thread (**www.thethread.com**) can provide the resources for apparel companies to create a Private Supply Chain™ with their sourcing partners to streamline the many process steps of transforming a styling concept into a product delivered to the customer. (See Figure 9.8.)

Logistics

The proper distribution and replacement of raw materials and garments involves servicing customers from the time the orders are received to delivery of product to the retailer. In today's market, this also includes important replenishment capabilities required by many retailers. For instance, the DAMA project found that men's cotton slacks were tied up in distribution and preparation for retail sale 10 to 16 days. Two to three weeks for garment distribution plus the increasing reliance on replenishment represent an additional opportunity for improvement in the overall textile and apparel supply chain. Quick response efforts have addressed the sweeping changes needed to improve the logistics of getting customers the right products at the right time.

- *Electronic communications*: In today's digital world, the apparel distribution process requires the use of bar codes and EDI. Purchase orders, product activity data for sales and inventory tracking, advance shipping notices, packing lists, and invoices processed through EDI transactions can substantially reduce distribution cycle time. UPC apparel bar-coding and bar-coding for shipping cartons are necessary to pro-

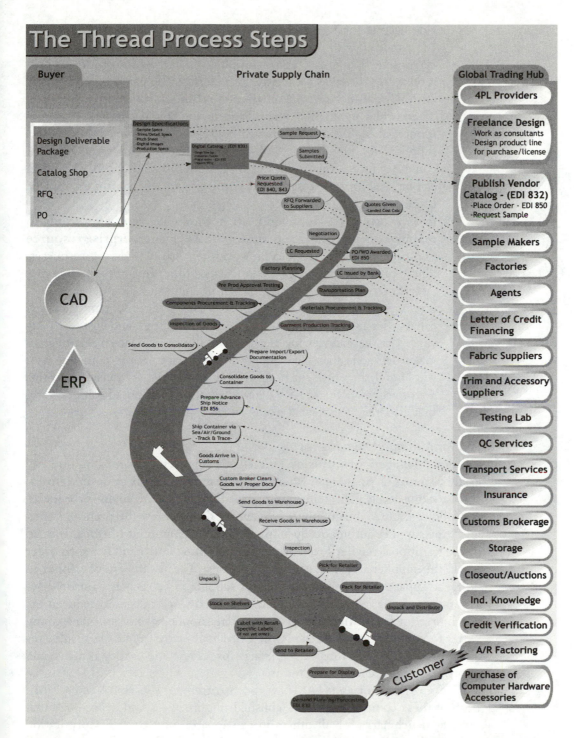

Figure 9.8 The Thread is a B2B company that utilizes customized software and the Internet to create a Private Supply Chain™, such as the one shown here, to streamline the sourcing process.

vide accurate fast communications of product distribution within a company and with retail customers.

- *Forecasting*: The greatest risk and potential for markdown losses is in forecasting the sales of apparel products by SKU. This is especially critical for fashions with dramatic style changes from season to season. There are a number of forecasting methods and strategies that are supported by QR. Collaboration between retailers and their apparel suppliers to provide point-of-sale data that are processed through computer forecasting models is a valuable forecasting tool. The data can be used for style testing and as the trigger mechanism for replenishment programs.

- *Resource planning*: More and more apparel companies are turning to **manufacturing resource planning (MRP)** and **enterprise resource planning (ERP)** systems to improve their use of logistical resources. These planning models give companies a total view of their changing operations. They encompass marketing and sales, line development, forecasting, raw materials inventories and positions, manufacturing capabilities and order status, distribution capacities, and customer service. This enterprisewide perspective allows company executives to make decisions that have the greatest impact on the company as a whole and therefore on bottom-line profits. Many consulting firms are offering MRP and ERP software that provide broad solutions and that also meet the special needs of the apparel industry.

Vendor Managed Inventories

Vendor Managed Inventories (VMI) is a high-level forecasting strategy used by some QR partners in which dynamic **model stocks** or desired inventory stocking levels for retailers and agreed upon replenishment procedures are followed. Once the amount of inventory drops below the predetermined level, the supplier automatically ships the necessary amount of stock. Instead of the traditional retailer's role of determining how much and when to order stock, the supplier now makes these decisions. The results are of benefit to both the apparel retailer and the apparel supplier. The retailer gains by having increased sales, smaller inventories, reduced stock outs, and reduced expenditures for forecasting and ordering. The supplier gains from developing better forecasting due to receiving their orders directly from POS results, reducing POS mistakes; thus saving charge backs and the cost of returns, and improving supply chain cooperation.

VF Corporation and TAL have been extremely successful using VMI. Both of these companies have established the processes and procedures that serve as benchmarks for all others in the apparel industry. VF Corporation will first determine what sizes are to be sent to a retail store. Next, they will send a selling floor plan that indicates how the product should be displayed.

Finally, VF Corporation will decide the weekly inventory levels required to generate the best return on investment. TAL follows the same approach. They collect and analyze POS data directly from each JCPenney store, determine what SKUs must be replenished, manufacture the required shirts, and then ship the new stock directly to the JCPenney store. Neither company could accomplish this supply chain miracle without the application of technology. JCPenney employed i2 Technologies (**www.i2.com**) and TAL used Intentia (**www.intentia.com**).

Radio Frequency Identification (RFID)

Radio Frequency Identification uses radio waves to transmit digital information that has been encoded on a RFID tag or label. This technology is similar to bar coding, except, instead of optically scanning the data from a label, a reader captures the data. Unlike bar coding, the stored information does not have to seen to be read. While the data used in bar coding is based upon the Universal Product Code (UPC), the data in RFID is based upon the **Electronic Product Code (EPC)**. The EPC assigns an individual number to each item and virtually unlimited identifying facts that differentiate one item from another.

The primary purpose when using this new technology is to improve the flow of product through the supply chain by keeping track of inventory at the retail, wholesale, or manufacturing level. It could also be used to locate the product after the consumer has purchased it. In 2004, the Voluntary Inter-Industry Commerce Standards (VICS) Association joined with the American Apparel and Footwear Association (AAFA) and Kurt Salmon Associates (KSA) to form the Apparel and Footwear RFID/EPC Committee. The purpose of this committee was to examine "how best to deploy RFID tagging of each item to benefit distributors, retailers and manufacturers. It will also look into the use of RFID not only to determine whether a product has been shipped or has arrived at the store, but also to match apparel with accessories." (Swedberg, 2005)

Although the technology has been available for quite some time, it is just beginning to be applied in the consumer products area. In 2003, Wal-Mart announced that beginning in 2005, they would mandate that their top 100 suppliers use RFID tags on all pallets and cases. As promised, they initiated the practice in 2004 for shipments destined to a Texas Distribution Center. Thirty-four smaller vendors have also volunteered to comply with the RFID requirements. In the meantime, VF Corporation prepared to meet the needs of Wal-Mart. In 2004 Target announced that by late spring of the following year, their top vendors must attach RFID information to pallets and cases destined for some of their DCs. They hoped to have all of their vendors comply by 2007. As with the adoption of EDI, once JCPenney and Mercantile Stores required their vendors to have EDI capabilities, it was only a few years later when most in the retailing community followed their lead. Now that Wal-Mart and Target have embraced RFID, can the other major retailers be far behind? In advance preparation for this eventuality, it has been reported that VF Corporation is preparing to meet the needs of Wal-Mart. While the benefits are many to supply chain management of apparel and footwear, one of the major drawbacks is cost. It is one thing to tag a pallet of merchandise, but it is a totally different thing to tag individual garments. Although RFID labels, when bought in mass quantities, have dropped from $.50 (when they were introduced) to $.25–.30, the cost is still burdensome for most apparel and footwear companies.

Collaborative Planning, Forecasting, and Replenishment

Quick response strategies took the apparel industry from a reactionary mode of design, forecast, manufacture, sell, and deliver to a collaborative mode of partnerships, visionary planning and control systems, consumer-driven product development, and more effective electronic communications. This created a more technology-driven merchandising function. Vendor-managed inventories focus on a unilateral response by apparel manufacturers to retail data relative to their product lines. The apparel manufacturer makes all replenishment decisions without input from the retailer. This one-sided approach to supplier responsibility for maintaining retail inventories misses many factors that could affect the ultimate sell-through of an apparel company's styles. Retailer promotions, multiple competitive inventory sources, and store sales fluctuations due to seasonality are a few of the factors that could alter a supply chain management decision.

The next step of evolution in supply chain management adds a proactive shared dimension to QR partnerships—**collaborative planning, forecasting, and replenishment** (**CPFR**). CPFR establishes a shared action and responsibility model for apparel manufacturers and their retail QR partners. Under CPFR the retailer and apparel manufacturer no longer share only data; they also share the total responsibility for creating forecasts and making commitments to produce specific SKUs. The partners collaborate on the critical decisions that will result in reduced inventories and increased sales.

Shared Business Plans
Apparel manufacturers and their retail QR partners must develop comprehensive business plans that address inventory levels, promotional programs, margin requirements, forecasting approaches, sales goals, manufacturing and distribution patterns, and replenishment strategies. The business plans must be integrated to establish common objectives that maximize both retail and manufacturing profit and operational goals.

Joint Development of Evaluation Criteria
The CPFR initiative should contain measurable criteria for evaluating the level of success for the program. These criteria should be developed jointly by the QR partners and contain quantifiable evaluation objectives. Average inventory levels, replenishment timetables, stock-out percentages, and maintained margins are examples of measurable criteria that can be established for CPFR programs. Many of the comprehensive CPFR software systems automatically compare the criteria to actual results.

Information Sharing
Partners in a CPFR effort must share information that could provide critical business intelligence. Effective CPFR programs must be custom-fitted for the particular QR partners and their specific business practices. This requires a complete sharing of company information and objectives. Exception reporting should be built into the CPFR management information systems to alert decision-makers in both the retail and manufacturing segments that some event has deviated from their expected standards. Regularly scheduled meetings between QR partners are needed to review progress and make adjustments to decision-making models. Accurate communications through dynamic connectivity is a key factor in successful CPFR programs.

Collaborative Forecasts
An effective CPFR program relies on accurate forecasting. A collaborative effort that supplies store-specific sales data and the apparel manufacturer's historical sales records is necessary to establish a solid forecasting base. Current market information and expertise from the retailer and the manufacturer will further refine the forecasting process. Many companies use pragmatic forecasting models (discussed earlier), which utilize style ranking from best selling to worst selling style by a select group of key company executives whose projections are weighted by the consistency and accuracy of their previous ranking results. This allows a company to project sales based upon the percentage of sales each ranking position achieved in previous seasons. Pragmatic forecasting is similar to key precinct analysis used to forecast elections, and due to the great fluctuations in fashion trends, must be used with care.

The outcome of the collaborative forecasting process is a single, shared forecast that is supported by both QR partners with a joint commitment to orders and delivery requirements.

Real Time Data Sharing
Retail POS data and SKU tracking of manufacturing in-process must be a continuous process communicated in real time through EDI to achieve maximum results from a CPFR program. This data must be shared by the retail and manufacturing CPFR partners.

Collaborative Analysis and Adjustment of Forecasts

The CPFR system evaluates the incoming data in order to isolate deviations from the plan so that forecasts can be fine-tuned and decision-making criteria can be adjusted to accommodate changing conditions.

Evaluation of Results

There must be an ongoing evaluation of program results based upon the joint evaluation criteria so that decision-makers from retail and manufacturing can make timely collaborative adjustments to the system.

FIGURE 9.9   COLLABORATIVE PLANNING, FORECASTING, AND REPLENISHMENT CYCLE

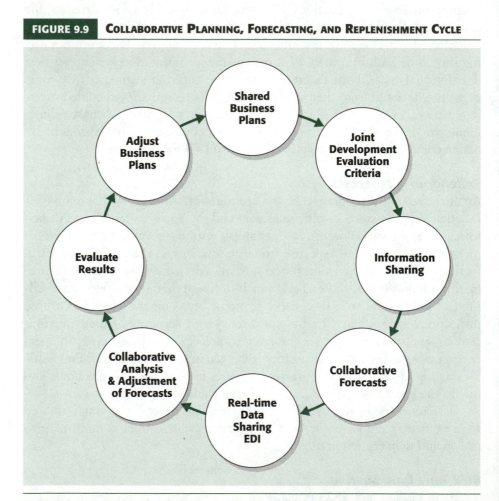

The Collaborative Planning, Forecasting, and Replenishment Cycle (CPFR) illustrates the process of sharing, evaluating, and adjusting information by apparel manufacturers and their retailing partners. Through CPFR the partners hope to make effective decisions in style forecasting and replenishment resulting in reduced inventories, and increased sales and profitability.

Adjustment of Business Plans

A final evaluation should be scheduled at the end of each fiscal period to adjust the shared business plans and reaffirm the partners' commitment to the CPFR program. (See Figure 9.9.)

CPFR systems bring a new perspective to QR partnerships by establishing shared information and decision-making networks. This collaborative, proactive approach to supply chain management provides optimal solutions to style forecasting and replenishment and allows both partners to achieve reduced inventory levels, increased sales, and improved profitability.

A total companywide effort fully supported by top management is necessary for an apparel company to succeed in QR. Each department within the company must provide their piece of the "puzzle" and support the total integrated QR strategy in order to achieve the return on investment and 20 percent to 40 percent or more added sales from quick response (KSA 1989). (See Figure 9.10.)

FIGURE 9.10   QUICK RESPONSE

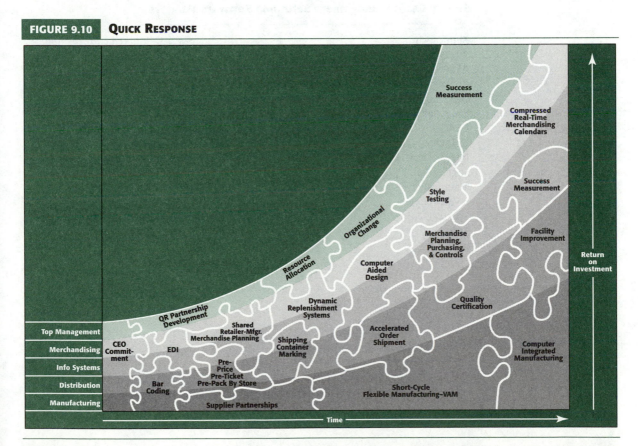

Figure 9.10 The financial success of Quick Response depends upon the cooperation and participation of everyone in the company. Each department must provide their piece of the puzzle and support the total integrated QR strategy.

Early pilot programs have demonstrated the many benefits of CPFR. For example, Wal-Mart conducted a pilot study with Sarah Lee Branded Apparel, which showed a substantial increase in underwear sales with a minimal increase in inventory. This resulted in dramatically improved ROI. Despite these results, the apparel industry has been very slow to adopt this strategy. In 2002, Tom Cole, chairman of Federated Logistics, expressed his loss of patience in getting CPFR started. In 2003, a spokesperson for Sears mentioned that it was difficult for CPFR to work with quickly changing fashions. Furthermore, in an October 2005 Newsletter from [TC][2], it was stated by one of the members of the Voluntary Inter-Industry Commerce Standards (VICS) Association that the apparel industry has focused its attention on price and not paid enough attention to inventory management.

TABLE 9.1

Supply Chain Management Solutions Software Vendors

3i Infotech	www.3i-infotech.com/fashion
7th Online	www.7thonline.com
ASAP of Georgia Inc.	www.asapofga.com
Computer Generated Solutions	www.cgsinc.com
Demand Solutions	www.demandsolutions.com
Exact Software	www.exactsoftware.com
GEAC	www.apparel.geac.com
I2 Technologies	www.i2.com
Intentia Americas, Inc.	www.intentia.com
Logility, Inc.	www.logility.com
Manugistics	www.manugistics.com
NSB Group	www.nsbgroup.com
Porini USA, Inc.	www.porini.it
SAP	www.sap.com

E. Lee Griffith III Experience—partner, The Context Group; principal, information technology, Kurt Salmon Associates

Channels of Distribution

"Today you have so many channels of distribution and so much dynamic distribution of product that the concept of seasons is just about disappearing from many companies. E-commerce has added yet another channel that has really complicated the process even further. Effective supply chain management is one of the keys to success in today's apparel and retail industries. You have to have the business processes and technologies to synchronize and optimize your supply chain. Also, the 'supply-chain' is no longer bound by your company's operations, but must include consideration of your suppliers and customers right through to point of sale. Collaboration and information exchange with customers and suppliers right across the supply chain is a winning strategy in the apparel industry today."

E-commerce

Initially, e-commerce was expected to have a huge impact on the apparel industry and it has, but to a large degree e-commerce has settled down to be viewed correctly as another storefront or channel of distribution. Frankly, my perspective is that some of the fundamental processes of E-commerce have been around for a long time. It began in the days when quick response was first conceptualized in the mid-1980s. E-commerce connects the supply chain from beginning to end so that you're essentially finding ways to electronically and immediately transmit information from the point-of-sale all the way back to the very first procurement of any raw materials and all points in between. Connecting the supply chain from beginning to end has been going on in quick response since the 80s; so in some respects, the only real new aspects from our perspective are the buzzwords applied to it, and also the fact that the Internet is enabling it. Some of the functions that have had to occur electronically business-to-business have been going on for quite some time, and we've been helping our clients to do that for quite a while.

"At the risk of oversimplification, E-commerce at the retail level is just another store possibly owned by the wholesaler or maybe by the retailer. There have been factory outlets for many years, and there was a lot of concern about the effect on the future of the retailer. I think E-commerce is just another augmentation, one more store out there in the mall similar to catalogs and

(continued)

mail order. It hasn't really eliminated stores; it opened up a new avenue. I know people who will go online to look at something and see it. But they still want to go to the store and check it out. In this way, E-commerce becomes an advertising or promotional vehicle.

"There's something about the Internet and E-commerce that raises people's expectations about performance. Manufacturers historically thought that 95 percent fulfillment of orders was good enough. Retailers might say that good enough is 97 percent to 98 percent, but the Internet raises that up to 99.999 percent. Nobody expects to see anything out of stock. The performance bar gets raised to a new level."

Technology

"We no longer have time for a production planner in a back office to sort out sales information to figure out what the next week's batch of production issues should be. There's some very sophisticated advance planning systems [APS] that can zero in on what should be issued next and for the next week. Technology's the name of the game in today's apparel industry and the software package industry has matured quite a bit. You also need an automated forecasting routine that's responding to the point-of-sale data and automatically changing the forecast, automatically changing the master schedule, and automatically

changing the next day's production orders. The whole chain needs to be run by automated, rule-based systems wih minimum manual intervention. The human intervention is only needed for exceptional situations highlighted by the system for attention. There's been a lot of progress in these technologies in the last few years."

Replenishment

"If you've got basic T-shirts, you can hoard some safety stock in the pipeline. But if you're in fashion products, you'd better be ready to produce what sells and get it back into the store within a week. Wal-Mart and Kmart have systems that require suppliers to provide weekly and, in some situations, daily replenishment. On a Monday the supplier has an order coming in on EDI, and that supplier had better be ready to fulfill at a rate of 95 percent by the next day, or they won't do business with the supplier.

"This is tough to do with fashion merchandise, real tough. The higher the fashion, the tougher it gets. Many advance merchants are getting away from any kind of replenishment of the fashion product. They're providing a new blast of merchandise every 3 weeks or every month, some of this through a collaborative design process on Web-based PDM/PLM systems. One of our current clients is a women's fashion apparel company that has no

(*continued*)

seasons. They're essentially selling the retailers a 6-month program that is a sequence of six assortments of fresh merchandise. With each period's sell-through of merchandise, they get more information on what they should be making with their next fashion hit 6 months out or if they should tweak something in one of their next two or three offerings.

"There are also vendor-managed inventory [VMI] programs where the inventory is essentially owned by the wholesaler. The vendor-managed system completely handles the assortment and replenishment of the merchandise. To be effective, this type of program requires careful management of the supply chain and rapid electronic feedback of point-of-sale data."

Data Mining

"It is critical to have access to your data and know what it's telling you. Data mining is a valuable tool that provides access to SKU level data by various attributes and allows the user to summarize the data quickly and easily. It can organize data in very flexible time periods and levels of detail. I think of it in two or three dimensions. There's the level of detail of the data elements whether it's shipments or orders or point-of-sale information. Then there's the characteristics or the many different attributes that describe the product such as model, fabrication, color, etc. Then you need the ability to

slice and dice those attributes in the database any way you want to and get meaningful results. The third dimension would be time. Whether you want to see the data in daily, weekly, or monthly increments and then be able to compare that with your line plan early in the season to tweak your strategy. The availability of this information to the merchant is mandatory in today's merchandising environment."

Electronic Data Interchange

"A standard way of doing business these days is electronic data interchange [EDI]. If a manufacturer wants to do business with the large chains, it's a requirement. With EDI you start with your most fundamental transaction sets like transferring purchase orders, acknowledgments, and shipping advices.

"The more a company does business with the mass merchants, the more EDI becomes a standard of doing business or else you're not going to be in business. Each retailer has it's own rules as to what transactions are required. Therefore, apparel manufacturers must be comfortable working with EDI. Smaller companies can actually use third-party providers for their EDI transactions if they can't afford an in-house capability.

"EDI is evolving from simple data exchange to collaborative planning and more frequent forecasting. It's advancing to a next level where

(*continued*)

instead of simply exchanging the raw data, companies are exchanging forecasts and plans. They're communicating data so the system of replenishment, forecasting, planning, and inventory information, and order status information actually starts to pass over the borders of corporations and firms and becomes a supply–chain-wide homogeneous system. The concept of collaborative planning and data exchange started in the early 80s with programs like Milliken's 'Partners for Profit.' The industry puts new names on the process every few years. It's a good direction, and companies are constantly making little tweaks and improvements to gain competitive advantage."

Supply Chain Management

"Supply chain management is going to be the key to making it all work. The logistics in fulfillment behind the Web site or the retail store is the real key to who's going to be successful and who's not. It's the procurement of the raw materials. It's the manufacturing to order by the unit. It's essentially getting it to the retailer or the E-commerce customer in a shorter and shorter lead time. Speed and accuracy are the bottom line for everything.

"T-shirts, jeans, basic apparel products . . . to me those producers should be lining up to integrate with their retailers. They should be receiving point-of-purchase informa-

tion as to what is selling and tracking data on how much inventory is in the full supply chain so that every time something is sold, they can literally react to what's the next item they want to issue into the supply chain.

"The consumer wants more and more, but wants to pay less and less. There's a sense that the supply chains have been squeezed as low as they can be on the inventory front, and that the next great frontier is both improving process speed and reducing administrative expenses—being able to run a company successfully on less and less. Doing more with less of your own internal resources is going to be the key to success.

"I'm a believer that American apparel manufacturing is going to return because of speed. It's already happening. Some people held onto their factories and didn't look at the almighty cost factors and are being successful because of their speed and responsiveness. Some of these factories found that even though their costs were higher than offshore, the cost was outweighed by the speed by which they could respond to the marketplace with effective supply chain management and agility.

"In most companies, the merchandiser is the key to managing the supply chain process. The merchandiser is typically responsible for ultimate production and procurement of goods and therefore forecasting and procurement of raw materials, as well as the bottom line."

Gus Whalen Experience— president/CEO, Warren Featherbone

Quick Response

"Our company defines quick response as replenishing our products at the SKU level within a week of the sale of the products at retail. The primary reason we use quick response is to improve the probability our products will be on the retailers' shelves in the proper SKUs for the needs of their consumers. It enables the retailers to operate more profitably because they have the right products at the right time, which maximizes their sales using less of our inventory.

"Right now about 70 percent of our total business is what we would call quick response or replenishable. Not all of our customers take advantage of our quick response capability because not all of them are set up electronically to do so. Some of the lines in our quick response program are replenished more rapidly than others. Our major customers are generally replenished within 2 weeks, while Dillard's is accomplished within 4 days. Dillard's was our first quick response partner. They actually came into our company and met with our supervisors, explaining their retailing challenges and our mutual objectives. Working together, we were able to make the concept work.

"Quick response makes us produce more sensibly because we're producing to actual sales as opposed to forecasts. If we try to produce to standard pre-season forecasts, we invariably make errors and end up with excess merchandise. Quick response requires a lot of hard work and effective electronic data communications, but it's a more efficient way of getting the right product to the end user.

"Today, we're really working hard in business-to-business via the Internet. What we're trying to do is get our smaller customers to order from us using quick response like our larger customers, except it'll be through the Internet."

Supply Chain Management

"I think right now, speed to market is one of the last differentiators in our industry. One of the interesting topics currently being discussed is logistics and the supply chain. I believe that we will shortly be able to demonstrate that the costs of actually moving piece goods to manufacturing and through manufacturing to retail is greater than, or very close to, the cost of manufacturing.

"The irony is that the farther we move manufacturing from the market, the more we aggravate the

(continued)

logistics costs, and those are going to be the ones that will rise faster than assembly. We produce all of our goods in domestic company-owned facilities. That allows us better control of our total supply chain.

"We are much more marketable because we are so much more responsive. Our customers are able to provide the ultimate consumer with the products that they want, when they want them. There's no dead stock and the retailer is not holding inventory very long, so it's extremely profitable for them. One of our top customers estimated that we're 26 percent more profitable for them than our competitors are. That's the benefit of quick response and supply chain management."

Summary

Improving supply chain management has become a primary objective of apparel companies wanting to compete in the expanding global marketplace of the twenty-first century. The apparel industry shifted its focus from reducing manufacturing direct labor costs in the 1970s and 1980s to quick response partnerships in order to reduce cycle times in the 1990s to proactive QR strategies of collaborative planning, forecasting, and replenishment in the early 2000s. To be effective at today's level of QR requires well-defined effective control systems, accurate and fast electronic communication, and collaboration through dedicated partnerships to share information and establish decision-making models that function within the supply chain management system.

The Crafted With Pride in U.S.A. Council and the demand-activated manufacturing architecture (DAMA) project laid the groundwork for developing QR strategies and applying new technologies. The DAMA project documented the process steps within the soft goods supply chain for a number of apparel products and developed software business tools and a supply chain architecture standard for collaborative business across the U.S. integrated textile complex.

Progressive companies are bringing a new perspective to QR partnerships as part of their overall supply chain management strategies. They are using a collaborative proactive approach to supply chain management by establishing shared information and decision-making networks for style forecasting and replenishment. This requires a much deeper commitment and trust by each partner and can result in reduced inventory levels, increased sales, and improved margins.

The merchandising function encompasses an apparel company's involvement across the broad scope of the integrated textile complex. Planning and control, line development, forecasting, materials management, and sourcing all are integrated in effective supply chain management systems. Primary merchandising responsibilities are the focus of the expanding scope of QR—line development, product sourcing, and materials management. This places merchandisers, or new specialized roles within the merchandising function, in very responsible and high profile positions within apparel companies. They must be adept at utilizing the emerging technologies of: EDI, PDS, CAD, Internet, World Wide Web, B2B commerce, forecasting models, VMI, MRP, RFID, ERP, and CPFR, while still being sensitive to the creative process.

Key Terms

blended sourcing

B2B (business-to-business)

collaborative planning, forecasting, and replenishment (CPFR)

demand-activated manufacturing architecture (DAMA)

enterprise resource planning (ERP)

electronic product code (EPC)

Fabric and Suppliers Linkage Council (FASLINC)

fast fashion

integrated textile complex (ITC)

inventory carrying costs

manufacturing resource planning (MRP)

model stocks

radio frequency identification (RFID)

short interval scheduling (SIS)

soft goods supply chain

Sundries and Apparel Findings Linkage Council (SAFLINC)

Textile Apparel Linkage Council (TALC)

theory of constraints (TOC)

Uniform Code Council (UCC)

Universal Product Code (UPC)

vendor-managed inventories (VMI)

vertical integration

Voluntary Inter-Industry Commerce Standards (VICS) Council

Discussion Questions and Learning Activities

1. What are the key components of current supply chain management strategies?
2. Select three different garment styles that come in two or more colors at a major department store or apparel chain store. Record the number of garments available for sale in the store for each style and color by size (SKU). Return to the store 1 week later and then 2 weeks later and record the same information. Compare the results of each visit and evaluate the effectiveness of the store's replenishment policy.
3. Replenishment is often effective for basic apparel products. What is an alternative strategy for fashion products?
4. Describe two factors that created the impetus for the development of quick response strategies in the apparel industry.

5. What new management strategies did the theory of constraints address that supported quick response as an effective means of improving the apparel industry?

6. Explain how the three Cs of quick response are applied by a manufacturer of apparel basics.

7. What two technologies have provided rapid and accurate product identification and the simultaneous transmission of that data to any global location? Give an example of how these technologies can aid in developing more accurate apparel forecasting.

8. Describe the primary differences between the "partner" relationships between apparel manufacturers and retailers in the early stages of quick response development and current collaborative efforts.

9. What steps would Southeast Asian contractors have to take to become more competitive as sourcing partners for U.S. apparel manufacturers and retailers?

10. What are two advantages of EDI over fax transmission of purchase orders between retailers and their apparel manufacturing QR partners?

11. Discuss the advantages of collaborative planning, forecasting, and replenishment over vendor-managed inventory systems.

12. In Case in Point 9.1, what was the primary reason that TSI was successful in implementing its QR program?

13. Discuss the role that information technology will play in the future of supply chain management.

14. What additional steps can be taken by apparel and retail companies to reduce the time it takes to create, produce, and then deliver seasonal merchandise?

References and Resources

Frazier, Robert. September 13, 1985. *Quick Response*. Presentation made at DUPAATCH.

Goldratt, Eliyahu M. 1994. *It's Not Luck*. North River Press.

Goldratt, Eliyahu M. 1998. *Essay on the Theory of Constraints*. North River Press.

Goldratt, Eliyahu M.; Cox, Jeff. 1992. *The Goal: A Process of Ongoing Improvement*. North River Press.

Kurt Salmon Associates. 1989. *Implementing VICS Technology & Quick Response*. VICS/Kurt Salmon Associates Publication.

Kurt Salmon Associates. 1997. *Quick Response—Meeting Customer Needs*. VICS/Kurt Salmon Associates Publication.

Lepore, Domenico; Cohen, Oded. 1999. *Deming and Goldratt*. North River Press.

Swedberg, Claire. 2005. *Apparel Footwear Groups Study*. RFID Journal. Available at www.rfidjournal.com/article.

Whalen, Charles E. ("Gus"). 1996. *The Featherbone Principle*. Gainesville, GA: The Featherbone Foundation.

Sourcing Strategies

- Examine the evolution of global sourcing.

- Discuss the role of merchandiser in the development of sourcing strategies.

- Analyze internal manufacturing, domestic sourcing, and offshore sourcing options.

- Identify the factors involved in the sourcing decision.

- Explore the role of technology in sourcing decisions.

- Evaluate the effect of international business paradigms in global sourcing.

One of the vital functions of the apparel process is **execution**—getting products of excellent quality made at the right time and for the right price.

Throughout the first half of the twentieth century, most U.S. apparel products were produced in company-owned domestic factories. After World War II, a retail buying frenzy took hold of the country. It put the focus squarely on mass production technologies. In addition the apparel industry profited greatly from the focus during the war on engineering and production efficiencies. Apparel conglomerates were formed, which combined men's, women's, and children's fashion divisions under a centralized corporate management structure. Large consolidated manufacturing plants with 300 to 600 workers sprung up in the U.S. South where they were closer to the textile mills and where labor rates were lower than in the North. The emphasis of these companies was on micromanagement. Massive engineering efforts were undertaken for the purpose of saving pennies per garment.

Up until the 1960s, apparel that was imported consisted of expensive, European designer fashions and garments made of high-quality raw materials. Couture fashions arrived from Paris and Milan, woolens from Ireland and Scotland, linens from Ireland and Belgium, leather goods and silk prints from Italy.

In the 1970s, the changing fashion scene, the introduction of new synthetic fibers, and increasing U.S. labor costs caused the apparel industry to reassess its traditional approach to manufacturing. Consumers wanted a greater variety of styles. At this time, a new generation of apparel companies evolved. Companies such as Esprit, Liz Claiborne, Calvin Klein, and Ralph Lauren were geared more toward branded merchandising than manufacturing.

Apparel companies needed to produce new products that required production skills not available in their own facilities. Furthermore, price competition forced them to seek less costly manufacturing opportunities. Many companies started looking outside the United States and found newly emerging low-cost labor markets. The process of procuring products to meet a company's marketing objectives is called *sourcing*. Sourcing determines where, when, and how a company's products will be manufactured. In the late 1990s and early 2000s, vertical retailers such as The Limited and GAP, as well as department stores developing private labels and private brands, followed the lead of national chains JCPenney and Sears and began to produce their apparel products using their own sourcing strategies.

Tom Ford, design director at fashion giant Gucci, said on the *Today Show* in 1998, "More and more we are a global culture, a global society." Sourcing in the fashion industry is a perfect example. In the 2000s, apparel products are imported into the United States from almost every country in the world.

■ Global Sourcing

Apparel products, which are labor-intensive, have provided a perfect opportunity for developing countries to move toward industrialization. Inexpensive equipment and simple infrastructure made the fashion business an attractive launching pad for emerging nations to develop a manufacturing base. U.S. apparel companies were initially attracted to Japan, Hong Kong, Taiwan, and South Korea because of five key attributes:

1. Labor rates were a fraction of those in the United States.
2. Strong political and social ties had been established through a U.S. military or industrial presence. Following World War II, the United States helped to strengthen the economies of these Asian countries as a defense against communist expansion.
3. The presence of large, English-speaking populations.
4. A developing infrastructure made it possible for raw materials to easily enter or be produced within the country and for finished goods to be shipped out of the country with little difficulty.
5. Governments had a positive attitude toward industrialization and investment of foreign capital.

There were other areas of the world with inexpensive labor, but these areas lacked the other attributes, thus making them unsuitable for development by the pioneers of a new burgeoning business practice, *global sourcing* (manufacturing products at the most effective locations around the world).

From the 1960s through the 1990s the apparel industry chased low-priced labor in more than 200 countries around the globe including the Far East, the Middle East, Asia, Mexico, Central and South America, and the Caribbean Basin. By 1996, the nearly $40 billion wholesale value of apparel imports almost equaled that of U.S. domestic apparel production (1997 TAC Report). Since 1996 imports have increased their penetration each year, reaching 91 percent of the apparel wholesale market in 2004. According to figures released by the American Apparel and Footwear Association, they represented 65 percent of apparel consumption in the wholesale market in 1997, 72.1 percent in 1998, 73.2 percent in 1999, 77.4 percent in 2000, 80.2 percent in 2001, 84.9 percent in 2002, 88.1 percent in 2003, and 91 percent in 2004. During the first six months of 2005, they have continued their dramatic growth and now represent close to 95 percent of apparel consumption.

This transition evolved in five phases:

Phase 1 took place in the 1960s when U.S. industries looked to Japan for lower-priced products, including textiles and apparel.

Phase 2 occurred in the 1970s and early 1980s when Hong Kong, Taiwan, and South Korea became the dominant "big three" apparel exporters.

Phase 3 developed in the late 1980s and early 1990s when the big three experienced industrial growth and skyrocketing labor rates. Apparel sourcing then migrated to the People's Republic of China, Thailand, Malaysia, Philippines, Saipan, the Middle East, and Central and South America.

Phase 4 occurred in the mid-1990s with a rapid growth of sourcing in Pakistan, India, Indonesia, Bangladesh, and Sri Lanka.

Phase 5 saw sourcing shift to Mexico and the Caribbean. This shift was a direct result of the North American Free Trade Agreement (NAFTA). This agreement made it possible for Canada, Mexico, and the United States to trade freely (without import duties or quotas) among one another. Similar trade incentives have been enacted through the Caribbean Basin Trade Partnership Act. President Clinton first signed it into law on May 18, 2000 as part of the Trade and Development Act. It was enhanced in 2002, and today it offers to 14 Caribbean countries the same preferential treatment for their apparel exports to the United States as Mexico and Canada under NAFTA.

Phase 6 took place during the first few years of the 21st Century in anticipation of the removal of quotas in 2005. Many companies initiated or expanded their sourcing relationships with China to the point that China was the largest exporter of apparel to the United States. India has also been the beneficiary of increased business and interest in the further development of their textile and apparel exports.

Many apparel executives found that chasing lower labor rates to the far reaches of the globe was not the panacea for sagging profit margins. The sourcing issue was far more complex than simply finding the cheapest labor. Product quality, government regulations, political and economic stability, cultural and language differences, availability and quality of raw materials and supplies, transportation and delivery time, and manufacturing support costs complicate the sourcing decision. Despite the problems, effective sourcing strategies are essential to the success of U.S. apparel companies.

■ Sourcing: Role of the Merchandiser

In many companies the apparel merchandiser plays a key role in the sourcing function. In small companies the merchandiser may have total responsibility for sourcing decisions; midsized companies may have buyers, production specialists, or sourcing agents who report to the merchandiser; larger companies may have a vice president of production, manufacturing, or sourcing and staff offices in the countries manufacturing their products.

Whatever the company structure, it is imperative that all those involved in the merchandising function understand the mechanics of global sourcing. There is a complex interrelationship between style development, fabric sourcing, and product sourcing. As the variety of fabrics and trims and the international sources of fabrics increase, the merchandiser is frequently involved in the complicated sourcing decision because fabrics are sourced from one country, trims from another, and production from yet another. This creates timing and logistics challenges, which are part of the overall sourcing decision. Merchandisers often develop whole segments of a line based upon materials available from the sourcing network.

No matter what role the merchandiser and product manager play in sourcing, from direct line responsibility to coordination with a specialized sourcing or production executive, merchandising and sourcing share a common goal— get the right product to the customer at the right price and at the right time.

■ Sourcing Options

Apparel companies have three options for sourcing: they can source internally, externally, or a combination of both. The decision as to which option is best suited for a specific company is based upon the company's financial resources, level of manufacturing expertise, and strategic objectives.

Internal Manufacturing

An apparel company can manufacture its products in its own domestic or international plants. Some companies have built offshore factories or set up strategic relationships with foreign companies as part owners of facilities in accordance with the offshore country's laws. (Many nations do not allow majority ownership of companies by foreign investors.) Internal manufacturing requires substantial capital investment for plant and equipment. However, internal manufacturing does provide the most control over production. In today's marketplace, internal manufacturing is most suitable for stable product lines, such as Levi Strauss jeans, and for companies that are quick response resources, able to respond rapidly to changing consumer demands.

Most companies that own manufacturing facilities use them as part of an overall sourcing strategy. They maintain a mix of internal manufacturing and external sourcing. The primary advantages of company-owned facilities are:

- *Control* over the flow of raw materials and trim items as well as production schedules and deliveries.
- *Quality* standards are more easily established and monitored in company-owned facilities.
- *Response* time through electronic data interchange with retailers and textile suppliers can be optimized since priorities are established and controlled by the owner of the facility.

Today's domestic apparel manufacturers are using QR technologies to reduce work-in-process inventories and maximize customer service and just-in-time strategies with their textile suppliers to minimize raw material inventories.

Domestic apparel manufacturers must consider the following hidden costs when they are tempted by offshore labor prices that are often only one tenth of those of domestic labor:

- Lower inventory turns (increased inventory carrying costs).
- Inability to replenish styles that create reorders (lost sales and margin dollars).
- Markdowns caused by inability to adjust orders placed 6 to 9 months in advance.
- Higher support costs (travel, communications, professional fees, brokers, insurance, etc.).
- Unexpected shipping delays and quota and customs problems (embargoes).
- Unexpected shipping delays due to imposition of temporary quotas, customs security inspections, and inability of port facilities to handle increased volume.

Even with the above factors on the side of domestic manufacturing, the United States continues to lose the manufacturing battle as more and more companies are increasing their offshore sourcing. By 2004 domestic production volume represented less than 10 percent of imported merchandise. As a result of imports and improved productivity, domestic apparel industry employment—which reached a peak of 1,438,100 in 1972—dropped to 629,000 in 1997, before falling to 284,800 in 2004. According to an article that appeared in *Women's Wear Daily* on October 10, 2005, employment declined further to 253,900 in September 2005. Table 1.2 (page 21) chronicles the annual employment levels from 1990 to 2004.

As a means of stemming the tide of foreign production, U.S. apparel producers are looking toward technology for a solution. Following are examples of how technology may advance domestic production:

1. **Automated sewing systems** using robotics to transfer highly skilled human functions to machines is one approach. Unfortunately, automation in the (soft goods) apparel industry has lagged far behind the hard goods industries (automotive and electronics) due to the extreme materials handling problems associated with great variations in the mechanical properties of fabric. Steel and plastics are rigid whereas cloth varies in degrees of limpness and elasticity and can be slippery or clingy, porous or dense. For example, suction pickup devices that can select and position one ply of newspaper stock are useless on porous cotton knits. A rigid electronic circuit board can be slid into perfect position in a fixture or jig, but a polyester microfiber fabric will crumple into a limp heap if shoved into the same fixture. De-

spite all our technological advances, we have not been able to duplicating the delicate sense of touch and manipulative abilities of human fingers.

2. **Computer-aided design (CAD)** and **computer-controlled cutting systems** are playing an increasingly important role in making U.S. producers more competitive. Designers are able to use CAD systems to create full color renderings of new design ideas, complete with draped fabric prints or woven designs. Once the styles are finalized, patterns can be drafted and graded; accurate, cost-effective markers can be made; and fabric can be cut using computer-controlled cutting systems. What once took days or weeks can now be accomplished in

Figure 10.1a By using pattern design software and automated marker systems, quick response manufacturers can react even faster to changes in market demand.

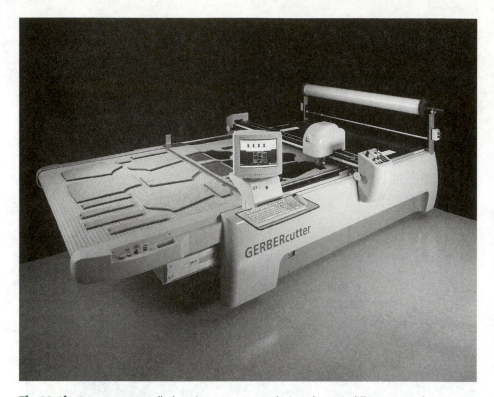

Fig.10.1b Computer controlled cutting systems are designed to suit different manufacturing requirements. This advanced technology allows domestic manufacturers to remain competitive in the global marketplace.

hours. These advances allow quick response manufacturers to react even more rapidly to market demands.

3. **Unit production systems (UPS)** are being used by U.S. apparel manufacturers to reduce labor and inventory carrying costs. A UPS overhead conveyor carries the components for a single garment from operation to operation, thereby reducing handling time (see Figure 10.2). This is in contrast to the bundle system, which moves bundles of components for 10 to 30 garments at a time, thereby dramatically increasing expensive work-in-process inventories and throughput time (the time it takes for a garment to move through the factory). Some factories using UPS have reduced throughput times from 3 and 4 weeks to days, or even hours. This short throughput time allows orders to be produced much closer to when they are required at retail, thereby allowing decisions of which styles to produce to be based upon actual sales data. This reduces the risk of producing garments that will not sell and eventually have to be marked down.

Figure 10.2 Installation of a unit production system (UPS) can reduce throughput time, labor, and inventory carrying costs. A UPS overhead transporter carries the components for a single garment from one sewing operator to the next without non-value added time being used for tying and untying bundles.

4. **Modular manufacturing systems (MMS)** are another technology used to reduce work-in-process with an added focus on improving quality. Operations requiring similar skills are grouped together in circular or arced stand-up sewing modules in which the sewing machines are raised so that operators can operate them standing up and the operators can easily move from machine to machine within the module. This production technique is comparable to techniques used by the automobile industry. By one operator performing a sequence of operations, material handling time and work-in-process are greatly reduced. Modules can be organized into teams that perform all the

operations required to produce a garment. With this team approach, quality can be a team responsibility and competition among teams for production and quality can reduce overall production costs and achieve improved quality.

If the U.S. apparel industry is to check the erosion of domestic production by imports, it must focus on new technology. The industry will have to follow the lead set by the textile industry, which invested millions in automating knitting and weaving facilities in the 1980s. Apparel companies must develop new generations of automated handling, cutting, and sewing equipment. This will require a change in management philosophy from relying on skilled labor to investing in capital-intensive manufacturing systems.

External Manufacturing

If an apparel company does not have or chooses not to use its own manufacturing facilities, it can us an outside contractor. This option eliminates the financial risk of owning plant and equipment and carrying overhead during downtimes. However, it puts the company at the mercy of its contractors. There are two general approaches to external manufacturing:

1. *Cut*, *make*, and *trim (CMT)* sourcing where the apparel company provides designs, fabrics, and trims, and the contractor provides labor and supplies.
2. *Full-package (FP)* sourcing [known in Asia as original equipment manufacturing (*OEM*)] where the contractor provides fabrics, trims, supplies, and labor.

It is easier for a small contractor to start with CMT than full-package sourcing because full-package contractors need up-front financing to purchase raw materials. Being a full-package contractor is even more difficult in developing countries. With labor rates of less than $1.00 per hour, the cost of the fabric and supplies could easily be ten times the amount the contractor would earn for labor. However, in the 21st Century, full package has become the preferred method when sourcing offshore.

The benefits of CMT contracting to the company outsourcing its production are:

- *Flexibility* since the outsourcing company controls raw materials, which allows for product and style changes to be made quickly and volume commitments to be adjusted to market needs.
- *Reduced investment* of the company's financial and human resources, which are needed for internal manufacturing. With CMT, the only initial investment is for fabric (which must be procured prior to man-

ufacturing) and for quality assurance and production follow-up personnel, who are needed to ensure that production deadlines will be met and quality standards will be achieved.

- *Control* over design and fabric resources can maximize material utilization and minimize the threat of having products copied by competitors (knockoffs).

The benefits of full-package contracting to the company outsourcing its production are:

- *Limited technical knowledge* about manufacturing is needed by the outsourcing company. This allows the outsourcing company to focus totally on product development and marketing. The downside of this benefit is that the contractor has full control over the manufacturing process from raw materials procurement through cutting, sewing, and finishing and therefore restricts the flexibility of the outsourcing company to make changes.
- *Limited investment* is required by the outsourcing company. Usually only a letter of credit is required, which is exercised (funds are transferred from the outsourcing company's bank account to the contractor's bank account) after the order is shipped.
- *Limited commitment* to a particular resource, thereby allowing the outsourcing company to make drastic style changes or change products from season to season. Some outsourcing companies do, however, try to develop long-term relationships with quality full-package contractors.

A variation of CMT is **offshore assembly**, also referred to as the **807 program**. As mentioned earlier, the term "807" refers to a paragraph published over 35 years ago in the Tariff Schedule of the United States Annotated (TSUSA), which allows components cut in the United States to be shipped offshore for assembly and then returned to the United States without incurring duties on the components. Duty is charged only for the value added in the offshore assembly process plus the cost of shipping. Item 807 is today's paragraph 9802.00.80 of the Harmonized Tariff Schedule of the United States Annotated (HTS). The key factor in this tariff clause requires that U.S. cut components be used that are: "(a) ready for assembly, (b) do not lose their physical identity in the assembly process by change in form, shape, or otherwise, and (c) have not been advanced in value except by operations directly related or incidental to the assembly process." This clause in the Harmonized Tariff Schedule specifically identifies "Assembly of cut parts of wearing apparel by sewing, hemming or stitching." Due to the restriction that the parts must be cut in the United States, most 807 production has occurred in locations in close proximity to the United States, such as Mexico, the

Caribbean, and Central America. This minimizes transportation costs and response times.

To complicate matters even more, there is also a **Special Regime Program 807a** (paragraph 9802.00.90) created in 1986 that allows garments made from parts cut in the United States and made of fabric formed in the United States to qualify for guaranteed access to the United States. The addition of 807a generated a rapid growth of assembly plants (*maquiladoras*) along the U.S. border with Mexico. These plants are *maquiladoras*, which are Mexican companies. They can be 100 percent foreign-owned, but they are restricted to assembling foreign merchandise for immediate export. For example, fabric is cut in Texas or California and shipped across the border and assembled in Mexico. This process of establishing a twin plant across the border from a U.S. city greatly reduces shipping costs and delivery time because of the close proximity to the United States. Major cutting operations opened in Florida for 807 and 807a sourcing where parts are shipped to nearby Caribbean countries for assembly.

Domestic Sourcing

Domestic sourcing still plays a minor role in the overall sourcing plans of many U.S. apparel companies, including those who do internal manufacturing as well as those who own no plant or equipment and exclusively use external manufacturing. The 1986 Report of the Technical Advisory Committee of the American Apparel Manufacturers Association (AAMA) highlights the following useful advantages that apply today when domestic contractors are used:

- *Additional output*: Domestic contracting can accommodate increased customer demand for manufacturing volume without new investment. Since fashion trends or fads often create dramatic fluctuations in consumer demand, outsourcing to domestic contractors can prevent costly investment in new plant, equipment, and workers that may become idle next season.
- *Added product-line flexibility*: In periods when even basic lines are affected by fashion trends, a domestic contracting program can provide for greater flexibility and reduce the costs incurred by style changes. This option allows an apparel company to focus its internal production on stable product lines and utilize external contractors for styles requiring specialized skills.
- *Coping with peak production requirements*: Domestic contractors can provide a means to meet the short-term requirements of peak production periods. Unfortunately, competitors will also be experiencing peak demands and, therefore, will be competing for the same contract resources.

- *Quick response and short throughput cycles*: Many domestic contractors specialize in specific product categories and use unit production systems to achieve much faster throughput times than most diversified, larger apparel manufacturers. This gives them the ability to quickly replenish stock that has experienced rapid sell-through.

- *Specialized equipment and skills*: A contractor may have specialized equipment, fabric specialties, or unique operator skills (for example, pleating, tucking, numerically controlled stitching, coverstitching, seam sealing, multineedle topstitching, silk or satin production capabilities).

- *Stabilizing in-house production*: A well-structured domestic contracting program not only handles peak production needs, but also helps stabilize the production mix of internal manufacturing. Quite often, the need for short runs and small reorders will upset a large plant's line balancing and production scheduling. Domestic contractors can help balance a manufacturer's overall production flow. Similarly, a reliable domestic contractor can help a manufacturer explore the potential of a new product category or market without making large commitments of capital and manpower. Using a number of contracting plants, each possessing its own special characteristics, can add immeasurably to the versatility and responsiveness of domestic sourcing. Where specialization is involved, some apparel companies take in contract work while contracting products out—all in the interest of realizing the full potential of their manufacturing strengths and maximizing the stability of their production mix. For example, a factory that specializes in denim shirts may contract out a new style made of microfiber fabric and take in a contract order for a cotton broadcloth shirt.

- *Quick start-up and turn-off abilities*: A smaller organization can turn on and off more quickly a large one. This is especially true in contracting. A domestic contractor usually has a management team focused on flexibility and reacting quickly to changing circumstances. Its success depends on adapting to variations in style content. This factor makes domestic contractors a valuable resource to be integrated into an effective overall sourcing strategy.

- *Union relations*: Increasing competition from offshore contractors has caused local unions to become more flexible in assisting companies in locating competitive domestic union contractors for specific products.

- *Access to 807 production*: The growth of offshore contracting has hurt domestic contracting, and some larger U.S. contractors have countered by developing their own 807 operations in the Caribbean and Mexico. Their experience and contacts can be used by apparel companies that are unable or unwilling to commit to their own 807 operations, but wish to take advantage of the lower wages and proximity offered by that sourcing option.

We support

CRAFTED WITH PRIDE IN U.S.A.

the textile and apparel industry.

Figure 10.3 This highly recognized label certifies that a garment was "Made In The USA." The prominent display of this label is an effort by the Crafted With Pride In USA Council to promote the purchase of products made entirely in this country and to compete with garments that are either made of foreign components or assembled offshore.

The U.S. fiber, textile, apparel, and home furnishings industries have spearheaded a program to help convince retailers and consumers to purchase textile and apparel products made in the United States. The Crafted With Pride In U.S.A. Council, Inc., was created to strengthen the competitive position of products made in the United States. The Council encourages retailers and manufacturers to prominently feature a "MADE IN USA" label and use the Council's highly recognizable red, white, and blue certification mark on labels and hang tags of domestically produced textiles and apparel (See Figure 10.3). The Council produced an eight year national television campaign to reinforce the positive value of purchasing "MADE IN USA" apparel and home furnishings and to encourage people to look for this label. The Council also sponsors prototype demonstrations of the effectiveness of quick response and distributes syndicated columns and newsletters stressing the importance of manufacturing, especially in the textile, apparel, and home furnishings industries, to the national economy.

Offshore Sourcing

Offshore sourcing (contracting outside of the United States) has become the dominant method of production. In 2004 more than 90 percent of apparel was manufactured offshore (American Apparel and Footwear Association, 2004). While the evolution of sourcing has seen the shifting of importance of various regions, the Big Four remains the leader in supplying clothing to the United States, followed by Central America. There has been a change in the principal exporting country, with China regaining their top spot from Mexico (see Table 10.1). With the removal of quotas among the members of the WTO on January 1, 2005, China's exports to the United States surged. Figures from OTEXA show that they increased from 8,717,844,729 to 12,727,939,521 square meter equivalents for the first nine months of 2004 versus 2005. This prompted the United States to begin imposing safeguard quotas in May 2005 limiting growth to 7.5 percent on nine categories of apparel as provided in the accession agreement that allowed China to enter the World Trade Organization. On November 8, 2005, the United States and China agreed bilaterally to limit the increase in exports in 2006 to 10 percent for apparel and 12 percent for textiles, and in 2007 to 12.5 percent across the board; in 2008, overall growth will be limited to between 15 percent and 16 percent (Clark; Ellis, 2005).

Extremely low-cost labor in developing countries has been the great attraction for the labor-intensive apparel industry. Table 10.2 shows a sampling of average hourly wages of apparel workers around the world. An analysis of workers' earnings is, however, only one element of the cost equation. Remember that support costs (overhead) in many developing countries are also

TABLE 10.1

U.S. Imports from Selected Regions and Countries

Region		1974	1984	1995	1999	2004
Big Four						
China		7	421	862	910	11,662
Hong Kong		309	848	821	841	862
Taiwan		353	808	598	637	1302
Korea		246	635	343	537	2301
	Region Subtotal	915	2712	2624	2925	16,127
	Percent of Imports	57	63	28	25.6	34
Japan	**Region Subtotal**	137	120	5	6	335
	Percent of Imports	8	3	0	0	0.7
Asean						
Indonesia		0	108	310	441	1275
Malaysia		0	54	152	178	364
Philippines		85	197	465	506	711
Singapore		75	107	84	73	49
Thailand		0	89	244	386	1113
	Region Subtotal	160	555	1255	1584	3512
	Percent of Imports	9.9	12.9	13.6	13.9	7.5
Other Far East						
Bangladesh		0	20	519	773	1109
India		23	112	258	337	1915
Sri Lanka		1	91	281	386	488
Pakistan		0	53	154	237	2970
Macau		0	54	155	211	448
	Region Subtotal	24	330	1367	1944	6930
	Percent of Imports	1.4	7.68	14.7	17	14.8
Mexico	**Region Subtotal**	76	72	774	2307	4101
	Percent of Imports	4.7	16.8	8.4	20.2	20.2
CBI						
Dominican Republic		5	79	632	858	772
Honduras		34	57	47	943	1209
Costa Rica		0	28	297	346	334
Guatemala		0	2	185	305	550
Jamaica		0	8	225	148	53
All other CBI		0	0	623	816	1250
	Region Subtotal	39	174	2009	3416	4168
	Percent of Imports	0	4	21.7	24.2	8.9
All Others	**Region Subtotal**	0	329	1221	1932	46,936
	Percent of Imports	0	8	13	14	28.1
TOTAL IMPORTS		1,619	4,292	9,255	11,410	46,936

The percentages of U.S. apparel imports from various regions of the world shifts as countries develop their economies, hourly labor costs increase, and trade regulations are modified.

Import quantities are stated in millions of SME (square meter equivalents).

Source: U.S. Department of Commerce, Office of Textiles and Apparel, (OTEXA).

TABLE 10.2	

Production Cost Index

Country	Percentage of U.S. Costs
China	26.41509
Costa Rica	39.62264
Dominican Republic	22.64151
Honduras	30.18868
Hong Kong	101.8868
India	32.07547
Israel	135.8491
Italy	186.7925
Malaysia	30.18868
Mexico	39.62264
Pakistan	20.75472
Philippines	50.9434
Poland	71.69811
South Korea	101.8868
Sri Lanka	35.84906
Taiwan	96.22642
Thailand	50.9434
Turkey	100
Vietnam	50.9434

The Production Cost Index takes into account the cost of production per SAM and includes: direct and indirect labor costs, average working time per year, industry specific productivity, depreciation for machinery and buildings, and interest rates. The calculated cost per SAM is then converted into an index with the U.S. being the basis and set at 100. Analysis based on 2005 data from KSA.

a fraction of the costs in the United States. The average number of hours worked also plays an important role in the overall value of labor and the final cost to manufacture apparel products. In many third-world countries, workers put in longer than 8-hour days and more than 5-day workweeks without a pay differential. Workers are also often required to work overtime during busy periods or risk losing their jobs. This additional output per worker absorbs greater overhead and fringe benefit costs, thereby reducing the final manufacturing cost per garment even more.

The biggest hurdle sourcing executives face is functioning on a global scale with many countries and many cultures. Over the past 20 years these executives have learned, often from trial and error, how to cope with the complexities of dealing with the global issues involved with offshore sourcing. Anyone contemplating a career that involves global sourcing should consider additional courses or training that focuses on international business practices, philosophies, and cultural issues.

Figure 10.4 The evolution of global sourcing has witnessed a constant shifting of production from one region of the world to another. Factories such as the one pictured here in Vietnam are representative of the growth in apparel manufacturing in Southeast Asia.

■ Factors in the Sourcing Decision

Deciding where, when, and how to source apparel products requires analysis of a complex variety of factors. Just as fashion is in a constant state of flux, so are the elements that go into the ultimate sourcing decision. In order for sourcing executives to make the correct decisions, they must carefully weigh each factor based upon their company's individual needs. Unfortunately there are no fail-safe computer models that a merchandiser or sourcer can use to determine the best sourcing alternative.

Cost Elements

The primary issue for most sourcing executives is cost. What will it cost to make a product in my own plant or at a domestic contractor or in an offshore facility? A typical mistake of newcomers to global sourcing is to make the decision based solely on a comparison of domestic manufacturing cost and the landed duty paid cost of importing the product using CMT, full package, or 807. However, there are a number of additional expenses involved in offshore sourcing that are not directly related to the manufacturing cost per unit.

"Not Just Price—Ortenberg Tells Why Claiborne Shops Abroad"

Unless there is a sharp change in the "mindset" of American textile and apparel manufacturers, Liz Claiborne, Inc., will have to continue to shop world markets for its fabrics and production, according to Arthur Ortenberg, cochairman.

In an unusual three-hour interview and demonstration at company headquarters here, Ortenberg went through Claiborne's spring-summer Lizsport collection and its men's wear collection piece by piece and explained why the firm had to reach to Japan for polyesters, China for silks, Hong Kong and Taiwan for cottons, Belgium for linens, Israel for knits, West Germany for yarns, and a multitude of other countries for its fabrics.

Ortenberg set up the meeting in response to charges by Du Pont and several converter and mill executives that American-made fabrics are as good as those made anywhere in the world and the sole reason for imports is low price. Any other reason is a "smokescreen," the American textile executives charged. The meeting in Claiborne's offices was designed to challenge that viewpoint. In addition to WWD, Ortenberg's guests included two Du Pont executives and Carl Rosen, president of Loomtex Corp., converter firm, who is former chairman of the Textile Distributors Association and a spokesman for the domestic textile industry.

There are many reasons why Claiborne sources more than 85 percent of its total ready-to-wear collection overseas, and price is only one of them," Ortenberg asserted, citing an interconnecting set of circumstances involving both textiles and apparel production.

These circumstances include lack of availability in the U.S. of certain types of fabrics, such as fine—50 denier or finer—silky polyesters and acetates like those available from Japan, lack of sewing capability in U.S. equipped to handle Claiborne's requirements of as much as 120,000 units at a clip, not enough fine-denier dyeing and printing capacity to tackle the firm's needs, and the superb quality of some overseas producers.

"We have zero problems when we bring goods out of Prato," he declared. Ortenberg lashed out at what he termed "short-term thinking" on the part of too many American textile producers who are so busy now that they do not want to try to produce goods to match Claiborne's demanding fashion and quality standards.

He charged that while a very few mills, such as Dan River, were eager and committed to working closely with Claiborne, for the most part American fabric producers are not.

"For several months we tried to run a fleece program here but three of the largest producers wouldn't even take our samples and try to make them. Obviously they were too busy with other work to bother to meet out standards. This is very frustrating," Ortenberg said.

"We often have to chase people domestically to get them to do business with us,"

(continued)

he said, "and when we can get the fabrics we need, the problem is we can't get the sewing . . . the number of units we require, the quality and the cost.

"Nobody makes denim any better than U.S. mills, but we have to send it to Hong Kong to have it made into jeans as we want them and this takes valuable time," he said.

Regarding apparel production, he said, "We do have a problem with fine-denier silk-like sewing capabilities in the U.S." To help develop nearby capacity in this skill, Claiborne has helped two contractor factories get started in New York's Chinatown. "We are planning to open another one there soon," he added.

Even in spun goods, Ortenberg feels overseas producers outstrip America.

"On spun goods there can be a world of difference also," he declared. "There's a tremendous difference in twist—and our customers look for the real thing."

He likened the difference to that of two bottles of wine, "a $100 prestigious bottle and a $1.79 lookalike."

"The bottles may appear similar on the outside, the corks and labels may look the same, but the contents inside these bottles are vastly different."

Of course, price is the number one reason Claiborne sources 100 percent of its men's wear lines and 99 percent of its dress division offshore, the executive admitted.

"On some of our goods it costs $15 a garment to stitch them in Hong Kong compared with $30 to $40 a unit to stitch them in the U.S.," he said.

Aside from price, however, Ortenberg declared workers in the Far East work better and are more dedicated than American workers.

"You better believe it," he said. "They make better garments overseas."

Ortenberg also cited "the growing concentration of power in fewer and fewer retail hands like Macy's" and other "super" large retail groups.

"We're fighting pressure from retailers who are turning to their own private label goods," he said.

Turning to another point, production, Ortenberg urged American industry to look to the Caribbean. "The entire Caribbean Basin is open to the U.S. textile-apparel complex," he declared. "They will have to establish a stitching capability there." On a positive note, Ortenberg had praise for the American textile industry, which he said had done an excellent job in modernizing equipment, improving technology and making its products better and more competitive.

"The problem really isn't with the textile industry as much as it is with the apparel industry. That's the rub," he explained.

"We're beginning to see a change in attitude of American mills. It's happening now but in a very small way."

As for knits, one of Claiborne's strong points, Ortenberg declared, "It would be a luxury to make more sweaters here. Yes, you can make more sweaters in America but not the type we need. The industry has the technology and the capability but the commitment is lacking."

He added with a smile: "When we show a new design to a Japanese sweater knitter, he says, 'ah how simple' but the American knitter says, 'oh how complicated.'"

However, he declared, "More and more we will be making sweaters here. It's a matter of properly using yarn along with a commitment to meet our needs. We have three domestic resources now and we'll have

(continued)

more next year. Sitting on top of this company is a tremendous responsibility," concluded Ortenberg, whose company had sales of $554,553,000 in 1985.

"We must have a close relationship with all our suppliers throughout all channels of the industry from fiber to fabric to finishing to cutting and sewing. Part of that commitment is to make sure our orders are fulfilled properly so the consumer can benefit—no shortcuts, no cheap dyes or finishing. Mindset is the key." ■

From Marvin Klapper. February 4, 1987. *Women's Wear Daily*, p. 1.

Case in Point 10.1 ## Summary

Liz Claiborne sources more than 85 percent of its ready-to-wear collection offshore for reasons other than price. Art Ortenberg, Claiborne cochairman, cited lack of availability of certain fabrics and the refusal of many American textile producers to create new fabrics to meet Claiborne's fashion and quality standards as a reason for sourcing offshore. Claiborne also experienced difficulty in acquiring the sewing quality and sewing cost needed for its products. To overcome these difficulties, the company has integrated domestic sourcing into its overall sourcing strategy by assisting contract factories in getting established in New York's Chinatown.

Price still plays an important factor in Claiborne's sourcing of men's wear and dresses in Hong Kong. Ortenberg sees the Caribbean Basin as a potential resource for apparel sourcing. His company is expanding its sweater production with domestic resources. No matter where Claiborne sources its products, it cites a close relationship with sourcing partners as the key to success. ■

To be successful in the global marketplace, a manufacturer needs a well-established **support structure** (personnel and service costs required to import products) in place, which generates the following expenses:

- *Computer and telephone links* with the contract manufacturing site to provide telephone, E-mail, and fax communications.
- *Courier service* to rush samples and approvals.
- *Buying office, agent, or staff* in the sourcing country to inspect quality and follow up on production progress and exportation.
- *Legal consultants* well versed in international law, trade agreements, U.S. customs regulations, and the regulations of the exporting countries.
- *Merchandising and manufacturing technical specialists* to visit the offshore contractor to establish appropriate manufacturing processes and quality standards.

A simplified version of a calculation sheet
used for the purposes of establishing the "cost per dozen"
for 807 garments is shown here:

807 Cost Per Dozen Calculation Sheet

Category		Annual $ Expense	Annual Dozens	Standard Per Doz.		Total Cost Per Dozen
General Cutting Supplies (includes 807 strapping/wrapping supplies)		10,000.00	200,000	.050		$ .050
Direct Labor	Additional - strapping/wrapping for 807	20,200.00	200,000	.101		$ .101
Indirect Labor	Cutting Room Manager	17,500.00	200,000	.088		
	Cutting Q. C.	15,240.00	200,000	.076		
	Marking/Plotting	6,240.00	200,000	.031		
	Piece Work Ticket Printing	3,000.00	200,000	.015		
	Label Printing	3,440.00	200,000	.017		
	Clerical (includes production control)	4,740.00	200,000	.024		
	Receive/Locate/Pull Piece Goods	15,500.00	200,000	.078		
	Plant Manager	18,720.00	200,000	.094		
	Count/Package/Stage Findings	13,460.00	200,000	.067		
	Stage/Load/Unload Containers	13,780.00	200,000	.069		
	Quality Audits	12,000.00	200,000	.060		
	Receiving Manager	7,420.00	200,000	.037		
	Fringe Benefits - (sub total Indirect labor)	131,040.00	200,000	.655 x 1.355		$ .888
Administrative Support	Quality Assurance	25,000.00	200,000	.125		
	Administrative/Clerical	51,220.00	200,000	.256		
	Engineering	14,760.00	200,000	.074		
	Mechanical	1,840.00	200,000	.009		
	Accounting	7,620.00	200,000	.038		
	Fringe Benefits (sub total Adm. Support)	100,440.00	200,000	.502 x 1.355		$ .680
Overhead	Telephone/Faxes	9,800.00	200,000	.049		$ .049
	Electricity	114,200.00	200,000	.571		$ .051
	Water	2,000.00	200,000	.010		$ .010
	Garbage Removal	6,200.00	200,000	.031		$ .031
	Insurance	17,400.00	200,000	.087		$ .087
Real Property Taxes		12,400.00	200,000	.062		$ .062
Depreciation		75,200.00	200,000	.376		$ .376
Air Freight/Expedites		260,000.00	200,000	1.300		$ 1.300
Shrinkage		62,400.00	200,000	.312		$ .312
Seconds		110,000.00	200,000	.550		$ .550
Travel/Lodging/Meals		187,000.00	200,000	.935		$ .935
Reserve Leased Equip.		84,000.00	200,000	.420		$ .420
Additional Work-In-Process		1,800.00	200,000	.009		$ .009
Transportation Expenses		28,000.00	200,000	.140		$ .140
						$ 6.051

Figure 10.5 Additional costs are generated by the support needed to run an 807 apparel sourcing program.

- *Customs brokers* to handle the exportation of raw materials and cut parts and the importation of finished goods into the United States.
- *Banking specialists* who understand the different types of financial documents necessary for doing business overseas. These may include irrevocable letters of credit, transferable letters of credit, back-to-back letters of credit, documents against payment, documents against acceptance, telegraphic transfer, and open accounts. (These financial instruments are described in Chapter 11.)
- *Freight and traffic specialists* to determine the best international carriers and freight forwarders and to establish realistic shipping schedules.
- *Oversight* by U.S. company executives to negotiate new orders, follow up on orders in process, and manage foreign support staff.

Thus we can see that decision makers must be cautious when they investigate international sourcing opportunities in order to fully evaluate all costs involved with the venture. Figures 10.5 and 10.6 illustrate the effect of the additional costs generated by a successful U.S.-based manufacturer in supporting an 807 apparel sourcing program. Figure 10.5 shows the additional support costs for the 807 operation, and Figure 10.6 shows the total manufacturing cost. Similar scenarios can be developed for supporting CMT or full-package international sourcing.

It is also important to factor in the cost of:

- *Risk* associated with doing business in the international marketplace where political, social, economic, and trade fluctuations are not con-

---

The final calculation in determining the total cost for producing a dozen garments of a particular style offshore on the 807 program might look something like this:

807 Cost Sheet

Style No._____   Date_____

Category		Standard Per Doz.		Total Cost Per Dozen
Fabric				$ 42.510
Sew/Trim/Finish (paid to O/S contractor) from 807 garment cost sheet				$ 21.456
Findings	Standard Findings (add 2 % for 807)	15.670	x 1.02	$ 15.983
Direct Labor	Onshore cutting cost (spread/cut/bundle)			$ 4.160
Offshore Cost (from 807 Calculation Sheet)				$ 6.051
				$ 90.160

Figure 10.6 The effect of the support costs of an 807 apparel program on the total manufacturing costs of producing an apparel product.

trollable, and time is critical to success in the ever-changing fashion scene.

- *Control* of quality and production.
- *Investment* requirements for management resources, support systems, and financing.

No matter which sourcing strategy is under consideration by an apparel company, the most critical issue involving cost is to be certain that *all cost elements* be identified and included in the decision. Identifying many costs involved in sourcing is difficult for companies that have not had extensive experience working in the global marketplace.

Capacity

Capacity is an important consideration when a potential sourcing alternative is being evaluated. Since most companies involved in sourcing stress that "relationship" is critical to a successful sourcing strategy, a new contract resource should be evaluated for both short- and long-term capabilities.

Liz Claiborne sourcing executive, Bob Zane, pointed out that, "In 1998 Liz will produce about 90 million apparel units (not including accessories) with a roster of 248 factories located in 30 countries throughout the world. Each vendor/partner averages 360,000 units per year. This is in contrast to 1994 production of 62 million units with a roster of 496 factories located in 38 countries. Our average producer accounted for 125,000 units per year. We want to become much more important to fewer people to enhance our manufacturing partnerships." In Claiborne's sourcing strategy it is critical that a vendor/partner have sufficient capacity to accommodate Claiborne's current and future needs.

A good sourcing executive should carefully evaluate a potential contract partner for:

- *Financial capacity* so that the partner will be able to invest in the necessary plant, equipment, and personnel to accommodate growth.
- *Plant space capacity* to support expanding needs.
- *Available workforce capacity* to properly staff for current and future production demands.

Minimums

Not only must a company be concerned about how much volume a contractor can handle, but it must also be concerned with how little—that is, minimum order quantities. Most domestic and offshore contractors will not accept orders for fewer than a specified number of units per style and color. This factor is particularly critical for smaller manufacturers of fashion-oriented apparel who cannot afford the high risk associated with issuing large orders.

Minimums vary by country and contractor. As new sourcing areas mature in sophistication, production capabilities, and quality, minimums tend to become higher and higher. The risk factor for potential markdowns associated with placing orders larger than can be supported by forecasts must be carefully weighed when making sourcing decisions. Companies with a mix of internal manufacturing and external sourcing end up producing the short run, smaller, initial orders in their own facilities, thereby driving up their manufacturing costs.

Labor Skills and Equipment Assessment

Since an apparel contractor is frequently selected to provide specialized sewing skills or equipment, the sourcer must carefully evaluate the contractor's *true capabilities*. This requires that the sourcing executive visit potential sourcing facilities and be well versed in manufacturing technology. Jack Listanowsky of The Limited remarked "The new philosophy is to bring an enhanced level of manufacturing expertise into the sourcing process. All actual factories and subcontractors must be approved by the sourcing department, not just the product as in the past. Professionals in manufacturing and sourcing are the ones who will be interfacing with the fashion contractor manufacturers." (See Executive Perspective 11.1 for more.)

Since performance in apparel manufacturing depends to a great degree on the skills of the sewing operators and the adequacy and quality of the equipment, the sourcing executive must carefully evaluate these factors. A formal **contractor evaluation form**, which lists an inventory of equipment, operator skills assessments, and production capacities, can be used to help the executive analyze the capabilities of the contractor. In some developing countries the apparel industry has not yet reached a level of sophistication to be able to apply industrial engineering principles to the production process. This results in inconsistencies in production methods. A careful assessment of operator training, methods analyses of each operation, and equipment evaluation are critical to making a quality sourcing decision. This may be done by a knowledgeable sourcing executive or a skilled engineer who is part of the sourcing team.

Some products may require specialized sewing skills and equipment as well as other factors that may influence the sourcing decision. An example would be a manufacturer of women's knit blouses deciding to expand into jeans production. Jeans require different sewing skills for handling heavy woven denims as well as specialized seaming equipment. Utilizing a domestic or international contractor specializing in denim jeans manufacturing should be considered in this sourcing decision. Since the United States is a major manufacturer of high-quality cotton denim, a domestic contractor or 807 contractor might be ideal options. Both of these local options would minimize the relatively high cost of transporting heavy denim fabric to and from distant locations.

Infrastructure

Many international contractors can provide low-cost labor, sufficient capacity, and appropriate skills and equipment. However, if their country doesn't have an adequate infrastructure, choosing them as a sourcing partner may prove costly. Infrastructure is taken for granted in the United States. Raw materials, trim, thread, packaging supplies, sewing machine parts and technicians, folders and work aids, reliable electrical power, and dependable shipping options are readily available to U.S. companies. Unfortunately, in most third-world countries the developing infrastructure lags behind sewing capability.

When an apparel company is considering a new global sourcing supplier, it must carefully analyze the infrastructure and other factors including the following:

- *Availability of quality raw materials, trim, findings, and packaging supplies* increases in importance as full package becomes the dominant method of offshore procurement. A qualified testing laboratory should analyze them. Samples of these items should be tested for tensile strength, color fastness, shrinkage, abrasion resistance, and seam compatibility. For example, thread or seam tape should not have greater shrinkage than the fabric to prevent seam puckering, and bathing suit fabric should be color fast to chlorine. No detail should be ignored when materials are analyzed. A major shirt manufacturer failed to test the pins that were used in packaging. A large percentage of its shirts were damaged when the pins rusted from humidity and temperature changes during the long sea voyage to the United States.
- *Availability and reliability* of electric power, material suppliers, and shippers should be determined. In many developing countries, electrical brownouts are often the rule rather than the exception. A backup power generator is a must in these countries if production schedules are to be maintained. Reliable suppliers of raw materials, trim, and findings are essential. The sourcer should identify qualified suppliers in the sourcing country or verify the ability to import needed items into the country without major difficulty, excessive cost, or lengthy delays.
- *Roads and transportation* can also be a critical factor in moving raw materials and finished products as well as getting workers from remote villages to factory sites. Some factories build dormitories to house employees and provide proper nutrition and medical care.

Jack Listanowsky of The Limited said, "It's not always just about price. Maybe I'll end up with an inferior quality label, and that's not acceptable." He also referred to logistics problems. "Did I pick the perfect country in the world that only has a boat coming in once a month? My traffic and logistics support mechanisms must be in place." Getting the finished product to the United States can be a major problem if the factory is located 6 hours through washed out jungle trails from the only seaport. A careful analysis of freight forwarders and trucking companies, and discussions with other manufacturers sourcing from the same country can provide valuable input.

Throughput Time and Lead Time

As fashions change more frequently than they used to, merchandisers must meet the needs of their customers by improving service and delivery with faster **total throughput times** (the time it takes for a production order to be processed from authorization to shipping). One factor that affects throughput time is the type of production system used, which affects factory throughput time. (**Factory throughput time** in hours equals work-in-process divided by average number of units produced per hour. Unit production systems and modular manufacturing reduce work-in-process, thereby lowering factory throughput time.) Other considerations are the distance from the distribution site to the factory, the transportation systems available, and the levels of government bureaucracy required to import raw materials into the manufacturing site and export finished product. Throughput times can vary from hours for domestic internal and external manufacturing, to weeks for 807 assembly operations, and months for CMT or full-package import programs.

The better international contract factories are usually fully booked early in a new production season. Therefore, orders must be placed with these factories well in advance of the actual start of production, which may add weeks or months to the total throughput time.

The lost income and customer dissatisfaction from stockouts and the markdowns created by having to authorize production far in advance of solid sales forecasts make throughput and lead times important elements in the sourcing decision. Many companies committed to offshore sourcing train their sourcing partners to utilize quick response technologies and the great advancements in communications (E-mail and the Internet) to shorten throughput times. Theoretically, with air transportation and electronic transfer of computer files containing pattern data, it should be possible to achieve throughput times in any part of the globe nearly as fast as those achievable in the United States. This increases the importance of developing automation systems and utilizing them in the United States to further reduce labor costs for the domestic apparel industry to survive.

Quality

Quality standards are of great concern to the executives making sourcing decisions. Historically, product quality has improved as developing countries mature as manufacturing resources. In the 1950s and early 1960s, the label "Made in Japan" denoted cheap prices and poor quality. Today, Japan is touted for its high-quality electronics, textiles, and automobiles. The same thing occurred in Hong Kong, Taiwan, and Korea with regard to apparel products. Over the years, the quality of garments produced in these areas improved to the point where many consumers look at a "Made in Hong Kong" label as a sign of high quality. As the quality improved, labor costs skyrocketed in these countries. From the time that Hong Kong, Taiwan, and Korea became resources for apparel imports, the average wages for sewing operators has increased by almost 900 percent.

Merchandisers must be very careful not to trade price for quality. Low cost cannot compensate for poor quality and the effect poor quality will have on a company's reputation. A careful audit of the quality in a factory under consideration as a sourcing partner is vital. Sample garments do not always reflect the production quality at a factory. At most offshore contractors, a sample department prepares samples. Therefore, a visit to the plant to inspect production in process is the only way to assess its ability to achieve the required quality standards. By the time the manufactured product arrives in the United States, it is usually too late for the apparel company to be compensated for an excessive number of quality rejects. Also there is rarely any time available to make repairs.

Liz Claiborne has established regional quality assurance centers in Hong Kong, Shanghai, Sri Lanka, Guatemala, Korea, Indonesia, the Dominican Republic, and the Philippines. Auditors inspect merchandise using the same formal audit procedures that are followed in Claiborne's domestic distribution center. "If an order fails, the vendor must take possession of the goods," says Bob Zane of Claiborne. "There's no excuse. There's no red tape involved because it's the vendor's country. This will be one of the most important things we have done to change the face of sourcing."

Competition

There is constant pressure to find the next "ideal" sourcing location. It is important to "keep an eye on the competition" when it comes to selecting the next sourcing opportunity. A company can be either a leader in developing new sourcing suppliers or a follower. A leader must find the next "virgin territory"—one that has low-cost skilled labor, is capable of meeting quality requirements, has a stable government, has qualified local management, has sufficient quota, has a good infrastructure, and is easily accessible by air and sea. A follower must know exactly when to jump into a new sourcing arena in order to keep up with the leaders. Deciding where a company should be positioned on the leader/follower sourcing tightrope is difficult in light of the myriad of complexities involved.

An executive may need courage to take the risk and assume the lead in finding and developing new sourcing locations. The downside can be catastrophic—late deliveries, quality disasters, or even government seizure of plant, equipment, and product. To take the lead in sourcing, a company must have a sophisticated, multilingual, development staff skilled in operator training, methods analysis, management training, and international business principles.

Emanuel Weintraub, president of Emanuel Weintraub Associates, Inc., a management consulting firm, summed it up in a *Bobbin* magazine article, "Solving the Sourcing Riddle," "What has a minimum of 10 sides to it and is creating an executive headache in the apparel industry? Answer: Figuring out an intelligent sourcing strategy for your company that won't jump up and bite you."

Distance

Another concern to sourcing executives is the distance from overseas contractors to domestic distribution centers and support personnel. The farther the production facility is from the United States, the greater the travel and shipping expenses become, and the longer the process takes. With the ever-increasing need for shortened delivery periods, distance becomes more important in the sourcing decision.

The North American Free Trade Agreement (NAFTA) and the Caribbean Basin Initiative (CBI) improved the competitiveness of Mexico and the Caribbean Basin, both of which have the benefit of being in the backyard of the United States. This advantage resulted in Mexican apparel imports increasing from 16.8 percent of total imports into the United States in 1984 to 20.2 percent in 2004. During this same period of time the imports from the Caribbean Basin increased from 4 percent to 8 percent (OTEXA, 2004).

The increase in sourcing in the Americas has not, however, put a halt to the constant search for cheaper labor, no matter what the distance. Apparel companies are continuing to search for new sourcing partners from as far away as Mongolia, Cambodia, Vietnam, and former Soviet republics to take advantage of low labor costs. Laura Jones, executive director of the U.S. Association of Importers of Textiles and Apparel has stated, "Mongolia could pose some logistical problems because of its location." She added, however, "Nothing is impossible where textiles are concerned. We have people making garments in very remote places" (Barrett, 1997).

Government Regulations

There are a myriad of government treaties, tariffs, quotas, laws, and complex reporting procedures related to the importation of apparel products. Constant changes in regulations and procedures make the sourcing executive's job even more of a challenge. In order to stay on top of these changes, many companies subscribe to the services of trade attorneys who provide weekly bulletins or monthly newsletters that focus on specific categories of trade issues. Since the cost of these services can be significant, some companies receive the information as members of specialized associations such as the National Knitwear and Sportswear Association.

Quota

Quotas place an annual limit on the number of units, kilograms, or square meters equivalent (SME) of imported products by category for each country. Since the end of World War II, world trade has been regulated by the **General Agreement on Tariffs and Trade (GATT)**, which was signed at the 1947 Geneva Trade Conference by 23 noncommunist nations. The objective of the current 116 signatory nations is to minimize trade barriers by reducing import quotas and tariffs and abolishing preferential trade agreements among member countries. All participating GATT members abide by a policy of **most-favored-nation (MFN)** status, which means that a participating country's exports to another participating country are charged the lowest tariff rates available to any nation.

In 1962 a **Long Term Arrangement (LTA)** permitting bilateral quotas was adopted by GATT members, which established formal mechanisms for voluntary restraint agreements on the flow of cotton textile exports. In 1971 the United States negotiated an extension of these restraint agreements to cover manufactured fibers and wool. These negotiations culminated in the **Multi-Fiber Arrangement (MFA)** in 1974 which allows industrialized nations to negotiate bilateral agreements with developing countries in order to control the rate of growth of textile and apparel imports. The MFA became the framework for quota negotiations between the United States and its apparel trading partners. The United States has negotiated bilateral textile and apparel quota agreements with over 40 countries covering 187 textile and apparel product categories. These import quotas are designed to protect domestic producers and maintain an orderly flow of trade.

The United States has different quotas for each product category for different countries. When a particular country reaches its limit for a product category, U.S. Customs places an embargo on the product category from that country from entering U.S. ports. Those products must then wait until the next quota year opens before they can be imported into the United States. There are many horror stories of apparel products arriving in U.S. ports in October and November destined for retail stores to accommodate holiday shoppers and being embargoed until after January 1 when they would be eligible for entry. It is the responsibility of the exporting country to control the amount of product that is shipped to the United States for each quota category. This is usually done by having the annual quota allocations (the amount of product that can be exported to the United States) issued to each factory in the country. Most quotas are based on the amount of the previous year's quota that was actually used by each factory. This results in many factories selling unused quota rights to other factories that have more orders than they can accommodate with their quota. This preserves the first factory's allotment for the following year. Some factories make substantial profits on "selling quota."

On December 15, 1993, GATT members completed the 7-year Uruguay Round of negotiations culminating in an agreement to phase out the MFA over a 10-year "integration" period. This agreement gradually "uplifted" (increased) quotas and reduced tariffs on clothing and textiles until all quotas were eliminated on January 1, 2005. This agreement was put into effect as a series of staged eliminations of quotas on various product categories. As an example, on January 1, 1998, the United States eliminated quotas on babies' apparel and apparel accessories of textile quota category 239 except for infants' cotton diapers, which will retain quota restrictions until the final deadline of January 1, 2005.

GATT was replaced as the overseer of world trade on January 1, 1995, by the World Trade Organization (WTO), which was established by a multilateral agreement in December 1993 to moderate trade disputes among its 116 member nations. The elimination of quotas under the Uruguay Round agreement affects only the products of WTO member countries. Quotas for countries such as Vietnam will not be eliminated because they are not currently members of the WTO. As part of the accession agreement when joining the WTO, China agreed to safeguards that would last until 2013. The safeguard provisions would allow the United States, countries in the European Union, and other members to impose restraints when an import surge resulted in a marketplace disruption.

A sourcing executive must not only be concerned about the availability of quotas for a specific category, but also how the quota will affect costs. In countries where quota is sold from factory to factory, in a sense, the price of quota is added to the contract price of the product. For product categories where demand is great and quotas are tight, the "cost of quota" can be equal to or greater than the cost of manufacturing the product. Some forward-thinking U.S. companies made substantial profits through quota negotiation. Stanley Tuttleman, cofounder of Mast Industries, states that "Mast hired a quota manager to investigate and negotiate quota. We were able to control large blocks of quota, which became valuable assets to our company."

Duty

Duty is a tax charged by a government on imported products. Another word for duty is **tariff**. Historically, the U.S. government has placed higher duty rates on products with fiber content that would create the greatest negative impact on U.S. fiber and textile companies. For example, apparel products constructed of manufactured fibers that have major producers in the United States have higher duty rates than cotton, which is a less important U.S. product; cotton has higher duty rates than silk, which has virtually no producers in the United States. The duty rates on textile and apparel products by category can be found in the **Harmonized Tariff Schedule of the United States Annotated (HTS)** (See Figure 10.7). The government maintains an updated version of this schedule on the World Wide Web at **www.usitc.gov/tata/hts.** Categories under the HTS are gender- and fiber-content-specific, for example, men's or boy's wearing apparel, not ornamented, not knit, of cotton, vests, valued over $2 each. The fiber content is determined by the "chief value" fiber such as chief value cotton (CVC) or chief value synthetic fiber (CVS).

Harmonized Tariff Schedule of the United States (2005) - Supplement 1
Annotated for Statistical Reporting Purposes

XI
61-6

Heading/ Subheading	Stat. Suffix	Article Description	Unit of Quantity	Rates of Duty		
				1		2
				General	Special	
6103		Men's or boys' suits, ensembles, suit-type jackets, blazers, trousers, bib and brace overalls, breeches and shorts (other than swimwear), knitted or crocheted: Suits:				
6103.11.00	00	Of wool or fine animal hair (443)	No. ..... kg	38.8¢/kg + 10%	Free (CA, CL, IL, JO, MX, SG)	77.2¢/kg + 54.5%
6103.12 6103.12.10	00	Of synthetic fibers: Containing 23 percent or more by weight of wool or fine animal hair (443)	No. ..... kg	60.3¢/kg + 15.6%	Free (CA, CL, IL, JO, MX, SG)	77.2¢/kg + 54.5%
6103.12.20	00	Other (643)	No. ..... kg	28.2%	Free (CA, CL, IL, MX, SG) 15.5% (AU) 14.4% (JO)	72%
6103.19		Of other textile materials: Of artificial fibers:				
6103.19.10	00	Containing 23 percent or more by weight of wool or fine animal hair (443)	No. ..... kg	Free		77.2¢/kg + 54.5%
6103.19.15	00	Other (643)	No. ..... kg	Free		72%
6103.19.20		Of cotton......................................	....	9.4%	Free (CA, CL, IL, JO, MX, SG)	90%
	10	Jackets imported as parts of suits (333).........	doz. kg			
	15	Trousers, breeches and shorts imported......... as parts of suits (347)	doz. kg			
	30	Waistcoats imported as parts of suits (359)	doz. kg			
6103.19.60	00	Containing 70 percent or more by weight of silk or silk waste (743)	No. ..... kg	0.9%	Free (AU, CA, CL, E, IL, J, JO, MX, SG)	45%

Figure 10.7 The Harmonized Tariff Schedule specifies rates of tariff for garments based upon the type of garment, fiber content of the fabric, and the construction of the garment. Source: **www.usitc.gov/tata/hts**

Duty rates are expressed as **ad valorem** (a percentage charged in proportion to product value) and in some cases also include a specific duty (a charge based on the product weight or on a per unit basis). Both these duty charges can fluctuate dramatically depending on the category. There are three rate classifications for each duty category: (1) the general rate for imports from countries with most-favored-nation status, (2) a special or preferential rate for imports from countries that qualify for special status, and (3) a rate for imports from countries that do not have most-favored-nation or special status. The advantage of 807 and 807a imports is not due to "special" duty rates, but rather to exemptions that reduce the ad valorem by the cost of the raw materials and labor for cutting in the United States and the freight for shipping those materials to the 807 assembly plant. Duty is charged only on the value added in the assembly operation. 807a imports, which are assembled from U.S. manufactured raw materials have the added advantage of qualifying for guaranteed access to the United States (no quota).

Since the HTS categories are extremely specific with regard to chief value, it is critical that sourcing executives carefully calculate the chief value fiber content. Body cloth, linings, interlinings, pocketing, thread, and stays must all be taken into account when sourcing decisions are made. Companies use a constructed value worksheet to determine the value of each fabric component and the associated labor before completing a duty statement for U.S. Customs. It is advisable to get customs rulings on any new products before they are imported in order to facilitate clearance. Because of the complexities of the HTS, companies involved in global sourcing should have experienced, qualified, import specialists on staff or available for consultation to guide them in making appropriate sourcing decisions.

North American Free Trade Agreement

In 1993, presidential candidate Ross Perot predicted that if NAFTA was passed by congress, the sound of U.S. jobs being drawn south would make "a giant sucking sound." The North American Free Trade Agreement (NAFTA) was passed by congress and went into effect on January 1, 1994. There hasn't been a mass migration of jobs to Mexico. Some labor analysts say that jobs were lost as a result of the agreement; others claim that jobs were actually created.

The goal of NAFTA was to:

- Progressively eliminate barriers to trade.
- Create new investment opportunities.
- Promote free competition.
- Stimulate U.S. trade with Mexico and Canada.

Under NAFTA, apparel products from Mexico or Canada are eligible for reduced duties or duty-free entry into the United States if they meet the textile "rules of origin." To qualify, apparel products must be processed in North America following the criterion of the "yarn forward rule." This means that yarn must be spun, the fabric woven or knit, the parts cut to shape, and the cut pieces sewn together into a finished garment in North America. There are some exceptions to the "yarn forward rule" that are covered by "tariff preference levels" (TPLs) that permit a specific number of apparel products to enter the United States at the preferential NAFTA tariff rates even though they do not qualify under the "rules of origin."

Another benefit of NAFTA for Special Regime Program 807a apparel products assembled in Mexico from U.S.-formed and cut fabric is that these previously quota-free products are now also duty-free. Since the passage of NAFTA, many U.S. apparel companies have reevaluated their positions on Mexico as a sourcing opportunity.

Caribbean Basin Trade Partnership Act

The Trade and Development Act was signed into law by President Clinton in May 2000. Title II of this law was the **Caribbean Basin Trade Partnership Act (CBTPA).** It entitled beneficiary countries to the same preferential tariff treatment as those granted to Canada and Mexico under NAFTA. The countries designated to receive these benefits were Belize, Costa Rica, Dominican Republic, El Salvador, Guyana, Haiti, Honduras, Jamaica, Nicaragua, Panama, Trinidad, and Tobago.

African Growth and Opportunity Act

Title I of The Trade and Development Act was the **African Growth and Opportunity Act (AGOA),** which provided preferential treatment to 35 designated countries in Sub-Saharan Africa. If apparel is made from U.S.A. fabric, yarn, and thread, it will have duty and quota free access to the markets of the United States. In 2002, AGOA II liberalized the requirements for U.S.A. components by allowing some garments to be made from regional and/or third country fabrics. In 2004, AGOA III extended life-bound preferences until 2015 and also extended the special treatment of apparel until 2008. In 2003, apparel imports reached 1.2 billion dollars.

Central America-Dominican Republic-United States Free Trade Agreement

In July 2005, Congress passed legislation that enabled the Central American countries of Costa Rica, El Salvador, Guatemala, Honduras, Nicaragua, and the Dominican Republic to enjoy the same benefits as NAFTA. Together this trade block only trails China in being the largest exporter of apparel to the United States. While there are remaining issues to be settled, the **Central America-Dominican Republic-United States Free Trade Agreement (CAFTA-DR)** will allow this region to grow in importance as a low-cost provider of apparel products. However, their growth will be limited by their ability to develop full-package capabilities. According to Will Duncan of [TC]², most of the contractors today do not have the technical or financial resources needed to become full-package suppliers. Until these contractors develop the required expertise, Central America will not reach its potential

Bi-Lateral Free Trade Agreements

The United States has completed Free Trade Agreements with Australia, Andean countries (Bolivia, Columbia, and Peru), Bahrain, Chile, Israel, Jordan, Morocco, Oman, Panama, and Singapore. The purpose of these agreements is to eventually eliminate any restrictions to free trade on apparel exports to the United States.

Political and Economic Environments

After experiencing the relative stability of Japan, Hong Kong, Taiwan, and South Korea, global sourcing has had to follow a risky path through developing nations in order to find the lowest labor costs. Developing countries are usually fraught with problems of political and economic instability.

"Borderline revolution is good; revolution is not good," said one senior sourcing executive. "A third world country where the needle trades are still the backbone of the economy is usually in a state of borderline revolution. As a country develops, hard goods and electronics take over the skilled labor market, pushing up the labor rates for the needle trades." The turmoil of a minor government revolution caught him in a country where borders were shut down for a number of weeks, and his products couldn't be shipped.

Economic crises hit Thailand, Singapore, Indonesia, Malaysia, and South Korea in 1997 and 1998. U.S. apparel companies with large import programs in these countries found themselves in a real dilemma. Some Asian contractors had spread themselves so thin financially that they could no longer afford to buy raw materials or make payrolls. Many apparel contracts were delayed or canceled as some Asian contractors were forced out of business. A few U.S. sourcing companies were hurt by late deliveries or lost production, but others looked upon the financial crises as opportunities for lower pricing from countries that experienced devaluation of their currency.

Economic crisis is truly a double-edged sword for the sourcing executive. When asked about the 1998 economic crisis in Indonesia, Jack Listanowsky of The Limited said, "Is it a crisis to run to, or a crisis to run away from? I have my own answers to that. If it's an Indonesian company, I'm less apt to run to it as I would be if it were a Taiwanese company. Half the factories in Indonesia are joint ventures because they get their money in Taiwan."

Global political and economic conditions must be constantly evaluated by sourcing executives and carefully factored into sourcing decisions. Some of the countries most recently under the watchful eye of global sourcing executives are China, Cambodia, Sri Lanka, Bangladesh, Lao People's Democratic Republic, and Vietnam. For these countries, political and economic environments and the effect of these conditions on infrastructures are major factors in their development as low-cost global apparel resources.

A major issue in recent years is the protection of intellectual property (IPR) rights. Some countries are more vigilant than others when enforcing the policies of the WTO. Counterfeit garments using counterfeit components are readily available in China as well as some other Far Eastern countries. This problem is compounded when U.S. Customs embargoes a shipment after being alerted to the presence of counterfeit merchandise.

Human Rights

Human rights are the basic rights of all human beings to be treated lawfully, humanely, and ethically. Human rights issues that are of specific concern to the apparel industry are:

- Child labor.
- Forced labor.
- Health and safety.
- Freedom of association and the right to collective bargaining.
- Discrimination.
- Disciplinary practices.
- Working hours.
- Compensation.

A tabloid TV show aired a three-part investigative series that purported to show private label apparel from JCPenney, Wal-Mart and Kmart being manufactured in three Nicaraguan sweatshops (Wilson 1997). Executives from JCPenney stated that the company takes allegations of human rights violations very seriously. Penney has a commitment to legal compliance and ethical business practices. Wal-Mart replied, "We have worked really hard on enforcing a code of conduct since 1992, which we have required all vendors to sign." A Kmart spokeswoman said, "Let there be no doubt that Kmart will not tolerate unlawful practices of human rights in factories that supply the products sold in our stores" (Wilson, 1997).

"Manufacturers must become more involved with labor and community issues in countries where they produce apparel and footwear, if they are to be successful," said Bruce J. Klatsky, chairman, president, and CEO of Phillips-Van Heusen Corp. (Owens, 1997).

The Gap, Liz Claiborne, and Levi Strauss have taken the lead in securing better treatment for workers employed by their import contractors. They have done so by incorporating labor conditions in their contracts with foreign companies or by using their economic weight to pressure third world states into implementing tougher labor-protection measures (Ramey and Barrett, 1997).

Media attention has brought human rights issues onto the front pages of our newspapers and onto television screens across our nation. Companies that do not carefully monitor the working conditions of their global sourcing suppliers are courting disaster. The White House has created an antisweatshop task force to monitor international apparel contractors for labor abuses. Under consideration is the use of a "no-sweat" label for countries meeting the task force guidelines.

Some apparel companies have gone as far as providing at-work medical care, nutritional programs, educational assistance, and child-care facilities for their global sourcing partners. This type of social responsibility is seen as an important investment in developing a strong vendor relationship and creating a positive consumer image for the company.

Human rights issues are being addressed by many apparel companies and organizations through social accountability statements and standards. The Worldwide Responsible Apparel Production (WRAP) Principles and Certification Program has been endorsed by the American Apparel and Footwear Association. WRAP is an independent, nonprofit corporation dedicated to the promotion and factory-based certification of lawful, human, and ethical manufacturing throughout the world. According to Steve Jesseph, Interim Executive Director, in a speech delivered at the AAFA Global Forum in March 2006, there are currently 1100 registered factories in 76 countries. The number of participants is growing by 30 percent annually. The Council on Economic Priorities Accreditation Agency (CEPAA) has developed Social Accountability 8000 (SA8000), which provides a verifiable, auditable standard that addresses the human rights concerns of the apparel industry.

■ International Business Paradigms

Retailers developing their own private labels and private brands and apparel manufacturers are sourcing more and more products offshore. With this increased focus on the international arena, it is important for sourcing executives to understand international business paradigms. When doing business in a foreign country, sourcing executives should be aware of the impact of language, culture, and differences in the processes of analysis and decision making. To develop successful business relationships in Asia, Eastern Europe, and Central and South America requires an understanding of proper business etiquette in each country that a sourcing executive wishes to operate. Unfortunately, there is no "one size fits all" when it comes to international business. Americans have a tendency to apply their own business paradigms to all international situations, and that can lead to disastrous results. Before venturing off to do business in a foreign country, a substantial amount of planning and research is necessary.

Among various cultures, some of the most difficult factors to understand are the differences in the thought processes used for analysis and decision making. Americans and most Europeans take a very systematic, linear approach to problem solving, while many East Asian cultures take a more holistic approach. In China and Thailand, business executives often rely on subjective feelings and personal experiences in solving problems and making decisions. Empirical evidence and objective analyses are often not the primary factors in decision making. This results in American executives finding it difficult to understand the reasoning behind decisions made by executives from different cultures or the changes in direction taken during business discussions. To be successful in the international arena, it is critical to understand that in different countries executive perspectives for doing business, analyzing problems, and making decisions can be based upon very significant cultural variables and key cultural values.

The area of international business paradigms is vast and complex and should be covered by full academic courses or extensive workshops and seminars. Examples of some of the fundamental differences in doing business in China, Thailand, and Mexico are presented in Figure 10.8.

■ Sourcing Technology

Researchers at North Carolina State University, working with Textile/ Clothing Technology Corporation [TC]² and the Demand-Activated Manufacturing Architecture (DAMA) Project of the AMTEX™ partnership sponsored by the Department of Energy addressed the sourcing problem. They have developed the **sourcing simulator**, a stand-alone PC tool that can aid retailer buyers by quickly and easily analyzing factors that affect sourcing decisions. This software allows buyers to conduct "what if" scenarios, comparing the overall financial results of sourcing apparel made in the United States under quick response programs with the costs of traditional sources, which can include domestic or offshore contractors. A user can assume different forecast errors and determine the gross margin return on investment (GMROI) under each scenario. The model provides a percentage of lost sales due to depleted stock, customer service level, percentage of goods sold at first price, percent of items marked down, and the percent of items remaining after markdown and sold to jobbers. Tabular and graphic displays show a buyer how a given level of forecast error will affect financial performance, inventory (turnovers, in-stock level), and customer service (lost sales, service level). As

| | FIGURE 10.8 | EXAMPLES OF DIFFERENCES IN DOING BUSINESS IN CHINA, THAILAND, AND MEXICO |

Factor	China	Thailand	Mexico
Time	Being late for an appointment is considered a serious insult. Lunch breaks take place from 12PM to 2PM and in large cities many services shut down.	Being late for an appointment in Bangkok is often unavoidable due to the unusually heavy traffic in the city. Punctuality is not a critical issue, but a courtesy call is a good policy if running late. Lunch breaks take place from 12PM to 1PM.	Punctuality is not a critical factor in Mexican business culture. Due to an American emphasis on being on time, Mexican business executives try to be punctual. Lunch breaks are used as key business meeting opportunities and may take place from 1:30PM to 3PM. An important word for Americans to understand is "mañana," which literally means "tomorrow." It often has a broader meaning of "later" and may also be used as a kind way of expressing "no."
Dress	Men should wear conservative business suits and ties in subdued colors. Bright colors are not appropriate. Women should wear conservative business suits with knee-length or longer skirts. Blouses should be in neutral colors with sleeves and high necklines. Women should also wear flat shoes or very low heels, especially if they are much taller than their hosts. In some factories, and when visiting someone's home, you may be asked to remove your shoes and put on slippers.	Men should wear Western-styled business suits and ties. Due to the extreme heat, many men wear undershirts to minimize sweat stains on dress shirts. Women should wear business suits with knee length or longer skirts. Blouses should have sleeves unless worn under a jacket. It is recommended to carry or wear a suit jacket since air conditioning in offices is set at low temperatures. In some factories, and when visiting someone's home, you may be asked to remove your shoes and put on slippers.	Men should wear dark, conservative suits and ties. Shirts should be neatly pressed and shoes highly polished. Women are encouraged to dress in feminine skirted suits or skirts and blouses. High heels are acceptable, especially for evening meetings or dinners. Both men and women are advised to refrain from wearing expensive jewelry or watches due to security risks in some Mexican cities.
Forms of Address	Address people by their professional or business title and their family name. Use official titles such as Chairman, General Manager, or Director. It is appropriate to skip the words "Deputy," "Vice," or "Assistant," when addressing	The word "Khun" is used in place of Mr., Mrs., or Ms. when addressing people. Instead of using their family or surname, they prefer to be addressed by their first name. Somchai Ratanaprayul would be addressed as Khun	Address professionals such as doctors, lawyers, professors, engineers, accountants, and architects by their professional titles and family names. This is important to proper Mexican business etiquette. Anyone without a

(continued)

FIGURE 10.8	CONTINUED		
Factor	**China**	**Thailand**	**Mexico**
Forms of Address	a Deputy Director, Vice Chairman, or Assistant General Manager. If a person does not have a professional title, use "Mr.," "Madam," or "Miss.," plus their family name.	Somchai. After you become acquainted with Thais, they may ask to be called by their nickname or shortened name. Khun Somchai could be called Khun Chai. Because of this form of address, Thais have a tendency to refer to Dan Jones as Mr. Dan instead of Mr. Jones.	professional title should be addressed by the Mexican terms for "Mr." (Señor), "Mrs." (Señora), or "Miss." (Señorita), followed by their family name.
Business Meetings	It is very important to bring an interpreter to business meetings to assist in understanding the nuances of discussions. Speak slowly and clearly using short, simple sentences. Avoid idiomatic expressions, jargon, and slang. If making a presentation, prepare printed copies for all parties present plus extras for those unable to attend. Copies of handouts should only be printed in black and white. Some bright colors have special negative meanings in this culture. Refrain from critical statements that could cause embarrassment. In the Chinese culture, "saving face" is critical to a person's reputation and social standing. Exchanging business cards is an important ritual. Your business cards should be printed with one side in English and the other in the local Chinese dialect. The use of gold ink has a benefit in Chinese culture since gold is the color of prestige and prosperity. Present your	An interpreter can be helpful in business meetings, but most Thais, especially in Bangkok, have a reasonable understanding of English. Speak slowly and clearly using short simple sentences. Avoid idiomatic expressions, jargon, and slang. Presentation materials should be colorful and contain graphics and photographs. Printed color copies of presentations should be made for all parties present, plus extras for those unable to attend. Business cards are exchanged at the beginnings of meetings, and allow identification of key decision makers. High quality business cards printed in English on one side and Thai on the other are important for making a good first impression. Thais will refrain from using the word "no" or referring negatively to any point under discussion. They will nod agreement even if they do not agree. This makes it very difficult to determine their true feelings about an issue. It can take a long time to reach an agreement because	Most Mexican business executives have a reasonable command of English so interpreters are usually not necessary. Mexicans prefer to do business only with people who they "know." This requires a lengthy period of cultivating a relationship. Your personal relationship with a potential business partner may be more important than professional expertise or some of the details of a business relationship. Mexicans focus on the particulars of each situation. Subjective feelings play a role in decision making. Presentations should focus on details and how the parties will achieve personal satisfaction from any agreements. Negotiations are usually lengthy and include a lot of bargaining to achieve a final agreement. Mexicans avoid directly saying "no." The terms "maybe" or "we'll let you know" may really mean "no." When a final deal is reached, always follow up with a written statement including all details of the agreement. In Mexican busi-

(continued)

FIGURE 10.8	CONTINUED		
Factor	**China**	**Thailand**	**Mexico**
Business Meetings	card with two hands and ensure that the side printed in Chinese is facing the recipient. The pace of business is often much slower than what Western executives are used to. Patience is an important virtue. Only the person of highest authority makes the final decisions, even if lower-level executives with a better command of English are the most active in the process.	Thais often need to consult with others before making a decision. To determine if a problem exists, it is necessary to ask questions concerning different details that could be part of the problem and then carefully analyzing the effect they have on the whole. The pace of business is often much slower than what Western executives are used to. Patience is an important virtue. Only the person of highest authority makes the final decisions, even if lower-level executives with a better command of English are the most active in the process.	ness culture, input from all levels is acceptable, but only the highest person in authority makes the final decisions.

can be seen in Figure 10.9, choosing the least expensive source may not always produce the best results in terms of profits or customer service.

Jim Lovejoy of [TC]^2 reports that an extension of this retail model has been developed for the apparel manufacturer and includes cut and sew times, fabric lead times, and manufacturing costs. He points out, "You can run many cases on domestic quick response and offshore manufacturing. The scenarios fre-

FIGURE 10.9		
	Vendor A	**Vendor B**
Wholesale Costs	$11.50	$13.50
Inventory Turns	1.7	2.6
Percent of Offering Sold	77%	91%
In Stock Percent	78%	93%
Lost Sales Percent	17%	4%
Gross Margin	$44,800	$50,229
Revenue Per Garment	$20.84	$23.25
GMROI	1.4	2.3

Simulation of sourcing an apparel product at offshore and domestic vendors.

quently lead to the conclusion that the best business model is a blend of the two, where the initial shipment comes from an inexpensive offshore supplier, and then a domestic quick response supplier fills in the rest of the program. That usually results in the best gross margin dollars. The other thing it can tell you is that if you are a manufacturer and have a retailer who has errors in forecasting, you can overcome the forecasting errors by shortening your lead times."

Most merchandisers and sourcing executives interviewed by the authors were of the opinion that financial modeling captures only one of the dimensions needed to make the sourcing decision. Jack Listanowsky of The Limited summarized it well, "Sourcing in today's ever-changing marketplace is anything but easy. It's category, it's labor, it's currency, it's price, it's quota, it's quality, it's timing, all bombarding your brain at one time."

Because of the complexity of the sourcing process, merchandisers and product managers should use the most sophisticated available digital technologies to capture and evaluate the data needed for making sourcing decisions and for communicating with their sourcing partners. Interactive data management systems, rapid Internet-based real-time data capture, and video-conferencing are technologies used by more and more merchandisers and product managers.

Bob Zane
Experience—senior vice president of manufacturing, sourcing, distribution, and logistics, Liz Claiborne Inc.

Vendor Consolidation

"Liz Claiborne has gone through vendor consolidation. In 1998 Liz will produce about 90 million apparel units (not including accessories) with a roster of 248 factories located in 30 countries throughout the world. Each vendor/partner averages 360,000 units per year. This is in contrast to 1994 production of 62 million units with a roster of 496 factories located in 38 countries. Our average producer accounted for 125,000 units per year. We want to become much more important to fewer people to enhance our manufacturing partnerships. Our goal is to take advantage of our purchasing power. With 90 million units we have a very powerful pencil and an equally powerful eraser.

"The consolidation process wasn't focused on simply reducing the number of countries Liz did business with. That wasn't as important as having a strategic overview with respect to sourcing. If there were a factory in Madagascar (there isn't), we would have to ask ourselves, 'If it is important for one division to be in Madagascar, isn't it important for more divisions to be in Madagascar?' If it is of strategic importance to the corporation to be in a location, then they should be there in force. We want to avoid the country of the month sourcing patterns which prevail in this industry. As we consolidated factories and countries, we were able to reduce our staffing requirements."

Vendor Certification

"Today we are focusing on purchasing the product instead of the process. We have gone from CMT [cut, make, and trim] to full-package contracts. We have gone into vendor certification, and I think we are ahead of the rest of the industry with respect to vendor certification. We have determined that in order to meet the requirements of the future, we want to buy packages from fewer vendors as opposed to processes from many vendors. We said that it's not enough to say to the vendors, you have to be better in order to earn more and more of our business. In many cases we have to teach them how, in fact, to be better. We set up our vendor certification teams. They visit the factories as well as the textile mills, and they determine where these people are with respect to the ability to be declared certified vendors of Liz Claiborne. Obvi-

(continued)

ously, some are more advanced than others. It's a multiyear program to get everyone where we want them to be. The goal is, however, that we will buy product from people who are certified, and certified means that they have demonstrated the financial ability to deal with our requirements, they have demonstrated the management organization and structure to deal with our communication requirements, and they have demonstrated adherence with our human rights initiatives. Vendor certification means all of these things as well as acceptable quality and acceptable delivery performance, etc. The goal is to work with more qualified vendors and have them give us the package we require, when we require it."

Great Roots and a Great Creed

"Art and Liz [Art Ortenberg and Liz Claiborne, the founders of Liz Claiborne] gave this company many, many great things. Great roots and a great creed, if you will. But the most important thing they gave this company was the inspiration not to invest in factories.

"The value of the relationship between the manufacturer and the contractor was instilled from day one by Art Ortenberg. It's not always easy, and it's not always automatic. It's a tough, tough business, but by and large we have excellent relationships with our vendors. We have some excellent attributes to

bring to the sourcing world. One of the most important is a sense of fairness. We have a strong balance sheet, so when we open a letter of credit, we fully intend to execute that letter of credit. We don't fool around. We're not interested in taking advantage of the fact that an *i* wasn't dotted or a *t* wasn't crossed. I mean, if the goods were shipped and the goods were fine, we pay and that's all there is to it. There are others who delay that. They look at discrepancies as an opportunity not to pay for goods that aren't selling."

Human Rights Is an Important Issue

"If you've been following the news of late, you know that human rights is an important issue. We've been sourcing in Saipan for a number of years. A group of us visited there last July or August and found some of the things were not acceptable. We spoke up. We spoke before the governor. We spoke before the manufacturers. We told them the importance we attach to conditions for people who produce our product. They promised they would be responsive. We committed to be back there in six months. On the return trip our staff found that the dormitories we had objected to were torn down, replaced with dormitories that none of us would feel badly about having our children use while in college. A

(*continued*)

couple of our people were walking down the aisle in one of the factories. When the workers found out that they were with Liz Claiborne, the workers cheered and thanked them.

"Human rights is a tough field. We believe that our code of conduct is right. We are trying very hard to take a leadership position. It's a very difficult assignment. There are people with different loyalties, with different points of view. There's a lot of protectionism going on. There's a union perspective. There's an anti-import perspective. There's a lot going on and we're trying to forge ahead in this environment. By and large we have been rewarded for our efforts. We feel that we have done the right thing."

Quality Assurance Centers

"Despite the quality coverage that we had with our QA's [quality assurance] stationed at various places around the world, goods that arrived in our domestic distribution centers were subjected to audit and were inspected. We realized that this was wrong from a number of different perspectives. Why inspect something here that was produced tens of thousands of miles away, and what do we do if there are problems? So we proceeded to open regional QA cen-

ters. The first one was opened in Hong Kong. We now have additional centers in Shanghai, Sri Lanka, Guatemala, Korea, Indonesia, and the Dominican Republic, with the Philippines coming on board shortly. Goods are delivered to the QA center, and the center uses the same statistical sampling procedures as are used in the United States. The people in these centers are Liz Claiborne people and have been trained by Liz Claiborne. The auditors look at the merchandise, and it is pass or fail. If it's fail, they call the vendor and the vendor must take possession of the goods. There's no excuse. There's no red tape involved because it's the vendor's country.

"This will be one of the most important things that we have done to change the face of sourcing. Not because it means better quality early in the game, but because it means, or will mean, that the goods, which are shippable from the QA centers are in the same condition as the goods that are shippable from the domestic distribution center. We will still have QA visits to the plants. The QA that is done at the center is a formal audit by dispassionate people. Once we can be assured that the goods we ship from overseas are equal to the quality of the goods we ship

(*continued*)

from our warehouses, the possibilities are limitless. Especially with advanced technologies, we could ship from overseas directly to stores. Directly to retailers' warehouses. It's more in line with our philosophy of dealing with our vendors. We're paying you top dollar. We want top product."

Corporate Centralized Umbrella

"Liz Claiborne was centralized; now we're not. We're divisionalized with a corporate centralized umbrella of sorts. We have a CEO, and reporting to the CEO is a president and four senior vice presidents. The senior VPs are responsible for manufacturing and sourcing, human resources, systems and logistics, and finance. Reporting to the president are the division heads. Those division heads have reporting to them the product people [merchandising] and a divisional manufacturing person. The divisional manufacturing person seeks to accomplish the sourcing requirements of the division acting within the umbrella of the corporation. It's the corporation that determines the basic policies. The corporation supervises the manufacturing facilities via the overseas offices and agencies—controls the numbers, reviews the allocations, participates in anything related to the strategic development of sourcing objectives. There is a close interface between the merchandiser

and the manufacturing/sourcing department on a divisional basis. Merchandising focuses on the development of the best product for their market.   Manufacturing/sourcing focuses on producing that product with the best quality at the most effective price."

Skills Needed to Be a Sourcing Executive

"The people of our generation all had factory operations as a base. They don't today. If you look at our people who are involved in sourcing, they started life as bundle boys, knitting engineers, production managers, on floor factory type technology. In Liz Claiborne most of our sourcing executives come from backgrounds like this. As far as the future is concerned, with fewer and fewer American factories of importance, you wonder what is going to happen. I suspect that more and more of the sourcing executives of the future will come from conventional business backgrounds. If you go through a factory with Liz Claiborne sourcing executives, they will recognize what is going on in the factory. They will be able to recognize the good from the bad, the wheat from the chaff. They won't be fooled by incorrect statements and will be capable of figuring out what is going on. That's a tremendous advantage. You have to concern yourself with what we and the industry do to preserve these skills with future sourcing executives.

(continued)

"Sourcing will be instrumental as long as we have an industry. And in order to do sourcing, you darn well have to know manufacturing."

5 Cs of the Liz Claiborne Sourcing Philosophy

"At Liz we believe that the things that have to take place for effective sourcing are:

Configuration: Know what it is that you have to do, where are you doing this, why are you doing this.

Consolidation: Make certain that you are using as relatively few vendors as is reasonable.

Certification: Make certain that those vendors are capable of doing all that you need done.

Concern: All the issues related to human rights and vendor relations.

Costs: If you take care of the first four, I think cost will take care of itself."

Changes on the Horizon

"The most important development will be 2004 and the preparations for 2004 when quotas are eliminated. Starting off with the premise, do we believe, or do we not believe that the politicians will deliver that which they have promised. We still have to see the development of western hemisphere sourcing. It should have been much further along than it is. We still have to see parity with respect to the CBI (Caribbean Basin Initiative). That's not happening fast enough. I have been hearing for many years that it's one year away, but it should have been here by now. Eastern hemisphere sourcing is so powerful. Asia is so powerful that any time we and any companies like us attempted to move west, Asia gave us reasons to stay east. When the West caught up with those reasons, we ran into this currency crisis which in the final analysis gave us still more reasons to stay in the East. Prices are going down. We are going into a deflationary period with respect to the sourcing of raw materials. But this will pass, and at the end of the day this industry will have a better developed western hemisphere than it has. That's very important to us. The CBI will help, but more than that it will require different attitudes or changing attitudes and changing financial arrangements. Our replenishment programs tend to be in the West, and we are continuously researching technologies like QR [quick response] to help us be even more responsive to the market."

Summary

Sourcing strategies are critical factors in the success of today's apparel companies. Determining where, when, and how a company's products will be manufactured is often the key to meeting the changing styling needs of fashion consumers while still meeting price requirements. Whether to manufacture in a company's own factories, source domestically, or source offshore requires a comprehensive evaluation of many complex factors. Cost, factory capabilities, infrastructure, time, quality, government regulations, political and economic environments, and human rights must all be considered in developing an effective sourcing strategy.

The weight and interaction of each element affecting sourcing varies greatly depending on a company's marketing plan, merchandising objectives, technical expertise, and product categories. The sourcing decision is based upon complex issues that are constantly changing in a vast global marketplace. The more factors that are taken into consideration, the greater the chance of making the most effective short- and long-term decisions. Because of time constraints and the number and complexity of factors involved, merchandisers must utilize the latest digital technologies to develop sound sourcing strategies.

Key Terms

ad valorem

African Growth and
  Opportunity Act (AGOA)

automated sewing systems

Caribbean Basin Trade
  Partnership Act (CBTPA)

Central America-Dominican
  Republic-United States
  Free Trade Agreement
  (CAFTA-DR)

computer-aided design (CAD)

computer-controlled cutting
  systems

contractor evaluation form

duty

execution

factory throughput time

General Agreement on Tariffs
  and Trade (GATT)

Harmonized Tariff Schedule of
  the United States Annotated
  (HTS)

Long Term Agreement (LTA)

maquiladoras

modular manufacturing systems
  (MMS)

most-favored nation (MFN)

Multi-Fiber Arrangement (MFA)

offshore assembly (807 program)

quotas

sourcing simulator

Special Regime Program 807a

support structure

tariff

total throughput times

unit production systems (UPS)

Discussion Questions and Learning Activities

1. What are two steps that need to be taken by the U.S. domestic apparel industry if it is to survive increased competition by imports?

2. Do products with the label "Made in the U.S.A." have special value in today's marketplace? If so, what is that special value?

3. Shop a specialty or better department store and select an exclusive designer garment. Where was this garment made? Explain why you think it was made where it was.

4. What part of the globe do you think will be the next likely candidate for apparel sourcing? Why?

5. What three skills or areas of expertise would you rank as most important for a sourcing executive?

6. What apparel product category would most likely be a candidate for domestic sourcing? Explain your answer.

7. Select your favorite article of clothing. Research the Harmonized Tariff Schedule of the United States to determine the current duty classification for this product.

8. Find two magazine articles with differing viewpoints on the effect of NAFTA on the U.S. apparel workforce. Summarize each article.

9. From the Executive Perspective of Bob Zane, senior vice president of manufacturing and sourcing, Liz Claiborne, Inc., what is the primary purpose of vendor certification?

10. Select three different countries involved in manufacturing and exporting apparel products, and research the impact of language, culture, and the processes of analysis and decision making in doing business in each country.

11. How would the sourcing strategy for an apparel company's national brands differ from the sourcing strategy for a retailer's private brands?

References and Resources

American Apparel and Footwear Association. Arlington, VA. 2004. Annual Report, p.6.

Barrett, Joyce. July 16, 1997. House Unit Backs LAO, Mongolia MFN. *Women's Wear Daily*, p. 10.

Clark, Evan; Ellis, Christy. November 8, 2005. Let's Make a Trade Deal: U.S.-China Sign Accord To Limit Surging Imports. *Women's Wear Daily*.

Clark, Kim. November 24, 1997. Apparel Makers Move South: The Fallout from Freer Trade. *Fortune*, p. 62.

Crafted With Pride in the U.S.A. Council, Inc. 1045 Ave. of the Americas, NY, NY 10018. (212) 819–4397.

Ford, Tom. April 28, 1998. *Today Show* interview. Design director, Gucci.

Owens, Jennifer. November 3, 1997. Global Firms: Commit to Overseas Workers. *Daily News Record*, p. 1.

Ramey, Joanna; Barrett, Joyce. March 18, 1997. Apparel's Ethics Dilemma. *Women's Wear Daily*, p. 10.

Scheines, Joseph. 1986. Planning & Implementing an Apparel Sourcing Strategy. *1986 Report of the Technical Advisory Committee.* American Apparel Manufacturers Association.

Scheines, Joseph. 1997. The Dynamics of Sourcing. *1997 Report of the Technical Advisory Committee.* American Apparel Manufacturers Association.

Textile/Clothing Technology Corporation. 211 Gregson Drive, Cary, NC 27511. (919) 380–2156.

U.S. Department of Commerce, Office of Textiles and Apparel. 2004.

Weintraub, Emanuel. June 1987. Solving the Sourcing Riddle. *Bobbin*, Reprint, pp. 32, 34.

Wilson, David. June 1987. PCT&S Gives Quick Response to CAD. *Bobbin*, pp. 170–173.

Wilson, Eric. November 12, 1997. *Hard Copy* Showing Report on Nicaragua Sweatshops. *Women's Wear Daily*, p. 13.

Web sites

http://www.agoa.gov

http://www.cbp.gov

http://www.usinfo.state.gov

http://www.usitc.gov/tata/hts

The Sourcing Process

After a company establishes sound short- and long-term sourcing strategies, it must develop an effective sourcing process with procedures that control the many functions involved in domestic or international sourcing. To cope with consumer and retail demand for a constant flow of new merchandise requires a nearly continuous product development process, which forces merchandisers to provide a continuous product sourcing capability. Since sourcing is a time-sensitive process, there must be well-defined control systems and procedures in place to maintain the critical schedules for placing production orders, delivery of those orders from the contractor, and shipment of customer orders.

■ The Domestic Sourcing Process

Because difficulties in sourcing usually arise when no structure is in place, specific procedures should be developed and followed by a company that chooses to source domestically. A "fire-fighting" philosophy of resolving problems as they occur is a guarantee that the sourcing executives will be constantly fighting fires rather than preventing them. Too many issues in sourcing have the potential for error. The following are processes and procedures that have been used effectively by companies that have had success in domestic sourcing.

Contract Procedures Manual

Most successful companies use a **contract procedures manual**, which contains all the steps to be followed and issues that must be addressed in the external sourcing function. The 1986 Report of the Technical Advisory Committee of the AAMA recommended that the following issues be covered in such a manual:

- **Materials**
  - Method of shipping and receiving; paperwork.
  - Freight costs.
  - Inventory control; paperwork.
  - Determination of who owns and who buys.
  - Care and condition.
  - What happens at the end of the contract.
- **Trim and findings**
  - Method of shipping and receiving; paperwork.
  - Inventory control; paperwork.
  - Standard usages.
  - Determination of who owns and who buys.
  - What happens at the end of the contract.

- **Material controls**
  - Spreading losses.
  - Standards by style.
  - Disposition of partial rolls and cutting waste.
- **Cutting tickets** (Authorization to cut a quantity of garments by style, size, color, and fabric.)
  - When and how issued.
  - Cuttings; material use reports.
  - Seconds and defective fabric.
- **Sewing schedule**
  - Sequence of tickets to be cut.
  - Projections of cut completion dates.
  - Weekly report of completed production.
- **Invoicing and shipping goods produced**
  - When, where, how to ship.
  - Limitations (invoices per cut ticket).
  - Packing instructions (SKU per carton).
  - Shipping cartons identification.
  - Separate invoices for quality audits.
  - How and where to ship goods.
- **Seconds procedures**
  - How packed.
  - How invoiced.
  - How shipped.
- **Quality**
  - Specifications; sample garments.
  - Weekly audits and reports.
  - Final acceptance audits; how performed; where performed; what to do if rejected.
- **Special factors**
  - Loan of equipment.
  - Insurance.
  - Governmental regulations—OSHA, EEOC, clean water.
  - Regular visits to provide assistance.
  - Employee working conditions.
- **Sourcing company personnel**
  - Contract manager name and phone number.
  - Other key contacts and phone numbers.
- **Documents and reports**
  - Examples of all documents and reports.
  - When to submit and to whom.

Research

The first step to take in finding the most effective domestic contractor is a thorough search of domestic sourcing options. In addition to finding the primary sourcing contractor, it is also critical to identify alternative and backup resources. There are a number of methods to follow for locating potential contractors.

Search the geographical areas with the greatest number of apparel contractors. The ten areas with the most apparel manufacturing facilities are: New York City, Los Angeles, Miami, Northern Georgia, Dallas, San Francisco, the Lehigh Valley of Pennsylvania, the Greenville area of South Carolina, the Greensboro triad in North Carolina, and the Charlotte metropolitan area (Moore, 1995).

Trade associations are often a good source of information about available contractors.

- The *American Apparel and Footwear Association (AAFA)* headquartered in Arlington, Virginia, will make inquiries of its extensive membership. The AAFA also cosponsors an international sourcing/contractors section at the annual Bobbin Show. Many domestic contractors are included.
- The *Atlantic Apparel Contractors Association* in Wind Gap, Pennsylvania, acts as a contractor liaison for its members.
- The *Garment Contractors Association of Southern California* with offices in Los Angeles, California, acts as a sourcing liaison for its members.
- *Garment Industry Development Corporation (GIDC)* of New York City represents over 100,000 apparel production workers.
- *San Francisco Fashion Industries Association* is the information center for the more than 400 factories located in San Francisco county.
- *Southeastern Apparel Manufacturers and Suppliers Association (SEAMS)* offers sourcing assistance. Based in South Carolina, this group offers a computer database and a sourcing bulletin. In addition, it sponsors an annual sourcing expo in Charlotte, North Carolina.

Some associations and services focus on specialized segments of the apparel industry.

- *National Knitwear and Sportswear Association (NKSA)*, headquartered in New York City, has five regional offices representing knit apparel and sportswear manufacturers and contractors.

- *Greater Blouse, Skirt and Undergarment Association*, located in New York City, can provide sourcing options in its specialized categories.
- *United Better Dress Manufacturers Association*, based in New York City, focuses on the upper end of the dress market.

Government agencies provide valuable data on manufacturing sources in their geographical area. State and local industrial development councils, chambers of commerce, economic development councils, labor and industry departments, and trade departments are good starting points. A careful scrutiny of the government pages of a local telephone directory is also an excellent source of information. The following are examples of what is listed there:

- Economic Development Corp. of Los Angeles County.
- Georgia Department of Industry and Trade, Atlanta, Georgia.
- California Trade and Commerce Agency, Pasadena, California.
- Beacon Council of Dade Country, Florida.
- South Carolina Department of Commerce, Charlotte, South Carolina.
- Florida Department of Commerce, Tallahassee, Florida.
- Charlotte Chamber of Commerce, Charlotte, South Carolina.
- North Carolina Department of Commerce, Business/Industry/Development Division, Raleigh, North Carolina.
- Tennessee Department of Economic and Community Development, Nashville, Tennessee.
- Mississippi Delta Developers' Association, Stoneville, Mississippi.

Registration numbers (RNs) are issued by the U.S. Federal Trade Commission to apparel manufacturers and must be listed on each product's garment or care label. A merchandiser or sourcing executive can locate the manufacturer of record for any garment by searching for the registered owner of the RN identification on the garment. Prior to 1960, **wool products label (WPL)** numbers (issued from 1941 to 1959 under the Wool Products Identification Act) were used and may still be found on many wool products. CA numbers refer to a Canadian manufacturing coding system. The RN or WPL numbers can be referenced in the *RN & WPL Encyclopedia* or the *RN WPL Directory* found in specialized libraries at major colleges and universities. CA numbers are cataloged by the Canadian Department of Industry, Consumer Products Division in Quebec.

Suppliers of apparel fabrics, findings, or trim are another good source of information about domestic manufacturers, as are *trade publications* such as

Women's Wear Daily, Daily News Record, and *Apparel* Magazine. Another excellent way to find sourcing contractors is by *networking* with other manufacturers. For example, attending trade shows such as the Material World Show in Miami or the Sourcing Expo in Charlotte are effective means of generating new sourcing contacts.

The *World Wide Web (WWW)* is quickly becoming a viable search tool for locating domestic contractors.

- *SourcingMall* at **www.sourcingmall.com** is an effort by the Demand-Activated Manufacturing Architecture (DAMA) project of the American Textile Partnership (AMTEX) to increase manufacturing competitiveness and regain domestic market share for the U.S. textile and apparel complex. This Web site provides links to various association Web sites and is an excellent starting point when initiating a search of the World Wide Web.
- The *American Apparel Producers' Network* is a nonprofit trade association for sourcing of designs, fabric, trim, supplies, and makers of apparel and sewn products. American Apparel Producers' Network can be found on the World Wide Web at **www.usawear.org**. Figure 11.1 shows a sample Web page from the American Apparel Producers' Network. It is the network home page for the American Apparel Producer's Network.

Review of Potential Sources

Based upon thorough research, companies seeking domestic sourcing partners should create a "short list" of contractors that meets their product, quality, price, and delivery criteria. A management team should then visit the domestic contract sites and prepare a formal comprehensive contractor evaluation. The following factors should be evaluated: building description and services, financial position, labor force, insurance coverage, process capability (verification of what type of garments can be made), warehousing and distribution capacity, spreading equipment, cutting equipment, sewing equipment, finishing capabilities, packing and shipping capabilities, quality control systems, and overall evaluation of facilities, staff, and management (1986 TAC Report).

The companies seeking domestic sourcing partners should review their contract procedures manuals with contractor candidates to determine whether they can comply with all procedure requirements.

Another important element in the review should be a careful check of the references for the contractors in question. The contractors should be asked to provide lists of current and past customers, and those customers should be

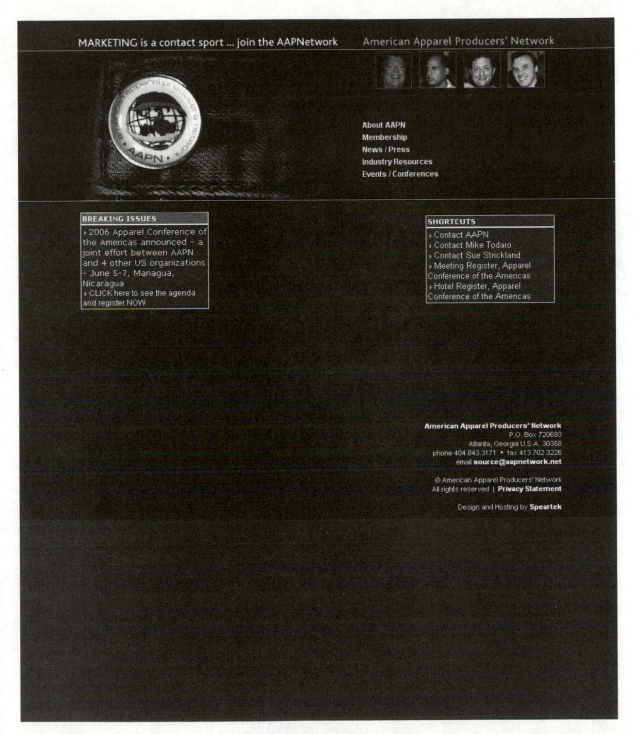

Figure 11.1 The homepage of The American Apparel Producers' Network outlines the mission of the trade association, explains how to search databases, and provides the links to the databases.

contacted to determine the contractor's record relative to on-time delivery, quality, and responsiveness.

Analysis of Factors in the Sourcing Decision

Once factors in the sourcing decision are researched, they should be evaluated for each source under consideration and the results compared. Each factor should be weighted based upon a company's particular needs. For example, a manufacturer of basic jeans destined for mass-market outlets would give more weight to price than to throughput time because price is a major consumer consideration when purchasing basic jeans. On the other hand, a women's designer dress manufacturer would put a greater value on throughput time. For the dress manufacturer, getting its newest styles to retailers before the competition is critical to success. After all factors have been analyzed, the contractors should be ranked in order of preference and a prime contractor selected.

Specifications, Preproduction Samples, and Price Quotes

Before final decisions are made, specification sheets complete with quality standards should be provided to the contractor. If the contractor is expected to produce initial patterns and prototypes, then merchandising should carefully monitor these processes. The contractor should then make preproduction samples (samples produced for analysis of construction and quality), preferably in the production line rather than in a sample department. This allows the contractor to develop accurate price quotes and enables the sourcing executive to evaluate production construction details (make) and quality. These preproduction samples are critical benchmarks for the actual production. The contractor should keep one of each style as a reference for production, and the sourcer should keep one of each style as a standard for quality.

Contract and Initial Order

If the contractor meets all the quantifiable expectations of the sourcer, a written contract should be negotiated and signed by both parties. In the apparel industry, far too many agreements between sourcer and contractor are oral and not specific enough to prevent conflict. Written communications procedures, areas of responsibility, delivery schedules, quality specifications and audit procedures, allowable defect levels and disposition of seconds, shipping procedures, pricing, and payment terms are critical to an enforceable contract. The primary purpose of the contract is to agree on specific procedures and responsibilities before any problems occur. The goal of an effective sourcing strategy is to build long-term relationships on a foundation of trust between sourcer and contractor. A written contract is the first step toward that goal.

After the contract is signed, the initial order is placed and the production process begins. In many cases, larger sourcing companies may provide technical assistance to improve methods, monitor quality, or even furnish specialized equipment to achieve pricing objectives. The sourcing process should always be looked upon as a partnership between sourcer and contractor with the common objective of achieving a quality product at a competitive price.

Follow-up

Follow-up is as critical to an effective sourcing strategy as the initial steps in evaluating a contractor and negotiating the contract. Without proper follow-up, production delays and deviations from quality or construction methods will be detected at delivery or during an inspection of finished garments. At this point, it is too late to take corrective action.

In-process inspections to monitor quality at the needle and evaluate progress toward order completion is the only method for ensuring that quality standards and delivery schedules will be met. These inspections should be unannounced as agreed to in the contract. If problems are detected during these inspections, there may be time to take corrective action and get the production orders back on track. A formal written inspection report should be reviewed with, and signed off on by, the contract manager.

Final Quality Inspection

If it is logistically feasible, a final statistical quality inspection should be performed at the contractor's production facility prior to shipment of the finished product. If quality problems are detected, it is much easier to get swift corrective action at the point of manufacture. The immediacy of such an inspection is also a valuable incentive for the contractor to pay extra attention to the sourcer's quality requirements. When the finished garments pass all quality criteria, they can be shipped to the sourcer's warehouse or even drop-shipped to customers, thus saving valuable time and money.

■ The International Sourcing Process

International sourcing carries with it a multitude of unique challenges. The mere scope of doing business on a global scale, where a contractor can be located 20 hours away by plane and another six hours away by four-wheel-drive vehicles through muddy jungle trails, is daunting. Add language barriers, cultural differences, laws of foreign countries, government regulations, volatile economies, undeveloped infrastructures, and human rights issues, and the task takes on monumental proportions. Just as with domestic sourcing, the key elements for successful international sourcing are proper planning and carefully developed procedures. The following processes and procedures apply to international sourcing.

Contract Procedures Manual

The same procedures for domestic sourcing apply to international markets with the addition of the following:

- **Testing**
    - Fabric performance.
    - Flammability.
    - Garment performance.
- **Labeling requirements**
    - Country of origin.
    - Content.
    - Special customs requirements.
    - Locations of labels.
- **Human rights**
    - Treatment of workers.
    - Social responsibility.
    - Environmental impact of production.
- **Quotas (as required for countries that are not members of the WTO)**
    - Availability.
    - Cost.
- **Shipping**
    - Special packing requirements for ocean and air containers.
    - International carton identification.
    - Accommodations for air shipment of late deliveries.
    - Anti-terrorist precautions.

Research

Locating international sources is more difficult and costly than finding domestic contractors. Information is not centralized as it is for domestic sourcing. However, information is provided by some foreign governments and manufacturers' associations in an effort to help the growth of national industries. Many of these groups have established agencies or service organizations in the United States. A sourcing executive must be careful when evaluating information provided by these foreign sources since they have a vested interest in presenting their factories in the best possible light.

Following are some suggestions for finding information about offshore sources:

- *Foreign consulates or trade missions* should be the first line of inquiry when researching new countries. They can be found in large trade centers such as New York City, Los Angeles, and Washington, D.C. A meeting with an apparel specialist from the consulate or trade mission can be a productive start of a search for international contractors. The Thai Department of Export Promotion (DEP) represents Thailand's apparel manufacturers. Bancomext, the National Foreign Trade Bank of Mexico, operates 40 trade commissions of Mexico throughout the world providing comprehensive export profiles on textile and apparel companies. There are also intergovernmental organizations that represent groups of small nations such as the Organization of Eastern Caribbean States (OECS). This organization has created the Eastern Caribbean Investment Promotion Service (ECIPS) to promote apparel manufacturing in the region.

Figure 11.2 The Italian Consulate is one of many foreign government offices in cities throughout the United States that will assist in the search for offshore sources of supply.

- *Associations, industrial developers, and foreign banks* are also good sources of leads for finding qualified international contractors. Many manufacturers in developing countries band together to form associations, such as the Malaysia Garment Manufacturers Association of the States of Malaysia. Industrial developers like Continental Industrial Zones of Honduras and Sinaloa Development Council, Mexico, are aggressive marketers who provide elaborate brochures and portfolios promoting their manufacturing clients. In most countries large trading banks are willing to connect a U.S. sourcing company with their apparel contractor clients.

- *Suppliers* can provide additional insight into potential sourcing partners in many countries. Jack Listanowsky of The Limited says, "I may contact every freight forwarder in a country and find out who is doing business there and what products they are sourcing. I will take the infrastructure industry and find out to whom they are selling labels, thread, etc. Then I'll identify who they are making goods for and get some sense of the tier level of customers. If they sell to Target Stores, it's a lot different from selling to Kenneth Cole." By contacting suppliers to the apparel factories in a country, a merchandiser can determine which U.S. companies are sourcing in that country and what product and fashion categories are being produced.

- *Traveling* to a region of the world targeted as a new sourcing site and visiting industrial zones is an effective means of locating new contractors. In the overall analysis this approach can save time because it provides immediate on-site evaluation of facilities and management staff.

- *Trade shows* such as Material World and Contempo are another means of locating contractors.

- The *World Wide Web (WWW)* is being used by more and more international companies to present their industrial capabilities to the world. An example of a Web site maintained by the Sinaloa Development Council of Mexico is **www.sinaloa-mex.com.mx**. It provides information on the manufacturing opportunities in Sinaloa, a northwestern state bordering the Pacific Ocean. In Thailand, the Thai Garment Manufacturers Association (TGMA) maintains a Web site that provides a listing of its member factories and their capabilities. The site is located at **www.thaigarment.org**. What is lacking is an international coordinating source to maintain a database of global apparel resources by country similar to that provided by the U.S. National Sourcing Database and the American Apparel Producers' Network for domestic contractors. Another growing Web source for locating apparel contractors are apparel trading networks. The Web sites **www.texyard.com**, and **www.thethread.com** provide search capabilities for contractors as well as B2B apparel trading opportunities.

If a company does not have the staff to investigate international sourcing, a sourcing agent or a trading company may be valid alternatives. **Sourcing agents** and **trading companies** represent multiple clients in locating contractors and providing follow-up and importing services. Sourcing agents who represent the apparel manufacturer in negotiating CMT or a package with contractors, may perform quality inspections, and may assist in the import process. Agents are paid fees, which are usually based upon a percentage of the FOB value of the orders processed. **FOB** (free on board) means ownership is transferred as designated [*FOB factory* means ownership is transferred when the goods are loaded on a transporting vehicle and the buyer (sourcer) is responsible for shipping costs. *FOB distribution center* means ownership is transferred when the goods arrive at the destination and the contractor is responsible for shipping costs]. Trading companies may sell complete packages to apparel manufacturers, handling all details of importing as the importers of record. They take ownership of the imported products and deliver them to their apparel manufacturing customers. Payment for trading companies is based upon a percentage of the landed, duty-paid value of the shipments. *Landed, duty-paid* means all costs associated with the product including the total product costs plus shipping costs to the customer and duty charges.

Review of Potential Sources

Visits to any international contractor sites under consideration are essential because of the complex variables involved in choosing an appropriate international sourcing partner. In addition to the evaluation criteria required of domestic contractors, the following factors must also be considered:

- *Infrastructure*: Does the country have appropriate transportation for shipping; availability of raw materials, findings, and supplies; an adequately trained labor force; and reliable electrical power?
- *Human rights and working conditions*: Does the factory follow international standards in its treatment of workers and does it provide safe and adequate working conditions?
- *Political and economic stability*: Does the country's political system and economy provide a stable environment for doing business?
- *Quota availability*: If the factory is located in a country that is not a member of the WTO, does it have sufficient quota available for the product categories being considered for production?
- *Communications*: Does the factory have qualified management who can communicate in English and understand product specifications and quality requirements? Does the factory have adequate telephone, fax, and Internet communications capabilities?
- *International Business Paradigms:* Are there any cultural variables or key cultural issues that must be considered before doing business in that country? Is there special training that must take place for personnel who will be representing your company in that country?
- *Consumer perception of the region*: Do consumers have a negative perception of the region of the world or country you are considering as a potential sourcing partner? For example, for many years apparel companies were reluctant to produce garments in Vietnam because of consumer sentiment about the Vietnam War.

When changing global economic conditions result in a reevaluation of a country's currency, a sourcer must be extremely careful to anticipate all potential effects. Mark Babbins, president of Southern Trading Company, relates, "With the devaluation of Thailand's currency in 1998, there was a rapid growth of exports, but at the same time imports diminished." Due to the imbalance of trade, there developed a tremendous shortage of shipping containers, causing severe delays in shipping and a dramatic increase in shipping costs." In 2005 the Chinese government was pressured by the United States to increase the value of their currency because the weakness of the yuan compared to other currencies made the price of Chinese products artificially low. The Chinese had to carefully weigh the effect of a higher valued yuan on the competitive value of their products in world markets against the possibility of additional U.S. restrictions on their exports. They initially raised the value of yuan by 2.5 percent and opened the door to further increases. Another situation arose when the euro increased in strength against the dollar. This resulted in European products becoming more expensive and less competitive.

The increased number and complexity of factors involved in doing business on a global scale make checking references for international contractors extremely critical. A major conflict with a company in a foreign country is not easily resolved due to the distance and the international legal ramifications.

Analysis of Factors in the Sourcing Decision

International sourcing requires detailed analysis of some of the factors involved in the sourcing decision.

- *Cost elements* must be given special attention because of the possibility of many hidden or less obvious expenses.
    - *Cost and productivity differentials* for apparel products produced in low-cost labor countries can reduce the direct cost of production by 35 percent to 45 percent compared to production costs in the United States. When the costs of providing a support structure and delivering the product to the United States are factored in, the advantage of the import product is reduced to from 2 percent to 23 percent. At the lower end of this range, risk factors could easily eradicate any direct production cost advantages. While quotas were eliminated for all members of the WTO, they still remain in place for those countries that are not members. When there are shortages of quota in specific categories from non-member countries, additional quota must be bought. This reduces the net cost advantage of importing.
    - *Raw material weight and bulk* require a product-by-product evaluation. Since shipping costs, and in some cases duty charges, are related to weight, garments made of lighter fabrics such as fine denier polyester or silk would be more suitable for distant sourcing locations. Heavyweight denim or bulky fleece (bulk is also a factor in ocean or air shipping costs) would be appropriate for sourcing in locations closer to the United States.
- *Equipment assessment* must include the technical support available. If specialized machines are necessary for creating a company's product, such as applying an embroidered logo to a shirt pocket, then the contractor must have skilled operators and technicians capable of maintaining the equipment. The same issue relates to the availability of spare parts.
- *Throughput time (lead time)* for international contractors must include buffers for weather-related shipping delays, appropriate allocations for customs entry and clearance, and shipment to domestic distribution sites. Wherever there is a connection that relies on two parties (factory and freight forwarder, freight forwarder and ship, broker and customs agent, broker and domestic freight forwarder), there is a risk of delay.
- *Quality* specifications must be quantifiable (measurable) in terms and language that are understood by the foreign contractor. When the

sourcer provides instructions or specifications for a garment, an accompanying diagram with numbered references is essential.

- *Government regulations* relative to quotas, terrorism and duties should be fully researched before a contractor is considered for evaluation. It is advisable to review any new products that do not fit into a specific classification category with U.S. Customs and Border Protection. A company can get either a **nonbinding ruling** as to the proper customs classification by an import specialist at a specific port (a quick response if time is of the essence). Unfortunately, under a nonbinding ruling the classification could be changed when the first shipment arrives in the United States for customs clearance. If there is sufficient time, a safer **binding ruling** issued by customs headquarters in Washington, D.C., prevents any possibility of change in classification.

- *International Business Paradigms* should be carefully researched to determine the affect on business negotiations and doing business in countries under consideration.

After carefully evaluating each factor based upon its impact on the overall sourcing decision, the contractors should be ranked in order of preference and a first choice and a backup contractor should be selected. In the aftermath of the terrorist attack on 9/11, the entire concept of risk has taken on new meanings. Major companies have redefined these exposures as one of the most important factors to consider when choosing their sources of supply. A dominant children's wear company has developed one successful approach. They have created a matrix based upon the following areas of concern: CSI Ocean Ports, Human Rights, Terrorist Risk, Political Stability, U.S. Customs Security Level, and Shipments Affected by Political Issues. Each area of concern is then assigned a point score with 1 the highest and 3 the lowest. Based upon their total point score, a country is determined to be low risk, moderate risk, high risk, unacceptable, or stay out.

Specifications, Preproduction Samples, and Price Quotes

When U.S. companies work with international contract resources, specification sheets and quality standards should be reviewed with key personnel at the factory to ensure that all critical elements are understood. A translator should be present for discussions and should be familiar with industry terminology.

In addition, a company technical representative or agent should be present when preproduction samples are made to evaluate the process as well as the product. A detailed product evaluation should be reviewed with factory management. One of each style of preproduction garment should be kept by both the factory and the sourcer as references. In the language of international business, a sample is really worth 1,000 words and eliminates almost as many headaches.

Price quotes should be in the currency chosen for the transaction. Years ago some companies negotiated prices in the foreign country's currency and hoped to make additional profit on the assumption that the U.S. dollar would increase in value by the time the payment came due thereby decreasing the real amount being paid. The advice to apparel manufacturers who want to play currency trader is *don't*! Leave currency trading to the professionals. Today most apparel manufacturers negotiate payment in U.S. dollars. This fixes their costs and eliminates surprises.

Contract and Financial Instruments—The Initial Order

An international contract should be prepared by knowledgeable international trade attorneys with apparel industry experience. A professional, comprehensive contract can prevent many conflicts and provide some protection for the sourcer in the event of disagreements. It is important to note that even the most detailed, airtight contract must still be adjudicated under international laws. When dealing with developing countries, this can be extremely difficult, sometimes requiring years of expensive legal costs. The best remedy is to have a well-defined legal contract in conjunction with a solid trusting relationship and open communications with a global sourcing partner.

An important element of any international contract is the means of payment. There are four basic methods of payment:

1. Letters of credit.
2. Documents against payment or acceptance.
3. Telex, wire, or electronic funds transfer.
4. Open account.

Letters of Credit

Letters of credit (L/Cs) are financial agreements between the sourcer (buyer) and its bank (issuing bank) to transfer responsibility for paying the seller (foreign contractor) to the issuing bank. This form of guaranteed payment based upon the credit worthiness of the issuing bank is the primary financial instrument used in international trade. Bank charges may include .25 percent to 1 percent of the total transaction price for issuing fees and negotiation fees, and flat fees per occurrence for discrepancies and amendments. A **discrepancy** requires that the bank investigate any difference between the documentation required by the L/C and the documentation presented. An **amendment** is any change made to the L/C after it is issued.

Marc Babins of Southern Trading Company had this to say about letters of credit: "When an L/C is created and issued, the financial liability to pay the contractor is shifted to the bank based upon the contractor meeting certain performance requirements. Along with this liability comes responsibility and

Application and Agreement for Irrevocable Commercial Letter of Credit
To: Wachovia Bank, National Association ("Bank")

Please **TYPE** information in the fields below. We reserve the right to return illegible applications for clarification.

Date:	12/1/05	Please issue an Irrevocable Commercial Letter of Credit substantially as set forth below and forward same through a selected correspondent by: ☒ Teletransmission ☐ Overnight Carrier ☐ Mail ☐ Other If Other, explain _____
L/C #: (Bank Use Only)		Advising Bank Name (optional): _____

Applicant (Full Name & Address)	Currency and Amount in Figures:
Lady Rams Sportswear Company School House Lane and Henry Avenue Philadelphia PA 19144	$1,000,000 Tolerance Amount (if applicable): 1% Currency and Amount in Words: one million U.S. Dollars
Beneficiary (Full Name & Address)	Expiration Date:
Perfect Quality Garment Company Ltd. Apparel Drive Bangkok Thailand	6/15/06 Latest Shipment Date: 5/1/06

Draft Tenor: ☒ Sight;   OR ____ Days from ☐ Sight or from ☐ Bill of Lading Date: OR ☐ Other ____
Draft for: ☒ 100%   OR ☐ ____ % of the invoice value, drawn at the Bank's option, on the Bank or its correspondent.
Charges: Wachovia's charges are for the: ☐ Applicant   ☒ Beneficiary
Discount: Discount charges, if any, are to be paid by the: ☒ Applicant   ☐ Beneficiary

Shipment From (Port of Loading):	**Shipment To** (Port of Discharge):
Bangkok, Thailand	Baltimore, MD

Brief Merchandise Description: ten thousand pair of women's cotton athletic pants

Terms of Shipment: ☒ FOB   ☐ C&F(CFR)   ☐ CIF   ☐ FAS   ☐ Other ____
Letter of Credit to be: ☒ Transferable   ☐ Non-Transferable
Partial Shipments are: ☒ Permitted   ☐ Non-Permitted
Transshipments are: ☐ Permitted   ☒ Non-Permitted

DOCUMENTS REQUIRED		
Transport Document (select <u>one</u>)	**Freight**	**Notify Party:**
☒ Full Set Clean Multi Modal Transport Bill of lading ☐ Full Set Clean on Board Marine Bill of Lading ☒ Air Waybill ☐ Other ____	☐ Collect ☒ Prepaid ☐ Issued or endorsed to the order of the issuing Bank.	Company Name: Lady Rams Sportswear Co., Inc. Contact Name: David Dean Address: School House Lane and Henry Avenue, Philadelphia, PA 19144 Phone: (215) 951-0000 Fax: (215) 951-1111

Insurance (select <u>one</u>)
☒ Insurance effected by Applicant. No insurance document is required.

☐ Air or Marine/War Insurance Policy or Certificate Covering "All Risks" for 110% Invoice cost.

Specify other risks as needed:

Figure 11.3 A sample copy of a Letter of Credit Application completed by a fictitious company, The Lady Rams Company, Inc. in the amount of $1,000,000 with Wachovia Bank. (This form contains the copyright notice ©2005 Wachovia Corporation).

authority for making sure the terms of the L/C are executed perfectly. Technically, the buyer [sourcer] has relinquished control over the agreement to the bank. Banks will confer with the buyer prior to accepting any discrepancies because the ultimate payment will come from the buyer's account. Most executives miss this very important factor, falsely thinking that they can withhold payment if they are not completely satisfied."

Since the issuing bank is responsible for payment, it requires substantial collateral from the sourcer. Banks often require that the sourcing company maintain a balance in its account or other collateral equal to the amount named in the L/C. That amount or collateral is frozen until the L/C is paid out.

If all the documents required of the L/C are in order, the payment usually cannot be stopped. If a sourcer wishes to stop a payment, a court order or injunction with proof of fraud may be required. This process takes considerable time to implement. Otherwise, the money transfer can be stopped only when a major discrepancy occurs; for example, timing, price discrepancies, or lack of proper documentation. Theoretically, if the contractor is 1 day late, the sourcer is no longer required to pay. However, in most cases the sourcer needs the merchandise and will file an amendment of the L/C with the issuing bank changing the delivery date.

The most common kind of letter of credit is an **irrevocable letter of credit**. Under this form of L/C the issuing bank forwards the L/C to the export contractor's bank (beneficiary), with a commitment to pay upon presentation by the export contractor of specified export documents as listed clearly in the L/C. Once these documents and a draft notice are presented to the sourcer's issuing bank, the L/C is executed by the bank and payment is made to the export contractor. The sourcer should be aware that the L/C is a guarantee that the bill will be paid, not a guarantee of quality. An L/C cannot be used as protection against fraud. A sourcer should require a quality release signed by themselves or their agent to be one of the requisite documents in the L/C.

Another form of L/C includes a transferable clause. This form of L/C allows the beneficiary (export contractor) the flexibility of transferring part, or all, of the letter of credit to another party maintaining the clauses except one document substitution (typically invoice). Most foreign contractors and intermediaries, such as trading companies, require this clause. Typically when a trading company is involved that has weak financial resources, it pursues the use of a back-to-back L/C. The buyer issues an L/C to the trading company's bank, which is generally very restrictive, and this L/C is used to back a new letter of credit from the trading company to the foreign contractor.

Another form of L/C is the **irrevocable standby letter of credit**. Instead of being triggered by performance by the beneficiary such as submission of all documentation required for payment, it is triggered by nonpayment by the sourcer. This type of L/C is usually used in domestic transactions. The standby L/C is normally set up as a source of collateral for a U.S. contractor when selling to a U.S. sourcer under an open account status. When the buyer fails to make payment according to the terms of the agreement, the contractor can draw against the standby letter of credit to receive payment.

Documents Against Payment or Acceptance

Documents against payment or acceptance are non-guaranteed forms of payment. This payment method is

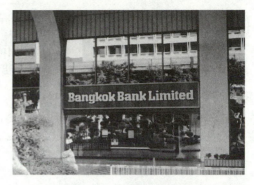

usually used when a sourcer does not want to tie up its finances for an extended period of time or cannot open a letter of credit because of financial problems. Using this form of payment requires an extremely trustworthy relationship between the sourcer and the contractor.

Figure 11.4 The Bank of Bangkok provides financial services that facilitate international commerce including the sourcing of apparel from Thailand.

Under a documents against payment transaction, the export contractor ships the goods, and the sourcer promises, but does not guarantee, to make payment when the goods arrive at the U.S. port of entry. The sourcer must show evidence of payment to U.S. customs in order to receive the documents necessary for importation since the exporter is listed as the owner of record. If the export contractor does not get paid, it retains possession of the import documents and can have the goods returned to the factory.

Under documents against acceptance, the sourcer receives and accepts the documents for a shipment and clears the goods, agreeing to pay at a future date. This procedure is very risky for the export contractor. Even if the transaction is handled through a bank, there is no guarantee of payment.

Telex, Wire, or Electronic Funds Transfer

Telex transfer (TT), **wire transfer (WT)**, and **electronic funds transfer (EFT)** are methods of making payment for a shipment when time is of the essence. These payment methods are usually used when payment is made in advance of shipment. The export contractor notifies the sourcer that the goods are ready for shipment, and the sourcer transfers the funds through its bank via telex, wire, or electronically by computer. When the funds are received by the export contractor's bank, shipment is made.

Open Account

An **open account** is the least used method of payment for international transactions. It is the riskiest for the export contractor since the contractor relinquishes control of the goods with only a promise to pay based upon terms of net payment due in 30, 60, 90, or 180 days. This arrangement creates an open line of credit for the sourcer in a specific amount against which purchases and payments are made. For example, under a $100,000 open account line of credit, the sourcer receives shipments of $50,000 and $20,000, leaving $30,000 open in the credit line. A new order valued at $45,000 will not be shipped until a payment of $15,000 or more is made.

The opening of a letter of credit or an alternative method of payment is the final step in completing an international sourcing contract. After finalization of the contract the initial production order starts being processed. As is the case with most new sourcing partnerships, the initial order is usually a trial order to test the reliability of a new contractor. If the new resource meets all expectations, a scheduled program offering production continuity for the contractor's factory is pursued. This is part of an overall sourcing strategy to develop long-term strategic relationships.

Follow-up

Because of the complexities of international sourcing, follow-up is difficult but essential. Delays in delivery are magnified by distance, and quality problems are too often discovered in an inspection at a domestic distribution center thousands of miles from the contract factory. Most sourcing companies have foreign offices or use agents or trading companies to perform in-process inspections as well as preshipment inspections. Communications are critical in the international follow-up phase. Because of language and cultural differences, the urgency and importance of quality and timing issues are often misinterpreted. In addition, it is important for the sourcing executive or representative to make sure the contractor has a clear understanding of how to deal with any problems that may arise. As with domestic sourcing, a formal written inspection report should be reviewed with, and signed off on by, the contract manager.

Final Quality Inspection

It is common practice for letters of credit to contain a clause requiring that a quality inspection certificate be signed by a representative of the sourcing company. This certificate is based upon a quality inspection performed in the contractor's factory prior to the goods being packed for export. After the merchandise arrives in the United States and is released by customs to the sourcing company, it is usually subjected to a more comprehensive quality inspection at the distribution center. This process is currently undergoing major changes at Liz Claiborne, which is opening regional QA (quality assurance) centers in major sourcing areas around the globe.

Bob Zane of Liz Claiborne explains, "Goods are delivered to the QA center, and the center uses the same statistical sampling procedures as are used in the United States. The people in these centers are Liz Claiborne people and have been trained by Liz Claiborne. The inspectors look at the merchandise, and it is pass or fail. If it's fail, they call the vendor and the vendor must take possession of the goods. There's no excuse. There's no red tape involved because it's the vendor's country. *This will be one of the most important things that we have done to change the face of sourcing.* Not because it means better quality early in the game, but because it means, or will mean, that the goods, which are shippable from the QA centers are in the same condition as the goods that are shippable from the domestic distribution center. We still have QA visits to the plants. The QA that is done at the center is a formal audit by dispassionate people. Once we can be assured that the goods we ship from overseas are equal to the quality of the goods we ship from our warehouses, the possibilities are limitless. Especially with advanced technologies, we could ship from overseas directly to stores. Directly to retailers' warehouses."

Shipping and Importation

There are three primary modes of transportation for imported apparel:

- *Trucking* is primarily used for products coming from Canada or Mexico. Trucking provides an easy transition to domestic delivery throughout the continental United States. Trucking is also used in conjunction with air or ocean freight by providing transport from the port of entry to the sourcing company's distribution site.

Figure 11.5 Containerized shipments off-loaded from ocean freighters at the Miami seaport await processing.

- *Ocean freight* offers containerized shipping using specially designed containers that can be locked for protection and sealed against the elements. Containers come in 20- and 40-foot lengths and hold large quantities of apparel goods. For smaller companies, there are importer consolidators who consolidate smaller shipments into container-sized loads. One drawback of ocean freight is the long time it takes for delivery. To save time, some companies ship products from the Far East to the West Coast of the United States and then transfer them to ground transportation for the trip east rather than continue by ship through the Panama Canal.

- *Air freight* is generally the most expensive long-range shipping alternative, but it is sometimes the most cost-effective for the apparel industry when other expenses are factored into the equation. For example, less packing is needed than for ocean transport, there is less opportunity for damage, and the travel time is much shorter (days rather than weeks). Furthermore, plane travel avoids the moisture, cold or warm air, and humidity that can plague ocean travel.

The U.S. Customs and Border Protection is the federal government agency that regulates imports and collects import duties. In 1996 the Customs Modernization Act (Mod Act) was passed, which transferred the responsibil-

Figure 11.6 U.S. Customs inspectors examining a truck shipment at the Los Angeles seaport to be sure it is in compliance with all government regulations.

ity of appraisal and classification from U.S. Customs to the importer. Before the Mod Act, customs had to validate imports on an entry-by-entry basis. The act changed the focus of customs from entry to importer. Customs specialists look at the importer on the whole to determine whether it has the capability to reasonably determine appraisal and classification for its products. The process for importing apparel involves:

- *Entry*: Within 5 working days of arrival of a shipment at a U.S. port of entry, entry documents must be filed. These documents are usually filed by a customs broker on behalf of the importer. Under the Mod Act, the broker as a professional consultant can be held liable, as can the importer, for any discrepancies (differences between what is stated in the documents and the actual goods) with the entry. The entry documents include:
  - Quota visa validating that the product is covered by quota from the country of origin. On July 1, 1996, the rules of origin for apparel changed to the country where the garments are sewn. Previously, country of origin was the country where the garments were cut. This has led to a rise in transshipping of apparel to avoid quota barriers for which China is the most flagrant violator. **Transshipping** involves China shipping sewn products to another country such as Malaysia where the goods are labeled and shipped under Malaysia's quota allotment. If customs suspects this to be the case, it can hold up the entry for validation of the country of origin.
  - When apparel is made in countries that are not members of the WTO, quota visas are required validating that the product is covered by quota from the country of origin (where the product was sewn). U.S. Customs and Border patrol check to see that there has not been transshipping of apparel to avoid quota barriers. If customs suspects this to be the case, it can hold up the entry for validation of the country of origin. **Transshipping** occurs when a product is made in one country, shipped to another country, and then shipped to a third country under the quota of the second country. Although China is a member of the WTO, and therefore free of quota, they signed an agreement on November 8, 2005 that in effect reestablished quotas on 34 types of apparel and textile products.
  - Commercial invoice or a pro forma invoice.
  - Packing list.
  - Bill of lading (a receipt given by a carrier for goods accepted for shipment).
  - Surety bond [importers and brokers must be bonded (insured against loss, damage, or default) to ensure payment of duties].
- *Examination and inspection*: Random examinations are made by the

port director. This involves a customs inspector and an import specialist. These inspections determine:

- The value of the goods for customs and their dutiable status.
- That the proper markings are on the goods including the country of origin.
- That the shipment has not been compromised by terrorists and includes materials that would harm the United States. To assist in removing this terrorist threat, CBP initiated **Customs-Trade Partnership Against Terrorism (C-TPAT),** which is a partnership with global trading companies who volunteer to secure their supply chains and facilitate the movement of legitimate cargo. These companies agree to put into practice increased security throughout their global supply chain. They also agree to require this of their service providers and business partners. In return for their collaboration, CBP will reduce the number of inspections of incoming cargo, reduce border wait times, provide the services of a C-TPAT supply chain specialists to assist in procedural and security issues, in addition to other benefits (**www.cbp.gov**).
- Whether the shipment contains prohibited items.
- Whether the shipment is correctly invoiced (for wearing apparel, license fees paid to a company in a foreign country are dutiable and must be listed on the invoice; license fees paid to a U.S. company like Disney or Warner Bros. are not dutiable).

- *Release:* The quota visa is input into the U.S. Custom and Border Protection's database to check if quota is still open for the product. If quota is still open, the goods are released to the importer. (There have been instances of counterfeit quota from some countries and the U.S. government placing an embargo on certain classifications, which may hold up release until the next quota year or the embargo is lifted.)
- *Liquidation:* The last step in the import process is liquidation of the entry. **Liquidation** involves customs verifying classification, valuation, and payment of duties. This must take place within one year but can be extended twice for a total of three years. During this process, customs verifies classification, valuation, and payment of duties.

Auditors, through a program of compliance assessments, review importers looking for deviations in classification or valuation. Import specialists are the classification experts on the audit team.

Unless a company has a well-staffed traffic department with customs specialists to handle global transportation and importation, the services of an international freight carrier or a customs broker are a must. These specialists handle the details of getting product from the international contractor's shipping dock to the sourcer's distribution center using the fastest, most cost-effective transportation. They process thousands of transactions per day and have a full-time staff at the major ports of embarkation and debarkation to ensure a smooth entry and customs clearance.

■ Managing the Sourcing Function

Because of the complexities involved, greater and greater specialized knowledge and skills are necessary to effectively manage global sourcing. In many small- to medium-sized companies, the merchandiser often shoulders this enormous responsibility. Frequently, merchandisers involve their global sourcing partners in creating the line. The merchandiser defines a line concept from which stylists create sketches, which are presented to the factory for prototype development. The merchandiser selects the final prototypes from which preproduction samples are made and production orders are issued.

In larger corporations, production executives or sourcing executives handle sourcing. These specialists coordinate with merchandisers and product managers to create any prototypes that need to be produced by the contractors. Under this type of structure, merchandising usually closely monitors production and approves fabric and product samples.

Marc Babins, president of Southern Trading Company, defines the skills needed for a sourcing executive as, "Understanding fabric and garment construction, having the ability to handle an enormous amount of very detailed information, organizational skills, openness for cultural exchange, sharp negotiating skills, and knowing the fair market value of products."

Mega apparel corporations such as Liz Claiborne, Tommy Hilfiger, Jones Apparel Group, and mega retail corporations such as JCPenney, Federated, and Sears have specialized sourcing departments, corporate staff executives with track records as leaders in global sourcing, and offices throughout the world. "We add value to each business unit as well as do strategic planning for the company," says Jack Listanowsky, vice president and chief sourcing and production officer for The Limited. "I focus on developing trust with my suppliers. We work together so we both make a profit, in the long run. The term 'partner relationship,' or 'vendor/partner,' is much more a part of our philosophy today as opposed to the way it was."

These corporate leaders are setting the direction for tomorrow's truly global companies where sourcing raw materials, manufacturing, and distribution to expanding international markets will be part of an integrated process encompassing the worldwide marketplace. To be an effective manager in this complex business environment will require unique individuals. The sample ad in Figure 11.7 may be very hard to fill, but it exemplifies the far-reaching skills required for global sourcing.

FASHION CAREER OPPORTUNITY
V.P. GLOBAL SOURCING

Major U.S. fashion manufacturer seeks professional take charge executive for challenging international position. The successful candidate must possess:

- In-depth knowledge of textile technology (mechanical properties of fabric, construction systems, dying, and finishing)
- Experience in international fabric markets
- Apparel manufacturing expertise (engineering background preferred, garment costing, constructions skills, and quality assurance required)
- Fluency in Spanish, Chinese, and Urdu
- Experience as world traveler with sensitivity to foreign cultures
- Expertise in apparel merchandising techniques (line planning, styling, product development)
- Excellent organizational and negotiating skills
- Working knowledge of U.S. Customs regulations (quotas, tariffs, and trade agreements)
- Computer literacy in database, spread sheet, Internet communications, and Web searching

The ideal candidate will be an entrepreneurial type who wants to be on the cutting edge of new technologies, will enjoy traveling for weeks at a time, loves international cuisines, and adjusts easily to jet lag.

Send résumé and photocopy of visa stamps to:
Fashions to Go, One Fashion Plaza, NY, NY.

Figure 11.7 The individual skills required to be a successful and effective sourcing executive are stated in this advertisement parody from a company seeking a qualified sourcing manager.

■ Future Trends

The future will see the nonstop migration of apparel production to the Orient. While China will increase their lead in supplying apparel to the U.S. market, India, Pakistan, and others also will improve their penetration. As more countries join the WTO, and as our government enacts more bi-lateral and regional agreements, the consumer will continue to benefit from low-cost labor. The availability and use of new technologies by apparel merchandisers and product managers will reduce the time it takes to bring apparel from concept to consumer. Fast fashion will be the prevalent mode of creation, execution, and delivery in a global marketplace.

"Hampton's Wake-up Call"

Managing Change

Evolving over the past decade from a mass merchant mindset to a better, more fashion-oriented business focus has been a learning experience for Hampton [Hampton Industries, producers of men's and children's sportswear, men's and children's sleepwear, loungewear, men's and boys' activewear, and private label products for leading U.S. retailers]. On the marketing side, for instance, Fuchs [Steven Fuchs, president of Hampton Industries] had to bring in division presidents with branded sourcing experience. He points out, "Because we are making a wide variety of product, we want the flexibility to outsource the majority of our products with the highest degree of control and visibility."

Distribution also has been overhauled to accommodate higher-value products, which are shipped in small pick-and-pack quantities and replenished. "Today," Fuchs adds, "price may be the third element to a retailer. You have to bring other values to the relationship like merchandise expertise and service expertise with shorter supply cycle times."

To tool up for this new level of service, Hampton had to scrap old legacy computer systems at a cost of $1.5 million. Moreover, a new approach was needed to ensure that the growing demands of retailers would be met. Fuchs stresses: "Our relationships with our factories and agents are changing dramatically. And it's primarily technologically driven—not because the technology is available, but because of the greater opportunities it represents to our retail customers and us. . . . The retailers are becoming very demanding, and rightfully so."

To illustrate the heightened pressure from stores, the company president tells of a meeting with Wal-Mart and its 200 top suppliers, during which the retailer said it expects its suppliers to increase inventory turns by one-half this year and by one turn or better next year. The mega-retailer then challenged the companies to figure out how to do it.

Those marching orders are OK with Fuchs, who observes: "[Wal-Mart] has given us the opportunity and ability to manage our business in their stores. And who cares more about our products in their stores than us? . . . Years ago, we felt our job ended when we shipped the goods, but today that is just the beginning of the responsibility," he urges. "The focus has to be on how our goods are selling at retail, and we now have the capability to help plan by specific retailer based on store information."

Hampton now collaborates with retailers to develop overall business plans and objectives for a given season at the SKU level. The company also has adopted retail development tools, including a demand management software package that allows Hampton to analyze sales data and make buying recommendations to retail customers. It currently is being used for both the branded and private label businesses.

"Talk is important and strategic plans are important," Fuchs states, "but actions speak louder than words. And we have to get to the point where we have a high degree of

(continued)

confidence not only in the quality of the garments, the cycle times and the delivery, but also in [ensuring] that all other compliance issues are adhered to 100 percent. If they're not, stores will not be able to receive the merchandise in an efficient manner and get it on the selling floor. And most importantly, they're not going to be able to report back to us what they sold."

On that score, Frank Simms, CFO and vice president of finance, who took part in the conversation with *Bobbin* via teleconferencing from the company's North Carolina corporate headquarters, speaks plainly, saying, "Over the last two years we've made some major systems conversions, somewhat painfully.

"But it was a necessity for us." Simms continues, "and we now have the ability to track our orders. And we can tie those orders in to our production requirements, fabric receipts, trim and binding receipts, and the status of the product on the production floor. [We can also tell] where goods are on the ocean, if they're coming that way."

To that end, the company is requiring its El Salvador plants (the company operates two sewing plants in El Salvador) and independent factories in Asia to provide advance shipping notices (ASNs). Fuchs explains that all the merchandise is bar coded and scanned, and the information is transmitted before it ships. At that point, the North Carolina facility is able to treat the merchandise as if it's in the building and handle logistics more effectively. And there's more. CFO Simms, who is quarterbacking the technology changes in Kinston, notes that the ASN requirements will begin to go downstream to components suppliers in November of this year.

Through 1990, and to a large extent until five years ago, all of Hampton's information systems and operations were focused on the company's ability to manufacture products. Now, Simms offers, the company is turning the emphasis toward improving the timeliness and accuracy of information

from its suppliers. "If there is going to be a problem, we want to address it early on so we can communicate accurately with our retailers," he adds.

And progress is being made along those lines. Simms estimates that in 1995 the company may have shipped 25 percent of its orders at the beginning of the shipping cycle. This year, that number is about 85 percent within the first week of the shipping window. Moreover, he reports that the company now has the visibility to realistically schedule work, saying, "If we have an order from a customer who wants delivery in 10 weeks, and we cannot meet that date, we will not accept the order."

Fuchs adds, "By having a dynamic tracking calendar that is very accurate, we can see very clearly what is possible, whereas before we might have rationalized, 'I can shave a week here or there,' with the end result being that nobody was happy."

In regard to the calendar, the president reports that about 40 stages are being tracked. "We can evaluate at what point something is occurring across the company. If a function is taking longer than it should, we can determine if it is our issue or a store issue," he says. "For example, with one private label customer we have consistently fallen five days behind at tracking step number five. Which is color approval. We recognized it's a problem with the retailer, but it isn't systemic throughout our organization."

With Hampton's new systems, from Online Data Systems (ODS) running on a network of IBM AS/400 servers, the company has also implemented the functionality to access its host computers through the Web. The firm is using that capability today with its sales group and the El Salvador factories, and it also is in a test mode with one of its agents. In the fall, the company expects all agents to be online, which will eliminate

(continued)

the need for manual updates, faxes, phone calls, etc. Says Simms, "We will all be talking the same language and [receiving the same] information. There won't be misunderstandings. We're very excited about that."

In conjunction with its host systems, Hampton also installed Manhattan associates' PkMS warehouse management system. Simms wryly comments, "It's a very good software program. It's also very complicated, which was one of our problems last year. But it allows our database of orders to be analyzed and sent to the warehouse. The orders are then arranged in a logical format for a process of picking, packing, staging and shipping. . . . Now we have active picking areas, reserve stock areas and automatic replenishment."

New Frontiers

On the manufacturing end of the business, one challenge that Hampton faced as it closed its U.S. factories was maintaining the ability to offer relatively fast turns on replenishment orders from private label customers. To compensate for the transit time to and from the company's El Salvador facilities, about a year ago the company implemented a new sewing procedure in the two plants called the "pull" system. It combines the elements of both modular manufacturing and a line operation (progressive bundle system).

Fuchs says that by the end of this year, the new method will reduce production time by approximately 25 percent, bringing cycle times at the facility down to the same levels as the firm's former U.S. plants. Additionally, the "pull" method has reduced work-in-process by 50 percent to 60 percent.

As he views the future, Fuchs says the next challenge will be more stores looking to control their own brands and source products directly to take the extra margin. He refers to Kmart's alliance with Martha Stewart and Target's new Mossimo line as examples, noting, "That is the beginning of the next evolution." ∎

Excerpt from Jules Abend. August 2000. *Bobbin*, pp. 1–8.

Case in Point 11.1   ## Summary

Hampton Industries adjusted to changing market conditions by developing a flexible outsourcing capability and enhancing its merchandising and service capabilities. This required a strategic plan to become more technology-driven to improve responsiveness to retail customers. The company adopted a software package to allow it to analyze sales data and make buying recommendations as well as developing systems that allow tracking of raw materials and the status of production orders. Hampton's information systems have shifted from a singular focus on manufacturing products to include improving timeliness and accuracy of information from its suppliers. Hampton is using a dynamic tracking calendar that allows tracking the critical stages of product development and sourcing. The company has also incorporated Web-based systems to communicate with its sales group, El Salvador factories, and sourcing agents.

Although Hampton Industries was forced to close its U.S. factories and utilize international sourcing to remain competitive, it has not lost sight of the importance of production throughput time to effective sourcing. It has implemented a "pull" system in its El Salvador plants to reduce production time and work-in-process.

Hampton Industries has adapted to change by embracing new technologies, hiring experienced branded sourcing executives, and developing enhanced management systems to improve its sourcing process. ∎

"Metropolis of Manufacturing"

With quotas lifted, China is rapidly flexing its muscles as a powerhouse of apparel production.

But China's industry is by no means monolithic. The world's most populous country is home to hundreds of apparel companies, ranging from small shops to sprawling megafactories, from state-owned reminders of China's communist history to temples of the country's growing embrace of capitalism. With their exports—at least for now—unrestrained, these enterprises are fighting tooth and nail to grow their sales.

Luen Thai Holdings Ltd. is betting its future on a model of a superfactory the company calls a "supply-chain city." Its first such 32-acre complex is now operating here in Dongguan and will employ 14,000 workers in 15 buildings when it is completed in early 2007.

The Dongguan complex, which currently employs 7,300 workers, aims to be a one-stop shop for Luen Thai's customers, where apparel brands can source entire season's worth of merchandise, tops and bottoms, knits and wovens.

"We offer everything in one area," said Lewis Leung, vice president and general manager of the Dongguan facility.

Beyond simple cutting and sewing, the facility houses a robust design department, sourcing operations—with office space for Luen Thai's major suppliers and customers—and logistics planning.

So far, the company has invested $51 million in the facility and plans to spend an additional $16.6 million in its expansion. It already represents a hefty part of Luen Thai, which has more than 20,000 employees at 12 manufacturing facilities and 14 offices in nine countries. The Dongguan factory last year produced 65 million garments. In the year ended June 30, 2004, the company's turnover came to $544.9 million.

But the Dongguan facility, massive as it is, will be dwarfed by the 115-acre complex Luen Thai plans to open next, in Qing Yuan, 30 minutes from Guangzhou.

Outside the Dongguan compound, one can feel overwhelmed by the noise and bustle of China's rapid industrialization.

Within the walls, the 24-hour facility has the feel of a college campus, where young, stylishly dressed workers can be seen taking their lunch breaks, and signs in English and Chinese offer directions to the various buildings.

The complex's centerpiece is a design and research center, where 22 designers—four from Hong Kong and 18 from China—work in a gallery-like area with a concrete floor and a central area for fabric displays. Graphics and prints for various clients serve as artwork on the walls.

Each season, the design department prepares trend forecasts that are tailor-made for each client, said Patricia Ho, senior manager of design and development. As well as design, the team works on sourcing and mock-up garments to show embroidery or beading options, Ho said. There also is a space for in-house training sessions and customer seminars.

The technical center is "the pentagon," where all the planning goes on, Leung said.

(continued)

This is where patterns are made and garments are fitted on mannequins that are shipped to Dongguan in different sizes from companies such as Liz Claiborne, Sears and Ann Taylor.

There are 452 staffers who work on patternmaking and samples. They produce 300 pieces a day and 2,500 styles a month.

The washing and color center is equipped with washing machines from all over the world, which Leung said allows the company to test how its garments will react to laundering, avoiding "surprise shrinkage" for consumers.

In some cases, completed samples are shipped out to potential customers, but two of Luen Thai's largest customers—Polo Ralph Lauren and Dillard's—have dedicated office space on site, with their own staffs.

Polo's space has carpets and wood floors that match the image. Leung said 105 Luen Thai employees whom he described as "baptized by Ralph Lauren" work in the 30,000-square-foot space, which includes a showroom, sales, merchandising and technical center.

Polo accounts for more than $150 million of Luen Thai's annual sales, Leung said.

Dillard's accounts for more than $60 million in annual sales, and Luen Thai has assigned 80 people to work solely on that account.

The Dongguan facility also provides space for clients to set up temporary offices to review samples if they wish. Leung noted that companies including Liz Claiborne have set up their own quality control offices in the city to allow for faster approval of garments.

For those who do make the trip to Dongguan, Building 15 of the complex is a 337-room hotel, from which they can walk to the sample room each morning.

For customers, it's a convenient setup. They can come to the supply-chain city and stay at its hotel as they follow a garment through its various stages. Amenities at the facility include a library, karaoke, gym with personal trainer and classes, computer room, snooker tables, mah-jong room, coffee shop, a theater that shows two movies a night—Chinese and English versions of "Alexander" and "Van Helsing" were on the schedule during a tour of the facility early this month.

The company's chief executive officer, Henry Tan, has the penthouse suite at the top of the tower, overlooking the complex of greenery and playing fields at the center of the complex, which Luen Thai calls "Central Park." Tan was not available for an interview.

In addition to offering work space to its customers, the complex features a Fabric and Trim Innovation Center, which serves as "a convention center" without the travel, Leung said.

This is a place where suppliers, such as Fountain Set Holdings Ltd., can exhibit their offerings in separate rooms. Luen Thai picked the 24 tenants, who don't pay for the space.

The complex's sewing buildings are designed to be focused and efficient. Each of the sewers has a "traffic light"—a collection of green, yellow and red plastic cards above their workstation. Green means all go; yellow means there's a quality problem and red means a "big problem" Leung said.

With this color system, a supervisor can simply look down a row to rate the productivity level. In addition, each row has a quality and efficiency percentage.

Dormitory buildings ring the property. When all are completed by the beginning of 2006, they will provide room for 14,000 workers.

(continued)

Leung said 95 percent of employees live at the complex, though they are offered a housing subsidy of $12 a month if they wanted to live outside. Leung acknowledged that sum in most cases would not be sufficient to pay for housing in the area.

Couples can live in the dorms, provided they both work for Luen Thai, Leung said, but children aren't allowed. Other rules include no smoking, no mixing of men and women in rooms and no gambling.

Staff also get a food stipend. There are four canteens at the facility, three of which are run by Café de Coral, a Chinese fast-food restaurant group based in Hong Kong.

A typical daily shift runs from 8 a.m. until 6 p.m. with an hour and a half lunch break, Leung said. Each person works one shift and gets paid a monthly minimum wage, worth $69. Those who work overtime receive additional pay, Leung said. There also are monetary incentives for high productivity and quality.

Leung insisted that managing a complex of 14,000 workers isn't a different challenge than managing a factory of 1,000. The essential task is to "make sure you preach the gospel" of the company culture, he added.

That gospel is plastered on walls throughout the complex, on signs that read "One Company, One Culture, One Team." It goes on to explain how unity is part of the corporate culture and how "luen" means "unity" in Cantonese and Mandarin Chinese.

Workers at the complex come from various Chinese provinces, as well as Hong Kong, Singapore, the Philippines, Mexico, Japan, the U.S. and the U.K.

To Luen Thai—and some of its largest customers — the advantage of the supply-chain city model is the economies of scale it allows.

Some of Luen Thai's competitors pooh-poohed that notion.

"In general, my experience—and there are exceptions—is that big factories equal big prices," said Steve Feniger, ceo of sourcing firm Linmark, which buys from a network of smaller factories. "The economies of scale we were all taught in business school turns out to be not so directly applicable to an apparel industry because of the changes in the last three years."

The changes hinge on timing. Previously, buyers might have bought twice a year, then four times a year to reflect the seasons. Now, Feniger said every single one of his clients is buying at least eight times a year and sometimes even as many as 12 times a year.

The increase, however, isn't necessarily reflected in the amount that is ordered.

"They aren't buying more, just smaller initial quantities, chasing what sells with repeats, changing to new styles where initial sales are weak," Feniger said. "All healthy for minimizing stock and increasing responsiveness, but very hard for megafactories to handle such small runs, without annual commitments."

But one Hong Kong apparel analyst suggested there are advantages beyond scale to the megafactories. By providing space and additional services to clients and suppliers, the analyst said, "You kind of lock up the relationship with your customers." ∎

From Vicki Rothrock. March 22, 2005. *Women's Wear Daily.*

Case in Point 11.2 **Summary**

Luen Thai's super factory that occupies 32 acres in Dongguan, China can be considered the one-stop shopping of sourcing. Their "supply chain city" of 14,000 workers enables apparel companies and retail companies to source an entire season. The process begins with seasonal trend forecasts, followed by design development, pattern making, and finally, full production and logistic capabilities. The number of employees dedicated to these processes dwarfs the number of personnel that any apparel company could employ for these purposes. Luen Thai will provide workspace and living accommodations for their customers while they are participating in the product development process. Luen Thai provides the ultimate in full-package sourcing, offering a viable alternative for apparel and retail organizations to meet the needs of the consumer by delivering the right product at the right price at the right time. ■

Jack Listanowsky Experience—vice president and chief sourcing and production officer, The Limited, Inc.

Selecting the Right Source

"Over the years there have been no major philosophical changes in thinking about sourcing, but the migration patterns have become wider. One still looks at sourcing, or should look at sourcing, from a wide variety of perspectives. You usually don't run to a country to get a particular product. You look for specific factories and a broad base of products to justify making an investment of time and resources in a particular country. Otherwise you might just as well take a dart and throw it at a map and say, 'Mongolia, let's go there.' A product or a factory may take you to a country and then you should look for justification to begin a program of sourcing from that country. I may contact every freight forwarder and find out who is doing business there and what products they are shipping out. I will take the infrastructure industry and find out to whom they are selling labels, thread, etc. Then I'll identify who is making goods there and get some sense of the tier level of customers. If they sell Target Stores, it's a lot different than if they're selling Ralph Lauren or Tommy Hilfiger.

"If I need to make a cotton T-shirt, I could run to Pakistan and show you that you can buy one cheaper than probably anywhere else in the world. They make fine quality cotton and have low labor costs. But then again, why go to Pakistan to save $0.20 per T-shirt if I don't have a concentration of other products I could buy there. In India I can buy anything from leather shoes to tailored clothing. The cost per unit of overhead and back end [support staff] is something you must think about. Many people only look at the FOB [free on board] cost, and that is only one factor and many times not the best picture. I look to be able to put a large enough investment into an area to make it pay off in the long term, not just a short-term profit margin on one product.

"There are major decisions to be made when searching for the right sourcing region:

1. Quota situation. Is there sufficient quota for my categories or no restrictions?
2. What's my time frame for delivery? For tailored clothing I can go to 25 percent of the world but not the other 75 percent. Casual and washed I can go to 75 percent of the world.
3. Product category. I won't go to Hong Kong to make complicated expensive merchandise. Quality is great but labor costs are high.

(continued)

4. Am I facing any logistics problems? Did I pick the perfect country in the world that has a boat coming in only once a month? My traffic and logistics support mechanisms must be in place. Does it have an infrastructure for all the back end pieces such as the trimmings, labels, boxes? This type of thinking process, of finding the best sourcing site, should be used.

5. What am I dealing with economically in the world? Today, should I be thinking of Indonesia, or not? Is it a crisis to run to, or a crisis to run away from? (I have my own answers to that.) If it's an Indonesian company, I'm less apt to run to it today as I would be if it were a Taiwanese company. (Many of the factories in Indonesia are joint ventures and they get their money in Hong Kong or Taiwan.)

6. What's my availability of labor in the country? For example, hand knits. Today I can't think of Korea because the women who used to do hand knitting have retired or passed away, and there are no young people who come out of high school or college and say, 'I think I'll be a hand knitter.'"

Accommodation

"I am prepared to pay another $.50 or $1.00 per garment for quality and speed. In the past it was much more all about price, delivery, quality, whereas now it is quality, delivery, price, as well as [speed]. I want the production facility close to my store cash register or warehouse! Now, I may be apt to go more domestic and discount margin emphasis. For example, if I schedule product in the stores by November 1 and by November 5 I've got a runaway seller, I'll never chase it for Christmas if my source is too far away. That's why I often give 40 percent of my total projection to a source that provides price and quality, and the next 60 percent goes to a source that provides quality, speed, and then price. Price can be the least important ingredient. That way I can replenish and take advantage of the runaway sellers. The extra sales that I capture easily compensate for the lower margin."

Team Approach

"At The Limited we have corporate roles such as the head of marketing, the head of merchandising and design, and myself as chief sourcing and production officer. We hope to add value to each business unit. The dotted line responsibility of the manufacturing people in the business unit comes to me. It is a support role, and if I'm not adding value, I'm not doing my job. Hopefully the phone will be ringing all the time because people want the support. I use each of the VPs of manufacturing within the business units as a team.

"I want to do a full court press in terms of Mexico. We're not heav-

(*continued*)

ily concentrated there so we're not as knowledgeable as we would want to be on day-to-day operations. I sent an E-mail to all eight VPs of the business units. 'Over the next three weeks put your thinking caps on and everybody list who's the best at every category in Mexico. Who's the best yarn spinner in cotton? Who's the best woolen spinner? Come down with the three you think are the best.' Then we'll network outside the business, and then I may commandeer a jet and three or four of us will fly to Mexico and we'll visit the three best in every category. Hopefully we'll understand who we should engage. Each business knows what the others are doing so you have multiple tests for all businesses at the same time. The team will create the answers."

Trust and Expertise

"I focus on developing a trust with my suppliers. We work together so we both can make a profit.

"Today I attempt to try and be vertical from raw materials to sewing through shipping. The term 'partner,' or 'vendor/partner,' is much more a part of our philosophy today as compared to the way it was. This is a learning process for the whole sourcing community.

"The Limited is reengineering itself and reinventing itself as far as sourcing is concerned. Our desire is to bring a world class level of manufacturing expertise into the businesses. All actual factories and subcontractors must be approved by the sourcing department. Professionals in manufacturing and sourcing are the ones who will be interfacing with the manufacturers.

"The best sourcing executives have a true manufacturing background and understand how a garment is constructed and produced. They need to know the variables that affect a garment in production and speak with knowledge.

"Country of origin issues [outsourcing] and human rights issues are very important in sourcing decisions.

"Strategic sourcing in today's ever-changing marketplace is anything but easy. It's category, it's labor, it's currency, it's price, it's quota, it's quality, it's timing, all bombarding your brain at one time."

Cheryl Nash
Experience—owner/
designer, Windridge

Target Market

"We're a women's wear manufacturer that produces related separates for the better women's sportswear market. Our target market is a broad range of women ages 25 to 60 with disposable income and a need to dress; typically a career customer or a suburban customer. We are clearly in the better market, not quite into bridge even though we use a lot of bridge fabrications. I always think of our styling as a "bridge" look but at a better price point."

Merchandising

"To me, merchandising is controlling the product mix (styling, fabrication, color, and pricing) to ensure the appropriate products are offered at the appropriate time and place. We produce a collection at a time, whereas many companies are constantly designing new product. We produce spring and fall coordinate groupings, developing these seasons in totality. That's the way our customers buy them and that's the way we are going to ship them. Our merchandising efforts in product development are focused on making sure that the product mix makes sense both for our customers and our company. We must be sure we are offering enough variety, not repeating ourselves, and that we've developed collections appropriate for both northern and southern climates and lifestyles."

Production Driven

"We outsource many of the production operations such as pattern making, marking, and grading. All of our manufacturing is outsourced through contractors under the responsibility of the production manager. We are very production-oriented as a company. My sales manager knows a great deal about production. My assistant designer is very knowledgeable in production so I like to say that our designs are production-driven. We also tend to be pretty common sense oriented. Production and sales usually define the common sense elements, which are relevent in the design phase."

Sourcing

"We do nearly all domestic sourcing for the manufacturing of our products. We have some factories that we have used for a number of years. There's always a situation when you need a faster turn time or you are

(continued)

using a new fabrication and the factory doesn't have the proper equipment. So we're always evaluating and interviewing new domestic manufacturing resources.

"We produce all our sweater knits and our leather goods offshore. For sweater knits we generally buy the whole package from an offshore contractor. My design department works with an agent in the United States to develop the yarn, the knit structure, and the rest of the product development. We go to the Orient to get the quality and full-fashioned construction we need for our sweaters.

"Sourcing for fabrics is both domestic and imported. For our cut and sew knits and our wovens, we do cut, make, and trim [CMT] contracting domestically. We primarily use one cutting facility and then send the cut work to a variety of sewing contractors. We are more important to our cutter if we give him all our work. Windridge is very quality driven and our cutter knows what our needs are."

Quality

"Our production manager goes over construction and quality details with our domestic contractors. We produce a sample line for our internal use. When we go into production, that house line is then marked up with instructions to point out specific quality concerns. Even if the contractor doesn't speak English, he can see that there is something that requires special attention.

"We don't produce a contract procedures manual per se. We have from time-to-time prepared manuals on quality control policies. Our best insurance is well organized pre-production work and having somebody in the factory to spot problems before they start. Our production and quality team are frequently in the factories. The last line of defense in our sourcing process is being in the factory to be certain the contractor is doing what we expect them to do. We solve problems in the factories. If we see a problem, we correct it immediately."

Summary

The continuous nature of product development requires a continuous sourcing effort as new styles are created. The sourcing strategies needed to perform continuous sourcing must be supported by effective sourcing processes that have well-developed control systems and procedures. One of the primary sourcing decisions is whether to choose domestic or international contract resources. Both domestic and international sourcing efforts should contain a contract procedures manual setting forth the steps that must be followed and the issues that must be addressed in the sourcing process.

The process for researching domestic contract resources involves searching geographical areas that have established apparel contractors, contacting trade associations and state and local government agencies, requesting information from materials suppliers, investigating trade publications and the World Wide Web, and networking with other manufacturers.

Merchandisers or other sourcing executives should carefully review the capabilities of potential sourcing contractors. The final sourcing decision should be based upon the company's specific needs and supported by a written contract covering all critical elements of the sourcing process. The actual production process should be preceded by the construction of preproduction samples based upon detailed specifications to evaluate the contract factory's capabilities and quality. Once production begins, in-process quality inspections and monitoring of production progress should be part of a comprehensive follow-up program.

The international sourcing process adds many new factors to be considered in the sourcing decision. The contract procedures manual for international sourcing should include foreign raw materials testing, human rights standards, labeling requirements, quota availability, and special shipping criteria.

Researching international sources is more difficult than locating domestic contractors. Foreign consulates and trade missions, industrial developers and foreign banks, international materials suppliers, apparel trading network Web sites, and traveling to international apparel contracting regions are effective methods for locating new international contract sources. Another option is to utilize sourcing agents or trading companies.

In reviewing potential international sources, it is important to include evaluation of a country's infrastructure, political and economic stability, a factory's human rights record, quota availability, communications capabilities, the effect of international business paradigms, potential risk, and U.S. consumer perception of the region or country under consideration. Special attention must also be given to evaluating all costs associated with international sourcing, not just the costs of materials and labor. All price quotes should be in U.S. dollars with payment usually stipulated to be made by a letter of credit.

After an international sourcing partner is selected, a contract should be prepared by qualified international trade attorneys. The follow-up process is critical to the success of international sourcing. Multiple visits should be made to the contract factory to review quality and production progress. A final pre-shipment quality inspection should be performed and stipulated as a requirement for payment of the letter of credit. Finally, the sourcing team must be prepared to handle the complex importation process.

Key Terms

amendment
binding ruling
contract procedures manual
Customs-Trade Partnership
   Against Terrorism (C-TPAT)
discrepancy
documents against payment or acceptance
electronic funds transfer (EFT)
free on board (FOB)
irrevocable letter of credit
irrevocable standby letter of credit

letters of credit (L/Cs)
liquidation
nonbinding ruling
open account
registration numbers (RNs)
sourcing agent
telex transfer (TT)
trading company
transshipping
wire transfer (WT)
wool products label (WPL)

Discussion Questions and Learning Activities

1. What is the primary value of using a contract procedures manual for domestic and international apparel sourcing?
2. What is the advantage of a World Wide Web database in researching sourcing options?
3. Why should the factors in the sourcing decision be weighted for different product categories?
4. Locate a garment labeled "Assembled in country X of U.S. components." Discuss what sourcing process was used to produce the garment and why the process was used.
5. What factors other than labor costs should be considered when an offshore contracting source is selected?
6. Since quotas are not a tax, why in some cases do quotas increase the cost of an imported garment?
7. What are three possible sources of information on apparel contractors in Tanzania?
8. Why is infrastructure important in evaluating a potential contract resource?
9. When using an irrevocable letter of credit as payment in a sourcing contract, who has the responsibility of paying the contractor?

10. What role does risk play in the sourcing decision?
11. What skills should a sourcing executive have?
12. From the Executive Perspective of Jack Listanowsky, vice president and chief sourcing and production officer, The Limited, Inc., under what circumstances would he pay a premium price for a garment?

References and Resources

Bianchi, Ray. November 1997. The Full Package Formula. *Bobbin*, pp. 32–34.

Gereffi, Gary. November 1997. Global Shifts, Regional Response. *Bobbin*, pp. 16–31.

Lardner, James. January 11, 1988. Annals of Business: The Sweater Trade—1. *The New Yorker*, pp. 39–72.

Lardner, James. January 18, 1988. Annals of Business: The Sweater Trade—2. *The New Yorker*, pp. 57–73.

Moore, Lila. September 1995. Home Is Where You Sew It. *Apparel Industry Magazine*, pp. 38–54.

Rothrock, Vicky. March 22, 2005. Metropolis of Manufacturing. *www.wwd.com*.

Scheines, Joseph. 1986. Planning & Implementing an Apparel Sourcing Strategy. *1986 Report of the Technical Advisory Committee*, American Apparel Manufacturers Association.

Shea, David. December 1993. Tracking the U.S. Contractor. *Bobbin*, pp. 52–54.

Staff Report. April 1996. Look Before You Leap. *Bobbin*, p. 71–74.

New innovations in computer technology and digital communications are changing the way apparel and retail companies research fashion trends, develop new styles, produce garments, and collaborate with their supply chain. Part 4 analyzes the new approaches apparel and retail companies are taking in research, product development, customization, and sourcing in this ever-changing technological age.

MERCHANDISING: THE FUTURE

Future Direction

- Explore the changes that are occurring in the apparel and retail industries as a result of new technologies.

- Examine the use of research technologies, data management software, and CAD systems in line and product development.

- Explore the effect of the elimination of quotas and the utilization of new technologies on sourcing.

The apparel and retail industries are undergoing rapid evolutionary changes that have resulted from consolidations, mergers, and acquisitions; the increasing competition for the consumer's apparel purchases between a retailer's private brands and an apparel company's national brands, the digital revolution, globalization, and the dedication to meeting the consumer's demands. Only a few years ago, fashion trends lasted a year or longer. Today, trend life cycles have shrunken to just one or two months. Progressive companies are providing fresh new styles to consumers on a continuous basis. European retailers Zara and H&M (Hennes and Mauritz) have adopted fast fashion, which brings new collections to their selling floors in a matter of days to satisfy the young consumer's insatiable appetite for the newest styles. This will energize more apparel and retail companies to accelerate the time required from concept to consumer. The traditional six to twelve month cycle will be replaced by a six to twelve week cycle and, in some cases, transformed into a six to twelve day cycle. Even the largest apparel and retail companies are reevaluating their roles as volume producers for the masses. They are seeing the need to address niche markets and even individual needs by continually expanding their capabilities for mass customization. Both industries are in a constant state of flux, which has placed tremendous pressure on the apparel merchandising and retail product managing functions. As a result, apparel merchandising has evolved in two distinct specialized areas:

- *Development:* defining a product line by picking up on the direction fashion is taking through high-speed digital communications. In addition, Internet capabilities, advanced CAD, PDS, and color management systems are being used to first develop and evaluate product alternatives, and then execute them.
- *Sourcing*: producing and distributing garments by utilizing interactive computer data management systems and QR strategies in a collaborative effort throughout the total supply chain.

Both areas require higher and higher levels of technical expertise and rely on improvements in information technology.

Merchandisers can no longer set a line development plan in motion and await the results at final adoption. Nor can they develop a comprehensive manufacturing and sourcing plan at the beginning of a season and expect it to meet customer demands with only midseason tweaking. Flexible planning systems, agile manufacturing, and quick response to evolving market trends are key elements in effective merchandising strategies.

■ Information Technology

Future merchandisers will be at the helm of vast information technology systems where they will make microadjustments in real time to maximize sell-through and minimize markdowns. Line development is becoming a "continuous styling" process that is in sync with the subtle changes in the marketplace. Feedback from consumer panels, test marketing, and point-of-sale data, as well as research from Internet design services provide information to merchandisers for fine-tuning products in the development process. Manufacturing and sourcing decisions are also becoming "continuous" processes. Quick response programs using collaborative planning, forecasting, and replenishment strategies make it possible to adjust production to better serve customer needs. George Q. Horowitz, chairman and CEO of Active Apparel Group Inc., sees technology reaching into all areas of the merchandising function. "The incredible technological revolution that's happening is going to affect the way we all do business in terms of designing, producing and distributing goods" (Abend, January 2000).

Planning and control software has changed the way merchandising calendars are created and utilized. As part of today's product development management systems, they provide standard templates that are customized by product category to establish who does what, what needs to be done, how long it should take to do, and when it is due. A proactive component alerts management to unfinished activities that are nearing their completion dates.

Figure 12.1 displays the execution portion of a merchandising calendar for offshore apparel, which establishes the schedule of activities based upon the critical path method. Figure 12.2 illustrates another report that monitors the status of the Product Development Cycle and alerts the merchandiser to the need for corrective action. Both of these documents use Justwin Web Connect™ software, which easily links together the enterprise's entire supply chain. As an advanced collaborative tool, it eliminates the artificial barriers of distance and time enabling everyone to closely follow all of the events that are critical to succeed in a truly global environment.

Global sourcing is moving toward more sophisticated communications and data sharing systems. New developments are being made in product data management software that can be translated into multiple languages, be customized to fit varying company requirements, and handle the complex logistics of working in a global environment. Some apparel manufacturers are even focusing on collaborative product development with their sourcing partners. E-sourcing using Internet- and Web-based platforms to locate new sourcing partners and manage the sourcing function is becoming a reality.

Digital technologies are creating the greatest impact on the merchandising function. E-commerce through B2B (business-to-business) communications and B2C (business-to-consumer) communication is changing the dynamics of developing and producing apparel. The electronic marketplace is in its infancy relative to apparel manufacturers offering products for sale directly

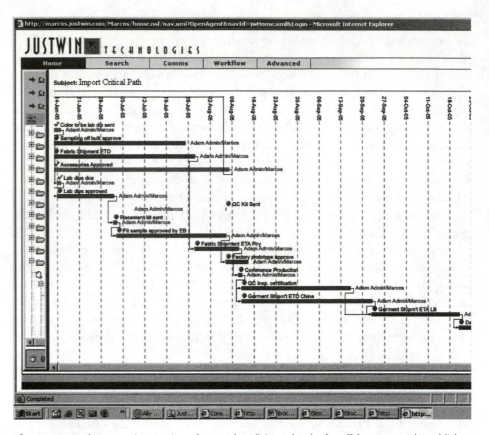

Figure 12.1 The execution portion of a merchandising calendar for offshore apparel establishes the schedule of activities based upon the critical path method.

to consumers. There is, however, a steady trend of firms testing the efficacy of shopping on-line for soft goods products that lend themselves more to classic brick and mortar retail establishments where customers can touch, feel, and try on garments. B2C communication provides the perfect platform for individualized service. Advanced body scanning to create a reusable digital blueprint that provides a perfect fit and allows consumers to personalize styles through customization are applications of digital technologies that are being given serious consideration by apparel producers. Table 12.1 lists apparel manufacturers, customization specialists, and retailers who have established their presence on the Web.

Information technology will continue to be critical to the future success of the apparel industry. The rapid acquisition, analysis, and communication of information and the effective use of the knowledge gleaned from it to make

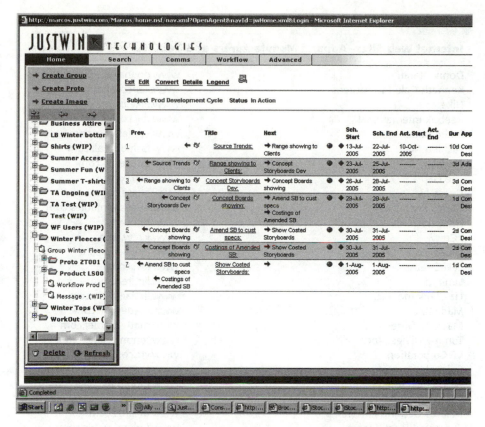

Figure 12.2 This report monitors the status of the Product Development Cycle and alerts the merchandiser to the need for corrective action.

accurate decisions is the driving force behind the apparel leaders in the first decade of the twenty-first century. Mackey McDonald, CEO of Vanity Fair Corporation, stressed the importance of knowledge in his keynote address at the 2000 CEO Summit. "At VF, we believe that knowledge will drive the apparel industry in the next 20 years, and our competitive advantage will come from the skill with which we gather and manage that knowledge. Either we and our partners will learn to add value through consumer knowledge or we just won't survive." Five years later, Michael D. Cole wrote the article "Technology's Next Frontier on Display at Tech Conference," which appeared in the November 2005 issue of *Apparel Magazine*. He wrote about the necessity of embracing the new technologies as a prerequisite for success. He states, "With the entire apparel industry deeply entrenched in global sourcing, technology is increasingly viewed as a competitive advantage . . . The offshore

---

TABLE 12.1

Internet Web Sites—Apparel Manufacturers and Retailers

Donna Karan	www.donnakaran.com
Kenneth Cole Productions	www.kencole.com
Nike	www.nike.com
Reebok International	www.rbk.com
Eddie Bauer	www.eddiebauer.com
Fashion Mall	www.fashionmall.com
Forever21	www.forever21.com
The Gap	www.gap.com
Guess Inc.	www.guess.com
Hanes Printables	www.hanesprintables.com
H&M (Hennes and Mauritz)	www.hm.com
J.Crew	www.jcrew.com
Lands' End	www.landsend.com
Levi Strauss	www.levi.com
Limited	www.limited.com
Liz Claiborne, Inc.	www.lizclaiborne.com
Made4Me	www.made4me.com
Made To Order	www.madetoorder.com
Tommy Hilfiger, Inc.	www.tommy.com
VF Corporation	www.vfc.com
Spiegel	www.spiegel.com
Bloomingdales	www.bloomingdales.com
Brooks Brothers	www.brooksbrothers.com
Dillards Department Stores	www.dillards.com
Federated Dept. Stores	www.federated-fds.com
Kmart	www.kmart.com
Macy's	www.macys.com
JCPenney	www.jcpenney.com
Sears Roebuck & Co.	www.sears.com
Target Stores	www.targetstores.com
Wal-Mart Stores	www.wal-mart.com
Zara	www.zara.com

A list of manufacturers, customization specialists, and retailers who may be found on the Internet.

movement to Asia, Central America, and other destinations has brought to focus new challenges—and the subsequent development of new high-tech tools—for achieving greater efficiencies and accelerating speed to market. Traditional methods of communication, for example, are now being eclipsed by better ways to collaborate on line accelerating design via digital samples, and improve the exchange of these files across the globe to reduce other costs such as for shipping. Accordingly, the apparel industry is embracing technological advances such as emerging PDM/PLM solutions, improved color management products, and new 3-D technologies" (Cole, 2005).

During the dynamic changes in the future of the apparel industry, the overall responsibilities of the merchandising function to develop, execute, and deliver product lines based upon the needs of a target market will remain the same, but new specialized subfunctions may evolve and job titles may change. Due to increasing technological demands and requirements for specific expertise, large and midsized companies are creating specialized positions in global sourcing, product information technology, product research, product data management, portfolio management, consumer information, Web site management, forecasting systems, product development, and communications systems.

■ Development

The future of line and product development in the apparel and retail industries will be a true blend of science, technology, and vision. There will always be a place for the creative genius of the true innovators of the fashion design world. Unfortunately those visionaries are limited to a very few at the top of the creative design chain. For the vast majority of successful companies, creativity will be defined by the ability of the merchandisers to tap into the fashion direction of their target market and direct their design team in developing a line that will define the leading edge of the fashion trends for their particular market. To do this effectively will require precise timing and an intimate knowledge of target consumers. The development of new and innovative research technologies, real-time data management software, and advanced CAD systems will provide the tools for the merchandisers of the future. For the vast majority of successful companies, creativity will be defined by the ability of the merchandisers and product managers to tap into the fashion direction of their target market. The merchandiser and product manager will direct their design teams in creating lines or groups of styles that not only define the leading edge of the fashion trends but also respond to the captured POS information of their particular market. To do this effectively will require precise timing, and an intimate knowledge of their consumers. The implementation of enhanced Product Development Management (PDM) and Product Life Cycle Management (PLM) systems will improve communications and speed line development by connecting through a centralized database the functions of design, costing, engineering, and sourcing. The application of the next generation of Computer Aided Design (CAD), Pattern Design Systems (PDS), Digital Printers, 3-D simulation, and Color Management Systems that improve on-screen visualization

Figure 12.3 An added dimension to global fashion research is the ability of a merchandiser to use the Internet for immediate access to fashion events such as catwalk shows.

and expedite approval of digital samples will all contribute to compress the time required to bring new lines to market (see Table 12.2 for software suppliers).

Research

The number of fashion-related Web sites is growing at a rapid pace. The latest European catwalk shows are only a mouse click away. Fashion research sites cover everything from color and fabric trends to niche market silhouette direction, and statistics on style category sales at retail sites around the world. Shopping the competition is as easy as clicking onto its Web site. As streaming video and high-speed Internet connections improve, it will be possible for merchandisers to research any and all fashion trends from their laptop anywhere in the world, thus dramatically reducing travel time and shrinking the research segment of line development.

Powerful Internet search engines like Alta Vista, AOL Search, Excite, Google, Hotbot, Infoseek, Lycos, Magellan, MSN Search, Netscape Search, Snap, Yahoo, and Webcrawler provide the opportunity for locating data on nearly any research topic. Many international museums and educational institutions are beginning to provide designers the opportunity to view parts of their historical costume, designer garment, textile, and art collections over the Internet. Search engines have the ability to crawl throughout the Internet looking for specific data or sites, download the information, and have it cataloged for use by the researchers at their convenience. The continued expansion of Internet-based research tools will provide future apparel merchandisers with instant access to valuable information and ideas, any time, any place.

Focus group discussions with consumer panels to evaluate new styling concepts are becoming feasible over the Internet. This instant feedback from target market consumers can provide an effective means for evaluating the potential for new styles. Concept and preference feedback from a company Web site via posted questionnaires is another effective tool for performing market research. Increasingly, more companies are utilizing real-time POS data capture for test marketing new products in key retail stores to create more accurate forecasts before placing initial production orders. Digital technology and the Internet will continue to shrink the world, thereby increasing the options and shortening the time it requires for apparel merchandisers to perform effective research.

Product Development

Digital systems are poised to play a major role in the future of product development. As computing speed continues to increase, three-dimensional design systems and virtual reality video simulations will transform much, if not all, of the product development process into high-speed digital applications. Realistic prototypes will be created using computer simulations, and advanced Internet-based audiovisual communications will allow the product development team to evaluate them from anywhere around the globe.

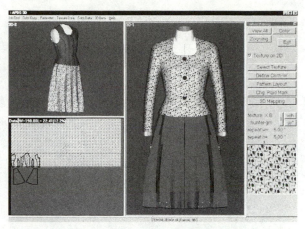

Figure 12.4 CAD/Cam software applications enable users to simulate three-dimensional draping on photographs or sketches.

More and more CAD/CAM applications are including two- and three-dimensional drape simulation tools so that designers can create computer-generated images to enable them to evaluate styling concepts without having to manufacture prototypes (see Figure 12.4). Textile CAD programs allow weave and knit generation of the fabrics used in creating even more realistic prototype simulations. The focus of CAD/CAM systems is on total production development solutions that provide suites of programs to accommodate all segments of the development process. These will include second generations of:

- Two- and three-dimensional creative drawing, modeling, and draping software to simulate style ideas as virtual prototypes for evaluation.
- Pattern design tools that can create two-dimensional garment patterns from three-dimensional simulations complete with accommodation for the mechanical properties of fabrics and ease allowances.
- Textile CAD systems that can create weave, knit, and print designs for application on virtual prototypes and then be electronically shared with weaving, knitting, and printing suppliers to shorten the fabric procurement cycle.
- Textile fabric digital printers that will allow actual prototypes to be created in fabric prints by the apparel designer (see Figure 12.5).
- E-commerce B2B communications access to suppliers that will allow merchandisers and designers to view fabrics and findings inventories on-line, integrate those raw materials into virtual prototypes, and place raw materials orders electronically.
- Data management systems that will capture all specification details, drawings, and sketches and maintain data integrity for any new styles in progress while making the information available via the Internet to the entire product development. (See Table 12.2 for Technology Software Vendors).

Figure 12.5 The MacDermaid ColorSpan Displaymaker FabriJet printer prints on unbacked fabric with a variety of textile or graphic inks. It is used for proofing designs, printing samples for displays and trade shows, and short run production.

Collaboration among the members of the product development team is becoming more of a digital experience than a person-to-person one as the availability of low-cost videoconferencing over the Internet is fast becoming a reality. A merchandiser in Los Angeles can link with designers in New York to view and discuss a garment prototype on a fit model in a sourcing partner's factory in Bangkok, Thailand. Through high-resolution video, data compression, and high-speed Internet transmission, the real time teleconference could allow the product development team to zoom in on the smallest construction detail or the smoothness of the garment drape on the model's body. Language translation software will be able to provide simultaneous translation in all languages. This will eliminate the language barrier that generates a large percentage of the problems associated with global apparel sourcing and deters collaborative product development.

Customization

As apparel companies focus more and more on providing personalized service to consumers, customization will continue to be a very important issue. **Customization** is the process of personalizing a garment by manufacturing it to an individual's specific body measurements or other specifications such as silhouette, fabric, color, and embellishments. In a **consumercentric** company, giving the customers exactly what they want is the primary focus. Kurt Salmon Associates consultants found that two thirds of the consumers they polled reported difficulty in finding clothes that fit well. About 36 percent of those people indicated that they would be willing to pay 12 percent to 15 percent more for customized clothes. These results and the ability of the Internet to reach individual consumers anywhere around the globe has many apparel manufacturers investigating the feasibility of customization.

In 1995, Levi Strauss first offered their Original Spin™ program for men and women, which allowed customers to create their own individual pair of jeans by modifying an authentic pair of Levi's. The customer's body measurements were generated from either a three-dimensional body scan (in the San Francisco Flagship store) or from measurements taken by a sales associate. The customer tried on a test pair of jeans suggested by the associate, and from there the fit could be modified to be tighter, looser, shorter, or longer. Once the fit details were finalized, the personalized jeans were produced and shipped to the store or directly to the customer within two or three weeks. Although Levi Strauss discontinued Original Spin™ in 2003, they maintained their interest in mass customization, and in 2005 installed the Intellifit System in selected stores. The Intellifit System uses kiosks that apply low power radio waves for 10 seconds to determine the consumer's body measurements. This information is then used to select the best fitting jeans that are available in the Levi's store. Intellifit kiosks have

Figure 12.6 A customer being measured for custom jeans under the Levis Strauss Original Spin™ program.

also been installed in several Macy's, David's Bridal stores, and other retail stores and shopping malls throughout the country. Once the consumer has been scanned, the information is embedded in a smart card. When the consumer swipes the smart card into a special reader, they access a database that allows them to compare their measurements with the sizing of products from many companies and then select those sizes that would provide the best fit.

Another pioneer in mass customization has been Lands' End, who first offered pants that could be purchased in a variety of styles, fabrics, and hem finishes, and then later offered custom dress shirts. Lands' End shirts could be purchased by sizing, profile, fabric, collar type, cuffs, and inclusion of pockets and back pleats. Today, Lands' End has developed a Virtual Model in which the consumer is asked to create a personal model by taking and registering body measurements. Based upon these measurements, the consumer can see how the various styles will fit and which will look best.

Brooks Brothers introduced "Digital Tailoring," which scanned the customer's body in 12 seconds and established exact measurements for critical tailoring points. The customer would then choose from a wide variety of fabrics and body styles. The finished suit, jacket, trousers, or shirt would be shipped in approximately three weeks. Other companies that have offered customized clothing include JCPenney, Southwick, Benchmark Clothiers, Lori Coulter, and Kathryn Chase Designs.

Couture designer Issey Miyake has experimented with customizable dresses by creating high-tech knits with perforations knit into the sleeves and hemlines to allow alterations. Web-based B2C sites from companies, large and small, offering customized garments are expected to increase in number dramatically in the coming years.

James Neal, a principal at Kurt Salmon Associates, agreed that goods aimed at smaller consumer clusters—more or less micromerchandising—and actual custom-made products would become a bigger piece of the apparel business in the years ahead. In the next 10 to 15 years, he suggested, goods that are in some way customized could grow to represent 30 percent of apparel sales (Malone, 1999).

E. Lee Griffith of The Context Group also sees customization as a key factor when he looks at the effect of future technologies on the apparel industry. "I think the information age is going to continue expanding exponentially, and there's a lot that is going to change. Personalization and customization are huge areas that consumers keep asking for. They want to customize their apparel, whether it's the fit or styling features. There's also a concept called 'Your Personal Agent,' where a firm will have your Internet profile that defines your needs, wants, and characteristics and 'Your Personal Agent' will find the products that you want. It will go shopping for you and come back to you with a personalized set of garments or other products that you might want to look at."

Body Scanning

A key element of customized clothing is fit, which requires critical body measurements. The technology that will allow fast and accurate body measurements to be taken is **body scanning**. A laser, white light, or other light source is used to illuminate the body, and cameras or sensors capture either specific body measurements or a three-dimensional digital image of the body (see Figure 12.7). One of the drawbacks of current technologies is that individuals being scanned must either strip to their underwear or wear a full body stocking and strike specific poses during the scanning process.

Another technological hurdle for body scanning was transforming the digital data from the scanning process into customized two-dimensional patterns that will create a garment that fits perfectly. Fit criteria differ based upon varying garment styles and the mechanical properties of fabrics. A tremendous amount of research has been done in developing algorithms for different categories of garments and fabrics that can transform body dimensions into custom garment patterns. The development of appropriate software systems that can accommodate the many variables in creating accurate

Fig. 12.7 A young women is having her body scanned by a multitude of white light beams that form patterns that record her measurements while she stands in a booth.

custom patterns will determine the future success of customization. The Textile and Clothing Technology Corporation continues as the price leader in developing technologically advanced body scanning. Their 3-D Body Scanner uses white light to scan the entire body in less than six seconds, and within a few minutes produces an exactly scaled 3-D model that accommodates the many variables in creating the accurate custom patterns that are required for mass customization.

Benefits

One of the major benefits is the use of body-scanning to capture data that will form the basis for better sizing throughout the apparel industry. In 2003, the SizeUSA survey was conducted by [TC²] and was based upon information that was gathered using their body scanning technology. This **anthropometric** (concerned with the measurement and study of the parts and capacities of the human body) survey showed major discrepancies between scanned body measurements and the size measurements that are used by the industry. The Director of the SizeUSA project, Jim Lovejoy, states, "If you look at the grade rules of most manufacturers today, they do not reflect what we are finding in our survey" (**www.tc2.com**). In addition, several universities, including Auburn, Central Michigan University, Cornell, Missouri, and North Carolina State, are conducting inter-disciplinary studies that focus on specific segments of society. The value of all this research is that it will allow merchandisers to develop apparel which comes closer to meeting the demands of their individual target markets. Customization offers many additional benefits to apparel

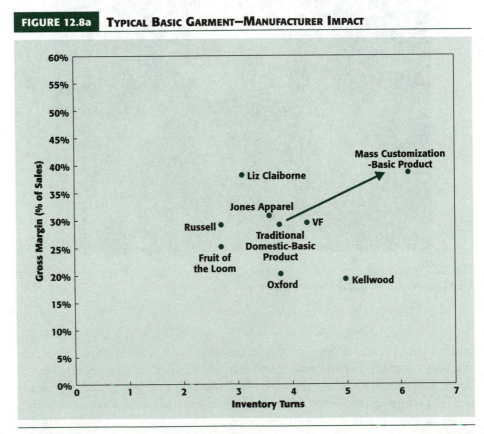

FIGURE 12.8a   TYPICAL BASIC GARMENT—MANUFACTURER IMPACT

Potential increase of gross margin percentages and inventory turns of traditional domestic basic producers who utilize mass customization.

manufacturers: increased gross profit margins, reduction of markdowns and charge-backs, lower inventories, increased customer satisfaction, and consumer loyalty. An analysis by the Textile/Clothing Technology Corporation and Kurt Salmon Associates determined that manufacturers of all garment categories could increase their gross margins and improve inventory turns through utilizing mass customization:

- Traditional domestic basic producers could increase gross margins (percent of sales) from 31 percent to almost 38 percent and inventory turns from 3.8 to over 6.
- Traditional domestic seasonal producers could increase gross margins from 46 percent to 55 percent and inventory turns from 2.8 to 4.4.
- Traditional domestic fashion producers could increase gross margins from 42 percent to 55 percent and inventory turns from 3 to 4.4. (See Figures 12.8a, b, and c.)

FIGURE 12.8b   **TYPICAL SEASONAL GARMENT—MANUFACTURER IMPACT**

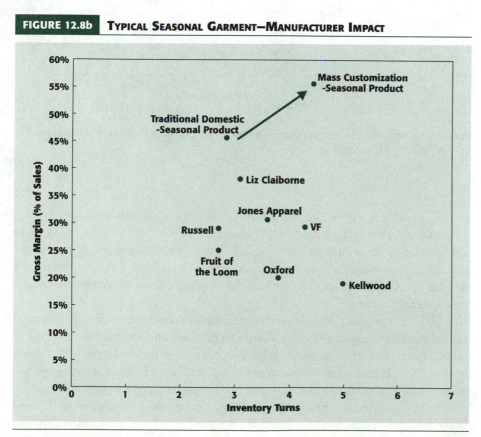

Potential increase of gross margin percentages and inventory turns of traditional domestic seasonal producers who utilize mass customization.

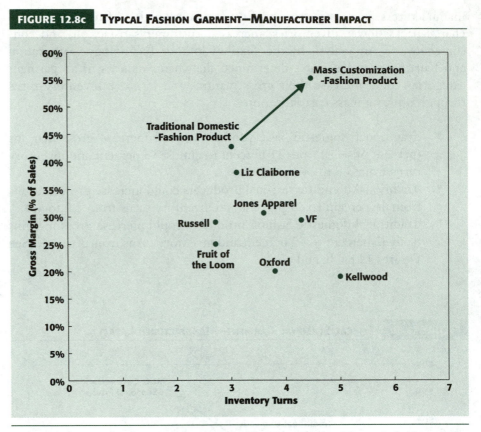

FIGURE 12.8c **Typical Fashion Garment—Manufacturer Impact**

Potential increase of gross margin percentages and inventory turns of domestic fashion producers who utilize mass customization.

Ultimately it will be the continued development of appropriate technologies that support high-quality customization and the ability of retailers to adapt to a new level of consumer service that will determine the degree of acceptance of customization. Apparel merchandisers will have to learn new technologies and refocus the product development team on consumercentric customizable styling.

The total product development function will continue to change dramatically through the expanded use of digital technology and improvements in communications. For merchandisers who adopt the new technologies, cycle times for the product development segments of the total apparel supply chain will become days rather than weeks, and true continuous styling will be a reality.

Someday apparel consumers will carry "smart cards" encoded with their body dimensions and personal fashion profiles, select and customize clothing styles using virtual reality to see themselves wearing the styles, and transmit their smart-card data to order their custom-fit garment. (See Figure 12.9.)

FIGURE 12.9   CUSTOM FIT GARMENT SYSTEM

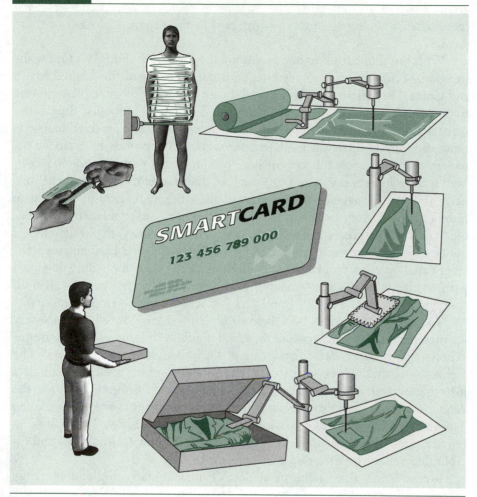

A consumer smart card used to transmit body measurements to a manufacturer who then produces a custom-fit garment.

We have seen the initial stages of this concept by apparel consumers who use "smart cards" with their individual body dimensions to select the proper sized merchandise. One thing is certain; the digital revolution is here and is gaining momentum every day.

■ Sourcing

The phase out of U.S. Customs quotas on apparel products by January 1, 2005, the continued focus on reducing the cycle of the total supply chain, new technologies, and collaborative planning, forecasting, and replenishment programs has had a dramatic effect on apparel sourcing. Merchandisers have reevaluated sourcing strategies with regard to the progress of each of these factors.

With the elimination of quotas among the members of the WTO, the institution of new and temporary safeguard quotas between the United States and China, the passage of CAFTA, and the expanding number of bilateral free trade agreements (recently concluded with Vietnam, Cambodia, Singapore, Australia, Chile, and Morocco), apparel merchandisers and product managers must carefully evaluate all global opportunities. They need to establish alliances with their most reliable offshore producers who can provide low cost, high quality apparel that meets the needs of their target market. Expert Product Life Cycle Management software will allow the merchandiser to evaluate orders against factory performance and capabilities, lead time, quantity, reliability, desired margin, risk assessment, and, when necessary, the availability of quota. The computer will recommend which factories would be the most efficient based upon past and current conditions. The creation of strategic global partnerships with the best sourcing organizations will remain critical in all sourcing efforts (see Tables 9.1 and 12.1 for Technology Software Vendors).

To gain the maximum benefit from global sourcing, it will be necessary for merchandisers to incorporate the latest digital technologies for communications and product data management with their sourcing partners. The technologies that will be vital to effective global sourcing are electronic data interchange and real-time tracking of orders as they progress through the vendor's factory. Web cams located in vendors' factories that send live video over the Internet will make viewing production live a reality. This will often require training global suppliers in the use of these new technologies and establishing vendor certification standards for them.

Robert Zane, Liz Claiborne senior VP of manufacturing and sourcing, sees technology and E-commerce as vital to future success. "We communicate electronically with our factories, and we transmit data and orders. Business-to-business communication is vital for success, and you will not survive as a manufacturer if you're not totally proficient and well equipped" (Abend, January 2000).

The increasing use of rapid replenishment programs for basic merchandise will continue to force merchandisers to reevaluate their sourcing strategies. The long lead times required for most production from the Far East make replenishment programs from them unfeasible and ordering excess quantities based upon longer range forecasts extremely risky. Therefore, merchandisers will continue to consider blended sourcing strategies using low-cost Far Eastern contractors for initial orders and higher-cost agile domestic factories or off-shore sources closer to home. In many cases, the reduced risk of markdowns and savings in transportation and duty will offset the increased

TABLE 12.2

Technology Software Vendors

3i Infotech	www.3i-infotech.com
AlvaProducts	www.alvaproducts.com
Blue Fox Porini USA	www.BlueFoxTA.com
Business Management Systems Inc.	www.bmsystems.com
Computer Generated Solutions	www.cgsinc.com
Datacolor	www.datacolor.com
Fashionware Solutions	www.fashionware.com
Freeborders	www.freeborders.com
GCS Software LLC	www.gcsnet.com
Geac	www.apparel.geac.com
GERBER TECHNOLOGY	www.gerbertechnology.com
Intentia Americas	www.intentia.com
Lectra	www.lectra.com
MATRIXONE	www.matrixone.com
New Generation Computing Inc.	www.ngcsoftware.com
OptiTex USA Inc.	www.optitex.com
PTC	www.ptc.com
Shapely Shadow Inc.	www.shapelyshadow.com
TUKAweb Inc.	www.tukaweb.com

production cost. As more apparel companies adapt to the fast fashion model and think in terms of offering fresh merchandise on a programmed delivery schedule, sourcing strategies will be developed in which the importance of timing supercedes the importance of cost. Tom Austin, president of Kellwood Co.'s Services Group addressed this issue at the Apparel Executive Forum 2005 hosted by *Apparel Magazine*. He explained that Kellwood's junior brands will source their core brands, which require five-month lead time from Asia; source Central America for their fashion injection styles, which require two to three month lead times; and use domestic suppliers for their hot fashion items, which require two to three week lead times. He added, "Being faster is always better," but Kellwood continuously evaluates if increased speed is worth the increase in cost (DesMarteau, 2005).

"McDonald's 2020 Vision"

Keynote: VF Corp.'s Mackey McDonald models a future in which intelligence about consumers is the most important commodity of all.

While many of the people speaking and attending the CEO Summit spoke in the abstract about the Internet's impact on retail, jeanswear and intimate apparel giant VF Corp. has a model up and running. It's called VF 2020, and it was the core of the keynote presentation given by Mackey McDonald, president, chairman and chief executive officer.

"Faced with a lot of choices to be made in this area, and with spending hundreds of millions of dollars, we made the decision to launch this project," he said. "We've had hundreds of people working on this in the company, we've talked to a lot of people outside the company. We've talked to futurists, to customers, and we designed a vision of what we think the retail industry will look like 20 years from now."

In essence, VF's vision of its own future is that of a big manufacturer that, through the advent of technology, will respond to needs at the niche level, and even at the level of individual consumers on the retail front lines.

Cindy Knoebel, the company's director of investor relations and one of the contributors to the project, joined McDonald in the presentation, narrating a video simulation of how the VF 2020 model would work in concrete terms, namely, to transform the acts of shopping and of selling in a future department store.

"We believe retailers in the future will need to create a more experience-based environment for shoppers," said Knoebel. Enter Ms. Lopez, a fictional shopper from the year 2020 who, in the video, is about to shop in a department store called Hometown Retail.

The fictional Lopez is heading for a theme boutique inside Hometown called "Hangar Up," which is merchandised to look like a 1920s aerodrome. "Here, shoppers can find the latest vintage fashion, experience the thrills and chills of single-engine flying and pick-up DVDs, eat in the pilot's lounge and browse through books," explained Knoebel.

Lopez's first move as she enters Hometown Retail is to swipe a card through a reader, imparting her precise body measurements as well as a history of her previous shopping visits into the store's database. When she enters Hangar Up, she's greeted by a robotic shopping aide that suggest styles she might like, based on her previous purchases. The robot can also shop for her if she decides instead to sit in the café and browse over the Internet.

The technology will enable her to customize products, say, changing a pattern on an existing blouse if she doesn't like it. And if, while on the Internet, she spots a jacket she likes during a virtual fashion show sponsored by Hometown, she can get a human sales assistant—they do still exist in the

(continued)

future—to determine exactly when the style will be manufactured and shipped to her home. Casual remarks about travel or social activities during this interaction can trigger contacts by travel agencies, group sales or hotels, and any sales of outside products or services made through such contacts will be partially credited to Hometown.

Knoebel said this kind of technology-supported shopping experience will fit VF because the vendor will have the flexibility to change as needed and will be equipped to help retailers pinpoint pertinent consumer information. The video simulation, for example, portrays a VF portfolio manager doing "collaborative forecasting" with Hometown's department manager; the two decide that Hanger Up should be reconfigured to reflect a coming trend for archaeologically inspired fashions.

"In coming decades, companies will compete on [the basis of] how well they know their customer base," said Knoebel. "VF is focused on new ways to gather and manage that information."

McDonald said he considered this 2020 model "an ambitious view of the future," and added that such ambition is necessary for a society that is now in a state of "permanent revolution," with new technologies arriving at an increasing pace.

"At VF, we believe that knowledge will drive the apparel industry in the next 20 years, and our competitive advantage will come from the skill with which we gather and manage that knowledge. Either we and our partners will learn to add value through consumer knowledge or we just won't survive. We know a lot about how consumers are changing today, and we can make some fairly secure guesses about what they'll be like tomorrow."

For one thing, said McDonald, the chunk of the population over the age of 65 will double between now and 2025. And that customer—who travels, entertains and spends time outdoors—is looking more for comfort and function in clothes than fashion."

Another fruitful customer base will be the 40-something segment, which is also on the increase. That group, said McDonald, spends more on apparel than any other. And the U.S. population will become increasingly diverse; Hispanic-Americans and Asian-Americans, for example, are the two fastest-growing subsets in the country.

However, in the electronic age, the significance of such population characteristics is shifting.

"We know that consumer taste is a moving target," said McDonald. "While immigration and multiculturalism tend to create a more diverse population, mass media will communicate the same product concepts to consumers around the world. Traditional marketing demographics of age and ethnic background may be less important in the future than true lifestyle differences.

"One thing we believe: Brands will dominate. They serve as a filter to make the shopping experience easier for consumers, who, faced with an avalanche of data on reliable and unreliable apparel choices, will stick with brands they know and trust."

While McDonald is convinced that stores aren't going anywhere, their various departments will become increasingly specific in their targeting, in order to fix on customers' current likes and dislikes. But while the look of departments might change more

(continued)

often, the product within those departments will still be branded.

"More and more retail outlets will be designed with easy-to-shop layouts and limited but targeted product choices, all based on their knowledge of the consumer," said McDonald. "They're using speed and flexibility to build competitive advantage."

McDonald also suggested that apparel stores will employ "Smartcards," which are shopping or debit cards that carry product profiles, home address, physical size and "choice of express delivery carrier."

Some such technology is already being tried out in stores, he said, such as Internet kiosks that allow customers to look at store inventory online. Other technology to come will include kiosks that would, for example, allow a parent to see what clothing would look like on a child without having to dress and undress the child.

"You can't put a price on that kind of convenience," said McDonald. "But we'll learn how."

Another convenience will be the ability to ring up purchases simply by swiping a card, rather than waiting to be checked out.

The Internet will figure prominently in this world of retail-enabling technology. "By 2020, the Internet will be accessible anywhere, anytime, through TVs, PCs, handheld PDAs and hybrid devices we don't even have yet like cell phone data stations," he said. But much is still barely in the hypothetical phase, including body scanning.

"The formula for a mass rollout remains elusive" he said. "We think retail innovators will learn how to adapt this technology as a means of offering service and convenience to consumers."

All this helps the retailer as well as the manufacturer, McDonald said, since order-ing and inventory will be completely automated, while forecasting will include point-of-sale data "to make sure customers never hear the words 'out of stock.'"

And it will be the responsibility of both retailer and manufacturer to keep alive the customers' interest in coming into stores, since most merchandise will be online much sooner than 2020. "When that happens, you won't go shopping because you have to, but because you want to. That means that retailers will have to offer more in terms of service, expertise and entertainment if they want to get you out of the house and into their store."

That's where McDonald foresees problems, since he feels the two sides are not yet prepared to share information readily, whether because of "competitive reasons" or technological barriers.

"Creating a new kind of relationship between our customers and suppliers—true, seamless communication—is the next phase in our permanent revolution," he said. VF plans to share information via all types of language, including text, images, voice and video.

McDonald also said that collaborative forecasting, planning and sourcing "must become a reality for tomorrow. Our new supply chain must adapt to a continuous process that can manage constant input from a variety of sources. Simulation and modeling technology will allow quick analysis of a greater variety of 'what if' scenarios and deliver predictions all the way down to the impact on profit and loss," he said.

"Imagine an entirely different kind of market week, where consumers participate online and vote on choices for the coming

(continued)

season. What about virtual focus groups, product chat groups and online fashion shows as a means of constantly communicating with the consumer?"

McDonald said that all of VF's suppliers and manufacturers will be connected globally so that orders can be tracked, and theoretically streamlined as consumer data is constantly monitored.

"We'll create hub-and-spoke transfer sites where we can gather, share, and sort product orders placed by consumers and retailers from a variety of sources," he said. "At the same time, our data warehouse will aggregate real time information from all supply chain participants, including consumers."

McDonald even foresees more custom-fit production becoming possible, as technology makes manufacturing smoother and customization becomes less cumbersome.

"And of course, all players will have the ability to track products and inventory through the supply chain from the cutting room to delivery, in real time," he said. "Imagine how this will impact how we interact with retailers 20 years from now. With this type of shared visibility, we'll both be able to focus on what really matters—managing customer wants." ■

From Janet Ozzard. June 14, 2000. *Women's Wear Daily*, p. 3.

Case in Point 12.1   Summary

VF Corp. has invested in developing a model of the retail apparel industry in the year 2020. Through that model the company sees its role as a large manufacturer responding to the needs of individual consumers through an experience-based shopping environment. VF's focus is on knowing its customer base and gathering and managing information about its target consumers. VF believes that knowledge will drive the apparel industry in the next 20 years and that success will be based upon how well companies gather and manage that knowledge.

VF Corp. is convinced that brands will dominate the market because consumers will stick with brands they know and trust. New technologies will make the shopping experience more convenient such as using smart cards to carry customer profiles and ring up purchases simply by swiping the card.

Ordering inventory will be automated based upon forecasts from point-of-sale data to eliminate stock-outs. Coordinated efforts between customers and suppliers will require sharing of information for collaborative forecasting, planning, and sourcing. Simulation and modeling technology will allow quick and accurate decision-making based upon impact on profit and loss.

Virtual focus groups, product chat groups, and on-line fashion shows will allow constant and instant communication with consumers. New technologies will make custom-fit production possible.

VF Corp.'s vision of the future embraces new technologies and focuses on managing customer demands and wishes. ■

Dr. Mike Fralix Experience—president, [TC]²

Digital Technologies

"At [TC]² we see the supply chain shifting once again into a new era. The modern day apparel industry started with a focus on mass production, and then went through an era of Quick Response. The focus then moved into an agile manufacturing era, then a mass customization era. The industry is now going beyond mass customization into the digital product supply era. The shift will require new digital technologies to be integrated with existing digital processes.

"Body scanning has become an enabler for digital product development for both mass customization and mass production. It is changing the way we think about fit and standard sizing. It is now feasible to find a fit model for each size in the range for a company's product line, scan them (instead of grading), create custom patterns for each of those fit models, and use the results as the size range for the product line. This creates the ability for a company to segment a population or a brand into its customer profile and provide them a more custom fit because there's no brand that fits every body shape.

"The entire product development process is going digital. It will be used from yarn formation and fabric creation, to designing silhouettes, and then draping those fabrics onto the silhouettes in three-dimensional form. The system will then create the requisite two-dimensional patterns and cut the garments using digitally controlled cutting machines. The apparel retail process is also changing. You will be able to source products from around the world and do it digitally over the Internet.

"The prevalence of Product Data Management (PDM) packages has already impacted the apparel process. You can embed patterns, cost sheets, bills of materials, specifications, fabric information, and trim information all under one set of data that can be accessed and distributed worldwide.

"While in Seoul, Korea, I recently saw two technologies under development. One (being developed in Japan) called a 'magic mirror' allowed a consumer wearing street clothes to stand in front of a mirror and select digital garments. Those garments appeared on the person while they were looking into the mirror. Another technology allowed virtual try-ons by scanning the consumer's face and then putting that face on one of four male or four female body models. They could then enter a virtual department store wearing 3-D glasses and could select and try on garments and see their

(continued)

virtual model in 3-D wearing those garments while walking down a virtual runway.

"In the digital world, product development, the marketing of products, and the interface with the consumer for the digital product are making great strides. Today we are beginning to see simulations that have the appearance of near reality. In the near future we'll be able to take a body scan, create a virtual, morphable body model and drape clothes on it. In addition, the ability to use technologies that were developed for the mass customization world in the mass market world is in sight."

Sourcing

"With the elimination of quotas, predictions indicate that somewhere between 60 percent and 70 percent of U.S. apparel is going to be sourced out of Asia. There is still going to be a substantial need for goods produced in Mexico, Central America, and South America and we are going to see some strengthening of sourcing from Central America over the next few years. We're going to see investments in textiles in Central America so that fabric availability is closer to the region, but we're not going to see it come back in any large degree to the U.S.

"We are beginning to see some changes in manufacturing and production systems to reduce cycle times. We are also seeing off-shore

sourcing partners investing in product development capabilities and taking on more responsibility for managing their customer relationships. They are moving away from being just suppliers of product. On a recent trip to Central America, we saw companies really shifting into value added and embellishments using screen printing or embroidery for high-end products."

Manufacturing

"There's been a real revolution in the apparel industry to reduce cycle times. For many companies the cycle time from fabric ready to cut with an order in hand to completing the order and having it in the warehouse ready to ship is eight weeks. We've seen companies decrease the cycle time to two weeks and in many cases less than a week. It is not uncommon for the cycle time to be 4-5 days from receipt of order to manufacture and ship. We're going to continue to see cycle times decrease until they get down to somewhere close to the cycle time of the product, which I believe will be a day and a half.

"I'd love to see more digital sewing, but I don't think we're anywhere near developing a tactile sensor that can effectively manipulate cloth and fold it, match seams, and control it during the sewing process. Systems that evaluate the mechanical properties of fabrics, like Kawabata and FAST, are being integrated

(*continued*)

into the sewing process so that we can begin to pre-program some components of sewing. Eventually a bar coded bundle ticket will get scanned at a work station and bring up at a terminal a sketch of the product with the quality specs and a detailed description of the particular operation.

"Manufacturing is also becoming more vertical. The world of textile producers, apparel manufacturers, and retailers that existed 20 years ago has changed. After NAFTA, many large textile producers started moving into apparel. Retailers have also blurred the lines by developing and sourcing apparel lines through their own private brands.

"Russell Corporation is completely vertical from fiber through to the finished knit product. In the case of woven products, nobody has been totally successful at controlling the entire supply chain from yarn through weaving, finishing, and cut and sew. On the other hand, joint ventures are being created where the textile mill and the apparel people are combining forces and becoming more partners rather than foes."

Digital Supply Chain

"At [TC]^2, about half of our demonstration is devoted to digital supply chain technologies. Body scanning is an enabling technology for 3-D product development. There has been much advancement in 3-D product development and the research is ongoing. Some of the newest developments relate to digital printing, which is now being used for more than just sampling. In the meantime, more and more companies will be designing and producing high-end digitally printed products. In addition, nano colorants will allow the digital application of solid colors to fabrics, thereby eliminating the need for traditional dye houses and dealing with the resulting effluents.

"Another potential application of nano colorants is coloring sewing thread on demand. While the ultimate would be to color the thread just before it enters the sewing needle, an interim step would be the ability to unwind, color, and rewind cone-to-cone and do that much closer to consumption. This would provide more flexibility for the supply chain and require less inventory of finished thread.

"I believe we are going to be able to apply solid colors digitally but not by using an inkjet print head. Imagine a coloring system that would allow solid colors to be applied to fabric without any pre- or post-treatment and the same colorants could be used on silk or cotton with the same appearance and the same performance results for light fastness, color fastness, and wash fastness. I believe that is where we are headed in the future.

"Great strides have been made in whole garment, full fashion digital knitting in both circular and flat bed knitting machines. They have not yet progressed to the point

(continued)

where I envision them—that is, becoming a plug and play device. Such a machine, where you download a file of a digital garment and convert it to the physical product automatically and seamlessly, is not yet available. One of the current limitations is the ability to change yarn colors.

"When we find an appropriate solution that allows design in 3-D and output in 2-D or 3-D without additional interface from a pattern maker, then a number of technologies will come together to enhance the digital supply chain."

Education

"A university student preparing for a future in the apparel industry can no longer focus on only one aspect of the business and expect to be successful. For example, a merchandising student also must understand sourcing, costing, garment construction, and the manufacturing process. They're also going to need a second language because of the global nature of sourcing. It is not necessary that one be conversant in any particular language other than English. It is more important to develop an appreciation for multi-culturalism and a second language allows one to communicate more effectively in a multi-cultural environment.

"Merchandising, marketing, and sourcing decisions are being made without enough knowledge of the fundamentals of manufacturing and operations. We need to maintain a focus on the basics when we are educating the future leaders of our industry. 'Basics' include an understanding of how pattern pieces go together, construction sequences, and the fundamentals of seams and stitches. This perspective might be surprising coming from someone who deals in high technology, but without the core knowledge, it is difficult to understand the bigger picture.

"There is also a need to better understand and apply technology and computer systems including the Internet, spreadsheets, and database software. The computer has become the primary work tool. A broader understanding of the implications of decisions is also needed, including where products are made and the relationship that has to cost, quality, delivery, and customer service.

"The world of apparel has become much more complex, and to be effective, students must be exposed to all aspects of the supply chain."

Summary

The future of the apparel industry will depend greatly on many factors. No time in the history of humanity has change been as rapid or dramatic as what has taken place in the first decade of the new millennium. It is extremely difficult to predict the exact course of events in the global economy. How will the trading nations of the world respond to the Chinese penetration of markets in the United States and Europe? How will terrorism impact the conduct of global trade? Will the fast pace of global consolidation continue in the apparel and retail industries? Will apparel and retail companies continue to expand into one another's traditional roles as exemplified by retailers increasing their product development activities of private label merchandise, and apparel companies adding to their retailing presence?

One thing is certain, however: the future of the apparel and retail industries will depend greatly upon the development of new technologies. Merchandisers and product managers must learn to use these new technologies to capture and manage information about their target markets, develop products using digital software, virtual systems, and mass customization; collaborate with customers to plan, forecast, and replenish products using interactive data management systems; and get those products made any place in the world that will deliver in the shortest possible time, with the best quality, at the lowest cost, and under humane working conditions.

Key Terms

anthropometric
body scanning
consumercentric
customization

Discussion Questions and Learning Activities

1. What do you believe the greatest challenge facing apparel merchandisers will be in the next 10 years? Explain why.
2. What role will E-commerce through B2B communications have in the future of the apparel industry?
3. What role can new technology play in improving the research function for line development?
4. What impact do CAD/CAM systems have on product development?
5. Which category of garments—basics, seasonal, or fashion—will be impacted most by new technologies and why?
6. Describe two impediments to customization in the apparel industry.

7. Locate three different companies on the Internet that offer customized apparel products and discuss the differences in each company's approach to customization.
8. What technological advancement do you foresee in the next five years that will have the greatest impact on the apparel industry? How will it affect the apparel industry?
9. Describe three uses of technology that improve global sourcing.

References and Resources

Abend, Jules. January 2000. 21st Century Ushers in Greater Technology Optimization. *Bobbin*, p. 54.

Cole, Michael. November 2005. Event Outlook: Technology's Next Frontier on Display at Tech Conference. *Apparel Magazine*. Retrieved November 28, 2005 from www.apparelmag.com/articles/nov/nov05_4.shtml</ref>.

DesMarteau, Kathleen. December 2005. Event Report: Apparel Executive Forum 2005, Forum Explores Supply Chain's Future. *Apparel Magazine*. Retrieved December 2, 2005 from www.apparelmag.com/articles/dec/dec05_1.shtml</ref>.

Kurt Salmon Associates/Textile Clothing Technology Corporation. August 8, 1997. Mass Customization: A Key Initiative of Quick Response. *Research Study*.

Malone, Scott. March 24, 1999. Cut It Out. *Women's Wear Daily*, pp. 24–25.

Textile Clothing Technology Corporation. June 2000. *The US National Size Survey*. Retrieved November 24, 2005 from www.tc2.com/what/sizeUSA/index.html.

Vitzthum, Carlta. May 18, 2001. Just-in-Time Fashion. *The Wall Street Journal*, pp. B1–B4.

Glossary

abnormal variations Measurements of the manufacturing process that fall outside the normal distribution curve.

absorption costing A method of costing that allocates fixed manufacturing overhead to each unit of production along with variable manufacturing costs. This method of costing absorbs all fixed and variable manufacturing costs into the cost of goods, which is used to establish inventory values.

acceptable quality level (AQL) The maximum number of each type of defect allowed before a garment is rejected.

accounting costing A measure of the actual costs derived from the cost control process of accounting used to create a company's financial statements.

active sportswear or **activewear** Functional as well as stylish clothing designed to improve the performance or comfort of the wearer while participating in a particular sport or activity.

activity-based costing A multistage costing process in which the manufacturing overhead and the general operating expenses are assigned to multiple cost pools rather than being assigned directly to departments. The cost pools are created for each activity that generates cost and then are assigned to garments styles based upon their use of these cost pools.

Ad Valorem A percentage charged in proportion to product value.

additive primary colors The colors red, green, and blue produced from emitted light.

adjusted gross margin (AGM) The gross margin minus inventory carrying costs and distribution costs.

African Growth and Opportunity Act (AGOA) An act that was signed by President Clinton in 2000 that provided preferential treatment to 35 designated countries in Sub-Saharan Africa. If apparel is made from U.S.A. fabric, yarn, and thread, it will have duty and quota free access to the markets of the United States.

alternate marketing Increasing market share or developing new products or new markets for an apparel company.

amendment A correction, revision, or change in a letter of credit.

anthropometric Concerned with the measurement and study of the parts and capacities of the human body.

apparel Clothing or attire.

apparel merchandising The development, execution, and delivery of an apparel product line based upon the needs of a target market.

apparel sector Companies that develop, manufacture, and distribute garments to the retail sector.

appearance retention An apparel product maintaining its original appearance and shape during use, storage, and care.

assortment plan A retailer's plan which first determines the dollar amount and quantities that should be invested in each classification, and then refines these figures into specific styles and indicates when they should be in stock on a monthly basis.

automated sewing systems Robotics used to transfer highly skilled human functions to machines.

B2B (business-to-business) Transactions performed over the Internet between businesses.

B2C (business-to-consumer) Transactions performed over the Internet between businesses and consumers.

balance The equal distribution of visual weight on a garment.

bill of materials Detailed listings of material requirements for each style.

binding ruling A customs ruling issued by customs headquarters in Washington, D.C. that prevents any possibility that the classification of imports will be changed.

blended costing The process of blending all the costs for manufacturing garments in all optional sourcing locations together into one cost formula.

blended sourcing Producing apparel styles at a far distant contractor to achieve lowest cost while producing the same styles at domestic, Mexican, or Caribbean Basin contractors to provide quick delivery for reorders.

blocks Sets of patterns for each basic garment type.

body scanning Technology that allows fast and accurate body measurements to be taken using a laser, white light, or other light source to illuminate the body, and cameras or sensors capture either specific body measurements or a three-dimensional digital image of the body.

bow Crosswise yarns arc as they go across the fabric.

care A product's response to the recommended procedures for cleaning.

care label A label on each article of apparel that must remain legible during the useful life of the garment with instructions on how to care for the garment. These instructions must provide warnings if a garment cannot be cleaned without harm to the product and, if followed, will cause no substantial harm to the product.

Caribbean Basin Trade Partnership Act (CBTPA) A law signed by President Clinton in 2002 that entitled Belize, Costa Rica, Dominican Republic, El Salvador, Guyana, Haiti, Honduras, Jamaica, Nicaragua, Panama, Trinidad, and Tobago to the same preferential tariff treatment granted to Canada and Mexico under NAFTA.

cash flow A statement of changes in a company's cash position.

Central America-Dominican Republic-United States Free Trade Agreement (CAFTA-DR) A law passed by Congress in July 2005 that entitles the Central American countries of Costa Rica, El Salvador, Guatemala, Honduras, Nicaragua, and the Dominican Republic to the same preferential tariff treatment as those granted to Canada and Mexico under NAFTA.

channel of distribution The process that moves products from the producer to the ultimate consumer.

collaborative planning, forecasting, and replenishment (CPFR) A shared action and responsibility model for apparel manufacturers and their retail quick response partners.

collection A term frequently used in Europe and by higher-priced designer and couture businesses for an apparel product line.

color story The array of color choices available for each garment style.

colorway The array of color choices available for each garment style.

comfort How the body feels in response to a garment.

computer-aided design (CAD) Computer systems used to create full color renderings of new design ideas, complete with draped fabric prints or woven designs.

computer-controlled cutting systems Automated cutting machines that are controlled by computer systems.

concept boards Large presentation boards that are created for themes; they contain photos, magazine clippings, 3-D elements, or sketches depicting the theme concept along with color palettes, fabric swatches, and stylized silhouette sketches.

conceptualization The ability to quickly and effectively visualize new styling ideas and communicate the concepts.

constant percentage sample The fixed percentage of a production lot that is inspected, no matter how many garments are in production.

consumer panels A select group of consumers that provides information on a continuing basis.

consumercentric A focus on giving the customers exactly what they want.

continuous production sample A sampling process used when there is continuous production of a style over a long period of time.

contract procedures manual A written list of all the steps to be followed and issues that must be addressed in the external sourcing function.

contractor evaluation form A form that lists an inventory of equipment, operator skills assessments, and production capacities that can be used to help an executive analyze the capabilities of a contractor.

contrast Use of dramatically different design elements to emphasize and attract the attention of the observer.

cost accounting An accounting system that maintains records of the cost of production and distribution.

cost of goods Cost of goods includes all costs required to produce a garment.

costing Estimating the associated costs for each style.

costing for sale A detailed calculation of the costs required to manufacture a style based upon available data.

count The number of yarns in the lengthwise and crosswise direction of the fabric (for woven materials the warp is listed first).

creation Developing finished garment styles that meet the expectations set forth in the conceptualization stage through an efficient design process.

creativity The ability to visualize a concept that will capture the essence of a consumer's buying urge.

critical defect A defect that would cause harm to the wearer when the garment is either worn or maintained.

critical path method (CPM) Determining the critical functions necessary to perform an activity or series of activities required to achieve an overall objective.

croquis Drawings of body silhouettes.

customization The process of personalizing a garment by manufacturing it to an individual's specific body measurements or other specifications such as silhouette, fabric, color, and embellishments.

Customs-Trade Partnership Against Terrorism (CTPAT) A partnership between U.S. Customs and Border Patrol and global trading companies who volunteer to secure their supply chains and facilitate the movement of legitimate cargo.

cut See *gauge*.

cut, make, and trim (CMT) The cost to cut, sew, and finish a garment including the cost of trim.

data mining Use of a variety of data analysis tools to discover patterns and relationships in customer and product data that may be used to make valid predictions.

data warehouses Databases with massive amounts of digital data about a company's products and sales.

dating The process of delaying payment for a specific time period.

delaminate Separate from the fabric shell.

demand-activated manufacturing architecture (DAMA) A collaborative research consortium of soft goods industry members, Department of Energy national laboratories, other federal agencies, textile universities, and industry associations to work on shrinking the supply chain, which links the U.S. fiber, textile, sewn products, and retail industries.

demographic Related to statistics of human populations.

designers People who interpret the concepts communicated by stylists into actual garments.

direct costing A method of costing that applies only the variable costs directly related to labor and materials as product costs or cost of goods. All other costs such as nonvariable factory expenses, marketing, product development, and general and administrative costs are allocated through gross margins as either a fixed cost per garment or as a target gross margin percentage.

direct labor Those costs related to changes in the condition or physical appearance of raw materials.

direct materials Fabric, thread, trim, and findings.

discrepancy Any difference between the documentation required by a letter of credit and the documentation presented.

documents against payment or acceptance Nonguaranteed forms of payment usually used when a sourcer does not want to tie up its finances for an extended period of time or cannot open a letter of credit because of financial problems.

draping The process of cutting, shaping, and draping fabric on a dress form or mannequin, thus allowing the designer to evaluate the way a fabric performs when it is shaped to conform to a three-dimensional silhouette.

durability The time a garment can be used for its intended purpose before it wears out. *Fabric durability* refers to strength and structural integrity such as resistance to abrasion, pilling, snagging, and color permanence.

duty A tax charged by a government on imports.

807 The original U.S. Customs category that allows garments to be cut in the United States from U.S. textiles and assembled in a foreign country with duty charged only on the value added in the foreign country.

electronic data interchange (EDI) The transfer of information between computers.

electronic funds transfer (EFT) Payment made for a shipment by the transfer of funds from bank to bank when time is of the essence.

electronic product code (EPC) Assigns an individual number to each item providing virtually unlimited identifying facts that differentiate one item from another.

emphasis The design principle that directs the viewer's attention to a specific area of a garment.

end ship date The last date that a season's orders can be shipped without incurring discounts or penalties from retailers.

enterprise resource planning (ERP) A software system that integrates key business and management processes and tracks company financial data, human resource data, and all manufacturing information including inventory management.

execution Getting products of excellent quality made at the right time and for the right price.

executive line reviews Analyses of the line during line development by executive committee; which is designed to keep the line development process on track and determine as soon as possible if the design team is deviating from the merchandiser's intended styling direction.

Fabric and Suppliers Linkage Council (FASLINC) A council created to improve communications and cooperation between textile companies and their fiber suppliers.

fabric-driven A design process in which companies base their lines around fabric and print design. The designers start by selecting fabrics and then create silhouettes for those fabrics.

factory throughput time Work-in-process divided by the average number of units produced in a time period.

fast fashion A supply chain initiative that collapses the cycle time required to create, develop, execute, and deliver an apparel product to the selling floor to three weeks or less.

fiber sector The agro-industry sector that produces natural fibers and the petrochemical sector that produces manufactured fibers also known as man-made or synthetic fibers.

final costing A detailed calculation of the costs required to manufacture a style based upon available data.

final line adoption The final selection of styles that will become part of a product line or collection by a company adoption committee made up of key executives.

financial accounting Accounting procedures that provide financial information to stockholders, creditors, and others who are *outside* an organization.

findings Functional nonfabric items such as zippers.

findings sector The manufacturers of a broad range of products that are integral to apparel production, such as buttons, zippers, labels, interfacings, pads, hook and loop fasteners, and thread.

fit model A model who has body measurements equal to those of the company's target market consumer.

flat pattern The process of altering basic pattern blocks or slopers to achieve the desired silhouette.

focus groups A cross section of consumers from a specific target market who meet with market research professionals to discuss their preferences.

free on board (FOB) Ownership for goods is transferred as designated [*FOB factory* means ownership is transferred when the goods are loaded on a transporting vehicle and the buyer (sourcer) is responsible for shipping costs. *FOB distribution center* means ownership is transferred when the goods arrive at the destination and the contractor is responsible for shipping costs].

frequency distribution A definite pattern created by normal measurements.

full-package sourcing Contracting to purchase a style where the contractor provides fabrics, trims, supplies, and labor.

fusibles Fabrics in which resin dots are applied with heat and pressed to the outer fabric.

Gantt chart A series of parallel horizontal graphs which show schedules for functions plotted against time.

garment pricing The calculation and determination of a wholesale selling price for a garment style that will meet the needs and expectations of customers and generate the intended profit for the company.

garment specifications Lists of raw materials, patterns, cutting instructions, construction guidelines, finished garment measurements, and quality expectations.

gauge For knit fabrics, the number of needles per inch in the knitting machine.

general and administrative expenses (G&A) All costs over and above those included in the total cost of goods of a product.

General Agreement on Tariffs and Trade (GATT) An agreement by 116 signatory nations designed to minimize trade barriers by reducing import quotas and tariffs and abolishing preferential trade agreements among member countries.

general operating expenses All costs over and above those included in the total cost of goods of a product.

Gestalt psychology The concept of perception, with the eye and brain defining visual images as a pattern or a whole rather than the sum of finite component parts.

global sourcing The contracting of production to factories in all parts of the world.

grade rules The formula for creating patterns of every size from the initial sample size patterns.

gross margin (GM) Net sales minus the total cost of goods sold.

gross margin return on inventory (GMROI) Gross margin divided by the average inventory investment.

Harmonized Tariff Schedule of the United States Annotated (HTS) The government list of duty rates on textile and apparel products by category.

harmony The combined result of the individual elements of design and their integration through the effective use of design principles.

hue The dimension of color that is referred to a scale of perceptions that ranges from red through yellow, green and blue, and circularly back to red.

income statement The financial statement that relates the company's sales revenues to the expenses resulting in a profit or loss for a specific period.

industry standard A standard adopted by an entire industry.

inspiration boards Large presentation boards that are created for themes; they contain photos, magazine clippings, 3-D elements, or sketches depicting the theme concept along with color palettes, fabric swatches, and stylized silhouette sketches.

integrated textile complex (ITC) The soft goods supply chain including fiber, yarn, textile, and apparel producers.

intensity The strength or weakness of color determined by its saturation or vividness of hue.

inventory carrying costs The costs to maintain inventories, such as interest charges on capital needed to purchase the materials and labor expended on inventory and the overhead expenses created by the space required to support inventory.

inventory turns The annual value of total inventory created divided by the average value of inventory throughout the year.

irrevocable letter of credit The most common kind of letter of credit in which the issuing bank forwards the letter of credit to the export contractor's bank (beneficiary), with a commitment to pay upon presentation by the export contractor of specified export documents as listed clearly in the letter of credit.

irrevocable standby letter of credit A letter of credit triggered by nonpayment by the sourcer instead of being triggered by performance by the beneficiary such as submission of all documentation required for payment. This type of letter of credit is usually used in domestic transactions.

isolation Placement of a styling element apart from other elements.

just-in-time (JIT) The purchasing and scheduling of raw materials programmed for delivery as close to their required usage as possible.

labor-intensive Requiring a large expenditure of labor in comparison to capital.

landed duty paid (LDP) The cost of a garment including the price paid to the contract manufacturer for the full package of labor and materials, plus the freight cost to get the product from the foreign factory to the U.S. distribution center, plus import duty charges and any associated brokerage expenses.

latent defect A defect that cannot be seen through normal testing and inspection and will become apparent only over the course of time.

letters of credit (L/Cs) Financial agreements between the sourcer (buyer) and its bank (issuing bank) to transfer responsibility for paying the seller (foreign contractor) to the issuing bank.

licensee A company that has the right to use intellectual property such as a designer name, brand name, or design owned by the licensor in return for payment of royalties to the licensor.

licensing An agreement for a licensee to use intellectual property such as a designer name, brand name, or design owned by the licensor in return for payment of royalties to the licensor.

licensor A company that agrees to allow a licensee to use its intellectual property such as a brand name or design in return for payment of royalties.

line The path the eye follows when viewing a garment.

line A group of styles produced for delivery during a specific time period.

line development The creation of a group of garment styles presented by apparel companies to their customers for sale and delivery during a specific time period.

line plan A detailed chart by product category of the number of styles, fabrics, colors, and sizes that should be included in a line.

line plan summary A written plan that establishes the number of fabrics, styles, constructions, and stock keeping units (SKUs) in a line by product group.

line preview date The date when management will review proposed styles to determine which ones will be adopted into the line.

line release date The date when the line will be available for sale to retailers.

line sheet A form for each style group in a line plan with space allocated for the number of styles planned for the group and sketches of each style with fabric swatches and pertinent prototype information.

liquidation Verifying classification, valuation, and payment of duties by U.S. customs.

Long Term Arrangement (LTA) An agreement permitting bilateral quotas adopted by GATT (General Agreement on Tariffs and Trade) members, establishing formal mechanisms for voluntary restraint agreements on the flow of cotton textile exports.

lot-by-lot sampling Selection of samples from each production lot.

major defect A defect that detracts from the attractiveness or the performance of a garment as with the misalignment or the malfunction of parts such as buttons and buttonholes.

mall intercepts At a mall, interviewers stop shoppers who fit a market segment profile and ask them to participate in a short survey.

managerial accounting The accounting process concerned with providing information to *managers*—that is, to those who are *inside* an organization and who are charged with directing and controlling its operations.

mandatory standard A standard required by statute.

maintained (margin) markup The final markup that is based upon all of the merchandise that has been sold at all prices compared to the cost of the merchandise.

manufacturing overhead All the costs of manufacturing except direct materials and direct labor.

manufacturing resource planning (MRP) Manufacturing specific software systems that focused on inventory management and tracking manufacturing systems.

mapping Indicating the location of holes, cuts, misprints, shade variances, and minimum widths of fabric.

maquiladoras Mexican companies that can be 100 percent foreign-owned, but are restricted to assembling foreign merchandise for immediate export.

markdown The reduction of the original wholesale or retail price.

market knowledge The comprehensive understanding of a company's market and products.

market segmentation Redefining a target market into smaller, more specialized segments.

market share The percent of the total sales that a company generates in a product category.

marketing calendar The basis for other company planning; it establishes the line preview date, line release date, sales plan, and shipping plan.

markup (gross margin) Net sales minus the total cost of goods sold.

master production plans A report showing, by style, the fabric needs by time period per available factory production capacity.

material utilization The percentage of fabric utilized in cutting garment parts.

materials management The planning, ordering, and follow-up of delivery and utilization of materials.

mechanical properties The properties of fabric created by the forces generated by the interaction of the fibers, yarns, and the fabric structure such as stretch, slipperiness, stiffness, compressibility, abrasion resistance, shear, bendability, and tensile strength.

merchandising To buy and sell commodities for a profit.

merchandising calendar The primary control tool in an apparel company. It establishes responsibilities for, and sets forth, starting dates and deadlines for completion of all key events for a season.

merchandising plan A plan developed by retailers to forecast sales by category within a specific time period.

metameric The effect created by different lighting such as fluorescent, incandescent, or natural sunlight causing fabric colors to take on different hues.

microfibers Modified, extremely fine, denier synthetic yarns that often have the feel and functionality of natural fibers.

minimum order quantities Smallest order quantity most textile companies require for each style and color of fabrics purchased.

minor defect A defect that will not affect greatly the intended use or the performance of a garment.

model stocks Desired inventory stocking levels for retail stores.

modular manufacturing systems (MMS) Operations requiring similar skills are grouped together in circular or arced stand-up sewing modules in which the sewing machines are raised so that operators can operate them standing up and the operators can easily move from machine to machine within the module.

most-favored-nation (MFN) A participating country's exports to another participating country are charged the lowest tariff rates available to any nation.

Multi-Fiber Arrangement (MFA) An agreement reached in 1974 by the members of the General Agreement on Tariffs and Trade, which allows industrialized nations to negotiate bilateral agreements with developing countries in order to control the rate of growth of textile and apparel imports.

net income The excess of revenues earned over the related costs incurred for an accounting period.

nonbinding ruling A customs classification set by an import specialist at a specific port (a quick response if time is of the essence). Under a nonbinding ruling the classification could be changed when the first shipment arrives in the United States for customs clearance.

nondurable goods Those products that have a short utility and must be replaced periodically.

normal distribution curve The curve created when most of the measurements of variations of a company's process or products fall close to the middle of the range of variations.

normal variation A variation that is a natural occurrence because no two products or processes are exactly the same.

offshore assembly (807 program) A paragraph published over 30 years ago in the Tariff Schedule of the United States Annotated (TSUSA), which allows components cut in the United States to be shipped offshore for assembly and then returned to the United States without incurring duties on the components.

open account The least used method of payment for international transactions. It is the riskiest for the export contractor since the contractor relinquishes control of the goods with only a promise to pay based upon terms of net payment due in 30, 60, 90, or 180 days.

open-to-buy The dollar amount a buyer can spend on purchases for a specific delivery period minus the dollar amount allocated to orders not yet delivered.

patent defect A defect that can be detected by examination, inspection, or testing.

payment terms The discount that is given if the total invoice amount is paid within a specified time period.

personal, fatigue, and delay (PF&D) Allowances for personal time, for reduction in production performance due to fatigue, and for normally expected work delays.

piece rate A payment of a fixed price for piece produced by workers.

placement The prominent positioning of a styling element or garment part that creates emphasis in a design.

point-of-sale The location, typically at the cash register, where a retail transaction takes place.

pragmatic forecasting Applying a merchandiser's experience to computer forecasting and style ranking to create adjusted projections.

precosting Estimating the manufacturing cost of a new style.

preproduction cycle The process of preparing a style for production including the development of production patterns and garment specifications.

pre-season planning The activity that coordinates product development and sales expectations with material purchases and production capacities.

pricing Establishing the wholesale selling price for each garment style in the line.

private brands A category of apparel that completely commits to a certain lifestyle and a specific consumer demographic. It has its own design integrity and identity.

private label Product development and production done directly by retailers.

product development The process of creating each individual style within the line.

product engineering Analysis of a style to determine whether any pattern adjustments or construction changes can reduce the cost of producing the style while still achieving the desired design results.

production costing The measure of actual variable manufacturing expenses for labor and materials.

production cycle The process of cutting, sewing, and finishing garments.

profit and loss statement The financial statement that relates a company's sales revenues to its expenses resulting in a profit or loss for a specific period.

proportion The relationship between the garment as a whole and the size and placement of parts and shapes.

prototype The first sample made to evaluate a new silhouette or fabric. The prototype is the first critical opportunity for the product development team to see an actual garment style and try it on a fit model.

prototyping The creation of the initial sample of a style in the actual fabric or a muslin for evaluation purposes.

pull-through marketing Promotion designed to get customers to search out and request products.

qualitative research Research that seeks open-ended responses to questions.

quantitative research Research that seeks responses to questions that can be summarized by objective, statistical results such as percentages, averages, or degrees of agreement or disagreement.

quick response (QR) A business strategy that is designed to promote responsiveness to rapidly changing consumer demand.

quickie costing Preliminary cost estimates used by merchandisers to evaluate different style alternatives during the early stages of product development (also called quick costing).

quotas An annual limit on the number of units, kilograms, or square meters equivalent (SME) of imported products by category for each country.

radio frequency identification (RFID) The use of radio waves to transmit digital information.

random sample A sample taken when each garment in the production of a style has an equal chance of being examined regardless of size, color, and so on.

real time Reference to actual point at which information is created or changed.

registration numbers (RNs) Numbers issued by the U.S. Federal Trade Commission to apparel manufacturers that must be listed on each of their product's garment or care label.

repetition The repeated use of a design element to create a unified look in a garment.

representative sample A sample that includes all sizes, colors, and other variations.

required departmental markup The required markup for the department that establishes the profit that must be generated after deducting the costs of the merchandise and the cost of all other expenses.

retail fashion merchandising The buying of apparel products and the selling of these products to the ultimate consumer for a profit.

retail sector The businesses that merchandise, promote, display, and sell products to the consumer.

rhythm A sense of movement and continuity created by repetition.

roving inspection An inspection process in which the inspector randomly goes from one sewing operator to another looking for the operation's correct seam allowance, the proper number of stitches per inch, the proper alignment of parts, and critical specifications.

sales forecasts Sales projection by category, style, color, and size based on historical data and statistical analysis.

scale The relationship between the garment as a whole and the size and placement of parts and shapes.

seasons Merchandising cycles that provide product offerings for sale at specific times of the year.

sell-through The percentage of items purchased from a specific manufacturer that are sold to consumers during a specific period of time.

shades The darkest values—colors mixed with black.

shading Color deviations.

shape An enclosed space or boundary produced in two or three dimensions.

shelf stock plan A plan of the styles and quantities by color and size that should be in stock on a weekly basis.

shippability Determination of whether or not a sufficient mix of SKUs are available to meet customer order minimum shipping requirements.

shippable-mix A complete assortment of styles required for a typical sales order including all sizes and colors for each style.

short interval scheduling (SIS) A strategy that establishes tight production control systems to decrease work-in-process inventories, thereby creating a leaner manufacturing process.

silhouette The three-dimensional outline or shape of a garment.

silhouette-driven A design process in which the designer creates silhouettes and then selects fabrics that are compatible with the silhouettes.

size scale The ratio of sales per size for a style.

skew When the filling yarn forms some angle other than 90 degrees with the warp.

skip-lot sampling Examination of selected production lots once a consistent level of quality has been proven over a period of time, when a high level of production has been reached, or when the same materials, construction, or design have been used.

slopers Sets of patterns for each basic garment type produced by a company.

soft goods supply chain The system that provides the raw materials and processes for getting textiles and apparel products from concept to consumer.

sourcing The process of deciding where and how to manufacture a product.

sourcing agent One who arranges an agreement with a contractor to produce products for a company in return for a commission.

sourcing simulator A stand-alone PC tool to enable retailer buyers to quickly and easily analyze factors affecting sourcing decisions.

Special Regime Program 807a Paragraph 9802.00.90 of the U.S. Harmonized Tariff Schedule created in 1986 that allows garments made from parts cut in the United States and made of fabric formed in the United States to qualify for guaranteed access to the United States.

specification sheet The document that communicates specifications both inside and outside the company.

specification (spec) writers Individuals who are specially trained to write specifications.

specifications Exact expectations that must be met in a product or by a service.

standard allowed minutes The time required for an average operator, fully qualified and trained and working at a normal pace, to perform an operation.

standard test methods Test methods approved by standards organizations such as the American Society of Testing and Materials and the American Association of Textile Chemists and Colorists.

standardization The process of developing and applying rules to establish consistency in the performance of a specific activity.

standards Descriptions of acceptable levels of performance.

start ship date The first date when a season's orders can begin to be shipped to retailers.

stationary inspection A method of inspection in which garment parts are brought to the inspector who visually assesses the critical points at a well-lit and properly equipped inspection station.

statistical process control (SPC) The application of statistics and control charts to monitor variations in the manufacturing process.

stock keeping unit (SKU) A garment inventory unit identified by style, color, and size.

storyboards Large presentation boards that are created for themes; they contain photos, magazine clippings, 3-D elements, or sketches depicting the theme concept along with color palettes, fabric swatches, and stylized silhouette sketches.

strategic planning Identifying where and how a company's resources should be allocated.

style An identifiable garment produced in a specific silhouette or body from a specific fabric and trims.

style number The alphanumeric code used to identify a garment style.

style ranking A forecasting system that uses key company personnel to rank styles from the top seller to the styles projected to generate the least sales.

style sales report A report developed and maintained by a retailer to indicate inventory on hand, inventory on order, sales for the past one, two, or three weeks, and sales-to-date. It alerts the buyer to the need to take action.

style status report A report showing actual sales versus forecasts, authorized fabric purchases and receipts, and authorized production for each style.

styling consultants Consultants who perform market and styling research and summarize the results in customized reports for a merchandiser.

styling services Services that may utilize large staffs located in key geographical areas to perform market and styling research and summarize the results in customized reports for a merchandiser.

stylists Individuals who create the styling concepts and theme directions for each line.

subjective pricing Pricing according to what the market will bear.

subtractive primary colors Hues that affect our perception of fabrics, which absorb light, are the subtractive (or pigment) primary colors yellow, blue, and red. When equal quantities of the subtractive primary colors are combined, the result is black.

Sundries and Apparel Findings Linkage Council (SAFLINC) A council of apparel companies and their trim and findings suppliers created to establish EDI standards to improve communications and product identification between their industry sectors.

supplier certification See **vendor certification**.

supply chain The system that provides the raw materials and processes necessary to get apparel products from concept to consumers.

support structure Personnel and service costs required to import products.

target market The ultimate consumers who will purchase a company's products, usually a homogeneous group of customers to whom a company wishes to appeal.

tariff A duty imposed by a government on imported or exported goods.

technical drawings Flat line drawings of a garment showing design details and special manufacturing instructions.

telex transfer (TT) The transfers of funds through a bank via telex.

Textile Apparel Linkage Council (TALC) A council established to develop voluntary standards to support quick response and just-in-time delivery between textile and apparel companies.

textile sector The businesses involved in yarn preparation, weaving or knitting, and fabric dyeing and finishing.

texture Surface variations of fabric that can be used as an effective element of design.

theory of constraints (TOC) A portfolio of management philosophies, management disciplines, and industry-specific "best practices."

tints The lightest values—colors mixed with white.

tolerances A range of acceptable quality values.

tones Darker values—colors mixed with gray.

total quality management (TQM) The process of directing all of a company's activities toward delivering a quality product to satisfy its target market and at the same time reaching its own business objectives.

total throughput time The time for a production order to be processed from authorization to shipping.

trading company A company that sources apparel production with an offshore contractor, opens the letter of credit, imports the garments, and sells them to an apparel firm for a profit.

transshipping One country shipping sewn products to another country where the goods are labeled and shipped under the second country's quota allotment.

trend boards Large presentation boards that are created for themes; they contain photos, magazine clippings, 3-D elements, or sketches depicting the theme concept along with color palettes, fabric swatches, and stylized silhouette sketches.

understanding Acquiring and maintaining a thorough sense of the market and target customer by the line development team.

Uniform Code Council (UCC) The administrative council that oversees issuance of manufacturer identification numbers and assists in implementing bar-code systems.

unit production systems (UPS) A manufacturing system in which an overhead conveyor carries the components for a single garment from operation to operation, thereby reducing handling time.

Universal Product Code (UPC) A twelve-digit number that identifies the product category, manufacturer, and merchandise item.

value The variation of light strength in a color. White is the total presence of light, and black is the total absence of light.

value added Any activity, over and above the direct cost of producing a garment, that adds to the value of the garment.

variable costing A method of costing that applies only the variable costs directly related to labor and materials as product costs or cost of goods. All other costs such as nonvariable factory expenses, marketing, product development, and general and administrative costs are allocated through gross margins as either a fixed cost per garment or as a target gross margin percentage.

vendor certification A formal certification between a buyer and seller that reduces the need for material inspections.

vendor-managed inventories (VMI) A high-level forecasting strategy used by some quick response partners in which dynamic model stocks or desired inventory stocking levels for retail stores and agreed upon replenishment procedures are used to control and rapidly replenish retail inventories by the apparel manufacturer thereby diminishing forecasting errors.

vertical integration Establishment of operations or joint ventures for apparel assembly by fiber and textile companies.

vertical retailers Retailers that develop and manufacture their own private label product lines.

videoconference A fast, efficient method of audiovisual communications over the Internet or through direct communications over high-speed digital phone lines.

Voluntary Interindustry Commerce Standard (VICS) An association established by retail, apparel, and textile firms to institute standards for product marking, computer-to-computer communications, and shipping container marking.

voluntary standard A standard that individual companies choose to develop and follow.

weekly sales plan A barometer for the sales department, financial planning, and manufacturing schedules. This plan shows season-to-date as well as sales statistics for a specific weekly or monthly time period.

weekly shipping plan A barometer for manufacturing, product sourcing, and finance. This plan shows season-to-date as well as shipping statistics for a specific weekly or monthly time period.

whole cost method Method of costing that absorbs all fixed and variable manufacturing costs into the cost of goods, which is used to establish inventory values.

wholesale net selling price The price, including discount, the manufacturer charges the retailer or wholesaler for each garment.

wholesale selling price The price the manufacturer charges the retailer or wholesaler for each garment.

wire transfer (WT) The transfers of funds through a bank via wire.

wool products label (WPL) Numbers (issued from 1941 to 1959 under the Wool Products Identification Act) that may still be found on many wool products.

work-in-process (WIP) The number of garments cut, but not finished and available for shipping.

Appendix

In order to accurately define the responsibilities of the position of merchandiser in an apparel company, a survey was conducted in 1994 involving over six hundred and seventy-five companies. Sixty-nine apparel companies responded and their answers are tabulated below according to their specific industry segment. If a company targeted more than one industry segment, their answers are represented in the row titled "multiple." The row titled "all" has the responses from all sixty-nine companies.

A second survey was conducted in 2002-2003 to see if the role and responsibilities of the merchandiser had changed in response to seven years of dramatic restructuring in the apparel industry as it responded to the retailer's demand for rapid replenishment, the consumer's desire for constant style change, the great advances in the application of technology, the increased consolidation of companies, and the rush to offshore outsourcing.

Over 700 surveys were sent to the members of the American Apparel and Footwear Association and a sampling of those apparel companies listed in the databases of OneSource Information Services and Harris InfoSource with sales in excess of two million dollars. Forty-three responses were tabulated and the mean and standard deviation calculated for each activity. In addition, the results were subjected to the "t" and "Chi Square" tests that established if any differences between the two surveys were statistically significant. To make the comparison between the 1995 and 2002-2003 surveys more meaningful, the results were analyzed from all respondents taken together as a group and not by industry segments.

In collaboration with Professor Doreen Burdalski, Coordinator of the Fashion Management Program at Philadelphia University, a companion survey was conducted in 2002-2003 for the purposes of comparing the role and responsibilities of merchandisers in an apparel company with product managers who create, develop, and execute private label apparel products in a retail organization. The questionnaire was mailed to 526 retailers in the United States from a list obtained from a database compiled by CareerSearch.net. This company compiles standardized data collected and formatted from major publishers of directories of approximately 30 major industry categories. The information is updated at least yearly, but in many cases quarterly. Surveys were sent only to the top executives listed in the database. The list of retailers in this database was limited to SIC codes 5311, Department Stores, and SIC code 56, Apparel Chain Stores. Forty-four retailers responded and of these 42 were used in this study. Twenty-nine of the 42 retailers actually carried private label merchandise. The results were tabulated, the mean and standard deviation calculated for each activity, and then subjected to the "t" and "Chi Square" tests. The findings are presented in the last study with the replies from apparel companies appearing in the row marked "A" and retail organizations in the row marked "R."

A. Please check the appropriate degree of responsibility the merchandiser has in your organization for the following activities:

1. defining the target market

	sole	major	equal	minor	none
all	3.1%	40.0%	41.5%	15.4%	0%
multiple	0	26.1	43.5	30.4	0
men	5.9	47.1	41.2	5.9	0
women	0	50.0	41.7	8.3	0
children	7.7	46.2	38.5	7.7	0

2. research of the target market

	sole	major	equal	minor	none
all	3.1%	47.7%	29.2%	18.5%	1.5%
multiple	4.3	43.5	13.0	39.1	0
men	5.9	52.9	35.3	5.9	0
women	0	41.71	50.0	8.3	0
children	0	53.8	30.8	7.7	7.7

3. knowledge of the marketplace

a. fashion forecasts of silhouettes, colors, fabrics, and trims

	sole	major	equal	minor	none
all	20.0%	66.2%	7.7%	4.6%	1.5%
multiple	26.1	60.9	8.7	4.3	0
men	23.5	64.7	5.9	5.9	5.9
women	8.3	75.0	16.7	0	0
children	15.4	69.2	7.7	7.7	0

b. current consumer preferences for silhouettes, colors, fabrics, and trims

	sole	major	equal	minor	none
all	15.4%	67.7%	13.8%	1.5%	1.5%
multiple	17.4	65.2	17.4	0	0
men	29.4	64.7	0	0	5.9
women	0	83.3	16.7	0	0
children	7.7	61.5	23.1	7.7	0

c. direction and performance of competitors

	sole	major	equal	minor	none
all	1.6%	54.0%	31.7%	9.5%	3.5%
multiple	0	47.8	34.8	17.4	0
men	6.3	56.6	25.0	6.3	6.3
women	0	54.5	45.5	0	0
children	0	61.5	23.1	7.7	7.7

4. planning and control of the merchandising process

a. develop a merchandising calendar

	sole	major	equal	minor	none
all	30.8%	53.8%	10.8%	1.5%	3.1%
multiple	43.5	47.8	8.7	0	0
men	23.5	70.6	0	0	5.9
women	25.0	50.0	25.0	0	0
children	23.1	46.2	15.4	7.7	7.7

b. develop a line plan summary

	sole	major	equal	minor	none
all	43.8%	35.9%	18.8%	1.6%	0%
multiple	56.5	30.4	13.0	0	0
men	52.9	35.3	11.8	0	0
women	25.0	41.7	33.3	0	0
children	25.0	41.7	25.0	8.3	0

c. develop a shelf stock plan

	sole	major	equal	minor	none
all	8.1%	25.8%	25.8%	21.0%	19.4%
multiple	4.3	17.4	26.1	30.4	21.7
men	18.8	37.5	18.8	0	25.0
women	8.3	33.3	33.3	16.7	8.3
children	0	18.2	27.3	36.4	18.2

d. other

	sole	major	equal	minor	none
all	12.5%	25.0%	62.5%	0%	0%
multiple	0	0	0	4.3	4.3
men	5.9	5.9	0	0	0
women	0	8.3	0	16.7	75
children	0	33.3	0	66.7	0

5. line development

a. conduct research

	sole	major	equal	minor	none
all	12.3%	64.6%	18.5%	4.6%	0%
multiple	13.0	65.2	13.0	8.7	0
men	23.5	58.8	17.6	0	0
women	0	75.0	16.7	8.3	0
children	7.7	61.5	30.8	0	0

b. direct designing activities

	sole	major	equal	minor	none
all	38.1%	33.3%	20.6%	3.2%	4.8%
multiple	45.5	27.3	18.2	4.5	4.5
men	41.2	35.3	17.6	5.9	0
women	16.7	25.0	41.7	0	16.7
children	41.7	50.0			

c. coordinate designing activities

	sole	major	equal	minor	none
all	40.6%	35.9%	12.5%	7.8%	3.1%
multiple	52.2	26.1	13.0	4.3	4.3
men	35.3	47.1	11.8	5.9	0
women	25.0	25.0	16.7	25.0	8.3
children	41.7	50.0	8.3	0	0

d. select raw materials

	sole	major	equal	minor	none
all	23.4%	37.5%	28.1%	7.8%	3.1%
multiple	34.8	30.4	30.4	0	4.3
men	35.3	47.1	5.9	11.8	0
women	0	25.0	58.3	8.3	8.3
children	8.3	50.0	25.0	16.7	0

e. purchase raw materials for design function

	sole	major	equal	minor	none
all	15.4%	29.2%	12.3%	29.2%	13.8%
multiple	17.4	43.5	17.4	13.0	8.7
men	23.5	35.3	0	29.4	11.8
women	8.3	8.3	33.3	33.3	16.7
children	7.7	15.4	53.8	23.1	0

f. preliminary or pre-cost of styles

	sole	major	equal	minor	none
all	10.8%	27.7%	35.4%	20.0%	6.2%
multiple	4.3	39.1	34.8	17.4	4.3
men	17.6	23.5	35.3	11.8	11.8
women	8.3	16.7	41.7	25.0	8.3
children	15.4	23.1	30.8	30.8	0

g. final cost of styles

	sole	major	equal	minor	none
all	12.3%	35.4%	15.4%	27.7%	13.0%
multiple	13.0	34.8	13.0	30.4	8.7
men	17.6	23.5	29.4	23.5	5.9
women	8.3	41.7	0	33.3	16.7
children	7.7	46.2	15.4	23.1	7.7

h. adjust styles to meet cost parameters

	sole	major	equal	minor	none
all	10.8%	49.2%	27.7%	9.2%	3.1%
multiple	8.7	60.9	17.4	13	0
men	17.6	29.4	47.1	5.9	0
women	0	50.0	25.0	16.7	8.3
children	15.4	53.8	23.1	0	7.7

i. establish selling price of styles

	sole	major	equal	minor	none
all	12.3%	43.1%	24.6%	15.4%	4.6%
multiple	8.7	47.8	13.0	30.4	0
men	5.9	41.2	29.4	17.6	5.9
women	25.0	25.0	41.7	0	8.3
children	15.4	53.8	23.1	0	7.7

j. select styles for seasonal line or collection

	sole	major	equal	minor	none
all	12.5%	57.8%	23.4%	6.3%	0%
multiple	13.0	52.2	26.1	8.7	0
men	25.0	50.0	25.0	0	0
women	0	75.0	16.7	8.3	0
children	7.7	61.5	23.1	7.7	0

k. maintain profit margins for seasonal lines

	sole	major	equal	minor	none
all	12.5%	31.3%	31.3%	18.8%	6.3%
multiple	13.0	39.1	26.1	13.0	8.7
men	12.5	31.3	25.0	18.8	12.5
women	16.7	25.0	33.3	25.0	0
children	7.7	23.1	46.2	23.1	0

B. Please check the appropriate answer for each of the following questions:

1. Does the merchandiser participate with the sales and marketing departments in the following activities:

a. presentation of seasonal line to sales staff?

	Yes	No
all	96.9%	3.1%
multiple	91.3	8.7
men	100	0
women	100	0
children	100	0

b. participate in line presentation to customers?

	Yes	No
all	93.8%	6.2%
multiple	91.3	8.7
men	100	0
women	91.7	8.3
children	92.3	7.7

c. monitor sales performance of styles in the current seasonal line?

	Yes	No
all	89.1%	10.9%
multiple	87.0	13.0
men	93.8	6.3
women	100	0
children	76.9	23.1

2. Does the merchandiser participate with the manufacturing or other departments in the following activities:

a. establish quality parameters?

	Yes	No
all	76.6%	21.9%
multiple	78.3	21.7
men	88.2	11.8
women	72.7	18.2
children	61.5	38.5

b. establish delivery schedules for specific styles?

	Yes	No
all	53.8%	46.2%
multiple	52.2	47.8
men	64.7	35.3
women	58.3	41.7
children	38.5	61.5

c. authorize production for individual styles?

	Yes	No
all	50.8%	49.2%
multiple	47.8	52.2
men	47.1	52.9
women	58.3	41.7
children	53.8	46.2

d. purchase of raw materials for stock?

	Yes	No
all	38.5%	61.5%
multiple	34.8	65.2
men	52.9	47.1
women	33.3	66.7
children	30.8	69.2

e. selection of manufacturing contractors?

	Yes	No
all	35.4%	64.6%
multiple	43.5	56.5
men	41.2	58.8
women	41.7	58.3
children	7.7	92.3

f. monitor manufacturing process?

	Yes	No
all	32.3%	67.7%
multiple	34.8	65.2
men	35.3	64.7
women	41.7	58.3
children	15.4	84.6

3. Please indicate below any other activities in which the merchandiser might be involved in addition to those mentioned in Sections "A" and "B."

no significant conclusions

4. Do you have more than one merchandiser?

	Yes	No
all	51.6%	48.4%
multiple	63.9	36.4
men	52.9	47.1
women	33.3	66.7
children	46.2	53.8

5. If you answered "Yes" to Question 4, please explain the need for more than one merchandiser.

a. more than one product line

all	75.0%
multiple	92.3
men	55.6
women	50.0
children	83.3

no other significant conclusions

6. If the responsibilities of the additional merchandiser(s) are different than those indicated above, please explain.

no significant conclusions

7. To whom does the merchandiser report?

	President (CEO)	Executive Vice President	Vice President Marketing	Other
all	43.8%	20.3%	15.6%	20.3%
multiple	26.1	17.4	30.4	26.1
men	62.5	12.5	6.3	18.8
women	33.3	33.3	16.7	16.7
children	61.5	23.1	0	15.4

8. What is the size of the merchandising staff that reports to your merchandiser?

	1–3	4–7	8–10	11–15	16–20	21–25	26–35	35 plus
all	64.5%	17.7%	4.8%	9.7%	0%	1.6%	0%	1.6%
multiple	50.0	31.8	4.5	9.1	0	0	0	4.5
men	86.7	0	6.7	6.7	0	0	0	0
women	75.0	25.0	0	0	0	0	0	0
children	53.8	7.7	7.7	23.1	0	7.7	0	0

9. What positions do you include in your merchandising staff?

no significant conclusions

C. Please check the appropriate answer for the following questions about your company.

1. What is your primary apparel market:

multiple	men	women	children
31.9%	27.2%	18.2%	22.7%

2. How would you define your primary target market?

a.	designer	better	moderate	budget	other
all	8.2%	44.3%	32.8%	13.1%	1.6%
multiple	9.1	45.5	36.4	9.1	0
men	3.3	46.7	33.3	6.7	0
women	8.3	33.3	33.3	16.7	8.3
children	0	50.0	25.0	25.0	0

b.	fashion leader	fashion conscious	fashion follower	traditional	basic
all	18.3%	38.3%	15.0%	21.7%	6.7%
multiple	15.0	25.0	25.0	25.0	10.0
men	31.3	31.3	6.3	18.8	12.5
women	18.2	54.5	9.1	18.2	0
children	7.7	53.0	15.4	23.1	0

3. Who are the retail customers in your primary target market? Please check all that are applicable.

	department stores	specialty stores	specialty chains	national chains	discount stores
all	50.8%	56.9%	32.3%	43.1%	91.7%
multiple	52.2	52.2	26.1	56.5	17.4
men	52.9	70.6	41.2	29.4	23.5
women	41.7	58.3	41.7	33.3	8.3
children	53.8	46.2	23.1	46.2	15.4

	mass merchandisers	other
all	32.3%	13.8%
multiple	26.1	8.7
men	29.4	23.5
women	33.3	16.7
children	46.2	7.7

4. What is the distribution in your primary target market?

	regional	national	international
all	1.5%	73.8%	24.6%
multiple	4.3	65.2	30.4
men	0	64.7	35.3
women	0	83.3	16.7
children	0	92.3	7.7

5. What is your approximate sales volume?

	less than $1,000,00	between $1,000,000 and $5,000,000	between $5,000,000 and $25,000,000	between $25,000,000 and $100,000,000
all	0%	4.8%	15.9%	47.6%
multiple	0	0	18.2	36.4
men	0	0	35.3	29.4
women	0	16.7	0	83.3
children	0	8.3	0	58.3

	between $100,000,000 and $250,000,000	over $250,000,000
all	22.2.%	9.5%
multiple	27.3	18.2
men	29.4	5.9
women	0	0
children	25.0	8.3

Comparison of Responsibilities of Apparel Merchandisers in 1995 and 2002

A. Please check the appropriate degree of responsibility the merchandiser has in your organization for the following activities:

1. defining the target market

	sole	major	equal	minor	none	mean	std deviation
2002	7.3%	70.7%	19.5%	0%	1%	2.20	.679
1995	3.1	40.0	41.5	15.4	0	2.69	.769

Significant statistical difference at the 5% level

2. research of the target market

	sole	major	equal	minor	none	mean	std deviation
2002	4.9%	61%	29.3%	2.4%	2.4%	2.37	.733
1995	3.1	47.7	29.2	18.5	1.5	2.68	.868

3. knowledge of the marketplace

a. fashion forecasts of silhouettes, colors, fabrics, and trims

	sole	major	equal	minor	none	mean	std deviation
2002	9.8%	61%	24.4%	4.9%	0%	2.24	.699
1995	20.0	66.2	7.7	4.6	1.5	2.02	.780

b. current consumer preferences for silhouettes, colors, fabrics, and trims

	sole	major	equal	minor	none	mean	std deviation
2002	12.2%	51.2%	36.6%	0%	0%	2.24	.663
1995	15.4	67.7	13.8	1.5	1.5	2.06	.704

c. direction and performance of competitors

	sole	major	equal	minor	none	mean	std deviation
2002	12.2%	46.3%	34.1%	7.3%	0%	2.37	.799
1995	1.6	54.0	31.7	9.5	3.5	2.59	.816

4. planning and control of the merchandising process

a. develop a merchandising calendar

	sole	major	equal	minor	none	mean	std deviation
2002	12.2%	58.5%	26.8%	2.4%	0%	2.20	.679
1995	30.8	53.8	10.8	1.5	3.1	1.92	.872

b. develop a line-plan summary

	sole	major	equal	minor	none	mean	std deviation
2002	14.6%	48.8%	31.7%	4.9%	0%	2.27	.775
1995	43.8	35.9	18.8	1.6	0	1.78	.806

Significant statistical difference at the 5% level

c. develop a shelf stock plan

	sole	major	equal	minor	none	mean	std deviation
2002	4.9%	9.8%	31.7%	34.1%	19.5%	3.54	1.075
1995	8.1	25.8	25.8	21.0	19.4	3.18	1.248

5. line development

a. conduct research

	sole	major	equal	minor	none	mean	std deviation
2002	12.2%	48.8%	26.8%	7.3%	4.9%	2.15	.976
1995	12.3	64.6	18.5	4.6	0	2.15	.690

b. direct designing activities

	sole	major	equal	minor	none	mean	std deviation
2002	14.6%	61.0%	9.8%	12.2%	2.4%	2.27	.949
1995	38.1	33.3	20.6	3.2	4.8	2.03	1.077

c. coordinate designing activities

	sole	major	equal	minor	none	mean	std deviation
2002	14.6%	48.8%	19.5%	17.1%	0%	2.39	.945
1995	40.6	35.9	12.5	7.8	3.1	1.97	1.069

d. select raw materials

	sole	major	equal	minor	none	mean	std deviation
2002	4.0%	41.5%	36.6%	7.3%	4.9%	2.56	.950
1995	23.4	37.5	28.1	7.8	3.1	2.30	1.019

e. purchase raw materials for design function

	sole	major	equal	minor	none	mean	std deviation
2002	7.5%	22.5%	10.0%	27.5%	32.5%	3.55	1.358
1995	15.4	29.2	12.3	29.2	13.8	2.97	1.334

Significant statistical difference at the 5% level

f. preliminary or pre-cost of styles

	sole	major	equal	minor	none	mean	std deviation
2002	10.0%	25.0%	25.0%	27.5%	12.5%	3.08	1.207
1995	10.8	27.7	35.4	20.0	6.2	2.83	1.069

g. final cost of styles

	sole	major	equal	minor	none	mean	std deviation
2002	12.5%	25.0%	27.5%	22.5%	12.5%	2.98	1.230
1995	12.3	35.4	15.4	27.7	13.0	2.86	1.223

h. adjust Cost of Goods styles to meet cost parameters

	sole	major	equal	minor	none	mean	std deviation
2002	12.5%	30.0%	27.5%	22.5%	7.5%	2.83	1.152
1995	10.8	49.2	27.7	9.2	3.1	2.45	.919

i. establish selling price of styles

	sole	major	equal	minor	none	mean	std deviation
2002	19.5%	41.5%	26.8%	2.4%	9.8%	2.41	1.140
1995	12.3%	43.1%	24.6%	15.4%	4.6%	2.57	1.045

j. select styles for seasonal line or collection

	sole	major	equal	minor	none	mean	std deviation
2002	9.8%	61.0%	22.0%	7.3%	0%	2.27	.742
1995	12.5	57.8	23.4	6.3	0	2.23	.750

k. maintain profit margins for seasonal lines

	sole	major	equal	minor	none	mean	std deviation
2002	12.2%	46.3%	24.4%	7.3%	9.8%	2.56	1.119
1995	12.5	31.3	31.3	18.8	6.3	2.75	1.098

B. Please check the appropriate answer for the following questions:

1. Does the merchandiser participate with the sales and marketing departments in the following activities:

a. presentation of seasonal line to sales staff?

	Yes	No
2002	87.8%	12.2%
1995	96.9	3.1

b. participate in line presentation to customers?

	Yes	No
2002	85.4%	12.5%
1995	93.8	6.2

c. monitor sales performance of styles in the current seasonal line?

	Yes	No
2002	78.0%	22.0%
1995	89.1	10.9

2. Does the merchandiser participate with the manufacturing or other departments in the following activities:

a. establish quality parameters?

	Yes	No
2002	82.5%	17.5%
1995	76.6	21.9

b. establish delivery schedules for specific styles?

	Yes	No
2002	64.1%	35.9%
1995	53.8	46.2

c. authorize production for individual styles?

	Yes	No
2002	41.0%	59.0%
1994	50.8	49.2

d. purchase of raw materials for stock?

	Yes	No
2002	25.0%	75.0%
1995	38.5	61.5

e. selection of manufacturing contractors/make sourcing decisions?

	Yes	No
2002	53.8%	46.2%
1995	35.4	64.6

f. monitor manufacturing process?

	Yes	No
2002	25.6%	74.4%
1995	32.3	67.7

Significant statistical difference at the 10% level

3. Do you have more than one merchandiser?

	Yes	No
2002	48.6%	51.4%
1995	51.6	48.4

4. To whom does the merchandiser report?

	President (CEO)	Executive Vice President	Vice President Marketing	Other
2002	55.6%	19.4%	2.8%	22.8%
1995	43.8	20.3	15.6	20.3

5. What is the size of the merchandising staff that reports to your merchandiser?

	1–3	4–7	8–10	11–15	16–20	21–25	26–35	35 plus
2002	20.0%	27.5%	22.5%	5.0%	2.5%	5.0%	2.5%	15.0%
1995	64.5	17.7	4.8	9.7	0	1.6	0	1.6

C. General Information

1. What is your primary apparel market?

	two or more	men's	women's	children's
2002	34.1%	12.2%	39.0%	14.6%
1995	31.9	27.2	18.2	22.7

2. How would you define the price range of your primary target market?

	designer	bridge	better	moderate	budget	other
2002	10.0%	15.0%	40.0%	58.0%	10.0%	3%
1995	8.2	NA	4.3	32.8	13.1	1.6

3. How would you define the level of fashion interest of your primary target market?

	fashion leader	fashion conscious	fashion follower	traditional/basic	other
2002	15.0%	53.0%	33.0%	45.0%	5.0%
1995	18.3	38.3	15.0	28.4	NA

4. Who are the retail customers in your primary target market? Please check all that are applicable.

	department stores	specialty stores	specialty chains	national chains	discount stores
2002	73.0%	83.0%	NA	58.0%	38.0%
1995	50.8	56.9	32.3	43.1	91.7

	mass merchandisers	other
2002	35.0%	18.0%
1995	32.3	13.8

5. What is the distribution in your primary target market?

	regional	national	international	national/international
2003	2.5%	75.0%	12.5%	7.5%
1995	1.5	73.8	24.6	0

6. What is your approximate sales volume?

	less than $1,000,000	between $1,000,000 and $5,000,000	between $5,000,000 and $25,000,000	between $25,000,000 and $100,000,000
2002	0%	9.6%	16.2%	32.4%
1995	0	4.8	15.9	47.6

	greater than $100,000,000
2002	40.4%
1995	31.7

Comparison of Responsibilities of Apparel Merchandisers and Retail Product Managers in 2002

(Please Note: Responses from apparel companies are presented in row "2002A" and from retailing organizations in row "2002R")

A. Please check the appropriate degree of responsibility the merchandiser/product manager has in your organization for the following activities:

1. defining the target market

	sole	major	equal	minor	none	mean	std deviation
2002A	7.3%	70.7%	19.5%	0%	1%	2.20	.679
2002R	0	55.2	34.5	10.3	0	2.55	.685

2. research of the target market

	sole	major	equal	minor	none	mean	std deviation
2002A	4.9%	61%	29.3%	2.4%	2.4%	2.37	.733
2002R	3.4	55.2	31.0	10.3	0	2.48	.738

3. knowledge of the marketplace

a. fashion forecasts of silhouettes, colors, fabrics, and trims

	sole	major	equal	minor	none	mean	std deviation
2002A	9.8%	61.0%	24.4%	4.9%	0%	2.24	.699
2002R	10.3	65.5	20.7	3.4	0	2.17	.658

b. current consumer preferences for silhouettes, colors, fabrics, and trims

	sole	major	equal	minor	none	mean	std deviation
2002A	12.2%	51.2%	36.6%	0%	0%	2.24	.663
2002R	3.4	62.1	31.0	3.4	0	2.34	.614

c. direction and performance of competitors

	sole	major	equal	minor	none	mean	std deviation
2002A	12.2%	46.3%	34.1%	7.3%	0%	2.37	.799
2002R	6.9	48.3	37.9	6.9	0	2.45	.736

4. planning and control of the merchandising/product managing process

a. develop a merchandising calendar

	sole	major	equal	minor	none	mean	std deviation
2002A	12.2%	58.5%	26.8%	2.4%	0%	2.20	.679
2002R	27.6	41.4	37.9	6.9	0	2.07	.842

b. develop a line-plan summary

	sole	major	equal	minor	none	mean	std deviation
2002A	14.6%	48.8%	31.7%	4.9%	0%	2.27	.775
2002R	27.6	55.2	17.2	13.8	6.9	2.59	1.053

c. develop a shelf stock plan

	sole	major	equal	minor	none	mean	std deviation
2002A	4.9%	9.8%	31.7%	34.1%	19.5%	3.54	1.075
2002R	13.8	65.5	13.8	3.4	3.4	2.17	.848

5. line development

a. conduct research

	sole	major	equal	minor	none	mean	std deviation
2002A	12.2%	48.8%	26.8%	7.3%	4.9%	2.15	.976
2002R	17.2	37.9	37.9	6.9	0	2.34	.857

b. direct designing activities

	sole	major	equal	minor	none	mean	std deviation
2002A	14.6%	61.0%	9.8%	12.2%	2.4%	2.27	.949
2002R	20.7	31.0	24.1	13.8	10.3	2.62	1.265

c. coordinate designing activities

	sole	major	equal	minor	none	mean	std deviation
2002A	14.6%	48.8%	19.5%	17.1%	0%	2.39	.945
2002R	20.7	34.5	20.7	10.3	13.8	2.62	1.231

d. select raw materials

	sole	major	equal	minor	none	mean	std deviation
2002A	4.0%	41.5%	36.6%	7.3%	4.9%	2.56	.950
2002R	24.1	27.6	17.2	24.1	6.9	2.62	1.293

e. purchase raw materials for design function

	sole	major	equal	minor	none	mean	std deviation
2002A	7.5%	22.5%	10.0%	27.5%	32.5%	3.55	1.358
2002R	NA						

f. preliminary or pre-cost of styles

	sole	major	equal	minor	none	mean	std deviation
2002A	10.0%	25.0%	25.0%	27.5%	12.5%	3.08	1.207
2002R	20.7	37.9	13.8	13.8	13.8	2.62	1.347

g. final cost of styles

	sole	major	equal	minor	none	mean	std deviation
2002A	12.5%	25.0%	27.5%	22.5%	12.5%	2.98	1.230
2002R	24.1	41.4	13.8	10.3	10.3	2.41	1.268

h. adjust Cost of Goods Solds to meet cost parameters

	sole	major	equal	minor	none	mean	std deviation
2002A	12.5%	30.0%	27.5%	22.5%	7.5%	2.83	1.152
2002R	13.8	44.8	24.1	10.3	6.9	2.52	1.090

i. establish selling price of styles

	sole	major	equal	minor	none	mean	std deviation
2002A	19.5%	41.5%	26.8%	2.4%	9.8%	2.41	1.140
2002R	17.2	58.6	20.7	0	3.4	2.14	.833

j. select styles for seasonal line or collection

	sole	major	equal	minor	none	mean	std deviation
2002A	9.8%	61.0%	22.0%	7.3%	0%	2.27	.742
2002R	13.8	65.5	13.8	3.4	3.4	2.17	.848

k. maintain profit margins for seasonal lines

	sole	major	equal	minor	none	mean	std deviation
2002A	12.2%	46.3%	24.4%	7.3%	9.8%	2.56	1.119
2002R	20.5	53.6	21.4	0	0	1.96	.693

B. Please check the appropriate answer for the following questions:

1. Does the merchandiser/product manager participate with the sales and marketing departments in the following activities:

a. presentation of seasonal line to sales staff?

	Yes	No
2002A	87.8%	12.2%
2002R	100	0

b. participate in line presentation to customers?

	Yes	No
2002A	85.4%	12.5%
2002R	NA	NA

c. monitor sales performance of styles in the current seasonal line?

	Yes	No
2002A	78.0%	22.0%
2002R	100	0

2. Does the merchandiser/product manager participate with the manufacturing or other departments in the following activities:

a. establish quality parameters?

	Yes	No
2002A	82.5%	17.5%
2002R	100	0

b. establish delivery schedules for specific styles?

	Yes	No
2002A	64.1%	35.9%
2002R	96.6	3.4

c. authorize production for individual styles?

	Yes	No
2002A	41.0%	59.0%
2002R	93.1	6.9

d. purchase of raw materials for stock?

	Yes	No
2002A	25.0%	75.0%
2002R	NA	NA

e. selection of manufacturing contractors/make sourcing decisions

	Yes	No
2002A	53.8%	46.2%
2002R	NA	NA

f. monitor manufacturing process?

	Yes	No
2002A	25.6%	74.4%
2002R	NA	NA

3. Do you have more than one merchandiser?

	Yes	No
2002A	48.6%	51.4%
2002R	51.7	44.8

4. To whom does the merchandiser report?

	President (CEO)	Executive Vice President	Vice President Marketing	Other
2002A	55.6%	19.4%	2.8%	22.8%
2000R	44.8	20.7	0	37.9

5. What is the size of the staff that reports to your merchandiser/product manager?

	1–3	4–7	8–10	11–15	16–20	21–25	26–35	35 plus
2002A	20.0%	27.5%	22.5%	5.0%	2.5%	5.0%	2.5%	15.0%
2002R	NA	NA	NA	NA	NA	NA	NA	NA

C. General Information

1. What is your primary apparel market?

	two or more	men's	women's	children's
2002A	34.1%	12.2%	39.0%	14.6%
2002R	36.3	14.6	39.0	NA

2. How would you define your primary target market?

a.	designer	bridge	better	moderate	budget	other
2002A	10.0%	15.0%	40.0%	8.0%	10.0%	3.0%
2002R	4.9	NA	22.0	19.5	NA	53.7

b.	fashion leader	fashion conscious	fashion follower	traditional/basic	other
2002A	15.0%	53.0%	33.0%	45.0%	5.0%
2002R	14.6	39.0	7.3	29.3	9.8

3. Who are the retail customers in your primary target market? Please check all that are applicable.

	department stores	specialty stores	specialty chains	national chains	discount stores
2002A	73.0%	83.0%	NA	58.0%	38.0%
2002R	NA	NA	NA	NA	NA

	mass merchandisers	other
2002	35.0%	18.0%
200R	NA	NA

4. What is the distribution in your primary target market?

	regional	national	international	national/international
2002A	2.5%	75.0%	12.5%	7.5%
2002R	56.1	31.7	9.8	2.4

5. What is your approximate sales volume?

	less than $1,000,000	between $1,000,000 and $5,000,000	between $5,000,000 and $25,000,000	between $25,000,000 and $100,000,000
2002A	0%	9.6%	16.2%	32.4%
2002R	NA	NA	NA	NA

	greater than $100,000,000
2002A	40.5%
2002R	NA

Credits for Figures

Chapter 1

1.2: National Income Accounts, as published by The American Apparel and Footwear Association. **1.4:** Courtesy of Fairchild Publications, Inc. **1.8:** Courtesy of Fairchild Publications, Inc. **1.9a and 1.9b:** National Cotton Council of America. **1.9d and 1.9e:** National Cotton Council of America.

Chapter 2

2.3: Photograph courtesy of Group Dynamics in Focus, Inc.

Chapter 3

3.2: Courtesy of VF Corporation. **3.6:** Photograph courtesy of WWD Magic International. **3.7a:** Courtesy of Fairchild Publications, Inc. **3.7m:** Courtesy of Fairchild Publications, Inc. **3.7p:** Reprinted with permission from *Seventeen* © 2006 Hearst Communications, Inc.

Chapter 4

4.3: Photograph courtesy of Gerber Technology, Inc. **4.6:** Courtesy of Healthtex and Lee.

Chapter 5

5.1: Courtesy of Fairchild Publications, Inc. **5.9–5.11:** Photograph courtesy of Gerber Technology, Inc.

Chapter 6

6.6: Courtesy of Katie McKensie. **6.8:** Photograph Courtesy of Gerber Technology, Inc.

Chapter 7

7.11–7.13: Reprinted with permission of Freeborders.

Chapter 8

8.1: Courtesy of Gerber Technology, Inc. **8.3:** Professor Melvin Wiener, Philadelphia University. **8.4:** Courtesy of Philadelphia University. **8.5:** Courtesy of Pincus Brothers Maxwell. **8.6:** Courtesy of Tung Mung Group. **8.7:** Published with permission of American Apparel and Footwear Association. **8.8:** Photograph courtesy of Tung Mung Group.

Chapter 9

9.1: Courtesy of Textile Clothing Technology Corporation. **9.2:** Reprinted with permission of Textile Clothing Technology Corporation. **9.8:** Courtesy of The Thread. **9.10:** Courtesy of Kurt Salmon Associates.

Chapter 10

10.1 and 10.2: Photographs courtesy of Gerber Technology, Inc. **10.3:** Courtesy of Crafted with Pride In USA Council. **10.4:** Photograph courtesy of Tung Mung International Group of Companies. **10.5 and 10.6:** Reprinted with permission of *Apparel Magazine*. **10.7:** Courtesy of Textile Clothing Technology Corporation.

Chapter 11

11.1: Reprinted with permission of American Apparel Producers Network. **11.3** © 2005 Wachovia is the registered trademark of Wachovia Corporation. Wachovia does not represent in any matter that this application and agreement are legally sufficient for any purpose. **11.5 and 11.6:** Photograph by James R. Tourtellotte, courtesy of U.S. Customs Service.

Chapter 12

12.1 and 12.2: Courtesy of Justwin Technologies. **12.4:** Photograph courtesy of Gerber Technology, Inc. **12.5:** Photograph courtesy of McDermid ColorSpan Corp. **12.7 and 12.8:** Courtesy of Textile Clothing Technology Corporation.

Company/Name Index

Subject Index